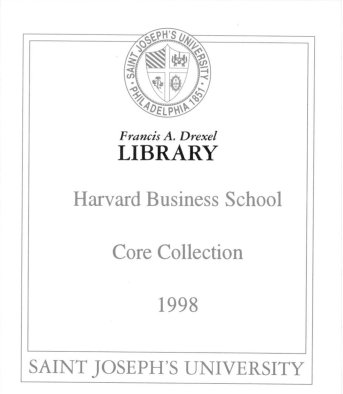

Business Forecasting Methods

Business Forecasting Methods

Second Edition

JEFFREY JARRETT

Basil Blackwell

Copyright © Jeffrey Jarrett 1991

First published 1987

Second edition, revised and updated,
First published 1991.

Basil Blackwell Ltd
108 Cowley Road, Oxford, OX4 1JF, UK

Basil Blackwell, Inc.
3 Cambridge Center
Cambridge, Massachusetts 02142, USA

British Library Cataloguing in Publication Data
A CIP catalogue record for this book is available from the British Library.

Library of Congress Cataloging in Publication Data
Jarrett, Jeffrey, 1940–
Business forecasting methods/Jeffrey Jarrett. — 2nd ed.
    p.   cm.
Includes bibliographical references.
ISBN 0-631-17329-3
1. Business forecasting.   I. Title.
HD30.27.J38 1990
658.4'0355—dc20   90-32587 CIP

Typeset in 10 on 11½ pt Times
by TecSet Ltd, Wallington, Surrey
Printed in Great Britain by The Alden Press Ltd., Oxford

Contents

Preface to the second edition

I intend this book for use as a one semester, or one or two quarter course, in introductory forecasting for business administration, economics, or applied statistics students. My aims are to present the theory and methods of forecasting at an introductory level and to illustrate clearly the application to management. Included in this book is a wide variety of features that make it unique among books on forecasting.

All chapters have a summary section in which the important concepts are presented. In these summaries, the reader is presented with a thorough review of the essential concepts illustrated in the chapter. Each chapter begins with a statement of objectives including a discussion of the important points to be learned. Readers are introduced at this time to what they will be able to do after studying the chapter. The chapter outline and list of key terms defined in the chapter follow. The key terms defined in the chapter are identified in italic type where they are introduced. These are the same key terms listed at the beginning of the chapter.

At the end of every chapter, exercises are included. Some exercises are of the drill type in that they give students experience with working with the many statistical formulas in forecasting. Word problems involving real-life forecasting problems are also amply included. Whenever possible, the data are real-life numerical information collected from applications in industry and government. The end of chapter exercises include some questions for review.

Throughout the book, illustrations of the output of SAS, Minitab and Micro-TSP computer software are given. In the advanced time series chapters, examples of IDA computer software output are included. Readers and students will see how these software systems implement statistically based forecasting methods and thus will be led to an understanding of the role of the computer in forecasting practice. Many of the problems in the book have data sets that are amenable to computer applications. Thus, these exercises emphasize how to obtain a numerical solution with the aid of computer software and indicate that the computer plays a significant part in the practice of forecasting. Answers to selected exercises appear at the end of the book.

Case material is included in the book in several ways. First, many short cases illustrate the application of a forecasting model in a variety of applications. Second, several sections of the book are cases with accompanying discussion. These are real applications in problem situations.

The book is divided into six parts. The initial portion (chapter 1) is an introduction to forecasting as a field of study in business. The importance of the computer is discussed along with methods for evaluating computer software. In the second part, the reader is introduced to moving average and smoothing methods. A chapter on classical decomposition follows. Causal and explanatory modeling techniques are presented in part III. This part includes a chapter on econometric models applied to forecasting problems. Part IV contains advanced time series modeling including model identification, estimation and diagnostic testing. Both seasonal and nonseasonal models are included. Part V introduces qualitative methods. A substantial discussion of forecasting by economic indicators is presented as well as the Delphi method. Finally, part VI contains a thorough discussion of forecast evaluation, revision and improvement, and the role of forecasting in business planning and control.

Instructors will often cover chapters 1–5 in sequence (some topics are optional). Chapter 6 is optional and may or may not be included at the discretion of the instructor. Chapters 7, 8, and 9 should be studied in sequence. However, chapter 10 could follow chapter 4, 5, 6, or 9 at the option of the instructor. Chapter 11 should be the last chapter studied regardless of the sequence followed. Thus there is a great deal of flexibility in the development of the course in business forecasting. Some sections in various chapters may also be omitted to meet the special desires of instructor and students.

Finally, the author wishes to dedicate this book to Ruth, Michael, Debra and Daniel. All of them contributed to this book in a very special way.

Jeffrey Jarrett
Kingston, Rhode Island

PART I

Introduction

CHAPTER I

Introduction

Objectives

The purpose of chapter 1 is to indicate the following:

1 Managers and administrators should study forecasting because it is an element in the process of decision-making in the face of an uncertain future.
2 Those involved in forecasting should be those who are involved in strategic planning and control.
3 There is a wide variety of forecasting methods to be discussed in this book.
4 Computer software for forecasting is widely available and extremely useful in the forecasting process.
5 Forecasts are classified according to their lead time and the rate of change in the data studied in the forecasting process.

Outline

1.1 Why Study Forecasting?

1.2 Who Should Forecast?

1.3 Methods of Forecasting

1.4 The Outline of this Book

1.5 Survey of Computer Software for Forecasting

1.6 Classifying Forecasts

1.7 Summary

Key Terms

• Forecasts

• Moving Average

• Exponential Smoothing

• Time Series Decomposition

• Regression models

• Econometric Models

• Advanced times series methods

• Qualitative forecasts

• Delphi technique

1.1   Why Study Forecasting?

In management and administration, the need for planning and control is important because the lead time for managerial decision-making ranges from several years or more, as in the case of capital construction in the electric utility industry, to a few days or even hours, as in the example of meeting production or inventory levels. Information about future events from forecasts are usually a critical input into a wide range of managerial and administrative decision-making, since today's plans are dependent on future expectations.

While forecasting is important, some people question the validity, reliability, and efficiency of a discipline involved in predicting future events. This often arises over the failure to recognize the progress that has been made in business forecasting over the last few decades. Many firms will not forecast because they hold false beliefs that either the future holds no important change or the future holds enough time to permit a firm or individual to react to a change in events after the fact. In addition, other firms may not forecast because they have simply ignored the need for predicting future events, or, for example, the firm has been fortunate not to have excess inventory or excessive lost sales. All organizations, however, operate in an atmosphere of uncertainty about future events, with decisions to be made in face of this uncertainty. Educated choices about future events are more valuable to decision-makers who operate in a climate of uncertainty than are uneducated guesses. Thus the ability to predict future events with accuracy is a necessary part of managerial planning and control.

1.2   Who Should Forecast?

Forecasts are numerical estimates of the future levels of sales, demand, inventories, costs, imports, exports, and prices, among others, for a firm, an industry, a sector of the economy, or the total economy. The objective of forecasting is to assist management to plan requirements for marketing efforts, materials, personnel, production, services, capital acquisition and construction and finances. Wise, educated, and well-prepared forecasts should be accurate enough to allow for better planning and control than could be accomplished without the forecast.

Example 1.1

A firm to manufacture weatherstripping and other insulation materials was formed to produce and market products developed from the founder's patents. The firm is largely family run and employs 25 with operations balanced throughout each calendar year. More than half of sales, however, are in the fall season. Inventories are increased during other seasons and are depleted in the fall. Sales from year to year are heavily related to changes, especially abrupt changes, in consumer prices for energy. Changes in building code laws and the variability in housing construction are also related to the firm's sales. Management feels that it needs more information about the size and changes in the market for its products.

The firm in the above example is faced with serious and complex problems. Forecasting is important to this firm because (a) the firm faces fluctuations in demand and inventory levels throughout the year, (b) the firm's sales are related to changes in the economic environment in which it operates, and (c) abrupt changes in economic conditions have serious consequences for the firm. Implementation of a forecasting program can enable the firm to plan and react promptly in the future and keep it on a profitable setting.

If the purpose of forecasting is to improve planning and control, accurate forecasts may reduce losses due to unsold inventory, losses due to unavailable inventory that could have been sold, costs associated with not having sufficient productive capacity, or costs associated with inefficient methods of production, among others. Who within a firm then should be involved in the forecasting efforts? Those involved in forecasting should include those responsible for managerial planning and control, and those in the support staff role who have the knowledge of modern forecasting methods. Thus the forecasting practitioners will typically be those well trained in forecasting who are in either decision-making responsibility or the support staff to those decision-makers. In the last chapter of this book, the role of forecasting in the overall business plan will be illustrated and discussed.

1.3 Methods of Forecasting

Forecasting methods to produce numerical estimates range from relatively simple to complex and sophisticated techniques. Most techniques described in this book are quantitative in nature; however, as we shall see, there are useful qualitative techniques.

We begin the study of forecasting methods by studying extrapolative or projective techniques, i.e. moving averages and exponential smoothing. A *moving average* is a trend method wherein each point of a moving average of a time series is the arithmetic mean (or weighted average) of a number of consecutive observations of the series. The number of observations in the moving-average computation is chosen to minimize the effects of seasonality or other disturbances in the series. Moving averages are often used to forecast low volume items as part of an inventory control program.

Exponential smoothing is a flexible trend method whereby past data observations are given different weights in computing the forecast. The method is similar to moving averages but permits the forecasters to adjust for previous inaccuracies in forecasts. Stated differently, it has the advantage of providing a simple up-to-date forecast, where the new forecast is equal to the previous one plus some stated proportion of the previous period's forecasting error. As we shall learn, the moving average and exponential smoothing methods are very similar. Furthermore, exponential smoothing methods are adaptable to adjustments to include trend and seasonal projections and adaptive types of optimum weighting procedures. Exponential smoothing methods are typically used to forecast large numbers of items, as in application of material requirements planning, sales monitoring, margin forecasting, and other financial data.

Time series decomposition methods are widely used to identify the systematic components of a time series, trend, cycle, and seasonal pattern, and the nonsystematic or random components. In making a trend projection, a mathematical expression, i.e. a straight line or slowly changing algebraic form, for the time series is projected ahead. The seasonal pattern is identified by first determining the seasonal indexes for each month or quarter of a year and, in turn, these patterns are projected ahead. The cyclical forecast may be prepared by other systematic projections or by economic judgement. Nonsystematic or irregular variation is usually assumed to be zero in a forecast but irregular adjustments may be needed for an anticipated stoppage in production or some other causal factors in the time period of the forecast.

An elaborate method for measuring seasonal variation is called the Census II or X-11 variant. This is a highly analytical method for measuring seasonal fluctuations. It analyzes changes in the seasonal patterns over time and provides a one-year-ahead forecast of the changing seasonal index. Typically, this method is used to deseasonalize and forecast monthly and quarterly time series compiled and published by agencies of the federal government of the United States (and other nations as well).

Regression models are those procedures for estimating linear relations, or polynomial relations, or multiple linear relations. These models express the past relationships among the item being forecast and the explanatory variables that are associated with the rise and fall of that item. These methods are very useful when adequate historical data are available on the major factors associated with variations in the item being forecast.

An extension of regression models are multi-equation systems that express the dynamic interrelationships of an economy, sector of an economy, or industry. These systems are called *econometric models* and are used to explain and predict the behavior of the variables in the model. Econometric models are considered causal models in that the equations are considered to have causal relationships that satisfy tests of economic theory. Typical applications include sales forecasting systems for large corporate entities, government agency revenue and expenditure forecasts, and sector or industry forecasts. Small simultaneous equation systems are also examples of econometric modeling techniques.

Advanced time series methods of filtering and Box–Jenkins procedures are powerful extensions of both exponential smoothing and decomposition methods. These techniques use the most recent observation as a starting value and analyze forecasting errors to determine the proper adjustments for future time periods. These methods are also highly complex, require large amounts of computer time, and may sometimes be more expensive to use. Box–Jenkins forecasts have proven to be very accurate for some sets of time series data. However, simpler techniques requiring less data have also proven to be successful in many forecasting applications.

Qualitative forecasts involve the use of judgement in analysis and prediction of future events. Predicting the cycle involves the use of knowledge obtained from past economic variables. The leading indicator approach involves time series that measure economic activity whose movement in either direction usually precedes another time series. As an example, the number of building permits issued is a leading indicator of sales of household durable equipment. Diffusion indexes are used in cyclical analysis to measure the spread of a cyclical turn throughout the economy or sector of an economy. Leading indicators, diffusion indexes, and other facets of qualitative cyclical analysis are used to predict demand for product by type.

The *Delphi technique,* which uses the subjective opinion of experts to predict technological change, demand, and long-term changes in business activity, is illustrated in chapter 10. Last, methods for forecast evaluation and revision are discussed in chapter 11. The forecast is also placed in the strategic plan of a business.

To forecast, a person will often study past internal data. A set of time-ordered observations on a variable during successive and equal time periods is referred to as a time series. Techniques which analyze the variation in the time series are referred to as time series methods. These methods are largely discussed in chapters 2, 3, 7, 8, and 9. Methods that attempt to explain the variation in a time series by studying its relationship to other time series data sets are called explanatory or causal modeling techniques (chapters 4, 5, and 6).

All the above methods for forecasting will be discussed, described, and analyzed in this book. A short summary is given in table 1.1

1.4 The Outline of this Book

Since the purpose of this book is to introduce a vast array of forecasting methods to the reader, the remaining chapters will detail all the procedures previously mentioned (see table 1.2). Part I is an introduction to the field of forecasting. In part II, the student is introduced to the simplest forecasting models. These include moving averages, exponential smoothing and extended forms of moving averages and exponential smoothing. The reader is then introduced to classical time series decomposition and the X-11 variant of the Census II methods.

In part III we discuss how the forecaster can study the relationship among variables. This enables the forecaster to establish regression models for forecasting. Simple linear models are introduced first (chapter 4), and then multiple regression and curvilinear models are considered (chapter 5). The reader learns to interpret computer output from useful software systems. Econometric models for forecasting are introduced to complete the regression-based procedures (chapter 6).

The general purpose autoregressive integrated moving average (ARIMA) time series methods are described in part IV. These forecasting methods are known as Box–Jenkins methods (chapters 7, 8, and 9) after their developers.

Part V introduces qualitative forecasting and its practical application to predicting business conditions. The concepts of leading, lagging, and roughly coincident indicators are introduced along with the general description of business cycles. Anticipation surveys, diffusion indexes, and methods for tracking cycles are discussed (chapter 10).

Finally, part VI will place forecasting in the global or strategic plan for a firm (chapter 11). Forecasts are also evaluated and revised. One last point concerns the use of the computer. Modern forecasting is rarely done without the computer. Hence, the use of computer techniques is integrated thoroughly throughout the book.

1.5 Survey of Computer Software for Forecasting

A large number of very useful and powerful computer software systems are now available for the purposes of forecasting. Table 1.3 is a summary of useful computer

TABLE 1.1 Forecasting methods

Method	Description	Applications	Chapter
Moving averages	Extrapolative technique based on mean of past observations.	Short-range forecasts for operations involving large number of items such as inventory control, scheduling, pricing and timing special promotions.	2
Exponential smoothing	Forecasts are weighted combinations of past observed and forecast values. More weight is given to most recent data.	Same as above.	2
Decomposition methods	Method assumes relationship between time and the variable being forecast. The time series variable is decomposed into systematic and nonsystematic components.	Long-range forecasting for capital construction, new product planning, etc. Short-term forecasting for advertising, planning, inventory, financing and production planning.	3
Regression analysis	Explanatory forecasting assumes association between dependent and one or more explanatory variables.	Short- and intermediate-term forecasting for established products and services; production, marketing, personnel and financing decisions.	4, 5
Econometric modeling	System of explanatory equations relating exogenous and endogenous variables.	Short- and intermediate-term forecasting for product demand, costs, prices, expenditures, and revenues.	
Box–Jenkins techniques	No pattern in the data is assumed. An iterative approach is used to identify a possibly useful model from a general class of models.	Same as above.	7, 8, 9
Economic indicators	Cyclical turning points can be predicted by examining its behavior over past business cycles.	Forecasting turning points in sales, demand, and general business activity.	10
Delphi method	Use of subjective opinion of experts to predict future direction of economy and sectors.	Forecasting technological change, demand, and business activity.	10
Forecast revision	Use of optimal linear correction procedure to revise forecasts and improve accuracy.	Improvement of forecast accuracy of extrapolative and other models.	11

TABLE 1.2 Outline of this book

Part no.	Chapter no.	
I	1	Introduction
II		Time series techniques
	2	Smoothing methods
	3	Methods for time series decomposition and analysis
III		Causal or explanatory modeling techniques
	4	Linear regression and correlation
	5	Multiple regression methods
	6	Econometric models
IV		Advanced topics in time series analysis
	7	Autocorrelation, autoregressive models, and time series analysis
	8	Additional time series models and identification
	9	Box–Jenkins methods and ARIMA modeling
V		Qualitative forecasting
	10	Forecasting business conditions – some qualitative approaches
VI		Issues in forecasting
	11	Forecast evaluation, revision, and business planning and control

software for forecasting. Most of these forecasting systems have been used by the author, many very extensively. Many examples of the output of these systems for various applications will be seen in subsequent chapters of this book. All the software is known to have a high degree of numerical analytic capability and a wide variety of algorithms, and has been used extensively in industry, in government, and at university level. The author wishes to thank the personnel of the firms whose software appears in this book for previous aid in the preparation of the forecasting applications.

SAS, which is a product of the SAS Institute of Cary, NC, is a widely used product for the purposes of forecasting. It is available for mainframe and minicomputers and there is a powerful version for personal computers (PCs). However, the PC version does not contain all the applications included in the versions for larger computers. SPSS-X, together with its companion product (TRENDS), is also a widely used system for data analysis, statistics, and forecasting. It is widely used on large computers and has a very good PC version. TRENDS is an add-on feature for the mainframe and minicomputer version which contains a large number of useful applications of the time series forecasting techniques discussed in this book. Many forecasters who already have knowledge of this software system should learn more about the forecasting features of this software.

TSP, and more importantly MICRO-TSP, has become one of the more widely used systems for forecasting in business and government. Practically all techniques discussed in this book are included in MICRO-TSP, although some of the introductory time series techniques may have slightly different algorithms. Furthermore, there is a student's version of this software system available for a fraction of the price

TABLE 1.3 Summary of useful computer software for forecasting

Title	Description
SAS, SAS/PC, and SAS/ETS	Statistical Analysis System – contains a large amount of statistical forecasting features. Extremely good data management and report writing features. Originally developed for IBM and plug compatible mainframe systems. Available on minicomputers with a new PC version.
SPSS-X, SPSS/PC, and TRENDS	Statistical Package for the Social Sciences – a large number of statistical and forecasting procedures coupled with new report writing features. System is generally available on most computers in batch and interactive modes.
TSP/MICRO-TSP	Time Series Processor – contains regression, econometric, and time series decomposition procedures. Available on mainframe and minicomputers. A smaller version Micro-TSP is available on personal computers and widely used.
TROLL	Time Shared Reactive On-Line Laboratory – econometrics and time series library of programs developed at the Massachusetts Institute of Technology. System is interactive with file editing and maintenance features.
STATGRAPHICS	APL-based system which is relatively device independent and interactive. Extremely good graphic features with ample selection of time series and smoothing techniques.
MINITAB	Interactive statistical system which is generally available on most computers. A PC version is also available. Easy to learn.
FOCUS	A comprehensive information control system with limited capabilities for statistical forecasting. Very good query and report writing features.
BMDP and BMDP/PC	One of the most comprehensive statistical software systems. Developed originally for mainframe computers but now available on smaller machines as well. A version called Desk Top BMDP is available for some microcomputers.
STATPRO	A comprehensive statistics, graphics, and database software system developed for personal computers. It is a complete system for data entry, storage, manipulation, and analysis with many forecasting features.
The Time Machine	Fits univariate ARIMA models by a complete Box–Jenkins analysis. Contains exponential smoothing, regression-based methods with a spreadsheet style for IBM PC/XT/AT or fully compatible computer. Available from Research Services, Ogden, UT.

TABLE 1.3 (continued)

Title	Description
FAME	Forecasting/Analysis/Modeling Environment is an interactive system to be implemented on a variety of 16-bit microprocessors as well as many mini and mainframe computers.
STATLIB	Interactive system and language for forecasting, statistical data analysis, econometric modeling, graphics and data management. Developed for VM/CMS and MVS/TSO operating systems.
Interactive Data Analysis (IDA)	Interactive data base and forecasting systems. Developed originally for large computers. Easy to learn with good interactive features and a comprehensive list of techniques. Good documentation.
MATHTAB/MATHSTAT	Data management and tabulation package comprising a wide variety of statistical systems. Product of Mathematica which can run on most business-size personal computers.
MODEL DECISION SUPPORT SYSTEM	A spread sheet based computational system for performing simulations and statistical analysis of data. Product of Lloyd Bush and Associates and available on Prime and other microcomputers and a PC version.
SCA Statistical System	A powerful and useful system for forecasting. Uses English-like statements as well as analytic statements for analysis. Largely used for regression and advanced time series methods. Has good automatic features.
AUTOBOX	PC software for advanced time series methods. Good automatic features. Product of Automatic Forecasting Systems, Hatboro, PA.
SMARTFORECASTS II	Automatic forecasting software designed to accompany Lotus 1-2-3 of Symphony. Contains moving average and exponential smoothing techniques in both automatic and nonautomatic modes. Regression-based methods are also included.
STATPLAN III	Permits data entry through Lotus 1-2-3 or Symphony files. Forecasting procedures include regression-based exponential smoothing, autocorrelation analysis, and trend and cycle decomposition.
SYSTAT	Interactive statistics and graphics software for IBM and MacIntosh computers. Contains wide variety of forecasting features. The instructional version is called MYSTAT and the graphics software is called SYGRAPH.

of the professional version. The producer of this software is Quantitative Micro Software, Irvine, CA.

The Interactive Data Analysis and Forecasting System (IDA) is a conversational system for statistical computation and forecasting that was designed and implemented at the University of Chicago Graduate School of Business, Chicago, Illinois. The software system is designed with user convenience in mind. The main emphasis of the software is on statistical tools associated with regression or linear models and related model-building techniques. IDA is also identified with those techniques used for time series model identification and diagnostic testing. Thus IDA has a range of capabilities, graphical and numerical, for suggesting models that may be appropriate and for assessing the adequacy of models that are tentatively entertained.

BMDP statistical software is not primarily a forecasting system. It is a system for performing a wide variety of statistical analysis including regression-based procedures and advanced time series techniques. There is also a PC version of this software for certain microcomputers.

STATGRAPHICS is an interactive time series computer software system designed to aid in forecasting. The software is APL based and is relatively device independent and interactive. Furthermore, it has good graphics features with a wide selection of forecasting algorithms available.

MINITAB is a large interactive system for data analysis and statistics. It is extremely easy to learn and contains the ability to produce output that is easy to understand. However, it does not contain algorithms for the exponential smoothing models nor does it have a routine for deseasonalizing data. Although these two features are very important, MINITAB is still useful for a variety of reasons. The syntax of MINITAB is so simple that a user can write his/her own macros for various algorithms not included in the various commands. In addition, the software is very easy to learn and a wide variety of books in elementary statistics are now including material on MINITAB in the text. Last, it is available on a wide variety of hardware.

SCA is a powerful statistical system available for many computers. Its forecasting features are good and many of its users praise it highly. The software, like many others, uses English-like statements as well as analytic statements for analysis. The software is mainly used only for regression-based and advanced time series methods.

AUTOBOX is an automatic forecasting system for the identification, fitting, and forecasting of advanced time series models of the Box–Jenkins variety. This program departs from the procedures used by SAS, MINITAB, and other software by incorporating a completely automatic feature performed without user intervention. For the readers of this book and "purists", the user does have the option of fitting advanced time series models in the usual way. However, the ability to have a software system achieve some labors of forecasting in an automatic manner is a watershed application of the techniques of artificial intelligence to time series analysis. Although one would argue that this software is not an expert system, it is at least comparable with other automatic techniques of the other software systems. AUTOBOX is designed to run on PC compatibles with PC-DOS or MS-DOS of 2.0 and higher.

Although there are a great many choices in obtaining forecasting software, the user should be aware of the usefulness of each type. Below, we offer a set of criteria for choosing among the various and increasing supply of computer software. Others have offered additional criteria, but this set is most useful for choosing forecasting software. Some of these criteria are also very useful for choosing other types of computer software. They include the following:

1   easy-to-use interface language;
2   ability to handle a variety of inputs;
3   wide selection of algorithms (forecasting procedures);
4   ability to move programs from one computer environment to another;
5   readable and usable output report features;
6   documentation that is readable and easy to follow;
7   cost to end-user and multiple users.

Criterion 1 refers to access control capabilities at the operating system level. Users desire an easy interface language with a simple and understandable syntax for describing the necessary tasks for forecasting. To be usable, a language should identify and control the capabilities of the software, build and retrieve data files according to user-specified data organizations, and specify selected forms of output and printable reports.

Criterion 2 suggests that software should be able to handle unrestricted quantities and types of input. This is an ideal which is not likely to happen; however, software should be able to handle multiple-input files with different formats. In addition, the user interface language should provide for data identification and labeling for immediate and subsequent use. If data are properly labeled by source, quality, editing conditions, and timeliness, it should be possible to retrieve, analyze, store, or repeat the data later according to these conditions. It is not likely that all software will achieve this ideal in the near future.

Criterion 3 states that a wide variety of forecast procedures should be available as part of the software's capabilities. End-users must be able to select the procedure that meets the needs of the forecasting problem. Software that focuses on only a few procedures may be undesirable for many users although it may otherwise have excellent features.

Criterion 4 refers to the desirability of portable data, programs, test cases, and documentation. Since operating systems vary, this goal may also be difficult to satisfy. End-users should recognize that hardware and some software producers deliberately limit the portability of programs for the purposes of creating market disadvantages for competitors.

Criterion 5 concerns the type of output reports which can be produced. Present-day equipment limits the type of output. Software should provide language to make specification of reports simple with respect to format, content layout, and particular hardware devices to be used. Finally, report control language should provide a convenient method of preparing clear and adequate titles and headings in tables and reports.

Criterion 6 is important because end-users simply cannot operate the wide variety of menu options without adequate and readable documentation. Different levels of documentation are necessary. New users need tutorials, adequate explanations, and an ample supply of illustrations. Casual users require detailed and self-contained documentation on the few options that they use most often. Advanced users require more details concerning performance evaluation, portability, ability to modify output reports and make forecast speculations, and maintenance of the forecast package.

Finally, criterion 7 refers to the expenses attached to acquiring the software. End-users are concerned with more than the vendor price. Does the software need additional equipment and what are the costs associated with it? Since there may be multiple users, the price and availability of multiple copies of the software may be crucial.

In evaluating software, the end-user or forecaster must be aware of the features of the software with respect to the above criteria. Only an informed and wise end-user can evaluate properly the usefulness of purchasing forecasting software. The above criteria can be invaluable aids. Finally, the foregoing list of computer software is not designed to be exhaustive but to give the forecaster a start in selecting the best software for his/her purpose. Forecasters should note that the author and his colleagues have extensively used many of the software products mentioned.

Note this book is neither a statistics text nor a guide to the use of any particular software system. To forecast, one needs only to have access to one or more of the publicly available software systems. One aim of this book is to teach students how to interpret the output of computerized forecasting programs. Therefore forecasting methods are emphasized but the mathematical underpinnings of the routines of various software systems are not emphasized. Although theory is important, the emphasis here is on methods and applications, and the use of these methods in solving specific forecasting problems is illustrated. Theory is discussed when appropriate.

1.6   Classifying Forecasts

If a forecast is prepared in December of one year for an action to be taken in June of the following year, the lead time for the forecast is said to be six months. The lead time for a forecast is the distance in time between the point at which the forecast is made and the point in time to which it refers. Lead time can be used as an aid for classifying forecasts.

Forecasts can be classified as short term, medium term, and long term. To classify forecasts, one must look at the rate of change of the time series as well as the lead time. For example, if one forecasts the position of a guided missile, the short-term forecast is a fraction of a second. A minute ahead is a long-term forecast and medium-term forecasts would be in between. In contrast, the short-term forecast of demand for a new electric power and light generating facility may be a ten year period and a long-term forecast would be over a 20 year period. Most forecasting problems, however, fall between these two extremes. A short-term forecast of the demand for canned vegetable products would lie between the extremes. Likewise, the medium- and long-term forecasts would also lie between the extremes (figure 1.1).

1.7   Summary

Forecasts are a critical input into a wide range of managerial and administrative decision-making. While forecasting is important, some people question the validity, reliability, and efficacy of a discipline involved in predicting future events. Forecasting is desirable, however, because it is a necessary part of managerial planning and control.

Accurate forecasting may reduce losses associated with unsold inventory and losses due to unavailable inventory that could have capacity or costs associated with inefficient methods of production among others.

Type of forecast	Short term	Medium term	Long term
Guided missile	1 second	1–60 seconds	1 minute or more
Canned vegetables	2 years	2–10 years	10 years
Electric power generating facility	10 years	10–20 years	20 years or more

FIGURE 1.1

Forecasting methods range from relatively simple techniques to many-dimensional and sophisticated techniques. The study of forecasting methods begins by examining extrapolative techniques such as moving averages and exponential smoothing. The study progresses to the methods of time series decomposition, regression, and econometric methods. In the last sections on quantitative techniques, the methods of time series autocorrelation analysis, adaptive methods, and Box–Jenkins procedures are considered. Finally, the concepts of leading indicators and other interpretative techniques are used to predict changes in business conditions.

In the last chapter, methods for evaluating and revising forecasts are introduced. Also, the role of forecasting in business planning and control is considered.

Forecasting usually requires the use of a computer software system to produce not only the forecasts but also to perform the model identification and diagnostic testing. In this chapter, a discussion of some of the more well-known software systems was made. The list was not exhaustive but all of them have reasonably good features. With few exceptions, all have been used extensively by the author and his colleagues. Three of them, SAS, Minitab, and Micro-TSP, will be used extensively in this book. The reader should note that statistical results may vary owing to the numerical analytic capabilities of the software, the features of the computer, and the mathematical formulas underlying the forecast methods used. Thus, we can expect differences between results unless the procedures, software, and computer configurations are exact.

Forecasts are classified as either long, medium, or short term. The term of the forecast is related to both the lead time and the rate of change in the time series. Thus forecasts are classified by consideration of both these factors since they indicate how crucial the timing of decisions based on forecasts can be.

Further Reading

Armstrong, J. S. (1985) *Long-Range Forecasting; From Crystal Ball to Computer.* New York: Columbia University Press.

Fildes, R. and Wood, D. (eds) (1978) *Forecasting and Planning*. New York: Praeger.

Firth, M. (1977) *Forecasting Methods in Business and Management*. Philadelphia, PA: International Ideas.

Granger, C. W. J. (1980) *Forecasting in Business and Economics*. New York: Academic Press.

Gross, C. W. and Peterson, R. T. (1983) *Business Forecasting*. Boston: Houghton Mifflin.

Hanke, J. E. and Reitsch, A. G. (1989) *Business Forecasting*. New York: Allyn and Bacon.

Jarrett, J. (1985) An evaluation of micro-computer software for forecasting, *Statistical Software Newsletter*, 11, November, 100–5.

Jarrett, J. (1987) Evaluating a PC software system for automatic statistical time series modeling and forecasting, *Statistical Software Newsletter*, 13, December, 115–17.

Levenbach, H. and Cleary, J. P. (1981) *The Beginning Forecaster; The Forecasting Process through Data Analysis*. Belmont, CA: Lifetime Learning Publications.

Robbinson, C. (1971) *Business Forecasting: An Economic Approach*. London: Thomas Nelson.

Sullivan, W. and Claycombe, W. W. (1977) *Fundamentals of Forecasting*. Reston, VA: Reston Publishing.

Wheelwright, S. C., Makridakis, S. and McGee, V. E. (1983) *Forecasting: Methods and Applications*. New York: Wiley.

Willis, R. E. (1987) *A Guide to Forecasting for Planners and Managers*. Englewood Cliffs, NJ: Prentice-Hall.

PART II

Time Series Techniques

CHAPTER 2

Smoothing Methods

Objectives

The purpose of this chapter is to introduce concepts used in the forecasting of numerical data called time series. In particular, by the end of this chapter you will be able to:

1 Graph a times series data set properly.
2 Understand the meaning of time series techniques for forecasting.
3 Evaluate the accuracy of a time series forecasting method.
4 Understand and apply the various time series forecasting methods.
5 Understand why one method may be more appropriate for one time series than another method.
6 Understand the differences between the various forecasting methods.

Outline

Key Terms

- Stationary
- Time Series

- Moving Average

- Exponential Smoothing

- Mean Square Error

- Root Mean Square Error

- Mean Absolute Percentage Error

- Adaptive-response-rate Single Exponential Smoothing

- Second Moving Average

- Double Exponential Smoothing

- Holt's Two-parameter Linear Exponential Smoothing

- Seasonal pattern

- Winters' model

2.1   Introduction

Statistical theory teaches that the arithmetic mean is an estimator that minimizes the error of estimating the value of a population mean. Specifically, the mean is an unbiased estimator and is the best one available if the results of a simple random sample are analyzed.[1] However, situations exist where the mean is not desirable for purposes of prediction. For example, if one is to estimate the sixth value in a simple series 1,2,3,4,5, the mean is equal to 3 and is obviously not a reliable estimator. If the mean is applied in this situation as an estimator for this series, clearly the result is a systematic pattern of forecast errors and these errors are not randomly distributed about zero.

If the arithmetic mean is to be used for forecasting then it is crucial to understand the conditions that determine its usefulness for predictive purposes. Firstly, the data must be randomly distributed and stationary (horizontal) over time. By *stationary*, we mean that the plot of the time series appears similar to a horizontal straight line with the x-axis being the time variable. If the data are not random, some pattern or trend in the data is implied. Existence of a pattern implies that a predictive method be used that can predict the pattern more accurately than the mean. Secondly, an arithmetic mean can only predict accurately when the series is stationary. For a nonstationary series like 1,2,3,...,9, the arithmetic mean will consistently overestimate the first half of the series and underestimate the last half of the series. Thus the mean is an adequate estimate for a stationary random series, that is, a series that does not exhibit a pattern, trend, or any evidence of periodicity. As we develop our knowledge of forecasting tools, we shall use the method of prediction by the arithmetic mean as a benchmark for comparison when other methods are to be analyzed.

One limitation of the arithmetic mean as a forecasting tool is that a large number of sample observations are required to use it as an estimator. For time series data, the sample size continually increases with time as new sample observations become

---

1   An estimator is unbiased if its expected value equals the value of the parameter being estimated.

available. New sample observations are included in the calculation of the arithmetic mean, creating storage and computational problems when forecasts for a large number of items are needed. Lastly, the arithmetic mean of a time series is not responsive to changes in the mean value over time. For example, if a step change occurs in the data, the arithmetic mean will not catch it and this forecasting method will be consistently inaccurate for a lengthy period of time. An approach to minimizing the inaccuracy in this method is to keep the same number of sample observations in calculating the mean. The result is a procedure of averaging the most recent constant number of sample observations. This procedure is called the method of moving averages.

In this chapter, two basic types of forecasting methods will be introduced: moving averages and smoothing. Moving averages are developed based on an average of weighted past observations. Smoothing methods are based on averaging past observations of a time series in a decreasing or exponential manner.

Figure 2.1 outlines the forecasting procedure for the methods discussed in this chapter. If you are at time period t in figure 2.1, you can observe past values of the variable of interest X_t or values forward in the future. One forecasting procedure is selected, the model is applied to the historical observations, and forecasted values F_{t+1} are obtained. Once forecast values are available, they can be compared with known values and the forecast error e can be calculated.

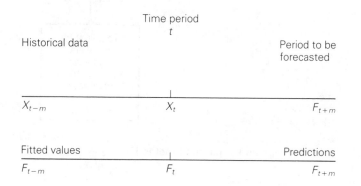

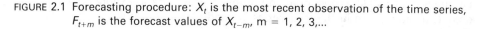

FIGURE 2.1   Forecasting procedure: X_t is the most recent observation of the time series, F_{t+m} is the forecast values of X_{t-m}, m = 1, 2, 3,...

To forecast, one can take the following steps:

1 Choose a forecasting method based on forecast knowledge about the observed pattern of the time series.
2 Use the forecasting method to develop fitted values of the data.
3 Calculate the forecast error.
4 Make a decision about the appropriateness of the model based on the measure of forecast error.

The procedures to be discussed in this chapter are summarized in figure 2.2. Each succeeding method models the pattern in the data beginning with the simplest methods, single moving averages and single-parameter exponential smoothing. Adaptive response rate single exponential smoothing (ARRSES) optimizes the

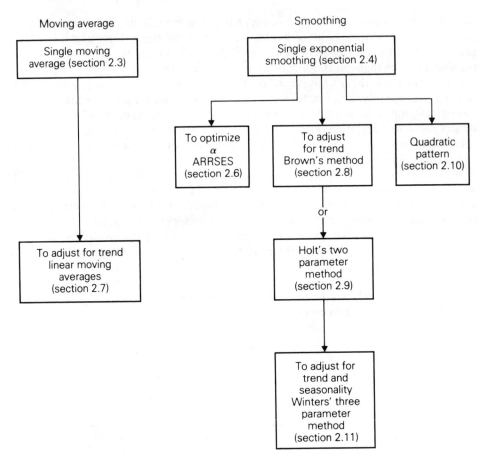

FIGURE 2.2 Moving average and smoothing method

parameters of single exponential smoothing and quadratic exponential smoothing models if the pattern in the time series is quadratic.

If the data pattern has a trend, the method of linear moving averages adjusts the single moving average for trend. Similarly, Brown's method adjusts single exponential smoothing for trend. Holt's method is another smoothing method with an adjustment for trend; however, Holt's method is a two-parameter model. Finally, Winters' method is a smoothing method with adjustments for trend and seasonality. It contains three parameters.

We shall begin our examination of these methods by studying how graphs or plots of data are presented and analyzed.

2.2   Graphing a Time Series

For the purpose of forecasting, we study a historical data set called a *time series*. A time series consists of the data of interest to a forecaster on a single variable which have been collected in a consistent way over time at equally spaced intervals.

Forecasters analyze time series to search for patterns. Many techniques are available to search for patterns, but all begin with the graphing or plotting of a time series data set.

In searching for patterns in the time series, plots and graphs can be particularly helpful. The forecaster will benefit greatly by learning how to interpret graphs properly. Even when working with computerized graphics procedures, an understanding of the structure and interpretation of graphs is a useful skill. A brief introduction to this important topic is given in this section.

A variety of graph papers are commercially available. The best results occur when using those types that are marked in small squares with bold lines at every fifth or tenth square. Do not confuse this graph paper with quadrule paper, which has light blue horizontal and vertical lines spaced four or five to an inch (or two to a centimeter). Although some refer to this as graph paper, the wider spacing of the lines makes accurate graphing more difficult. Paper that has the bold lines marked every sixth or twelfth line in both the horizontal and vertical directions should not be used; this is intended for architectural drafting, not forecasting. If working with monthly time series data is desirable, then special paper is available with the horizontal scale divided in groups of 12 and often with months premarked. Computerized techniques are available for use with all these special characteristics. Software user guides should be consulted to learn how to use these special graphing techniques.

Forecasters have developed a number of conventions to help in the drawing and interpreting of graphs. Although these conventions are not sacrosanct, they can be useful in helping others interpret an analysis of the data and in turn the forecast.

Every graph should have a heading such as "Manufacturing and trade inventories in 1972 dollars". The heading can be at either the top or bottom. In addition, information concerning the geographic area or organized group that is represented and the period of time that the data cover should be disclosed. In figure 2.3, the geographic area is the United States (USA) for the year 1981 where the data were seasonally adjusted. This last phrase will become clearer when we study the next chapter. Use of headnotes and footnotes is advisable to insure understanding and give clarity to the graph.

The source note should show the source of the data and should appear below the graph. The information in the source note should be detailed enough to permit the reader to obtain the original data easily. It is not necessary for the source note to follow bibliographic reference format. Note that the source of the data is given in figure 2.3. However, if the data were referenced in a previous table, they need not be re-referenced.

The scales on the graph should be easy to read and understand. Vertical and horizontal scale lines should be marked on all graphs. For computerized graphing techniques, the scale marking may be plotted automatically by the software. However, when the forecaster becomes accustomed to the software, he/she can usually override the automatic features to produce the graph which is easiest to read. For example, each scale should be labeled in a prominent place with the name of the variable and units of the scale. Often automatic features may not give desirable results. Hence a great deal of practice is advisable in the use of the graphics and forecasting software. In plotting time series, the horizontal scale refers to historical or chronological time. In this case, the scale units are shown, but the scale is not otherwise labeled. In figure 2.3, the year 1981 is the horizontal scale with marks for each month.

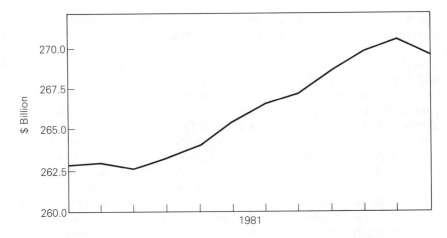

FIGURE 2.3 Manufacturing and trade inventories (in billion US 1972 dollars), seasonally
adjusted
Source: Survey of Current Business, March 1982, p. S-3

For the vertical scale, show the base line. Points on a graph are plotted relative to a base line that is normally zero or for ratios or index numbers at 100. Occasionally, other values could stand for the base line. With rare exceptions, the horizontal base line should always be shown on the graph. Frequently, when all the values of the variable lie above the base line, it will be the same as the horizontal scale line. One shortcoming of computer graphics software is that it shows the horizontal scale line and not the base line. Figure 2.3 is plotted by computer graphics software with the horizontal scale in billion dollars beginning with 260.0 and increasing to 270.0.

Scale units should be chosen such that the graph shows adequate detail. If this requires an excessive amount of blank space between the base line and the lowest plotted values of the variable, an exception is made. In this situation, the vertical scale can begin above the zero point.

The intent of the graph should be made clear. Whenever possible, the plotting of the data points should be connected by straight lines. Occasionally, certain software systems will not connect points and thus the forecaster is constrained. In plotting residuals from forecasts where the randomness of the points is to be emphasized, the points may be left unconnected.

Separate graphs should be plotted for each time series studied. Several different variables can be plotted on the same graph when it is necessary to compare patterns. Some form of difference in the plotting symbols should be used when plotting two or more times series on the same graph. Computer graphics programs generally use different symbols to mark the data points for the different series. Always be cautious when using different colors. They look attractive on the original but will not be distinguishable when reproduced in a monochrome format.

2.3   Single Moving Averages

Forecasting time series by the method of moving averages involves calculating the average of the sample observations and then employing that average as the forecast for the next period. The number of sample observations included in the calculation of the average is specified at the initiation of the forecasting process. We use the term *moving average* because as each new sample observation becomes available a new average is calculated by dropping the oldest sample observation and including the newest one. As each new average is calculated, it becomes the forecast for the next period. Consequently, each forecast employs the same number of sample observations from the time series and includes only the most recent observations.

Example 2.1

Data for manufacturing and trade inventories in constant (1972) dollars (seasonally adjusted, total (billion dollars)) for the United States for 1981 are collected. It is decided to forecast by the method of moving averages. Since the appropriate method to employ is not known, both a three and a five month moving average will be calculated and used to forecast. The purpose is to analyze and determine the usefulness and limitations of this method for the set of data given in table 2.1.

TABLE 2.1 Forecasting using moving averages

| (1) | | (2) | (3) | (4) | (5) |
| | | Time | Observed | Three-month | Five-month |
Year	Month	period	values	moving average	moving average
1981	Jan	1	262.8		
	Feb	2	262.9		
	Mar	3	262.6		
	Apr	4	263.2	262.8	
	May	5	263.9	262.9	
	Jun	6	265.4	263.2	263.1
	Jul	7	266.5	264.2	263.6
	Aug	8	267.1	265.3	264.3
	Sep	9	268.5	266.3	265.2
	Oct	10	269.7	267.4	266.3
	Nov	11	270.4	268.4	267.4
	Dec	12	269.4	269.5	268.4

Note: Observed values are manufacturing and trade inventories in constant (1972) dollars end of year (seasonally adjusted) total ($ billions) for 1981.
Source: Survey of Current Business, March 1982, p. S-3.

Table 2.1 illustrates the application of the technique of moving averages to the time series of manufacturing and trade inventories in the United States for 1981 (seasonally adjusted). Both a three and a five month moving average are calculated.

The three month moving average for April is simply the sum of the observations for January, February, and March, that is, 262.8 + 262.9 + 262.6 = 788.3, divided by three to equal 262.8. Thus, this average becomes the forecast for April.

To forecast for May, we subtract the value for January (262.8) from the total (788.3) and add the actual value for April (263.2) to equal 788.7. Divide the new total by three to find the forecast for May, which is 262.9. This method is continued to forecast for all the months of the year. The last figure in column 4,269.5, is the average for the period of September through November. Last, the actual value for December would not be used in a calculation until we forecast for January 1982.

Similarly, the result of employing a five month moving average is contained in column 5. The forecast for June is the sum of the observed values for January through May divided by five. The final entry in column 5 is the sum of the observed values for July through November. Last, as each new observation for manufacturing and trade inventories becomes available, the moving average can be easily recalculated and updated.

The values for manufacturing and trade inventories, the three month moving average (MA3), and the five month moving average (MA5) are plotted in figure 2.4. Note that the five month moving average has a greater smoothing effect than the three month moving average. Obviously, if all the observations were used (a 12 month moving average), the arithmetic mean of all the data would be used to forecast. However, when only one month is used to forecast, the most recent period is the forecast value.

In general, the arithmetic mean is the best estimator when the sample observations are random; thus a large number of periods should be used when the actual values are random. The effect of using a large number of periods will be to utilize a nearly horizontal line to forecast, which smooths the fluctuations associated with randomness. Similarly, a small number of periods can be used when there is a pattern in the sample observations. Using only a few periods to forecast permits the moving average to approximate and follow the pattern in the observations. These forecasts will trail the pattern in the actual data, lagging the movements by several periods.

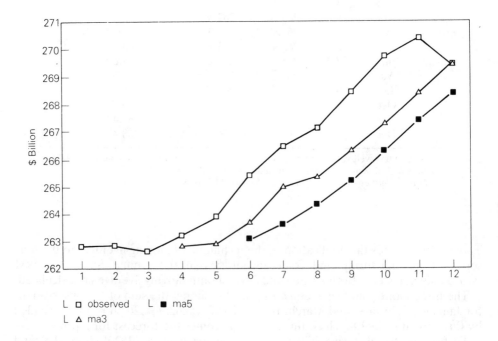

FIGURE 2.4 Observed values and forecasts by moving-average method

The moving average method is stated algebraically as follows:

$$F_{t+1} = \frac{X_t + X_{t-1} + \ldots + X_{t-n+1}}{n}$$

$$= \frac{1}{n}\left(\sum_{i=t-n+1}^{t} X_i \right) \tag{2.1}$$

where t is the most recent observation and $t + 1$ is the next period. This formula requires that the forecaster has the values of the past n observations.

Applying the concept of adding a new observation and dropping the oldest observation, we can restate the formula as

$$F_{t+1} = \frac{1}{n}\left(\sum_{i=t-n}^{t-1} X_i \right) + \frac{1}{n}(X_t - X_{t-n})$$

$$= F_t + \frac{X_t}{n} - \frac{X_{t-n}}{n} \tag{2.2}$$

Note that the formula for the moving average is simply an adjustment of the forecast F_t in the previous period. Obviously, if n is increased, the smoothing effect becomes greater because a much smaller adjustment is made for each new time period. If the data are highly volatile, this is an attractive characteristic.

The method of moving averages is a very attractive procedure for forecasting since the data requirements are small. However, this technique is not as widely used as the next procedure we shall study, exponential smoothing, since the requirement that data be stationary is very limiting. However, the method of moving averages is more attractive than simply using the arithmetic mean of an entire time series to forecast. It is more flexible because n can be changed to respond to observable patterns in the data.

2.4 Single Exponential Smoothing

There are major limitations to the use of moving averages. First, for purposes of computation, the past n sample observations must be available. If a large number of items are to be forecast, these data can require considerable storage space. Second, equal weights are given to all past observations and no weight is given to observations earlier than period $t-n+1$. Recent observations, however, may contain more information than older ones in forecasting future movements. Thus, we may wish to give more weight in forecasting to the recent observations than to the older ones.

A method that simplifies forecasting calculations and has small data requirements is entitled *exponential smoothing*. This method also produces self-correcting forecasts with built-in adjustments that regulate forecast values by changing them in the opposite direction of earlier errors.

To develop this method we begin with equation (2.2) and rewrite it as

$$F_{t+1} = \frac{X_t}{n} - \frac{F_t}{n} + F_t \tag{2.3}$$

by making the substitution $F_t = X_{t-n}.$[2] Furthermore, this equation can then be rewritten as

$$F_{t+1} = \frac{1}{n} X_t + \left(1 - \frac{1}{n}\right) F_t \tag{2.4}$$

Equation (2.4) is a forecast based on weighting the most recent observation with a weight of value $1/n$ and weighting the most recent forecast with a weight of $1-1/n$. Since the number of periods n is a constant, the fraction $1/n$ must be greater than zero and less than unity. If we substitute α for $1/n$, the basic model is written as

$$F_{t+1} = \alpha X_t + (1-\alpha)F_t \tag{2.5}$$

where t is the current time period, F_{t+1} and F_t are the forecast values for the next and the current periods, and X_t is the current observed value. α is called the *smoothing constant* and it takes values between zero and unity. Since the above equation contains only one constant, it is the model for single exponential smoothing.

Example 2.2

Data on manufacturing inventories in constant (1972) dollars by month (seasonally adjusted, total (billion dollars)) for the United States in 1981 is collected from the *Survey of Current Business*. These data are to be used to forecast by the method of single exponential smoothing. Since we are uncertain as to the best value of α to use for forecasting, three values (0.2, 0.5, and 0.8) are chosen. These data and forecasts are contained in table 2.2.

For the month of March 1981, assuming $\alpha = 0.2$, the forecast is

$$F = \alpha (X_{\text{Feb}}) + (1 - \alpha)F_{\text{Feb}}$$
$$= 0.2 (145.8) + (1 - 0.2)(145.5)$$
$$= 145.6$$

Note also that the initial forecast (February) is the value of the observation in the previous time period (January).

  Single-parameter exponential smoothing is very simple since only one value, the last period's forecast, must be saved. In essence, the entire time series is embodied in that forecast. If we express F_t in terms of the preceding observed X_{t-1} and the forecast F_{t-1} values, then the equivalent for the next period's forecast becomes

---

2 We assume that the forecast in period t is equal to the observed value of the time series in period $t - n$. This is a reasonable assumption in the development of exponential smoothing models.

TABLE 2.2 Forecasting by single parameter exponential smoothing

(1)		(2)	(3)	(4)	(5)	(6)
			Observed	*Exponentially smoothed*		
		Time	*values*	*Alpha 2*	*Alpha 5*	*Alpha 2*
Year	*Month*	*period*	X_t	$\alpha = 0.2$	$\alpha = 0.5$	$\alpha = 0.8$
1981	Jan	1	145.5	—	—	—
	Feb	2	145.8	145.5	145.5	145.5
	Mar	3	146.1	145.6	145.7	145.7
	Apr	4	146.4	145.7	145.9	146.0
	May	5	146.6	145.8	146.2	146.3
	Jun	6	146.3	146.0	146.4	146.5
	Jul	7	146.8	146.1	146.2	146.3
	Aug	8	146.9	146.2	146.5	146.7
	Sep	9	147.7	146.3	146.7	146.9
	Oct	10	148.1	146.6	147.2	147.5
	Nov	11	148.1	146.9	147.7	148.0
	Dec	12	147.5	147.1	147.9	148.1

Note: Observed values are for manufacturing inventories in constant (1972) dollars, by month (seasonally adjusted), total ($ billions) for 1981.
Source: *Survey of Current Business*, March 1982, p. S-3.

$$F_{t+1} = \alpha X_t + (1 - \alpha)\left[\alpha X_{t-1} + (1 - \alpha)F_{t-1}\right] \tag{2.6}$$

which simplifies to

$$F_{t+1} = \alpha X_t + \alpha(1 - \alpha)X_{t-1} + (1-\alpha)^2 F_{t-1} \tag{2.7}$$

This new equation is a second-degree single exponential smoothing model. We can continue this for several earlier periods which shows that all preceding values of X are reflected in the current forecast. Thus the name for this procedure is derived from the successive weights α, $\alpha(1 - \alpha)$, $\alpha(1 - \alpha)^2$, $\alpha(1 - \alpha)^3$,..., which decrease exponentially. More recent periods in the time series receive greater weight in computing the forecast. Progressively less forecasting importance is assigned to older data values of X. In fact, the oldest observed value for X is eventually wiped out. The forecasting procedure can be modified at any time by changing the value of α.

The effect of the value of α on the amount of smoothing that is done can be observed in figure 2.5. A large value of α (0.8) yields little smoothing in the forecast. Alternatively, a small value of α (perhaps 0.20, 0.10, or 0.05) yields considerable smoothing. The result stems from the following.

We can rewrite equation (2.5) as follows:

$$F_{t+1} = F_t + \alpha(X_t - F_t) \tag{2.8}$$

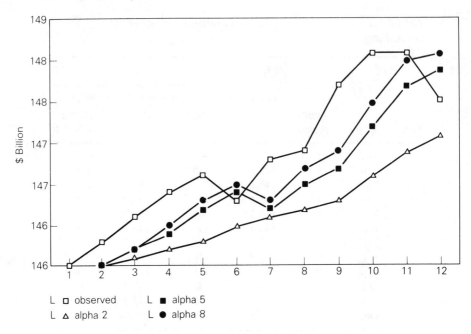

FIGURE 2.5 Observed values and forecasts by single exponential smoothing

and this is simply

$$F_{t+1} = F_t + \alpha e_t \qquad (2.9)$$

where the forecast error e_t for period t, is just the actual minus the forecast. Thus we see that the forecast provided by exponential smoothing is the old forecast plus an adjustment for the error occurring in the last forecast.

When α is close to unity, the new forecast includes a substantial adjustment for the error in the previous forecast. However, if α is too close to zero, the new forecast will include only a small adjustment for error. Thus the effect of the size of α is similar to the effects of different values for the number of sample observations when computing a moving average. Finally, single exponential smoothing produces forecasts that trail the pattern in the sample data. This occurs because the procedure only adjusts the next forecast for some percentage of the most recent forecast error and cannot predict changes in direction of the series.

The question regarding the best smoothing constant is still not answered. We shall address this question next.

2.5 Evaluating the Error in Forecasting

The major advantage of single exponential smoothing is its limited data requirements and relative simplicity. Despite the attractiveness of exponential smoothing, there are several important limitations. First, forecasts generated by exponential smoothing are sensitive to the specification of the smoothing constant. The choice of α is based on a trial-and-error process. Second, exponential smoothing techniques result in forecasts that lag behind the turning points in actual time series data. To evaluate the usefulness of this technique, we are required to evaluate the error in forecasting.

In equation (2.9), the error in period t was defined as the actual value X_t less the predicted value F_t:

$$e_t = X_t - F_t \tag{2.10}$$

An examination of the error in forecasting permits the forecaster to evaluate whether the technique accurately mirrors the patttern exhibited in the sample observations. An evaluation of the reliability of any technique requires the specification of criteria; however, there is no generally acceptable best measure. There are a number of measures for assessing forecast accuracy. One generally accepted technique for evaluating exponential smoothing (and many other) techniques is the *mean square error* (MSE):

$$\text{MSE} = \frac{\Sigma(e_t)^2}{n} = \frac{\Sigma(X_t - F_t)^2}{n} \tag{2.11}$$

This measure defines error as the sum of squares of the forecast errors e_t divided by the sample size, that is, the number of forecast periods. To indicate the computation of MSE consider the next example.

Example 2.3

Continuing with example 2.2, the forecaster is asked to evaluate the forecasts prepared by the methods of exponential smoothing. Each set of forecasts is to be evaluated to determine which smoothing constant α is best, that is, has the smallest measurable error. Table 2.3 exemplifies the computation of MSE for $\alpha = 0.2$.

Applying the formula for MSE to the data of table 2.3, we find

$$\text{MSE} = \frac{\Sigma(e_t)^2}{n}$$

$$= \frac{8.35}{11}$$

$$= 0.759$$

Thus, for the forecast based on smoothing constant $\alpha = 0.2$, the sum of the squared forecast errors divided by the number of forecasts (MSE) is 0.759. If we calculate the MSE for the other constants, we find

$$\text{MSE} = 0.302 \quad \text{when} \quad \alpha = 0.5$$

and

$$\text{MSE} = 0.200 \quad \text{when} \quad \alpha = 0.8$$

TABLE 2.3 Computation of MSE and RMS for exponential smoothing model where $\alpha = 0.2$

Period	(1) Observed value X_t	(2) Forecast F_t	(3) Error e_t	(4) Square of error $(e_t)^2$
1	145.5	—	—	—
2	145.8	145.5	0.3	0.09
3	146.1	145.6	0.5	0.25
4	146.4	145.7	0.7	0.49
5	146.6	145.8	0.8	0.64
6	146.3	146.0	0.3	0.09
7	146.8	146.1	0.7	0.49
8	146.9	146.2	0.7	0.49
9	147.7	146.3	1.4	1.96
10	148.1	146.6	1.5	2.25
11	148.1	146.9	1.2	1.44
12	147.5	147.1	0.4	0.16

$$8.35 = \Sigma(e_t)^2$$
$$\text{or} \quad = \Sigma(X_t - F_t)^2$$

Note: Data taken from table 2.2

The relatively wide range of MSE values indicates the important role of α in exponential smoothing.

Since MSE is a measure of the squares of individual forecast errors, forecasters often find it convenient to compute the square root of MSE. This measure, which is referred to as the *root mean square error* (RMS), thus measures error in terms of units which are equal to the original values studied. It is defined as follows:

$$\text{RMS} = \left[\frac{\Sigma(e_t)^2}{n}\right]^{1/2} = (\text{MSE})^{1/2} \tag{2.12}$$

and for the above example is equal to 0.871, 0.550, and 0.447 for the smoothing constants 0.2, 0.5, and 0.8 respectively.

A third method for calculating forecast error, *mean absolute percentage error* (MAPE), is based on the assumption that the severity of error is linearly related to its size. It is defined by

$$\text{MAPE} = \frac{\Sigma \lvert e_t \rvert / x_t}{n} \times 100 \tag{2.13}$$

and is the sum of the absolute values of the errors divided by the corresponding observed values all divided by the number of forecasts. For the data of table 2.4, we obtain MAPE = 0.53%.

As a measure of forecast error, MAPE is less valid than either MSE or RMS except for the simplifying assumption made before. However, many computer

TABLE 2.4 Computation of MAPE for exponential smoothing model where $\alpha = 0.2$

Period	(1) Observed value X_t	(2) Absolute error $|e_t|$	(3) Proportion calculation $|e_t|/X_i$
1	145.5	—	—
2	145.8	0.3	0.0021
3	146.1	0.5	0.0034
4	146.4	0.7	0.0048
5	146.6	0.8	0.0055
6	146.3	0.3	0.0021
7	146.8	0.7	0.0048
8	146.9	0.7	0.0048
9	147.7	1.4	0.0095
10	148.1	1.5	0.0101
11	148.1	1.2	0.0081
12	147.5	0.4	0.0027

$$0.0579 = \Sigma |e_t|/X_t$$

$$\text{MAPE} = \frac{0.0579}{11} \times 100 = 0.53\%$$

Note: Data are taken from tables 2.2 and 2.3.

programs for forecasting contain code for the automatic calculation of MAPE as well as MSE or RMS. We shall return to the analysis of MAPE as a method for evaluating forecasts in chapter 11. For the most part, MSE and RMS are more useful and statistically more sound measures of forecast error. The choice between these two is simply whether we wish to have units in squared errors or in the square root of the sum of the squared errors. They both measure error in the same way.

As noted above, a very useful application of measuring forecast accuracy is the determination of the appropriate smoothing constant α to be used in exponential smoothing. This constant determines the extent to which past observations influence the forecast. Small values for α dampen out remote observations in the time series slowly and result in a slow response to changes in the parameters describing the mean level of the time series. A forecast using a large value for α, however, quickly dampens out remote observations in the time series and results in a more rapid response. Unfortunately, this can cause the forecasting procedure to respond to irregular movements in the time series. These irregular movements do not reflect changes in the parameter describing the time series. Thus such a situation is no better than a forecasting procedure which reacts very slowly to changes in the parameter of time series.

To solve the problem of choosing α, a sensitivity analysis of the historical time series is performed with different values for the smoothing constant. For each value over a range of values, an exponential smoothing module forecast is prepared and the appropriate measure of forecast accuracy is calculated. In practice, studies have found that values of from 0.05 to 0.30 work very well in exponential smoothing modules. Values of α greater than 0.30 usually indicate that an alternative forecasting model would be more appropriate.

As an example, sensitivity analysis was applied to a set of historical data to determine the appropriate smoothing constant. The results are given in table 2.5. The lowest MSE and RMS occur for $\alpha = 0.20$. This would indicate that this smoothing constant is "best" for the historical time series. If the "best" smoothing constant was greater than 0.3 this may indicate that a particular type of time series behavior such as seasonality is present. Thus, forecasting models that recognize these other forms of behavior would provide a better forecast.

To sum up, the forecasting process is thoroughly integrated with the measurement of forecasting accuracy. As indicated in the preceding paragraph, the process requires the forecaster to generate a series of forecasts over an interval and to calculate the MSE or RMS for each forecast. The smoothing constant that results in the lowest MSE or RMS is the value that should be chosen for forecasting. As new data are obtained, the process is repeated to generate other new "best" smoothing constants. If the "best" smoothing constant is greater than 0.3 then another forecasting model is suggested. Thus, a problem with exponential smoothing is that in almost all cases the smoothing constant must be supplied by the model user and that it is often chosen by the trial-and-error methods illustrated in this section.

TABLE 2.5

α	MSE	RMS
0.02	39.3	6.27
0.04	39.2	6.26
0.06	38.6	6.21
0.08	38.4	6.20
0.10	38.2	6.18
0.12	38.1	6.17
0.14	37.9	6.16
0.16	37.4	6.12
0.18	37.4	6.12
0.20	37.2	6.10
0.22	37.6	6.13
0.24	37.8	6.15
0.26	37.9	6.16
0.28	38.1	6.17
0.30	38.3	6.19

2.6   Adaptive-response-rate Single Exponential Smoothing

Since specification of the smoothing constant is a problem associated with exponential smoothing, a method that does not require specification of α has a distinct advantage. *Adaptive-response-rate single exponential smoothing* (ARRSES) is attractive when a great many items have to be forecast. By the term "adaptive", we mean that this method can change the value of an unspecified α on an ongoing basis. ARRSES changes the value of α when there is a change in the basic pattern requiring a different smoothing constant.

The formula for ARRSES forecasting is

$$F_{t+1} = \alpha_t X_t + (1-\alpha_t)F_t \tag{2.14}$$

where

$$\alpha = \left| \frac{E_t}{M_t} \right| \tag{2.15}$$

$$E_t = \beta e_t + (1-\beta)E_{t-1} \tag{2.16}$$

is the smoothed error,

$$M_t = \beta|e_t| + (1-\beta)M_{t-1} \tag{2.17}$$

is the absolute smoothed error,

$$e_t = X_t - F_t \tag{2.18}$$

is the error, and

$$\beta = 0.2$$

Note that equation (2.14) indicates that the forecast F_{t+1} is a linear combination of the previous period's observed value and forecast. The smoothing constant is the absolute value of E_t divided by M_t. E_t is a linear combination of the forecast error e_t and the smoothed error e_{t-1} in the previous period. M_t is the absolute smoothed error and is a linear combination of the forecast error and the absolute smoothed error in the previous period. Generally, β is assigned the value 0.2, indicating that in equations (2.16) and (2.17) the first term is given a much smaller weight than the second term. With $\beta = 0.2$, the second term is given four times more importance.

Example 2.4

Data on manufacturing inventories in constant (1972) dollars by month (seasonally adjusted for the United States (billion dollars)) in 1981 is to be forecast by ARRSES. These are the same data as employed and forecast in example 2.3. The data and method are described in table 2.6

For period 9, for example, the computations are as follows:

$$F_9 = \alpha_8 X_8 + (1 - \alpha_8)F_8$$

$$= (0.590)(146.9) + (1 - 0.590)(146.7)$$

$$= 146.8$$

TABLE 2.6   Forecasting using adaptive-response-rate single exponential smoothing

1981	Period	(1) Observed value X	(2) Forecast F	(3) Error e_t	(4) Smoothed error E_t	(5) Absolute smoothed error M_t	(6) α_t value
Jan	1	145.5					
Feb	2	145.8	145.5	0.3	0.060	0.060	1.000
Mar	3	146.1	145.5	0.6	0.108	0.108	1.000
Apr	4	146.4	146.1	0.3	0.146	0.146	1.000
May	5	146.6	146.4	0.2	0.157	0.152	1.000
Jun	6	146.3	146.6	−0.3	0.066	0.186	0.355
Jul	7	146.6	146.3	0.3	0.113	0.209	0.541
Aug	8	146.7	146.5	0.2	0.130	0.207	0.678
Sep	9	147.7	146.8	0.9	0.284	0.346	0.821
Oct	10	148.1	147.5	0.6	0.347	0.397	0.874
Nov	11	148.1	148.0	0.1	0.298	0.338	0.882
Dec	12	147.5	148.1	−0.6			

Note: Manufacturing inventories in constant (1972) dollars by month (seasonally adjusted) total ($ billions) for 1981.
Source: Survey of Current Business, March 1982, p. S-3.

When the observed value for period 9 becomes known, the following computations are made:

$$e_9 = 147.7 - 146.8 = 0.9$$

$$E_9 = 0.2(0.9) + 0.8\,(0.130) = 0.284$$

$$M_9 = 0.2|0.9| + 0.8(0.207) = 0.346$$

and

$$\alpha_9 = \left| \frac{0.284}{0.346} \right| = 0.821$$

After each value is calculated, the new forecast is made and then the ARRSES model parameters are re-estimated. When all new observed values are exhausted, the forecast is completed.

ARRSES forecasts can be compared with other exponentially smoothed forecasts by computing the MSE for all forecasts for a given time series. For the data of table 2.6, the calculation is

$$MSE = \frac{\Sigma e_t^2}{n}$$

$$= \frac{0.3^2 + 0.5^2 + ... + (-0.6)^2}{11}$$

$$= 0.057 \ (RMS = 0.239)$$

Recall from example 2.3 that the MSE for the single-parameter exponentially smoothed model with $\alpha = 0.8$ was equal to 0.200. Hence, for this set of time series data and for the time period covered, the ARRSES technique outperformed the single-parameter exponential models for the smoothing constants studied. A different time series, or data for a different time period, may have different results. However, for this time series, the fitted values are quite close to the observed values.

   Another question with respect to ARRSES relates to the appropriate value for the constant β. In general, β is usually set at 0.1 or 0.2; these values reduce the effects of previous errors e and allow the response to occur gradually. At times a forecaster may generate ARRSES forecasts for values of β over the interval from 0.1 to 0.2 and choose the value that minimizes MSE. This is similar to the procedure for choosing the constant; α is computed for period $t+1$ instead of for period t to allow the system to "settle" by not being overly responsive to changes in the time series.

2.7   Linear Moving Averages

Applying the method of moving averages to a set of sample observations (time series) containing a pattern gives forecasts that consistently underestimate the observed value. Re-examination of example 2.1 and figure 2.4 indicates how a time series exhibiting a consistent upward pattern results in moving-average forecasts that underestimate the observed value. In example 2.1, randomness is present; however, to observe more clearly how a consistent upward pattern or trend affects the results, consider the next example where no randomness is present.

Example 2.5

A hypothetical series with a pattern of growth is to be forecast by the method of moving averages ($n = 3$) (see table 2.7).

TABLE 2.7

Period	Observed value	Forecast	Error
1	2.5	—	—
2	5.0	—	—
3	7.5	—	—
4	10.0	5.0	5.0
5	12.5	7.5	5.0
6	15.0	10.0	5.0
7	17.5	12.5	5.0
8	20.0	15.0	5.0
9	22.5	17.5	5.0
10	25.0	20.0	5.0

In the example (table 2.7), note that the forecast lags the observation by two periods consistently. The error for each period that is forecast is the same, 5. A perfect linear trend in the series results in a systematic error that cannot be avoided unless an alternative technique is attempted.

To avoid this error, forecasters may apply the method of linear moving averages. This method requires the calculation of a *second moving average*, that is, a moving average of the moving average of the observed values. These second moving averages will lag behind the single moving average by the same amount as the single moving average lags the observed values. Therefore differences between observed values and single moving averages will be the same as the differences between single and second moving averages.

To forecast with the absence of systematic error, the following formulas apply:

$$\text{(single moving average)} \quad S_t = \sum_{i=t}^{t-n+1} \frac{X_i}{n} \tag{2.19}$$

$$\text{(second moving average)} \quad S_t' = \sum_{i=t}^{t-n+1} \frac{S_i}{n} \tag{2.20}$$

$$\text{(overall forecast)} \quad a_t = S_t + (S_t - S_t') = 2S_t - S_t' \tag{2.21}$$

$$\text{(trend in observations)} \quad b_t = \frac{2}{n-1}(S_t - S_t') \tag{2.22}$$

Table 2.8 contains the application of the linear moving average procedure to the hypothetical data of example 2.5. Note that column 3 is the result of applying single moving averages ($n = 4$) to the observed time series. Column 4 is the error associated with this initial forecast.

Equation (2.20) is similar in form to calculating single moving averages but is the equation of the second moving average; the result is in column 5. Equation (2.21) permits one to forecast by adding to the single moving average, the difference between the single and second moving averages. Equation (2.22) permits a direct estimate of the trend in the data. The moving averages are the average of n observations which are centered in the middle of the n observations, $(n-1)/2$. If the single moving average was used for prediction, it would follow the observed value by $(n-1)/2b$ where b is the trend change or pattern in each period. However,

$$\frac{n-1}{2}b_t = S_t - S_t'$$

which is the difference in the two moving averages. We can rewrite the formula for b_t in the form of equation (2.22).

Finally, to forecast for any period, the formula for the forecast is

$$F_{t+m} = a_t + b_t m \tag{2.23}$$

where m is the number of periods ahead to be predicted.

To illustrate the method of linear moving averages, consider the next example.

TABLE 2.8   Forecasting by linear moving averages – time series with consistent upward pattern and no random component

(1)	(2)	(3) Single moving average	(4)	(5) Second moving average	(6)	(7) Overall	(8)
Period	Observed value	n = 3	Error	n = 3	Error	forecast	Error
1	2.5	—	—				
2	5.0	—	—				
3	7.5	—	—				
4	10.0	5.0	5.0				
5	12.5	7.5	5.0				
6	15.0	10.0	5.0				
7	17.5	12.5	5.0	7.5	5.0	17.5	0
8	20.0	15.0	5.0	10.0	5.0	20.0	0
9	22.5	17.5	5.0	12.5	5.0	22.5	0
10	25.0	20.0	5.0	15.0	5.0	25.0	0
Key to formulas	(X_t)	(S_t)	(e_t)	(S'_t)	(e'_t)	a_t	

Note: Column 4 = column 2 − column 3
        Column 6 = column 3 − column 5
        Column 7 = column 3 + column 6
        Column 8 = column 2 − column 7

Example 2.6

Observed values on exports of goods and services for the United States (exclusive of transfers under military grants) by year (billion dollars) exhibit both trend and randomness over the period 1971–82. The data are to be forecast by linear moving averages with $n = 3$. Table 2.9 presents data for the time series (column 2) and the results of the steps of the linear moving-average procedures.

As a point of departure let us consider the computations for one row of the table:

$$F_{1978} = a_{1977} + b_{1977} \times 1$$

$$= 203.7 + 49.0 \times 1$$
$$= 252.7 \qquad \text{(by equation (2.23))}$$

where

$$a_{1977} = 2S_{1977} - S'_{1977}$$
$$= 2(154.7) - 105.7$$
$$= 203.7 \qquad \text{(by equation (2.21))}$$

$$b_{1977} = \frac{2}{3-1}(S_{1977} - S'_{1977})$$

$$= 1 \times (154.7 - 105.7)$$

$$= 49.0 \qquad \text{(by equation (2.22))}$$

$$S_{1977} = \frac{X_{1974} + X_{1975} + X_{1976}}{3}$$

$$= \frac{145 + 148 + 171}{3}$$

$$= 154.7 \qquad \text{(by equation (2.19))}$$

$$S'_{1977} = \frac{S_{1974} + S_{1975} + S_{1976}}{3}$$

$$= \frac{79.7 + 106.0 + 131.3}{3}$$

$$= 105.7 \qquad \text{(by equation (2.20))}$$

All rows of table 2.9 are calculated using the methods outlined above. The result of this procedure is to have improved forecasts when a consistent pattern exists in the time series when compared with the results of simple moving averages. Specifically, the mean square error will be smaller for the results of linear moving averages than for the results of simple moving averages.

For the above problem, we can calculate the MSE for the comparable forecasts from 1978 to 1981. The results are

$$\text{MSE} = 1599.2 \text{ for simple moving averages} \qquad (\text{RMS} = 39.99)$$

and

$$\text{MSE} = 3323.7 \text{ for linear moving averages} \qquad (\text{RMS} = 57.65)$$

TABLE 2.9 Forecasting a series with a trend and randomness with a linear moving average $(n = 3)$

(1)	(2) Observed value	(3) Single moving average	(4) Second moving average	(5)	(6)	(7) F
Year	X_t	S_t	S'_t	a	b	m = 1
1971	66					
1972	72					
1973	101					
1974	145	79.7				
1975	148	106.0				
1976	171	131.3				
1977	185	154.7	105.7	203.7	49.0	
1978	221	168.0	130.7	205.3	37.3	252.7
1979	229	192.3	151.3	233.3	41.0	242.6
1980	345	211.7	171.7	251.7	40.0	274.3
1981	376	265.0	190.7	339.3	74.3	291.7
1982						413.6

Note: Observed values are exports of goods and services for the United States (exclusive of transfers under military grants) by year ($ billions). Values are rounded to the nearest billion dollars.
Source: Survey of Current Business, various issues, p. S-1.

Hence the error associated with linear moving averages for this time series and for the time period covered is greater than the error associated with the simple moving average approach. It is not an appropriate model for these data.

2.8   Brown's Linear Exponential Smoothing

When a consistent pattern is evident in the time series, single exponential smoothing, like simple moving averages, becomes less useful.[3] A forecaster can resort to other methods for smoothing and forecasting a time series. One method is to extend the single exponential smoothing technique to *double exponential smoothing*. This technique is simply the exponential smoothing of the single exponential values.

The single exponential series is given by

$$S_{t+1} = \alpha X_{t+1} + (1 - \alpha)S_t \tag{2.24}$$

which is a rewriting of equation (2.5). In turn, the double exponential smoothing equation is

$$S'_{t+1} = \alpha S_{t+1} + (1 - \alpha)S'_t \tag{2.25}$$

However, the application of double exponential smoothing to time series yields results that generally lag the movements in observed values of the time series. Thus, both single and double exponentially smoothed values have the same property of lagging the actual values.

Brown's linear exponential smoothing method provides an additional correction similar to that of linear moving averages. In this method, the difference between the single and double smoothed values is added to the single smoothed value and adjusted for the pattern in the data. The equations for these adjustments are

$$a_t = S_t + (S_t - S'_t) = 2S_t - S'_t \tag{2.26}$$

$$b_t = \frac{\alpha}{1 - \alpha}(S_t - S'_t) \tag{2.27}$$

$$F_{t+m} = a_t + b_t m \tag{2.28}$$

where m is the number of periods ahead to be forecast.

Example 2.7

Data on the dollar value of real estate loans, total for the United States, is to be forecast by Brown's single-parameter linear exponential smoothing method. These data are for 1980 and 1981 by month and are presented in column 1 of table 2.10. To demonstrate this forecasting technique, the calculation for one row will be presented next, assuming a smoothing constant of $\alpha = 0.2$. Finally, for period 1, the initial values for single exponential smoothing (column 2) and double exponential smoothing (column 3) are set at the value of the observation for period 1 (January 1980 in this example).

---

3   As an alternative to trend-adjusted exponential smoothing, we can use a mathematical transformation of the original time series to adjust for trend. For example, we could use a single exponential smoothing model of first differences of the time series. Differencing is discussed in chapter 7.

TABLE 2.10 An application of Brown's linear exponential smoothing

			(1)	(2)	(3)	(4)	(5)	(6)
				$\alpha = 0.2$	$\alpha = 0.2$			
				Single	Double			
			Observed	exponential	exponential			
		Period	values	smoothing	smoothing			
Year	Month	t	X_t	S_t	S'_t	a	b	F
1980	Jan	1	101	101.0	101.0	101.0	0.000	
	Feb	2	102	101.2	101.0	101.4	0.050	
	Mar	3	103	101.6	101.0	102.2	0.150	101.5
	Apr	4	105	102.3	101.3	103.3	0.250	102.4
	May	5	105	102.8	101.6	104.0	0.300	103.6
	Jun	6	105	103.2	101.9	104.5	0.325	104.3
	Jul	7	106	103.8	102.3	105.3	0.375	104.9
	Aug	8	107	104.4	102.7	106.1	0.425	105.7
	Sep	9	108	105.1	103.2	107.0	0.475	106.6
	Oct	10	109	105.9	103.7	108.1	0.550	107.6
	Nov	11	110	106.7	104.3	109.1	0.600	108.7
	Dec	12	112	107.8	105.0	110.6	0.700	109.8
1981	Jan	13	113	108.8	105.8	111.8	0.750	111.4
	Feb	14	114	109.8	106.6	113.0	0.800	112.6
	Mar	15	114	110.6	107.4	113.8	0.800	113.8
	Apr	16	115	111.5	108.2	114.8	0.825	114.6
	May	17	117	112.6	109.1	116.1	0.875	115.7
	Jun	18	118	113.7	110.0	117.4	0.925	117.0
	Jul	19	119	114.8	111.0	118.6	0.950	118.4
	Aug	20	120	115.8	112.0	119.6	0.950	119.6
	Sep	21	122	117.0	113.0	121.0	1.000	120.6
	Oct	22	123	118.2	114.0	122.4	1.050	122.1
	Nov	23	124	119.4	115.1	123.7	1.075	123.5
	Dec	24	125	120.5	116.2	124.8	1.075	124.8
1982	Jan	25						125.9

Note: Observed values are for real estate loans, total for the United States (rounded to the nearest billion dollars).
Source: Survey of Current Business, various issues, p. S-15.

The computations for period 4 are as follows:

$$S_4 = 0.2X_4 + 0.8S_3 \qquad \text{(column 2)}$$

$$= 0.2(105) + 0.8(101.6) = 102.3$$

$$S'_4 = 0.2S_4 + 0.8S'_3 \qquad \text{(column 3)}$$

$$= 0.2(102.3) + 0.8(101.0) = 101.3$$

$$a_4 = 2S_4 - S'_4 \qquad \text{(column 4)}$$

$$= 2(102.3) - 101.3 = 103.3$$

$$b_4 = \frac{0.2}{0.8}(S_4 - S'_4) \qquad \text{(column 5)}$$

$$= \tfrac{1}{4}(102.3 - 101.3) = 0.250$$

$$F_5 = a_4 + b_4(1) \qquad\qquad\qquad\qquad\qquad \text{(column 6)}$$

$$= 103.3 + 0.25 = 103.55 \text{ or } 103.6$$

The results of table 2.10 indicate that both the single and double exponential smoothing techniques are less than the actual values when the trend is growing. If the trend was falling, then the exponential values would be greater than the actual values. In general, the degree of difference between the actual and single exponential values is the same as the degree of difference between the single and double exponential values. Thus, if we add the difference between the single and double exponential values, we arrive at the value of *a* (column 4).

To refine the forecast further, we calculate *b* (column 5) and equation (2.27) and add it to *a* for one-period-ahead forecasts (column 6 and equation (2.28)).

If we desired to forecast more than one period ahead, we would substitute the appropriate number of periods ahead that we wish to forecast for the value of equation (2.28). However, the further ahead the forecast is required, the greater is the inaccuracy that can be expected. Also, we should remember that the degree of forecasting accuracy is dependent on the appropriateness of the smoothing constant α used in calculating the single and double exponential smoothing values.

When we measure MSE, we find it is smaller for this technique in comparison with single exponential smoothing or linear moving averages. In general, Brown's single exponential smoothing is more accurate than either single exponential smoothing or the method of second moving averages. Furthermore, the data requirements for this method are no greater than for single exponential smoothing and considerably less than for second moving averages.

2.9   Two-parameter Linear Exponential Smoothing

Holt's two parameter linear exponential smoothing is an extension of Brown's method whereby a growth factor is added to the smoothing equation. The method smooths the trend values directly. Three equations and two smoothing constants are included in this technique:

$$S_t = \alpha X_t + (1 - \alpha)(S_{t-1} + b_{t-1}) \qquad\qquad\qquad (2.29)$$

where *b* is the growth factor, and

$$b_t = \gamma(S_t - S_{t-1}) + (1 - \gamma) b_{t-1} \qquad\qquad\qquad (2.30)$$

where γ is the new smoothing constant for the trend, and

$$F_{t+m} = S_t + b_t m \qquad\qquad\qquad\qquad\qquad (2.31)$$

Equation (2.29) adjusts S_t directly for the growth b_{t-1} of the previous period, by adding it to the smoothed value S_{t-1} for the previous period. Thus the previous smoothed value is adjusted in line with the trend directly and eliminates the lag in smoothing. The trend is updated by equation (2.30) and is expressed as the difference between the last two smoothed values. When growth exists in the observed values of a time series, new observations will be greater than the previous ones. Furthermore, there still remains some randomness which can be eliminated by smoothing the growth $(S_t - S_{t-1})$ in the last period by γ and adding it to the previous estimate of growth b_{t-1} multiplied by $1 - \gamma$. Thus, equation (2.30) is a smoothing expression for updating a trend. Last, equation (2.31) is employed to predict m periods ahead by adding to the base value S_t the growth factor b_t times m.

Example 2.8

Data on average hourly earnings of nonsupervisory workers in hospitals in the United States (S1C 806) is collected every quarter by the Bureau of Data Management and Strategy of the Health Care Financing Administration/DHHS. Observations are made every quarter, and table 2.11 contains the data for the 12 month period ending March for the years 1977–82. These data are to be forecast by linear exponential smoothing adjusted for trend. The smoothing parameter α for single exponential smoothing is assumed equal to 0.2, and the smoothing parameter γ for the trend is assumed to be equal to 0.3. For period 1, the smoothing value is equal to $4.42, the observed value for that period. The trend for period 1 is zero.

TABLE 2.11 An application of two-parameter linear exponential smoothing to data on earnings

Twelve-month period end March	Period	(1) Observed value $X_t(\$)$	(2) $\alpha = 0.2$ Smoothing of data $S_t(\$)$	(3) $\gamma = 0.3$ Smoothing of trend b_t	(4) Forecast $m = 1$ $F_{t+m}(\$)$
1977	1	4.42	4.42	0	—
1978	2	4.75	4.49	0.021	4.42
1979	3	5.16	4.64	0.061	4.51
1980	4	5.60	4.88	0.114	4.70
1981	5	6.23	5.24	0.188	4.99
1982	6	7.01	5.75	0.284	5.43
1983	7	—	—	—	6.03

Note: Observed values are for average hourly earnings of nonsupervisory workers in hospitals (S1C 806) in the United States.
Source: US/DHHS, Health Care Financing Administration, Bureau of Data Management and Strategy, *Health Care Financing Trends*, 3(1), June 1982, p. 15; 2(3), Summer 1981, p. 16.

To illustrate the computations, consider period 3.

column 2

$$S_3 = 0.2X_3 + 0.8(S_2 + b_2) \quad \text{(by equation (2.29))}$$
$$= 0.2(5.16) + 0.8(4.49 + 0.021) = 4.64$$

column 3

$$b_3 = 0.3(S_3 - S_2) + 0.7b_2 \quad \text{(by equation (2.30))}$$
$$= 0.3(4.64 - 4.49) + 0.7(0.021) = 0.061$$

column 4

$$F_4 = S_3 + b_3 m \qquad \text{(by equation (2.31))}$$
$$= 4.64 + (0.061 \times 1) = \$4.70$$

As with all exponential smoothing techniques, the accuracy of the forecasts is dependent on the appropriateness of the smoothing constants used. In this procedure, there are smoothing parameters in the model and hence two sources of variation. When compared with single exponential smoothing, Holt's method is better when the measures of forecast error are smaller. The MSE for Holt's procedure is 1.323, the RMS is 1.150, and the MAPE is 17.83 percent. If single exponential smoothing is applied with a constant of 0.2 to the observed values of table 2.11, the forecast for 1983 would be $5.48, the MSE would be 1.434, the RMS would be 1.198, and the MAPE would be 17.49 percent. Thus the forecast would show less upward growth, the MSE and RMS would be larger, and the MAPE would be fractionally smaller. Obviously, the MAPE would be of limited value in this application. By all other standards, Holt's procedure would be preferred over single exponential smoothing.

2.10 Quadratic Exponential Smoothing

A higher form of exponential smoothing is appropriate when the underlying pattern of the observed time series is quadratic, cubic, or of a higher order. In this section, only quadratic exponential smoothing is presented.

To incorporate the quadratic term in the forecasting equation, a third level of smoothing (triple smoothing) enters the estimation process. The third level of smoothing permits the estimation of the quadratic term of the forecasting equation.

The equations for quadratic exponential smoothing are as follows:

$$S_t = \alpha X_t + (1-\alpha)S_{t-1} \tag{2.32}$$

$$S_t' = \alpha S_t + (1 - \alpha)S_{t-1}' \tag{2.33}$$

$$S_t'' = \alpha S_t' + (1 - \alpha)S_{t-1}'' \tag{2.34}$$

$$a_t = 3S_t - 3S_t' + S_t'' \tag{2.35}$$

$$b_t = \frac{\alpha}{2(1 - \alpha)^2} [(6 - 5\alpha)S_t - (10 - 8\alpha)S_t' + (4 - 3\alpha)S_t''] \tag{2.36}$$

$$c_t = \frac{\alpha^2}{(1 - \alpha)^2} (S_t - 2S_t' + S_t'') \tag{2.37}$$

$$F_{t+m} = a_t + b_t m + 0.5c_t m^2 \tag{2.38}$$

The detailed statistical derivation of the above equations is explained by Brown (1963, pp. 140–2). These equations are considerably more complicated than those for single and double exponential smoothing techniques. Except for these additional computational problems, the approach is similar to the procedures presented for the simpler methods. As a point of departure, we shall illustrate this technique for the earnings data of example 2.8. These data are presented in table 2.12 along with the computations of the parameters of the quadratic exponential model. Initial estimates for columns 2, 3, and 4 are set equal to the observed value for period 1. To illustrate the computations for period 3, with $\alpha = 0.20$, consider the following:

TABLE 2.12 An application of quadratic exponential smoothing for the data of example 2.8, $\alpha = 0.2$ and $m = 1$

		(1)	(2)	(3)	(4)	(5)	(6)	(7)	(8)
			Single	Double	Triple				
Twelve-month		Observed	smooth-	smooth-	smooth-				
period ending	Period	value ($)	ing	ing	ing				
March	t	X_t	S_t	S_t'	S_t''	a	b	c	F
1977	1	4.42	4.42	4.42	4.42				
1978	2	4.75	4.49	4.43	4.42	4.60	0.266	0.003	
1979	3	5.16	4.62	4.47	4.43	4.94	0.714	0.008	4.62
1980	4	5.60	4.82	4.54	4.45	5.44	1.310	0.014	4.98
1981	5	6.23	5.10	4.65	4.49	6.12	2.088	0.023	5.46
1982	6	7.01	5.48	4.82	4.56	7.04	3.046	0.032	6.11
1983	7								6.94

Note: Data are average hourly earnings of nonsupervisory workers in hospitals in the United States (SIC 806). See note to table 2.11.

column 2

$$S_3 = 0.2X_3 + 0.8S_2 \quad \text{(by equation (2.32))}$$
$$= 0.2\,(5.16) + 0.8\,(4.49) = 4.62$$

column 3

$$S_2' = 0.2S_3 + 0.8S_2' \quad \text{(by equation (2.33))}$$
$$= 0.2(4.49) + 0.8(4.42) = 4.43$$

column 4

$$S_2'' = 0.2S_3' + 0.8S_2'' \quad \text{(by equation (2.34))}$$
$$= 0.2(4.43) + 0.8(4.42) = 4.42$$

column 5

$$a_2 = 3S_3 - 3S_3' + S_3'' \quad \text{(by equation (2.35))}$$
$$= 3(4.49) - 3(4.43) + 4.42 = 4.60$$

column 6

$$b_2 = \frac{0.2}{2(1 - 0.2)^2}[(6-1)\,S_3 - (10 - 1.6)S_3' + (4 - 0.6)S_3''] \quad \text{(by equation (2.36))}$$

$$= 0.15625[5(4.49) - (8.4)(4.43) + (3.4)(4.42)] = 0.266$$

$$c_2 = \frac{0.2^2}{(1 - 0.2)^2}[4.49 - 2(4.43) + 4.42] = 0.003 \quad \text{(by equation (2.37))}$$

$$F_{2+1} = 4.60 + 0.266 + 0.5(0.003)^2 = 4.62 \quad \text{(by equation (2.38))}$$

Note that the mere sophistication of a forecasting procedure does not guarantee increased accuracy. To evaluate this procedure, we have to obtain the magnitude of the forecast error and compare it with the results of other procedures. Furthermore, as with all exponential smoothing procedures, the accuracy of the results is strongly associated with the appropriateness of the smoothing constants selected.

When the pattern of the data is quadratic, then quadratic exponential smoothing is most useful. If the pattern in the time series is not quadratic, the forecast error will be large, indicating poor performance of the quadratic model. A plot of the observed and fitted and forecast values (figure 2.6) will indicate that the quadratic model will tend to follow the pattern in this time series. In comparison with the results of using Holt's method, the quadratic model produces fitted and forecast values which more closely approximate the observed values. In addition, we can compare the statistics of forecast error shown in table 2.13.

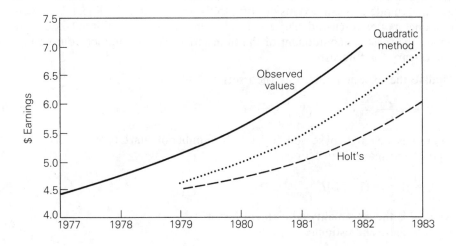

FIGURE 2.6 Hourly earnings and forecasts. Data from tables 2.11 and 2.12

TABLE 2.13

	Quadratic model	Holt's two-parameter model
MSE	0.519	1.323
RMS	0.720	1.150
MAPE	11.68%	17.83%

For all three measures of forecast accuracy, MSE, RMS, and MAPE, the quadratic exponential smoothing model performed better than Holt's two-parameter method for the smoothing constants chosen. Thus, for the time series studied – hourly earnings of nonsupervisory workers in hospitals – the quadratic method produced better results. However, the quadratic model will not apply for time series with a consistent linear pattern. For those situations, Holt's method will outperform the quadratic model.

2.11 An Application of Exponential Smoothing to Seasonal Data

One last form of exponential smoothing deserves special consideration at this time. Economic statisticians found that time series data exhibit regular repeating patterns within a calendar year. This *seasonal pattern* occurs consistently from year to year. Although this phenomenon will be examined more thoroughly in chapter 3, we should point out that Winters (1960) developed a method for adjusting for seasonal or periodic movement within the framework of linear exponential smoothing. Hence, the procedure can be employed to forecast for a time series exhibiting both a trend and seasonal pattern.

The *Winters' model*, which is a three-parameter linear and seasonal exponential smoothing model, is an extension of Holt's two-parameter linear exponential smoothing model discussed earlier. The extension is an additional equation to estimate the seasonal component of the time series. For this model, four equations are necessary for forecasting.

1 Update the exponentially smoothed series

$$S_t = \alpha \frac{X_t}{I_{t-L}} + (1 - \alpha)(S_{t-1} + b_{t-1}) \tag{2.39}$$

where L is the length of seasonality, i.e. the number of quarters or months in a year.

2 Update the seasonality estimate

$$I_t = \beta \frac{X_t}{S_t} + (1 - \beta)I_{t-L} \tag{2.40}$$

where I is the seasonality adjustment factor.

3 Update the trend estimate

$$b_t = \gamma(S_t - S_{t-1}) + (1 - \gamma)b_{t-1} \tag{2.41}$$

4 Forecast m periods into the future

$$F_{t+m} = (S_t + b_t m)I_{t-L+m} \tag{2.42}$$

Equation (2.39) updates the smoothed series; it is only a slight variation of equation (2.29) of Holt's two-parameter model. In equation (2.29), X_t is divided by I_{t-L} which adjusts the original observations X_t for seasonality and, in turn, removes the effects of seasonality, as best as can be measured, from the time series.

Equation (2.40) is the estimate of the seasonal component X_t/S_t multiplied by the constant β plus the old seasonal estimate I_{t-L} multiplied by $1 - \beta$. Thus the updating of the seasonal estimates is itself an exponential smoothing process. Also, X_t is divided by S_t to express the value as an index, rather than in absolute terms. This permits the averaging of the new seasonal estimate with the seasonal index for the previous period.

Equation (2.41) is the update of the trend component and is arrived at by the usual exponential smoothing process. This equation is the same as equation (2.30) of Holt's model.

Finally, after equation (2.39), equation (2.40) is obtained for m periods into the future by equation (2.42). It is very similar to Holt's equation (2.31). The difference is that this estimate for the future period $t+m$ is multiplied by I_{t-L+m}. This is the final seasonal index available, and therefore becomes the forecast adjustment for seasonality.

The flexibility and power of Winters' seasonal exponential smoothing is best illustrated through an actual application to a time series that has both a seasonal and trend component.

Example 2.9

Data on new plant and equipment expenditures, total nonfarm business (billion dollars, unadjusted) exhibits both a seasonal and trend pattern. These data are exhibited in table 2.14 for the period covering the first quarter of 1979 through the first quarter of 1982. Note that the first quarter of each year is the smallest value for that year and the fourth quarter is the largest value for that same year.[4]

TABLE 2.14 An application of three-parameter seasonal exponential smoothing to data on expenditures for new plant and equipment ($ billions) (Winters' model)

Year	Quarter	(1) Period	(2) Observed values X_t	(3) Single smoothing S_t	(4) Seasons I_t	(5) Trend b_t	(6) Forecast F_{t+m}
		−3			0.897		
		−2			1.006		
		−1			1.001		
		0		63.6	1.096	1.60	
1979	1	1	57.3	64.9	0.889	1.54	
	2	2	66.8	66.4	1.006	1.53	66.8
	3	3	68.4	68.0	1.004	1.54	67.9
	4	4	78.0	69.9	1.108	1.61	76.2
1980	1	5	65.2	71.9	0.900	1.69	63.9
	2	6	74.0	73.6	1.006	1.69	74.1
	3	7	74.1	75.0	0.994	1.63	75.7
	4	8	82.3	76.2	1.091	1.54	84.6
1981	1	9	69.8	77.7	0.899	1.53	69.8
	2	10	79.6	79.2	1.005	1.52	79.7
	3	11	81.8	81.0	0.998	1.58	80.6
	4	12	90.4	82.6	1.093	1.58	90.4
1982	1	13	73.8				75.3

Note: Data are for new plant and equipment expenditures, total nonfarm business in the United States ($ billions, unadjusted). Smoothing constants are $\alpha = 0.2$, $\beta = 0.6$, and $\gamma = 0.2$. Computations have been rounded for printing in this table. MSE = 1.345, RMS = 1.160, and MAPE = 1.07%.
Source: Survey of Current Business, various issues, p. S-1.

---

4 Larger data sets are usually suggested for estimating the seasonal pattern; however, for illustrative purposes this smaller data set is used.

To carry out this exponential smoothing technique requires an initialization phase. This phase uses past data to start the forecasting process. After initialization, the updating phase is begun where forecasts are altered as each new observation becomes available.

The purpose of initialization is to start the forecasting system with reliable estimates of S_t, I_t, and b_t. Furthermore, the initialization method presented here is a variation of Winters' (1960) original method. An alternative procedure is presented by Johnson and Montgomery (1976).

1 First, we estimate the trend by calculating the mean of the time series for the first year and last year of the observed value X_t:

first year

$$\tfrac{1}{4}(X_1 + X_2 + X_3 + X_4) = \tfrac{1}{4}(57.3 + 66.8 + 68.4 + 78.0)$$

$$= 67.6$$

last year

$$\tfrac{1}{4}(X_9 + X_{10} + X_{11} + X_{12}) = \tfrac{1}{2}(69.8 + 79.6 + 81.8 + 90.4)$$

$$= 80.4$$

To estimate the initial slope b_0, of the trend equation we calculate

$$b_0 = \frac{80.4 - 67.6}{8} = 1.6$$

2 Note that the change from the middle of the first year (1979) to the middle of the third year (1981) occurs over eight quarters. The mean of the first year is quarter 2.5 (i.e $(1 + 2 + 3 + 4)/4 = 2.5$).

Hence the deseasonalized level at time $t = 0$ is now estimated by

$$S_0 = \frac{X_1 + X_2 + X_3 + X_4}{4} - 2.5b_0$$

$$S_0 = 67.6 - 2.5(1.6)$$

$$= 63.6$$

Thus the initial trend line is

$$\hat{S}_t = S_0 + b_0 t \tag{2.43}$$

$$= 63.6 + 1.6t$$

3 To estimate the initial seasonal factors, we set up table 2.15. Column 1 is the original data X_t. Column 2 is the result of using equation (2.43) to find trend values for each period. These trend values are derived in an identical fashion. For example, consider period 3:

$$\hat{S}_3 = 63.6 + 1.6(3) = 68.4$$

Seasonal factors are determined by first dividing the observed values X_t by the estimated trend values $\hat{S}_t$. These ratios are presented in column 3. The second step

TABLE 2.15 Finding initial estimates of seasonal factors for input into Winters' model

	(1)	(2)	(3)	(4) Initial seasonal factors	(5) Revised initial seasonal factors
Period	X_t	$\hat{S}_t$	$X_t/\hat{S}_t$		
0		63.6			
1	57.3	65.2	0.879	0.895	0.897
2	66.8	66.8	1.000	1.004	1.006
3	68.4	68.4	1.000	0.999	1.001
4	78.0	70.0	1.114	1.094	1.096
5	65.2	71.6	0.911		
6	74.0	73.2	1.011		
7	74.1	74.8	0.991		
8	82.3	76.4	1.078		
9	69.8	78.0	0.895		
10	79.6	79.6	1.000		
11	81.8	81.2	1.007		
12	90.4	82.8	1.092		

Note: Observed values are the same as in table 2.14.

is to average these ratios for each quarter to determine initial factors. For this example, the initial seasonal factor for period 1 is

$$\frac{0.879 + 0.911 + 0.895}{3} = 0.895$$

These initial factors are presented in column 4.

4 Finally, the sum of the seasonal factors must sum to 4 (4×1.0). Since the factors in column 4 total 3.992, we revise these initial factors by the ratio of 4/3.992. This ratio (1.002) is multiplied by each quarterly seasonal factor to produce the revised initial seasonal factors of column 5. These last seasonal factors will be part of the input to the forecasting model.

Once the initial estimates of trend and seasonality are made, Winters' model incorporates them into the exponential smoothing process of equations (2.39) – (2.42). Thus the initial estimates of the trend, the observed value at time $t = 0$, and seasonal factors can be continuously updated. By returning to table 2.14, the updating process can be explained.

For period 1, we update as follows

$$S_1 = \alpha \frac{X_1}{I_{-4}} + (1 - \alpha)(S_0 + b_0) \qquad \text{(column 3)}$$

With $\alpha = 0.2$, we have

$$S_1 = 0.2 \left(\frac{57.3}{0.897} \right) + 0.8(63.6 + 1.6) = 64.9$$

$$I_1 = \beta \frac{X_1}{S_1} + (1 - \beta)I_{-4} \qquad\qquad \text{(column 4)}$$

With $\beta = 0.6$, we have

$$I_1 = 0.6 \left(\frac{57.3}{64.9} \right) + 0.4(0.897) = 0.889$$

$$b_1 = \gamma(S_1 - S_0) + (1 - \gamma)b_0$$

With $\gamma = 0.2$, we have

$$b_1 = 0.2(64.9 - 63.6) + 0.8(1.6)$$

$$= 1.54$$

Finally, for one-period-ahead forecasts,

$$F_2 = (S_1 + b_1 (1))I_{-3}$$

$$= (64.9 + 1.54)(1.006) = 66.8$$

The updating process (table 2.15) continues until all the data are exhausted. As new observations are collected, the updating process continues. The statistics for measuring forecast error with Winters' model were calculated and compared with those for Holt's method where the smoothing constants for the data and trend were kept the same (0.2 and 0.2). These statistics are shown in table 2.16

As the statistics indicate, the forecast error when forecasting this data set by Winters' model is small compared with that obtained with Holt's model. The difference in the accuracy is because Winters' model incorporates an adjustment for the seasonal pattern in the data whereas Holt's model does not. Figure 2.7 shows the results graphically. Note that Winters' model closely approximates the movement of the data across the graph, whereas Holt's model merely follows the general upward pattern in the data and does not change when the seasons of the year change.

There are two principal limitations associated with this three-parameter exponential smoothing process. First, as with all exponential smoothing processes, the selection of the smoothing constants (α, β, and γ) is made by finding the smallest MSE (or RMS or MAPE). Since there are three parameters, this can be a very expensive process. The constants used in table 2.14 are those recommended by Winters, but they are not universally acceptable. Second, as we shall see in the next chapter, a cyclical component exists in many observed time series. It is extremely difficult to build a cyclical factor into Winters' model. Hence, this source of variation is not accounted for except to note the level S and rate of change b.

TABLE 2.16

	Winters' model	Holt's model
MSE	1.345	60.463
RMS	1.160	7.776
MAPE	1.07%	8.53%

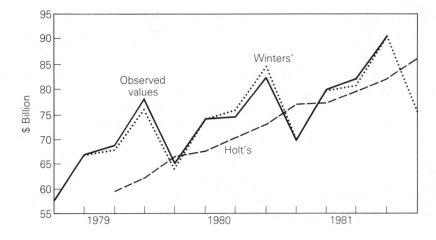

FIGURE 2.7 Comparison of Winters' and Holt's forecasts for new plant and equipment expenditures, United States

2.12 Summary

If a time series is stationary, one appropriate method for predicting future values is the method of moving averages. This method involves the calculation of the average of the sample observations, using this average as the forecast for the next period.

When recent observations contain more information than do earlier ones for forecasting future values, exponential smoothing may provide good forecasts. This method produces self-correcting forecasts with built-in adjustments that regulate forecast values by changing them in the opposite direction of earlier errors.

Forecasts generated by exponential smoothing are sensitive to the specification of the smoothing constant. Also, exponential smoothing techniques result in forecasts which lag behind the movements in the observed time series which it is predicting. The smoothing constant should lie in the range from 0.05 to 0.30.

A general measure of the reliability of a forecast is the mean square error (MSE), which is the sum of squares of the differences between the time series observations and the predictions divided by the number of observations predicted. The square root of MSE is the root mean square error (RMS) which indicates forecast error in terms of the original units and not the squares. The two measures are numerically related and yield the same results when two methods of forecasting are compared. The mean absolute percentage error (MAPE) is a relative measure of forecast error. It assumes that the severity of forecast error is proportional to the size of the error.

Adaptive-response-rate single exponential smoothing (ARRSES) does not require specification of the smoothing constant and it is attractive when a large number of items have to be predicted. ARRSES changes the value of the unspecified smoothing constant on an ongoing basis.

If a pattern exists in a time series, the method of linear moving averages will account for this pattern in its forecasts. When a trend is evident in the time series, single exponential smoothing becomes less useful. Extending the procedure to double exponential smoothing permits the forecaster to adjust for trend in the process. Brown's method for forecasting finds the difference between the single and double smoothed values. This difference is added to the single smoothed value and is adjusted for the exhibited pattern in the data.

Holt's two-parameter linear exponential smoothing is an extension of Brown's method in which a growth factor is added to the smoothing equation.

A higher form of exponential smoothing is appropriate when the underlying pattern of the observed time series is quadratic or of a higher order. Quadratic exponential smoothing incorporates the quadratic term in the smoothing process.

When a seasonal pattern is exhibited in data, triple exponential smoothing is a method for correcting the forecast for this source of variation. Winters' three-parameter linear and seasonal exponential smoothing model is an extension of Holt's two-parameter method. The extension is an additional equation to estimate the seasonal component of the time series.

2.13 Exercises

1 The equation

$$F_{t+1} = \frac{1}{n} X_t + \left(1 - \frac{1}{n} \right) F_t \tag{2.4}$$

is another form of the formula for simple moving averages. What weight is assigned to the observed value in time period t if $n = 3$? If $n = 10$? As n becomes larger, what happens to the weight assigned to the forecast in period t?

2 (a) How do the α values of 0.1, 0.3, and 0.7 weight the past observations in forecasting with single exponential smoothing?

(b) How do the same values of α, weight the past observations in forecasting by Brown's linear exponential smoothing method?

3 In a single exponential smoothing application to a time series of shipments of goods from inventory, the results in table 2.17 were obtained.

TABLE 2.17

α	MSE	MAPE(%)
0.2	40	26.2
0.4	60	33.4
0.6	75	29.4
0.8	79	28.5

(a) Based on the MSE or RMS results, which value for α would lead to the most accurate forecasts? Why?

(b) Based on the MSE or RMS results, should the forecaster investigate other values for the smoothing constant? Why?

(c) Answer parts (a) and (b) with respect to the MAPE calculations.

4 In ARRSES, the smoothing constant is given by

$$\alpha = \left| \frac{E_t}{M_t} \right| \tag{2.15}$$

As the smoothed error increases in value with respect to the absolute smoothed error, what happens to α? Why?

5 In Brown's linear exponential smoothing method, the difference between the smoothed value in period t and the double smoothed value in the same period is weighted by the fraction $\alpha/(1 - \alpha)$. If $\alpha = 0.2$, what is the weighting? If $\alpha = 0.8$, what is the weighting? What is the importance of $S_t - S'_t$ as α is increased?

6 Holt's method is an extension of Brown's linear exponential smoothing method. As the growth factor b_t is updated, what relative importance is given to the growth factor in period $t-1$? Explain fully.

7 In Winters' three-parameter exponential smoothing, a factor for seasonality is included in the forecasting equation. Explain how the seasonal component is updated to account for new observations?

8 The unemployment rate in the United States (all civilian workers) as a percentage of the civilian labor force (seasonally adjusted) between January 1986 and December 1987 is shown in table 2.18.

TABLE 2.18

Year	Month	Unemployment rate	Year	Month	Unemployment rate
1986	Jan	6.8	1987	Jan	6.7
	Feb	7.2		Feb	6.6
	Mar	7.2		Mar	6.5
	Apr	7.1		Apr	6.3
	May	7.2		May	6.3
	Jun	7.1		Jun	6.1
	Jul	7.0		Jul	6.1
	Aug	6.8		Aug	6.0
	Sep	7.0		Sep	5.9
	Oct	6.9		Oct	5.9
	Nov	6.9		Nov	5.8
	Dec	6.7		Dec	5.7

(a) Prepare an estimate for the unemployment rate in January 1988 based on a single moving average with $n = 3$. Plot the forecasts and observations.

(b) Prepare an estimate for the unemployment rate in January 1988 based on single exponential smoothing with $\alpha = 0.25$. Plot the forecasts and observations.

(c) In January 1988, the unemployment rate was 5.8 percent. Which method more closely approximates the observed value?

(d) Calculate the MSE or RMS for the methods of parts (a) and (b).

(e) Based on MSE or RMS, which procedure provides more accurate forecasts?

(f) Repeat parts (d) and (e) using MAPE.

TABLE 2.19

Year	Paid admissions per game (thousands)
1969	22.6
1970	19.7
1971	21.0
1972	18.5
1973	18.3
1974	19.3
1975	21.6
1976	23.4
1977	25.9
1978	28.3
1979	29.4
1980	24.1

Data were privately secured.

9 In table 2.19, data on the number of paid admissions per game at Fenway Park for Boston Red Sox home games are listed for the years 1969–80.
   (a) Prepare an estimate for paid admissions per game for 1981 by single moving averages ($n = 3$).
   (b) Prepare an estimate for paid admissions per game for 1981 by single exponential smoothing ($\alpha = 0.2$).
   (c) Prepare an estimate for paid admissions per game for 1981 by single exponential smoothing ($\alpha = 0.3$).
   (d) Based on the above estimates, calculate the MSE or RMS for the methods of parts (a), (b), and (c).
   (e) Based on MSE or RMS, which method was most accurate?
   (f) Based on MAPE, which method was most accurate?
10 (a) For the data of exercise 8, forecast the unemployment rate for January 1982 by ARRSES ($\beta = 0.2$).
   (b) Calculate the MSE for this method.
   (c) Is ARRSES more accurate than the methods of problem 1 based on MSE?
11 (a) For the data of exercise 9, forecast the number of paid admissions per game for 1981 by ARRSES ($\beta = 0.2$).
   (b) Calculate the MSE or RMS for this method.
   (c) Is ARRSES more accurate than the methods of exercise 1 based on MSE?
   (d) Answer part (c) using MAPE.
   (e) Plot the forecasts and actual values.
12 Table 2.20 contains data on annual wine production in millions of gallons for the years 1970–88.
   (a) Forecast for 1989 by the method of single exponential smoothing. Choose your own α.
   (b) Forecast for 1989 by Brown's method of linear exponential smoothing. Choose your own α.
   (c) Forecast for 1989 by the linear moving-averages method.
   (d) Which of the three methods is most appropriate? Why?

TABLE 2.20

Year	Production
1970	149.2
1971	155.8
1972	150.2
1973	157.3
1974	164.7
1975	167.1
1976	165.8
1977	175.3
1978	181.5
1979	197.2
1980	217.0
1981	247.0
1982	269.6
1983	273.1
1984	280.0
1985	300.3
1986	298.3
1987	310.4
1988	319.0

13 Apply single exponential smoothing to the following series 3, 6, 9, 12, 15, 18, 21, 24, 27, 30. From this application, would you conclude that Brown's linear exponential smoothing method would produce better results?

14 A business conditions newsletter is asked to prepare forecasts of the Consumer Price Index (All Urban Consumers) (CPI-U) for its monthly publication. The data are presented in table 2.21.

TABLE 2.21

Month	1986	1987
Jan	290.1	286.3
Feb	287.4	287.7
Mar	283.7	289.5
Apr	281.2	291.4
May	282.1	292.3
Jun	282.8	292.8
Jul	281.9	292.8
Aug	281.9	294.2
Sep	283.5	296.1
Oct	283.6	297.3
Nov	284.0	297.9
Dec	284.2	297.2

(a) Forecast for January 1988 by Holt's double-parameter linear exponential smoothing. Assume $\alpha = 0.2$ and $\gamma = 0.3$.

(b) Interpret the meaning of the smoothing constants $\alpha = 0.2$ and $\gamma = 0.3$.

(c) Calculate the MSE or RMS for the forecasting procedure of part (a).

(d) Compute a forecast using the method of linear moving averages with 12 observations in each average

(e) Compute the MSE or RMS for the forecasting procedure in part (d).

(f) Which method achieved more accurate forecasts for this data set for the time period covered? Why?

(g) Using Winters' model ($\alpha = 0.2$, $\gamma = 0.3$, $\beta = 0.3$), repeat parts (c)–(f).

15 (a) Forecast for the randomless series 1, 5, 10, 17, 26, 37, 50, 65, 82 by single exponential smoothing.

(b) Apply Brown's quadratic exponential smoothing to the data set of part (a).

(c) Which method does a better job of forecasting? Why?

16 Data on new plant and equipment expenditures, United States (total nonfarm business, billion dollars, 1982=100) are given in table 2.22.

TABLE 2.22

Year	Observed value
1978	304.42
1979	327.08
1980	332.66
1981	337.11
1982	310.58
1983	306.71
1984	352.88
1985	377.28
1986	379.47
1987	388.60
1988	430.23

(a) Apply single exponential smoothing to the above data ($\alpha = 0.3$).

(b) Apply Holt's procedure to the above data ($\alpha = 0.3$, $\gamma = 0.5$).

(c) Apply Brown's linear exponential smoothing method to the above data ($\alpha = 0.3$).

(d) From the *Survey of Current Business* (US Department of Commerce, 1990) find the value of new plant and equipment expenditures for 1989.

(e) Which method provided the best estimate?

17 Table 2.23 contains data on exports of goods and services, United States (billion dollars).

(a) Apply Winters' model to the above data, years 1982–87, and forecast for the first quarter 1988 ($\alpha = 0.4$, $\beta = 0.4$, and $\gamma = 0.3$).

(b) Apply single exponential smoothing to the same data set and forecast for the first quarter 1988 ($\alpha = 0.3$).

(c) Which forecast provides better estimates? Why?

TABLE 2.23

Quarter	1982	1983	1984	1985	1986	1987	1988
1	89.5	81.5	89.7	87.9	92.8	98.8	118.7
2	92.9	83.6	90.9	91.6	95.7	102.4	
3	85.1	82.4	88.3	88.4	90.8	102.7	
4	82.1	87.1	91.8	92.7	95.7	120.9	

18 Data on US merchandise trade (billion dollars) are contained in table 2.24.
  (a) Apply Winters' model to the following data and forecast for the first quarter of 1988 ($\alpha = 0.2$, $\beta = 0.6$, and $\gamma = 0.2$).
  (b) Apply single exponential smoothing to the following data and forecast for the first quarter of 1988 ($\alpha = 0.3$).
  (c) Which method forecasts better? Why?

TABLE 2.24

Quarter	1985	1986	1987
1	55.2	53.0	57.8
2	55.0	55.4	62.7
3	49.7	51.6	62.3
4	52.9	56.5	70.9

19 The data in table 2.25 represent the annual sales for single family dwellings by Gross Built Construction.

TABLE 2.25

Year	Number of dwellings
1970	435
1971	561
1972	780
1973	921
1974	922
1975	970
1976	978
1977	1005
1978	1091
1979	1264
1980	1201
1981	1638
1982	1321
1983	1320
1984	1766
1985	1875
1986	1981
1987	2002
1988	2043

(a) Plot the time series.
(b) Apply single exponential smoothing to the above data. Let the smoothing constant be 0.15.
(c) Apply Holt's method with smoothing constants of 0.15 and 0.15.
(d) Which procedure is best when you compare the MSE or RMS? Are the plots of the forecasts reasonably close to the actual values?

20 The data in table 2.26 are sales of a small manufacturer over a three year period.
(a) Plot the time series.
(b) If a seasonal pattern is present use Winters' model to forecast. Choose your own smoothing constants. If a seasonal pattern is not present, use Holt's model and choose your own smoothing constants.

TABLE 2.26

Month	1984	1985	1986
Jan	17.4	17.9	18.3
Feb	17.0	17.1	17.8
Mar	17.8	18.4	19.2
Apr	17.1	17.4	17.9
May	17.0	16.2	18.0
Jun	16.8	16.4	17.5
Jul	15.8	16.3	16.9
Aug	16.4	16.8	18.5
Sep	17.7	18.4	19.2
Oct	18.9	20.1	20.8
Nov	17.9	18.2	20.1
Dec	17.3	18.0	18.8

References

Brown, R. G. (1963) *Smoothing, Forecasting and Prediction*. Englewood Cliffs, NJ: Prentice-Hall.

Johnson, L. A. and Montgomery, D. C. (1976) *Forecasting and Time Series Analysis*. New York: McGraw-Hill.

Bureau of Economic Analysis, *Survey of Current Business*, March 1982. Washington, DC: US Department of Commerce.

US/DHHS/Health Care Financing Administration, Bureau of Data Management and Strategy, *Health Care Financing Trends*, 3(1), June 1982; 2(3), Summer 1981.

Winters, P. R. (1960) Forecasting sales by exponentially weighted moving averages. *Management Science*, 6, April, 324–42.

Further Reading

Bails, D. G. and Peppers, L. C. (1982) *Business Fluctuations; Forecasting Techniques and Applications*, Englewood Cliffs, NJ: Prentice-Hall.

Benton, W. K. (1972) *Forecasting for Management*. Reading, MA: Addison-Wesley.

Bowerman, B. L. and O'Connell, R. T. (1979) *Forecasting and Time Series.* North Scituate, MA: Duxbury.

Farnum, N. R. and Stanton, L. W. (1989) *Quantitative Forecasting Methods,* Boston: PWS-Kent, ch. 2.

Firth, M. (1982) *Forecasting Methods in Business and Management.* Philadelphia, PA: International Ideas.

Granger, C. W. J. (1980) *Forecasting in Business and Economics,* New York: Academic Press.

Hanke, J. E. and Reitsch, A. G. (1989) *Business Forecasting,* Boston, MA: Allyn and Bacon, ch. 4.

Holt, C. C., Modigliani, F., Muth, J. F. and Simon, H. A. (1960) *Planning Production Inventories and Work Force.* Englewood Cliffs, NJ: Prentice-Hall, ch. 14.

Levenbach, H. and Cleary, J. P. (1981) *The Beginning Forecaster.* Belmont, CA: Lifetime Learning Publications.

Makridakis, S., and Wheelwright, S. C. (1983) *Forecasting Methods and Applications.* New York: John Wiley, ch. 3.

Makridakis, S., Wheelwright, S. C. and McGee, V. (1985) *Forecasting Methods for Management,* 4th edn. New York: John Wiley.

Thomopoulos, N. T. (1980) *Applied Forecasting Methods,* Englewood Cliffs, NJ: Prentice-Hall.

Appendix A Forecast-1 Computer Program

The following computer program designed for IBM and fully compatible computers will make computations for forecasting and measurement of forecast error for all the models discussed in chapter 2. The program is interactive with supporting error messages. The output of computations can be saved for future use with a software package for producing graphics.

```
5 CLEAR
10 '
20 ' PROGRAM: FORECASTING
30 '
40 ' DATE: 05/29/85
50 '
60    VER$="2.2"
70 '
80 '
90' ----------------------------------------------------------------
100 ON ERROR GOTO 59000 :  ' Error handler
110 GOSUB 1000 :  ' Initialize system variables
190 T$="FORECASTING MODELLING SYSTEM"
200 GOSUB 20000 :  ' heading
210 TH=5
215 MM = 10 :  ' no. of menu items
220 PRINT "Available options :"
230 PRINT
240 PRINT TAB(TH) "1. Create/edit data files"
245 PRINT TAB(TH) "2. Single Moving Average"
250 PRINT TAB(TH) "3. Exponential Smoothing"
260 PRINT TAB(TH) "4. Adaptive-Response-Rate Single Exponential Smoothing"
270 PRINT TAB(TH) "5. Linear Moving Average"
280 PRINT TAB(TH) "6. Brown's One-Parameter Linear Exponential Smoothing"
290 PRINT TAB(TH) "7. Holt's Two-Parameter Linear Exponential Smoothing"
```

```
300 PRINT TAB(TH) "8. Brown's Quadratic Exponential Smoothing"
310 PRINT TAB(TH) "9. Winters' Linear and Seasonal Exponential Smoothing"
350 PRINT TAB(TH) "10. Finished"
400 PRINT : PRINT
410 PRINT"Please enter the number of option : "; :
420 LINE INPUT IN$
430 AN=VAL(IN$)
440 IF AN<1 OR AN>MM THEN GOTO 190
450 ON AN GOSUB 10000, 30500, 30000, 31000, 32000, 33000, 34000, 35000, 36000, 64000
460 '
470 GOTO 190
990 ' ----------------------------------------------------------------
991 ' sub: initialize system variables
992 '
1000 DIM AN$(4),PA(4)
1010 ME = 100 : ' max no. of periods allowed
1020 DIM X(ME), F(ME+1), E(ME+1), S1(ME+1), S2(ME+1), S3(ME+1)
1030 '
1040 LP = 80 : ' characters per line-display
1050 PP = 80 : ' characters per line-printer
1060 '
1070 EN$ = CHR$(13) : ' ascii carriage return
1080 '
1090 T1 = 5 : ' tab 1
1100 T2 = 20 : ' tab 2
1110 T3 = 40 : ' tab 3
1115 T4 = 60 : ' tab 4
1120 '
1130 ' possible answers
1140 '
1150 AN$(0) = "no"
1160 AN$(1) = "n"
1170 AN$(2) = "yes"
1180 AN$(3) = "y"
1270 '
1280 ' numeric values corresponding to answers
1290 '
1300 PA(0) = 0
1310 PA(1) = 0
1320 PA(2) = 1
1330 PA(3) = 1
1410 '
1420 TF$ = CHR$(12) : ' form feed - top of form
1430 '
1440 MC = 20 : ' max lines - display
1450 ML = 55 : ' max lines - printer
1460 '
1470 D1 = 1 : ' data file no. 1
1700 '
1710 ' disable soft keys and clear line 25
1720 '
1730 FOR I = 1 TO 10
1740   KEY I, ""
1750 NEXT
1760 KEY OFF
1770 '
1800 RETURN
9990 ' ----------------------------------------------------------------
9991 ' sub: create/edit database
9992 '
10000 T$="CREATE/EDIT DATABASE"
10010 GOSUB 20000 : ' heading
10020 PRINT: PRINT
10030 PRINT "Available options: "
```

```
10040 PRINT
10050 OPT = 6 :  'options available'
10060 PRINT TAB (TH) "1. Create a new database"
10070 PRINT TAB (TH) "2. Edit an existing database"
10075 PRINT TAB (TH) "3. Delete a database"
10080 PRINT TAB (TH) "4. Display a database (on screen)"
10090 PRINT TAB (TH) "5. Print a database"
10100 PRINT TAB (TH) "6. Finished"
10110 PRINT
10120 PRINT
10130 INPUT "please enter your selection : "; IN
10140 IF IN<1 OR IN > OPT THEN GOTO 10000
10150 IF IN=OPT THEN RETURN
10160 ON IN GOSUB 11000, 12000, 12500, 13000, 14000
10170 GOTO 10000
10990 ' ------------------------------------------------------------------------
10991 ' sub: create new database
10992 '
11000 T$="CREATE A NEW DATABASE"
11010 GOSUB 20000 :  ' heading
11020 '
11030 LINE INPUT "enter file name (8 characters maximum, no extension) : "; IN$
11040 L = LEN (IN$)
11050 IF L=0 THEN GOTO 11030
11060 IF L>8 THEN PRINT "*** ERROR *** File name too long": GOTO 11000
11070 OPEN "0", D1, IN$+". dat"
11080 CLOSE D1
11090 '
11100 DF$=IN$ :  ' save file name as default
11110 '
11120 ' start input of data
11130 '
11140 T=0 :  ' periods
11150 GOSUB 20000 :  ' heading
11160 '
11170 ' do until input = "done" or max. obs. entered
11180 '
11185 IF T>=ME THEN GOSUB 20000: PRINT: PRINT : PRINT "MAXIMUM NUMBER OF OBSERVA
        TIONS ENTERED ": PRINT : GOSUB 62000 : GOTO 11300
11190 IF DL>MC THEN GOSUB 20000
11200 PRINT "input data for period "; T+1; ": ";
11210 LINE INPUT IN$
11220 IF IN$="done" OR IN$="DONE" THEN GOTO 11300
11230 X (T) =VAL (IN$) :  ' save observation
11240 T=T+1           :  ' increment no. of periods
11250 DL=DL+1         :  ' increment display count
11260 GOTO 11185
11270 '
11280 ' finished input processing
11290 '
11300 XL=T-1 :  ' last observation in array
11305 XN = T :  ' no. of observations
11310 '
11320 GOSUB 16000 :  ' write data
11330 '
11340 RETURN
11990 ' ------------------------------------------------------------------------
11991 ' sub: edit database
11992 '
12000 T$="EDIT DATABASE"
12010 GOSUB 20000 :  ' heading
12020 '
12030 PRINT : PRINT
12040 PRINT "Available options : "
```

```
12050 PRINT
12060 OPT=4 :  ' total no. options
12070 PRINT TAB(TH) "1. Edit data for a period"
12080 PRINT TAB(TH) "2. Delete a period"
12090 PRINT TAB(TH) "3. Insert a new period"
12100 PRINT TAB(TH) "4. Finished"
12110 PRINT : PRINT
12120 INPUT "please enter your selection : "; IN
12130 IF IN<0 OR IN>OPT THEN GOTO 12000   : ' check for valid input
12140 IF IN=OPT THEN RETURN            : ' exit condition
12150 ON IN GOSUB 17000, 17400, 17700
12160 GOTO 12000
12490 ' -----------------------------------------------------------
12491 ' sub: delete a database
12492 '
12500 T$="DELETE A DATABASE"
12510 GOSUB 20000 :  ' heading
12520 '
12530 GOSUB 21000 :  ' query – filename
12540 '
12545 D$=DF$+".dat"
12550 KILL D$
12560 '
12570 PRINT : PRINT "****** File deleted from diskette ******"
12580 PRINT
12590 GOSUB 62000 :  ' operator wait
12600 '
12610 RETURN
12990 ' -----------------------------------------------------------
12991 ' sub : display database
12992 '
13000 T$="DISPLAY DATABASE"
13010 GOSUB 20000 :  ' heading
13020 '
13030 GOSUB 21000 :  ' query – file name
13040 '
13050 GOSUB 20000 :  ' heading
13060 GOSUB 13500 :  ' subheading
13070 '
13080 FOR T = XS TO XL
13090   IF DL>=MC THEN GOSUB 62000: GOSUB 20000: GOSUB 13500
13100   PRINT TAB(T1) T+1; TAB(T2) X(T)
13110   DL=DL+1 :  ' line count
13120 NEXT
13130 '
13140 GOSUB 62000 :  ' operator – wait
13150 '
13160 RETURN
13490 ' -----------------------------------------------------------
13491 ' sub: subheading display
13492 '
13500 PRINT TAB(T1) "PERIOD"; TAB(T2) "OBSERVATIONS"
13510 PRINT TAB(T1) "------"; TAB(T2) "------------"
13520 PRINT
13530 DL=DL+3 :  ' increment line count
13540 RETURN
13990 ' -----------------------------------------------------------
13991 ' sub: print database
13992 '
14000 T$="PRINT DATABASE"
14010 GOSUB 20000 :  ' heading
14020 '
14030 GOSUB 21000 :  ' query – file name
14040 '
```

```
14050 GOSUB 20000 :  ' heading
14060 PRINT : PRINT : PRINT : PRINT
14070 PRINT "****** PRINTING "; DF$; " FILE — PLEASE WAIT ******"
14080 '
14090 GOSUB 20500 :  ' print heading
14100 GOSUB 14500 :  ' print subheading
14110 '
14120 FOR T = XS TO XL
14130   IF PL>=ML THEN GOSUB 20500 : GOSUB 14500
14140   LPRINT TAB(T1) T+1; TAB(T2) ×(T)
14150   PL=PL+1 :  ' increment line count
14160 NEXT
14170 '
14180 RETURN
14490 ' -----------------------------------------------------------
14491 ' sub: subheading
14492 '
14500 LPRINT TAB(T1) "PERIOD"; TAB(T2) "OBSERVATIONS"
14510 LPRINT TAB(T1) "------"; TAB(T2) "------------"
14520 LPRINT " "
14530 PL=PL+3
14540 RETURN
14990 ' -----------------------------------------------------------
14991 ' sub: read database
14992 '
15000 INPUT "enter 1 for NORMAL file; 2 for DIF file"; AN
15005 IF AN<>1 AND AN <>2 THEN GOTO 15000
15010 ON AN GOTO 15020, 15150
15017 ' -----------------------------------------------------------
15018 'sub: input NORMAL file
15019 '
15020 PRINT : PRINT "*** reading data from file : "; DF$+". dat"
15030 OPEN "I", D1, DF$+". dat"
15040 '
15050 INPUT#D1, XN, Z$:  ' read no. of observations
15052 '
15054 XL=XN−1 :  ' last position in array
15060 FOR T = 0 TO XL
15070   INPUT#D1, X(T), Z$
15080 NEXT
15090 '
15100 CLOSE D1
15110 '
15120 RETURN
15147 ' -----------------------------------------------------------
15148 'sub: input DIF file
15149 '
15150 PRINT : PRINT "***reading data from file : "; DF$+". dif"
15160 OPEN "I", D1, DF$+". dif"
15165 '***header section
15170 WHILE T$<>"DATA"
15175    GOSUB 15350 : 'read
15180    IF T$<>"VECTORS" THEN GOTO 15190
15185       IF V2>1 THEN PRINT "ERROR: more than 1 series in file; can't read" : X
N=0 : FOR I=1 TO 2000 : NEXT : GOTO 15300
15190       IF T$<>"TUPLES" THEN GOTO 15220
15200          XN=V2
15210          IF XN>100 THEN PRINT "ERROR: more than 100 obs. in series; reading onl
y 100" : XN=100
15220 WEND
15221 '
15230 '***data section
15240 XL=XN−1
15260 FOR T=0 TO XL
```

```
15270    GOSUB 15400 :  'read BOT flag (garbage)
15280    GOSUB 15400 :  X(T)=V2
15290 NEXT
15291 '
15300 CLOSE D1 :  IF XN=0 THEN RETURN
15310 T2$="do you want to save data under NORMAL format (y/n - default: n) : "
15315 GOSUB 22000 :  'QUERY -Y/N
15320 IF CK<>1 THEN RETURN
15325 GOSUB 16000 :  'save under NORMAL format
15340 RETURN
15341 '
15342 '
15349 '***read header item
15350 INPUT#D1, T$
15360 GOSUB 15400
15365 RETURN
15366 '
15399 'read data item
15400 INPUT#D1, V1$, V2$ :  INPUT#D1, S$
15410 V1=VAL(V1$) :  V2=VAL(V2$)
15420 RETURN
15990 ' -------------------------------------------------------------
15991 ' sub: write database
15992 '
16000 PRINT
16010 PRINT "*** saving data in file : ";DF$+".dat"
16020 '
16030 OPEN "0",D1,DF$+".dat"
16040 '
16050 PRINT#D1, XN;EN$: ' no. of observations
16060 FOR T = 0 TO XL
16070   PRINT#D1, X(T);EN$
16080 NEXT
16090 '
16100 CLOSE D1
16110 '
16120 RETURN
16990 ' -------------------------------------------------------------
16991 ' sub: edit a line
16992 '
17000 T$="EDIT DATA FOR A PERIOD"
17010 GOSUB 20000 :  ' heading
17020 '
17030 GOSUB 21000 :  ' query - file name
17040 '
17050 T1$="enter number of period you want to change : "
17060 GOSUB 18000 :  ' common edit processing
17070 '
17080 INPUT "enter new value : ";X(T-1)
17090 PRINT
17100 T2$="do you wish to change any more values (y/n - default: n) : "
17110 GOSUB 22000 :  ' query - y/n
17120 IF CK=1 THEN GOTO 17050 :  ' yes - change more values
17130 '
17140 ' finish update processing
17150 '
17160 GOSUB 16000 :  ' save changed values
17170 '
17180 RETURN
17390 ' -------------------------------------------------------------
17391 ' sub: delete a period
17392 '
17400 T$="DELETE A PERIOD"
17410 GOSUB 20000 :  ' heading
```

```
17420 '
17430 GOSUB 21000 :  ' query – file name
17440 '
17450 T1$="enter number of period you want to delete :  "
17460 GOSUB 18000 :  ' common edit processing
17470 '
17480 PRINT : PRINT "**** DELETING PERIOD "; T; " ****"
17490 PRINT
17500 '
17510 FOR I = T–1 TO XL
17520    X(I)=X(I+1) :  ' delete period t
17530 NEXT
17540 '
17550 ' adjust pointers
17560 '
17570 XL=XL–1 :  ' last observation in x
17580 XN=XN–1 :  ' total number of observations
17590 '
17600 T2$="do you want to delete any more periods (y/n – default: n) :  "
17610 GOSUB 22000 :  ' query – y/n
17620 IF CK=1 THEN GOTO 17450 :  ' yes – delete more periods
17630 '
17640 ' finished deletions
17650 '
17660 GOSUB 16000 :  ' save changes
17670 '
17680 RETURN
17690   --------------------------------------------------------------
17691 ' sub :  insert another period
17692 '
17700 T$=" INSERT A PERIOD"
17710 GOSUB 20000 :  ' heading
17720 '
17730 GOSUB 21000 :  ' query – file name
17740 '
17750 T1$="enter number of period at which data is to inserted :  "
17760 GOSUB 18000 :  ' common edit processing
17770 '
17790 INPUT "enter new value :  "; XT
17800 PRINT
17810 PRINT "**** Inserting data at period "; T; " ****"
17815 PRINT
17820 '
17830 FOR I = XL TO T–1 STEP –1
17840    X(I+1)=X(I) :  ' move each period forward
17850 NEXT
17860 X(T–1)=XT :  ' new data for period t
17870 '
17880 ' adjust pointers
17890 '
17900 XL=XL+1 :  ' last observation in x
17910 XN=XN+1 :  ' total observations
17920 '
17930 T2$="do you want to insert any more periods (y/n – default: n) :  "
17940 GOSUB 22000 :  ' query – y/n
17950 IF CK=1 THEN GOTO 17750 :  ' yes – more insertions
17960 '
17965 ' finished
17970 '
17975 GOSUB 16000 :  ' save changes
17980 '
17985 RETURN
17990 ' --------------------------------------------------------------
17991 ' sub :  common edit routines processing
```

```
17992 '
18000 GOSUB 20000 :  ' heading
18010 '
18020 ' current status of default file
18030 '
18040 PRINT : PRINT "Data file "; DF$; " currently has "; XN; " observations "
18050 '
18060 ' request period processing
18070 '
18080 PRINT : PRINT T1$; :  INPUT T
18090 T+INT(T) :  ' take integer portion
18091 '
18092 IF T<=0 THEN PRINT : PRINT "*** ERROR *** period entered is less than one":
GOTO 18080
18094 '
18100 IF T>XN+1 THEN PRINT : PRINT "*** WARNING *** period entered is greater than
the number of observations":
18110 PRINT
18120 PRINT "current value for period ";T;" is ";X(T-1)
18130 PRINT
18140 '
18150 RETURN
19990 ' --------------------------------------------------------------------------
19991 ' sub: display heading
19992 '
20000 CLS
20010 TL = LEN(T$) :  ' length of title
20020 MD = INT(LP/2) :  ' display midpoint
20030 TB = MD-INT(TL/2) :  ' title tab
20040 LOCATE 1, 1 :  ' position cursor
20050 PRINT TAB(TB) T$
20052 TL=LEN(VER$)+8
20054 TB=MD - INT (TL/2) :  ' version tab
20056 PRINT TAB(TB) "VERSION ";VER$
20060 PRINT
20070 PRINT STRING$(LP-1, "-")
20080 PRINT
20090 DL = 5 :  ' LINE COUNT
20100 RETURN
20390 ' ----------------------------------------------------------------
20391 ' sub: display subheading
20392 '
20400 PRINT TAB(T1-2) "PERIOD"; TAB(T2-2) "OBSERVATION"; TAB(T3-2)
"FORECAST"; TAB(T4-2) "ERROR"
20410 DL=DL+1
20420 RETURN
20490 ' ----------------------------------------------------------------
20491 ' sub: print heading
20492 '
20500 GOSUB 60100 :  ' top of form
20510 TL = LEN(T$) :  ' length of title
20520 MD = INT(PP/2) :  ' printer line midpoint
20530 TB = MD - INT(TL/2) :  ' title tab
20540 LPRINT TAB(TB) T$
20542 TL=LEN(VER$)+8
20544 TB=MD - INT (TL/2) :  ' version tab
20546 LPRINT TAB(TB) "VERSION ";VER$
20550 TL = LEN(DF$)+12
20560 TB = MD - INT(TL/2) :  ' tab
20570 LPRINT TAB(TB) "INPUT FILE : " +DF$
20580 LPRINT " "
20590 LPRINT STRING$ (PP-1, "-")
20600 LPRINT " "
20610 PL = 6 :  ' lines printed
```

```
20620 RETURN
20790 ' ------------------------------------------------------------
20791 ' sub: print subheading
20792 '
20800 LPRINT TAB (T1-2) "PERIOD"; TAB (T2-2) "OBSERVATION"; TAB (T3-2) "FORECAST";
TAB (T4-2) "ERROR"
20810 PL=PL+1
20820 RETURN
20990 ' ------------------------------------------------------------
20991 ' sub: obtain input file name
20992 '
21000 PRINT "enter data file name ";
21010 IF DF$="" THEN GOTO 21040
21020 PRINT "(default file: "; DF$; ") ";
21030 '
21040 LINE INPUT ": "; IN$
21045 IF IN$="" AND DF$="" THEN PRINT : PRINT "*** ERROR *** Invalid file name ":
PRINT : GOTO 21000
21050 IF IN$="" THEN GOTO 21060 ELSE DF$= IN$ : GOSUB 15000 : ' read new data
21060 RETURN
21990 ' ------------------------------------------------------------
21991 ' sub: query - y/n responses
21992 '
22000 PRINT T2$;: LINE INPUT IN$
22005 IF IN$="" THEN CK=0: RETURN : ' default response is no
22010 FG=0
22020 PRT=0
22030 FOR II = 0 TO 3
22040   IF IN$=AN$ (II) THEN CK=PA (II) : FG=1
22050 NEXT
22060 IF FG=0 THEN GOTO 22000
22070 RETURN
22990 ' ------------------------------------------------------------
22991 ' sub: display results
22992 '
23000 GOSUB 20000 : ' display heading
23010 GOSUB 20400 : ' display subheading
23020 '
23030 FOR T = PS-1 TO PF-1
23040   IF DL>=MC THEN GOSUB 62000 : GOSUB 20000 : GOSUB 20400
23050 '
23055   PRINT TAB (T1) T+1;
23060   PRINT TAB (T2) ;
23070   IF T<XS OR T>XL THEN PRINT STRING$ (6, "-") ; ELSE PRINT X (T) ;
23080   PRINT TAB (T3) ;
23090   IF T<FS OR T>FL THEN PRINT STRING$ (6, "-") ; : ELSE PRINT F (T) ;
23095   PRINT TAB (T4) ;
23096   IF T<FS OR T>XL THEN PRINT STRING$ (6, "-") ; : ELSE PRINT E (T)
23100   DL = DL + 1
23110 NEXT
23120 '
23130 GOSUB 62000 : ' wait
23140 '
23150 GOSUB 50000 : ' display performance statistics
23160 '
23170 RETURN
23990 ' ------------------------------------------------------------
23991 ' sub: print results
23992 '
24000 GOSUB 20000 : ' heading
24001 T2$="do you want to print the results (y/n - default: n) : "
24002 GOSUB 22000 : ' print results ?
24004 '
24006 IF CK=0 then return
```

```
24008 '
24010 GOSUB 20500 : ' print heading
24015 GOSUB 20800 : ' print subheading
24020 '
24030 FOR T = PS-1 TO PF-1
24040   IF PL>=ML THEN GOSUB 20500 : GOSUB 20800
24050 '
24060   LPRINT TAB (T1) T+1;
24070   LPRINT TAB (T2) ;
24080   IF T<XS OR T>XL THEN LPRINT STRING$ (6, "-") : ELSE LPRINT X (T) ;
24090   LPRINT TAB (T3) ;
24100   IF T<FS OR T>FL THEN LPRINT STRING$ (6, "-") : : ELSE LPRINT F (T) ;
24104   LPRINT TAB (T4) ;
24105   IF T<FS OR T>XL THEN LPRINT STRING$ (6, "-") : ELSE LPRINT E (T)
24110   PL=PL+1
24120 NEXT
24130 '
24140 GOSUB 50500 : ' print performance statistics
24150 '
24160 RETURN
26990 ' -------------------------------------------------------------
26991 ' sub: perform heading, query file name, query periods to forecast
26992 '
27000 GOSUB 20000 : ' heading
27010 GOSUB 21000 : ' query – file name
27015 IF XN=0 THEN RETURN : ' in case unable to read DIF file
27020 GOSUB 28000 : ' query – periods to forecast
27030 RETURN
27990 ' -------------------------------------------------------------
27991 ' sub: query – periods to forecast
27992 '
28000 PRINT"number of observations in this database : "; XN
28005 INPUT"enter period number to starting forecasting (default is 1) : "; PS
28010 DL = DL + 1 : ' increment line count
28020 IF PS <= 0 THEN PS =1
28030 IF PS > XN+1 THEN PRINT "*** ERROR *** cannot forecast this number of peri
ods"
28040 PRINT"enter period number to stop forecasting (default is"; XN+1; ")";
28050 INPUT PF
28060 IF PF = 0 THEN PF= XN+1
28070 IF PF<=PS THEN PRINT "*** ERROR *** last period to forecast must be great
er than "; PS: GOTO 28040
28090 IF PF > XN+1 THEN PRINT "*** ERROR *** last period to forecast is greater than
"; XN+1
28100 RETURN
28490 ' -------------------------------------------------------------
28491 ' sub: query – constant
28492 '
28500 PRINT "input value for "; TC$; " (default : 0.2) : ";
28510 LINE INPUT AL$
28520 IF AL$="" THEN CN=. 2 ELSE CN=VAL (AL$)
28530 '
28540 IF CN<0 OR CN>1 THEN PRINT "*** ERROR *** "; TC$; " is not in 0–1 range": PRI
NT : GOTO 28500
28550 RETURN
28990 ' -------------------------------------------------------------
28991 ' sub : query – periods ahead
28992 '
29000 LINE INPUT"number of periods ahead (default: 1) : "; M$
29005 IF M$="" THEN M=1 ELSE M=VAL (M$)
29010 IF M<=0 THEN PRINT"*** ERROR *** number of periods must be greater than ze
ro ": PRINT : GOTO 29000
29020 '
```

```
29030 IF M>XN THEN PRINT"*** ERROR *** number of periods specified is too large
": PRINT : GOTO 29000
29040 '
29050 RETURN
29490 ' -------------------------------------------------------------
29491 ' sub: query - request moving average period
29492 '
29500 INPUT "number of periods needed to compute moving average : "; N
29510 '
29520 ' check answer
29530 '
29540 IF N<=0 THEN PRINT : PRINT "*** ERROR *** number of periods must be greater
than zero ": PRINT : GOTO 29500
29550 '
29560 IF N>XN THEN PRINT : PRINT "*** ERROR *** number of periods specified is to
o large": PRINT : GOTO 29500
29570 '
29580 RETURN
29990 ' -------------------------------------------------------------
29991 ' sub: exponential smoothing
29992 '
30000 T$ = "EXPONENTIAL SMOOTHING"
30010 GOSUB 27000 : ' heading, input file, periods to forecast
30015 IF XN=0 THEN RETURN : 'in case unable to read DIF file
30020 '
30030 TC$="alpha"
30035 GOSUB 28500 : ' query - alpha
30040 AL=CN          : ' save alpha
30042 '
30044 GOSUB 62500 : ' wait message
30046 '
30050 ' initialize values
30060 FS = PS    : ' forecast start
30070 FL = PF-1 : ' forecast end
30080 F(FS-1) = X(FS-1) : ' initialize forecast
30090 '
30100 ' forecast
30110 '
30120 FOR T = FS TO FL
30130    F(T) = X(T-1) * AL + F(T-1) * (1-AL)
30140    E(T) = X(T) - F(T)
30150 NEXT
30160 '
30165 GOSUB 51000 : ' computer performance statistics
30166 '
30170 GOSUB 23000 : ' display results
30180 GOSUB 24000 : ' print results
30190 GOSUB 58000 : ' query -save data for plotting
30210 RETURN
30490 ' -------------------------------------------------------------
30491 ' sub: single moving averages
30492 '
30500 T$="SINGLE MOVING AVERAGES"
30510 GOSUB 27000 : ' heading, input file, periods to forecast
30515 IF XN=0 THEN RETURN : 'in case unable to read DIF file
30520 '
30530 GOSUB 29500 : ' query - moving average period
30540 '
30550 GOSUB 62500 : ' wait message to operator
30560 '
30570 '    initialize variables:
30580 '
30590 FS=PS-1+N   : ' forecast start
```

```
30600 F1=PF-1      : ' forecast end
30610 '
30620 '     initial forecast
30630 '
30640 FT=0
30650 FOR T = PS-1 TO PS-1+N-1
30660    FT=FT+X(T)
30670 NEXT
30680 F(FS) = FT/N
30690 E(FS) = X(FS) - F(FS)   : ' initial error term
30700 '
30710 '  compute remainder
30720 '
30730 FOR T = FS TO FL-1
30740    F(T+1) = ((X(T) - X(T-N))/N) + F(T) : ' forecast
30750    E(T+1) = X(T+1) - F(T+1)           : ' error term
30760 NEXT
30770 '
30780 GOSUB 51000 : ' performance statistics
30790 '
30800 GOSUB 23000 : ' display results
30810 GOSUB 24000 : ' print results
30815 GOSUB 58000 : ' query -save data for plotting
30820 '
30830 RETURN
30990 ' -------------------------------------------------------------
30991 ' sub: adaptive-response-rate single exponential smoothing
30992 '
31000 T$="ADAPTIVE-RESPONSE-RATE SINGLE EXPONENTIAL SMOOTHING"
31010 GOSUB 27000 : ' heading
31015 IF XN=0 THEN RETURN : 'in case unable to read DIF file
31020 '
31030 TC$="alpha"
31040 GOSUB 28500 : ' query alpha
31050 AL=CN        : ' save alpha
31060 '
31070 TC$="beta"
31080 GOSUB 28500 : ' query beta
31090 BETA=CN      : ' save beta
31100 '
31102 GOSUB 62500 : ' wait message
31104 '
31110 '           initialize :
31120 FS = PS    : ' start of forecast
31130 FL = PF-1 : ' end of forecast
31140 F(FS-1)=X(FS-1) : ' initial forecast value
31150 ET = 0     : ' smoothed error
31160 MT = 0     : ' absolute smoothed error
31170 '
31180 FOR T = FS-1 TO FL-1
31190    E(T) = X(T)-F(T)
31200    MT = BETA * ABS(E(T)) + (1-BETA)*MT : ' absolute smoothed error
31210    ET = BETA * E(T) + (1-BETA)*ET      : ' smoothed error
31220 '
31230    F(T+1) = AL*X(T) + (1-AL)*F(T)      : ' forecast
31240 '
31250    IF MT=0 THEN AL=0 ELSE AL=ABS(ET/MT)
31260 '
31270 NEXT
31280 '
31290 GOSUB 51000 : ' compute performance statistics
31300 GOSUB 23000 : ' display results
31310 GOSUB 24000 : print results
31315 GOSUB 58000 : query -save data for plotting
```

```
31320 '
31330 RETURN
31990 ' ----------------------------------------------------------------
31991 ' sub: linear moving average
31992 '
32000 T$="LINEAR MOVING AVERAGE"
32010 GOSUB 27000 :  ' heading, input file, periods to forecast
32015 IF XN=0 THEN RETURN :  'in case unable to read DIF file
32020 '
32030 GOSUB 29500 :  ' query – request moving average
32040 '
32070 GOSUB 29000 :  ' query – no. of periods ahead
32100 '
32102 GOSUB 62500 :  ' wait message
32104 '
32110 SS = PS + N −2: ' initial value for St'
32120 SF = PF −2     : ' final value for St' (xl)
32130 DS = SS + N −1: ' initial value for St''
32140 DF = PF −2     : ' final value for St'' (xl)
32150 FS = (PS−1) + 2 * (N−1) +M: ' initial value for forecast
32160 FL = PF −1      : ' final value for forecast
32170 '
32180 ' n month moving average
32185 '
32190 FOR T = SS TO SF
32200    MA=0
32210    FOR TA = T TO T−N+1 STEP−1
32220     MA = MA + X(TA)
32230    NEXT
32240    S1(T)=MA/N
32250 NEXT
32260 '
32270 ' n month double moving average
32280 '
32290 FOR T = DS TO DF
32300    MA=0
32310    FOR TA = T TO T−N+1 STEP −1
32320     MA = MA + S1(TA)
32330    NEXT
32340    S2(T) = MA/N
32350 NEXT
32360 '
32370 ' compute forecast
32380 '
32390 FOR T = FS TO FL
32400    A = 2*S1(T−M) − S2(T−M)
32410    B = (S1(T−M) − S2(T−M)) * (2/(N−1))
32420    F(T) = A + B*M
32430    E(T) = X(T) − F(T)
32440 NEXT
32450 '
32460 GOSUB 51000 :  ' compute performance statistics
32470 '
32480 GOSUB 23000 :  ' display results
32490 GOSUB 24000 :  ' print results
32495 GOSUB 58000 :  query –save data for plotting
32500 '
32510 RETURN
32990 ' ----------------------------------------------------------------
32991 ' sub; Brown's one-parameter linear exponential smoothing
32992 '
33000 T$="BROWN'S ONE-PARAMETER LINEAR EXPONENTIAL SMOOTHING"
33010 GOSUB 27000 :  ' heading
33015 IF XN=0 THEN RETURN :  'in case unable to read DIF file
```

```
33020 '
33030 TC$="alpha"
33040 GOSUB 28500 :  ' query - alpha
33050 AL=CN          :  ' save alpha
33060 '
33070 GOSUB 29000 :  ' query - no. of periods ahead
33080 '
33082 GOSUB 62500 :  ' wait message
33084 '
33090 FS=PS+M :  ' forecast start
33100 FL=PF-1 :  ' forecast end
33110 S1(FS-M-1) = X(FS-M-1) :  ' initialize single exp. smooth.
33120 S2(FS-M-1) = X(FS-M-1) :  ' initialize double exp. smooth
33130 '
33140 FOR T = FS-M TO FL-M
33150   S1(T) = AL*X(T) +  (1-AL)*S1(T-1)
33160   S2(T) = AL*S1(T) +  (1-AL)*S2(T-1)
33170   AT = 2*S1(T) - S2(T)
33180   BT =  (AL/(1-AL)) *  (S1(T)-S2(T))
33190   F(T+M) = AT + BT*M
33195   E(T+M) = X(T+M) - F(T+M)
33200 NEXT
33210 '
33220 GOSUB 51000 :  ' compute performance statistics
33230 '
33240 GOSUB 23000 :  ' display results
33250 GOSUB 24000 :  ' print results
33255 GOSUB 58000 :  ' query -save data for plotting
33260 '
33270 RETURN
33990 ' -------------------------------------------------------------
33991 ' sub: Holt's two-parameter linear exponential smoothing
33992 '
34000 T$="HOLT'S TWO-PARAMETER LINEAR EXPONENTIAL SMOOTHING"
34010 GOSUB 27000 :  ' heading
34015 IF XN=0 THEN RETURN :  'in case unable to read DIF file
34020 '
34030 TC$="alpha"
34040 GOSUB 28500 :  ' query alpha
34050 AL=CN          :  ' save alpha
34060 '
34070 TC$="gamma"
34080 GOSUB 28500 :  ' query - gamma
34090 GAMMA=CN       :  ' save gamma
34100 '
34110 GOSUB 29000 :  ' query - periods ahead
34120 '
34122 GOSUB 62500 :  ' wait message
34124 '
34130 '      initialize :
34140 BT=0   :  ' trend
34150 FS=PS+M :  ' forecast start
34160 FL=PF-1 :  ' forecast end
34170 S1(FS-M-1)=X(FS-M-1) :  ' initial smoothed value
34180 '
34190 FOR T = FS-M TO FL-M
34200   S1(T) = AL*X(T) +  (1-AL)* (S1(T-1)+BT)
34210   BT = GAMMA*(S1(T) - S1(T-1)) +  (1-GAMMA)*BT
34220   F(T+M) = S1(T)+BT*M
34230   E(T+M) = X(T+M) - F(T+M)
34240 NEXT
34250 '
34260 GOSUB 51000 :  ' compute performance statistics
34270 '
```

```
34280 GOSUB 23000 :  ' display results
34290 GOSUB 24000 :  ' print results
34295 GOSUB 58000 :  ' query —save data for plotting
34300 '
34310 RETURN
34990 ' -------------------------------------------------------------
34991 ' sub: Brown's quadratic exponential smoothing
34992 '
35000 T$="BROWN'S QUADRATIC EXPONENTIAL SMOOTHING"
35010 GOSUB 27000 :  ' heading
35015 IF XN=0 THEN RETURN :  'in case unable to read DIF file
35020 '
35030 TC$="alpha"
35040 GOSUB 28500 :  ' query — alpha
35050 AL=CN         :  ' save alpha
35060 '
35070 GOSUB 29000 :  ' query — periods ahead
35080 '
35082 GOSUB 62500 :  ' wait message
35084 '
35090 '        initialize :
35100 FS=PS+M :  ' forecast start
35110 FL=PF—1 :  ' forecast end
35120 T=FS—M—1: ' temp. index
35130 S1(T) = X(T) :  ' sing. exp. smooth
35140 S2(T) = X(T) :  ' double exp. smooth
35150 S3(T) = X(T) :  ' triple exp. smooth
35160 '
35170 ' forecast
35180 '
35190 FOR T = FS—M TO FL—M
35200   S1(T) = AL*X(T) + (1—AL)*S1(T—1)
35210   S2(T) = AL*S1(T) + (1—AL)*S2(T—1)
35220   S3(T) = AL*S2(T) + (1—AL)*S3(T—1)
35230   AT = 3*S1(T) — 3*S2(T) + S3(T)
35240   BT = (AL/(2*(1—AL)^2))*((6—5*AL)*S1(T)—(10—8*AL)*S2(T)+(4—3*AL)*S3(T))
35250   CT = ((AL*AL)/(1—AL)^2)*(S1(T)—2*S2(T)+S3(T))
35260   F(T+M) = AT + BT*M + .5 * CT * M * M
35270   E(T+M) = X(T+M) — F(T+M)
35280 NEXT
35290 '
35300 GOSUB 51000 :  ' compute performance statistics
35310 '
35320 GOSUB 23000 :  ' display results'
35330 GOSUB 24000 :  ' print results
35335 GOSUB 58000 :  ' query —save data for plotting
35340 '
35350 RETURN
35990 ' -------------------------------------------------------------
35991 ' sub: Winters' linear and seasonal exponential smoothing
35992 '
36000 T$="WINTERS' LINEAR AND SEASONAL EXPONENTIAL SMOOTHING"
36010 GOSUB 27000 :  ' heading
36015 IF XN=0 THEN RETURN :  'in case unable to read DIF file
36020 '
36030 TC$="alpha"
36040 GOSUB 28500 :  ' query — alpha
36050 AL=CN         :  ' save alpha
36060 '
36070 TC$="beta"
36080 GOSUB 28500 :  ' query — beta
36090 BETA=CN       :  ' save beta
36100 '
36110 TC$="gamma"
```

```
36120 GOSUB 28500 : ' query - gamma
36130 GAMMA=CN    : ' save gamma
36140 '
36150 GOSUB 29000 : ' query - forecast periods ahead
36160 '
36170 INPUT"enter length of seasonality : ";L
36180 IF L<=0 THEN PRINT :PRINT "*** ERROR *** seasonality must be greater than
zero":PRINT :GOTO 36170
36190 IF L>PF-PS+1 THEN PRINT :PRINT "*** ERROR *** seasonality is greater
than the forecast interval of interest":PRINT :GOTO 36170
36200 '
36205 GOSUB 62500 : ' wait message
36206 '
36210 '           initialize:
36220 '
36230 FS=PS+M-1   : ' initial forecast period
36240 P=INT(PF/L) : ' no. of periods
36250 K=P*L-1     : ' index of last observation
36260 FL=K+M      : ' index of last forecast
36270 PF=FL+1     : ' reset last period to forecast
36280 '
36290 GOSUB 37000 : ' initialize s0,b0, s3(i)
36300 '
36310 ' forecast
36320 '
36330 FOR T = PS-1 TO PF-1
36340   S1(T) = (AL*X(T))/S3(T) + (1-AL)*(SO+BO)    : ' exp. smooth series
36350   S3(T+L) =BETA*X(T)/S1(T) + (1-BETA)*S3(T)   : ' seasonality estimate
36360   BO=GAMMA*(S1(T)-SO) + (1-GAMMA)*BO          : ' trend estimate
36370   F(T+M) = (S1(T)+BO*M)*S3(T+M)               : ' forecast
36380   E(T+M) =X(T+M)-F(T+M)                       : ' error term
36390   SO=S1(T)                                    : ' save prior estimate
36400 NEXT
36410 '
36420 GOSUB 51000 : ' compute performance statistics
36430 '
36440 GOSUB 23000 : ' display results
36450 GOSUB 24000 : ' print results
36455 GOSUB 58000 : ' query -save data for plotting
36460 '
36470 RETURN
36990 ' ------------------------------------------------------------
36991 ' sub: initialization for Winters' method
36992 '              based on Johnson & Montgomery technique (1976)
36993 '
37000 '
37010 ' mean of first period
37020 '
37030 M1=0
37040 FOR T = PS-1 TO PS+L-2
37050   M1=M1+X(T)
37060 NEXT
37070 M1=M1/L
37080 '
37090 ' mean of last period
37100 '
37110 M2=0
37120 FOR T = K-L+1 TO K
37130   M2=M2+X(T)
37140 NEXT
37150 M2=M2/L
37160 '
37170 ' initial slope of trend
37180 '
```

```
37190 BO=(M2-M1)/(L*2)
37200 '
37210 ' mean of first season period
37220 '
37230 M3=0
37240 FOR T = PS TO PS+L-1
37250   M3=M3+T
37260 NEXT
37270 M3=M3/L
37280 '
37290 ' initial trend estimate
37300 '
37310 S0=M1-M3*BO
37320 '
37330 ' trend estimates
37340 '
37350 FOR T = PS-1 TO PF-1
37360   S1(T)=S0+BO*(T+1)
37370 NEXT
37380 '
37390 ' seasonality estimates
37400 '
37410 FOR T = PS-1 TO PF-1
37420   S2(T)=X(T)/S1(T)
37430 NEXT
37440 '
37450 ' initial trend seasonal factors
37460 '
37470 FOR T = 0 TO L-1
37480   FOR TA = 0 TO K STEP L
37490     S3(T)=S3(T)+S2(T+TA)
37500   NEXT
37510   S3(T)=S3(T)/L
37520 NEXT
37530 '
37540 ' adjust initial seasonal trends
37550 '
37560 S=0
37570 FOR T = 0 TO L-1
37580   S = S+S3(T)
37590 NEXT
37600 F=L/S : ' adjustment factor
37610 FOR T = 0 TO L-1
37620   S3(T)=S3(T)*F
37630 NEXT
37640 '
37650 RETURN
49990 ' -------------------------------------------------------------
49991 ' sub: display performance statistics
49992 '
50000 GOSUB 20000 : ' heading
50010 T1$="PERFORMANCE STATISTICS"
50020 TL=LEN(T1$)
50030 MD=INT (LP/2)
50040 TB=MD-INT(TL/2) : ' tab for subtitle
50050 PRINT TAB(TB) T1$
50060 PRINT TAB(TB)STRING$(TL,"-")
50070 PRINT
50080 PRINT"MEAN SQUARED ERROR (MSE) :"; MSE
50090 PRINT
50100 PRINT"MEAN ABSOLUTE PERCENTAGE ERROR (MAPE) :";MAPE
50110 PRINT
50120 PRINT"THEIL'S U-STATISTIC : ";TU
50130 PRINT
```

```
50140 GOSUB 62000 :  ' WAIT
50150 RETURN
50490 ' -------------------------------------------------------------
50491 ' sub: print performance statistics
50492 '
50500 GOSUB 20500 :  ' heading
50510 T1$="PERFORMANCE STATISTICS"
50520 TL=LEN(T1$)
50530 MD=INT(PP/2)
50540 TB=MD-INT(TL/2) :  ' tab for subtitle
50550 LPRINT TAB(TB) T1$
50560 LPRINT TAB(TB) STRING$(TL,"-")
50570 LPRINT " "
50580 LPRINT "MEAN SQUARED ERROR (MSE) :  ";MSE
50590 LPRINT " "
50600 LPRINT "MEAN ABSOLUTE PERCENTAGE ERROR (MAPE) :";MAPE
50610 LPRINT " "
50620 LPRINT "THEIL'S U-STATISTIC : ";TU
50630 RETURN
50990 ' -------------------------------------------------------------
50991 ' sub: compute all performance statistics
50992 '
51000 GOSUB 51500 :  ' determine periods of performance
51005 GOSUB 52000 :  ' mean squared error
51010 GOSUB 52500 :  ' mean absolute percentage error
51020 GOSUB 53000 :  ' theil u-statistic
51030 RETURN
51490 ' -------------------------------------------------------------
51491 ' sub: determine period of performance
51492 '
51500 IF FS+1<PS THEN TS=PS-1 ELSE TS=FS
51510 IF XL+1>PF THEN TF=PF-1 ELSE TF=XL
51520 RETURN
51990 ' -------------------------------------------------------------
51991 ' sub: mean squared error
51992 '
52000 D=0 :  ' initialize summation
52010 '
52020 FOR I=TS TO TF
52030   D = D+ E(I)*E(I)
52040 NEXT
52050 '
52060 MSE= D/(TF-TS+1)
52070 RETURN
52490 ' -------------------------------------------------------------
52491 ' sub: mean absolute percentage error
52492 '
52500 PE=0 :  ' initialize percent error
52510 '
52520 FOR I = TS TO TF
52530   PE = PE + ABS((E(I)/X(I))*100!)
52540 NEXT
52550 '
52560 MAPE = PE/(TF-TS+1)
52570 RETURN
52990 ' -------------------------------------------------------------
52991 ' sub : theil u statistic
52992 '
53000 FPE = 0 :  ' predicted relative change
53010 APE = 0 :  ' actual relative change
53020 S1 = 0  :  ' initialize summation
53030 S2 = 0  :  ' initialize summation
53040 '
53050 FOR I = TS TO TF-1
```

```
53060    FPE = (F(I+1)-X(I))/X(I)
53070    APE = (X(I+1)-X(I))/X(I)
53080    S1 = S1 + (FPE-APE)^2
53090    S2 = S2 + APE * APE
53100 NEXT
53110 '
53120 TU = (S1/(TF-TS))/(S2/(TF-TS))^.5
53130 RETURN
53990 ' --------------------------------------------------------------
53991 ' sub: compute autocorrelation coefficients
53992 '
54000 GOSUB 54500 : ' compute mean
54010 '
54020 ' compute p-order autocorrelation
54030 '
54040 FOR K = 1 TO P
54050 ' initialize working variables
54060    C1=0
54070    C2=0
54080    C3=0
54090    C4=0
54100    FOR T = K1 TO K2 - K
54110       C1=X(T)-XB
54120       C2=X(T+K)-XB
54130       C3=C3+C1*C2  : ' numerator
54135    NEXT
54140    FOR T = K1 TO K2
54145       C4=C4+(X(T)-XB)^2 : ' denominator
54150    NEXT
54160 '
54170    R(K) = C3/C4   : ' autocorrelation coefficient
54180 NEXT
54190 '
54200 RETURN
54490 ' --------------------------------------------------------------
54491 ' sub: compute mean
54492 '
54500 ' determine last period
54510 IF PF-1>=XL THEN K2=XL ELSE K2=PF
54520 ' determine first period
54530 K1=PS-1
54540 '
54550 ' compute mean
54560 '
54570 XB=0
54580 FOR I = K1 TO K2
54590    XB=XB+X(I)
54600    NEXT
54610 '
54620 XB=XB/(K2-K1+1)
54630 '
54640 RETURN
57990 ' --------------------------------------------------------------
57991 ' sub: output file
57992 '
58000 T2$="do you want to save the data (y/n - default: n) :"
58002 GOSUB 22000 : ' query y/n
58004 IF CK=1 THEN 58010 ELSE RETURN
58010 INPUT "enter 1 for ASCII file; 2 for DIF file"; AN
58015 IF AN<>1 AND AN<>2 THEN GOTO 58010
58020 ON AN GOTO 58030, 58150
58027 ' --------------------------------------------------------------
58028 ' sub: output ASCII file
58029 '
```

```
58030 PRINT :PRINT "*** saving data in file : ";DF$+".prn"
58040 OPEN "O",D1,DF$+".prn"
58050 FOR I = PS-1 TO PF-1
58060  PRINT#D1, STR$(I+1);",";
58070  IF I<XS OR I>XL THEN PRINT#D1, " ";",";: ELSE PRINT#D1, STR$(X(I));",";
58080  IF I<FS OR I>FL THEN PRINT#D1, " ";",";: ELSE PRINT#D1, STR$(F(I));",";
58090  IF I<FS OR I>XL THEN PRINT#D1, " ": ELSE PRINT#D1, STR$(E(I))
58100 NEXT
58110 '
58120 CLOSE D1
58130 '
58140 RETURN
58147 ' -------------------------------------------------------------------------
58148 'sub: output DIF file
58149 '
58150 PRINT : PRINT "***saving data in file : "; DF$+".dif"
58160 OPEN "O",D1,DF$+".dif"
58170 '***header section
58180 V1=0 : S$=""
58185 T$="TABLE" : V2=1 : GOSUB 58400
58190 T$="VECTORS" : V2=3 : GOSUB 58400
58195 T$="TUPLES" : V2=PF-PS+1 : GOSUB 58400
58200 DIM LB$(3) : LB$(1)="observ" : LB$(2) ="forecast" : LB$(3)="error"
58210 FOR I=1 TO 3
58215    V1=I
58220    T$="LABEL" : V2=0 : S$=LB$(I) : GOSUB 58400
58225    T$="MAJORSTART" : V2=1 : S$="" : GOSUB 58400
58227    T$="MINORSTART" : GOSUB 58400
58230    T$="PERIODICITY" : GOSUB 58400
58233    T$="TRUELENGTH" : V2=PF-PS+1 : GOSUB 58400
58235 NEXT
58240 T$="DATA" : V1=0 : V2=0 : GOSUB 58400
58249 '
58299 '***data section
58300 FOR I=PS-1 TO PF-1
58305    GOSUB 58500 : 'BOT flag
58310    V1=0 : S$="V"
58315    IF I<XS OR I>XL THEN V2=0 ELSE V2=X(I)
58317    GOSUB 58600 : 'write data item
58320    IF I<FS OR I>FL THEN V2=0 ELSE V2=F(I)
58322    GOSUB 58600
58325    IF I<FS OR I>XL THEN V2=0 ELSE V2=E(I)
58327    GOSUB 58600
58330 NEXT
58335 V1= -1 : V2=0 : S$="EOD"
58340 GOSUB 58600 : 'EOD flag
58345 '
58350 CLOSE D1
58355 '
58360 RETURN
58361 '
58362 '
58398 '***write header item
58400 PRINT#D1, T$
58405 PRINT#D1, STR$(V1);",";STR$(V2)
58410 PRINT#D1, CHR$(34); S$; CHR$(34)
58415 RETURN
58416 '
58498 '***write BOT flag
58500 V1= -1 : V2=0 : S$="BOT" : GOSUB 58600
58505 RETURN
58506 '
58598 '***write data item
58600 PRINT#D1, STR$(V1);",";STR$(V2) : PRINT#D1, S$
```

```
58610 RETURN
58611 '
58990 ' -----------------------------------------------------------------
58991 ' Error Handler
58992 '
59000 IF ERR=53 THEN PRINT :PRINT "*** ERROR *** File not found on diskette":
PR
INT : INPUT "re-enter data file name : ";DF$: RESUME
59010 '
59020 IF ERR=61 THEN PRINT :PRINT "*** WARNING *** Disk is full ":PRINT "Please
delete old files from diskette":CLOSE:END
59030 '
59040 PRINT "ERROR NO. ";ERR;" ON LINE "; ERL
59050 PRINT
59060 PRINT "Program aborted"
59070 CLOSE
59080 END
60090 ' -----------------------------------------------------------------
60091 ' sub: top of form
60092 '
60100 LPRINT TF$
60110 RETURN
61990 ' -----------------------------------------------------------------
61991 ' sub: query — wait for operator response
61992 '
62000 PRINT : PRINT"press <(ENTER)> to continue"
62010 IF INKEY$<>EN$ THEN GOTO 62010
62020 RETURN
62490 ' -----------------------------------------------------------------
62491 ' sub: wait message for operator
62492 '
62500 PRINT
62510 PRINT"********* PLEASE WAIT — PERFORMING COMPUTATIONS *********"
62520 RETURN
62990 ' -----------------------------------------------------------------
62991 ' sub: prompt — feature not implemented
62992 '
63000 PRINT
63010 PRINT
63020 PRINT
63030 PRINT "********* THIS FEATURE HAS NOT BEEN IMPLEMENTED **********"
63040 PRINT
63050 PRINT
63060 GOSUB 62000
63070 RETURN
63990 ' -----------------------------------------------------------------
63991 ' sub: end
63992 '
64000 CLOSE
64010 END
```

Appendix B User Manual for FORECAST-1 for the IBM Personal Computer

Table of Contents

I.0 Introduction

FORECAST-1 is a group of commonly used forecasting models which operate on the IBM personal computer (PC). The models incorporated in FORECAST-1 can be found in most current texts on forecasting. Because of this fact, this manual will not discuss the advantages or disadvantages associated with each model or make recommendations as to the appropriate technique to use in specific circumstances. Rather, this manual will explain how to use the program – FORECAST-1 – on the IBM PC. Section 2.0 describes how to get started and how to set up.

Presently, FORECAST-1 contains the following models:

- single moving-average model
- exponential smoothing model
- adaptive-response-rate single exponential smoothing model
- linear moving-average model
- Brown's linear exponential smoothing model
- Holt's two-parameter linear exponential smoothing model
- Brown's quadratic exponential smoothing model
- Winters' linear and seasonal exponential smoothing model

Section III.0 describes each of these models in more detail as well as the various parameters that the operator is expected to provide.

FORECAST-1 was designed for the novice user – more specifically, for a user who is more interested in forecasting and analysis. Consequently, there are very few things a user must remember in order to use FORECAST-1.

FORECAST-1 is entirely menu driven. This means that the program will ask the user for a parameter whenever one is required. If the user enters an incorrect value, the program will simply display an error message (in English) and allow the user to re-enter the value correctly.

Another user-friendly feature that was implemented was the use of default values. Oftentimes, there exists a parameter value which is repeatedly used. Rather than have the operator continually enter these types of values, FORECAST-1 will display the system default value. If the user wants to use the default value, he/she simply presses the ⟨ENTER⟩ key and the program will use the default value. Otherwise, the user can enter any value that he/she desires. Hopefully, this will minimize the amount of data that the operator has to enter and make the use of FORECAST-1 less error prone.

In terms of hardware/software requirements, FORECAST-1 was designed to use as a minimum the following:

> IBM PC with 128k memory
> >1 double-density disk drive
> >monochrome display monitor
> >80 column printer
> >IBM PC DOS with disk BASIC

OKAY!! . . . . . . NOW LET's GET STARTED . . . . . .

II.0 Getting Started

Once the IBM PC has been powered on, the diskette with FORECAST-1 has been inserted into the drive, and the initial prompts for the date/time have been entered, then type the following (in response to the DOS prompt A>):

> A> BASICA

This will load the disk version of BASIC.

After disk BASIC has been loaded, type the following:

> RUN"FORECAST/BAS"

This will load FORECAST-1 and start execution. The next thing you should see is the menu shown in figure II-1.

```
                    FORECASTING MODELLING SYSTEM
                            VERSION 2.2

 Available options:

     1. Create/edit data files
     2. Single Moving Average
     3. Exponential Smoothing
     4. Adaptive-Response-Rate Single Exponential Smoothing
     5. Linear Moving Average
     6. Brown's One-Parameter Linear Exponential Smoothing
     7. Holt's Two-Parameter Linear Exponential Smoothing
     8. Brown's Quadratic Exponential Smoothing
     9. Winters' Linear and Seasonal Exponential Smoothing
    10. Finished

 Please enter the number of the option : ___
```

FIGURE II.1 Main menu

We are now ready to create a database. To do this, select menu option number 1 – Create/edit data files – by typing 1 in response to the query at the bottom of the display. You should now see the menu shown in figure II-2.

We want to create a new database, so select menu item number 1 – Create a new database. You should now see the menu shown in figure II-3. The first thing the program wants the user to provide is the name of the database in which data is to be stored. As an example, type in

TESTDATA

Please note two things: (1) the database file name cannot be greater than eight characters; (2) do not put a file extension such as .dat or .bas onto the file name (FORECAST-1 will automatically put a file name extension of .dat onto the file name).

Now type in your data in response to the prompts. When you are all done and you have no more data, simply type

done

Figure II-4 is an example of a typical user session.

After typing <done>, the menu shown in figure II-2 is again displayed. At this point the user can do a variety of things, namely display the items of the database on the CRT, print the items of the database on the printer, edit items in a database,

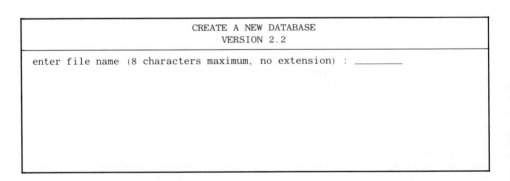

```
                    CREATE/EDIT DATABASE
                        VERSION 2.2

 Available options:

        1. Create a new database
        2. Edit an existing database
        3. Delete a database
        4. Display a database (on screen)
        5. Print a database
        6. Finished

 Please enter your selection : ____
```

FIGURE II.2   Database management functions

```
                    CREATE A NEW DATABASE
                        VERSION 2.2

 enter file name (8 characters maximum, no extension) : _____
```

FIGURE II.3   Create a new database meu

```
                    CREATE A NEW DATABASE
                        VERSION 2.2

   enter file name (8 characters maximum, no extension) : TESTDATA

   input data for period  1  :  4.42
   input data for period  2  :  4.75
   input data for period  3  :  5.16
   input data for period  4  :  5.6
   input data for period  5  :  6.23
   input data for period  6  :  7.01
   input data for period  7  :  done


   *** saving data in file : TESTDATA.dat
```

FIGURE II.4   Typical user session

delete an entire database from the diskette, or return to the main menu (shown in figure II-1). Whatever function is selected, the user simply has to respond to the prompts.

At this point, we now have a database which we can analyze using the various forecasting models. This is the topic of Section III.0.

III.0   Forecasting Models

This section describes each of the forecasting models, their input parameters, and their output displays. All error messages and their meanings are listed in section IV.0.

As noted earlier, the operator can select any model from the main menu (see figure II.1). Depending upon the model selected, the appropriate display will appear and the operator will be asked to answer a series of questions that are pertinent to that model.

The operation of any of the models is essentially the same. The only difference is that the operator is required to answer more questions in the case of some models. Typically, the sequence of events is something like the following:

- the operator selects a specific forecasting model;
- the operator must answer a series of questions;
- in response to the questions and data, the model forecasts are computed and displayed along with the performance statistics (if desired, the operator can print the results);
- after the display or printing of the results, the main menu is again displayed for the operator and the operator can continue or can stop.

Figure III.1 is an example of some questions that are common to all the models. An explanation of these questions follows:

1. "enter data file name" –
The name of the data file which contains the data you want to analyze must be

```
                    SINGLE MOVING AVERAGES
                         VERSION 2.2

enter data file name :   TESTDATA

*** reading data from file : TESTDAT.dat
number of observations in this database : 6
enter period number to start forecasting (default is 1) :
enter period number to stop period forecasting (default is 7) :
```

FIGURE III.1   FORECAST-1 questions common to all models

supplied here. The name must be 1–8 characters and must not have an extension. The data file to be analyzed must presently exist and must have been created by FORECAST-1 (see section II.0).

If there is a default file name in existence due to a previous operator action, then the question will appear as follows:

        enter data file name (default name: TESTDATA) :

In this situation, the operator can enter a new file name if desired or can use the default file simply by pressing ⟨ENTER⟩.

If the default file is not selected, a message will appear on the display screen telling the operator that the appropriate file is being read into memory from the diskette.

After the selection of the database, FORECAST-1 will display the following message for the operator:

        number of observations in this database :

This will remind the operator of the size of this database

2. "enter period number to start forecasting (default is 1) : "
The operator has the option to analyze only a portion of his/her database. The operator can start forecasting at a period other than period number 1. Again, the operator can simply press ⟨ENTER⟩ if the default is okay.

3. "enter period number to stop forecasting (default is XX) : "
The operator can specify the period to stop the forecasting. The default value (i.e. XX) is set to the number of periods of data in the database plus 1, that is, FORECAST-1 will forecast one period ahead.

Sections III.1 – III.8 will explain in greater detail those input parameters required for each specific forecast model.

After the operator has provided all the appropriate input parameters, the following message should appear:

********* PLEASE WAIT – PERFORMING COMPUTATIONS *********

This means exactly what it says – FORECAST-1 is computing the forecast for this model.

Once the computations have been completed, the results are displayed as shown in figure III.2. If there are a lot of data to be displayed, FORECAST-1 will stop displaying data when the entire screen is full. To see the next few periods, press ⟨ENTER⟩. Continue this until you have seen all the forecasted periods. This procedure insures that the operator has the opportunity to review the results at his/her pace.

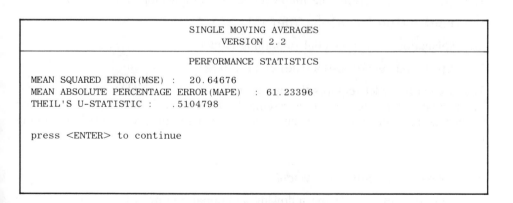

```
                        SINGLE MOVING AVERAGES
                            VERSION 2.2

     PERIOD          OBSERVATION          FORECAST          ERROR

        1               4.42              ------           ------
        2               4.75              ------           ------
        3               5.16              ------           ------
        4               5.6               ------           ------
        5               6.23              4.9825           1.2475
        6               7.01              5.435            1.575
        7               ------            6.0              ------


  press <ENTER> to continue
```

FIGURE III.2   Example display of the results of a forecast

```
                        SINGLE MOVING AVERAGES
                            VERSION 2.2

                       PERFORMANCE STATISTICS

  MEAN SQUARED ERROR (MSE)  :    20.64676
  MEAN ABSOLUTE PERCENTAGE ERROR (MAPE)   :  61.23396
  THEIL'S U-STATISTIC :    .5104798


  press <ENTER> to continue
```

FIGURE III.3   Example performance statistics

After all the periods and results have been reviewed by the operator, performance statistics associated with the results obtained from the model will be displayed (for example, see figure III.3). The performance statistics include:

> mean squared error (MSE)
> mean absolute percentage error (MAPE)
> Theil's U-statistic

Consult your text in order to understand the advantages/disadvantages associated with each performance statistic as well as how to interpret the results.

This section discussed that portion of FORECAST-1 that is common to the operation of all the forecasting models. The remaining sections will examine those things that are unique to the operation of each forecast model.

III.1   Single Moving-averages Model

For this model, the operator must answer the following additional questions:

1. "number of periods needed to compute moving average : "

The single moving average model requires that the operator specify the number of periods that should be used to compute the moving average. It should be noted that this is the only parameter in FORECAST-1 that the operator must always enter.

III.2   Exponential Smoothing Model

The operator must answer the following additional questions for this model:

1. "input value for alpha (default : 0.2) : "

The exponential smoothing model requires that a "weight" be specified. This weight or alpha must be between zero and unity. A typical value of 0.2 was used as a default value. Again, the operator can vary the range of alpha and observe the results by examining the forecasted values.

III.3   Adaptive-Response-Rate Single Exponential Smoothing Model

The operator must answer the following additional questions for this model:

1. "input value for alpha (default : 0.2) : "

See explanation for exponential smoothing model.

2. "input value for beta (default : 0.2) : "

The ARRSES model requires the operator to enter two weights: alpha and beta. The meaning and range of beta is essentially the same as in the case of alpha. For further explanation, see the explanation of alpha for the exponential smoothing model.

III.4   Linear Moving-Average Model

The operator must answer the following additional questions for this model:

1. "number of periods needed to compute moving average : "

As in the case of the single moving average, the operator must enter the number of periods needed to compute a moving average. For more information, see the explanation for the single moving-average model

2. "number of periods ahead (default: 1) : "

The operator can specify the number of periods ahead this model is to forecast. That is, after specifying the number of observations (i.e. periods) to be used in the forecast, the operator can specify the number of periods into the future which the model is to forecast. If the operator selects the default value, the model will forecast one period into the future.

III.5   Brown's One-Parameter Linear Exponential Smoothing Model

The operator must answer the following additional questions for this model:

1. "input value for alpha (default : 0.2) : "

See explanation of alpha for the exponential smoothing model.

2. "number of periods ahead (default : 1) : "

See explanation of this value for the linear moving average model.

III.6   Holt's Two-Parameter Linear Exponential Smoothing Model

The operator must answer the following additional questions for this model:

1. "input value for alpha (default : 0.2) : "

See explanation of this value for the exponential smoothing model.

2. "input value for gamma (default : 0.2) : "

This value is a weight and has essentially the same meaning and range as that defined for alpha. See the explanation of alpha defined for the exponential smoothing model.

3. "number of periods ahead (default: 1): "

See the explanation of this value for the linear moving model.

III.7 Brown's Quadratic Exponential Smoothing Model

The operator must answer the following additional questions for this model:

1. "input value for alpha (default : 0.2) "

See the explanation of this value for the exponential smoothing model.

2. "number of periods ahead (default : 1) : "

See the explanation of this value for linear moving-average model.

III.8   Winters' Linear and Seasonal Exponential Smoothing Model.

The operator must answer the following additional questions for this model:

1. "input value for alpha (default: 0.2) : "

See the explanation of this value for the exponential smoothing model.

2. "input value for beta (default: 0.2) :"

See the explanation of this value for the exponential smoothing model.

3. "input value for gamma (default: 0.2) :"

See the explanation of this value for the exponential smoothing model.

4. "number of periods ahead (default : 1) :"

See the explanation of this value for the linear moving-average model.

It should be noted that this model's initialization was based on the Johnson and Montgomery (1976) technique.

IV.0 FORECAST-1 Error Messages and Descriptions

1. File-Related Error Messages

(a) *** ERROR *** File Not Found On Diskette

The file name specified cannot be found on this diskette. There are several possible reasons for this : (1) you mis-spelt the file name; (2) you may have previously deleted this file; (3) you have inserted the wrong diskette and your file is not on this diskette.

(b) *** ERROR *** File Name Too Long

The file name must be less than eight characters. Remember – do not include an extension such as .dat to the file name. FORECAST-1 will do this for you.

(c) *** WARNING *** Disk is full
    Please delete old files from diskette

This warning indicates that the diskette on which you want to save your data file is already full. There is no more room left on this diskette. You will have to save your data on another diskette which has space available on it or you will have to delete files from the current diskette.

(d) *** ERROR *** Invalid File Name

This error message will occur if you pressed ⟨ENTER⟩ in response to a request for a file name and there is currently no default file specified. FORECAST-1 does not know what file you want to use.

2. Errors Relating To Incorrectly Specifying Forecasting Periods.

(a) *** ERROR *** Period Entered Is Less Than One

The period that you wish to use to start your forecast must be greater than zero. A period number less than unity is meaningless.

(b) *** ERROR *** Cannot Forecast This Number of Periods

The period that you wish to use to start your forecast must be less than the number of periods or observations in your current data file. For example, you cannot start your forecast at period 12 if there are only 11 periods of data in your database.

(c) *** ERROR *** Last Period To Forecast Must Be Greater Than XX

The period that you wish to use to stop your forecast must be greater than the number of the period you specified to start the forecast. For example, you cannot stop your forecast at period 6 if you previously specified that the forecast would start at period 7.

(d) *** ERROR *** Last Period To Forecast Is Greater Than XX

For this model, you cannot forecast more than one period beyond the last period of your data. For example, you cannot forecast to period 15 if your database only contains 10 periods of data.

3. Errors Relating To Incorrectly Specifying The Number of Periods Ahead.

(a) *** ERROR *** Number of Periods Must Be Greater Than Zero

For this model, the number of periods into the future you want to forecast must be greater than zero.

(b) *** ERROR *** Number of Periods Specified Is Too Large

For this model, the number of periods into the future you want to forecast is greater than the number of observations in your database.

4. Errors Relating to Incorrectly Specifying Smoothing Constants.

(a) *** ERROR *** (Alpha, Beta, Gamma) is not in 0–1 Range

All of the three smoothing constants – alpha, beta, or gamma – must be in the range between zero and unity. The value entered was not in this range.

5. Errors Relating To Incorrectly Specifying Seasonality.

(a) *** ERROR *** Seasonality Must Be Greater Than Zero

The length of the seasonality constant must be greater than zero. A value less than zero is meaningless.

(b) *** ERROR *** Seasonality Is Greater Than The Forecast Interval Of Interest

The length of the seasonality constant is greater than number of periods being used in this forecast. For example, a seasonality constant of 12 is incorrect if you are only using 10 periods of data in this forecast.

CHAPTER 3

Methods for Time Series Decomposition and Analysis

Objectives

This chapter introduces the notion of the decomposition of economic time series into systematic and nonsystematic components. The systematic components are trend, cycle, and seasonal variation, and the nonsystematic component is the irregular variation. Knowledge of these components permits forecasts to decompose time series and forecast each component on an individual basis. By the end of this chapter, you will be able to:

1 Isolate the seasonal component by the ratio-to-moving-average method.
2 Estimate both linear and exponential trends.
3 Isolate the cyclical component by a centered moving-average method.
4 Estimate the irregular variation in a time series.
5 Forecast each component to arrive at a prediction for the entire time series.
6 Understand the importance of the X-II procedures.

Outline

Key Terms

- Time Series Decomposition
- Systematic Components

- Seasonal Patterns
- Trend
- Cyclical Movements
- Irregular Variations
- Ratio-to-moving-average method
- Constant Seasonals
- Relative Seasonals
- Absolute Seasonals
- Exponential Trend
- Trading Day Adjustment

3.1 Introduction

In chapter 2 simple extrapolatory methods were employed to predict future values for a series of observed values of a time series. The time period was either years, quarters of a year, or months. Time series are studied under the implicit assumption that past behavior can predict the future course of variation in the observed variable. Although predicting future conditions is not without error, the procedures of analyzing and decomposing time series are valuable in the forecasting process because they may reduce forecast error.

Recall that it is impossible to forecast the future with complete precision and that there will always be some degree of error in the forecast. Methods for *time series decomposition* and analysis are statistical techniques for improving predictions by breaking down the pattern in time series into subpatterns called components.

Decomposition assumes that the data are made up as follows:

$$data = pattern + error$$

$$= f(\text{systematic components}) + error$$

This error or residual variation is assumed to be the difference between the combined effect of the subpatterns of the time series (*systematic components*) and the observed values for the time series. In this chapter, we shall study the nature and scope of these components. The decomposition techniques used to study these components do not consist of only one body of statistical theory. Also, the conditions necessary for scientific statistical investigation, such as random sampling, are not totally present. Hence, time series decomposition procedures are often evaluated by judgmental criteria.

The remainder of this chapter is devoted to a discussion of time series analysis and its application to forecasting. Unlike smoothing methods, there is no one body of statistical theory developed for this subject matter. Thus good judgment is required in applying these methods to forecasting problems. However, by pointing out the statistical limitations of these techniques we can reduce the area over which judgment must operate and thus improve the forecasting process.

3.2 The Nature of Economic Time Series

Movements of an economic time series are related to a number of factors called components. We study these components to explain the movements and direction of the observations of the time series. There are four general components which explain the behavior of economic time series. Three are called systematic or recurring factors. They are (a) the seasonal factor, (b) the trend and (c) the cyclical component. The fourth factor is nonrecurring and is referred to as the random, irregular, or residual component, i.e. the error.

Forecasters analyze these components to determine their effect on the movement in the time series. The four components interact to account for the variation in the data values over time. These influences account for the often erratic behaviour in the economic time series.

Seasonal

Seasonal patterns can be found in data classified as quarterly, monthly, or weekly. They take place and recycle within a period of one year, repeat themselves year after year, and are predictable.

An example of seasonal variation is presented in figure 3.1 where monthly data on initial claims on state unemployment insurance programs are presented. Claims are high in January and fall off until about May, reach another peak usually in July, fall off again and then start climbing from September until January of the following year. These movements result from fluctuations in the demand and supply of labor. Obviously, unemployment insurance claims are very high in January as people are laid off from seasonal employment during the December holiday period. The claims diminish until the warmer weather arises. At that time, the supply of labor is increased as schools and colleges end their terms. Unemployment claims continue high until September when schools and colleges begin their academic year again. For other time series, the nature and causes of seasonal fluctuations differ. These causes can be natural or man-made. Man-made causes are those resulting from (a) customs such as giving gifts at Christmas, Mother's Day and Father's Day, (b) the change of style in clothing during climatic seasons of the year, and (c) the dates of the introduction of new model automobiles which influence sales.

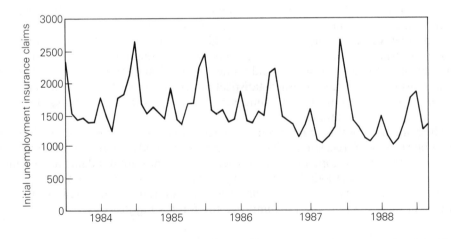

FIGURE 3.1 Time series of initial unemployment insurance claims, state programs (totals in thousands)
Source: US Department of Labor, Washington, DC

Note that in figure 3.1 we portray a monthly seasonal movement. If annual data were plotted, the monthly seasonal fluctuations would be obliterated. Similarly, an economic time series of deposit behavior at a financial instituation may show a recycling pattern within a month. Data on weekly or daily deposit behavior would show this; however, this seasonal pattern would be obliterated if only monthly data were observed.

When data are observed over a longer period of time than one year, the forecaster may focus on the other components.

Trend

Trend is the continuous movement of the time series over an extended period of time. It may appear in linear or curvilinear form. Usually, the forces affecting or producing these movements include changes in technology, changes in productivity, and changes in foreign competition among others.

Cyclical

Cyclical movements refer to wave-like fluctuations (often irregular) of more than one year's duration resulting from changes in general economic activity. It is the difference between the expected value of the time series resulting from the trend and the actual value of the time series. Thus, it can be viewed as the residual variation fluctuating around the trend associated with changed general economic activity.

Irregular

The nonsystematic components or *irregular variations* are those caused by non-periodic or unpredictable events. These events include strikes, earthquakes, wars, weather changes and the passage of legislation having economic effects, among others. These events do not repeat themselves where business cycles are repetitive.

3.3   Decomposition of Time Series

In analyzing economic time series, the assumption is made that the three systematic components and the random component result from different causes. Isolating the three systematic components throws some light on the nature of the factors affecting them. This knowledge permits us to project the effect of the systematic component into the future. After allowances for the irregular component, a forecast can be made.

If Y_t symbolizes the actual observation at time t, we express Y_t in terms of the series trend T_t at time t, the seasonal factor S_t at time t, the cyclical component C_t, and irregular factors I_t. We can assume that the relationship is of the following form:

$$Y_t = S_t \, T_t \, C_t \, I_t \tag{3.1}$$

This equation states that the value of the economic variable at time t is the product of the four components considered. Alternatively, the relationship can be assumed to be additive as follows:

$$Y_t = S_t + T_t + C_t + I_t \tag{3.2}$$

In this relationship the components are not interrelated. The magnitude of one component is not related to the magnitude of any other.

Of the two decomposition models, the additive model is more difficult to work with. Also, the additive model assumes that the individual factors are independent. As an example, if the additive model were used, the model would assume that the trend has no impact on the seasonal factor no matter how high or low it becomes. This assumption is not tenable except for very short-term forecast horizons. Thus in this chapter we shall emphasize the multiplicative model since virtually all users of decomposition analysis find it more plausible.

As noted, the analysis of time series involves the isolation of the S, T, and C components from the original data. In subsequent sections of this chapter and in the two following chapters, we shall discuss many of the techniques that are used to isolate these components. Last, we shall utilize some of the techniques of Micro-TSP and the SAS Econometric and Time Series Library Programs for handling large amounts of data by computerized methods.

3.4   Analyzing and Isolating Seasonal Movements

Knowledge of seasonal patterns is a vital factor in business planning. The knowledge that flower sales will be high in May in the United States (March in the United Kingdom) because of Mother's Day tells the florist that the stock of flowers and floral arrangements should be increased to meet the demand. The knowledge that production will be high during the warm weather aids the toy manufacturer to plan for working capital requirements, machine maintenance, recruitment of labor, and purchase of new raw materials.

As well as enabling one year business plans to be made, knowledge of seasonal movements permits us to analyze past performance, change the pattern of production and distribution, and perhaps even alter the pattern of seasonal variation itself. Although there are various methods to measure seasonal variation, we shall focus on one, the *ratio-to-moving-average method*. The logic behind this and other methods is to eliminate the influence of trend, cyclical, and irregular elements from the original time series data to insure that only the influence of the seasonal element remains. Although the name of this procedure is similar to that of moving averages of chapter 2, we shall see that there are substantial differences.

For quarterly data, a four-quarter moving average is constructed to estimate the seasonal factors from the time series observations. If monthly data were used, a 12 month moving average would be constructed. The idea is to eliminate the other components so the only fluctuations left are seasonal. These moving averages would eliminate the recurring movements due to seasonality that exist in the data. The basic assumption behind the moving average is that the seasonal pattern recurs on a regular basis in each succeeding year. While the seasonal pattern is not exact in succeeding years, it does exist within reasonable limits and the moving average minimizes the effect to a certain extent.

To explain the theory, we shall assume that the components in the time series are of a multiplicative form (equation (3.1)). The ratio-to-moving-average term arises because we take the time series variable Y_t and divide it by the moving average as follows:

$$\frac{Y_t}{\text{MA}} = \frac{S_t T_t C_t I_t}{T_t C_t I_t} = S_t \tag{3.3}$$

The resulting quantity S_i is the seasonal component in the time series data as best we can measure it.

Example 3.1

During the year 1988, the President and his Council of Economic Advisors studied employment figures carefully as indicators of the state of the economy. The study was reported in the *Economic Report of the President, 1989*. Information used in this report came from several sources, one of which is total employment on nonagricultural payrolls and is reported in a number of publications including the *Monthly Labor Review of the US Department of Labor*. The data for two months of 1988 are presented in table 3.1.

TABLE 3.1

Month	Number employed (thousands)	Seasonal index	Number employed Seasonally adjusted (thousands)
March	10 4161	99.182	10 5020
April	10 4559	99.314	10 5281
Change	+398		+261

Source: US Bureau of Labor Statistics.

In the above example, the increase in the number employed between March and April 1988 was 398 thousand. However, to assess the change properly, the two figures must be adjusted for seasonal variation. When this is accomplished by dividing each figure by the appropriate seasonal index, the change in employment on a seasonally adjusted basis is 261 thousand.

In the above example, we see the importance of seasonal adjustment. In this application, we would conclude that employment increased by less on a seasonally adjusted basis than if the seasonal adjustment was not made. If the seasonal adjustment was not made the conclusion would overstate the increase in employment by 137 thousand and our interpretation would be in error. In conclusion, we can only examine seasonally adjusted data to determine meaningful changes in monthly (or quarterly) economic time series.

A number of methods have been developed to measure and isolate seasonal variation. We shall describe only the ratio-to-moving-average method for isolating seasonality, since it is most widely applicable.

Example 3.2

Data on new plant and equipment expenditures (total nonfarm business) was taken from the *Survey of Current Business*, various issues (table 3.2). Quarterly seasonal indices are to be computed using the method of comparing actual values with a four-quarter moving average.

TABLE 3.2 Calculation in steps 1–4 for finding seasonal indices of new plant and equipment expenditures – total nonfarm business ($ billions)

Year	Quarter	(1) Actual data	(2) Four-quarter moving total	(3) Centered moving total	(4) Centered average	(5) Column 1 as a percentage of column 4
1971	1	17.7				
	2	20.6				
			81.2			
	3	20.1		164.1	20.5	98.0
			82.9			
	4	22.8		167.2	20.9	109.1
			84.3			
1972	1	19.4		170.4	21.3	91.1
			86.1			
	2	22.0		174.6	21.8	100.9
			88.5			
	3	21.9		179.1	22.4	97.8
			90.6			
	4	25.2		183.9	23.0	109.6
			93.3			
1973	1	21.5		189.7	23.7	90.7
			96.4			
	2	24.7		196.1	24.5	100.8
			99.7			
	3	25.0		202.0	25.3	98.8
			102.3			
	4	28.5		208.1	26.0	109.6
			105.8			
1974	1	24.1		214.8	26.9	89.6
			109.0			
	2	28.2		221.4	27.7	101.8
			112.4			
	3	28.2		226.5	28.3	99.6
			114.1			
	4	31.9		228.4	28.6	111.5
			114.3			
1975	1	25.8		228.2	28.5	90.5
			113.9			
	2	28.4		226.6	28.3	100.4
			112.7			
	3	27.8		225.5	28.2	98.6
			112.8			
	4	30.7		226.9	28.4	108.1
			114.1			
1976	1	25.9		230.8	28.9	89.6
			116.7			
	2	29.7		237.2	29.7	100.0
			120.5			
	3	30.4		244.3	30.5	99.7
			123.8			
	4	34.5		251.6	31.5	109.5
			127.8			
1977	1	29.2		260.0	32.5	89.8
			132.2			
	2	33.7		268.0	33.5	100.6
			135.8			
	3	34.8		290.2	36.3	95.9
			154.4			
	4	38.1		332.5	41.6	91.6
			178.1			
1978	1	47.8		379.9	47.5	100.6
			201.8			
	2	57.4		433.1	54.1	106.1
			231.3			
	3	58.5		472.1	59.0	99.2
			240.8			
	4	67.6		491.0	61.4	110.1
			250.2			
1979	1	57.3		510.3	63.8	89.8
			260.1			
	2	66.8		530.6	66.3	100.8
			270.5			
	3	68.4		548.8	68.6	99.7
			278.3			
	4	78.0		563.8	70.5	110.6
			285.5			
1980	1	65.1		576.7	72.1	90.3
			291.2			
	2	74.0		586.7	73.3	101.0
			295.5			
	3	74.1				
	4	82.3				

There are six steps in the solution process for finding the seasonal indices of new plant and equipment expenditures.

1 Obtain a four-quarter moving total as shown in column 2. The first entry in this column, 81.2, is the sum of the four-monthly figures for 1971, and it is recorded at the middle of the period between the second and third quarter 1971. The second entry in this column, 82.9, is obtained by subtracting the first quarter 1971 figure from 81.2 and adding the first quarter 1972; that is, 82.9 is the sum of the four quarters from the second quarter 1971 to the first quarter 1972, and it is recorded at the middle of this period. All succeeding entries in the column are found by continually subtracting and adding quarterly values.
2 Calculate the centered moving total of the entries in column 2. These are shown in column 3, with the first entry being the sum of the first two values in column 2, the second entry being the sum of the second and third values in column 2, and so on. The entries in column 3 are recorded between those of column 2, and thus they are in line with (or centered on) the original data.
3 Each item in column 3 is divided by 8 (twice the number of quarters) to find the centered moving average. These moving-average values are the trend cycle estimates, and are used to eliminate the TC components from the original series.
4 Divide column 1 (the $STCI$ data) by the corresponding value in column 4 (TC estimate) and multiply these ratios by 100. In this way, we arrive at the percentages of moving average shown in column 5. All that remains is to eliminate the irregular component, and to this end we arrange the data as in table 3.3.

TABLE 3.3 Calculations for steps 5 and 6 in finding seasonal indices for new plant and equipment expenditures

	Quarter					
Year	1	2	3	4		
1971			98.0	109.1		
1972	91.9	100.9	97.8	109.6		
1973	90.7	100.8	98.8	109.6		
1974	89.6	101.8	99.6	111.5		
1975	90.5	100.4	98.6	108.1		
1976	89.6	100.0	99.7	109.5		
1977	89.8	100.6	95.9	91.6		
1978	100.6	106.1	99.2	110.1		
1979	89.8	100.8	99.7	110.6		
1980	90.3	101.0				
Total	822.8	912.4	887.3	969.7	Sum	
Mean	91.4	101.4	98.6	107.7	399.1	Step 5
Seasonal index	91.6	101.6	98.8	108.0	400.0	Step 6
		$400/399.1 = 1.002\ 256$				

5 For each quarter, find the average (mean) percentage value over all the years. For the first quarter, the average percentage is 91.4. However, this and the other average percentages cannot be used as seasonal indices themselves. This is because the four average percentages must sum to 400. They sum to 399.1. Thus a final calculation is necessary to obtain the seasonal index.
6 Adjust the average percentages so that they sum to 400 by multiplying each percentage by an adjustment factor of 400/399.1 or 1.002 256. The end result is a new percentage figure which varies from a base of 100 and represents the seasonal index.

The data can be deseasonalized or adjusted for the seasonal influences by dividing the original quarterly data value by the seasonal index. The deseasonalized data represent an average value that would have occurred if the year had operated at the same level as the first quarter 1971. The deseasonalized value for the first quarter 1971 would be

$$\frac{\text{first quarter 1971}}{\text{first quarter seasonal index}} = \frac{17.7}{91.6} \times 100$$

$$= \$19.3 \text{ billion}$$

To adjust for the seasonal component in all the time series data of example 3.2, each observation is divided by the appropriate seasonal index and multiplied by 100. The resulting time series would contain the trend, cycle, and irregular components only. By removing this seasonal component, analysts can seek to determine and identify the other factors which explain the variation in time series data. All this can be done by computer and an illustration is given in figure 3.2. Note that the results are identical except that the seasonal factors are presented. The seasonal factor is the index divided by 100.

The steps outlined above are very similar to those that would be followed in calculating monthly seasonal indices. The minor modifications that would be made can be seen by comparing the steps above with the following procedure.

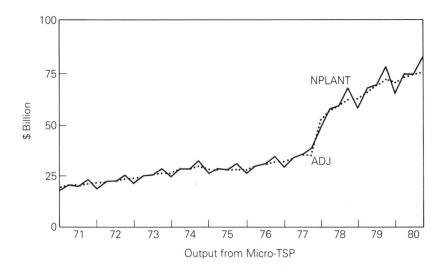

Output from Micro-TSP

FIGURE 3.2 New plant and equipment expenditures and seasonally adjusted series

1 Determine a 12 month moving total.
2 Center the moving total on each month.
3 Calculate the centered moving average by dividing the centered moving total by twice the length of seasonality ($2 \times 12 = 24$).
4 Divide each value in column 1 by the corresponding value in column 4, that is, express each month's actual value as a percentage of the moving average in step 3.
5 For each month (January, February,...,December) find the average percentage value from step 3 over all years.
6 Adjust the average percentages so that they sum to 1200.

The difficulty of calculating seasonal indices by this last method is usually not a serious problem. As we shall see when dealing with large databases, computer software procedures, such as TSP and SAS, are available to perform the calculations.

In figure 3.2, new plant and equipment expenditures (NPLANT) and the seasonally adjusted series (ADJ) are plotted against time. The series ADJ is the result of dividing each value in the NPLANT series by the appropriate seasonal index and remultiplying by 100 as illustrated above. Note the larger fluctuations in NPLANT in comparison with ADJ. This is the result of removing the serial variation from the original time series (NPLANT). Thus a result of deseasonalizing time series is to reduce the total variation in the data. In turn, a forecaster can more easily focus on understanding the movement in the series associated with the other components.

In the problems discussed up to now, the seasonal indices considered are called *constant seasonals*. Stated differently, the seasonal index for each month is assumed to be the same from year to year. Often, this assumption is not valid since seasonal indices may exhibit movements. The methods of this section steps can be applied to determine a moving seasonal. Winters' exponential smoothing model of chapter 2 was one example of a procedure producing moving seasonals.

Seasonal indices computed in this section are described as *relative seasonals* since they are expressed as a percentage. Relative seasonals assume that the seasonal effect is proportional to the level of the series. For example, at higher levels the amplitude of seasonal fluctuations will be greater. The seasonal index for the second quarter in example 3.2 was 101.6. Thus, on the average, the actual values are 1.6 percent larger ($C_t T_t I_t$). Alternatively, the seasonal fluctuations are not proportional to the level of the time series but remain about the same in absolute amount for all levels. The index which describes such movements is known as an *absolute seasonal*. Obviously, the method for deriving this last type of seasonal index differs slightly from the method described above. Thus, seasonal indices can be either constant or moving, and can be stated in either relative or absolute terms.

Finally, the moving-average method of chapter 2 does not center the data as in the ratio-to-moving-average method.

3.5 Trend Fitting and Analysis

The second component of a time series, the trend, is the subject area of interest in this section. We study trends to determine the long-term direction in a time series. In general, these movements result from a variety of causes including changes in technology, prices, population, and productivity.

The total savings deposits in a mutual savings bank, savings and loan institution, or credit union may rise from year to year for a period of time because the number of depositors continues to grow. Furthermore, each depositor tends to have greater dollar savings associated with a general increase in depositors' incomes. In part, this results from the general increase in prices called inflation.

A laser manufacturer may see an increase in sales revenues due to technological change. The development and improvement of lasers accompanied by wider application of their use has increased the number of lasers sold each year.

Changes in productivity, which, in turn, may result from technological change, give an upward slope to many economic time series.

Finally, the general upward pattern in revenues of a hospital is associated with the general increase of the prices or reimbursement rates for hospital services. It is the increase in the amount and use of more sophisticated medical technology that has contributed to the general increase in the prices charged by the hospital for the services performed in that institution.

A first step in the analysis of the trend component is to determine the purpose of analyzing it. We may wish either to project the trend or to eliminate it from the original series. Naturally, we may wish to do both. Having the purpose in mind guides the forecaster in choosing which method to use and in the length of the time series to analyze. If the purpose is to project the trend into the future, it is important to know for how far into the future the projection is to be made. A trend projection for 15 years ahead usually requires the use of a time series of longer duration than a projection of only three years.

In trend analysis, the initial step is to chart the time series on both arithmetic and ratio (semilogarithmic) scales before choosing the method of measurement. Specifically, consider the next example. Although there are statistical tests for determining the "significance" of the trend, i.e. the Runs test, an examination of the plot of the time will suffice.

Example 3.3

The data in table 3.4 are average weekly earnings of production of nonsupervisory workers on private nonagricultural payrolls. During the period 1950–60, average weekly earnings increased by $27.54. For the period 1960–70, the increase was $39.16 and for the 1970–80 period it was $115.27. Note that the arithmetic increase in average weekly earnings was about the same for the first two ten year periods but increased by a much larger absolute amount in the last ten year period. The relative increases and ratio from period to period are given in table 3.5. Observing the data in these two tables indicates that relative changes were roughly the same over the

TABLE 3.4

Year	Average weekly earnings
1950	53.13
1960	80.67
1970	119.83
1980	235.10

first 20 years but increased substantially in the last decade. The absolute changes were not the same over the three decades.

The X axis (horizontal) is ruled with an arithmetic scale and the Y axis (vertical) is ruled with a logarithmic scale. The logarithmic scale is ruled in a way that the actual plot is the logarithm of the data (Y value) rather than the actual data. When data are plotted on such a scale, equal vertical distances represent equal relative changes rather than equal absolute changes.

TABLE 3.5

Year			
From	To	Increase (%)	Ratio
1950	1960	51.84	1.52:1
1960	1970	48.54	1.49:1
1970	1980	96.19	1.96:1

In figure 3.3, data on average weekly earnings for the time period are displayed for both arithmetic and logarithmic scales. Note that, on the arithmetic chart, the distances from A to B and B to C are smaller than the distance from C to D. This reflects the absolute changes from 1950 to 1960, 1960 to 1970, and 1970 to 1980.

On the semilogarithmic scaled graph the vertical distance between A and B is greater than that between B and C. The vertical distance from C to D is greatest. These results reflect the relative changes observed for the three time periods. Furthermore, these relative changes cannot be seen clearly in the arithmetic chart, but are shown vividly on the semilogarithmic scale.

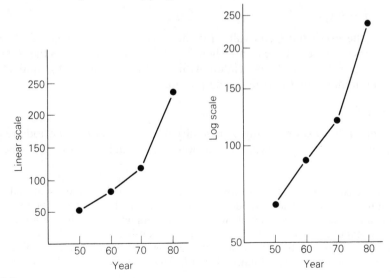

FIGURE 3.3

To understand why we have a different picture on a semilogarithmic graph and an arithmetic graph requires some understanding of logarithmic scales. Logarithmic scales vary due to tiering. The scale may be single tiered, i.e. 1 to 10, double tiered, i.e. 1 to 10 to 100, or tiered at higher levels, i.e. 1 to 10 to 100 to 1000. Since equal distances represent equal ratios, the distance from 1 to 2 is the same as the distance from 2 to 4, 10 to 20, 100 to 200, and so on. For the same reason, the distance from 1 to 2 (ratio 2:1) is greater than the distance from 2 to 3 (ratio 3:2) or from 3 to 4 (ratio 4:3). Thus, the greater the relative change, the greater is the vertical distance.

For the data of example 3.3, we note that the ratio of earnings between each ten year period varies from 1.49:1 to 1.96:1. This relatively narrow range in the ratios indicates that the semilogarithmic scale would appear more like a straight line than if the same data were plotted on an arithmetic graph. Hence we can conclude that the nature of the economic time series determines whether an arithmetic or a semilogarithmic scale is most appropriate.

In addition to depicting relative change, semilogarithmic plots are also used to present data that vary greatly in absolute amounts. Forecasters may display two sets of data where the size of one series varies more widely than the second. Finally, we must take great care in interpreting and explaining that equal vertical distances on the semilogarithmic plot represent equal ratios or equal relative changes.

3.6   The Linear Trend Model

Judgement is often the criterion used to determine which model constitutes the best fit. At times, a forecaster will simply draw a line through the series of observations to reveal the shape and direction of a trend in the time series. In drawing the freehand trend, the forecaster must be able to recognize the repeating seasonal fluctuation and cycles through which the trend passes. Unless the forecaster is very familiar with the particular time series, this process can be very difficult. Thus forecasters usually rely on the objective method of least squares to avoid the subjectivity involved in the freehand method.

To begin, we shall define the estimated linear equations as follows:

$$\hat{Y}_t = a + bX_t$$

where $\hat{Y}_t$ is the predicted trend value for the Y variable for a selected coded time period X,[1] a is the value of the trend when $X = 0$ (the intercept), b is the slope of the equation (the change in $\hat{Y}$ associated with a unit change in X), and X is the observation number for the coded time period.

Example 3.4

Actual data on the cost of heating a university over a 15 year time period are plotted as shown in figure 3.4. The symbol Y denotes the actual values of the time series.

---

1   The predicted or forecast value for Y is denoted $\hat{Y}$. This is the usual and common nomenclature of classical time series decomposition analysis. In chapter 2, the forecast value was denoted as F which is common nomenclature for application of the methods of moving averages and exponential smoothing. This apparent inconsistency is usual practice in the field of forecasting. Thus in this book we shall follow the usual practices of forecasters remembering at all times the meaning of $\hat{Y}$ and F. Thus $\hat{Y}$ is the predicted value for the trend factor T_t .

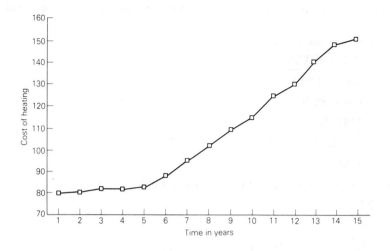

FIGURE 3.4 Plot of heating cost against time

Although some variation in the series is observed, the heating cost appears to increase by a constant amount over the time period. Hence a linear trend is appropriate and can be estimated by least squares methods (table 3.6).

TABLE 3.6 Worksheet for least squares

Period X	Heating cost ($ hundreds) Y	X^2	XY
1	80	1	80
2	81	4	162
3	82	9	246
4	82	16	328
5	83	25	415
6	88	36	528
7	95	49	665
8	102	64	816
9	110	81	990
10	115	100	1150
11	125	121	1375
12	130	144	1560
13	140	169	1820
14	148	196	2072
15	151	225	2265
Total 120	1612	1240	14 472
ΣX	ΣY	ΣX^2	ΣXY

In computing the trend equation, the formulas and computations are as follows.

1 The formula for the slope is

$$b = \frac{n\Sigma XY - \Sigma X \Sigma Y}{n\Sigma X^2 - (\Sigma X)^2} \qquad (3.4)$$

By substitution we find

$$b = \frac{15(14472) - (120)(1612)}{15(1240) - (120)^2}$$

$$= 5.6286$$

2 The slope is now substituted in the formula for the intercept

$$a = \frac{\Sigma Y}{n} - b\frac{\Sigma X}{n} \qquad (3.5)$$

$$= \frac{1612}{15} - 5.6286\left(\frac{120}{15}\right)$$

$$= 62.44$$

Limiting the significant digits to two decimal places, we write the estimating equation as

$$\hat{Y}_t = 62.44 + 5.63X_t$$

(origin at $X = 0$; one unit of X = one year).

   To interpret the above equation, we say that for every change of one year (or time period) there is on the average a change of $5.63 thousand in heating cost. At year (time period) zero, the costs are estimated to be $62.44 thousand.
   An alternate procedure for calculating trend values by hand is to code the time periods (X values) in another way. In this second method, the calculations are made easier because the time periods are coded so that the X values sum to zero. When $\Sigma X = 0$, the formula for the slope becomes

$$b = \frac{n\Sigma XY}{n\Sigma X^2} \qquad (3.6)$$

Furthermore, the formula for the intercept becomes

$$a = \frac{\Sigma Y}{n} \qquad (3.7)$$

Try it yourself by letting the time periods range from −7 to +7 instead of from 1 to 15. The former $X = 8$ becomes the new coded value $X = 0$. Finally, the interpretation of the estimated slope is the same as before; only the interpretation of the intercept changes. It is still the value of $\hat{Y}$ when $X = 0$ but there is now a new position for $X = 0$ and the intercept is the former value of $\hat{Y}$ when $X = 8$. Thus the equation arrived at is the same except for an adjustment for the shift in the origin.
   Last, if we examine figure 3.5, we observe the same trend line calculated by a computer program (SAS software system). The equation of the trend line is found under the column marked ESTIMATE and the rows for INTERCEPT and TIME. Note that the equation of the trend line would be

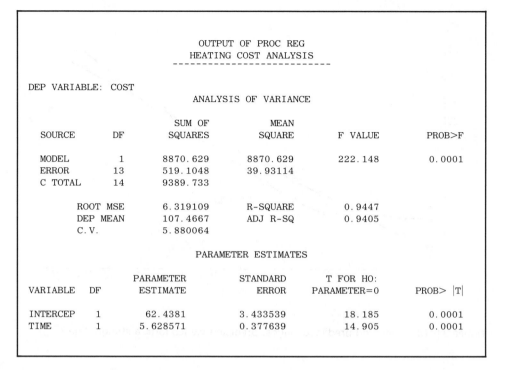

OUTPUT OF PROC REG
HEATING COST ANALYSIS

DEP VARIABLE: COST

ANALYSIS OF VARIANCE

SOURCE	DF	SUM OF SQUARES	MEAN SQUARE	F VALUE	PROB>F
MODEL	1	8870.629	8870.629	222.148	0.0001
ERROR	13	519.1048	39.93114		
C TOTAL	14	9389.733			

ROOT MSE	6.319109	R-SQUARE	0.9447	
DEP MEAN	107.4667	ADJ R-SQ	0.9405	
C.V.	5.880064			

PARAMETER ESTIMATES

VARIABLE	DF	PARAMETER ESTIMATE	STANDARD ERROR	T FOR H0: PARAMETER=0	PROB> |T|
INTERCEP	1	62.4381	3.433539	18.185	0.0001
TIME	1	5.628571	0.377639	14.905	0.0001

FIGURE 3.5 Output of PROC REG heating cost analysis

$$\hat{Y}_t = 62.44 + 5.63X$$

(parameter estimates rounded to two decimal places).

If we wish to forecast one period ahead, that is, time period 16, substitute this number in the trend equation:

$$\hat{Y}_{16} = 62.44 + 5.63(16) = 152.52$$

Therefore, for period 16, the heating cost is estimated to be $152 520.

Finally, the same computer program produced a scatter diagram of fitted and actual values. Observe the close proximity of the fitted and actual values in figure 3.6. In later chapters we shall evaluate how good this fit is. However, we can observe the mean square error (MSE) term for this procedure. The MSE is the value under the column MEAN SQUARE and across the row ERROR in figure 3.5, which is 39.93 (rounded to two decimals). If we compare this MSE with the MSE measure for another forecasting technique, we can evaluate whether trend fitting by least squares techniques is more accurate than other forecasting techniques.

Although the linear trend line is more often applied to time series than any other model to describe long-term movements, the use of other models to describe change is often advisable.

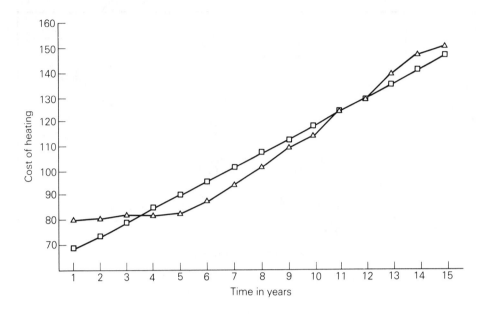

FIGURE 3.6 Observed and predicted values: predicted values form a straight line

3.7 Exponential Trend Analysis

A time series which does not appear linear on an arithmetic graph may appear linear on a semilogarithmic graph. In this case, the equation of the line is

$$\hat{Y}_t = (AB^{X_t}) \tag{3.8}$$

where Y and X are variables, and A and B are constants. This latter model is referred to as an *exponential trend*. If the trend is linear on a semilogarithmic graph, the trend is best fitted by an exponential trend.

For computational purposes, the following equivalent expression in logarithmic terms is

$$\log \hat{Y}_t = \log a + X_t \log b \tag{3.9}$$

To fit an exponential trend by the method of least squares, we estimate $\log a$ and $\log b$ from the following formulas:

$$\log a = \frac{\Sigma \log Y}{n} \tag{3.10}$$

$$\log b = \frac{\Sigma(X \log Y)}{\Sigma X^2} \tag{3.11}$$

which are provided by coding the X values so that we make $\Sigma X = 0$. Consider the next example.

Example 3.5

Sales for the Tri-State Cable and Interconnector Control Corporation for the years 1974–80 were as shown in table 3.7. The above set of data is linear in a semilogarithmic scale but is not linear in an arithmetic scale. The worksheet in table 3.8 is set up to permit the hand computation of the exponential equation. Year 1977 is coded at $X = 0$.

TABLE 3.7

Years	Sales ($ thousands)
1974	10.7
1975	13.9
1976	18.1
1977	23.5
1978	30.6
1979	39.8
1980	51.7

TABLE 3.8 Worksheet for semilog least squares (common logarithms)

X	log Y	X log Y	X²
−3	1.029	−3.087	9
−2	1.143	−2.286	4
−1	1.258	−1.258	1
0	1.371	0	0
1	1.486	1.486	1
2	1.600	3.200	4
3	1.713	5.139	9
Total 0	9.600	3.194	28
ΣX	$\Sigma \log Y$	$\Sigma X \log Y$	ΣX^2

Fitting the above computations into the formula for log a, we have

$$\log a = \frac{\Sigma \log Y}{n} = \frac{9.600}{7} = 1.371$$

Substituting the above values in the formula for log b, we have

$$\log b = \frac{\Sigma(X \log Y)}{\Sigma X^2} = \frac{3.194}{28} = 0.114$$

Writing the trend equation in semilogarithmic form yields

$$\log \hat{Y}_t = 1.371 + 0.114X_t$$

(origin at year 1977; one unit of X = one year).

When the numbers whose logarithms are 1.371 and 0.114 are found, the exponential trend line is written

$$\hat{Y} = 23.50(1.300)^{X_i}$$

(origin at year 1977; one unit of X = one year). To interpret this equation, we say that 23.50 is the value of Y when $X = 0$ (the year 1977) and 1.300 is 1 plus the average rate of growth in sales over the time period studied. Note, also, that the Y values are in thousands of dollars and hence 23.50 indicates $23 500. Last, on an annual basis, the growth rate per year on the average is 30 percent. The observed and predicted values are displayed in figure 3.7. Note that the values are identical and the trend line is not straight but is curved on this graph.

For purposes of forecasting, some may find the semilogarithmic form of the equation more accurate. For example, if we wish to forecast sales for 1982, we substitute 5 for X in the equation as follows:

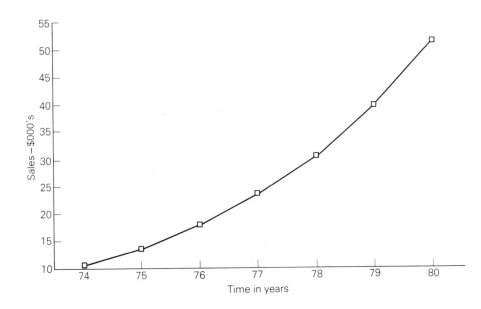

FIGURE 3.7 Observed and predicted values – semilogarithmic trend; observed and predicted are identical

$$\log \hat{Y}_5 = 1.371 + 0.114(5) = 1.941$$

and

$$\hat{Y}_5 = 87.297$$

or $87 297 is the estimate of sales revenues for the year 1982 based on the exponential trend in the time series.

The SAS output for producing the exponential trend for the data of table 3.8 is illustrated in figure 3.8. Note that the estimated parameters for the INTERCEPT

```
                    OUTPUT OF PROC REG
                  EXPONENTIAL TREND MODEL
                  --------------------------

DEP VARIABLE: LOGS           LOG OF SALES -BASE 10
                            ANALYSIS OF VARIANCE

                    SUM OF            MEAN
SOURCE          DF  SQUARES          SQUARE      F VALUE       PROB>F

MODEL           1   0.3643669       0.3643669   999999.990    0.0001
ERROR           5   4.96315E-07     9.92631E-08
C TOTAL         6   0.3643674

        ROOT MSE   0.0003150604        R-SQUARE    1.0000
        DEP MEAN   1.371463            ADJ R-SQ    1.0000
        C.V.       0.02297258

                     PARAMETER ESTIMATES

                    PARAMETER         STANDARD        T FOR HO:
VARIABLE        DF  ESTIMATE          ERROR           PARAMETER=0

INTERCEP        1       3.15791       0.0002741956    11516.998
PERIOD          1       0.2626674     0.0001370978     1915.913

                                        VARIABLE
VARIABLE        DF  PROB > |T|           LABEL

INTERCEP        1       0.0001          INTERCEPT
PERIOD          1       0.0001
```

FIGURE 3.8 Exponential trend by common logarithms

TABLE 3.9 Worksheet for semilogarithmic least squares (base e logarithms)

X	$ln(Y)$	X $ln(Y)$	X^2
-3	2.370	-7.110	9
-2	2.632	-5.264	4
-1	2.896	-2.896	1
0	3.157	0	0
1	3.421	3.421	1
2	3.684	7.368	4
3	3.945	11.836	9
Total 0	22.105	7.355	28
ΣX	$\Sigma \ln(Y)$	$\Sigma X \ln(Y)$	ΣX^2

and PERIOD are equal to 1.371 and 0.114 after rounding to three decimal places. Therefore, the exponential trend model is easily estimated by this software system.

The exponential trend model can also be estimated by the use of logarithms to the base e (natural logarithms). Table 3.9 contains the worksheet for semilogarithmic least squares (base e logarithms). By substituting in equations (3.10) and (3.11) we find $\ln a = 3.158$ and $\ln b = 0.263$. Writing the trend equation in semilogarithmic form yields

$$\ln \hat{Y}_t = 3.158 + 0.263X_t$$

(origin at year 1977; one unit of X = one year)

When the numbers whose logarithms are 3.158 and 0.263 are found, the exponential trend equation is written

$$\hat{Y}_t = 23.50(1.300)$$

with the same origin and unit value as above. The interpretation of this equation is exactly the same as noted for the exponential trend equation arrived at by using common logarithms (base 10 logarithms).

For purposes of forecasting, we can use either the semilogarithmic or exponential trend form to predict for any future year. For example, if we wish to forecast for 1982, we substitute 5 for X in the equation as follows:

$$\ln \hat{Y}_5 = 3.158 + 0.263(5) = 4.473$$

and

$$\hat{Y}_5 = 87.297$$

or $87 297. This estimate for 1982 is the same as achieved by the results noted before for the case of common logarithms (logarithms to base 10).

Finally, the results of using SAS to solve this problem are illustrated in figure 3.9. The parameter estimates for the INTERCEPT and PERIOD are 3.158 and 0.263 rounded to three decimal places. Thus a forecaster has the choice of working with either natural (base e) or common (base 10) logarithms when computing the equation for the exponential trend. The choice is best made by each forecaster based on how easy it is for him/her to use either logarithm system.

3.8   Monthly or Quarterly Trend Estimates

To compute trend values for monthly or quarterly data, least squares procedures coupled with the computer can produce equations of the type discussed earlier in this chapter. In this section, only trend estimates for yearly data will be converted to trend estimates for periods of less than a year. Previously, trend was defined as the long-term movement in a time series. Following from this definition, the approach of this section is to develop a short-term trend equation from an already computed yearly trend equation. These estimates are done simply by calculating the parameter estimates in annual terms and either dividing by 12 for monthly estimates or by 4 for quarterly estimates.

```
                        OUTPUT OF PROC REG
                      EXPONENTIAL TREND MODEL

DEP VARIABLE: LY                 LOG OF SALES -BASE E
                                  ANALYSIS OF VARIANCE

                          SUM OF            MEAN
SOURCE           DF       SQUARES           SQUARE        F VALUE        PROB>F

MODEL             1       1.931836         1.931836      999999.990      0.0001
ERROR             5       .00000263141    5.26282E-07
C TOTAL           6       1.931839

            ROOT MSE   0.0007254533       R-SQUARE        1.0000
            DEP MEAN        3.15791        ADJ R-SQ        1.0000
            C.V.        0.02297258

                         PARAMETER ESTIMATES

                          PARAMETER          STANDARD        T FOR H0:
VARIABLE         DF        ESTIMATE           ERROR        PARAMETER=0

INTERCEP          1         3.15791       0.0002741956      11516.998
PERIOD            1        0.2626674      0.0001370978       1915.913

                                              VARIABLE
VARIABLE         DF      PROB > |T|             LABEL

INTERCEP          1        0.0001            INTERCEPT
PERIOD            1        0.0001
```

FIGURE 3.9 Exponential trend by natural logarithms

Example 3.6

Data for American Hospital Supply Inc. for the years 1965–80 is provided to find the trend component of the time series for net income ($ million). Based on the actual value, the trend equation is estimated to be

$\hat{Y}_t = -10.877 + 7.056X_t$ (origin at year 1964) calculated by least squares methods. Note that $X = 0$ will represent 1 July 1964, the midpoint of the year 1964.

Changing the scale of the equation from annual to monthly totals, divide the equation by 12:

$$\hat{Y}_t = \frac{-10.877 + 7.056X_t}{12}$$

$$= -0.90642 + 0.5880X_t \quad (\text{\$ million})$$

If we wish to convert net income from $ million to $ thousand, we multiply the equation by 1000 and obtain

$$\hat{Y}_t = -906.42 + 588.0X_t \quad (\text{\$ million})$$

The X in the equation still refers to units in terms of years. Thus X is converted to represent months by dividing it by 12 as follows:

$$\hat{Y}_t = -906.42 + 588.0\,\frac{X_t}{12}$$

$$= -906.42 + 49.0X_t$$

If we wish to convert the origin from 1 July 1964 to 15 January 1965, we substitute as follows:

$$\hat{Y}_t = -906.42 + 49.0(X_t + 6.5)$$

$$= -587.92 + 49.0X_t$$

(origin at 15 January 1965; one unit of x = one month). Last, to forecast for the first month of 1991 ($X_t = 300$), we set

$$\hat{Y}_{300} = -587.92 + (49\times300)$$

$$= \$14112.08 \text{ thousand}$$

The above prediction is therefore the trend prediction for the first month of 1991. Similarly, quarterly forecasts are derived from annual trend prediction equations by dividing by a factor of 4 to reflect quarters, rather than by 12 as in this example.

3.9   Isolating Cyclical Movements and the Irregular Variation

In this section, we shall consider an application of the method of moving averages to isolate the cyclical component. This isolation process is similar to the notion of isolating trend and seasonal components earlier. We should note that predicting cyclical movements and turning points in economic activity is subject to a very different type of analysis. This second approach was developed by the National Bureau of Economic Research (NBER), and we shall study their methods in a later chapter. At this point, however, we shall consider another approach.

Isolation of the cyclical component is achieved by first deseasonalizing the data as follows:

$$\frac{Y_t}{\text{seasonal index}} = \frac{T_t C_t S_t I_t}{S_t}$$

$$= T_t C_t I_t \qquad (3.12)$$

The above deseasonalized data is then detrended as follows:

$$\frac{T_t C_t I_t}{T_t} = C_t I_t \qquad (3.13)$$

The resulting series now contains only variation associated with the cyclical component and irregular variation.

The cyclical component can be elicited from the time series via a moving-average process that smooths irregular variations out of the data. In turn, by dividing the cyclical–irregular series by the cyclical component, the irregular variation is found. To illustrate this process, let us consider the next example.

TABLE 3.10 Isolation of the cyclical component for new plant and equipment expenditures ($ billions)

Year	Quarter	(1) Deseasonalized values $T_t \times C_t \times I_t$	(2) Trend $\hat{Y}_t = T_t$	(3) $C_t \times I_t$ as percentage of trend	(4) Weighted period moving total	(5) Cyclical component C_t	(6) Irregular variation I_t
1971	1	19.3	9.6	201.0	—	—	—
	2	20.3	11.1	182.9	727.9	182.0	100.5
	3	20.3	12.6	161.1	654.7	163.7	98.4
	4	21.1	14.1	149.6	596.2	149.1	100.3
1972	1	21.2	15.6	135.9	548.5	137.1	99.1
	2	21.6	17.0	127.1	510.1	127.5	99.7
	3	22.2	18.5	120.0	483.6	120.9	99.3
	4	23.3	20.0	116.5	462.3	115.6	100.8
1973	1	23.5	21.5	109.3	440.7	110.2	99.2
	2	24.3	23.0	105.6	423.8	106.0	99.6
	3	25.3	24.5	103.3	413.7	103.4	99.9
	4	26.4	26.0	101.5	401.9	100.5	101.0
1974	1	26.3	27.5	95.6	388.9	97.2	98.4
	2	27.8	28.9	96.2	381.8	95.5	100.7
	3	28.5	30.4	93.8	376.3	94.1	99.7
	4	29.5	31.9	92.5	363.2	90.8	101.9
1975	1	28.2	33.4	84.4	341.2	85.3	98.9
	2	27.9	34.9	79.9	321.4	80.4	99.4
	3	28.1	36.4	77.2	309.2	77.3	99.9
	4	28.4	37.9	74.9	298.8	74.7	100.3
1976	1	28.3	39.4	71.8	290.1	72.5	99.0
	2	29.2	40.8	71.6	286.6	71.7	99.9
	3	30.3	42.3	71.6	287.6	71.9	99.6
	4	31.9	43.8	72.8	287.6	71.9	101.3
1977	1	31.9	45.3	70.4	284.5	71.1	99.0
	2	33.2	46.8	70.9	285.1	71.3	99.4
	3	35.2	48.3	72.9	287.6	71.9	101.4
	4	35.3	49.8	70.9	316.5	79.1	89.6
1978	1	52.2	51.3	101.8	381.7	95.4	106.7
	2	56.5	52.7	107.2	425.4	106.4	100.7
	3	59.2	54.2	109.2	438.0	109.5	98.7
	4	62.6	55.7	112.4	443.4	110.9	99.7
1979	1	62.6	57.2	109.4	443.1	110.8	101.4
	2	65.7	58.7	111.9	448.2	112.1	98.7
	3	69.2	60.2	115.0	458.9	114.7	99.8
	4	72.2	61.7	117.0	461.5	115.4	100.3
1980	1	71.0	63.1	112.5	454.7	113.7	101.4
	2	72.8	64.6	112.7	451.4	112.9	98.9
	3	75.0	66.1	113.5	452.4	113.1	99.8
	4	76.2	67.6	112.7	—	—	100.4

Source: Original data from *Survey of Current Business*, various issues.

Example 3.7

Data on new plant and equipment expenditures (total nonfarm business) were previously collected from the *Survey of Current Business* in example 3.3. Quarterly data were, in turn, deseasonalized and that result is reported in column 1 of table 3.10. The deseasonalized data are then used to estimate the trend component by the method of least squares. Column 2 of table 3.10 is the trend component. The data are now ready for analysis by the moving-average techniques.

Column 3 of table 3.10 represents the cyclical–irregular component as a percentage of the trend which is column 2. Note that this component C_tI_t is now ready to be smoothed by a process such as the moving-average method.

The moving-average methodology assumes that the pattern exhibited in time series can be represented by an average of past observations. The presence or absence of cyclical forces in the moving average depends on the length of the moving average, that is, three, four, or five or more previous periods.

A simple moving average model M_t is set forth in the following equation:

$$M_t = \frac{Z_t + Z_{t-1} + Z_{t-2} + \ldots + Z_{t-n+1}}{n} \tag{3.14}$$

where M_t is the moving average at time t, Z_t is the value in period t (in equation (3.14), the deseasonalized and detrended value, i.e. $Z_t = C_tI_t$), and n is the number of terms in the moving average. For ease of computation, the equation can be restated as

$$M_t = M_{t-1} + \frac{Z_t - Z_{t-n}}{n} \tag{3.15}$$

Thus, for time period t, the moving average is the arithmetic mean of the n most recent observations.

In the above equations, equal weights are assigned to each of the n most recent observations. Zero weights are assigned to all other historical observations. If weight W_t were attached to each observation Z_t, the formulas would be rewritten as

$$M_t = \frac{W_tZ_t + W_{t-1}Z_{t-1} + W_{t-2}Z_{t-2} + \ldots + W_{t-n+1}Z_{t-n+1}}{n} \tag{3.16}$$

and

$$M_t = M_{t-1} + \frac{W_tZ_t - W_{t-n}Z_{t-n}}{n} \tag{3.17}$$

Thus, for time period t, the moving average is the arithmetic mean of the n most recent observations.

In the above equations, equal weights are assigned to each of the n most recent observations. Zero weights are assigned to all other historical observations. If weight W_t were attached to each observation Z_t, the formulas would be rewritten as

$$M_t = \frac{W_tZ_t + W_{t-1}Z_{t-1} + W_{t-2}Z_{t-2} + \ldots + W_{t-2}Z_{t-2} + \ldots + W_{t-n+1}Z_{t-n+1}}{n} \tag{3.18}$$

and

$$M_t = M_{t-1} + \frac{W_tZ_t - W_{t-n}Z_{t-n}}{n} \tag{3.19}$$

where W_t is the weight assigned to observation Y_t at t.

As each new data value becomes available, it is included in the average and the data value for the nth period preceding it is discarded. Hence M_t is an updated version of the immediately preceding estimate. The second form of M_t highlights this point.

Moving averages will respond to changes in the underlying data pattern depending on both the number of periods included in the moving average and the weights assigned in the formula. Note that if the weights are assigned equally, then the formulas for the weighted and unweighted moving average are equivalent. If large weights are given to current periods and very small weights to older periods, then the recent observation will affect the moving average more. Also, the more periods are included in the moving average (larger values of n), the less sensitive the moving average will be to changes in the pattern of the cyclical movement. In contrast, a small value of n leads to a moving average that responds very rapidly to changes.

Last, if we were to predict for periods beyond the current period t, the predictive equation would become

$$\hat{Z}_{t+1} = M_t = \frac{W_t Z_t + W_{t-1} Z_{t-2} + \ldots + W_{-n+1} Z_{t-n+1}}{W_t + W_{t-1} + W_{t-2} + \ldots + W_{t-n+1}} \tag{3.20}$$

where $\hat{Z}$ is the predicted value of Z at $t + 1$.

To illustrate the usefulness of moving averages, we shall return to example 3.7 and its accompanying table 3.10. In the example, the smoothing process will be a weighted moving average with weights 1, 2 and 1. The current period has double the weight of the preceding and succeeding periods. For example, for the second period of the second quarter of 1971, the weighted moving total of 727.9 is found by adding the products of the weights and values in column 3. Thus

$$727.9 = (1 \times 201.0) + (2 \times 182.9) + (1 \times 161.1)$$

In turn, the cyclical component is derived by dividing the weighted three-quarter moving total (column 4) by the sum of the weights (4). A cyclical component of 182.0 indicates that cyclical forces are increasing economic activity by a factor of 82 percent above the trend level. If no cyclical component was present, the trend level would be smaller. However, a cyclical component of 72.5 (first quarter of 1976) implies that actual new plant and equipment expenditures were being depressed by 27.5 percent because of the downturn in economic activity.

Finally, the identification of the irregular component is accomplished by dividing each of the values already adjusted for seasonality and trend (table 3.10, column 3) by the values representing the effect of only the cyclical component (table 3.10, column 5) and multiplying by 100. The resulting index aids in identifying the contribution of the irregular component in the quarterly values of the time series, as shown in column 6 of table 3.10 (labeled I_t).

The irregular component is calculated in the following manner:

$$I_t = \frac{C_t I_t}{C_t} \times 100$$

For example, for 1971, quarter 2,

$$C_t I_t = 182.9$$
$$C_t = 182.0$$

$$I_t = \frac{C_t I_t}{C_t} \times 100 = \frac{182.9}{182.0} \times 100 = 100.49$$

The irregular variations in a time series, especially those that are sizable, can usually be explained. For example, large irregularities can be due to work stoppages due to strikes and/or lockouts, earthquakes, extreme weather conditions, and the like. The irregular component of a time series is composed of fluctuations that are a result of unpredictable and/or nonsystematic events.

The decomposition of the new plant equipment expenditures is now complete. The short-term quarterly data have been separated into components. For example, for the first quarter of 1980,

$T_t = 63.1$ (table 3.10, column 2)

$S_t = 91.8$ (seasonal index for first quarter calculated for these data)

$C_t = 113.7$ (table 3.10, column 5)

$I_t = 98.9$ (table 3.10, column 6)

To put the series back together, we return to the original multiplicative decomposition model and substitute the appropriate components.

$Y_t = T_t S_t C_t I_t$

Y (quarter 1, 1980) $= 63.1 \times 0.918 \times 1.137 \times 0.989$

$$= 65.1 \quad \text{(table 3.2)}$$

The multiplicative model is often used to develop a short-term forecast. Again, each component is estimated by the methods discussed previously and illustrated in the next section.

Knowledge of the contribution of each of the systematic components, seasonal, trend and cyclical factors, called classical decomposition, permits the forecaster to achieve a principal goal of time series analysis. The goal is to explain the variation in the data observations over time. In the next section, we shall return to this notion with reference to a procedure which adjusts data for seasonal variation.

3.10   Time Series Decomposition Results and Forecasting

Up to this point, we have considered methods of analyzing time series data for the purpose of separating the series into its components of trend, seasonal, cyclical, and irregular variation. While the analysis of time series to identify its components is important, the effort involved is justifiable only if the results permit better forecasting. This section considers one method for utilizing decomposition results to predict the future values of a series. The section is limited, however, to the use of decomposition results obtained from analysis of the multiplicative model.

Example 3.8

In January of 1989, the budget officer of a certain county was given the task of predicting revenues from an increase in the county sales tax for 1990. To forecast, the budget officer utilized a quarterly trend–cycle equation and seasonal indices supplied by the staff of the budget office. The trend–cycle equation and indices had been developed using county sales tax collection data over the past 15 years. The data were adjusted to eliminate differences in the county sales tax rate over the 15 year interval.

The equation was

$$\hat{Y}_t = \$14.5 + 1.5X_t$$

where all figures are in millions of dollars and $X = 1$ occurred in the first period of 1974. Since the first quarter of 1990 is $X = 65$, the second quarter is $X = 66$, and so on. Also, the indices of quarterly sales tax collection were as follows:

first quarter	85
second quarter	95
third quarter	108
fourth quarter	112

The budget officer proceeded to develop the forecast using

$$\text{forecast} = T_t C_t \frac{S_t}{100}$$

To proceed, the budget officer combined the above forecasting expression with the trend–cycle equation developed by the budget office staff to arrive at the following predictive formula:

$$\hat{Y} = \frac{(\$14.5 + 1.5\ X_t)S}{100}$$

The forecast sales tax revenues by quarter are

$$\hat{Y}_{65} = \frac{(14.5 + 1.5(65))85}{100} = 95.200$$

$$\hat{Y}_{66} = \frac{(14.5 + 1.5(66))95}{100} = 107.825$$

$$\hat{Y}_{67} = \frac{(14.5 + 1.5(67))108}{100} = 124.200$$

$$\hat{Y}_{68} = \frac{(14.5 + 1.5(68))112}{100} = 130.480$$

The sum of the quarterly forecasts is the annual forecast (million dollars) in sales tax collections for the year 1990, which is $457.705 million.

The above method for forecasting consists of employing a trend–cycle projection and seasonal indices. This method can be used to predict far into the future. However, projections into the future become more unreliable as one predicts further into the future. Projections of more than five years into the future can only be made for those time series that are highly stable and regular. The greater the time between the present and the future period the less confidence we have in the reliability of the forecast.

In the next example, a forecaster can break down the multiplicative model even further by examining the trend and cycle components independently.

Example 3.9

In this example, we return to the problem of forecasting the new plant and equipment expenditures. This time series was decomposed using the methods of this chapter in section 3.9. To develop the one-quarter-ahead short-term forecast, each individual component was estimated on an accurate basis. The process is as follows:

1 *Trend:* the quarterly trend estimated using the appropriate linear trend model is

$$Y = 8.1100 + 1.4873X$$

Since a one-period-ahead model would be for quarter 41, this X-coded value is substituted in the trend equation:

$$Y = 8.1100 + 1.4873(41) = 69.09$$

2 *Seasonal:* the adjusted seasonal index from the US Department of Commerce for the first quarter ahead is 91.8. Alternatively, we could have used the ratio-to-moving-average method of this chapter which gave a similar result.

3 *Cyclical:* the cyclical component must be estimated using the methods outlined in section 3.9. Subjectively, we must use the data of table 3.10 and all available information on the future direction of economic activity and this time series to come up with a reliable estimate. (More details of this subjective approach will be examined in chapter 10.) The result is that an estimate for the cyclical component for the first quarter of 1981 is 111.5

4 *Irregular:* the irregular index component must also be estimated from past experience. Since irregular fluctuations are often unpredictable, an estimate of 100 (a factor of 1.0) will commonly be used. On occasion, a forecaster will vary from this practice if an irregularity is anticipated. For example, one may anticipate a work stoppage due to a strike or other job action or some government action that may be relevant. In this example, an estimate of 100 for this component will be appropriate as this series is an aggregate.

For the one-period-ahead projection, we have

$$Y_t = T_t S_t C_t I_t$$

$$Y(\text{period } 41) = 69.09 \times 0.918 \times 1.115 \times 1.0 = 70.18$$

The importance of each component dictates their use in forecasting. If the time series is extremely seasonal, the seasonal variation analysis will provide important, if not complete, information for the forecasting process. Finally, knowledge of all the components of the time series are important in forecasting by decomposition techniques.

3.11　Forecasting and the X-11 Procedures

The X-11 version of the Census Method II Seasonal Adjustment Program is a principal procedure for decomposing economic time series and was developed by the Bureau of the Census.[2] The Census technique is a refinement of NBER techniques for decomposing time series for systematic components.

2　For a full discussion of this set of procedures see US Department of Commerce, US Bureau of the Census (1967).

There are four distinct phases of the X-11 procedures. First, monthly time series data can be adjusted to account for variation in the number of trading days in a month. *Trading day adjustments* are desirable since a given month usually has a varying number of business or trading days from year to year. For many industries or sectors of the economy, this source of variation may have altered the observed value of the series in different years. To illustrate this source of variation, consider the next example.

Example 3.10

Data on new construction expenditures (million dollars) in the United States for the period January 1984 to March 1989 was obtained from the US Department of Labor. Data for the month of May (five observations) are given in table 3.11. The trading day adjustment can be explained from these data.

TABLE 3.11 Trading day adjustment for new construction expenditures in the United States ($ millions)

Year	(1) New construction expenditures	(2) Adjustment factors	(3) Adjusted new construction expenditures
1984	1367	1.01960	1341
1985	1488	1.03165	1442
1986	1391	0.99823	1393
1987	1143	0.96714	1182
1988	1084	1.00002	1084

To find the adjustment factor for each month of each year, the X-11 system performs a least squares trend analysis to produce adjustment factors (column 2). The observed values for new construction expenditures (column 1) are then divided by the adjustment factors to arrive at the adjusted values for expenditures (column 4). For quarterly data, the trading day adjustment is unnecessary. Figure 3.10 contains the SAS computer output of the original series and figure 3.11 contains the trading day adjusted series.

After trading day adjustments are made, the next phase of the X-11 system is to adjust the original data for seasonality. Also, adjustments for extreme values associated with unusual and unpredictable events are made. This process of adjustments for extremes is made by calculating the standard deviations. The extreme right-hand column, TOTAL, contains the row-wise totals in the original and adjusted series (figures 3.10 and 3.11).

The third phase of X-11 recalculates the original seasonal factors as a result of extreme adjustments. A special adjustment process recalculates these new seasonal factors (seasonal index numbers). Also, the cycle and trend components are estimated by a centered moving average of the original time series. These estimates of the components are then used to arrive at the final seasonal factors which are moving seasonals and different from the constant seasonals of the ratio-to-moving-average method. Figure 3.12 contains these final seasonal factors (moving seasonal index numbers) including one year ahead seasonal factors for forecasting. By

```
B 1 ORIGINAL SERIES
YEAR    JAN      FEB      MAR      APR      MAY      JUN
1984    2355     1528     1424     1432     1367     1367
1985    2627     1667     1507     1637     1488     1422
1986    2447     1581     1508     1574     1391     1427
1987    2205     1476     1385     1349     1143     1319
1988    2041     1418     1301     1153     1084     1200
1989    1856     1258     1360    *******  *******  *******
AVG     2255     1488     1414     1429     1295     1347


YEAR    JUL      AUG      SEP      OCT      NOV      DEC      TOTAL
1984    1766     1457     1243     1758     1816     2074     19587
1985    1909     1453     1343     1668     1664     2249     20634
1986    1831     1392     1361     1530     1464     2164     19670
1987    1591     1098     1050     1179     1321     2650     17766
1988    1465     1189     1031     1120     1357     1763     16122
1989 *******  *******  *******  *******  *******  *******     4474

AVG     1712     1318     1206     1451     1524     2180

TOTAL —          98253 MEAN             1560 S.D. —           374
```

FIGURE 3.10

Source: US Department of Labor, Washington, DC

```
C19 ORIGINAL SERIES ADJUSTED FOR FINAL COMB.  TD.  WGTS.
YEAR    JAN      FEB      MAR      APR      MAY      JUN
1984    2355     1486     1427     1464     1341     1364
1985    2577     1682     1558     1580     1442     1527
1986    2372     1595     1593     1537     1393     1459
1987    2209     1489     1385     1352     1182     1273
1988    2110     1362     1276     1151     1084     1202
1989    1856     1269     1318    *******  *******  *******
AVG     2246     1481     1426     1417     1288     1365


YEAR    JUL      AUG      SEP      OCT      NOV      DEC      TOTAL
1984    1766     1412     1334     1696     1762     2190     19597
1985    1842     1456     1373     1636     1661     2249     20583
1986    1796     1439     1314     1483     1572     2088     19641
1987    1542     1160     1025     1181     1351     2599     17748
1988    1515     1147     1000     1183     1325     1766     16122
1989 *******  *******  *******  *******  *******  *******     4443

AVG     1692     1323     1209     1436     1534     2178

TOTAL —          98134 MEAN             1558 S.D. —           366
```

FIGURE 3.11

```
D10 FINAL SEASONAL FACTORS
YEAR      JAN       FEB        MAR       APR       MAY       JUN
1984    145.600   95.723    91.852    91.854    83.382    87.368
1985    145.844   95.962    91.912    91.886    83.064    87.584
1986    145.610   96.341    92.508    91.836    82.429    87.819
1987    145.323   96.609    93.346    91.687    81.960    88.247
1988    144.896   96.883    94.160    91.621    81.652    88.439
1989    144.929   97.024    94.432    91.587    81.498    88.535
1990    144.946   97.094    94.567   *******   *******   *******
AVG     145.307   96.519    93.254    91.745    82.331    87.999

YEAR      JUL       AUG        SEP       OCT       NOV       DEC       AVG
1984    108.207   85.443    79.228    95.463    99.320   136.128    99.964
1985    108.603   85.402    78.773    95.030    99.400   136.345    99.984
1986    109.219   85.360    78.103    94.288    99.670   136.479    99.972
1987    109.489   85.451    77.854    93.487    99.642   136.633    99.977
1988    109.656   85.464    77.615    92.957    99.606   136.693    99.970
1989    109.739   85.470    77.495    92.693    99.589   136.723    99.976
1990   *******   *******   *******   *******   *******   *******   112.202

AVG     109.152   85.431    78.178    93.986    99.538   136.500

TOTAL  —          7534.727
```

FIGURE 3.12

```
D11 FINAL SEASONALLY ADJUSTED SERIES
YEAR    JAN      FEB       MAR       APR       MAY       JUN
1984    1617     1552      1553      1594      1608      1562
1985    1767     1753      1695      1720      1736      1743
1986    1629     1656      1721      1674      1690      1662
1987    1520     1541      1484      1474      1442      1443
1988    1456     1406      1355      1256      1328      1359
1989    1281     1308      1396     *******   *******   *******
AVG     1545     1536      1534      1544      1561      1554


YEAR    JUL      AUG       SEP       OCT       NOV       DEC       TOTAL
1984    1632     1653      1684      1777      1774      1609      19615
1985    1696     1704      1743      1721      1671      1649      20600
1986    1644     1686      1682      1573      1577      1530      19725
1987    1409     1357      1317      1263      1356      1902      17508
1988    1381     1342      1289      1272      1331      1292      16068
1989 *******  *******   *******   *******   *******   *******     3985

AVG     1552     1549      1543      1521      1542      1597

TOTAL  —         97500 MEAN           1548 S.D.  —          167
```

FIGURE 3.13

dividing the original series (figure 3.10) by the seasonal factors (figure 3.12) and remultiplying by 100, we arrive at the final seasonal adjusted series (figure 3.13).

For purposes of comparison, month-to-month changes in the original and final seasonally adjusted series are presented in figures 3.14 and 3.15 and labeled tables E-5 and E-6 by the X-11 system. These changes can be compared for the purposes of both economic analysis of the time series and forecasting future movements in the time series.

Finally, X-11 generates summary statistics. These summaries are useful to forecasters in determining the success of the technique in isolating the seasonal factors and in developing future estimates of the trend–cycle factor. In particular, the X-11 routine provides a tool for measuring the relative contributions of the S_t, C_tT_t, and I_t components to percentage change in the original time series. Also, the relative contribution of the S_t, C_tT_t, and I_t components over a 1,2,3,...,12 month span can be measured.

A portion of this output appears in figure 3.16. Note that for one-month-ahead forecasts, 88.37 percent of the variation in the original series is associated with seasonality(s), 0.307 percent with the trend–cycle component C, 4.66 percent with the random or irregular component and 6.66 percent with the trading day variation. For forecasts up to nine months ahead, at least 90 percent of the variation in the original series is associated with seasonality. Of course, for 12 months-ahead forecasts, seasonality does not account for any variation in the original series.

The X-11 version illustrated in this section is usually carried out by using a standard software system. The SAS Econometrics Library (SAS Institute, 1984) is the system used in providing the various tables shown in figures 3.10–3.16.

In recent years a new variant of X-11 is becoming popular as a method for producing moving seasonal index numbers. The new procedure called X11ARIMA is a result of criticism of the X-11 system. The criticism centers on the unreliability of

E 5 MONTH-TO-MONTH CHANGES IN ORIGINAL SERIES

YEAR	JAN	FEB	MAR	APR	MAY	JUN
1984	*******	−35.117	−6.806	0.562	−4.539	0.000
1985	26.663	−36.544	−9.598	8.626	−9.102	−4.435
1986	8.804	−35.390	−4.617	4.377	−11.626	2.588
1987	1.895	−33.061	−6.165	−2.599	−15.271	15.398
1988	−22.981	−30.524	−8.251	−11.376	−5.984	10.701
1989	5.275	−32.220	8.108	*******	*******	*******
AVG	3.931	−33.809	−4.555	−0.082	−9.305	4.850

YEAR	JUL	AUG	SEP	OCT	NOV	DEC	AVG
1984	29.188	−17.497	−14.688	41.432	3.299	14.207	0.913
1985	34.248	−23.887	−7.571	24.200	−0.240	35.156	3.126
1986	28.311	−23.976	−2.227	12.417	−4.314	47.814	1.847
1987	20.622	−30.987	−4.372	12.286	12.044	100.606	5.866
1988	22.083	−18.840	−13.288	8.632	21.161	29.919	−1.562
1989	*******	*******	*******	*******	*******	*******	−6.279
AVG	26.890	−23.037	−8.429	19.793	6.390	45.540	
TOTAL −	102.529						

FIGURE 3.14

```
E 6 MONTH-TO-MONTH CHANGES IN FINAL SEASONALLY ADJ. SERIES
YEAR        JAN       FEB       MAR       APR       MAY       JUN
1984     *******    -4.038     0.063     2.651     0.859    -2.873
1985      9.799     -0.790    -3.271     1.451     0.961     0.381
1986     -1.242      1.641     3.973    -2.767     0.994    -1.705
1987     -0.645      1.411    -3.747    -0.647    -2.179     0.068
1988    -23.434     -3.476    -3.607    -7.306     5.687     2.401
1989     -0.886      2.153     6.715   *******   *******   *******
AVG      -3.282     -0.516     0.021    -1.324     1.264    -0.346


YEAR        JUL       AUG       SEP       OCT       NOV       DEC       AVG
1984      4.501      1.281     1.901     5.490    -0.179    -9.285     0.034
1985     -2.700      0.495     2.292    -1.259    -2.936    -1.286     0.261
1986     -1.050      2.551    -0.230    -6.501     0.256    -2.985    -0.589
1987     -2.385     -3.662    -2.934    -4.083     7.310    40.311     2.402
1988      1.616     -2.828    -4.008    -1.254     4.569    -2.892    -2.878
1989    *******    *******   *******   *******   *******   *******     2.661

AVG      -0.004     -0.433    -0.596    -1.521     1.804     4.773

TOTAL -             -1.291
```

FIGURE 3.15

```
REL. CONTRIBUTIONS OF COMPONENTS TO VARIANCE IN ORIG. SERIES
SPAN IN     D13      D11      D10       A2       C18                RATIO
MONTHS       I        C        S        P       TD      TOTAL      (X100)
   1       4.660    0.307   88.372    0.000    6.662   100.000    84.032
   2       3.055    0.512   93.808    0.000    2.626   100.000    90.774
   3       2.705    1.079   95.053    0.000    1.163   100.000    89.709
   4       2.268    1.709   92.443    0.000    3.580   100.000    82.301
   5       2.327    2.664   92.460    0.000    2.549   100.000    95.359
   6       1.915    3.955   92.747    0.000    1.382   100.000    92.800
   7       2.177    3.618   91.356    0.000    2.850   100.000    87.891
   8       2.748    4.654   90.964    0.000    1.635   100.000    87.189
   9       2.652    5.781   90.715    0.000    0.852   100.000    96.425
  10       2.120    6.199   88.431    0.000    3.250   100.000    94.192
  11       4.233   15.121   77.260    0.000    3.387   100.000    86.241
  12      18.090   67.765    0.120    0.000   14.025   100.000    99.161
```

FIGURE 3.16

seasonal estimates for the most recent observations of a time series. X11ARIMA is said to produce more reliable seasonal estimates for recent observations. It does this by extrapolating for one year (12 months) new observations at both ends of the data set using ARIMA methods. (These methods will be studied in chapter 9.) The modified series is then filtered by the X-11 system discussed before. The resulting seasonal factors and deseasonalized series are said to be more reliable than the original X-11 system. The X11ARIMA system is now being incorporated in many seasonal adjustment programs and is currently the method used exclusively for seasonal adjustment by the Federal Government of Canada.

3.12 A Final Note on Decomposition

Decomposition methods originated around 1900 and are one of the oldest forecasting procedures in use today. This work came under the direction of economists who were concerned with the impacts of severe downturns in business activity and sought ways to predict and perhaps prevent them. They felt that the elements of economic activity were such that changes in business cycles could be isolated from the seasonal components of time series. In 1911, French economists presented a report analyzing the causes of the 1907 business and economic depression. This government-appointed group introduced the notion of leading and coincidental indicators and attempted to separate trend from cycle to follow the movement of the latter component. Today, the NBER has greatly increased our knowledge of economic indicators. In chapter 10, we shall return to this notion.

A second direction of time series decomposition recognized the need to study the serial correlation within or between variables. Spurious correlation of time series could result in erroneous forecasts. Hence, much work was done to eliminate patterns in time series to permit better forecasts. We shall return to this notion in chapters 4 and 5.

Finally, decomposition permits us to isolate the systematic elements in a time series. How are we able to combine these elements for forecasting purposes?

In long-range forecasting we are concerned mainly with trend. An electric light and power company may desire to predict demand for electric power 10, 20, or 30 years ahead for purposes of making wise generating plant construction decisions. The power company will predict the trend in annual demand to decide on the extent of an expansion program and make plans for its long-range financing. There is little need and it is not standard practice to predict the seasonal pattern of demand 10, 20, or 30 years ahead because this knowledge would be of little value in decision-making today.

At times, it would be desirable to predict the cyclical influence in a long-range forecast. However, such predictions are beyond our ability. Even short-run cyclical effects are not predicted with accuracy in any consistent manner. Thus a practical rule is to reassess the usefulness of a long-range forecast of trend regularly. As the period for which the forecast was made approaches, the revised trend forecast can be modified on the basis of a qualitative analysis of the cyclical influence.

Let us now look at an illustration of a short-run forecast.

Example 3.11

A firm wishes to predict demand for the upcoming year. The forecast is to be used as a basis for decision on the financial budget, production and inventory control, sales quota, advertising and promotional schemes, procurement policy, and labor needs. For short-run forecasting, however, the firm must know the seasonal pattern in product demand. The following procedure is often followed.

1 The firm extrapolates the past trend in product demand.
2 The trend forecast is modified for possible cyclical and random effects and for

possible changes in the past trend. The possible change may occur for any one or combination of the following factors:
(a) general business conditions;
(b) changes in the competitive position of the company;
(c) current dealer inventory situation;
(d) marketing policy;
(e) product research and development;
(f) anticipated price change;
(g) capacity problems;
(h) influence of government regulations.

The analysis of the influence of these factors on past trends is the basis for adjustment. After the annual forecast is made, it is then necessary to allocate this forecast among the months (or quarters) of the year on the basis of the seasonal pattern. If the annual forecast for a product is $5.4 million, then the average monthly demand is $450 000. Furthermore, if the seasonal index for January is 120, then the forecast of January demand is $450 000 × 1.20 = $540 000. In turn, product demand forecasts are derived by multiplying $450 000 by the appropriate seasonal factors.

We should note that forecasting based on time series decomposition leans heavily on judgment. Merely projecting a trend a year ahead is only one step in product demand forecasting. Subsequent adjustment of projections is a key factor in developing the final forecast. The use of judgment is not wholly within the province of the theory of prediction. Hence the risks of an error in the forecasting procedure cannot be measured in a classical statistical sense. In chapter 10, we shall return to the notion of the use of qualitative forecasting.

3.13   Summary

Decomposition assumes that time series data are made up of a pattern (or patterns) and error. These patterns are called systematic components; trend, seasonality, and cycle.

Seasonality or seasonal fluctuations are variations which occur regularly during the period of a year and are the result of customs and climatic conditions. The trend of a time series is the result of long-term economic forces affecting the series being studied. Cycles are oscillatory movements of more than one year in duration resulting from changes in aggregate business and economic activity. (Figure 3.17 summarizes the components of a time series.)

Time series are also subject to random or irregular fluctuations. The ratio-to-moving-average method eliminates the influence of trend, cyclical, and irregular elements from the original time series data to insure that only the influence of the seasonal element remains.

Seasonal index numbers are used to eliminate the seasonal component from time series data. These index numbers may be constant or moving and may also, be relative or absolute.

The trend of a time series can be graphically presented on arithmetic scale charts or on semilogarithmic scale charts. Many methods can be used to fit the trend of a time series. One such method is the method of least squares. Trend estimates for a year can be converted to trend estimates for periods of less than a year.

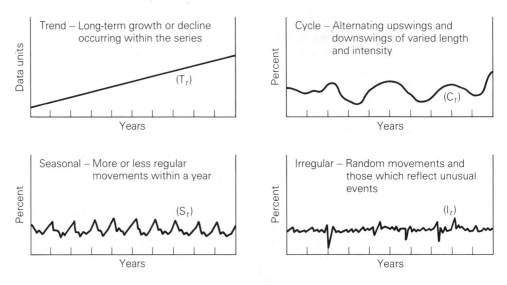

FIGURE 3.17 Components of a time series. A typical time series is influenced by four types of movement. To forecast, one decomposes the time series into its components. In turn, a forecaster then predicts each component separately. Finally, using the multiplicative model, each prediction is multiplied together to arrive at the final forecast

The cyclical component is best forecast on the basis of sound economic knowledge of the current state of the economy. However, the cyclical component can be isolated by a moving-average process for data that were previously deseasonalized and detrended.

By dividing the cyclical–irregular series by the estimated cyclical component, the irregular variation is found. Finally, by breaking down the multiplicative model into its components, forecasts can be prepared by remultiplying the predicted values for each component. The importance of each component dictates their use in forecasting.

The X-11 version of the Census Method II Seasonal Adjustment process is a principle procedure for decomposing economic time series. The procedure contains four lengthy processes which permit a forecaster to adjust for variation due to trading days, the cycle–trend component, and extreme values. Finally, summary data indicating the proportionate shares of each source of variation in the time series are presented in the printed results of this method.

A new variant of X-11 called X11ARIMA is said to provide better estimates of the seasonal component. Use of X11ARIMA is said to provide more reliable seasonal index numbers leading to more reliable deseasonalized time series.

Finally, decomposing time series into its systematic components, we can make both long-run and short-run forecasts based on both the quantitative analysis of this chapter and the use of expert and wise judgment.

3.14 Exercises

1 In each of the following forecasting situations indicate what systematic component(s), seasonal, trend, cyclical, of the time series must be measured to provide a basis for forecasting.

(a) An estimate of the demand for natural gas in 1995 is required as a basis for decisions on how much of an increase in transmission lines should be planned.

(b) A state tax commissioner wishes to estimate the yield of a sales tax in the coming fiscal year for budgetary purposes.

(c) An investor wishes to decide, on the basis of past price and earnings movements, whether or not to buy common stock of a listed company as a long-term commitment.

(d) Monthly production levels and inventory levels for the upcoming years must be prepared for a manufacturing company.

(e) A health planning agency must plan for future capacity of health care delivery systems to provide sufficient health care services to meet a community's needs.

(f) A speculative investor wishes to decide on the basis of past price and earnings movements whether or not to buy a firm's common stock for a quick payoff.

(g) A businessman must determine whether this month's sales indicate that business improved over the past month.

2 Suppose that a forecaster collected sales data for a department store in San Diego, an apple orchard owner in Michigan, and a clothing manufacturer in Pennsylvania. For each of these businesses, categorize the seasonal, cyclical, trend, and irregular forces that would be expected to affect sales.

3 A retail store chain had its statistical section prepare the data shown in table 3.12 on sales and seasonal index numbers.

TABLE 3.12

Month	Sales ($ thousands)	Seasonal index
Jan	140	105
Feb	145	80
Mar	130	85
Apr	150	104
May	160	108
Jun	150	102
Jul	155	98
Aug	145	90
Sep	170	105
Oct	165	102
Nov	180	107
Dec	195	114

(a) Interpret the meaning of the seasonal indexes for January and February.

(b) Find the percentage change from month to month in actual sales.

(c) Deseasonalize the actual data by the seasonal index numbers.

(d) Find the percentage change from month to month in deseasonalized sales.
(e) Compare the results of parts (b) and (d).
4 The quarterly seasonal index numbers in table 3.13 were determined for shipments from inventories (dollars) for a furniture manufacturer in Georgia.
(a) Interpret the meaning of the index for each quarter.
(b) If shipments from inventories were $250 000 in quarter 2 and $310 000 in quarter 3, what was the deseasonalized change in shipments?

TABLE 3.13

Quarter	Seasonal index
1	90
2	100
3	110
4	100

5 The following trend forecast for sales of a manufacturer was made by the method of least squares:

$$\hat{Y} = 100\ 000 + 25\ 000X$$

(origin at $X = 1985$; one unit of X = one year)
(a) What is the forecast for 1990?
(b) For each change of one year, what is the change in sales?
6 Two trend forecasts were made for sales (dollars) of a laser manufacturer. The first forecast was linear,

$$\hat{Y} = \$5000 + 10\ 000X$$

and the second forecast was loglinear,

$$\log \hat{Y} = 3.699 + 0.50X$$

(origin at $X = 1985$; one unit of X = one year).
(a) Forecast for 1989 by each of two trend equations.
(b) Interpret the slope coefficient for the linear trend forecast.
(c) Interpret the slope coefficient for the loglinear trend forecast.
7 An economic statistician produced cyclical components for quarterly data on electric light and power usage by a machine tool and dye manufacturer.
(a) The cyclical factor for the first quarter of 1987 was 71.5. Interpret the meaning of this number.
(b) The cyclical factor for the third quarter of 1989 was 115. Interpret the meaning of this number.
8 Data on shipments of goods from inventory were examined to determine the trend in the time series. The following represents a partial output of a computer program to measure the linear trend:

TABLE 3.14

	I	II	III	IV	I	II	III	IV	I	II	III	IV
						End of period						
		1979				1980				1981		
Canada	108.1	108.7	108.1	108.8	110.9	107.2	109.0	112.2	110.5	111.8	112.4	110.4
France	77.8	77.6	74.3	72.8	74.0	74.0	76.1	81.8	89.8	103.6	100.8	104.1
Germany (West)	51.4	50.7	48.0	47.7	48.0	48.4	49.9	53.9	57.9	65.8	63.9	62.1
		1982				1983				1984		
Canada	111.2	114.3	115.4	109.6	110.5	112.4	113.5	111.2	114.5	116.2	114.3	112.5
France	106.5	108.3	111.0	112.5	108.7	109.6	110.5	114.2	118.3	109.6	108.7	104.5
Germany (West)	64.5	68.3	69.2	62.5	69.7	72.4	74.5	75.6	78.5	69.5	62.5	65.5

Dep. variable: Y	Shipments ($ thousand)
Variable	Parameter estimate
Intercept	48.534
Time	12.453

(time = years with 1981 = 0; one unit of X = one year).

(a) Write out the equation of the trend line.
(b) Interpret the meaning of the intercept coefficient.
(c) Interpret the meaning of the slope coefficient.
(d) Forecast the trend for 1990.

9 The data in table 3.14 are the indexes of some foreign currency price of the US$.

  (a) Plot one of the above time series on arithmetic scale paper (by hand or computer). Qualitatively describe the seasonal pattern.

  (b) Compute quarterly seasonal index numbers for the same time series by hand or by computer (i.e. TSP seasonal index program).

  (c) Deseasonalize the data and plot the deseasonalized data on the graph prepared in (a). Do the results of (b) and (c) bear out your description of the seasonal pattern?

  (d) If you were asked to find the trend of this series, would you fit the trend line to the observed values or the deseasonalized data? Explain.

  (e) What assumptions would you make if you were to apply these index numbers after 1989?

10 The data in table 3.15 are bankers' acceptances (total, billion dollars) in the United States by month.

  (a) Compute monthly seasonal factors (by computer if available) for these data.

  (b) Deseasonalize the data.

  (c) Plot the original and deseasonalized series and comment on the seasonal pattern.

  (d) In January 1988 bankers' acceptances were $63.0 billion. Deseasonalize this value.

11 For the data of exercise 10, estimate the linear trend of this time series. Do this for the deseasonalized data and find the trend estimate for each monthly period. (Hint: create a table similar to table 3.10.)

TABLE 3.15

	1984	1985	1986	1987
Jan	73.5	72.3	68.3	65.0
Feb	74.4	76.1	67.2	65.1
Mar	73.2	73.7	66.9	66.0
Apr	78.5	72.8	66.2	66.8
May	79.5	69.7	66.8	67.7
Jun	82.1	68.4	67.1	69.6
Jul	81.0	68.5	66.4	68.5
Aug	79.8	66.8	64.5	68.6
Sep	77.9	68.7	67.0	68.8
Oct	75.7	69.3	65.9	71.9
Nov	75.2	67.9	65.0	71.1
Dec	75.5	68.1	65.0	70.6

Source: Survey of Current Business, various issues.

12 Use the method of moving averages to find the cyclical component of the time series of exercise 10. Find the irregular component.
13 The data in table 3.16 are sales revenue for the Rhode Island Group Health Association (thousand dollars).

TABLE 3.16

Year	Revenue	Year	Revenue
1972	1011	1977	6615
1973	1808	1978	8891
1974	2200	1979	10 442
1975	2940	1980	11 799
1976	4612	1981	13 823

(a) Plot the data on both an arithmetic and a semilogarithmic scale.
(b) Estimate the linear trend by least squares. Forecast for 1982.
(c) Estimate the loglinear trend by least squares. Forecast for 1982.
14 The data in table 3.17 are per capita gross state product (1972 dollars) in million dollars for the state of New Hampshire.
(a) Plot the time series on an arithmetic scale.
(b) Estimate the trend in the observed values.
(c) Forecast for January 1987.
(d) Forecast for the years 1987–90.
15 The data in table 3.18 are indices of output per hour of all persons (or labor productivity) in manufacturing (1977 = 100).
(a) Plot the observed values on a semilogarithmic chart.
(b) Estimate the loglinear trend. Interpret the coefficients.
(c) Forecast the index for 1990 and 1991.

TABLE 3.17

Year	GSP	Year	GSP	Year	GSP
1969	2890	1975	4812	1981	10370
1970	3050	1976	5570	1982	11065
1971	3294	1977	6400	1983	12493
1972	3668	1978	7438	1984	14181
1973	4189	1979	8368	1985	15888
1974	4483	1980	9276	1986	17887

Source: Federal Reserve Bank of Boston (1988) *Gross State Product – New England 1969–1986*, p. 8.

TABLE 3.18

Year	Index	Year	Index	Year	Index
1970	79.2	1976	97.7	1982	105.9
1971	86.6	1977	100	1983	112.0
1972	91.0	1978	100.9	1984	118.1
1973	93.1	1979	101.4	1985	123.6
1974	90.9	1980	101.7	1986	127.7
1975	93.5	1981	103.6	1987	132.0
				1988	136.2

Source: *Monthly Labor Review*, various issues.

16 For the linear trend estimated in exercise 11, convert to estimate bankers' acceptances. Estimate the bankers' acceptances for the first quarter of 1988.
17 The data in table 3.19 represent millions of cases of Pepsi-Cola beverages sold.
   (a) Estimate the linear trend by least squares.
   (b) Convert the estimate of the yearly trend to a monthly trend estimating equation.

TABLE 3.19

Years	Sales	Years	Sales
1971	803.7	1976	1045.4
1972	857.0	1977	1171.9
1973	910.5	1978	1281.0
1974	924.8	1979	1377.0
1975	926.0	1980	1435.0

Source: Lehman Bros, Kuhn Loeb Research, *The Soft Drink Industry in 1981*, pp. 4–5.

(c) Forecast for January 1982.
18 The data in table 3.20 are exports of goods and services of the United States (billion dollars, not seasonally adjusted).
   (a) Deseasonalize the data.
   (b) Estimate the trend by the method of least squares and complete columns 1, 2, and 3 of the table in a similar way to table 3.10.
   (c) By the method of moving averages complete columns 4 and 5 of the table for these data in a similar way to table 3.10.
   (d) Interpret the cyclical component for the second quarter of 1985 and the third quarter of 1986.
   (e) Find the irregular component.
   (f) Forecast for the first quarter of 1988.

TABLE 3.20

Year	Quarter	Observed values	Year	Quarter	Observed values	Year	Quarter	Observed values
1982	1	89.3	1984	1	89.5	1986	1	90.9
	2	97.7		2	90.5		2	95.4
	3	84.8		3	87.9		3	90.4
	4	81.8		4	92.1		4	95.2
1983	1	81.1	1985	1	87.6	1987	1	98.5
	2	83.3		2	91.0		2	102.4
	3	82.1		3	87.6		3	102.7
	4	87.8		4	92.4		4	120.9

Source: *Survey of Current Business*, various issues.

19 (a) For the data of exercise 10, apply an appropriate computer program to perform the decomposition of the time series by the X-11 variant of the Census II method. (Hint: SAS ETS library.)
   (b) Interpret the one-year-ahead monthly seasonal index numbers.
   (c) From the *Survey of Current Business*, find the values for bankers' acceptances for 1989. Deseasonalize these data by the one-year-ahead seasonal index numbers.
   (d) Recompute the decomposition with the newly observed data. Do the one-year-ahead monthly seasonal index numbers change? Why?
20 (a) For the data of exercise 18, apply the appropriate computer program to perform the decomposition of the time series by the X-11 variant of the Census II method.
   (b) Interpret the one-year-ahead quarterly seasonal index numbers.
   (c) From the *Survey of Current Business* find the values for new plant and equipment expenditures in durable goods industries.
   (d) Recompute the decomposition with the newly observed data. Do the one-year-ahead seasonal index numbers change? Why?
21 (a) Collect data on sales (or revenues) for any firm you wish for a period of at least ten years.

(b) Plot the data on both arithmetic and semilogarithmic charts. Which chart indicates a better fit?

(c) Estimate the trend for these data. Interpret the meaning of the intercept and slope coefficients.

(d) Forecast for the year 1991

22 Collect data for a five-year period by month for any time series (not previously seasonally adjusted). Decompose the series by the X-11 variant of the Census II forecasts and the summary statistics on the relative contribution of components to the percentage change in the original series.

23 A comptroller for a large manufacturer estimated the following linear trend equation for sales revenue of the firm:

$$Y_t = 10.2 + 0.87X_t$$

(sales in million dollars). Seasonal index numbers were estimated to be as shown in table 3.21. Prepare quarterly and annual forecasts for 1991 ($X = 10$).

TABLE 3.21

Quarter	Index number
1	95
2	111
3	92
4	101

References

Federal Reserve Bank of Boston (1988) *Gross State Product – New England, 1969–1986,* Boston, MA.

Lehman Bros, Kuhn Loeb Research (1982) *The Soft Drink Industry in 1981.* New York.

Monthly Labor Review, various issues, Washington, DC: US Department of Labor, Bureau of Labor Statistics.

SAS Institute (1984) *SAS/ETS User's Guide; Econometric and Time Series Library.* Cary, NC: SAS Institute.

Survey of Current Business, various issues. Washington, DC: US Department of Commerce.

US Department of Commerce, Bureau of the Census (1967) The X-11 variant of the Census Method II seasonal adjustment program. Technical Paper No. 15, 1967 Version, US Department of Commerce, Bureau of the Census, Washington, DC.

Further Reading

Dagum, E. B. (1983) The X11-ARIMA seasonal adjustment method. Statistics Canada, Catalogue 12-563E, Ottawa.

Hall, R. E. and Lillien, D. M. (1988) *Micro-TSP User's Manual,* Version 6.5. Irvine, CA: Quantitative Micro Software.

Hanke, J. E. and Reitsch, A. G. (1989) *Business Forecasting.* Boston, MA: Allyn and Bacon, ch. 8.

International Monetary Fund, *International Financial Statistics Yearbook,* 1980–2.

Jarrett, J. E. (1989) Forecasting monthly earnings per share-time series models. *OMEGA International Journal of Management Science,* 17(1) 37–44.

Jarrett, J. E. and Kraft, A. (1989) *Statistical Analysis for Decision Making.* Boston, MA: Allyn and Bacon, ch. 15.

Makridakis. S., Wheelwright, S. and McGee, V. (1983) *Forecasting: Methods and Applications,* 2nd edn., New York: Wiley, ch. 4.

Thomopoulos, N. T. (1980) *Applied Forecasting Methods.* Englewood Cliffs, NJ: Prentice-Hall.

Willis, R. E. (1987) *A Guide To Forecasting for Planners and Managers.* Englewood Cliffs, NJ: Prentice-Hall, ch. 4.

Appendix

The following tables are output from Minitab and Micro-TSP. They represent how output from these programs would appear if they were applied to the data of examples 3.4 and 3.5.

TABLE 3. A1

Y = 62.4 + 5.63 X

Predictor	Coef	Stdev	t-ratio	p
Constant	62.438	3.434	18.18	0.000
X	5.6286	0.3776	14.90	0.000

s = 6.319   R-sq = 94.5

Table 3.A1 shows the partial output of Minitab software for the data of example 3.4. The dependent variable, cost, is denoted by the letter Y. The variable for time is denoted X and its coefficient is equal to 5.6286 (5.63 in the equation). Note that the constant or intercept is equal to 62.438 (62.4 in the equation).

TABLE 3. A2

The regression equation is
logY = 1.37 + 0.114 X

Predictor	Coef	Stdev	t-ratio	p
Constant	1.37146	0.00012	11516.44	0.000
X	0.114075	0.000060	1915.82	0.000

s = 0.0003151   R-sq = 100.0

Table 3.A2 shows the partial Minitab output of example 3.5 with common logarithms. The exponential trend analysis is similar to that above except that the dependent variable is in logarithms (log Y). The dependent variable is log Y, the common logarithm of sales. The constant or intercept is equal to 1.37146 (1.37 in the equation). The coefficient for the variable for time, denoted X, is 0.114075 (0.114 in the equation).

Table 3.A3 shows the partial Minitab output for the exponential trend problem (example 3.5) using natural logarithms. Note that the estimate of the constant or intercept is 3.15791 (3.16 in the equation). The estimate of the coefficient of the time variable X is 0.262667 (0.263 in the equation). Finally, ln Y denotes the natural logarithm of sales.

TABLE 3. A3

The regression equation is
lnY = 3.16 + 0.263 X

Predictor	Coef	Stdev	t-ratio	p
Constant	3.15791	0.00027	11516.79	0.000
X	0.262667	0.000137	1915.88	0.000

s = 0.0007255   R-sq = 100.0

Table 3.A4 shows the partial output of using Micro-TSP personal computer software. The data is from example 3.4, the trend analysis for cost-of-heating data. The dependent variable is cost, the independent variable is period, and there are 15 observations. The estimated constant (or intercept) is 62.438 (rounded to three decimals) and the estimated slope coefficient is 5.629. Finally this solution is consistent with the other solutions to example 3.4 obtained using SAS and Minitab.

TABLE 3. A4

LS // Dependent Variable is COST
Date: / Time: 0:04
SMPL range: 1 -   15
Number of observations: 15

VARIABLE	COEFFICIENT	STD. ERROR	T-STAT.	2-TAIL SIG.
C	62.438095	3.4335393	18.184762	0.000
PERIOD	5.6285714	0.3776390	14.904636	0.000

Table 3.A5 shows the partial Micro-TSP output for the data of example 3.5 using natural logarithms. The dependent variable is LNY (natural logarithm of sales in

TABLE 3. A5

```
LS // Dependent Variable is LNY
Date:                    / Time:  0:10
SMPL range:  1974 - 1980
Number of observations: 7
================================================================================
     VARIABLE      COEFFICIENT      STD. ERROR       T-STAT.       2-TAIL SIG.
================================================================================
        C          3. 1579100      0. 0002742      11516. 113        0. 000
        X          0. 2626673      0. 0001371      1915. 7650        0. 000
================================================================================
```

thousand dollars), the independent variable is X (coded values for the period from −3 to +3), and there are seven observations. The estimated constant (intercept) is 3.158 (rounded to three decimals) and the estimated slope coefficient is 0.263 (rounded). The estimated trend equation is consistent with previous solutions to example 3.5 obtained using SAS and Minitab.

PART III

Causal or Explanatory Modeling Techniques

CHAPTER 4

Linear Regression and Correlation

Objectives

This chapter introduces the statistical theory of regression with emphasis on simple linear regression. The purpose of regression is to determine the nature of the relationship between one variable, called the dependent variable, and a second variable, called the independent variable. The method for estimating a regression is called the least squares method. Also, the methods of correlation analysis will be examined to permit a forecaster to determine the degree of a relationship between two variables. Knowledge of regression and correlation permit forecasters to predict the behavior of any entity studied and for which data have been collected. By the end of this chapter, you will be able to:

1 Estimate the parameters of a regression model.
2 Calculate the standard error of regression.
3 Test hypotheses concerning the presence of regression and regression parameters.
4 Calculate the coefficients of correlation and determination.
5 Construct both point and interval estimates from regression models.
6 Examine the residuals from regression to determine whether the model assumptions are present.
7 Estimate a model when serial correlation (autocorrelation) is present.
8 Interpret the output of useful computer software.

Outline

Key Terms

- Dependent variable
- Independent variable
- Multiple relationship
- Simple relationship
- Incomplete theory
- Imperfect specification
- Errors of measurement
- Conditional mean
- Homoscedasticity
- Serial correlation (autocorrelation)
- Y intercept
- Slope of the regression
- Direct relationship
- Indirect relationship
- Standard error of regression
- Coefficient of determination
- Explained sum of squares
- Error sum of squares
- Coefficient of correlation
- Durbin–Watson test

4.1 Introduction

In the previous chapters, two major classes of time series methods, exponential smoothing and decomposition, were considered. Models appropriate for different patterns under different conditions were presented. Smoothing methods appeared suitable for short-term forecasting where often large numbers of items are forecast. Alternatively, decomposition methods can be employed for both short- and long-term forecasting. However, these methods require a multitude of computations and a great deal of personal judgment by the forecaster. This is particularly true when predicting the cyclical component. Thus decomposition is often limited to forecasting fewer items than the less restricting smoothing models.

This and the next chapter will consider simple and multiple regression and correlation methods. As will be seen, there is more than one reason for studying regression methods.

One purpose for studying regression is to estimate the nature of the relationship between a *dependent variable* and an *independent variable*. The dependent variable, Y for example, is the one that we wish to predict. (It was the dollar value of mortgage loans made by a savings and loan association.) The independent variable X, the one used to aid us in prediction, could, for example, be the average interest rates on home mortgages. The goal of forecasting is to predict the dollar value of mortgage loans based on the measured association with average interest rates. The nature of association and prediction is made if we have a sample of values for the two variables.

The purpose of linear correlation is to answer the question concerning the degree of linear association between the two variables. Although there may be plausible reasons for a relationship, correlation says nothing about these reasons. It indicates only whether two variables vary together. This may be because one variable is the cause and the other the effect, or perhaps they both vary together as a result of a third variable's being the cause. Correlation, however, only indexes the degree of association.

When there is more than one independent variable, such relationships are called *multiple relationships*. In this chapter, we limit our study to *simple relationships* which include only one independent variable X and one dependent variable Y. Furthermore, in this chapter we shall study only those relationships that are expressed by a straight line. In the next chapter, our study will focus on other mathematical relationships such as those expressed by a nonlinear equation.

4.2   The Simple Linear Regression Model

The simple regression model expresses the relationship between a variable Y, e.g. dollar value of mortgage loans, and a variable X, e.g. average mortgage interest rates, in the form of a straight line. The population regression line of Y on X is the association of mortgage loans on interest rates. Underlying the regression is a certain set of assumptions which this two-variable population must satisfy for the simple linear regression model to apply.

If we assume that the relationship is linear, a straight line describes the relation between mortgage loans Y and interest rates X. Mathematically, the linear regression model can be expressed as follows:

$$Y = \beta_0 + \beta_1 X + e \tag{4.1}$$

In this equation e is the random error, which measures the vertical deviation of each value of the dependent variable from the population regression line for an associated value of the independent variable.

In trying to predict mortgage loans for a particular interest rate, our prediction is subject to error. This error can arise from one or more possible causes.

1 *Incomplete theory:* certain variables related to mortgage loans may have been omitted. A more complete theory might have required the inclusion of information on consumer incomes or housing market conditions. Thus more independent variables could possibly be added to the regression relationships.
2 *Imperfect specification:* a linear relationship is estimated when actually the relationship may be nonlinear, such as that expressed by the equation of a parabola.
3 *Errors of measurement:* even though the relationship was carefully prepared, computational errors may occur in the measurement of the variables. Thus the forecasting experiment must include a set of controls to limit the computation and nonstatistical errors.

Basically, the model assumes that if the set of causes giving rise to the random error term are controllable it would be possible to predict mortgage loans precisely, when the interest rate is known. When all these factors account for "error", they have very different theoretical implications for the model specified. These implications will be discussed later.

In a statistical experiment the same distribution of X values will appear in any replication of the experiment. However, the distribution of the Y values for given X

values may vary from experiment to experiment because of the effect of the random error term. Thus, for our illustration in figure 3.1, we had ten observations with mortgage loans ranging from 8 to 16 percent. If the experiment were repeated, ten observations would again be made with mortgage loans ranging from 8 to 16 percent. However, the distribution of the Y values could change from experiment to experiment. The values of the independent variable X are said to be predetermined, while the dependent variable Y is a random variable.

Values of predetermined variables are determined independently of the current model. These values, such as the range of interest rates, may be determined prior to the current time period when the experiment is conducted. The potential range of values for the mortgage loans was established when the test was designed. In contrast, the mortgage loan data could only be determined when the experiment was conducted to observe the mortgage loans and interest rates for a sample of thrift institutions. The dependent variable Y is associated with the values of the predetermined variable, but the predetermined variable X is not associated with the values for the dependent variable Y. There are four assumptions concerning the error term.

1 The expected value of the random error is zero or

$$E(e) = 0 \qquad (4.2)$$

On the average, the value of the random error is equal to zero. To understand this assumption consider the expected value of both sides of the model equation for a given value of X. The expected value of the sum

$$E(Y|X) = E(\beta_0 + \beta_1 X + e) \qquad (4.3)$$

can be reduced to the sum of the expected values:

$$E(Y|X) = E(\beta_0) + E(\beta_1 X) + E(e) \qquad (4.4)$$

β_0 and β_1 are constants and X is given; therefore it can be treated as a constant. Thus the equation reduces to

$$E(Y|X) = \beta_0 + \beta_1 X \qquad (4.5)$$

since the expected value of a constant is a constant and $E(e)$ is zero. This expectation is the *conditional mean* because it measures the mean or average value of Y that is associated with a particular value of X. Therefore this assumption implies that for a given value of X, the mean of the Y values is on the regression line.

2 The variance of the random error term is the same for each X value. This assumption is called *homoscedasticity:*

$$\text{var}(e) = E[e - E(e)]^2 = E(e^2) = k \qquad (4.6)$$

where k is a constant term. However, from the model

$$e = Y - (\beta_0 + \beta_1 X) \qquad (4.7)$$

Therefore, this assumption implies that $E[Y - (\beta_0 + \beta_1 X)]^2 = k$, or that the variance and standard deviation are the same for each X value in the population. Var (e) measures the variability in the value of the dependent variable Y about the regression line for given values of the independent variable X.

3 The values of e are independent of each other or $E(e_i e_j) = 0$. This means that the error in mortgage loans for any given interest rate is not related to the error for any

other interest rate. When these errors are related, *serial correlation* (or *autocorrelation*) is present.

4 The error term for each X value is normally distributed. Since the Y values for a given X vary from experiment to experiment only because of the random error term (the X values are the same from experiment to experiment), the Y values must of necessity also be normally distributed. Thus e is also normally distributed.

To illustrate the meaning of these assumptions, let us consider an illustration in forecasting savings deposits for a family.

Example 4.1

A common problem in the application of economic theory to understanding the savings behavior of families is to relate savings deposits to family income. For a particular location over a fixed time period, the simple linear regression model relating personal income X for a family of four, to the monthly contributions Y to savings deposits is expressed as follows:

$$\mu_Y = -100 + 0.07X$$

where μ_Y is the mean or conditional mean of the Y values for a given X.

The above linear regression of Y on X is linear with normally distributed Y values for given X and an independent random error term with a mean of zero and a constant standard deviation. If the family personal income is $2000 a month ($X = 2000), the monthly increase in savings would be $40. This is expressed symbolically by

$$\mu_Y = -100 + 0.07(2000) = \$40$$

Similarly, if family personal income per month is $3000, then

$$\mu_Y = -100 + 0.07(3000) = \$110$$

This application of the regression model produces a straight line with particular geometric definitions for the parameters B_0 and B_1. In the above application β_0 is usually called the Y *intercept* of the equation; if $\beta_1 X = 0$, $\mu_Y = \beta_0$ (− 100 in this application). This is the monthly contribution to savings regardless of the level of monthly personal income.

In the example $\beta_1 = 0.07$. This is the *slope of the regression* line or the change in savings associated with a dollar (unit) change in personal income. On average, each dollar change in personal income is associated with a 7 cent increase in savings. The relationship is said to be *direct* or to have a positive slope. However, if an increase in one of the variables is associated with a decrease in the other variable, the relationship is said to be *indirect* or to have a negative slope.

Before we go on, we should note one area of concern in the application of regression theory. If an assumption is not true, how do we identify this problem? At times the methods are robust, that is, a small divergence from the assumptions will not seriously affect the use of regression. However, there are situations where we as forecasters must adjust the results or use other techniques for forecasting. Many of these problems will be considered in the remainder of this chapter and the next chapter.

4.3　Estimating the Simple Linear Regression Model

Observation of a b_0 sample of Y values for a fixed sample of X values permits one to estimate a linear equation of the form

$$\hat{Y} = b_0 + b_1 X \tag{4.8}$$

where b_0 and b_1 are estimates of the regression parameters β_0 and β_1. $\hat{Y}$ is the estimated value of μ_Y, the conditional mean of Y for given X. To find b_0 and b_1 for a given set of sample data we can use the following formulas for b_1 and b_0:[1]

$$b_1 = \frac{n\Sigma XY - (\Sigma X)(\Sigma Y)}{n\Sigma X^2 - (\Sigma X)^2} \tag{4.9}$$

and

$$b_0 = \frac{(\Sigma Y)(\Sigma X^2) - (\Sigma X)(\Sigma XY)}{n(\Sigma X^2) - (\Sigma X)^2} \tag{4.10}$$

A more convenient formula for b_0 is often used. This formula is

$$b_0 = \frac{\Sigma Y - b_1 \Sigma X}{n} \tag{4.11}$$

Example 4.2

The sample data in table 4.1 were obtained in a study of the relationship between mortgage loans Y in Buckeye Savings and Loan Association and average contract interest rate on conventional new home mortgages over a ten year period (1971–80).

TABLE 4.1　Worksheet for regression

Interest rate X	Mortgage loans ($ millions) Y	X²	XY	Y²
7.60	7.50	57.760	57.000	56.250
7.45	7.44	55.502	55.428	55.354
7.78	7.93	60.528	61.695	62.885
8.71	8.41	75.864	73.251	70.728
8.75	9.21	76.563	80.587	84.824
8.76	12.03	76.738	105.383	144.721
8.80	14.33	77.440	126.104	205.349
9.30	16.25	86.490	151.125	264.063
10.48	17.99	109.830	188.535	323.640
12.25	21.73	150.063	266.192	472.193
89.88 ΣX	122.82 ΣY	826.778 ΣX^2	1165.300 ΣXY	1740.007 ΣY^2

1　The derivation of these formulas can be found in Younger (1985, ch 2).

To estimate the regression line for these data, the data are arranged and calculated as indicated in the worksheet. The original data for the X and Y variables are listed and their totals are calculated. The remaining two columns are designed to find the other summation values required for calculating the regression coefficients b_0 and b_1. By substitution, we find

$$b_1 = \frac{n\Sigma XY - (\Sigma X)(\Sigma Y)}{n\Sigma X^2 - (\Sigma X)^2}$$

$$= \frac{10(1165.300) - 89.88(122.82)}{10(826.778) - (89.88)^2}$$

$$= 3.242$$

This regression coefficient indicates that on average an increase of one percentage point in the interest rate is associated with an increase of \$3.242 million in savings deposits with Buckeye Savings and Loan. The regression coefficient for the Y intercept is found from

$$b_0 = \frac{\Sigma Y - b_1\Sigma X}{n}$$

$$= \frac{122.82 - 3.242(89.88)}{10}$$

$$= -16.859$$

Thus the estimated regression equation of the line is

$$\hat{Y} = -16.859 + 3.242X$$

Since the X values in the sample range from 7.45 to 12.25, the Y intercept does not necessarily estimate saving deposits when the interest rate is outside that range. We have no sample Y observations for the fixed value $X = 0$, and thus we cannot conclude that the regression equation holds at that point. It can be seen from figure 4.1 that the regression line is the best estimate that can be made of the mortgage loan size based on the assumptions of the simple linear regression model.

In this section we have considered only the problem of fitting a straight line to paired data. The methods of regression analysis can also be used to fit other kinds of equations and to estimate predicting equations in more than two unknowns. The problem of fitting some curves other than straight lines and equations having more than two variables will be treated in the next chapter.

4.4   Standard Error of Regression

The *standard error of regression*[2] provides us with an estimate of the accuracy of the predictive equation. Note from figure 4.1 how the actual values of Y scores vary about the line of prediction. The more widespread the scatter of the Y values about the regression line, the greater is the probability of error in making predictions from that equation.

---

2   The standard error of regression has various synonyms such as the standard error of residuals, the standard error of the estimates, and the root mean square error.

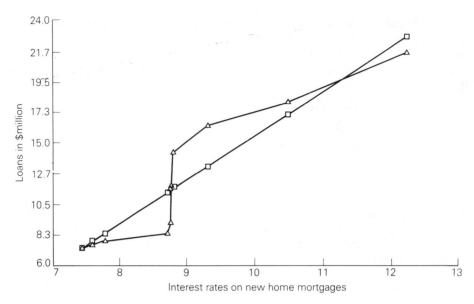

FIGURE 4.1 Mortgage loans by interest rates (observed and predicted); predicted values
         form a straight line

If we consider the simple linear regression model we note that

$$Y = \beta_0 + \beta_1 X + e \tag{4.12}$$

and

$$\mu_Y = \beta_0 + \beta_1 X \tag{4.13}$$

The difference between the actual value Y and the conditional mean μ_Y is the error
term e. The standard error of regression which measures the scatter of the observed
values of Y about the regression line is defined by

$$S_e = \left(\frac{\Sigma e^2}{n - 2} \right)^{1/2} \tag{4.14}$$

The sum of the squared deviations is divided by $n - 2$ because this divisor makes S_e
an unbiased estimator of the standard deviation about the true population regression
line. In general, the denominator is $n - k$ where k is the number of coefficients
(parameters) in the regression equation. Last, note that this formula is similar to the
formula for mean square error (MSE) of chapter 2.

A convenient form or short formula for calculating the standard error of
regression is

$$S_e = \left(\frac{\Sigma Y^2 - b_0 \Sigma Y - b_1 \Sigma XY}{n - 2} \right)^{1/2} \tag{4.15}$$

All quantities required by this formula were calculated for example 4.2.[3] Hence

---

3   These calculations were performed using a computer and have all been rounded to three
decimal places; thus there may be rounding errors in some cases.

$$S_e = \left[\frac{1740.007 - (-16.859)(122.82) - 3.242(1165.300)}{8} \right]^{1/2}$$

$$= 2.015$$

As implied by its name, the S_e is interpretable as a standard error score on a normal curve. It is therefore interpretable in terms of probability values. Stated differently, we would expect about 95 percent of the Y values to fall within ± 2 standard errors of the regression line.

An easy way of visualizing the standard error of regression is to plot it along with a regression line as in figure 4.1 (see figure 4.2). The fitted regression line is the same as in figure 4.1, but now we have added a line above and below the regression line to represent the 95 percent probability that estimates of Y will be within 1 standard error of the regression line. We are reminded in figure 4.2 that in applying regression analysis, estimates are made and that all have calculable margins of error.

4.5 Statistical Significance for Regression

Is there evidence of a linear association between the dependent variable Y and the independent variable X? If no association exists then the value of the slope B is zero. Stated differently, if there is sample evidence to reject the hypothesis that there is no presence of regression, then X and Y are not associated with each other. Consider the next example.

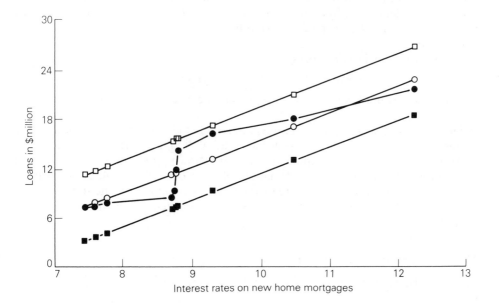

FIGURE 4.2 Observed, predicted, and two standard error limits; predicted values and limits form straight lines

Example 4.3

To determine if the slope of the regression of mortgage loans and interest rates is statistically significant, we wish to determine if the slope is zero or not. If a risk of 5 percent of α is assumed, the critical t scores for eight $(n - 2)$ degrees of freedom are ± 2.306. Hence the decision rule is as follows: reject the hypothesis of $B = 0$ if t based on sample evidence is greater than -2.306 or less than $+2.306$; otherwise, accept it.

The standard deviation of the slope is

$$S_{b1} = \frac{S_e}{[\Sigma \bar{X}^2 - (\Sigma X)^2/n]^{1/2}} = \frac{2.015}{[826.778 - (89.88)^2/10]^{1/2}} = 0.463$$

Since the hypotheses to be tested are

$$H_0 : \beta_1 = 0$$
$$H_A : \beta_1 \neq 0$$

we have

$$t = \frac{b_1 - \beta_1}{S_{b1}} = \frac{3.242 - 0}{0.463} = 7.00$$

Since the computed t score is 2.306, the null hypothesis is rejected at the 0.05 level of significance. Thus β_1 does not equal zero and there is a significant relationship between mortgage loans and interest rates on new home mortgages.

There is an alternative strategy for testing the statistical significance of a simple regression analysis. The alternative is a form of the F test called the analysis of variance for regression. This F ratio reveals how the variation in one group can be the same as or different from the variation in a second group. Given a calculated F ratio and the degrees of freedom associated with its components, we can then make probability estimates that the F occurred by chance. Hence we can test hypotheses with this F.

In regression analysis F represents

$$\frac{\text{sums of squares associated with regression/degrees of freedom}}{\text{sums of squares not associated with regression/degrees of freedom}}$$

If the variance associated with regression exceeds the variance not associated with regression, the less we would expect the value of F to have arisen by chance.

As in all F tests, the components of F are drawn from sums of squares. The numerator is the sum of squared deviations of the predicted variable about its mean, that is, the sum of squares due to regression. The denominator is the sum of squared deviations of differences between the actual and predicted values, that is, the sum of squares of the error term.

Our hypotheses are stated as

H_0: there is no evidence of regression (a relationship)

H_A: there is evidence of regression (a relationship)

If we wish to take a 5 percent chance of rejecting a true H_0 with no evidence of regression, the critical F score is 5.32 (see table A.3 at the end of the book). We can now compute the F ratio for the mortgage loan problem:

$$F = \frac{\Sigma(\hat{Y}_i - \overline{Y})^2/(m - 1)}{\Sigma(Y_i - \hat{Y})^2/(n - m)} \tag{4.16}$$

where m is the number of parameters. Note that the numerator of the equation is the sum of the squared deviations of the regression line from the average Y value, and the denominator is the sum of the squared deviations of the actual Y values from the corresponding position on the regression line. Stated differently, the entire denominator is the square of the standard error of regression. The F ratio can be rewritten as follows:

$$F = \frac{b_1^2(\Sigma X_i^2 - n\overline{x}^2)}{S_e^2} \tag{4.17}$$

For the data of example 4.3, the substitutions are made in the above formula as follows:

$$F = \frac{(3.242)^2 (826.795 - 10(8.988)^2)}{(2.015)^2} = 49.03$$

Since F computed from the data is greater than 5.32, the critical F score, the analysis indicates that H_0 should not be accepted and there is evidence of a relationship.

As will be shown in later chapters, F tests of the above forms are particularly useful in regression models with more than one independent (predictor) variable. For example, F tests can ascertain whether additional independent variables contribute significantly to the model.

Finally, we noted that t and F tests as applied in the situation discussed in this section are two ways of looking at the same thing. They involve dividing variation into components representing variation associated with regression and components representing variation not associated with regression. Further, they permit us to estimate the likelihood that the variation associated with the regression is greater than could occur by chance alone. Mathematically, the F ratio is equal to the square of t and thus our observation as to their similarity of use is not unwarranted.

4.6   Significance of the Y Intercept

In this section, we question the validity of the estimate of β_0 which is denoted by b_0 in the predictive equation. Remember that $b_0 = -16.859$ in example 4.3 is based on sample data, and if an alternative sample of ten observations were made, regression methods would probably have led to a different value of b_0.

At best, the Y intercept (or regression constant) gives the average Y value at a specified X; $X = 0$. However, often β_0 does not have any physical meaning in the problem. In some problems, if $X = 0$, it is reasonable that $Y = 0$. If X is the number of items sold and Y is the sales revenue (price times items sold), then it is only logical that Y be zero. Because of sampling variability or specification error, the predicted regression line could show an intercept different from zero. Alternatively, in some relationships where the slope coefficient is negative, we would expect that the regression constant would not be zero. For example, if interest rates on mortgage loans were zero, there would be a nonzero demand for mortgage dollars. In both illustrations, the null hypothesis is stated in the same manner, that is,

$$H_0: \beta_0 = 0$$

The alternative hypothesis is

$$H_A: \beta_0 \neq 0$$

The t statistic for the test is stated as

$$t = (b_0 - \beta_0) \bigg/ \left\{ S_e \left[\frac{1}{n} + \frac{n \bar{X}^2}{n(\Sigma X_i^2) - (\Sigma X_i)^2} \right]^{1/2} \right\} \tag{4.18}$$

with $n - 2$ degrees of freedom. The t value (from table A.2 at the end of the book) at $\alpha = 0.01$ is 3.355. Hence if the computed t statistic results in a value greater than 3.355 or less than -3.355, we would be led to reject the null hypothesis and to conclude that β_0 is not zero.

Based on the numerical values of examples 4.2 and 4.3, we find

$$t = (-16.859 - 0) \bigg/ \left\{ 2.015 \left[\frac{1}{10} + \frac{10(8.988)}{10(826.778) - (89.88)^2} \right]^{1/2} \right\} = -4.00$$

and we should conclude that β_0 is *not* equal to zero. Such a result adds validity to our predictive regression model.

4.7   The Degree of Association

Correlation characterizes the existence of association between variables. Although there may be a large number of reasons for an association, correlation says nothing about these reasons. Correlation indicates only whether two or more variables vary together either positively or negatively. Thus correlation tells us nothing about causation but only indicates the degree of association or relationship existing between variables. Also, in this section we focus only on the linear association between two variables.

To begin, we define the *coefficient of determination* ρ^2 as the measure of the relative amount of the variation in the dependent variable Y that is explained by the linear regression relationship between Y and X. The coefficient indicates how closely the least squares regression line fits the data points in the scatter diagram. From sample evidence, the sample coefficient of determination r^2 is used to estimate the population coefficient of determination ρ^2.

The coefficient of determination r^2 is analyzed in terms of variation in the dependent variable Y. It indicates the proportion of this variation that is accounted for by the regression relationship between X and Y. For a single data point, if we think of $\bar{Y}$ as the mean value of the dependent variable, then $Y - \bar{Y}$ would represent the total deviation of Y. The deviation is composed of two parts:

$$Y - \bar{Y} = (\hat{Y} - \bar{Y}) + (Y - \hat{Y}) \tag{4.19}$$

A portion of the total deviation is explained by the least squares estimated regression line. $\hat{Y} - \bar{Y}$ represents the explained deviation. The remainder of the deviation, $Y - \hat{Y}$, is associated with random error and is unexplained.

The above analysis can also be extended to apply to the total variation of the dependent variable, measured by $\Sigma(Y - \bar{Y})^2$. Variation can be divided into two elements. First, the variation of the estimated values of the regression line $\hat{Y}$ about the mean $\bar{Y}$ is measured by

$$\Sigma(\hat{Y} - \overline{Y})^2$$

This is called the explained variation or the *explained sum of squares*. The second element is the residual or *error sum of squares*. It reflects the variation in the actual values Y of the dependent variable about the estimated values $\hat{Y}$ of the regression line and is measured by $(Y - \hat{Y})^2$. This is called the unexplained variation. Thus we have

total variation = explained variation + unexplained variation

$$\Sigma(Y_i - \overline{Y})^2 = \Sigma(\hat{Y}_i - \overline{Y})^2 + \Sigma(Y_i - \hat{Y}_i)^2 \tag{4.20}$$

The coefficient of determination is defined as

$$r^2 = \frac{\Sigma(\hat{Y}_i - \overline{Y})^2}{\Sigma(Y_i - \overline{Y})^2} \tag{4.21}$$

It will take on values in the range between zero and unity, and indicates the proportion of the variation in the dependent variable explained by the regression of Y on X.

When $r^2 = 0$, it implies that there is no linear association between X and Y, that is, there is no linear relationship between these variables. In terms of our formula for r^2, this would imply that the estimated regression line exactly coincides with the mean Y of the dependent variable. Thus $\Sigma(\hat{Y} - \overline{Y})^2 = 0$ and $r^2 = 0$.

When $r^2 = 1$, there is a perfect linear relationship between X and Y. All the sample data points fall exactly on the predicted line.

For the purpose of illustration, we return to example 4.3, and ask what proportion of the total variation in mortgage loans Y is associated with the regression on interest rates X. For the purposes of computation, the following formula for the coefficient of determination applies:

$$r^2 = \frac{[n\Sigma XY - (\Sigma X)(\Sigma Y)]^2}{[n\Sigma X^2 - (\Sigma X)^2][n\Sigma Y^2 - (\Sigma Y)^2]}$$

By substitution, we find

$$r^2 = \frac{[10(1165.30) - 89.88(122.82)]^2}{[10(826.778) - (89.88)^2][10(1740.007) - (122.82)^2]}$$
$$= 0.860$$

Thus 86 percent of the total variation in mortgage loans is associated with the regression on interest rates.

Another measure of the association between two variables is the *coefficient of correlation* ρ. It is the square root of the coefficient of determination:

$$\rho = \pm (\rho^2)^{1/2}$$

where the sign is not indeterminate. The estimator of the population coefficient of correlation is r, the sample coefficient of correlation. The coefficient of correlation can take on values in the range between -1 and $+1$. When $\rho = 0$, there is no correlation between X and Y. Thus there is no linear relationship between X and Y. A value of $\rho = +1$ implies that there is a perfect direct linear relationship between X and Y. Likewise, when $\rho = -1$, it implies a perfect inverse linear relationship between X and Y.

Since $r^2 = 0.860$, then $r = 0.927$. Note that the sign of the coefficient of correlation is always the same as the regression coefficient (slope) for the independent variable X. Since the slope has a positive sign, the correlation coefficient is also positive.

Can we test for the significance of correlation? The answer is "yes", but a word of caution is worth noting here. The test for the significance of the correlation coefficient is equivalent to the test for significance of regression. Hence the results are and must be the same.

For the Buckeye Savings and Loan Association (examples 4.2 and 4.3), we wish to test the null hypothesis, $\rho = 0$, that no correlation exists versus the alternative that $\rho \neq 0$. Symbolically, we write

$$H_0: \rho = 0$$

$$H_A: \rho \neq 0$$

The t statistic for this problem is given by

$$t = \frac{r}{[(1 - r^2)/(n - 2)]^{1/2}} \tag{4.22}$$

for $n - 2$ degrees of freedom. For the data of examples 4.2 and 4.3, the critical t score at $\alpha = 0.05$ for eight degrees of freedom is ± 2.306. Hence, the decision rule is as follows: accept the hypothesis of $\rho = 0$ if t based on the sample evidence is greater than -2.306 or less than $+2.306$; otherwise, reject it.

By substitution, we find

$$t = \frac{0.927}{[(1 - 0.860)/(10 - 2)]^{1/2}} = 7.00$$

Hence we reject the null hypothesis and conclude that there is evidence of correlation. Note that this is the same t score as that computed in example 4.3.

4.8   Another Look at the Regression Model

If we re-examine the regression model, we find that the predictive model states that increases in mortgage loans by Buckeye Savings and Loan are associated with increases in interest rates on new home mortgages. Although the fitted regression model is shown to have a statistically significant regression coefficient (slope), the sign of the coefficient may be puzzling. Economic theory indicates that higher interest rates are associated with a decline in new home mortgages, and this is at odds with the results of the regression.

The indication here is that the assumption made in the simple regression model that the relationship is linear does not hold. Stated differently, the model implemented here is incomplete. There may be an additional variable which can both improve the predictive ability of our model and also explain why our result is the way it is. This additional variable may be associated with both mortgage loans and interest rates, and thus is complicating the understanding of our result. In the next chapter, we shall attempt to find the independent variable when we study multiple regression analysis.

The estimating equation in regression analysis is established on the basis of a sample of observations. A great deal of care must be exercised in making forecasts of values of the dependent variable based on values of the independent variable outside the range of the observed data. Such extrapolations are risky. For example, if interest rates are 20 percent, it would be unwise to use the predictive equation to estimate mortgage loans. To do so would imply that the simple linear regression model could be projected up to a value of 20 percent for the independent variable. Without additional information, we do not know whether the linear form is valid outside the range of the sample data. In some instances, extrapolations have to be made, but the limitations and risks involved should always be kept in mind. We shall re-examine this problem in later chapters.

4.9 Output of Computer Programs

Numerous interactive statistical computer systems and software language systems are available for many computer installations. One such system, SAS, is particularly useful and the output of a sample program will be discussed next.

For most installations, the SAS log printout reproduces the instructional part of the program, checks for errors and denotes the type of error, and tells the user how much CPU time and memory were used at each step.

The list output (figure 4.3) produces the simple linear regression results. Notice that SAS produces the following:

```
DEP VARIABLE: Y                    MORTGAGE LOANS
                                ANALYSIS OF VARIANCE

                          SUM OF          MEAN
   SOURCE        DF       SQUARES         SQUARE       F VALUE      PROB>F

   MODEL         1        199.0535       199.0535      49.032       0.0001
   ERROR         8         32.4773       4.059663
   C TOTAL       9        231.5308

            ROOT MSE        2.01486      R-SQUARE       0.8597
            DEP MEAN        12.282       ADJ R-SQ       0.8422
            C.V.            16.40499

                          PARAMETER ESTIMATES


                          PARAMETER       STANDARD       T FOR HO:
      VARIABLE      DF     ESTIMATE        ERROR         PARAMETER=0

      INTERCEP      1      -16.8585       4.210066       -4.004
      X             1        3.242159     0.4630143       7.002

                                          VARIABLE
   VARIABLE       DF      PROB > |T|        LABEL

   INTERCEP        1        0.0039         INTERCEPT
   X               1        0.0001       INTEREST RATE
```

FIGURE 4.3 Output of PROC REG. Mortgage loans by interest rates regression

1 an overall analysis of variance table;
2 sundry statistics;
3 parameter estimates and tests.

The overall analysis of variance breaks down the total sums of squares into its components, that is, the portion attributable to the model (regression) and the portion not accounted for by the model (error). The mean square is simply the sum of squares divided by the corresponding degrees of freedom. The mean square (MS) error term is the square of the standard error of estimate of regression defined earlier in this chapter.

The various statistics include a great many useful items for analytical purposes. The MODEL F is the ratio of the MS (model) to the MS (error). In the problem illustrated, the value is 49.032 and is significant (labeled PR > F) at the 0.0001 level. R-SQUARE is the estimate of the coefficient of determination. For this problem 0.8597 of the total variation in loans is accounted for by the regression. In general, large values of R^2 indicate a better model fit.

CV is the coefficient of variation and is an indicator of the variation in the population of Y values (the loans). It is equal to the standard deviation of the Y values divided by the mean of the Y values times 100.

ROOT MSE is the standard deviation of the dependent variable and is equal to the square root of MS (error). Dep Y is the mean of the dependent variable. In this example, it is the overall mean of the variable Mortgage loans.

The parameter estimates and tests section of the output indicates the estimates of the regression model parameters, that is, the Y intercept and slope (regression coefficient). In figure 4.3 the INTERCEPT estimate is -16.8585 and the estimate of the interest rate (X) coefficient is 3.242 159. T for HO: PARAMETER = 0 means the t value for testing the hypothesis that the regression coefficient (slope) equals zero. The t value for testing the hypothesis that the intercept is zero is -4.00 and the t value for testing the hypothesis that the regression coefficient (slope) is zero is 7.002.

The next column to the right in the table labeled PR > 1T1 answers the following question: If the parameter equals zero, what is the probability of finding a larger absolute value of t? For the problem illustrated these probabilities are 0.0039 and 0.0001. Hence it is very unlikely that rejecting the hypothesis that the parameters equal zero will be an error. The Y intercept is not likely to cross the origin, nor is it likely that the slope is zero.

The remaining column, STD ERROR, gives the estimates of the standard error of the Y intercept (4.210 066) and the standard error of the slope (0.463 014 3). These values are used in the computation of the t value discussed earlier.

4.10   An Analysis of the Sequence Plots

Plottings of actual and predicted values and of residuals provide a very useful way of detecting violations of the assumptions of the regression model. Plots are most useful for models having an economic interpretation as in the example of this chapter. In reviewing the plots, we want to observe no systematic pattern about the predicted values or about the zero line on the plot of residuals. If there is a systematic pattern in the plot of residuals, the residuals are said to be serial correlated (or autocorrelated) and are not independent of one another. Examination of figures 4.1 and 4.4

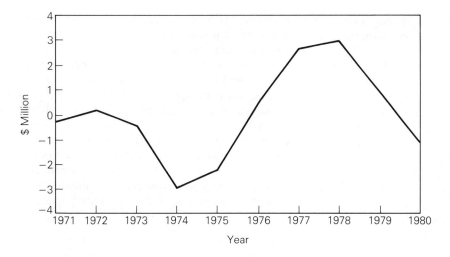

FIGURE 4.4 Plot of residuals

indicates that serial correlation may be present. In the next section, we shall consider
how to solve the problem of serial correlated observations.

Returning to the plot of residuals, three general patterns indicate violation of one
or more assumptions of simple linear regression. The three patterns are summarized
in figure 4.5. The pattern of variation shown in figure 4.5(a) indicates that a trend

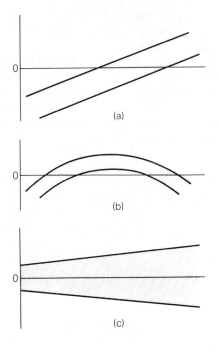

FIGURE 4.5 Examples of various residual patterns

variable has not been included in the model. Stated differently, the demand for loans is slowly changing, perhaps because of changing tastes, social conditions, styles of living and other factors. A possible solution is to consider a multiple linear regression with a variable for time as well as interest rates in the regression model.

If the sequence of plots indicates a trend that is not constant over time, the rate of change in the trend is either increasing (as in figure 4.5(b)) or decreasing. In this case, the inclusion of a new time variable in quadratic terms (a nonlinear or curvilinear model) may be appropriate.

Finally, a sequence plot such as that shown in figure 4.5(c) indicates a more serious problem. In figure 4.5(c), the plotted residuals indicate a nonconstant standard error about the expected mean value of regression which is called heteroscedasticity. This violation of the regression assumption invalidates the model of this chapter and calls for another technique called weighted least squares regression.

4.11   Serial Correlation (Autocorrelation)

Now, let us return to one of the original assumptions of the linear regression model underlying trend analysis. The regression model

$$Y = \beta_0 + \beta_1 X + e \tag{4.1}$$

assumes that e is a variable with $E(e) = 0$ and that the variance of e is constant. If e is no longer assumed to be fully random and successive values of e are considered not to be statistically independent, the errors are said to be serial or autocorrelated.

When autocorrelation is present, least squares regression procedures still result in unbiased and consistent estimates. However, the procedure is not fully efficient; the standard error formula and tests of significance do not apply. Often, the fitted regression line fits the sample data values more closely than does the population regression line. In turn, an artificially high coefficient of determination results, indicating that the estimated regression model is more reliable than it actually is.

Several procedures for measuring the magnitude of autocorrelation and tests for its presence exist. The most universally accepted testing criterion is provided by the *Durbin–Watson* test. This test involves the determination of whether or not the correlation between residuals is zero. Consider

$$e_t = \rho e_{t-1} + d_t \tag{4.23}$$

where ρ is the autocorrelation parameter that measures the correlation between residuals and the d_t are independent random variables (or disturbances). Each error term consists of a portion of the previous error term, when ρ is greater than zero, and a new random disturbance term denoted d_t. If $\rho = 0$, $e_t = d_t$, and the successive error terms are independent since the disturbance terms are independent.

The null and alternative hypotheses for the Durbin–Watson test are

$$H_0{:}\rho = 0$$

$$H_A{:}\rho > 0$$

Note that the alternative hypothesis is one-sided since residuals in time series tend to show positive autocorrelation.

The following formula (Durbin and Watson, 1951) is used to calculate the Durbin–Watson statistic:

$$DW = \frac{\Sigma(e_t - e_{t-1})^2}{\Sigma e_t^2} \tag{4.24}$$

where e_t is the error or difference between the actual and fitted values at time t and e_{t-1} is the error or difference between the actual and fitted values during the previous time period $t - 1$.

The Durbin–Watson procedure provides upper and lower critical values U and L as criteria of choice between the null and alternative hypotheses. The decision is stated as follows:

1 if $DW > U$, conclude H_0;
2 if $DW < L$, conclude H_A;
3 if $L < DW < U$, the test is inconclusive.

The critical values for L and U are included in the tables at the end of the book. To locate the appropriate L and U values, we need to know the sample size, level of significance, and number of independent variables. To analyze an actual set of observations, let us consider the next example.

Example 4.4

Data for American Hospital Supply Inc. for the years 1965–80 are provided to find the relationship between net income (million dollars) and time. The data for this regression are estimated by regression (least squares). The output of the SAS is shown in figure 4.6. The regression equation is

$$\hat{Y}_t = -10.877 + 7.056X$$

(origin at 1964; one unit of X = one year) and net income is in million dollars.

The actual, fitted, and residual values for this regression are presented in table 4.2. These values are necessary for calculation of the DW statistic. First, the square of the individual differences between the residual in time period t and the residual in the previous time period is calculated. For time period 2, we have

$$e_2 - e_1 = 9.25 - 13.67 = -4.42$$

and

$$(e_2 - e_1)^2 = (-4.42)^2 = 19.5364$$

The value in the numerator of the formula for the DW statistic is

$$\Sigma(e_t - e_{t-1})^2 = 331.7922$$

The sum of the squared residuals is

$$\Sigma(e_t)^2 = 1674.0475$$

By substitution into the numerator and the denominator of the DW formula, we find

$$DW = \frac{331.7922}{1674.0475} = 0.198$$

```
DEP VARIABLE: Y                          NET INCOME
                              ANALYSIS OF VARIANCE

                          SUM OF              MEAN
    SOURCE        DF      SQUARES            SQUARE       F VALUE         PROB>F

    MODEL          1     16926.92          16926.92      141.559         0.0001
    ERROR         14      1674.047         119.5748
    C TOTAL       15     18600.97

              ROOT MSE     10.93503        R-SQUARE        0.9100
              DEP MEAN     49.0975         ADJ R-SQ        0.9036
              C.V.         22.27207

                              PARAMETER ESTIMATES

                          PARAMETER            STANDARD        T FOR H0:
       VARIABLE      DF    ESTIMATE              ERROR        PARAMETER=0

       INTERCEP       1    -10.8773            5.734377         -1.897
       X              1      7.055853          0.5930351        11.898

                                                              VARIABLE
       VARIABLE      DF      PROB > |T|                         LABEL

       INTERCEP       1        0.0787                          INTERCEPT
       X              1        0.0001                          PERIOD

    DURBIN-WATSON D                  0.198
    (FOR NUMBER OF OBS.)              16
    1ST ORDER AUTOCORRELATION  0.723
```

FIGURE 4.6 Output of PROC REG, Durbin–Watson statistic calculated

Checking with the table for the upper and lower bounds for a sample of 16 with one independent variable, and letting the level of significance equal 0.05, we find

$$L = 0.98$$

$$U = 1.24$$

Since DW = 0.198 is less than $L = 0.98$, the sample evidence indicates that we cannot accept the null hypothesis. Hence the conclusion is that the error terms are positively correlated ($\rho > o$).

It is important to note that adjacent error terms e_t and e_{t-1} are usually of the same sign, resulting in relatively small values for the individual differences. When positive correlation is present, the individual differences tend to be small resulting in a small value for the DW statistics. Finally, DW is a check for first-order serial correlation only.

The SAS output shown in figure 4.6 calculates, among other things, the DW statistic for the regression of net income on time. Note that the DW statistic is the same. Our next problem is to recognize that a solution to the problem of autocorrelation is required.

TABLE 4.2 Actual, fitted, and residual values
for regression of net income on time for
American Hospital Supply Inc., 1965–1980

	(1)	*(2)* *Fitted*	*(3)*
Time *period*	*Actual* Y	*($ millions)* $(\hat{Y})$	*Residual* (e)
1	9.85	−3.82	13.67
2	12.48	3.23	9.25
3	15.19	10.29	4.90
4	20.92	17.35	3.57
5	25.00	24.40	0.60
6	26.65	31.46	−4.81
7	29.16	38.51	−9.35
8	35.60	45.57	−9.97
9	40.81	52.62	−11.81
10	46.33	59.68	−13.35
11	55.18	66.74	−11.56
12	66.27	73.79	−7.52
13	77.92	80.85	−2.93
14	92.60	87.90	4.70
15	109.40	94.96	14.44
16	122.20	102.02	20.18

4.12   Correcting for Autocorrelation (Serial Correlation) (Optional Topic)

Specifically, autocorrelation indicates that a major portion of the variation in the dependent variable (net income of American Hospital Supply Inc.) is not explained by the trend analysis. Thus the best solution is to search for those explanatory variables which explain the remaining portion of the variation in the dependent variable; this is a multiple regression problem which will be discussed in chapter 5. In the case of the net income of American Hospital Supply, including a variable for demand for their services, such as the number of patient-days or hospital expenses, or a variable for the price of hospital expenses, or a variable for the price of hospital input services, may reduce the autocorrelation to an insignificant level.

When no additional variables which will reduce autocorrelation to an insignificant level can be identified easily, a number of mathematical procedures which can reduce the autocorrelation to a manageable level are available. Some techniques for phasing out autocorrelation are to fit a least squares model to the percentage change from year to year, to correlate the absolute amounts of change from year to year, to lag the dependent variable one period and include it as an independent variable, and to use the rho correction technique.[4] From the computational point of view, this last technique is simplest and will be considered next.

---

4   In chapters 7, 8, and 9 we shall investigate ARIMA modeling techniques to account for autocorrelation.

The rho correction is a factor equal to half the difference between the DW statistic and 2.0. For the data of example 4.4, we have

$$\text{rho} = \frac{2 - \text{DW}}{2} = \frac{2 - 0.198}{2}$$

$$= 0.901$$

To adjust for autocorrelation, the residual for period $t-1$ is multiplied by the rho correction factor and added to the estimate for period t. If 1981 is to be estimated ($X = 17$) we find

$$\hat{Y} = -10.877 + 7.056(17)$$

$$= 109.075$$

and

$$\text{rho} \times C_{1980} = \text{correction factor}$$

$$(0.901)(20.183) = 18.185$$

$$\text{forecast } (1981) = \hat{Y} + \text{correction factor}$$

$$= 109.075 + 18.185$$

$$= 127.260$$

Hence the forecast for the 1981 net income for American Hospital Supply Inc. is $127.260 million. This procedure will tend to reduce autocorrelation and improve predictions whenever the forecaster cannot easily find a new variable to be included in the predictive equation for trend.

In a commonly used estimation procedure known as first differencing it is assumed that rho = 1. In this case the transformed model becomes

$$\nabla Y_t = \beta_0(1 - \text{rho}) + \beta_1 \nabla X_t + e_t \tag{4.25}$$

$$= \beta_0(1 - 1) + \beta_1 \nabla X_t + e_t$$

and

$$Y_t = \beta_1 \nabla X_t + e_t \tag{4.26}$$

Thus the regression coefficient β_1 is estimated by using least squares regression through the origin with the transformed variables

$$\nabla Y_t = Y_t - Y_{t-1}$$

$$\nabla X_t = X_t - X_{t-1}$$

Note that these transformed variables are first differences. This approach is effective in a variety of applications.

Table 4.3 contains the transformed variables ∇Y_t and ∇X_t based on the first-difference transformation for the net income of American Hospital Supply Inc. The table contains the calculations for estimating the linear regression through the origin. Figure 4.7 contains the SAS output for the above model. Note that the standard error S_{b_1} of the parameter estimate is 1.252 with a t statistic of 5.984. This new standard error is probably more accurate than the original standard error of 0.593 for the ordinary least squares applied to the original variables. Furthermore, the original

TABLE 4.3 First differences of net income of American Hospital Supply Inc.

Y	X	XY	X^2
2.63	1	2.63	1
2.71	1	2.71	1
5.73	1	5.73	1
4.08	1	4.08	1
1.65	1	1.65	1
2.51	1	2.51	1
6.44	1	6.44	1
5.21	1	5.21	1
5.52	1	5.52	1
8.85	1	8.85	1
11.09	1	11.09	1
11.65	1	11.65	1
14.68	1	14.68	1
16.80	1	16.80	1
12.80	1	12.80	1
		112.35	15
		$\Sigma\nabla Z\nabla Y$	$\Sigma\nabla X^2$

$$b_1 = \frac{\Sigma\nabla X\nabla Y}{\Sigma\neq X^2} = \frac{112.35}{15} = 7.49$$

```
DEP VARIABLE: YD              FIRST DIFFERENCE OF Y
                              ANALYSIS OF VARIANCE

                       SUM OF          MEAN
SOURCE        DF       SQUARES         SQUARE      F VALUE       PROB>F

MODEL         1        841.5015       841.5015     35.812        0.0001
ERROR         14       328.965         23.4975
U TOTAL       15       1170.467

         ROOT MSE     4.847422        R-SQUARE      0.7189
         DEP MEAN         7.49        ADJ R-SQ      0.6989
         C.V.         64.71858
NOTE: NO INTERCEPT TERM IS USED.  R-SQUARE IS REDEFINED.

                       PARAMETER ESTIMATES

                       PARAMETER        STANDARD      T FOR HO:
VARIABLE      DF        ESTIMATE          ERROR      PARAMETER=0

XD            1           7.49          1.251599        5.984

                                        VARIABLE
VARIABLE      DF       PROB > |T|         LABEL

XD            1          0.0001        FIRST DIFFERENCE OF X
```

FIGURE 4.7 First-differences regression model. Output of PROC REG

standard error most likely understates the magnitude of the true standard error because of the presence of autocorrelation.

To forecast for period 17, we substitute in the first-difference model:

$$Y_{t+1} - Y_t = b_1(X_{t+1} - X_t)$$
$$Y_{t+1} = b_1(X_{t+1} - X_t) + Y_t$$
$$Y_{17} = (7.49 \times 1) + 122.20$$
$$Y_{17} = \$129.69 \text{ million}$$

Hence the forecast for 1989 is $129.69 million. This technique is more reliable than predicting with a least squares model that does not attempt to correct for autocorrelation.

There are a variety of more sophisticated methods for correcting for autocorrelation. One of the most popular methods involves a series of iterations, each of which produces a better estimate of rho than the previous one. This is called the Cochrane–Orcutt procedure (Cochrane and Orcutt, 1949) and it utilizes the notion that rho is a correlation coefficient associated with errors of adjacent time periods. First, the original model is estimated using ordinary least squares. Second, the residuals from the estimated equation are used to perform the regression of equation (4.23). The estimated value of l(rho) is used to perform the generalized differencing transformation process, and a new regression is run. The transformed equation is

$$Y_t^* = \beta_0(1 - l^*) + \beta_1 X_t^* \tag{4.27}$$

where

$$Y_t^* = Y_t - l^* Y_{t-1}$$
$$X_t^* = X_t - l^* X_{t-1}$$

The estimated transformed equation yields estimated values for the original intercept β_0 and the slope parameter β_1. These revised parameter estimates are substituted into the original equation, and new regression residuals are obtained. The new estimated residuals are

$$\hat{e}_t^* = Y_t - b_0 - b_{1t} X_t \tag{4.28}$$

Furthermore, the re-estimated residuals can now be employed to re-estimate rho and l, and the iterative process can be carried out for as many steps as the forecaster desires. Typically, the iterations should cease when the new estimates differ from the old ones by less than 0.005 or after a sufficiently large number of iterations are accomplished, usually 20.

The iterative technique is generally performed using a computer program because of the large number of computations involved. One such routine is available under Micro-TSP, but there is a wide selection of statistical and forecasting programs which provide for such routines. SAS software produces a Cochrane–Orcutt solution in a manner similar to that described above to produce forecast models.

The output of the SAS time series procedure (AUTOREG) contains five parts (figure 4.8). First, the least squares parameter estimates (1) are printed; these estimates are identical with the output of other SAS regression procedures. Second estimates of the autocorrelation of the residuals of the least squares trend line are calculated. Since the independent variable is lagged only one year (NLAG = 1), the first-order autocorrelation is estimated and is equal to 0.723 402(2). The parameter of the regression of residuals

```
                    A U T O R E G   P R O C E D U R E

DEPENDENT VARIABLE = Y NET INCOME


                    ORDINARY LEAST SQUARES ESTIMATES

           SSE          1674.047    DFE                  14
           MSE          119.5748    ROOT MSE        10.93503
           SBC          125.3578    AIC             123.8126
           REG RSQ        0.9100    TOTAL RSQ         0.9100
           DURBIN-WATSON  0.1982


VARIABLE DF   ①    B VALUE       STD ERROR      T RATIO   APPROX PROB

 INTERCPT 1      -10.8772500    5.73437660      -1.897      0.0787
 X        1        7.0558529    0.59303511      11.898      0.0001

                    ESTIMATES OF AUTOCORRELATIONS

              LAG     COVARIANCE     CORRELATION
               0       104.628        1.000000
               1        75.6881       0.723402   ②

                 PRELIMINARY MSE=       49.87509

          ESTIMATES OF THE AUTOREGRESSIVE PARAMETERS
          LAG     COEFFICIENT      STD ERROR      T RATIO
           1     -0.72340175  ③   0.19149009    -3.777750

                    YULE-WALKER ESTIMATES

           SSE          455.2216    DFE                  13
           MSE          35.01705    ROOT MSE         5.91752
           SBC          108.0358    AIC             105.7181
           REG RSQ  ④     0.8742    TOTAL RSQ         0.9755
                        ⑤
VARIABLE DF        B VALUE       STD ERROR      T RATIO   APPROX PROB

 INTERCPT 1       -8.78025528    8.01059446      -1.096      0.2929
 X        1        7.29979523    0.76796803       9.505      0.0001
```

FIGURE 4.8 Output of PROC AUTOREG

$$\dot{e} = \rho e_{t-1} + d_t$$

where ρ is the autocorrelation coefficient as estimated in (3). The AUTOREG
procedure uses this estimate to produce various statistics including the coefficient of
determination of the new predictive equation (4). Note that REGRSQ is 0.8742
indicating that 87.42 percent of the total variation in net income is associated with
the variation in time for an autocorrelated adjusted predictive equation. Finally,
estimates of parameters and their standard errors are printed (5). The t ratios are
only approximately valid in this case. However, the time variable X is significant at
the 0.0001 level. The predictive equation is (rounded to three decimal places)

$$\hat{Y}_t = l^* Y_{t-1} + b_0(1 - l^*) + b_1(X_t - l^* X_{t-1}) \tag{4.29}$$

(origin at $X = 1964$; one unit of $X =$ one year). To forecast for the year 1981, we substitute $X_{17} = 17$, $X_{16} = 16$, $l^* = 0.723$, and $Y_{16} = 122.2$. Then

$$\hat{Y} = 0.723(122.2) + (-8.780)(1 - 0.723) + 7.300(17 - (0.723)(16))$$

$$= \$125.572 \text{ million}$$

Thus this equation predicts that the net income in 1981 is expected to be \$125.572 million. Note that the prediction of this equation is different from those of the hand-calculated rho procedure and the TSP Cochrane–Orcutt procedure.

One last comparison may be of interest at this point. Table 4.4 gives a comparison of the initial least squares regression and the autocorrelation corrected regression. Note that the corrected regression reduces the values for the MSE and the coefficient of determination (R-SQUARE). The values of b_0 and b_1 change but not by very much. However, the estimated standard errors of these estimates do increase and in turn, they decrease the t ratios for testing the hypothesis that the parameter equals zero. The results of these t tests are the same. However, it is obvious that least squares regression underestimates standard error in the presence of serial correlation. In turn, this could result in the use of an unimportant independent variable for prediction because of the inflated t ratio.

The estimated value of l is -0.723, and an approximate t test[5] for $l = 0$ yields a t ratio of -3.78. With 14 degrees of freedom, this ratio is significant at less than the 0.01 level. This result corroborates the Durbin–Watson test applied previously, that is, there is evidence of autocorrelation.

All four of the autocorrelation correction procedures produce different forecasting equations. No one procedure is without error. Each procedure has a standard error of regression (root mean square error). In a later chapter, we shall return to the problem of adjusting for forecasting error. The best solution to this problem of autocorrelation is to improve the predictive equation by searching for additional

TABLE 4.4 Comparison of least squares and corrected regression

	Least squares	Corrected
MSE	119.575	35.018
R-SQUARE	0.910	0.874
b_0	-10.877	-8.780
S_{b_0}	5.734	8.011
t ratio	-1.90	-1.10
	$(P < 0.079)$	$(P < 0.293)$
b_1	7.056.	7.300
S_{b_1}	0.593	0.768
t ratio	11.90	9.805
	$(P < 0.0001)$	$(P < 0.0001)$
l(rho)	—	-0.723
t ratio	—	3.78

Note: Corrected regressions of this type are often called autocorrelated models.

---

5 This test is omitted from the discussion; see Box and Jenkins (1976) for a test of this type.

equation by searching for additional explanatory variables to include in the predictive model. In chapter 5 on multiple regression we shall examine those methods for reducing forecast error by including additional explanatory variables in the predictive equation. When missing variables are not readily available, one or more of the above techniques will provide useful results.

Finally, we can suggest a four-step approach to fit time series models by regression techniques.

1 Use least squares to obtain initial estimates.
2 Use Durbin–Watson to determine whether there is evidence of serial correlation.
3 If serial correlation is present, construct a re-estimated model by a correction technique. Do diagnostic tests.
4 If serial correlation is not present, use initial estimates for forecasting after diagnostic tests are performed.

4.13   The Simple Linear Regression Model and Forecasting

We have seen that for a given value of X, designated X_0, the estimated regression model becomes

$$\hat{Y} = b_0 + b_1 X_0$$

Since b_0 and b_1 are random variables which have values that change from sample to sample and have a joint probability distribution, the standard error of the estimate $\hat{Y}_0$ can be calculated as follows:

$$SE(\hat{Y}_0) = S_e \left[\frac{1}{n} + \frac{(X_0 - \overline{X})^2}{\Sigma(X_i - \overline{X})^2} \right]^{1/2} \tag{4.30}$$

Further, this standard error is for the mean forecast for the given value of X, denoted X_0; we denote the standard error as SE(mean). In equation (4.30) the only item to change on the right-hand side is X_0, the new value of X. If X_0 equals the mean of the n known X values, then equation (4.30) yields the smallest possible value for the standard error of the mean forecast. As X_0 departs from the mean $\overline{X}$ of the X values, the standard error increases. This is easily seen if you observe the numerator $X_0 - \overline{X}$ indicates to how far X_0 departs from the mean X. The denominator value $\Sigma(X_i - \overline{X})^2$ refers to the n known X values.

The above equation considers the forecast $\hat{Y}_0$ as if it were a mean or expected value. Often, interest may center on how far a particular (individual) forecast may differ from the observed value. The extent of the differences of particular forecasts from observed values is found by combining the effects of the joint distribution of b_0 and b_1 and the observed pattern of dispersion around the estimated regression, the standard error of regression $\hat{\sigma}_e$. The standard error of an individual (particular) forecast is given by

$$SE(\text{individual}) = S_e \left[1 + \frac{1}{n} + \frac{(X_0 - \overline{X})^2}{\Sigma(X_i - \overline{X})^2} \right]^{1/2} \tag{4.31}$$

As in equation (4.30), if $X_0 = \overline{X}$, equation (4.31) yields the smallest value for the standard error of the individual forecast. Furthermore, if $X_0 = \overline{X}$, equations (4.30) and (4.31) become

$$SE(\text{mean}) = S_e\left(\frac{1}{n}\right)^{1/2} \tag{4.32}$$

and

$$SE(\text{individual}) = S_e\left(1 + \frac{1}{n}\right)^{1/2} \tag{4.33}$$

In turn, the ratio of SE (individual) to SE (mean), which is $(n + 1)/1$, indicates that the standard error of individual forecasts is greater than the standard error of mean forecasts. To illustrate the points made above, consider the next example.

Example 4.5

In the above study of the relationship of mortgage loans Y in the Buckeye Savings and Loan Association (example 4.2), the estimated regression equation was found to be

$$\hat{Y} = -16.859 + 3.242X$$

where mortgage loans were in millions of dollars. The F statistic ($F = 49.03$ with one and eight degrees of freedom) was significant at the 0.05 level. The decision-maker wishes to forecast the value of mortgage loans associated with interest rates of 10, 11, or 12 percent.

To solve the above problem, we substitute the given values into the regression equation and obtain the following results (in million dollars):

$\hat{Y} = -16.859 + 3.242 \times 10 = 15.561$ when the interest rate is 10 percent

$\hat{Y} = -16.859 + 3.242 \times 11 = 18.803$ when the interest rate is 11 percent

$\hat{Y} = -16.859 + 3.242 \times 12 = 22.045$ when the interest rate is 12 percent

If interest centers on estimating mortgage loans on the average, we would use equation (4.30) to estimate the standard error of the mean forecast:

$$SE(\text{mean}) = \left[\frac{1}{10} + \frac{(X_0 - \overline{X})^2}{\Sigma(X_i - \overline{X})^2}\right]^{1/2}$$

The only value not specified on the right-hand side is the given value X_0 for the interest rate X. For the three interest rates, the standard errors are as follows:

$SE(\text{mean}) = 0.392$ when $X = 10$ percent

$SE(\text{mean}) = 0.454$ when $X = 11$ percent

$SE(\text{mean}) = 0.509$ when $X = 12$ percent

In turn, if we wish to be certain that 95 out of every 100 confidence intervals contain the true mean forecast, we refer to the t tables (see table A.2 at the end of the book); with eight degrees of freedom and $t = 2.306$, there is 0.025 of the area in the right tail of the t distribution. Thus $-2.306 \leq t \leq 2.306$ represents 0.95 of the area under the t distribution (a 95 percent confidence interval). To calculate the 95 percent confidence interval for the mean mortgage loans forecast, the appropriate standard error is multiplied by ± 2.306. The interval is thus

$$\hat{Y}_0 - 2.306 \text{ SE(mean)} < \mu Y_0 < \hat{Y}_0 + 2.306 \text{ SE (mean)} \qquad (4.34)$$

By substitution, we find

$X = 10$: $14.657 < \mu_{Y_0} < 16.465$

$X = 11$: $17.750 < \mu_{Y_0} < 19.850$

$X = 12$: $20.871 < \mu_{Y_0} < 23.219$

Similarly, we use equation (4.31) to calculate standard errors of forecast for specific savings deposits at a given rate of interest. The general form for this equation is

$$\text{SE(individual)} = \left[1 + \frac{1}{10} + \frac{(X_0 - \overline{X})^2}{\Sigma(X - \overline{X})^2} \right]^{1/2}$$

where X_0 is the assumed interest rate to forecast. For the three interest rates, the standard errors are

SE(individual) = 1.074 when the interest rate is 10 percent

SE(individual) = 1.764 when the interest rate is 11 percent

SE(individual) = 2.028 when the interest rate is 12 percent

Of course, the point estimates for mortgage loans at the three interest rates are the same as for the previous computations; however, the confidence interval estimates differ. The 95 percent confidence interval estimates for the individual forecasts are

$X = 10$: $13.084 < Y < 18.038$

$X = 11$: $16.326 < Y < 21.280$

$X = 12$: $17.368 < Y < 26.722$

Note that the confidence interval estimates for the individual forecasts are much wider. Also, as is true for the confidence or prediction interval for individual forecasts, the further the X_0 value is from $\overline{X}$, the wider is the prediction interval.

A number of factors affect the size of the standard error of regression and hence the standard error of forecast and confidence interval. The larger the sample size n, the smaller are these standard errors and, in turn, the narrower are the confidence intervals. This agrees with intuitive notions that larger sample sizes produce greater precision in forecasts.

Second, as noted above, the greater the deviations of X_0 from $\overline{X}$ the wider are the confidence intervals. Confidence interval estimates may be very wide for very small or very large values of X compared with the analogous intervals for X values very close to the mean value $\overline{X}$.

Third, the less uniform are the data the greater is the standard error of regression and the wider are the confidence intervals. Predictions would be less precise.

Finally, the more variable the sample of X values (in our illustration, the interest rates), the larger is $\Sigma(X_i - \overline{X})^2$. Thus the smaller are the standard errors and the more accurate (narrow) are the confidence intervals. This is consistent with the notion that if we observe a relationship for an institution with a wide variety of interest rates, we would be able to predict mortgage loans better than if the variation in interest rates was very small.

The usefulness of confidence intervals depends on the purpose for which they are to be used. For long-term forecasts, relatively wide limits can be appropriate and useful. In contrast, short-term planning decisions usually require narrow and precise intervals. If a two-variable regression analysis produces large standard errors which prohibit narrow intervals, this type of analysis may not be useful. In such an instance, more independent variables must be introduced to obtain greater precision of estimation and prediction. In the next chapter, we shall discuss multiple regression and correlation which deals with the use of two or more independent variables.

4.14   Summary

The purpose of regression is to estimate the nature of the relationship between a dependent variable and an independent variable.

The purpose of correlation is to answer questions concerning the degree of association between the two variables. Although there may be plausible reasons for a relationship, correlation says nothing about these reasons. It only indicates whether or not two variables vary together.

Firstly, in the simple regression model we assume that the relationship is linear. Error of prediction can arise from (a) incomplete theory (certain variables related to the dependent variables may have been omitted from the regression), (b) imperfect specification (a linear relationship is estimated when the relationship is nonlinear) or (c) errors of measurement (computational error may occur in the measurement of the variables). In addition, for forecasting the same distribution of X values appears in any replication of the experiments.

The assumptions concerning the error term are as follows:

1 The random error term has a mean of zero.
2 The variance of the random error term is the same for each X value; this is known as homoscedasticity.
3 Error terms are independent of each other, that is, there is no serial correlation.
4 The error term for each X value is normally distributed.

The standard error of regression provides an estimate of the accuracy of the productive equation. It is the sum of squared deviations of the residuals from the regression line divided by $n - k$ where k is the number of coefficients in the regression equation, that is, the root mean square error.

A regression is meaningful if the slope of the line is shown to be different from zero. Also, a significant F ratio indicates that the variance associated with regression is greater than the variance not associated with regression.

The intercept of the regression model indicates the value of Y when $X = 0$.

The coefficient of determination is a measure of the relative amount of variation in the dependent variable that is explained by the regression on the independent variable. Correlation is positive if the X and Y values vary in the same direction. If they vary in opposite directions, correlation is said to be negative.

Plotting of actual and predicted values and of residuals provides a very useful way of detecting violations of the assumptions of the regression model. Various residual patterns can indicate serial correlation, nonlinearity, or heteroscedasticity.

The Durbin–Watson test indicates whether successive error values are serially correlated. Various procedures exist to correct for serial correlation. These include a hand-calculated correction procedure, the Cochrane–Orcutt procedure, and the method of first differences.

Interest often centers on the observed pattern of dispersion around the estimated regression estimates. Confidence intervals for the mean value and the individual value permit forecasters to account for the dispersion in estimates.

4.15 Exercises

1 The following equation measures the relationship between family income X and family savings Y:

$$Y = -1750 + 0.065X$$

(a) Interpret the meaning of the intercept.
(b) Interpret the meaning of the slope.
(c) If a family has an income of $25 000, what is the estimate of family savings?

2 Two regressions are performed to find the best predictive relationship. The following are the results of measuring the accuracy of prediction:

Regression	S_e
1	7.50
2	27.50

Which regression is best? Why?

3 (a) A study of the relationship between sales and cost of goods sold resulted in a correlation coefficient of 0.856. What proportion of the total variation in sales is associated with the regression on cost of goods sold? Does this indicate that variation in sales is caused by the variation in cost of goods sold? Why or why not?

(b) A study of the relationship between bituminous coal production and the price per tonne resulted in a correlation coefficient of 0.653. What proportion of the total variation in bituminous coal production is associated with the price per tonne of coal? Does this indicate that variation in production is caused by variation in prices? Why or why not?

(c) Two studies of the variation in savings deposits in thrift institutions resulted in coefficients of determination of 0.75 and 0.82. The first study employed interest rates on new home mortgages as the independent variable and the second study employed family income as the independent variable. Interpret the coefficients of determination for each study. Do you have enough information to conclude which study would lead to a better predictive model?

4 The data in table 4.5 indicate the age and the maintenance and repair expenses for the materials-handling vehicles of a large-scale parts manufacturer. The information is to be used to estimate expenses and to determine a replacement policy for its fleet of materials-handling vehicles.

(a) Plot the scatter diagram for these data.

TABLE 4.5

Vehicle	Age (years)	Expense (dollars)
1	1	45
2	1	125
3	1	50
4	1	75
5	2	90
6	2	165
7	2	210
8	2	125
9	3	79
10	3	140
11	3	220
12	3	245
13	4	175
14	4	295
15	4	335
16	5	725
17	5	895
18	5	520

(b) Estimate the regression to describe the relationship between expenses Y and age X.
(c) Test to determine whether the slope coefficient is different from zero (at a significance level of 0.01).
(d) Test to determine whether there is evidence of regression at the 0.01 level. (Hint: calculate the F ratio.)
(e) Test to determine the significance of the intercept at the 0.01 level. What do the results mean?
(f) Plot the residuals on a graph. Is there evidence of heteroscedasticity, nonlinearity, or serial correlation? Why or why not?
(g) What proportion of the variation in expenses is associated with the variation in age?
(h) Calculate the Durbin–Watson statistic and test for serial correlation.

5 The data in table 4.6 are gross premium revenues for Rhode Island Group Health Association (thousand dollars) and Rhode Island per capita income (dollars).
(a) Plot the scatter diagram for these data.
(b) Estimate the regression to describe the relationship between revenues and per capita income.
(c) Test to determine whether the slope coefficient is different from zero (at the 0.01 level).
(d) Test to determine whether there is evidence of regression at the 0.05 level. (Calculate the F ratio.)
(e) Test to determine whether the intercept equals zero at the 0.05 level.
(f) Plot the residuals on a graph. Is there evidence that one or more of the assumptions of simple linear regression is violated? Why or why not?
(g) What is the coefficient of determination? Interpret this coefficient.

TABLE 4.6

Year	Revenue	RI per capita income
1972	1011	4433
1973	1808	4779
1974	2200	5287
1975	2940	5709
1976	4612	6186
1977	6615	6775
1978	8891	7526
1979	10 443	8371
1980	11 799	9429
1981	13 823	10 466

6 (a) Calculate the Durbin–Watson statistics for the data of exercise 5.
  (b) Is there evidence of serial correlation?
  (c) Use the hand-calculated rho technique to correct for serial correlation and
     forecast for $X = \$12\ 000$.
  (d) Use the method of first differences to correct for serial correlation.
  (e) Use a computer software system to correct for serial correlation by the
     Cochrane–Orcutt method.
7 The data in table 4.7 are annual indexes of productivity and related data

TABLE 4.7

Year	Private business sector		Manufacturing	
	Output per hour	Compensation per hour	Output per hour	Compensation per hour
1970	86.1	58.2	80.8	57.4
1971	90.8	61.7	86.6	61.1
1972	93.9	65.6	91.0	64.4
1973	94.8	71.3	93.4	68.8
1974	92.7	78.0	90.9	76.4
1975	94.8	85.5	93.5	85.5
1976	97.9	92.9	97.1	92.1
1977	100.0	100.0	100.0	100.0
1978	99.8	108.4	101.5	108.2
1979	99.5	119.3	102.1	118.7
1980	99.3	131.5	101.4	132.4
1981	100.7	143.7	103.6	145.2
1982	100.3	154.9	105.9	157.5
1983	103.0	161.4	112.0	162.4
1984	105.5	167.9	118.1	168.0
1985	107.7	175.5	123.6	176.4
1986	110.1	183.1	127.7	183.0
1987	111.0	190.4	132.0	186.9

Source: *Monthly Labor Review*, various issues.

(1977 = 100) for various sectors of the US economy. Answer the following for either set of data.

(a) Plot a scatter diagram for these data with output per hour on the X axis and compensation per hour on the Y axis.
(b) Estimate the regression. Interpret the meaning of the predictive equation.
(c) Is there evidence that the slope coefficient is different from zero?
(d) Is there evidence that the intercept is different from zero?
(e) What is the coefficient of determination and coefficient of correlation? Interpret.
(f) Does the Durbin–Watson statistic give evidence of serial correlation?
(g) Using one of the techniques requiring computer software, correct for serial correlation.

8 For the data of example 4.4 in the text, plot the residual on a sequence plot. What is the shape of this sequence plotting? Interpret the sequence plotting and determine what kind of regression should be re-estimated?

TABLE 4.8

Year	(1) Demand	(2) CPI	(3) Income per capita
1971	803.7	118.3	3763
1972	857.0	123.2	3880
1973	910.5	139.5	4112
1974	924.8	158.5	4050
1975	926.0	172.1	4101
1976	1045.4	177.4	4216
1977	1171.9	188.0	4332
1978	1281.0	206.3	4487
1979	1377.0	228.3	4584
1980	1435.0	250.0	4567

9 The data in table 4.8 are (1) quantity demand for Pepsi-Cola beverages (millions of cases), (2) the Consumer Price Index (CPI) for processed foods and beverages (1967 = 100), and (3) per capita disposable personal income (1972 dollars).

(a) Estimate the regression of demand on (i) CPI and (ii) income per capita.
(b) Based on the standard error of regression, which regression is better?
(c) Based on the coefficient of determination, which regression is better?
(d) Do either or both regressions show evidence of serial correlation?
(e) If serial correlation is present in either regression, correct by one of the methods requiring computer use.
(f) Based on the root mean square error (standard error of regression) after the correction for serial correlation, which regression results in the better equation?

10 The data in table 4.9 are the gross state product in Massachusetts for several industries in 1982 (million dollars).

(a) Plot the scatter diagram.
(b) Estimate the regression on time (1969 = 0).
(c) What is the standard error of regression and coefficient of determination?

TABLE 4.9

Year	Manufacturing	Trade	Services	Year	Manufacturing	Trade	Services
1969	15 327	10 963	10 790	1978	19 024	12 512	13 351
1970	14 490	11 206	11 056	1979	19 559	12 829	14 041
1971	14 232	11 555	11 255	1980	19 614	12 775	14 381
1972	15 352	12 174	11 664	1981	20 115	12 892	15 263
1973	16 826	12 650	12 165	1982	19 739	13 016	15 693
1974	16 149	11 938	12 115	1983	21 424	14 412	16 764
1975	15 274	11 781	11 885	1984	25 321	16 388	17 968
1976	16 856	11 934	12 263	1985	27 177	17 841	19 059
1977	17 715	12 337	12 489	1986	27 649	19 613	20 558

Source: Federal Reserve Bank of Boston (1988) *Gross State Product – New England 1969–1986.*

(d) For the regression diagnostic tests, what can be concluded about the slope and intercept coefficients?
(e) If linear exponential smoothing was applied to the same data set, what is the mean square error of this forecast?
(f) Which method has a smaller mean square error, regression or linear exponential smoothing?
(g) Does the regression of part (b) show evidence of serial correlation?
(h) If serial correlation is present, correct for it by one of the computerized techniques described in this chapter.
(i) What is the mean square error for the results of part (h)? Is this MSE smaller than the MSE for the linear exponential smoothing forecast?

11 The data in table 4.10 are mortgage loans (million dollars) for two savings and loans associations in the state of Ohio.
(a) Collect data for the years 1980–9 for disposable personal income in the state of Ohio.
(b) Using a computer, calculate the linear regression of loans on income for each association. Interpret the coefficient of each equation.

TABLE 4.10

	Association	
Year	1	2
1980	13.9	161.8
1981	15.1	194.4
1982	16.1	207.4
1983	19.8	231.6
1984	23.2	251.5
1985	26.4	316.4
1986	26.4	387.2
1987	28.2	454.4
1988	29.3	481.3
1989	30.4	508.8

(c) Calculate the standard error of regression for each predictive equation.

(d) On the basis of the standard error of regression, which equation is better for purposes of forecasting?

12 (a) For the data of exercise 9, estimate demand if the CPI is 280, 290, and 300. (Ignore serial correlation.)

(b) Calculate the 95 percent interval estimate of the mean value if the CPI is 280, 290, and 300.

(c) Calculate the 95 percent interval estimate of the individual value if the CPI is 280, 290, and 300.

13 (a) For the data of exercise 9 estimate demand if income per capita is $5000, $6000, and $7000. (Ignore serial correlation.)

(b) Calculate the 95 percent interval estimate of the mean value if income per capita is $5000, $6000, and $7000.

14 (a) For the data of exercise 4, estimate expenses if age is equal to 5.

(b) Calculate the 95 percent and 99 percent interval estimates for a mean value of expenses given age is equal to 5.

(c) Calculate the 95 percent and 99 percent interval estimates for the individual value of expenses given age is equal to 5.

(d) Repeat parts (a), (b), and (c) for age equal to 6.

15 Data collected from a sample of British industrial workers for personal income and personal savings (rounded to the nearest thousand pounds) are given in Table 4.11.

TABLE 4.11

Income	Savings	Income	Savings
8.8	0.36	16.7	0.91
9.4	0.21	17.7	0.95
10.1	0.10	18.6	0.92
10.6	0.20	19.7	1.05
11.9	0.11	21.1	1.54
12.7	0.12	22.8	1.91
13.5	0.41	23.9	1.87
15.5	0.50	25.4	2.01

(a) Estimate the linear regression of savings on income.

(b) Test for overall regression.

(c) Is the Y intercept different from zero?

(d) Is the slope coefficient different from zero?

(e) If a British worker's income is £24 000, what is the expected level of personal savings? Calculate the 99 percent interval estimate for the mean value of savings, and for the individual level of savings.

(f) Plot the residuals and comment on the assumptions of regression.

(g) What is the coefficient of determination? What is the coefficient of correlation?

16 A sample of supervisory workers in the health care industry produced information on their income and mortgage loans to the nearest $000s which is shown in table 4.12.
(a) Estimate the linear regression of loans on income.
(b) Test for the presence of regression, the Y intercept.
(c) Plot the residuals and comment on the assumptions of regression.
(d) Estimate the size of the mortgage loan for an income of $70 thousand.
(e) What is the coefficient of determination? What is the coefficient of correlation?

TABLE 4.12

Income	Loan	Income	Loan
42	130	57	177
46	127	61	184
48	184	64	211
49	128	67	224
51	144	68	231
53	205	72	230
48	164	78	195
49	193	79	240
47	208	80	225
54	190	80	264

References

Box, G. E. and Jenkins, G. M. (1976) *Time Series Analysis, Forecasting and Control*. San Francisco, CA: Holden-Day.

Cochrane, D. and Orcutt, G. H. (1949) Application of least squares regression to relationships containing autocorrelated error terms, *Journal of the American Statistical Association*, 44, March, 749–809.

Durbin, J. and Watson, G. S. (1951) Testing for serial correlation in least-squares regression II, *Biometrika*, 38, 159–78.

Federal Reserve Bank of Boston (1988) *Gross State Product – New England 1969–1986*.

Monthly Labor Review, various issues. Washington, DC: US Department of Labor, Bureau of Labor Statistics.

Younger, M. S. (1985) *A First Course in Linear Regression*. North Scituate, MA: Duxbury.

Further Reading

Berensen, M. L., Levine, D. M. and Goldstein, M. (1983) *Intermediate Statistical Methods and Applications; A Computer Package Approach.* Englewood Cliffs, NJ: Prentice-Hall.

Farnum, N. R., and Stanton, L. W. (1989) *Quantitative Forecasting Methods.* Boston, MA: PWS-Kent, ch. 4.

Fox, K. A. (1968) *Intermediate Economic Statistics,* New York: John Wiley.

Jarrett, J. E. and Kraft, A. (1989) *Statistical Analysis for Decision Making.* Boston, MA: Allyn and Bacon, ch. 11.

Kleinbaum, D. G., Kupper, L. I. and Muller, K. E. (1988) *Applied Regression Analysis and Other Multivariable Methods.* North Scituate, MA: Duxbury.

Mendenhall, W. and McClave, J. T. (1986) *A Second Course in Business Statistics: Regression Analysis.* San Francisco, CA: Dellen.

Neter, J., Wasserman, W. and Kutner, M. H. (1985) *Applied Linear Statistical Models.* Homewood, IL: Irwin.

Pindyck, R. S. and Rubinfeld, D. L. (1976) *Econometric Models and Economic Forecasts.* New York: McGraw-Hill, chs 2, 4.

SAS Institute (1984) *SAS/ETS User's Guide: Econometric and Time Series Library.* Cary, NC: SAS.

Appendix

The output of Minitab software for personal and minicomputers is presented for the least squares regressions performed in this chapter.

TABLE 4. A1

```
The regression equation is
Y = -16.9 + 3.24 X
```

Predictor	Coef	Stdev	t-ratio	p
Constant	-16.859	4.210	-4.00	0.004
X	.3.2422	0.4630	7.00	0.000

```
s = 2.015    R-sq = 86.0%
```

Table 4.A1 is a partial computer output of an ordinary least squares regression for the data for example 4.2. There are ten observations, the dependent variable Y is mortgage loans in million dollars, and the independent variable is the interest rate X. The estimated regression is written out in equation form by Minitab and the coefficient of determination is expressed as a percentage. The t statistics for each coefficient aid in determining the usefulness of the fitted regression model. Their interpretation is the same as that shown in figure 4.3. Additional tests and graphs can be performed by Minitab and this information is available in the Minitab Users' Guide.

Table 4.A2 is the Minitab output associated with the regression of net income on time. This table is similar to figure 4.6. Y is the net income of American Hospital

TABLE 4. A2

```
The regression equation is
Y = -10.9 + 7.06 X

Predictor             Coef         Stdev        t-ratio            p
Constant           -10.877        5.734         -1.90         0.079
X                   7.0559        0.5930        11.90         0.000

s = 10.94    R-sq = 91.0%

Durbin-Watson statistic = 0.20
```

Supply Inc. and X is the time (period) in years. The output is interpreted in the same way as the previous table with one additional item. DW is the calculated Durbin–Watson statistic and is roughly equal to the value reported in figure 4.6 in the text.

The output of Micro-TSP personal software is presented in table 4.A3 for the data of example 4.2. There are ten observations, the dependent variable (MORT) is mortgage loans in million dollars, and the independent variable is interest rates (INT). The estimate regression equation is

$$\hat{Y} = -16.80392 + 3.235081X$$

and the coefficient of determination R^2 is 0.859760. The t statistics for each coefficient along with the two-tail significance level aid in determining the usefulness of the fitted model. Their interpretation is the same as in figure 4.3. Finally, the F statistic is roughly the same as indicated in figure 4.3 for determining the overall regression.

TABLE 4. A3

```
LS // Dependent Variable is MORT
Date:                 / Time: 0:05
SMPL range:   1971 - 1980
Number of observations: 10
==============================================================================
     VARIABLE       COEFFICIENT      STD. ERROR       T-STAT.      2-TAIL SIG.
==============================================================================
        C          -16.803792       4.2003069      -4.0006105       0.004
       INT           3.2350681      0.4619411       7.0032052       0.000
==============================================================================
R-squared            0.859760
```

The output of Micro-TSP for the data of example 4.4 (American Hospital Supply Inc.) is presented in table 4.A4. The computer output in this table presents the solution to the problem using the Cochrane–Orcutt method. The value for AR(1) is the estimated autocorrelation coefficient after six iterations and is used to forecast one period ahead. The forecast using this model for period 17 is 135.1131 and is thus

TABLE 4. A4

```
LS // Dependent Variable is NETINC
Date:                    / Time: 0:12
SMPL range:  2 — 16
Number of observations: 15
Convergence achieved after 6 iterations
==================================================================================
      VARIABLE      COEFFICIENT      STD.ERROR        T-STAT.       2-TAIL SIG.
==================================================================================
         C         −438.43388       1036.2608      −0.4230922        0.680
        TIME         23.613523       24.248951       0.9737957        0.349
----------------------------------------------------------------------------------
        AR(1)         0.9451174       0.0775050      12.194278         0.000
==================================================================================
R-squared              0.995127    Mean of dependent var.      51.71400
Adjusted R-squared     0.994315    S.D. of dependent var       34.80344
S.E. of regression     2.624201    Sum of squared resid        82.63717
Durbin-Watson stat     0.868843    F-statistic               1225.255
```

different from, although similar to, the previous solutions. The dependent variable is net income (NETINC) and the independent variable is time in years (TIME).

CHAPTER 5

Multiple Regression Methods

Objectives

This chapter presents the model and application of multiple linear regression for forecasting. Multiple regression is the study of the nature of the relationship between a dependent variable and two or more independent variables. The concept of multicollinearity is explained as well as the tests for the presence of regression and whether or not model parameters are equal to zero. In addition, methods for finding the "best" regression are considered. By the end of this chapter, you will be able to:

1 Estimate a multiple regression model by least squares.
2 Test the parameters of the model.
3 Use dummy variables in a regression model.
4 Interpret the computer output of various regression-based procedures such as all the possible regressions and stepwise methods.

Outline

Key Terms

- Multiple linear regression
- Polynomial model
- Multiple coefficient of determination
- Sum of squares due to regression

- Total sum of squares
- Error sum of squares
- Adjusted coefficient of multiple determination
- Multicollinearity
- Dummy variable
- Stepwise regression

5.1   Introduction

In simple linear regression the relationship between one independent variable and one dependent variable is investigated for the purposes of forecasting. Previously, we noted that simple linear regression can frequently lead to accurate forecasts. However, more than one independent variable is usually necessary to predict the values of a dependent variable accurately. Regression problems involving more than one independent variable are called multiple regression.

5.2   Assumptions of the Multiple Linear Regression Model

The *multiple linear regression* model is of linear form:

$$Y = \beta_0 + \beta_1 X_1 + \beta_2 X_2 + .. + \beta_m X_m + e \tag{5.1}$$

where Y is the dependent variable, X_1, X_2,...,X_m are the independent variables, e is the random error term, β_0 is the intercept, and β_1, β_2,...,β_m are the regression coefficients explaining the association between the independent and dependent variables. Random error exists for the same reason as in the simple linear regression model of chapter 4, that is, incomplete theory, imperfect specification, and errors of computation.

In regression analysis, we can ask whether or not we could significantly improve our prediction by increasing the complexity of the fitted model. Specifically we can ask whether or not a model of the form

$$Y = \beta_0 + \beta_1 X + \beta_2 X^2 + ... + e \tag{5.2}$$

that is, a *polynomial model* (or curvilinear model), is a better fit than a multiple linear model. Or, we can ask whether a model of the form

$$Y = \beta_0 + \beta_1 X_1 + \beta_2 X_2 + \beta_3 X_3^{0.5} + ...e \tag{5.3}$$

for example, is a better fit for predictive purposes. Equation (5.3) is one example of a polynomial model with nonlinear variables. The random error term e is in part a result of choosing a multiple linear model when a model is similar to equations (5.2) or (5.3). Thus, in multiple linear regression we assume that the best-fitting model is linear.

Also, the same distribution of values for the independent variables appears each time the experiment is performed. However, the distribution of Y values for given values of the independent variables may vary for each experiment because of the effect of the random error. The values of the independent variables are predetermined while the dependent variable is a random variable.

Four assumptions are made for the error term.

1 The expected value of the random error term is zero:

$$E(e) = 0 \tag{5.4}$$

On average the random error term is equal to zero. If we take the expected value of the linear multiple regression equation, for given values of the independent variables, say $X_1, X_2, ..., X_n$, we have

$$E(Y|X_1, X_2, ..., X_n) = E(\beta_0 + \beta_1 X_1 + \beta_2 X_2 + ... + \beta_n X_m + e) \tag{5.5}$$

$$= E(\beta_0) + E(\beta_1 X_1) + E(\beta_2 X_2) + ... + E(\beta_m X_m) + E(e)$$

and

$$\mu_Y = \beta_0 + \beta_1 X_1 + \beta_2 X_2 + ... + \beta_m X_m \tag{5.6}$$

since $E(e) = 0$. The above regression model simply says that for the given values of $X_1, X_2, ..., X_m$, the mean $\overline{Y}$ of the Y values, is the point determined by the multiple regression model.

2 The variance σ_e^2 of the random error term is constant for each set of values of the independent variables in a multiple regression model. σ_e^2 measures the variability in the value of the dependent variable about the regression plane for given values of the independent variables.

3 The random error terms are independent of each other for the multiple regression model.

4 The error term e for each set of values for the independent variables is normally distributed.[1]

Example 5.1

In a study of the riskiness in investing in for-profit nursing homes, an analyst investigates those factors that determine the relative risk measure beta of a security.[2] The predicting equation for beta, as the dependent variable Y contains certain financial ratios as independent variables. These are as follows: X_1, ratio of interest on debt to total revenue; X_2, average annual change in net earnings; X_3, coefficient of variation of net earnings; X_4, profit margins.

The predictive equation is

$$\hat{Y} = 0.759 + 0.580 X_1 - 0.012 X_2 + 0.034 X_3 - 7.244 X_4$$

For purposes of prediction, we substitute for each independent variable as follows:

$$\hat{Y} = 0.759 + 0.580(0.309) - 0.012(10.967) + 0.034(2.859) - 7.244(0.013)$$

$$= 0.810$$

Thus, on the average, a nursing home with financial characteristics that are the same as the values substituted in the predictive equation will have a beta estimated to be equal to 0.810. From the predictive equation, we observe that increases in the financial characteristics X_1 and X_3 increase the estimate of beta whereas increases in the financial characteristics X_2 and X_4 decrease the estimate of beta. Note that the regression coefficients measure the net change in the beta associated with a per unit change in the independent variable. Finally, the number of degrees of freedom of the model is equal to the number of observations minus the number of parameters estimated.

---

1   Note that these assumptions are the multiple regression version of the assumptions of the simple linear regression model.

2   This study has been published as a report by the US Department of Health and Human Services/Health Care Financing Administration/Office of Research, Demonstrations, and Statistics (1981).

5.3   Estimating the Multiple Linear Regression Model

As in the simple linear regression model, estimation follows from observation of random samples of the dependent variable for fixed values of the independent variable. The dependent variable is a random variable whereas the independent variables are predetermined.

The method of least squares is the mathematical procedure for fitting the multiple regression equation to the sample data. We estimate the regression parameters (β_0, β_1, β_2,..., β_m) so that the resulting statistical relation provides the best possible fit to the data. The procedure is to minimize the sum of the squared vertical deviations between the actual sample values of the dependent variable Y and the estimated values $\hat{Y}$. The procedure is merely an extension of the least squares technique for simple linear regression relationships.

The following example illustrates the method of least squares for a multiple regression problem of the form

$$\hat{Y} = b_0 + b_1X_1 + b_2X_2 \tag{5.7}$$

where b_0 is the estimated intercept and b_1 and b_2 are the estimated regression coefficients.

Example 5.2

Buckeye Savings and Loan wished to improve its forecast of the dollar value of mortgage loans by adding an additional predictor variable (Ohio personal income in billion dollars) to the predictive equation. In previous examples, only interest rates on home mortgages were included in the predictive equation. Computations for the multiple linear regression are given in table 5.1.

TABLE 5.1   Worksheet for multiple regression

Mortgage loans ($ millions) Y	Ohio personal income ($ billions) X_1	Interest rates X_2	X_1Y	X_2Y	X_1X_2	X_1^2	X_2^2	Y^2
7.50	44.80	7.60	336.00	57.000	340.48	2007.0	57.760	56.250
7.44	49.00	7.45	364.56	55.428	365.05	2401.0	55.502	55.354
7.93	54.47	7.78	431.95	61.695	423.78	2967.0	60.528	62.885
8.41	58.90	8.71	495.35	73.251	513.02	3469.2	75.864	70.728
9.21	62.75	8.75	577.93	80.587	549.06	3937.6	76.563	84.824
12.03	68.37	8.76	822.49	105.383	598.92	4674.5	76.738	144.721
14.33	75.87	8.80	1087.22	126.104	667.66	5756.3	77.440	205.349
16.25	84.00	9.30	1365.00	151.125	781.20	7056.0	86.490	264.063
17.99	93.50	10.48	1682.06	188.535	979.88	8742.3	109.830	323.640
21.73	101.24	12.25	2199.95	266.192	1240.19	10249.5	150.063	472.193
122.82	692.90	89.88	9362.51	1165.300	6459.24	51260.4	826.778	1740.007

The three equations that must be solved to determine the values of b_0, b_1, and b_2 are[3]

$$\Sigma Y = nb_0 + b_1\Sigma X_1 + b_2\Sigma X_2$$

$$\Sigma X_1 Y = b_0\Sigma X_1 + b_1\Sigma X_1^2 + b_2\Sigma X_1 X_2$$

$$\Sigma X_2 Y = b_0\Sigma X_2 + b_1\Sigma X_1 X_2 + b_2\Sigma X_2^2$$

The computations of the required summations are in the worksheet of example 5.2.

Substituting into the above equations yields

$$122.82 = 10b_0 + 692.90b_1 + 89.88b_2$$

$$9362.51 = 692.90b_0 + 51\ 260.4b_1 + 6459.24b_2$$

$$1165.300 = 89.88b_0 + 6459.24b_1 + 826.78b_2$$

Solving the three equations simultaneously gives

$$b_0 = -7.025$$

$$b_1 = 0.242$$

$$b_2 = 0.279$$

In the Buckeye Savings and Loan example, the b_1 value of 0.242 indicates that each increase of 1 billion dollars of personal income in Ohio when interest rates are held constant is associated with an increase of $0.242 million in mortgage loans on average. Similarly, the b_2 value of 0.279 indicates that each increase of 1 percent in interest rates, when Ohio personal income is held constant, is associated with an increase in mortgage loans of $0.279 million on the average.

5.4 Least Squares Solutions and Significance Tests

Since least squares solutions to multiple regression are generally solved by use of computer software, it is not worthwhile to write down the precise algebraic equations for b_0, b_1, b_2,.... However, a great deal of emphasis should be placed on studying some properties of the least squares regression. Equation (5.1) is the unique linear combination of the independent variables X_1, X_2,..., X_n, which has the maximum possible association with the dependent variable. Stated differently, of all choices of linear combinations of the form in equation (5.1), the linear estimator $\hat{Y}$ is such that the *multiple coefficient of determination* is

$$R_{Y.\hat{Y}}^2 = \frac{\Sigma(\hat{Y} - \overline{Y})^2}{\Sigma(Y_i - \overline{Y})^2} \tag{5.8}$$

The numerator is the *sum of squares due to regression* or the model sum of squares and the denominator is the *total sum of squares* where $\hat{Y}_i$ is the predicted value of Y for the ith observation, $\overline{Y}_i$ is the mean of the predicted values and is equal to the

---

3 For the solution of a system of three equations with three unknown values in regression see Mendenhall and Sincich (1986, ch. 4).

mean $\overline{Y}$, of the observed values. For the data of example 5.2, we estimate R^2 (R-SQUARE) by

$$R^2 = \left(\begin{array}{c} \text{sum of squares} \\ \text{due to regression} \end{array}\right) \Big/ \left(\begin{array}{c} \text{total sum} \\ \text{of squares} \end{array}\right)$$

$$= \frac{223.7570}{231.5307} = 0.9664$$

Hence 96.64 percent of the total variation in mortgage loans of Buckeye Savings and Loan is associated with the linear regression on Ohio personal income X_1, and interest rates on new home loans X_2. We should note that the multiple coefficient of correlation is the positive square root of R^2 ($R = 0.983$). The multiple correlation coefficient is a measure of the strength of the linear association between Y and the best-fitting linear combination of independent variables in equation (5.1). Further-more, it can be shown that the multiple correlation coefficient is always nonnegative and is a direct generalization of the simple correlation coefficient to the case of two or more independent variables.

As with the simple linear regression model, the F distribution and test can be used to provide an overall summary of a multiple regression analysis. These tests can be summarized in a table (see table 5.2) called an analysis of variance (ANOVA) table after the general title given to this class of diagnostic tests.

Denote SSY as the total sum of squares; then

$$\text{SSY} = \Sigma(Y_i - \overline{Y})^2 \tag{5.9}$$

which is the total variability in the Y observations before accounting for the joint effect of the independent variables X_1, X_2. The term SSE, the *error* (or residual) *sum of squares*, is defined by

$$\text{SSE} = \Sigma(Y_i - \hat{Y}_i)^2 \tag{5.10}$$

TABLE 5.2   ANOVA for mortgage loans regressed on two independent variables

Source	DF	SS	MS	F
Model	2	223.7570	111.8785	100.74
Error	7	7.7738	1.1105	
	9	231.5308		

Notes: F is significant at less than the 0.01 level.
R-SQUARE = 0.9664
Model SS = SSY − SSE = 223.7570
Error SS = SSE   = 7.7738
Total SS = SSY   = 231.5308

This measures the amount of variation in the dependent variable Y which is not explained after the independent variables have been used to estimate the regression model to predict Y. Finally,

$$\text{SSY} - \text{SSE} = \Sigma(\hat{Y}_i - \overline{Y})^2 \tag{5.11}$$

is called the model (or regression) sum of squares and measures the reduction in variation (or explained variation) due to the independent variable in the regression equation. Thus we now have the familiar expression

total sum of squares = model sum of squares + error sum of squares

or

$$\Sigma(Y_i - \overline{Y})^2 = \Sigma(\hat{Y}_i - \overline{Y})^2 + \Sigma(Y_i - \hat{Y}_i)^2 \tag{5.12}$$

To test for significant overall regression, we state the following null hypothesis:

H_0: there is no evidence of association (regression)

H_A: there is evidence of association (regression)

The above hypothesis is tested by the following F ratio:

$$F = \frac{\text{model sum of squares/number of independent variables}}{\text{error sum of squares/total} - \text{number of regression coefficients}}$$
$$= \frac{(SSY - SSE)/m}{SSE/(n - m - 1)} \tag{5.13}$$

where m is the number of independent variables.

The above F ratio is compared with the critical F ratio with m and $n - m - 1$ degrees of freedom at the significance level α. An equivalent expression for F is

$$F = \frac{R^2/m}{(1 - R^2)/(n - m - 1)} \tag{5.14}$$

For the above example,

$$F = \frac{0.9664/2}{(1 - 0.9664)/(10 - 2 - 1)} = 100.74$$

The critical F, with two degrees of freedom in the numerator and seven degrees of freedom in the denominator at $\alpha = 0.01$, is 9.55. Hence, at the 0.01 level, we can reject H_0 and conclude that there is sufficient evidence of association. We should note that the calculated F ratio is the same as that calculated in table 5.2

In addition to the test for the overall significance of the model, several additional questions concerning the model are of interest. First, do each of the independent variables alone explain a significant portion of the variation in Y? Second, does the addition of an additional variable significantly contribute to the prediction of Y after controlling for the contribution of the independent variables which are already included? Third, does the fitted regression model make sense from the point of view of what we believe to be true, that is, does it explain behavior correctly?

These and other questions of importance require many more statistical computations. Such computations are usually made by using appropriate computer software. In the next section, we shall consider the output of one particularly useful computer program for computing multiple regression.

We should note that R^2 increases with the number of independent variables, which reduces the number of degrees of freedom. A statistic $\overline{R}^2$ takes account of the number of degrees of freedom. This statistic is given by

$$\overline{R}^2 = 1 - \left(\frac{n - 1}{n - m}\right)(1 - R^2) \tag{5.15}$$

and is called the *adjusted coefficient of multiple determination*. This coefficient may actually become smaller when another independent variable is introduced into the model, because the increase in R^2 may be more than offset by the loss of a degree of freedom in the denominator $n - m$. Most computer software refers to this measure as adjusted R-square.

For the data of example 5.2, we find

$$\overline{R}^2 = 1 - \left(\frac{10 - 1}{10 - 2} \right) (1 - 0.9664) = 0.9622$$

Hence, 96.62 percent of the total variation in mortgage loans is associated with linear regression on the independent variables, Ohio personal income and interest rates, adjusted for degrees of freedom. The reduction from R^2 to $\overline{R}^2$ is often only slight.

5.5   An Example of Computer Software Output (SAS)

The output of the linear regression models procedure of SAS (figure 5.1) consists of three sections as follows:

1 overall analysis of variance table;
2 sundry statistics;
3 report on parameter (regression coefficients) estimates.

```
DEP VARIABLE: MORT                MORTGAGE LOANS
                               ANALYSIS OF VARIANCE

                       SUM OF        MEAN
   SOURCE      DF      SQUARES       SQUARE      F VALUE      PROB>F

   MODEL       2       223.757       111.8785    100.743      0.0001
   ERROR       7       7.773751      1.110536
   C TOTAL     9       231.5308

        ROOT MSE          1.05382     R-SQUARE      0.9664
        DEP MEAN          12.282      ADJ R-SQ      0.9568
        C.V.              8.580196

                         PARAMETER ESTIMATES

                       PARAMETER             STANDARD      T FOR HO:
   VARIABLE     DF     ESTIMATE              ERROR         PARAMETER=0

   INTERCEP     1      -7.025                3.032435      -2.317
   PERINC       1      0.2424147             0.05139792    4.716
   INT          1      0.2792712             0.6732662     0.415

                                             VARIABLE
   VARIABLE     DF     PROB > |T|            LABEL

   INTERCEP     1      0.0537               INTERCEPT
   PERINC       1      0.0022               PERSONAL INCOME
   INT          1      0.6907               INTEREST RATES
```

FIGURE 5.1 Buckeye Savings and Loan. Regression on two variables

Firstly, the overall analysis of variance breaks down the total sum of squares for the dependent variable (mortgage loans) into the portion associated with the model and the portion associated with error. The mean square for error is an estimate of the mean square error (MSE) for the multiple regression. The standard error of multiple regression S_e is the square root of this number:

$$S_e = (1.110\ 536)^{1/2} = 1.053\ 82$$

The F value, that is, the ratio of the mean square (model) to the mean square (error), is 100.74. It is significant at 0.0001, indicating that the variation in Y values (mortgage loans) is associated with the regression on Ohio personal income and interest rates. Thus the model accounts for the behavior of mortgage loans.

The R-SQUARE (coefficient of determination) indicates that 0.9664 (or about 96.6 percent) of the variation in Y values (mortgage loans) is explained by the regression on Ohio personal income and interest rates. Recall that the larger the value of the coefficient of determination, the better is the model's fit. Also, this is the multiple coefficient of determination and thus is the ratio of the variation in Y explained by X_1 and X_2 divided by the total variation in Y.

Note that there is not much sense in defining a multiple correlation coefficient, the square root of R-SQUARE. No meaningful sign could be attached indicating the direction of the multiple relationships. Although in the Buckeye Savings and Loan Association example, Y is directly related to X_1 and X_2, in other examples Y might be related to X_1 and X_2 in different directions. Hence we would not know which sign to attach to the square root, and thus this statistic, although often reported, is a meaningless measure.

CV (coefficient of variation), and ROOT MSE (standard error of regression) are defined in the same manner as in the simple linear regression model.

The report on parameter estimates permits us to write out the estimated regression model. Under the column PARAMETER ESTIMATE the estimated regression coefficients are given, yielding the predictive equation

$$\hat{Y} = -7.025 + 0.242X_1 + 0.279X_2$$

(note that the coefficient values are rounded to three decimal places). These coefficients were interpreted earlier when we discussed the hand computation of these values. The estimates of the model parameters are tested for significance:

T FOR H0: PARAMETER = 0

indicates the t statistic for testing the null hypothesis that the parameter is zero.

The t statistic for the test for significance of the Y intercept is -2.32 and is significant at the 0.0537 level. Recall that a significant Y intercept may indicate that other variables can be used to explain the behavior of the Y variable (mortgage loans). We shall investigate this later.

The t statistic for the test for significance of the regression coefficient for X_1 (Ohio personal income) is 4.72. It is significant at the 0.0022 level, indicating that the variation in the independent variable is associated with the variation in the dependent variable. Knowledge of Ohio personal income will explain, at least in part, the behavior in mortgage loans made by Buckeye Savings and Loan. Furthermore, since the coefficient has a positive sign, increases in Ohio personal income are associated with increases in Buckeye mortgage loans.

Finally, the t statistic for the test for significance of the regression coefficient for X_2, (interest rates on new home mortgages) is only 0.415. Furthermore, the significance level is listed at 0.6907, which should lead to acceptance of the hypothesis that the parameter is zero. The inclusion of a variable for interest rates does not 'significantly' increase the explanatory power of the regression model. Recall that in the simple linear regression model of mortgage loans on interest rates, the independent variable (interest rates) was significant. Is there a dilemma? This is a profound question that requires further investigation by examination of a scatter diagram and a plot of residuals. Is there an explanation of the apparent paradox of having a variable significant in one predictive equation but not in another?

The scatter diagram is presented in figure 5.2. Note that MORT refers to the observed Y values and PRED refers to predicted Y values. Examination of the predicted and actual values indicates a scatter of variation that may be associated with time. At first (1971), the actual value is greater than the predicted values. Then (1973–5) the predicted values are greater than the actual values followed by another period when actual values are larger than predicted values (1977–80, with the exception of 1979).

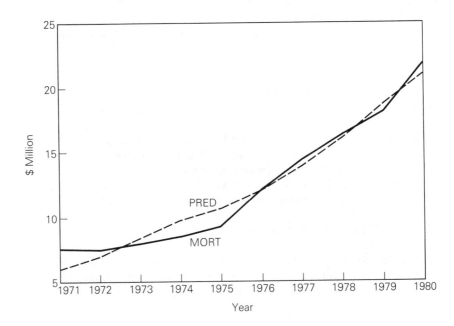

FIGURE 5.2 Observed and predicted values

An examination of figure 5.3, the plot of residuals, indicates the same phenomenon that is indicated on the previous scatter diagram. The apparent wave-like pattern indicates that a trend variable may not have been included in the model. Stated differently, the model explaining the behavior of mortgage loans is slowly changing over time. Thus it is possible to improve the model by explicitly recognizing trend as a variable to be included in the predictive regression model.

We should point out that these diagnostics of the residuals test for the first-order autocorrelation discussed in the previous chapter when the Durbin–Watson test was presented. Correlated residuals are quite common when the dependent variable is a

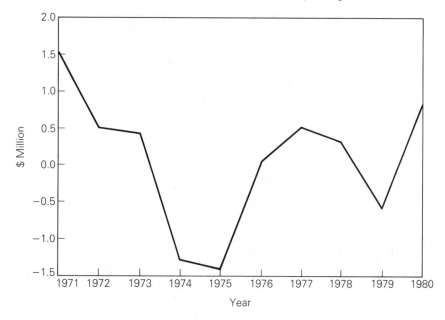

FIGURE 5.3 Plot of residuals from forecast

time series variable. In chapter 7, we shall see that this type of autocorrelation, which is called first-order autocorrelation, is only one form of autocorrelation. The subject of chapter 7 will be to measure and examine the behavior of higher-order autocorrelated residuals, and this will be important in the development of other types of forecasting methods.

5.6   Predictive Model with Trend Factor

Example 5.3

Buckeye Savings and Loan Association wished to improve its forecasting accuracy by including an independent variable for time (in years). Since the data for mortgage loans Y, Ohio personal income X, and the interest rates X_2 are for years 1971–80, they included the trend variable in the equation by specifying a new variable X_3 with that sequence of values. SAS procedures are then followed to estimate the predictive model.

Figure 5.4 contains the REG procedure output for the SAS computer program of the form

$$Y = f(\text{Ohio personal income, interest rates, time})$$

expressed in linear form as follows:

$$Y = \beta_0 + \beta_1 X_1 + \beta_2 X_2 + \beta_3 X_3 + e \tag{5.16}$$

where X_3 is time in years. The F statistic for the overall analysis of variance is 86.01. This statistic is significant at 0.0001, indicating that the variation in Y values

```
DEP VARIABLE: MORT                    MORTGAGE LOANS
                                    ANALYSIS OF VARIANCE

                                SUM OF           MEAN
        SOURCE          DF       SQUARES         SQUARE      F VALUE       PROB>F

        MODEL            3      226.2694       75.42314      86.012        0.0001
        ERROR            6        5.261332      0.8768887
        C TOTAL          9      231.5308

                     ROOT MSE    0.9364234     R-SQUARE      0.9773
                     DEP MEAN      12.282       ADJ R-SQ      0.9659
                        C.V.       7.624356

                             PARAMETER ESTIMATES

                            PARAMETER            STANDARD       T FOR H0:
        VARIABLE        DF   ESTIMATE             ERROR       PARAMETER=0

        INTERCEP         1    -11.9504          3.965876       -3.013
        PERINC           1      0.4850539       0.1504466       3.224
        INT              1     -0.24604         0.6739679      -0.365
        YEAR             1     -1.30283         0.769685       -1.693

                                                VARIABLE
        VARIABLE        DF    PROB > |T|          LABEL

        INTERCEP         1     0.0236          INTERCEPT
        PERINC           1     0.0180          PERSONAL INCOME
        INT              1     0.7276          INTEREST RATES
        YEAR             1     0.1415          TIME PERIOD
```

FIGURE 5.4 Buckeye Savings and Loan. Regression on three variables

(mortgage loans) is associated with the regression on Ohio personal income, interest rates, and time. Also, the R-SQUARE of 0.9772, or about 97.7 percent of the total variation in mortgage loans, is explained by the predictive model specified above.

Examination of the parameter estimates yields the equation (1970 = 0)

$$\hat{Y} = -11.9504 + 0.485X_1 - 0.246X_2 - 1.303X_3$$

The intercept, of course, is the value of Y when X_1, X_2, and X_3 are zero and has no meaningful behavioral explanation. A value of 0.485 for the regression coefficient of the Ohio personal income variables indicates that an increase of $0.485 million in mortgage loans is associated with a $1 billion increase in Ohio personal income. Similarly, a $0.246 million decrease in mortgage loans is associated with a 1 percent increase in interest rates, and a $1.303 million decrease is associated with an increase of 1 (one year) in the time variable.

For the first time, a negative regression coefficient is reported for the interest rate variable. This is important because economic theory teaches us that increases in mortgage loans are associated with a decrease in interest rates. Previously the regressions did not show this (see example 5.2), and thus this equation is the only one with the correct specification.

The report on the tests for the parameter estimates permits us to determine the statistical significance of the various coefficients of the predictive model. The Y intercept of the equation has a t statistic of 1.68 and is not significant at a reasonably small level. Thus, we would accept the null hypothesis that the Y intercept is zero.

The t statistic for the variable (PERINC) for Ohio personal income is 3.224 and is significant at 0.00180. This variable was also significant in the previous regression of example 5.2.

The t statistic for the variable interest rates (INT) is -0.365 and is not significant. Also, the t statistic for the time variable (YEAR), which is equal to -1.693, is not significant at a reasonably small level. Hence we cannot conclude that the data have demonstrated evidence of association between the mortgage loan variable and these two variables acting independently.

There are a number of possible explanations for this phenomenon. First, there is the likelihood that the error of overfitting the model is occurring. Overfitting may mean that too many independent variables are included in the model, given the sample size. Experience has shown that small sample sizes cannot permit us to show statistical significance for independent variables when theory indicates that these independent variables should be significantly associated with the dependent variable. Only larger sample sizes will solve this problem. Second, two or more of the independent variables are highly interrelated with each other. If this occurs, the coefficients of the predictive equation become meaningless. This problem is discussed in the next section.

5.7 Multicollinearity

Multicollinearity exists when two or more independent variables are linearly related and they will contribute redundant information. The effects of multicollinearity can be seen in several ways.

1 A regression coefficient that has a positive sign in a two-variable regression model may change to a negative sign in a multiple regression model containing three variables or more. The direction of change could be reversed.
2 The estimate of regression coefficients varies considerably from sample to sample.
3 Since multiple regression has an additional aim of explaining and interpreting behavior as well as predicting behavior, highly intercorrelated variables do not allow the individual influences of each of the independent variables to be separated out.

All these effects are the result of the large variances for the correlation coefficient between the pairs of variables.

In this chapter two multiple regression models were developed to predict the mortgage loans of Buckeye Savings and Loan Association. The first regression model produced the equation

$$\hat{Y} = -7.025 + 0.242X_1 + 0.279X_2$$

where X_1 is Ohio personal income and X_2 is interest rates on new home mortgages. Similarly, a second multiple regression model containing a third independent variable X_3 for time (in years) was estimated with the following result (1970 = 0)

$$\hat{Y} = -11.9504 + 0.485X_1 - 0.246X_2 - 1.302X_3$$

Note that the sign of the coefficient for the interest rate variable X_2 changed on going from one model to the other. This phenomenon suggests the presence of multicollinearity. If multicollinearity exists, the regression coefficients b_1, b_2, and b_3 are not completely reliable measures of the effects of the associated independent variables. Better indicators may be available.

One method by which we can determine whether multicollinearity is present is to produce a correlation matrix. A correlation matrix is simply a printout of the individual linear correlation coefficients of each pair of variables. Under SAS and other software languages (SPSS-X or Minitab, for example), the correlation matrix is produced easily and is similar to the output of figure 5.5. Figure 5.5 contains the correlation matrix of coefficients and significance levels. A quick examination of the four variables leads to the following observations.

```
PEARSON CORRELATION COEFFICIENTS
/ PROB > |R| UNDER HO: RHO=0 / N = 10
```

	MORT	PERINC	INT	YEAR
MORT MORTGAGE LOANS	1.00000 0.0000	0.98265 0.0001	0.92722 0.0001	0.95545 0.0001
PERINC PERSONAL INCOME	0.98265 0.0001	1.00000 0.0000	0.93307 0.0001	0.98855 0.0001
INT INTEREST RATES	0.92722 0.0001	0.93307 0.0001	1.00000 0.0000	0.89740 0.0004
YEAR TIME PERIOD	0.95545 0.0001	0.98855 0.0001	0.89740 0.0004	1.00000 0.0000

FIGURE 5.5 Correlation matrix, Buckeye Savings and Loan

1 Ohio personal income (PERINC), interest rates (INT), and time (YEAR) are potentially good predictor variables with simple correlation coefficients paired with mortgage loans of 0.983, 0.927, and 0.955 respectively.
2 Personal income and interest rates are highly interrelated at 0.933.
3 Personal income and time (year) are interrelated at 0.989.
4 Interest rates and time (year) are interrelated at 0.897.
5 All these coefficients are significant at very small significance levels (0.0004 or less).

All this indicates that some variation in mortgage loans is explained by personal income, interest rates, and time.

Existence of multicollinearity indicates that the regression model is unable to separate the specific relationship between each independent variable and the dependent variable. Although this problem is troublesome and no simple solution exists, the model may still, as a whole, demonstrate a significant relationship between the dependent variable and the independent variables as a group. However, we may wish to remove from the predictive model one of the mutually correlated variables. In that event, the remaining predictive equation can be used for forecasting but, perhaps, not for the purposes of explaining the behavior of the dependent variable.

5.8   Dummy Variables in Regression Models

Categorical variables (those on a nominal scale) are included in regression models by using *dummy variables*, where classes are coded often by use of 0 and 1 or −1 and 1. This approach is useful whenever we wish to index the relationship of a group or treatment variable with a dependent variable.

Example 5.4

A manufacturer wishes to measure how well a particular aptitude test predicts job performance. Ten women and ten men are to take the test which measures manual dexterity. Both the job performance rating Y and the score on the aptitude test X are continuous variables. Each observation will be given a score of 0 for male and 1 for female. This coding creates the dummy variable X_2.

The above example will enable the forecaster to assess the overall predictability of the aptitude test from sex data. Furthermore, the statistical significance of the categorical variable can be tested and the relative contribution of the gender variable to predictive accuracy can be estimated.

   To illustrate the use of dummy variables, consider the use of 0 for males and 1 for females where the multiple regression is

$$\hat{Y} = b_0 + b_1 X_1 + b_2 X_2$$

where X_1 is the job performance rating and

$$X_2 = \begin{cases} 0 & \text{for males} \\ 1 & \text{for females} \end{cases}$$

The single equation is equivalent to the following two equations:

$$\hat{Y} = b_0 + b_1 X_1 \quad \text{for males}$$

$$\hat{Y} = b_0 + b_1 X_1 + b_2 X_2 \quad \text{for females}$$

   Note that b_2 represents the effect of a female on job performance and b_1 is the effect of job performance rating differences (the b_1 value is assumed to be the same for males and females). The important implication is that a single multiple regression of the above type will yield two estimated lines, one for males and one for females. We can view X_2 as a switching variable that is on when an observation is for a female and off for a male.

Example 5.5

A manufacturer's representative administers a one hour aptitude test to aid in the selection of salespeople for an expensive sales training program. The test is designed to measure and predict the ability of each person to be influenced positively by the training program. To determine the influence of gender, if any, each respondent is recorded as a 1 if they are female and 0 if they are male. For evaluation of the effectiveness of this approach, sales records for the past two months are collected for 15 salespeople chosen at random. These data along with aptitude test scores and gender are evaluated using the following model:

$$\hat{Y} = b_0 + b_1 X_1 + b_2 X_2$$

where X_1 is the aptitude test score and X_2 indicates gender (0 = male, 1 = female).

Figure 5.6 contains the SAS output for this sample. The estimated model equation is

$$\hat{Y} = -259.26 + 29.3978 X_1 - 37.0021 X_2$$

The coefficient of determination is 0.8208 and the adjusted coefficient is 0.7909. Furthermore, since the F value for the test for overall regression is 27.479, we can reject the hypothesis that there is insufficient evidence of regression at the 0.0001 level.

```
DEP VARIABLE: SALES           MONTHLY SALES IN UNITS
                              ANALYSIS OF VARIANCE

                        SUM OF          MEAN
SOURCE          DF      SQUARES         SQUARE      F VALUE      PROB>F

MODEL            2       573470         286735      27.479       0.0001
ERROR           12      125215.7      10434.65
C TOTAL         14      698685.7

              ROOT MSE      102.1501      R-SQUARE      0.8208
              DEP MEAN      508.8667      ADJ R-SQ      0.7909
              C.V.           20.07404

                         PARAMETER ESTIMATES

                      PARAMETER            STANDARD        T FOR HO:
VARIABLE        DF    ESTIMATE             ERROR           PARAMETER=0

INTERCEP         1     -259.26             107.1975         -2.419
SCORE            1       29.3978             4.046371         7.265
GENDER           1      -37.0021            55.18514         -0.671

                                          VARIABLE
VARIABLE        DF    PROB > |T|           LABEL

INTERCEP         1      0.0324             INTERCEPT
SCORE            1      0.0001             APTITUDE TEST SCORE
GENDER           1      0.5152             0=MALE 1=FEMALE
```

FIGURE 5.6 Regression with dummy variable

The t statistic for the parameter for the aptitude test score is 7.265. Hence we can reject the hypothesis that $\beta_1 = 0$ at any reasonable level. The t statistic for the parameter for gender is −0.671. Hence we cannot reject the hypothesis that $\beta_2 = 0$ at any reasonable level.

The statistical analysis of the estimated predictive model indicates that sales is associated with aptitude test score but cannot be shown to be associated with gender. The use of the dummy variable indicates whether or not gender is a legitimate indicator variable to predict sales performance.

Dummy variables are useful whenever a variable is desired to determine whether some nonquantifiable variable can influence the prediction of the variable that we wish to predict. In production processes, we can test whether the number of nonconforming units is associated with whether the units are made during the first or second shift.

The above analysis can also be applied to fitting an equation to explain and interpret seasonal variation. Applying multiple linear regression to a monthly time series gives the model

$$Y = \beta_0 + \beta_1 X_1 + \beta_2 X_2 + \ldots + \beta_{12} X_{12} + e$$

where X_1 is time, from 1 to n, X_2 is the February dummy variable (1), X_3 is the March dummy variable (2), and so on to the December dummy variable X_{12} (11), and e is the error term. The regression coefficients of the dummy variables are interpreted as the effect of a change from one month to another, that is, the seasonal component. Lastly, since there are a large number of independent variables, a large amount of data is required for this application. Usually about ten years' data (120 observations) are advisable.

Finally, for quarterly data, we have

$$Y = \beta_0 + \beta_1 X_1 + \beta_2 X_2 + \beta_3 X_3 + \beta_4 X_4 + e$$

where X_1 is time, from 1 to n, X_2 is the spring dummy variable, X_3 is the summer dummy variable, X_4 is the fall dummy variable, and e is the error term. The interpretation refers to the effect of a change from one season (quarter) to another.

5.9   The "Best" Regression Model

In forecasting and prediction, the achievement of a high degree of prediction, that is, a coefficient of determination close to unity, is not always an end in itself. We are interested in selecting a complete set of potential independent variables all of which add to the predictive accuracy of the forecast model. Only those variables that may add to the predictive accuracy of the model should be included. Furthermore, we are faced with the dilemma of providing the most accurate forecast for the smallest cost. Since it costs money to obtain and monitor information on a large number of independent variables, the model should include as few independent variables as possible. The simplest equation is the best. Equations with a large number of independent variables require relatively large sample sizes. Large sample sizes require more expense in the accurate prediction of the dependent variable.

Selection of the "best" regression model generally requires a compromise between achieving the highest coefficient of determination and selecting a minimum number of predictor variables. No unique statistical procedure exists for developing this compromise but several suggestions can be made.

To begin, a forecaster should list those potential independent variables that are thought to be useful in prediction. Following this compilation, a second step is to screen out those predictor variables which do not seem appropriate. Some criteria used to screen out these variables are as follows:

1 drop the variable where plausible causality is not present;
2 drop the variable which may duplicate other variables (collinearity);
3 drop the variable which may be subject to large errors of measurement or is unable to measure.

The final step is to reduce the list of potential independent variables to obtain a reasonably good predictive model comprising higher coefficients of determination and cost. Although personal judgement is very important, there are several techniques available to us that are worthy of discussion. However, these selection techniques included in the SAS system cannot create new independent variables. They can only aid us in the shortening of the list of potential independent variables. The two statistical procedures are called all possible regressions and stepwise regression and are usually performed with good statistical software (such as SAS, SPSS-X, or Minitab).

5.10   All Possible Regressions

All possible regressions calls for the investigation of all possible models involving the list of potential independent variables. The first procedure under SAS and other computer software procedures for examining the list of potential independent variables fits every possible regression model with every possible combination of the independent variables. For the problem of forecasting mortgage loans made by Buckeye Savings and Loan Association (example 5.3) there were three independent variables. Since each independent variable can either be or not be included in the equation, there are altogether $2^3 - 1$ regression models including one or more of the listed variables. Thus there are seven possible regression models to be considered. Applying this concept to example 5.3, we can produce the SAS output table of figure 5.7. Note that the output table is divided into three sets of regression model outcomes. This breakdown coincides with the number of independent variables contained in the predictive model.

N = 10	REGRESSION MODELS FOR DEPENDENT VARIABLE: MORT MODEL: MODEL1	
NUMBER IN MODEL	R-SQUARE	VARIABLES IN MODEL
1	0.85972792	INT
1	0.91288099	YEAR
1	0.96559926	PERINC
2	0.93790717	INT YEAR
2	0.96642454	PERINC INT
2	0.97677114	PERINC YEAR
3	0.97727588	PERINC INT YEAR

FIGURE 5.7 All possible regressions, Buckeye Savings and Loan

Observe from the SAS output the set of independent variables (or variable) for each parameter grouping. Let the equation with the highest R-square be considered 'best'. These last equations from each set are given in table 5.3.

In the last step in this analysis, we can ask ourselves which model is best for predictive purposes. Recall that the closer the coefficient of determination R^2 is to 1.0, the better is the fit of the regression model to the observations. However, a forecaster desires the simplest model possible. This is because for every additional variable in the predictive equations, there is an added need for additional sample observations.

In this approach, the goal is to find out when a forecast should no longer add additional independent variables to the model. If the cost of including an additional variable is greater than the increase in R^2, the new variable should not be added. This can only be answered on an individual case-by-case approach. There is no hard and fast decision rule with a clear cut answer in every situation.

In the Buckeye Savings and Loan example, the coefficient of determination for the regression on Ohio personal income is 0.9656. Very little improvement is gained by adding additional variables to the equation. However, is the cost of adding an additional variable greater than the marginal benefit of the higher R^2? Adding the time variable (YEAR) cannot have much of an incremental cost. It should probably enter the regression. However, adding the INT (interest rate) variable is not as clear cut. We should point out that achieving the highest R^2 is not always considered good statistical practice for model fitting. Hence, another procedure for choosing the best model, called stepwise regression, is considered next.

TABLE 5.3

Number in model	R-square	Variables in model
1	0.9656	PERINC
2	0.9768	PERINC YEAR
3	0.9773	PERINC INT YEAR

5.11   Stepwise Regression Techniques

Under *stepwise regression* techniques, there are various methods for solution. In this section, we shall focus on one type of stepwise regression. However, all stepwise procedures do have certain common elements. First, the stepwise method requires use of a computer since a large number of regressions, F statistics, and independent variables are involved. Second, the stepwise approach adds and often deletes independent variables at each stage of the analysis as various sequences of regression are computed. Finally, the stepwise procedure is easy to use because the computer program will produce the "best" regression equation. Unfortunately, stepwise techniques can be easily abused because the computer program produces an "automatic" solution. In this section we focus on one option under the general title of stepwise techniques under SAS which is entitled STEPWISE.

Example 5.6

The data of Buckeye Savings and Loan Association is processed by SAS stepwise techniques. The predictive model is of the form

$$MORT = f(YEAR, PERINC, INT)$$

The variables MORT, YEAR, PERINC, and INT are defined as in previous examples (see example 5.3).

Stepwise regression is initiated by the identification of the dependent variables and the set of potentially important independent variables. The independent and dependent variables are then entered into the computer and the stepwise procedure begins. The computer fits all possible one-variable models of the form

$$\hat{Y} = \beta_0 + \beta_1 X + e$$

to the data. For each model, the regression coefficient β_1 is tested to determine whether it differs from zero. The F statistic (or equivalent t statistic) is calculated to test this hypothesis. In turn, the independent variable that produces the largest F statistic (or equivalent t statistic) is identified as the "best" one-variable predictor of Y. Note also that the independent variable with the largest F statistic will also be the one with the largest coefficient of correlation.

   After the initial step, the stepwise program searches for the best two-variable model, then for the best three-variable model, and so on. The stepwise option under SAS and other software systems and languages adds and deletes variables from the regression model as each step is processed. Each step considers adding one independent variable at a time. The variable is added if the F ratio for a variable to be added is significant at some specified level. In this example, the specification is the risk level $\alpha = 0.15$

   After each variable is added, the stepwise method examines all the variables already included in the model and deletes any variable that does not produce an F statistic significant at the 0.15 level. (An option is also available to change this level if desired.) Only after this checking is finished, and the necessary deletions made, can another variable be considered for the model.

   When no variable has an F statistic that can meet the 0.15 significance level for entry, or when the variable to be added to the model is one just dropped from it, the STEPWISE process ends. Hence the computer has generated the "best" predictive model.

   The output of the STEPWISE procedure prints a complete report on the final regression, and each step from the addition of the first independent variable. The output for the Buckeye Savings and Loan problem is shown in figure 5.8. Note that the printout includes the analysis of variance table, the regression coefficients, and related statistics.

   For each step the analysis of variance includes the source of variation (i.e. regression, error, and total), the degrees of freedom, the sum of squares and the mean square for each source. Note that for the final step the F statistic is defined as

$$F = \frac{\text{estimated variance accounted for by regression}}{\text{estimated variance not accounted for by regression (error)}}$$

$$= \frac{113.077}{0.768}$$

$$= 147.17$$

```
        STEPWISE REGRESSION PROCEDURE FOR DEPENDENT VARIABLE MORT

     ????:  SLENTRY AND SLSTAY HAVE BEEN SET TO  ?????????????????????

STEP 1      VARIABLE PERINC ENTERED       R SQUARE = 0.96559926
                                          C(P)  =     3.08305594

                    DF        SUM OF SQUARES    MEAN SQUARE       F       PROB>F

REGRESSION           1        223.56593053     223.5659305     224.55     0.0001
ERROR                8          7.96482947       0.9956037
TOTAL                9        231.53076000

                 B VALUE        STD ERROR       TYPE II SS        F       PROB>F

INTERCEPT      -5.89329859
PERINC          0.26230767      0.01750457      223.5659305     224.55     0.0001

BOUNDS ON CONDITION NUMBER:                          1,            1
------------------------------------------------------------------------------

STEP 2     VARIABLE YEAR ENTERED        R SQUARE = 0.97677114
                                        C(P)  =     2.13326998

                    DF        SUM OF SQUARES    MEAN SQUARE       F       PROB>F

REGRESSION           2        226.15256462     113.0762823     147.17     0.0001
ERROR                7          5.37819538       0.7683136
TOTAL                9        231.53076000

                 B VALUE        STD ERROR       TYPE II SS        F       PROB>F

INTERCEPT     -12.2469126
PERINC          0.4471474      0.10190576       14.79253432      19.25     0.0032
YEAR           -1.1734425      0.63953390        2.58663409       3.37     0.1092

BOUNDS ON CONDITION NUMBER:                     43.918,        175.672
------------------------------------------------------------------------------

NO OTHER VARIABLES MET THE 0.1500 SIGNIFICANCE LEVEL FOR ENTRY
```

FIGURE 5.8 Stepwise regression procedure, Buckeye Savings and Loan

which is significant at the 0.0001 level. Hence the variables YEAR (1970=0) and PERINC significantly account for the variation in mortgage loans.

The R-SQUARE for step 2 is 0.977 which indicates that 97.7 percent of the total variation in mortgage loans is associated with regression on time (YEAR) and Ohio personal income (PERINC).

The names of the independent variables included in the model are printed below the analysis of variance table. The corresponding estimates of the regression coefficients (b values) are given next, yielding the "best" predictive model (1970 = 0)

$$\hat{Y} = -12.247 + 0.447X_2 + 1.173X_3$$

where X_2 is Ohio personal income (PERINC) and X_3 is time (YEAR). The TYPE II sum of squares (SS) for each variable, which is the SS that would be added to the error SS if that one variable were removed from the model, is reported next. The F statistic is defined as

$$F = \frac{\text{(SS that would be added to error SS if the one variable were removed from the model)/df}}{\text{error mean square}}$$

This F statistic for the variable YEAR is

$$F = \frac{2.587}{0.6395} = 3.7$$

and is significant at the 0.1092 level. For the variable PERINC, this F statistic is

$$F = \frac{14.793}{0.1019} = 19.25$$

and is significant at the 0.0032 level. Both variables are entered into the final regression model since these F statistics were significant at a level less than 0.15.

At this point, the "best" or final predictive model is *best* in a limited sense. First, the model is limited to the original set of independent variables selected for possible inclusion. If the potential independent variables are selected unwisely, then the stepwise process cannot possibly produce a useful predictive model. Second, the particular significance levels chosen to include or drop independent variables from the equation will, in part, determine the "best" predictive equation. Finally, we could choose an alternative selection technique than the one considered in this section. For example, an alternative stepwise procedure is to begin with all variables included in the regression. In successive steps, the least useful independent variables are removed in a step-by-step fashion. This alternative technique may have another result. Thus we must conclude that the stepwise procedure is extremely useful, but is one among many procedures for finding a predictive model for forecasting purposes.

5.12 Summary

Regression methods involving more than one independent variable are called multiple regression methods. Error exists in multiple regression predictions as a result of incomplete theory, imperfect specification, and computation errors.

Coefficients estimated in multiple regression measure the net change in the dependent variable associated with a per unit change in the independent variable.

The method of least squares for fitting the multiple regression equation provides the best fit by minimizing the sum of the vertical deviations between the observed values of the dependent variable and the estimated values.

A measure of goodness of fit is the coefficient of determination. This is the sum of squares due to regression divided by the total sum of squares or total variation in the Y values. The multiple correlation coefficient is always nonnegative and is a direct generalization of the simple correlation to the case of two or more independent variables.

To test the overall significance of a multiple regression model, an analysis of variance (ANOVA) is performed to indicate whether the model sum of squares is significantly greater than the error sum of squares.

In addition to testing for overall significance, diagnostic tests indicate whether (a) each of the independent variables alone explain a significant portion of the variation in the dependent variable and (b) the fitted regression model explains behavior correctly.

The standard error of multiple regression is the square root of the mean square error for the model. In the ANOVA for regression, the F ratio is the mean square of the regression model divided by the mean square error.

Plots of residuals in multiple regression analysis indicate the same phenomenon as in simple linear regression analysis.

Multicollinearity results when pairs of independent variables are correlated with each other and the independent variables contribute redundant information. Existence of multicollinearity indicates that the regression model is unable to separate the specific relationships between each independent variable and the dependent variable

Categorical variables (those on a nominal scale) are included in regression models by using dummy variables where classes are coded by numerical values.

Selection of the "best" regression model may require a compromise between achieving the highest coefficient of determination and selecting a minimum number of predictor variables.

Under stepwise selection of the best predictive model, the method examines all the variables and deletes any variable that does not produce a significant F statistic. The final predictive model is best in a limited sense. The model is limited to the original set of independent variables; the particular significance levels chosen to include or drop independent variables will, in part, determine the final predictive equation; and an alternative selective technique would probably result in another predictive model.

5.13   Exercises

1 A study was made relating the cost Y per patient day in a hospital to the average length of stay X_1 and the hospital occupancy rate X_2. The equation was

$$\hat{Y} = 75.00 + 12X_1 + 110X_2$$

  (a) Interpret the meaning of the regression coefficients for X_1 and X_2.
  (b) If the average length of stay is eight days and the occupancy rate is 0.80, what is the estimated cost per patient day?
2 Table 5.4 represents the results of a regression model.
  (a) Write out the equation of the model.
  (b) Interpret the meaning of the intercept.
  (c) Interpret the meaning of the estimate of the coefficient for each independent variable.
  (d) For each estimated coefficient taken separately, can we reject the hypothesis that the parameter equals zero? At what significance level?
3 The data in table 5.5 are the results of applying F tests to test for the overall significance of regression.
  (a) Complete the mean square column of table 5.5.
  (b) Complete the F column of the table.
  (c) At the 0.05 significance level, can we reject the hypothesis that all indepen-

TABLE 5.4

Parameter	Estimate of coefficient	t-ratio	PR > T
Intercept	3.94	9.07	0.0001
X_1	−1.05	−1.44	0.2021
X_2	0.93	3.57	0.0118
X_3	0.18	0.61	0.5646
X_4	−0.32	−1.66	0.1473

TABLE 5.5

Source	DF	Sum of squares	Mean square	F
Model	4	0.0119		
Error	6	0.004		
Total	10	0.0123		
R-square = 0.9667				

dent variables considered together do not explain a significant amount of the variation in Y?
(d) Interpret the meaning of the R-square value.
4 A study was made to regress the demand for crude oil in the United States on crude oil prices, real gross national product, oil heating units, and registered motor vehicles. The results are summarized in table 5.6 (adapted from Hutchinson and Ferrone, 1977).
(a) Interpret the meaning of each coefficient.
(b) Write out the equation of the predictive model.
(c) Explain in words the meaning of R-square.
(d) What does the table say about the overall significance of the model?

TABLE 5.6

Dependent variable: barrels of crude oil consumed in US		
F = 14.38[a]	R-square = 0.709	
Independent variable	Estimated coefficient	t-ratio
----------------------	-----------------------	---------
Intercept	−0.007	
Price	85.51	1.05
Real GNP	4.92	2.75[b]
Heating oil units	0.163	5.17[a]
Registered motor vehicles	1.59	0.10

Notes: [a] Significant at 0.01 level.
[b] Significant at 0.05 level.

(e) Interpret each of the t ratios in the table.

5 Table 5.7 shows the results of a regression model estimation and the associated diagnostics.

(a) Write out the equation of the regression equation.

(b) What is the meaning of the estimate of the coefficient for the intercept?

(c) Interpret the meaning of the net regression coefficients for each independent variable.

(d) Can we reject the hypothesis

H_0: net regression coefficient = 0

for any of the independent variables? At what level?

(e) Complete the F column of the ANOVA table.

(f) Can we reject the hypothesis that all independent variables considered together do not explain a significant amount of the variation in the dependent variable? At what level?

(g) What proportion of the total variation in the dependent variable is explained by the regression on the independent variables?

TABLE 5.7

Dependent variable: Y

Parameter	Estimate of coefficient	t-ratio	$PR > |T|$
Intercept	3.014		
X_1	−0.214	3.29	0.011
X_2	1.027	5.18	0.001
X_3	0.479	1.25	0.246

Source	DF	Sum of squares	Mean square	F
Model	3	0.045	0.015	
Error	8	0.008	0.0009	
Total	11	0.053		

6 The following study was performed to find the "best" possible regression to relate sales of baseball tickets for the Boston Red Sox to the number of wins X_1, the price X_2, and time X_3. The data in table 5.8 were calculated.

(a) What proportion of the total variation in ticket sales is explained by the "best" one-independent-variable regression model?

(b) What proportion of the total variation in ticket sales is explained by the three-independent-variables regression model?

7 The multiple coefficient of determination can be defined by

$$\overline{R}^2 = 1 - \frac{\Sigma e^2/(n - m)}{\Sigma(Y_i - \overline{Y})^2/(n - 1)}$$

where e is the error, m is the number of independent variables, and n, Y_i, and $\overline{Y}$ have their usual definitions.

(a) If the sum of the squared error terms equals zero, how do we interpret the coefficient of determination?

TABLE 5.8

Number in model	R-square	Variables in model
1	0.226	X_1
1	0.626	X_2
1	0.268	X_3
2	0.375	X_3, X_1
2	0.662	X_2, X_1
2	0.828	X_3, X_2
3	0.856	X_1, X_2, X_3

(b) The above formula can be rewritten as follows:

$$\bar{R}^2 = 1 - \frac{n - 1}{n - m}(1 - R^2)$$

If $1 - R^2$ decreases more slowly than $n - m$ because of the addition of more variables, what will happen to $\bar{R}^2$?

8 The data in table 5.9 show mortgage loans for a Savings and Loan Association located in Ohio, Ohio personal income, and interest on new home loans in the US (average).

(a) Develop a regression model that relates mortgage loans to personal income, interest rates, and time.

(b) Interpret the estimates of the net regression coefficients.

(c) Test the following hypothesis for each regression coefficient:

H_0: regression coefficient = 0

Can we reject the hypothesis? At what level?

(d) By analysis of variance for regression, is there sufficient evidence that the model explains a significant amount of the variation in mortgage loans?

TABLE 5.9

Year	Mortgage ($ millions)	Ohio personal income (income $ billions)	Interest rates
1972	161.8	49.00	7.45
1973	194.4	54.47	7.78
1974	207.4	58.90	8.71
1975	231.6	62.75	8.75
1976	251.5	68.37	8.76
1977	316.4	75.87	8.80
1978	387.2	84.00	9.30
1979	454.4	93.50	10.48
1980	481.3	101.24	12.25
1981	508.8	111.8	14.16

(e) What proportion of the total variation in mortgage loans is explained by the regression on the independent variables?

(f) If Ohio personal income is $140 billion, interest rates are 15 percent, and the year is 1984, what are the estimated mortgage loans?

9 The data in table 5.10 contain information on automobile tire sales Y (thousands), number of automobile registrations X_1 (millions), and disposable income X_2 (million dollars, constant 1967 dollars).

(a) Determine the regression model that best fits the above data.

(b) Interpret the meaning of the estimated net regression coefficients for each independent variable.

(c) Test the hypothesis that each regression coefficient taken individually is equal to zero. (Hint: at what significance level can you reject the hypothesis?)

(d) What proportion of the total variation in sales is explained by the regression model?

(e) Test whether the overall regression adequately explains the variation in Y? (At what level?)

(f) Determine whether each new variable should *not* be included in the regression model.

(g) Plot the residual values and see if there is any pattern in residual terms.

TABLE 5.10

Y	X_1	X_2
10 170	112.9	307.50
11 314	117.6	310.73
13 188	125.4	341.28
15 181	129.9	713.44
15 305	132.9	621.63
16 393	138.5	764.49
18 481	143.8	829.06
20 278	148.8	1052.26
21 744	154.1	1496.84
21 289	155.2	1937.13

10 The data in table 5.11 are for cost of heating per day for a manufacturing plant, direct labor hours (DLH), machine hours (MH), degree days (DD), and the producer price index for oil products (PPI). Find the highest coefficient of determination for all possible regressions of all sizes. What would be the best regression for each size model?

11 For the data of exercise 10, use the methods of stepwise regression to find the best regression. Explain the meaning of the net regression coefficients for the best equation.

12 Determine the correlation matrix for the data of exercise 10. Is there evidence of multicollinearity?

13 The data in table 5.12 concern unit sales (in thousands), price per unit, and gender of the person in charge of sales.

(a) Using the methods of regression, estimate the relationship between the quantity of products sold, price, and gender.

TABLE 5.11

Obs	Cost	DLH	MH	DD	PPI
1	80	56	160	30	100
2	81	54	161	40	101
3	82	55	162	38	102
4	82	57	158	22	103
5	83	60	160	45	103
6	88	60	158	55	104
7	95	62	150	65	105
8	102	65	170	40	105
9	110	63	180	69	105
10	115	70	168	75	106
11	125	70	180	80	107
12	130	75	175	90	107
13	140	80	185	50	108
14	148	80	170	96	108
15	151	60	165	110	109

(b) Test for overall regression at the 0.05 level and the 0.01 level.
(c) Test whether the parameters of the regression are equal to zero.
(d) Interpret the results of the tests of significance.

14 The marketing research department of a firm believe that cosmetics use scores move linearly with quarterly sales patterns. From experience, the over-the-counter sales are highest in the springtime and follow a seasonal pattern, that is,

TABLE 5.12

Quantity	Price ($)	Gender
3.6	8.80	M
5.5	7.90	F
7.4	7.20	F
8.0	6.80	F
11.2	6.10	M
13.0	5.40	M
14.0	5.20	M
15.0	5.00	F
15.0	5.10	F
15.2	4.90	M

actual sales exhibit a discernible seasonal pattern. To solve the problem we set up three dummy variables: X_1 for spring, X_2 for summer, and X_3 for winter. A value of 1 is given if sales are in the appropriate quarter and 0 if sales are in another quarter. Data on aptitude test scores for sales personnel are also collected to determine whether sales are also associated with aptitude as measured by the test.

TABLE 5.13

Sales	Test score	Season
40	35	Fall
41	42	Fall
48	47	Fall
49	45	Winter
73	48	Spring
74	52	Spring
68	59	Winter
51	49	Summer
55	53	Summer
63	49	Summer
75	42	Spring
70	43	Spring
38	39	Winter
43	49	Winter
57	61	Summer
76	48	Spring

The data are given in table 5.13.
(a) Estimate the linear regression of sales on test score and the dummy variables for spring, summer and fall.
(b) Test for overall regression.
(c) Test the parameters of the model to see if they are equal to zero.
(d) Estimate sales if the test score is 52 and sales are in the spring.
(e) Interpret the results of the statistical tests in (b) and (c).

15 By the methods of stepwise regression, find the "best" multiple regression of sales of refrigerators (electric, 6.5 cubic feet and over) associated with new housing units X_1, consumer credit X_2, personal consumption expenditures for durable goods (per capita) X_3, expenditures for national advertising of household

TABLE 5.14

Year	Y (thousands)	X_1 (thousands)	X_2 ($ billions)	X_3	X_4 ($ millions)	X_5	X_6
1	5286	1469	61.6	$415	24.3	$274	$222
2	5691	2085	64.2	474	28.6	271	216
3	6315	2379	66.1	533	31.5	270	217
4	6774	2057	76.0	588	33.8	279	221
5	5982	1352	82.0	576	32.6	295	234
6	4582	1171	85.7	621	30.4	311	244
7	4817	1548	94.5	731	38.9	350	273
8	5707	1990	93.5	825	50.3	425	307
9	5890	2023	110.1	916	53.7	548	328
10	5701	1749	123.4	966	46.7	559	376

equipment X_4, average price of refrigerators X_5, and average price of freezers X_6 (data given in table 5.14).

16 For the data in exercise 15, is there evidence of multicollinearity among the variables?

References

Hutchinson, P. M. and Ferrone, D. D. (1977) An alternative estimation of the demand for crude oil. *Review of Business and Economic Research*, 13, Fall, 11–107.

Mendenhall, W. and Sincich, T. (1986) *A Second Course in Business Statistics: Regression Analysis*, 2nd edn. San Francisco, CA: Dellen.

US Department of Health and Human Services Health Care Financing Administration/Office of Research, Demonstrations, and Statistics (1981) *Profits, Growth and Reimbursement Systems in the Nursing Home Industry*, Washington, DC.

Further Reading

Berensen, M. L., Levine, D. M. and Goldstein, M. (1983) *Intermediate Statistical Methods and Applications; A Computer Package Approach*. Englewood Cliffs, NJ: Prentice-Hall.

Draper, N. and Smith, H. (1986) *Applied Regression Analysis*. New York: John Wiley.

Farnum, N. R. and Stanton, L. W. (1989) *Quantitative Forecasting Methods*. Boston, MA: PWS-Kent, ch. 4.

Fogler, H. R. and Garapathy, S. (1982) *Financial Econometrics for Researchers in Finance and Accounting*. Englewood Cliffs, NJ: Prentice-Hall.

Fox, K. A. (1967) *Intermediate Economic Statistics*. New York: John Wiley.

Fruend, R. J. and Minton, P. D. (1979) *Regression Methods: A Tool for Data Analysis*, New York: Marcel Dekker.

Hanke, J. E. and Reitsch, A. G. (1989) *Business Forecasting*. Boston, MA: Allyn and Bacon, chs 7, 9.

Kerlinger, F. N. and Pedhazur, E. J. (1973) *Multiple Regression in Behavioral Research*. New York: Holt, Rinehart and Winston.

Kleinbaum, D. G., Kupper, L. L. and Muller, K. E. (1988) *Applied Regression Analysis and Other Multivariable Methods*. Boston, MA: PWS-Kent.

Neter, J., Wasserman, W. and Kutner, M. H. (1985) *Applied Linear Statistical Models*. Homewood, Il: Irwin.

Younger, M. S. (1985) *A First Course in Linear Regression*. North Scituate, MA: Duxbury.

Appendix A   Polynomial Regression Models

So far the analysis has been restricted to regression models of linear form, i.e. simple linear and multiple linear regression models. In this appendix, we study the method of curvilinear regression analysis. Curvilinear regression differs from the linear regression model because the independent variable is raised to a certain power. The regression is often called a polynomial power. The degree of the polynomial is the highest power to which the independent variable is raised. The equation

$$Y = \beta_0 + \beta_1 X + \beta_2 X^2 + e \qquad (5.A1)$$

is a second-degree polynomial since X is raised to the second power; e is the error term. The equation

$$Y = \beta_0 + \beta_1 X + \beta_2 X^2 + \beta_3 X^3 + e \qquad (5.A2)$$

is a third-degree polynomial equation with e as the error term.

The degree to which the independent variable is raised indicates the number of bends in the regression equation. For example, a first-degree polynomial

$$Y = \beta_0 + \beta_1 X + e$$

describes a straight line. A second-degree polynomial describes a single bend in the regression curve and is referred to as a quadratic equation or parabola. Similarly, a third-degree polynomial has two bends and is referred to as a cubic equation (see figure 5.A1). For any given equation, the highest order it can take is equal to the number of distinct observations in the independent variable.

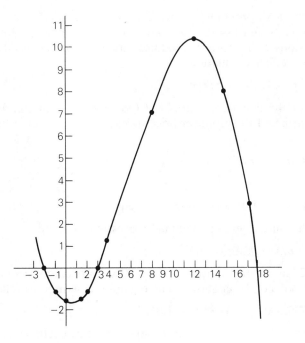

FIGURE 5.A1 Third-degree polynomial model

Recall that the purpose of forecasting is to predict the value of the dependent variable with a minimum degree of error and to describe a set of data as well as possible. Hence we seek the highest-degree polynomial equation required to explain the variation in the dependent variable.

The methods of curvilinear regression can best be described as a series of steps, testing at each one whether a higher-degree polynomial adds significantly to explaining the variation in the dependent variable. Stated differently, does the addition of another order to the equation add significantly to the explanatory power of the equation? In SAS, if the F statistic for TYPE I SS is significant at a small probability level, then the addition of the higher order is adding to the predictive and explanatory power of the equation. However, if the F statistic for the highest order is not significant at a small probability level, then the equation should be reduced to the next lowest order.

Example 5.A1

In a study of the cost of heating a building, the producer price index for energy was utilized as an independent variable to predict the cost of energy. The experimenter decided to estimate both a second-degree and third-degree polynomial equation to forecast the cost of energy. An SAS computer program was written to process the data and to calculate the regression estimates of the two predictive equations.

Note that, in the SAS program, the REG procedure is used again to calculate the regression estimates and associated analysis of variance for performing the poly-nomial regressions. The SAS procedures are used to begin the processes of computing the predictive equations.

$$COST = f(PPI, PPI\text{-squared})$$

will produce for the dependent variable COST (cost of heating, Y variable), and independent variable PPI (producer price index, X variable) an estimated equation denoted by

$$\hat{Y} = b_0 + b_1 X + b_2 X^2$$

Similarly, a model of the form

$$COST = f(PPI, PPI\text{-squared}, PPI\text{-cubed})$$

will produce the third-degree polynomial regression estimate

$$\hat{Y} = b_0 + b_1 X + b_2 X^2 + b_3 X^3$$

Figure 5.A2 shows the output of the REG procedure (from SAS) for the second-degree polynomial equation. The equation is written as follows:

$$\hat{Y} = 10\ 798.690 - 213.681X + 1.065X^2$$

The t statistics for the intercept and for the b_1 and b_2 coefficients are statistically significant at very small probability levels (0.0002 and 0.0001). To interpret the coefficients, we say that cost $\hat{Y}$ equals 10 798.690 when X is zero; for every change of one unit in the product price index there is a concurrent change of 213.681 in one direction and 1.065 in the other direction in cost. The change, as measured by the first derivative of the equation, is $-213.681 + 2.130X$.

The coefficient of determination (R-SQUARE) is 0.968, indicating that about 96.8 percent of the total variation in cost Y is associated with second-degree

```
DEP VARIABLE: COST                     HEATING COST
                                  ANALYSIS OF VARIANCE

                          SUM OF             MEAN
   SOURCE        DF       SQUARES           SQUARE      F VALUE        PROB>F

   MODEL         2        9092.259          4546.13     183.389        0.0001
   ERROR        12        297.4739          24.78949
   C TOTAL      14        9389.733


            ROOT MSE       4.978905       R-SQUARE       0.9683
            DEP MEAN       107.4667       ADJ R-SQ       0.9630
              C.V.         4.632976

                              PARAMETER ESTIMATES

                          PARAMETER              STANDARD          T FOR HO:
   VARIABLE      DF        ESTIMATE                 ERROR        PARAMETER=0

   INTERCEP      1         10798.69              2084.119            5.181
   PPI          1         -213.681              39.87072           -5.359
   PPISQ        1         1.064795              0.190599            5.587

                                               VARIABLE
   VARIABLE      DF       PROB > |T|            LABEL

   INTERCEP      1         0.0002               INTERCEPT
   PPI          1         0.0002               PRODUCER PRICE INDEX
   PPISQ        1         0.0001               PPI SQUARED
```

FIGURE 5.A2 Output of PROC REG

polynomial regression with PPI. For both X and X^2, the coefficients b_1 and b_2 are significant at 0.0001. Hence, both X raised to the first power and X raised to the second power should be included in the regression equation.

The results of the third-degree polynomial regression are presented in figure 5.A3. We find that, of the total sums of squares (9389.733), the sums of squares associated with the cubic term X^3 is 75.829 (calculated from another SAS procedure). Thus the proportion of the total sums of squares accounted for by the cubic term is

$$\frac{75.829}{9389.733} = 0.0081$$

Hence the cubic term accounts for only 0.81 percent of the variation in the dependent variable. Furthermore the F statistic associated with adding the cubic term is 3.76 and is significant at only 0.0785. Since this probability level is not a very small value, we can argue that the cubic term does not account for a significantly large enough portion of the variation in the dependent variable to be included in the regression model. Each term in a polynomial regression can be examined in the way we have used in examining the cubic term.

If a fourth-degree term was included in the regression model, it is likely that the proportion of the total sums of squares accounted for by the quartic term, X^4 would be very small. Furthermore, the F statistic would not be significant. For purposes of

```
DEP VARIABLE: COST                   HEATING COST
                               ANALYSIS OF VARIANCE

                         SUM OF          MEAN
   SOURCE        DF       SQUARES         SQUARE      F VALUE       PROB>F

   MODEL          3      9168.115       3056.038     151.686       0.0001
   ERROR         11      221.6187       20.14715
   C TOTAL       14      9389.773


            ROOT MSE      4.488558      R-SQUARE       0.9764
            DEP MEAN      107.4667      ADJ R-SQ       0.9700
                C.V.      4.176698


                          PARAMETER ESTIMATES

                         PARAMETER           STANDARD        T FOR HO:
   VARIABLE      DF       ESTIMATE             ERROR        PARAMETER=0

   INTERCEP       1       169903.5          82018.42          2.072
   PPI            1       -4785.15          2356.246         -2.031
   PPISQ          1       44.82974          22.55554          1.988
   PPICU          1       -0.139603         0.07194649       -1.940

                                           VARIABLE
   VARIABLE      DF      PROB > |T|         LABEL

   INTERCEP       1       0.0626            INTERCEPT
   PPI            1       0.0672            PRODUCER PRICE INDEX
   PPISQ          1       0.0723            PPI SQUARED
   PPICU          1       0.0784            PPI CUBED
```

FIGURE 5.A3

forecasting, it is extremely rare to find a significant F statistic beyond the third degree. Moreover, the higher the degree of the polynomial, the more it is affected by the unreliability of the measure involved, and the more difficult it is to interpret. Often it is recommended to test the quadratic term and then the cubic term for linearity. If the cubic term is not significant, the regression is terminated at the quadratic term. Similarly, if the quadratic term is not significant, the analysis is terminated at the linear term. The results indicate that a quadratic forecasting equation is appropriate.

Exercises

A1 The data in table 5.A1 are net income for American Hospital Supply Inc. (million dollars) for the years 1965–80 (1965 = 1).
  (a) Calculate the linear regression of net income on time.
  (b) Calculate the quadratic regression of net income on time.
  (c) Calculate the cubic regression of net income on time.
  (d) Which regression has the smallest standard error of regression?
  (e) Which regression has the highest coefficient of determination?
  (f) Is the cubic term significant? At what level?

TABLE 5.A1

Year	Net income
1	9.85
2	12.48
3	15.19
4	20.92
5	25.00
6	26.65
7	29.16
8	35.60
9	40.81
10	46.33
11	55.18
12	66.27
13	77.92
14	92.60
15	109.40
16	122.20

(g) Is the quadratic term significant? At what level?
(h) On the basis of the above result which is the best functional form for forecasting?
(i) Forecast for the years 1981, 1982, and 1983 by each equation.
(j) Find the actual net income for the years 1981–3 and compare with the forecasts.

A2 A regression analysis was performed to find the best polynomial relationship between costs of goods sold Y and units produced X. The quadratic term is identified by XX. Table 5.A2 is the output of a computer program.
(a) Write out the equation of the polynomial equation.
(b) Interpret the meaning of the quadratic and linear terms.
(c) Can we reject the hypothesis that each parameter coefficient equals zero? At what level?

TABLE 5.A2

Parameter	Coefficient estimate	t-ratio	PR > T
Intercept	12 250	4.75	0.005
X	75.50	6.83	0.002
XX	1.05	6.50	0.002

A3 A regression analysis was performed to find the best polynomial relationship between the net asset value of a common stock mutual fund (NAV) and years (TIME) (1974 = 0). The quadratic term is identified by TIMESQ. Table 5.A3 is the output of a computer program (Micro-TSP).

TABLE 5. A3

```
LS // Dependent Variable is NAV
Date:                    / Time: 10:26
SMPL range:  1974 - 1989
Number of observations: 16
```

VARIABLE	COEFFICIENT	STD. ERROR	T-STAT.	2-TAIL SIG.
C	8.2278031	3.1472762	2.6142616	0.021
TIME	-2.5172432	0.8521025	-2.9541553	0.011
TIMESQ	0.4814373	0.0487274	9.8802204	0.000

R-squared	0.985804	Mean of dependent var	31.84562

(a) Write out the equation of the polynomial equation.
(b) Interpret the meaning of the quadratic and linear terms.
(c) Can we reject the hypothesis that each parameter coefficient equals zero? At what level?

A4 A second polynomial regression was estimated for the data of exercise A3. This time the cubic term is identified by TIMECU in table 5.A4.
(a) Write out the polynomial equation.
(b) Interpret the meaning of the cubic, quadratic, and linear terms.
(c) Can we reject the hypothesis that each parameter coefficient equals zero? At what level?

TABLE 5. A4

```
LS // Dependent Variable is NAV
Date:                    / Time: 10:27
SMPL range:  1974 - 1989
Number of observations: 16
```

VARIABLE	COEFFICIENT	STD. ERROR	T-STAT.	2-TAIL SIG.
C	0.5270066	3.9502707	0.1334102	0.896
TIME	2.2166142	1.9514667	1.1358709	0.278
TIMESQ	-0.1940712	0.2625905	-0.7390638	0.474
TIMECU	0.0264905	0.0101742	2.6036978	0.023

R-squared	0.990929	Mean of dependent var	31.84562

Appendix B   Output of Minitab and Micro-TSP

At this point we introduce computer output from Minitab software for the data of example 5.2 (Buckeye Savings and Loan). In this example (figure 5.B1) the regression of mortgage loans Y is on Ohio personal income X1 and interest rates X2.

```
The regression equation is
Y = - 7.03 + 0.242 X1 + 0.279 X2

Predictor           Coef        Stdev      t-ratio           p
Constant          -7.025        3.032        -2.32       0.054
X1               0.24241      0.05140         4.72       0.000
X2                0.2793       0.6733         0.41       0.691

S = 1.054        R-sq = 96.6

Analysis of Variance

SOURCE             DF           SS          MS          F           p
Regression          2       223.76      111.88     100.74       0.000
Error               7         7.77        1.11
Total               9       231.53
```

FIGURE 5.B1 Buckeye Savings and Loan. Regression on income and interest rates

Note that the output is similar to the SAS output of figure 5.1. The list of variables is presented in a similar manner except that the term Constant is used instead of INTERCEPT. Coef indicates the estimates of the regression coefficients. Stdev Coef

```
The regression equation is
Y = - 12.0 + 0.485 X1 - 0.246 X2 - 1.30 time

Predictor           Coef        Stdev      t-ratio           p
Constant         -11.950        3.966        -3.01       0.024
X1                0.4851       0.1504         3.22       0.018
X2               -0.2460       0.6740        -0.37       0.728
time             -1.3028       0.7697        -1.69       0.141

S = 0.9364       R-sq = 97.7

Analysis of Variance

SOURCE             DF           SS          MS          F           p
Regression          3      226.269      75.423      86.01       0.000
Error               6        5.261       0.877
Total               9      231.531
```

FIGURE 5.B2 Buckeye Savings and Loan. Regression on three variables

is the standard error of the regression coefficients. T-ratio is associated with the test that the parameter equals zero and is the coefficient divided by the standard deviation of the coefficient. The probability that the null hypothesis can be rejected is then given. Some additional statistics include $R^2 = 96.6$ (in percent) and the standard error of regression $s = 1.054$.

The output of Minitab for the data of example 5.3 is presented in figure 5.B2. The list of variables is similar to that of figure 5.4 which was output from SAS. The term Constant is used instead of INTERCEPT. Coef indicates the estimates of the regression coefficients, Stdev Coef is the standard deviation of the coefficients, t-ratio is defined as before, and the probability associated with rejecting a true null hypothesis is also included. As noted before additional statistics include the coefficient of determination R^2 and the standard error of regression s.

```
LS // Dependent Variable is MORT
Data:              / Time:  0:27
SMPL range: 1971 - 1980
Number of observations:  10
========================================================================

    VARIABLE      COEFFICIENT     STD.ERROR       T-STAT.      2-TAIL SIG.
========================================================================

       C         -7.0250052      3.0324356      -2.3166214       0.054
    PERINC        0.2424147      0.0513979       4.7164289       0.002
     INT          0.2792716      0.6732663       0.4148011       0.691
========================================================================

R-squared                   0.966425   Mean of dependent var      12.28200
Adjusted R-squared          0.956832   S.D. of dependent var       5.072045
S.E. of regression          1.053820   Sum of squared resid        7.773753
Durbin-Watson stat          0.994504   F-statistic               100.7428
```

FIGURE 5.B3 Output of Micro-TSP. Regression on two variables

```
LS // Dependent Variable is MORT
Date:              / Time:  0:27
SMPL range: 1971 - 1980
Number of observations:  10
========================================================================

    VARIABLE      COEFFICIENT     STD.ERROR       T-STAT.      2-TAIL SIG.
========================================================================

       C        -11.950434       3.9658776      -3.0133139       0.024
    PERINC        0.4850539      0.1504466       3.2240941       0.018
     INT         -0.2460393      0.6739678      -0.3650608       0.728
     YEAR        -1.3028279      0.7696852      -1.6926763       0.141
========================================================================

R-squared                   0.977276   Mean of dependent var      12.28200
Adjusted R-squared          0.965914   S.D. of dependent var       5.072045
S.E. of regression          0.936423   Sum of squared resid        5.261333
Durbin-Watson stat          1.575731   F-statistic                86.01221
```

FIGURE 5.B4 Output of Micro-TSP. Regression on three variables

The previous figures are illustrations of partial output of Micro-TSP which is one of the more useful programs for personal computers. The output of example 5.2 is included in figure 5.B3. Note that the output is similar to the standard outputs of mainframe and minicomputer software. The list of variables is the same as in the outputs of other software systems. Instead of the term INTERCEPT, the letter C is used to express the estimate of A. COEFFICIENT indicates the estimates of the regression coefficients. STD. ERROR is the standard error for the estimated regression coefficients. T-STAT is the t ratio for the test that the parameter equals zero and is the coefficient divided by the standard error. 2-TAIL SIG is the significance level at which the null hypothesis that the parameter equals zero can be rejected. Additional statistics include R^2 (0.966), the overall F statistic (100.748) and the standard error of regression (1.054). The Micro-TSP output of example 5.3 is shown in figure 5.B4.

Appendix C   Further notes on model fitting

As discussed in this and the previous chapter, the trend in a time series may be nonlinear. This requires the specification of appropriate nonlinear models and the fitting of these models to the observed data. The fitting of nonlinear models is usually done with lengthy time horizons and is usually coupled with only a limited number of data points. Although the fitting of nonlinear models can be very helpful to a forecaster and business planner, it must be done with great caution since tenuous assumptions must be made about the model.

There are many different shapes of curves that can be used to fit historical data. One frequently used form is the S curve. The model implies a slow start, a steep growth, and a leveling off to a plateau. This model may characterize, for example, sales of a new innovative product, usually characterized by the introduction of new technology.

Mathematically, there are many different equations that represent S curves. The most common of these are as follows:

$$Y = e^{(b_0 - b_1/x)} \tag{5.C1}$$

$$Y = L/(1 + b_0 e^{-b_1 x}) \tag{5.C2}$$

$$Y = L/e^{-b_0 e - b_1 x} \tag{5.C3}$$

$$Y = 1 - b_0 e^{-b_1 x} \tag{5.C4}$$

Estimation of these functional forms is accomplished by transforming both sides of the equation into logarithmic form. In turn, the equation is estimated by least squares regression using conventional computer software. Sometimes special software such as SAS NLIN (for nonlinear regression) can be used to estimate the parameters of the equation directly. A better fit is often obtained if a direct nonlinear regression procedure is applied.

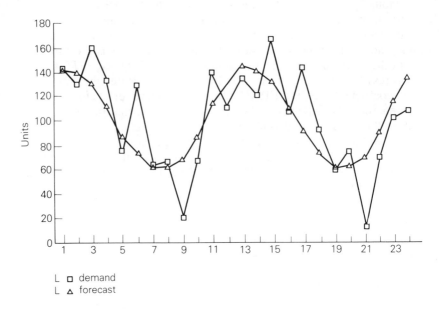

L □ demand
L △ forecast

FIGURE 5.C1 Observed (demand) values and forecast – three-term trigonometric model

In addition to the above models, trigonometric functions are used for a variety of purposes. These models are often applied if demand for a product is seasonal and data are collected on a monthly or quarterly basis. The models are called trigonometric because the model includes a series of sine and cosine terms. One such model is as follows:

$$Y = b_0 + b_1 \sin x + b_2 \cos x \tag{5.C5}$$

where b_0 is the intercept, b_1 is the coefficient of sin x, and b_2 is the coefficient of cos x. The above model may fit a situation where demand for a product has a pattern which flows up and down in an oscillating manner, and where the average level is the same from year to year (see figure 5.C1). In this application, the demand is seasonal within a business cycle and is stationary (horizontal) over the long run. The value of X is determined by the number of time periods that are observed in one cycle (usually one year). Since three terms are used to express the demand pattern, the trigonometric model is referred to as a three-term model.

Estimation of the trigonometric model is carried out in a straightforward manner by use of the sine and cosine functions available in standard statistical software. Much care must be taken when specifying the model to insure that the pattern in the data is approximated by the model.

CHAPTER 6

Econometric Models

Objectives

By the end of this chapter, you will understand that econometrics is the science of economic measurement with the goal of establishing quantitative relationships between economic variables with the aid of statistics. An econometric model is an explicit system in which a forecaster can assemble and weigh economic information in a systematic and meaningful manner. By the end of this chapter, you will be able to:

1 Understand the structure of an econometric model.
2 Understand the limitations and problems associated with constructing large scale econometric models.
3 Evaluate the usefulness of econometric models for forecasting.
4 Be able to estimate elasticities to evaluate and predict the effects of business policy.

Outline

Key Terms

- Econometrics
- Exogenous
- Endogenous
- Structural Equations
- Structural Coefficients
- Full Information Maximum Likelihood

- Limited Information Maximum Likelihood
- Indirect Least Squares
- Two-stage Least Squares
- Specification Problem
- Identification Problem
- Reduced-form Equations
- Elasticity
- Point elasticity
- Multiplicative form
- Constant Elasticity

6.1   Introduction

Literally, *econometrics* means economic measurement, and measurement is a very important element of econometrics. Not all economic measurement, however, is econometrics. The estimation of national income or the construction of the consumer price index are very important problems of economic measurement that are not econometric problems.

Econometrics is regarded as the discipline which attempts to establish quantitative relationships between economic variables with the aid of the theory of statistics. In the previous two chapters, we studied how simple regression theory is a special case of multiple regression. Now, we shall see that multiple regression is an important special case of econometrics. An econometric model usually contains several relations with one or more of the variables appearing in more than one of the equations of the model.

Problems arise when we estimate one equation at a time and, in turn, estimate the parameters appearing in it by regression methods. The mere mechanical application of this method can lead to meaningless results. For example, regression methods may result in regression coefficients which are not good estimators of the true values of the parameters of the econometric equations. Also, a multiple regression may result in a parameter estimate for a coefficient of an independent variable in one equation of the model. However, the variable appears in more than one equation and the estimated coefficient may make no sense in the second equation.

In a set of equations which comprise an econometric model, some of the explanatory (independent) variables recur. In some cases, such as demand relations for a number of different commodities, no identification or simultaneous estimation problem arises. Thus the econometric equations can be dealt with one by one.

Whereas in previous chapters the distinction between dependent and independent variables was very important, this distinction is not valid for a system of two or more equations having interdependent variables. Instead, the important distinction is between jointly dependent variables and predetermined variables. The latter exert an influence on the jointly dependent variables but are not influenced by them in return.

A lagged variable, referring to a previous period, is a variable treated as predetermined, but current values of some variables may also be predetermined. Such variables are called *exogenous* since they are determined from outside the equation system. Variables determined within the system are called *endogenous*.

Current values of the endogenous variables then constitute the jointly dependent variables, and the term endogenous can be used instead of jointly dependent.

The theoretical scheme of the econometric model determines whether a variable is classified as exogenous or endogenous. A noneconomic variable will usually be considered to be exogenous, but economic variables such as price or costs of production may be treated as either endogenous or exogenous.

A complete econometric model consisting of a system of simultaneous equations will contain as many equations as there are endogenous variables. However, there may be any number of exogenous variables and they may be more or less numerous than the endogenous ones.

In this chapter, the purpose is not to provide the detailed knowledge required to utilize econometric models fully. Instead, the aim of this chapter is to consider those ideas necessary (a) to present the advantages and limitations of econometric models, (b) to describe the statistical methods necessary for estimations and (c) to discuss econometric models as a tool for forecasting.[1]

6.2   The Simultaneous Equation Basis of Econometric Modeling

To begin, let us consider a simple linear supply–demand system for a price p and a quantity q which are determined by the following system of two simultaneous equations: the demand relation

$$q = b_{01} + b_1 P + e \tag{6.1}$$

and the supply relation

$$q = b_{02} + b_2 P + u \tag{6.2}$$

The terms e and u are the error or disturbance terms, the b_{0i} are intercepts and the b_i are regression coefficients for the right-hand side variables. Each equation is a function of price, and we can regard p and q as endogenous variables. If there are two endogenous variables, the values of their coefficients are determined from two simultaneous equations.

The above equations are called the *structural equations* of the model. They show the relationships between variables on grounds of an established or a new economic theory explaining behavior of economic entities. The regression coefficients are referred to as the *structural coefficients* in the model.

To consider further an econometric model of price determination in a single market, let us examine the following system of equations:

$$q_d = b_{01} + b_1 P + c_1 I + e \tag{6.3}$$

$$q_s = b_{02} + b_2 P + c_2 R + u \tag{6.4}$$

$$q_d = q_s \tag{6.5}$$

where q_d is the quantity demanded for a good, q_s is the quantity supplied, P is the price, I is income, R is rainfall, and e and u are error terms. The endogenous variables are q_d, q_s, and P, and the exogenous variables are I and R. Random error

---

1   In addition, this chapter focuses on making the reader aware of econometric modeling, and which consulting firms engage in such activities. Hence, this chapter could be considered later if the reader wishes.

(disturbance) terms e and u are included in the equation for one or more of the following reasons.

1 Variables that may influence demand or supply have been omitted from the simultaneous equations.
2 Equations may be misspecified in that the particular functional forms chosen should be nonlinear rather than linear.
3 Variables included may be measured inaccurately and there may be some basic randomness in behavior on the part of both demanders and suppliers.[2]

Six explicit parameters are contained in the model: b_{01} and b_{02} are intercepts (constants); b_1 and b_2 multiply P (price); c_1 multiplies I (income); and c_2 multiplies R (rainfall). The model also contains implicit assumptions concerning the probability distributions for the error terms of each equation.[3]

The demand equation specifies that demand is a linear function of price, income, and error. Parameter b_1 would be negative (indicating a downward-sloping demand curve) and parameter c_1 is generally positive (added income increases demand).

For the supply equation, b_2 is positive (quantity supplied is an upward-sloping function with respect to price) and c_2 is generally positive, indicating that rainfall increases supply of the marketable goods.

The right-hand sides of equations (6.3) and (6.4) include two random variables. The first are the error terms (e and u) and the second is P which is endogenous and hence influenced by both error terms. Thus the left-hand sides q_d and q_s are also random. One assumption of the error term is that

$$E(e) = 0 \qquad E(u) = 0 \tag{6.6}$$

Thus the expectations of equations (6.3) and (6.4) become

$$E(q_d) = b_{01} + b_1 \, E(P) + c_1 I \tag{6.7}$$

$$E(q_s) = b_{02} + b_2 \, E(P) + c_2 R \tag{6.8}$$

Equation (6.5) is the equilibrium condition stating that demand equals supply. This equation does not contain an error term (it is an identity). Thus the equilibrium solution can be found by equating the two simultaneous equations and expressing the endogenous variables as a function of all exogenous variables and error terms. This method, called the reduced form, permits the solution of the system.

The following example illustrates how a firm can use a system of equations to forecast.

Example 6.1

The following five-equation system is a simple method for employing an econometric model for forecasting sales for a firm based on general business conditions. Although many such forecasting models may be much more complex, this model provides a point of departure:

---

2 Note that these are a restatement of the general regression assumptions of chapters 4 and 5.

3 See chapter 5, sections 5.1 and 5.2, for a discussion of these assumptions.

$$C_t = b_{01} + b_1 Y_t + e_{1t} \tag{6.9}$$

$$I_t = b_{02} + b_2 P_{t-1} + e_{2t} \tag{6.10}$$

$$Y_t = C_t + I_t + G_t \tag{6.11}$$

$$(DY)_t = Y_t - A_t - T_t \tag{6.12}$$

$$S = b_{03} + b_3 (DY)_t \tag{6.13}$$

where C is personal consumption expenditures, I is capital investment (net), P is profits; G is government purchases of goods and services, Y is gross national product (GNP), DY is disposable personal income, A is capital consumption allowances, T is taxes and transfer payments, S is sales of product X, and e_1 and e_2 are error terms. Equations (6.9), (6.10), and (6.13) are behavioral hypotheses. The first states that current period consumption is a function of the current level of GNP. The second states that current capital investment is related to previous period's profits. Finally, (6.13) indicates that sales of product X (or firm X) are related to disposable personal income. Equation (6.11) states that GNP is equal to consumption, investment, and government purchases, and equation (6.12) indicates that disposable personal income equals GNP less capital consumption allowances and taxes and transfer payments.

The basic notion of the econometric forecasting model is that sales of a firm (or product) are related to general economic and business conditions expressed in the multi-equation forecasting model. This interdependence puts great pressure on forecasting services to collect data, perform statistical computations, and estimate the parameters of the forecasting model. In the end, the forecast is no better than the underlying econometric model which forms the central core of the forecasting (decision) system.

The tasks involved in econometric model-building are similar to those of multiple regression but extended to the case of simultaneous equations. These forecasting tasks include (a) determining which variables to incorporate in each equation, (b) assessing the functional form for the estimating equations, (c) using a simultaneous estimation procedure to measure the regression coefficients, (d) examining the validity of the assumptions of the error terms and re-estimating when advisable, and (e) diagnostic testing of the results by statistical techniques. Tasks (a) and (c) are new, but tasks (b), (d), and (e) have been examined in previous chapters. We should note, however, that these tasks are all interrelated and are not totally separable. Finally, economic theory has an increased role.

6.3   Benefits and Limitations of Econometric Models for Forecasting

One of the foremost benefits of econometric models is that they provide the forecaster with an explicit system in which economic information can be assembled and weighed in a systematic and meaningful manner. Assembling, collecting, and presenting data permits the forecaster to communicate findings easily, and clarifies for the forecast users the types of information required. Also, the influence or weight of the information as measured by the regression coefficients is formally presented in the model. Thus if the forecast user does not agree with the measured coefficients, he/she could substitute different values for the coefficients and examine the consequences. In this manner, various scenarios can be examined through this use of econometric models as a simulation process.

Economic relationships in the model are explicit and objective. Forecasters can use alternative assumptions concerning variables which are exogenous to the model. In the forecasting model of example 6.1, we can examine the effects of a proposed change in personal income taxes on sales. Although the prediction may not be accurate, the effects of a change in an exogenous variable can be assessed.

Econometric models provide forecasters with a detailed account of their predictions. It is possible to trace and reproduce the causes of both successful and inaccurate forecasts when the assumptions concerning exogenous variables and the model solution are known. When errors are studied, improvements in future forecasts can be made by adjusting the model appropriately. However, without studying past mistakes, the forecaster will not be able to change and alter models based on discredited hypotheses.

Forecasting is not the only use of econometric models. Intelligent use of such models includes the feature that they lend themselves to improving our understanding of economic relationships. They permit us to verify and refine testable hypotheses concerning the theory of business behavior. These tests may permit the forecaster to find new and more refined hypotheses that may ultimately lead to a better understanding of the economic system and business fluctuations for the purposes of forecasting.

Although large-scale econometric models are here to stay, the forecaster must recognize their limitations. The basic problem is that the traditional methods of regression require us to use dependent variables from some equations as independent variables in other parts of a multidimensional equation system. Regression analysis of experimental data indicates that bias would result if we used the dependent variable from the experimental regression as an independent variable in a second regression. Random errors from the dependent variable of the first experimental regression would cause its behavior in the second regression to be different from that of a controlled variable. A controlled variable would have values fixed by the experimenter and would not contain random elements.

Multicollinearity, a serious problem in a single time series equation, is even more acute when dealing with an econometric model. When many structural coefficients between aggregated variables in a model are consistently estimated, these problems are multiplied and expanded.

In many cases large-scale and heavily aggregated models do not incorporate readily detailed information concerning developments within individual sectors of the economy. For example, leading economic statisticians in a particular agency may have at their disposal an elaborate network of economic and statistical information concerning a particular sector of the economy. However, the econometric model may contain only one simple (often extrapolative) equation representing that sector. Thus the model ignores a large amount of important evidence concerning that sector of the economy.

Finally, econometric models cannot be left alone to run without continuous monitoring of the results. Periodic changes are necessary and require skilled specialists who are knowledgeable and involved with the very skillful application of econometrics. Medium- and small-size firms do not employ people capable of understanding and implementing econometric forecasts. Thus econometric consulting firms, such as Chase Econometrics, Data Resources Inc, Wharton Econometrics, and the like, have been established to aid firms in their econometric forecasting.

6.4 Econometric Estimation Problem

A goal of estimation is to obtain unbiased estimators of population parameters. Furthermore, as the sample size becomes larger, the accuracy of the estimators must increase also. If the sample size is equal to a complete count of the sampling frame for the population, the estimators would be the same as the value for the population parameters.

Estimators of the parameters $b_0, b_1, b_2,...,b_m$ of a multiple regression can be shown to be unbiased under suitable conditions. In multi-equation econometric models, this is not the case. This can be illustrated by re-examining equations (6.9) and (6.11). Recall

$$C_t = b_{01} + b_1 Y_t + e_1$$

and

$$Y_t = C_t + I_t + G_t$$

where all the terms are defined in example 6.1.

The independent variable Y_t of equation (6.9) is determined partly by the level of consumption C_t, which is an endogenous variable, and partly by the exogenous variables I_t and G_t. These variables can now be classified in a system of equations as either endogenous (C_t, Y_t) or exogenous (I_t, G_t). A problem arises because the endogenous variables are related to each other in equation (6.9). Hence the relation causes dependence between the dependent variable C_t and the error term e_{1t} which appears as a dependence among successive values of e_{1t}. Thus the assumption that the error term is independent is violated.

To examine this closely, we substitute equation (6.11) into equation (6.9) as follows:

$$C_t = b_0 + b_1(C_t + I_t + G_t) + e_{1t}$$

$$C_t - b_1 C_t = C_t(1 - b_1) = a_1 + b_1(I_t + G_t) + e_{1t} \tag{6.14}$$

$$C_t = \frac{b_{01}}{1 - b_1} + \frac{b_1 I_t}{1 - b_1} + \frac{b_1 G_t}{1 - b_1} + \frac{e_{1t}}{1 - b_1}$$

By substituting,

$$b_0 = \frac{b_{01}}{1 - b_1} \quad \text{and} \quad b = \frac{1}{1 - b_1}$$

we have

$$Y_t = b_0 + b(I_t + G_t) + \frac{e_{1t}}{1 - b_1} \tag{6.15}$$

Equation (6.15) implies the existence of a relation between the dependent variable C_t and the error term e_{1t}. The result is a biased estimation of the coefficients b_0 and b in (6.15) as well as biased coefficients for b_{01} and b_1 in equation (6.9). Bias exists for both small and large samples, and can be predicted if we are willing to assume that the population variance is known. Thus the method of least squares (or ordinary least squares (OLS) cannot generally be used reliably to forecast for a simultaneous equation system.

6.5   Econometric Estimation Procedures

To avoid simultaneous equation bias, a number of statistical estimation procedures were developed to reduce and eliminate this bias. Relative advantages and disadvantages of these methods depend on the sample studied and the time period covered. Our purpose in this section is not to debate the issues but only to provide a short description of several important ones. Furthermore, one or more of these procedures are available on most computer software systems, such as TROLL, SPSS, SAS, TSP, and BMDP, and on other software written for special purpose situations.

Full information maximum likelihood (FIML) utilizes a concept called maximum likelihood. This concept, which is a highly complex mathematical process, results in estimators obtained by minimizing the determinant of the covariance matrix associated with the residuals of the reduced form of the equation system.[4] The system is also referred to as least generalized residual variance (LGRV) and is quite complex both theoretically and computationally. Hence, we shall not pursue this method further.

The method of *limited information maximum likelihood* (LIML) is similar to FIML. This method recognizes only a portion of the interdependence by estimating the parameters for each equation one at a time but only with respect to the exogenous variables. By successive estimation, the estimated values are substituted into the equation being estimated. Thus, in a limited way, LIML accounts for the existing dependence among the variables.

The method of *indirect least squares* (ILS) is at the opposite extreme of computational difficulty and theoretical rigor. Although similar to OLS, ILS is applied to the reduced form of the equation system. The reduced form of an econometric model is obtained by successive substitutions of the original equations until all endogenous variables are expressed as functions of only the exogenous variables. To illustrate this technique, let us return to equations (6.9) and (6.11) of example 6.1. Equation (6.9) was changed into equation (6.14) which is the reduced form:

$$C_t = \frac{b_{01}}{1 - b_1} + \frac{b_1}{1 - b_1} I_t + \frac{b_1}{1 - b_1} G_t + \frac{e_{1t}}{1 - b_1}$$

since the dependent variable C_t is in terms of the exogenous independent variables I_t and G_t. Equation (6.11) can also be expressed in a reduced form by substituting (6.9) into (6.11):

$$Y_t = b_{01} + b_1 Y_t + I_t + G_t + e_{1t}$$

$$Y_t(1 - b_1) = b_{01} + I_t + G_t + e_{1t}$$

---

4   See Goldberger (1964) or Kmenta (1986) for a discussion of this and other estimation techniques.

$$Y_t = \frac{b_{01}}{1 - b_1} + \frac{1}{1 - b_1}(I_t + G_t) + \frac{e_{1t}}{1 - b_1} \tag{6.16}$$

Equations (6.14) and (6.16) are the reduced forms of equations (6.9) and (6.11). By substituting

$$b_0 = \frac{b_{01}}{1 - b_1} \qquad b = \frac{b_1}{1 - b_1} \qquad c = \frac{1}{1 - b_1}$$

in (6.14) and (6.16), the following are obtained:

$$C_t = b_0 + b(I_t + G_t) + \frac{e_{1t}}{1 - b_1} \tag{6.17}$$

$$Y_t = b_0 + c(I_t + G_t) + \frac{e_{1t}}{1 - b_1} \tag{6.18}$$

Equations (6.17) and (6.18) can now be solved by OLS since variables I_t and G_t are exogenous. The resulting estimators of coefficients b and c are unbiased and consistent as the sample size increases. However, the values of b_0 and b_1, which are functions of b_0 and b, are biased but not inconsistent. Although the methods of ILS are relatively simple, its computational complexities have led most econometricians and forecasters to use alternative procedures.

The *two-stage least squares* (2SLS) method combines some of the advantages and limitations of both FIML and ILS. The procedure is practical, the estimators are consistent, and the bias is small for larger sample sizes. The first step is to choose one of the endogenous variables as the independent variable. In the previous model Y is the independent variable and we would try to eliminate the dependence of C on e. This is accomplished by applying OLS to the reduced form of equation (6.18) to estimate the coefficients b_0 and c. The results are, in turn, substituted into the original equation (6.9) as follows:

$$C_t = b_{01} + b_1 Y_t + e_{1t} \tag{6.19}$$

$$Y_t = b_0 + c(I_t + G_t) \tag{6.20}$$

Substituting (6.20) into (6.19) yields

$$C_t = b_{01} + b_1 a + b_1 c(I_t + G_t) + e_{1t}$$

or

$$C_t = b_{03} + b_3(I_t + G_t) + e_t \tag{6.21}$$

where

$$b_{03} = b_{01} + b_1 b_0$$

$$b_3 = b_1 c$$

The equation (6.21) contains exogenous variables and C_t is not related to the error term e_t. Therefore the procedure results in both unbiased and consistent estimators. One important disadvantage of 2SLS is that it ignores the full extent of interdependence among the various equations. This occurs because 2SLS is a sequential estimation procedure resulting in a loss of some of the dependence.

An extension of 2SLS is three-stage least squares (3SLS) which in most cases results in more efficient estimators. Although the method accounts for the interdependence more fully and for large samples results in more asymptotically efficient estimators, it is not used as extensively as 2SLS. 3SLS is computationally far more difficult requiring more code in computer programs and greater use of computer memory at higher costs.

6.6 The Specification Problem

One of the limiting problems associated with all regression-based procedures is that the omission of an important explanatory variable will result in greater forecast error. In an econometric model, nonrandom error results from the misspecification of an equation. The error is magnified in econometric models because all equations are affected when an important variable is missing from one equation. Furthermore, autocorrelation of the error terms results and there is little indication of the source of this problem. Finally, since the econometric model contains many equations, there is a greater likelihood that misspecification will occur.

Exogenous variables are required in the above estimation procedures and the choice of such variables is not without problems. Forecasters will choose those exogenous variables which are not determined within the system and these choices may often be arbitrary. For example, in the econometric model of example 6.1, government purchases of goods G_t was an exogenous variable. In a more detailed model of the economy, the level of G_t may be influenced by changes in aggregate economic conditions as measured by GNP. The government purchases variable is thus endogenous, and other variables such as tax rates or monetary policy should be treated as exogenous.

Additionally, a requirement of econometrics is that one equation is necessary for each endogenous variable specified in the model. If this is not done, the model is underspecified and at least one endogenous variable must be treated as exogenous to facilitate the estimation process. However, when there are more endogenous variables than equations in the system, the model is said to be overspecified. Such overspecification can lead to other errors of estimation and reduce the significance of the parameters estimated in the simultaneous equation system. All this is referred to as the *specification problem*.

6.7 The Identification Problem

Related to the problem of specification and the choice of endogenous and exogenous variables for multi-equation models is the problem of identification. To see what this problem is, let us return to the model of equations (6.1) and (6.2):

$$q = b_{01} + b_1 p + e$$

$$q = b_{02} + b_2 p + u$$

Equation (6.1) is the demand relation and (6.2) is the supply relation, where q is the quantity demanded or supplied, p is the price, and e and u are error terms. When data are collected from a sample, the observed values are the combined results of both equations and do not represent observations about either equation taken separately. Pairs of (p,q) values are the points of intersection (or equilibrium) of the supply–demand schedules since they are the only points recorded. In figure 6.1(a) the supply relation is fixed and the demand relation is shifting. Similarly, in figure 6.1(b) the demand relation is fixed and the supply relation is shifting. Thus, alternative methods for identifying supply and demand relations separately must be developed, and this is known as the *identification problem*.

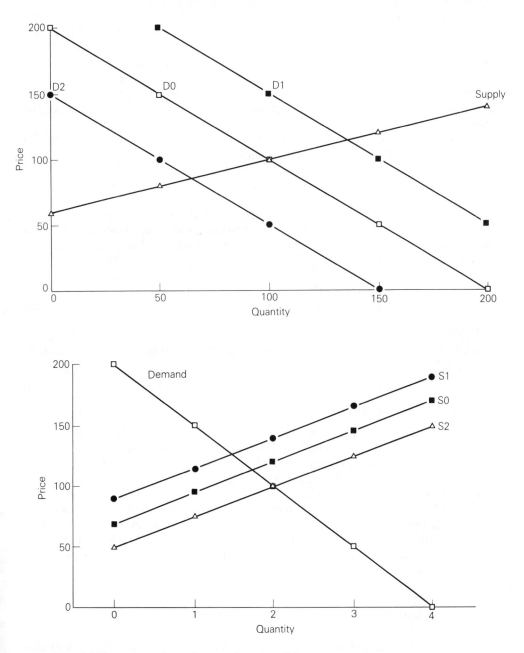

FIGURE 6.1 (a) Movement along the supply curve; (b) movement along the demand curve

One method is to identify, through a market experiment, where there are one or more explanatory variables. In a retail experiment, we could vary the price p of a product in a number of stores according to a carefully planned experimental design. The effects of differences in incomes among the customers of each retail enterprise would also have to be accounted for. Estimates of the demand relation as a regression of per capita quantities purchased by customers upon the predetermined retail prices would be obtained. The supply relation of producers (or sellers) would simply not be relevant for this type of controlled experiment.

To estimate the supply relation, another controlled experiment would be performed. The second experiment would concern decisions by producers. These decisions would involve changes in production levels for different prices.

In both experiments the supply and demand relations would be estimated independently. There would be no way for customers to influence the observations made in the supply experiments and producers would not be able to influence the observations in the demand experiment.

An alternative to the controlled experiment is the method of *reduced forms*. To consider this method, study the next example.

Example 6.2

In a study to show that common stocks do not perform as well as bonds during periods of inflation, a simultaneous equation model is specified. Structural equations include returns to bonds R_b and returns to common stocks R_s. These are endogenous variables. The two structural relations are

$$R_b = b_{01} + b_1 R_s + b_2 I + e_1 \qquad (6.22)$$

$$R_s = b_{02} + b_3 R_b + b_4 E + e_2 \qquad (6.23)$$

where I is interest rate and E is earnings.

We can solve the above equations to estimate the interdependence of R_b and R_s simultaneously to find

$$R_b = b_{03} + b_5 E + b_6 I + e_3 \qquad (6.24)$$

$$R_s = b_{04} + b_7 E + b_8 I + e_4 \qquad (6.25)$$

These equations are called the *reduced-form equations* of the model. These equations expressly show how the endogenous variables (R_s, R_b) are jointly dependent on the exogenous variables (E, I) and the error terms of the system. By applying the methods of 2SLS, the simultaneous equations can be solved minimizing the simultaneous equation bias.

As with the specification problem, the identification problem is both well documented and solvable. Neither problem is as serious as estimation problems; however, the problems can be costly to solve. These problems coupled with those of obtaining reliable sample data are the greatest obstacles to the development and implementation of econometric models.

6.8   An Application of Econometric Models

One of the great difficulties in judging the suitability of firm-specific econometric models for forecasting is that they are proprietary and details of the model are not publicly available. However, there are some publicly available applications (generally supported by research funds from agencies of the US Government). One very good example was developed for the Social Security Administration (Hambor, 1979).

Example 6.3

An econometric model is developed to provide a framework for analysis and prediction of the short-term behavior of the OASDI (Old Age, Survivors, and Dependents Insurance – Social Security Insurance) system. Annual time series data are employed to specify and estimate the parameters of a multi-equation– simultaneous system econometric model of the benefit and contribution components of the OASDI system. The proposed structural specifications are confirmed by the observed time series data. One particular result is that some evidence indicates "that labor market conditions and benefit payments (per beneficiary) relative to the wage rate are important factors in determining both retirement and disability beneficiary status".

The general form of the model consists of three estimating equations with dependent variables: (a) the number of awards to new beneficiaries, (b) average benefit award, and (c) the total benefit payments from a given trust fund. Data were collected over an eight year period and subjected to a one-year-ahead test to assess forecast accuracy. Although one predictive observation is not sufficient to assess a model's forecast accuracy, it does provide some evidence as to how the model should be updated in the future.

Table 6.1 contains data for 19 of the endogenous variables in the OASDI model. Although the variables are not identified here, they are important measures of the impact of economic variables on the OASDI sector.

Columns 2 and 3 are actual and predicted values for these 19 endogenous variables. Column 4 is the error or difference between columns 2 and 3. Column 5 reports the forecast error E_n when the predicted values are obtained from a solution which sets all independent variables equal to their actual values. This solution is called a null solution. The null solution values are equal to the values in column 3 if there are no endogenous independent variables determining that particular variable. When column 3 and the null solution are the same, columns 4 and 5 are the same.

Column 6 reports the estimated standard error of regression σ_R, where relevant. Finally, column 7 reports the percentage error $\%E$, that is, the error in column 4 as the absolute percentage value of the actual values in column 2.

One method of assessing the forecast accuracy is to compare the percentage error with the standard error of regression. Thirteen of the nineteen values of $\%E$ are less than 2 percent and nine are less than 1 percent. Thirteen absolute values are less than twice the standard error or regression ($2\sigma_R$) and six values are less than σ_R. Sixteen of the nineteen values of E_n in column 5 are less than $2\sigma_R$ and seven are less than 1 standard error of regression.

Although the above analysis is not conclusive, it appears that for most variables the forecasts are relatively accurate. Stated differently, if we are willing to accept forecasts that are within two standard errors of the actual value, the econometric model will forecast accurately most of the time. Predictions within two standard errors indicate that we are willing to take about a 5 percent chance of the forecast being in error.

TABLE 6.1 Actual and predicted results, errors, standard errors, and percentage error for econometric model

(1) Variable	(2) A	(3) P	(4) E = A − P	(5) E_n	(6) σ_R	(7) %E
DB62 (million)	0.092	0.152	−0.060	−0.049	0.027	65.2
DB65 (million)	0.537	0.529	0.008	−0.008	0.030	1.5
TR (million)	0.932	0.986	−0.054	−0.054	0.030	5.8
CR (million)	0.149	0.149	0	0	0.003	0
ABA$_R$ ($/mo.)	205.9	203.7	2.20	2.20	1.57	1.1
VOAS ($ billion)	58.51	58.88	0.370	0.040	0.207	0.6
U65 (%)	5.3	4.9	0.4	0.4	0.26	7.5
U604 (%)	4.7	5.15	−0.45	−0.45	0.40	9.6
ND (million)	0.592	0.587	0.005	0	0.014	0.8
ND (million)	0.592	0.566	0.026	0.023	0.012	4.4
ABA$_D$ ($/mo.)	233.6	234.6	−1.00	−1.00	1.36	0.4
VD ($ billion)	8.414	8.330	0.084	0.084	0.049	1.0
VD ($ billion)	8.414	8.246	0.168	0.073	0.049	2.0
U25 (%)	6.1	5.8	0.3	0.3	0.060	4.9
WS ($ billion)	801.6	800.9	0.7	0.6	0.460	0.1
TESL ($ billion)	31.61	31.87	−0.260	−0.210	0.097	0.8
TSL ($ billion)	4.294	4.235	0.059	0.059	0.012	1.2
TLSE ($ billion)	3.405	3.414	−0.009	−0.009	0.018	0.3
TSE ($ billion)	3.335	3.335	0	0.001	−0.021	0

Source: Hambor (1979, p. 16).

In addition to the ability to forecast, econometric models can be used to perform extensive analysis relevant to the issues of business and managerial decision-making. For example, in the case of the OASDI model, there may be developments in environmental economic factors or changes in social security laws which will affect the beneficiary status or size of benefits received by current and future beneficiaries. Such changes can be incorporated into the model and tested in terms of the sensitivity of the model to these changes. This last use adds substantially to the benefits associated with building econometric models.

6.9 How Does an Econometric Model Fit into the Practice of Forecasting?

In the previous section, an illustration of a microeconometric model was described. The model of the OASDI sector permits one to forecast a large number of endogenous variables including beneficiary status and the average benefit value per beneficiary. However, the development of sector- or firm-specific econometric models have been found to be too complex and too costly for all but the largest of firms or organizations.

In example 6.1, one method for incorporating an econometric model into a firm's forecast was suggested. This suggestion is based on the notion that business managers are better educated than in the past. Specifically, this can be attributed to a growth in the number of personnel trained in statistics and the increased power and distribution of computers. At present most econometric work is carried out by economic statisticians in government and at large universities. Also, there has been a rapid growth in the number of econometric consulting firms. These econometric consultants permit a firm to link their decision-making and forecasting to the simultaneous equation models built by the consultant. Thus econometric forecasting can be a process whereby a firm links its own regression-based forecast to the explanatory variables estimated by the econometric model of the forecaster consultant.

In this manner, the econometric model expresses the relationship between what a firm may wish to forecast and a variety of economic indicators estimated by the consultant. These indicators may include such variables as disposable personal income, business capital spending, interest rates, and money supply, among others. The linkage is often expressed by a second model at the firm-specific level which may provide smoothed estimates of monthly sales by product or division and forecast seasonal factors if desirable. Finally, a third level of forecasting based on a model expressing a relationship between such variables as company sales and advertising and promotional policies could be developed. Thus the impact of advertising and promotional policies could be assessed in an intelligent manner.

6.10   The Econometric Forecasting Industry

In the past 25 years, a new industry, econometric forecasting, has grown from infancy to an industry having gross revenues in excess of $100 million. The econometric model-building firms include Data Resources Inc. (DRI), Chase Econometrics (CE), Wharton Econometrics (WE), and the Kent Economic and Development Institute (KEDI). DRI, started by Professor Otto Eckstein (of Harvard University and formerly of the President's Council of Economic Advisors) and later purchased by McGraw-Hill Inc, is by far the largest of these firms. All these firms, and others, have grown substantially.

Services provided by these firms and bureaus include the following:

1 analysis of structural relationships among economic variables to see how they are related to each other;
2 production of forecasts of general economic and business activity (macroeconomic forecasts);
3 production of forecasts of firm-, industry-, or sector-specific economic and business variables (microeconomic forecasts);
4 evaluation of the economic and financial impact of changes in federal fiscal and monetary policy;
5 by sensitivity analysis and simulations, development of econometric models to determine the effects of different policy scenarios on macroeconomic variables.

A comparison of the salient features of the econometric models produced by the four firms mentioned above is presented in table 6.2. The number of simultaneous equations included in the model varies from 455 (CE) to about 22 500 (KEDI). The number of macroeconomic variables forecast varies from 700 (CE) to about 10 000 (WE). All the econometric models have a database consisting of survey data (primary sources) and government sources (secondary sources).

TABLE 6.2   Characteristics of four econometric models

Model	DRI	CE	WE	KEDI
Number of equations used	1000+	455	669	22 500
Number of macroeconomic variables forecasted	1000	700	10 000	1714
Data base	Survey and gov't sources	Survey and gov't sources	Survey and gov't sources	Survey and gov't sources
Classification of forecasts	Sectors and two-digit industries	Sectors and two-digit industries	Sectors and two-digit industries	Sectors and two-digit industries
Approximate weights given to forecasting methods (%)				
1 Econometric model	55	70	60	60
2 Judgment	30	20	30	20
3 Time series	10	5	–	10
4 Current data analysis	5	5	10	–
5 Interaction among variables	–	–	–	10

Sources:: Lee (1978, p. 2), Chen (1982, p. 32).

The forecasts for each of the four models are for sectors and two-digit industries. Lead times range from two to eight years ahead to 20 years ahead. All the service release their forecasts on a monthly basis. The techniques used to forecast differ among the service bureaus since the econometric models alone are not adequate for producing forecasts. The econometric model makes up about 55–70 percent of the forecast analysis. Judgment (to be considered in chapter 10) makes up about 20–30 percent of the analysis. Time series analysis (to be considered in chapters 7, 8, and 9) make up 5–10 percent of the analysis. Current data analysis makes up 5–10 percent of the analysis, and, finally, in one model 10 percent of the forecast analysis is the interaction among variables.

How well do econometric models perform? There is no simple answer to this question since a large number of economic variables are forecast. In one large study (McNees, 1981, pp. 5–21), 13 econometric models of private and nonprofit econometric forecasting services were evaluated. The overall performance was evaluated by focusing on 15 variables and considering the data used to measure errors and alternatives for summarizing them. In turn, the study explained why a definitive ranking of the forecasters is so difficult.

Users of econometric forecasts would usually like to know whose current forecast will be most accurate. Statistically, there is no rigorous way to determine whether past differences in forecasting accuracy are significant. Since past forecast errors for a particular economic variable are likely to be correlated with their own past values, with errors for other variables, and with the errors of other forecasters, it is not reasonable to try to draw rigorous inferences about the rankings of the forecasters' past performance.

The forecasters' past performance could be ranked from best to worst if all forecast users had well-known, precise, and identical interests in terms of forecast variables and time horizons. Unfortunately, forecast users have very different interests. Business managers are often interested in a two- or three-year time horizon in capital acquisition problems, whereas those involved in financial markets are interested in very short-term horizons. A solution to this dilemma is to focus on a single variable and one time horizon. Thus no forecast evaluator can state which forecaster is best but can only evaluate a single variable for one time horizon.

Even if evaluation focuses on a single variable and horizon, data for econometric forecasters are not entirely comparable. Gaps exist in the forecasts and data are not complete because some forecasters do not issue a forecast in each quarter or include all horizons in the forecast sets. In addition, the comparison is difficult because forecasters issue their forecasts on different dates within each quarter and also have access to different amounts of information. Hence there is no simple clear-cut way of stating who is the best econometric forecaster. Some forecasters are clearly superior in forecasting some variables but not others.

Thus, at the present time it is not possible to state definitively which econometric forecasting service will perform best. For forecast users, the choice of an econometric forecaster is, therefore, not a simple one.

6.11   Measuring the Elasticity of Demand (Optional Topic)

One of the important applications of econometrics or statistical science applied to economics is the measurement of the effectiveness of business policy. To examine effectiveness, one must define what constitutes the utility of actions of firms. For example, what is the optimal amount of money that a firm should spend for advertising a product or service? It is through econometric measurement that one can answer this or similar questions.

There is a wide-ranging and rich literature concerning the importance of demand theory. Some interesting aspects of this theory with respect to the importance of advertising in maximizing a firm's profits was set forth by Dorfman and Steiner (1954) and Ward (1975). To understand this theory requires us to review microeconomic concepts such as the *demand function*. For example, the demand Y for a product is associated with variables for price X_1, price of a competitive good X_2, consumer income X_3, and advertising expenditures X_4. The demand function could include other variables, but for the moment this will suffice for our consideration.

The *demand curve* is that part of the demand function above which expresses the relation between the price charged for the product and the quantity demanded when the effects of all other predictor variables are held constant. Knowledge of the distinction between movement along the demand curve (figure 6.1(b)) and a change in the demand function (figure 6.1(b)) is imperative in understanding the meaning of elasticity. Furthermore, knowledge of the effect of changing prices on demand is essential in establishing or altering price policy.

Elasticity measures the responsiveness of a percentage change in quantity demanded with respect to a percentage change in price with all other factors (variables) held constant. Elasticity can be defined in terms of point or arc elasticity. For arc elasticity

$$E = \frac{\text{change in } Y/\overline{Y}}{\text{change } X_i/\overline{X}_i}$$

$$= \frac{\Delta Y/\overline{Y}}{\Delta X/\overline{X}_i}$$

$$= \frac{\Delta Y}{\Delta X_i} \frac{\overline{X}_i}{\overline{Y}} \qquad (6.26)$$

where Y is the quantity demanded and X is any variable such as price. Arc elasticity measures responsiveness over a range of values of X_i. *Point elasticity* is defined as the responsiveness of quantity demanded at a particular value (point) for X_i, which is given by the partial derivative with respect to the predictor variable multiplied by the ratio of the variable to the quantity demanded:[5]

$$E = \left(\begin{array}{c} \text{partial derivative} \\ \text{of } Y \text{ with respect to } X_i \end{array} \right) \frac{X_i}{Y} \qquad (6.27)$$

Example 6.4

A manufacturing firm estimated its demand function for one of its product lines to be

$$Y = -10\ 000X_1 + 2000X_2 + 0.025X_3 + 3\ 000\ 000X_4 + 0.10X_5$$

The above demand function relates quantity demanded to the associated variables price X_1, consumer incomes X_2, population X_3, index of credit terms X_4, and advertising expenditures X_5. This demand relationship can be used to demonstrate the point elasticity of demand. The derivative of quantity demanded with respect to advertising is 0.10, if all other variables are held constant. Furthermore, if the advertising expenditure X is \$20 million and the quantity demanded Y is 100 million units, then the point elasticity is

$$E = 0.10 \frac{20}{100} = 0.02$$

Thus a 1 percent change in advertising expenditure will result in a 2 percent change in product sold.

In a similar manner, management can determine the elasticity of the other factors associated with quantity demanded. For example, what is the price elasticity of demand? To answer this, management finds the derivative with respect to price to be $-10\ 000$. If $X = \$15\ 000$ and $Y = 100$ million units, then elasticity is

$$E = -10\ 000 \frac{15\ 000}{100\ 000\ 000} = -0.10$$

Thus a 1 percent change in price will result in a 10 percent change in quantity demanded. Management should note that the elasticity is negative in this instance, indicating that a decrease in price will result in an increase in quantity demanded.

---

5   In calculus notation this equation is written $E = (\partial Y/\partial X_i)(X_i/Y)$.

Elasticities are usually quoted in absolute terms. Thus the sign of the elasticity coefficient is usually ignored. However, managers and forecasters should always be aware of the direction of the change that is predicted.

Finally, the relationship between price elasticity (quoted in absolute terms) and revenue should be noted. If elasticity is greater than unity in absolute terms ($E>1$), then demand is said to be elastic. Total revenue will decline with price increases and rise with price decreases. If elasticity equals unity in absolute terms ($E = 1$), demand is said to be unitary. Total revenue is unaffected by changes in price. If elasticity is less that the absolute value of unity ($E<1$), total revenue rises with price increases and declines with price decreases. If $E = 0$, then demand is perfectly inelastic and no change in price will be associated with a change in quantity demanded. If $E = -\infty$, then demand is perfectly elastic and there is a market-determined price for all units of the product sold by the firm. This last case occurs under the limiting condition of pure and perfect competition.

The techniques of econometric estimation are employed to estimate elasticities. Information concerning demand for product and those factors that are associated with demand are carried out to find a useful econometric relationship. Consumer interviews or surveys using scientific sampling techniques are often carried out. Their purpose is to obtain information by questioning potential customers. However, such surveys often provide poor results because consumers are unwilling or incapable of giving accurate answers to hypothetical or anticipatory questions concerning key economic variables such as price. For short-term demand and sales forecasting, consumer attitudes and expectations about the future frequently make the difference between an accurate estimate and a large forecasting error. Market studies often try to identify important economic variables in the demand function. However, difficulties arise when certain key variables are uncontrollable and make the results of these studies less than reliable.

Regression-based techniques usually provide the most reliable methods of estimating elasticities and predicting demand. As noted in previous chapters, regression requires (a) the specification of variables for the predictive model, (b) the specification of the functional form of the relationship, and (c) obtaining data for model building. By specification, we refer to the problems noted earlier in this chapter and those discussed in chapter 5. However, we should always take care in the specification stage to try to understand completely the nature of the demand for the product or service being studied. Misspecification is a key problem in all econometric studies of demand and should be kept to a minimum.

Once the variables are specified, a decision must be made on the functional form of the relationship. The most common form is the multiple linear relationship discussed previously. Linear relations have a great deal of appeal in empirical work because many demand relationships are in fact approximately linear over the range for which the data are collected. In addition, the method of least squares provides a useful technique for estimating these relationships and interpreting the coefficients to find the elasticities.

A second useful functional form is to specify a multiplicative demand relationship. The *multiplicative form* is written as follows:

$$\hat{Y} = b_0 X_1^{b_1} X_2^{b_2} \tag{6.28}$$

where $\hat{Y}$ is the quantity demanded, X_1 and X_2 are independent variables, and b_0, b_1, and b_2 are the estimated parameters of the model. This model is popular because it is frequently the most logical form for the demand relationship. Its intuitive appeal emanates from the fact that the marginal effects of each independent variable on demand are not constant, but usually depend on the value of the variable as well as the values of all other variables in the model. For those who understand calculus, this is seen easily by finding and interpreting the partial derivative with respect to any variable in the demand model. Thus the marginal effect of a change in price on product demand, for example, depends on the level of income, advertising, and all the other independent variables. In addition, the elasticity of any factor in the model is equal to the exponent of the variable in the multiplicative demand model. The elasticity of price is simply equal to the value of b estimated by the multiplicative model and is therefore a constant value over the demand function. This *constant elasticity* relationship holds for all the variables in any multiplicative demand relationship.

The last consideration in measuring elasticities is to obtain data on price, credit terms, output-to-capacity ratios, advertising expenditures, incomes, and similar variables. Obtaining data for these items is not often easy nor is it likely to be available for public consumption when it is proprietary information kept by for-profit enterprises. Data on consumer attitudes toward product and service quality is often even more difficult to acquire. Data on consumer attitudes and expectations are usually acquired by scientific samples of human populations which can be expensive and, if not carried out properly, will err and lead to forecasts with huge errors. Nonscientific samples should always be avoided since they may introduce bias in the results. Furthermore, it is not even possible to measure the magnitude of the bias in nonscientific surveys.

Example 6.5

The manufacturer of a new piece of office equipment in the Detroit, Cleveland, and Chicago areas established a service plan for its most popular model. Any customer could purchase a one-year contract covering labor and parts to take effect at the end of the usual 90 day manufacturer warranty period.

The director of service marketing decided to evaluate sales of these contracts in order to estimate the utility of the service contracts with respect to sales volume in the various market areas served by the firm. The director treated the relationship between quantity demanded of the service contracts and contract premium and promotion expenses as a multiplicative model. Thus the least squares solution to the problem would be to estimate the model in the form

$$\hat{Y} = b_0 X_1^{b_1} X_2^{b_2}$$

To use least squares estimation, the data for the dependent variable Y, the number of one year contracts purchased, and the two predictor variables, i.e. the promotion expenses X_1 and the premium X_2 for the one year contract, must be obtained. To estimate the model the variables must be converted to natural logarithms:

$$\ln \hat{Y} = b_0 + b_1 \ln X_1 + b_n \ln X_2$$

After the conversion, the director used a computer program (SAS) for the estimation and obtained the results shown in figure 6.2. The independent variables are given in natural logarithms. The parameter estimates are equal to the point elasticities which are constant. The independent variables are denoted LX1 (logarithm of promotion expenses) and LX2 (logarithm of the premium for one year contracts).

```
DEP VARIABLE: LY         ONE-YEAR CONTRACTS PURCHASED
                             ANALYSIS OF VARIANCE

                        SUM OF          MEAN
SOURCE          DF      SQUARES         SQUARE      F VALUE        PROB>F

MODEL           2     0.002953644    0.001476822    12.391        0.0020
ERROR          10     0.001191834    0.0001191834
C TOTAL        12     0.004145478

          ROOT MSE      0.01091712      R-SQUARE      0.7125
          DEP MEAN      9.210951        ADJ R-SQ      0.6550
             C.V.       0.1185232

                          PARAMETER ESTIMATES

                        PARAMETER        STANDARD       T FOR HO:
VARIABLE        DF       ESTIMATE          ERROR       PARAMETER=0

INTERCEP        1       7.294419        0.5596109       13.035
LX1             1       0.1390282       0.05351421       2.598
LX2             1       0.0771621       0.03380768       2.282

                                        VARIABLE
VARIABLE        DF      PROB > |T|        LABEL

INTERCEP        1        0.0001        INTERCEPT
LX1             1        0.0266        PROMOTION EXPENSES
LX2             1        0.0456        PREMIUM FOR 1-YEAR CONTRACT
```

FIGURE 6.2 Multiplicative model for estimating elasticities. Data all in natural logarithms. Output of PROC REG

Since the parameter estimates are shown to have t statistics large enough to reject the hypothesis that the parameter equals zero (at levels less than 0.05), the equation can be written out as follows:

$$\ln \hat{Y} = 7.294 + 0.139 \ln X_1 + 0.077 \ln X_2$$

The equation can then be converted to multiplicative form as follows:

$$\hat{Y} = 7.294 X_1^{0.139} X_2^{0.077}$$

Thus the exponent for the variable X for promotions expenses is the constant elasticity value 0.139. A change of 1 percent in promotion expenses will lead to a change of 13.9 percent in the number of contracts purchased. Similarly, the constant elasticity of price is 0.077. Thus a change of 1 percent in the premium (price) of the contract will result in a 7.7 percent change in the contracts purchased.

In a similar manner, one can estimate multiple linear as well as multiplicative models to estimate the elasticity with respect to some associated variable. A word of caution concerning this technique should be noted. The problems associated with least squares estimation of multiple relationships cannot be ignored. A forecaster should always be aware of the common pitfalls associated with these techniques which have been discussed before.

6.12   Summary

Econometrics is the science of economic measurement which attempts to establish quantitative relationships between economic variables with the aid of the theory of statistics. Econometric models are systems of simultaneous equations linking economic variables with the purpose of forecasting and explaining economic behavior.

A jointly dependent variable is called an endogenous variable and a predetermined variable is called an exogenous variable. The theoretical scheme of the econometric model determines whether a variable is classified as exogenous or endogenous.

A complete system of simultaneous equations will contain as many equations as there are endogenous variables.

Structural equations show the relationship between variables on the grounds of an established or a new economic theory. Coefficients of these equations are called structural coefficients.

An econometric model provides the forecaster with an explicit system in which economic information can be assembled and weighed in a systematic and meaningful manner. Econometric predictions provide forecasters with a detailed account of their predictions. These models also enable testable hypotheses concerning the theory of business behavior to be verified and refined.

Limitations of econometric models include the multicollinearity of variables and the error associated with the simultaneous estimation of the model equations. Also, large-scale econometric models which are heavily aggregated do not readily incorporate detailed information concerning developments within individual sectors of the economy. Finally, these models need continuous monitoring to implement necessary periodic changes.

To avoid simultaneous equation bias, one or another of the following estimation techniques is employed: FIML, LIML, 2SLS or 3SLS, or ILS. 2SLS is the most commonly used technique.

Other problems associated with econometric model building are those of specification and identification.

Firms often employ econometric models by linking a sales forecast to one or more economic indicators produced by a consulting firm's proprietary econometric model. The linkage permits firms to employ large-scale models without having to build one themselves.

At the present time, there is no clear-cut and simple way of assessing the overall forecasting performance of the vast array of econometric forecasters.

Measurement of elasticities is a very useful application of econometric methods. Use of the multiplicative form for the demand relationship permits a forecaster to estimate easily the elasticities of each variable associated with demand for a product or service.

6.13 Exercises

1 The following firm-specific simultaneous model was developed for forecasting:

$$Y = a + bX + cZ + e_1$$

$$M = d + eX + fU + e_2$$

$$N = g + hZ + iY + e_3$$

(a) Which variables are endogenous?
(b) Which variables are exogenous?

(c) Explain how the simultaneous equations are interdependent.

2 The following econometric model for a firm was developed, based on accounting statement information (adapted from Elliot and Uphoff, 1972).

$$GM = NS\text{-}COGS \qquad\qquad I$$

$$TOTSE = MKT + ADV + MER \qquad II$$

$$GAIR = GM + GAIR1 + TIME \qquad III$$

$$OP = GM - TOTOTHER \qquad\qquad IV$$

$$TOTOTHER = TOTSELL + GAIR \qquad V$$

$$MS = COGS + TUS \qquad\qquad VI$$

For simplicity, the coefficients, constants and error terms are not included in the above system.

(a) Identify the exogenous variables.

(b) Identify the endogenous variables.

3 Consider the following simple two-equation model:

$$Y_1 = a_1 Y_2 + e_1$$

$$Y_2 = b_1 Y_1 + b_3 Z_1 + b_4 Z_2 + e_2$$

(a) If b_3 and b_4 equal zero, explain why the first equation is overidentified.

(b) Reduce the above two-equation models to a single equation to be estimated by ordinary least squares.

4 Suppose that we have a model of the following form:

$$Y_t = A_1 X_{1t} + A_2 X_{2t} + A_3 X_{1,t-1} + e_1$$

$$Y_t = b_1 X_{1t} + b_2 X_{2t} + b_3 X_{2,t-1} + e_2$$

$$Y_t = c_1 X_{1t} + c_2 X_{2t} + c_3 X_{3t} + e_3$$

where X_3 is exogenous, and Y, X_1, and X_2 are endogenous.

(a) Explain why OLS cannot be used to estimate the parameters of the above model.

(b) What solutions are open to the econometric investor?

5 An econometrician fits the following two-equation models to sample data:

$$I_t = a + bC_t + e$$

$$C_t = c + dI_{t-1} + fG_t + u$$

where I is investment at time t, C is consumption at time t, and G is government expenditure at time t. The coefficients are $a = 0.05$, $b = 0.82$, $c = 0.45$, $d = 0.25$, and $f = 0.60$. The errors e and u are assumed to be random with expected values equal to zero.

(a) If $I_0 = 600$ and $G_1 = 500$, forecast I_1 and C_1.

(b) If $G_2 = 540$, what is the forecast of C_2 and I_2?

(c) What are the endogenous and exogenous variables?

6 A company econometrician built the following model to relate firm revenues R from product sales with wages W paid to the sales and marketing professionals and disposable personal income Y:

$$R_t = 0.55 S_{t-1} + 0.25W + 0.03Y$$

$R^2 = 0.75 \qquad \text{DW} = 1.95$

$W = 100 + 0.30R + 0.015Y$

$R^2 = 0.80 \qquad \text{DW} = 0.80$

(a) The second equation of the model was criticized as being poorly specified. Why?

(b) How should the model be used to forecast revenues in the next period?

TABLE 6.3

Variable	E	S_E	$\%E$
x_1	0.05	0.045	40
x_2	0.25	0.125	25
x_3	0.30	0.40	5
x_4	0.75	0.375	3
x_5	0.01	0.02	7
x_6	0.05	0.03	2
x_7	0.06	0.04	4

7 Based on an econometric model, the analysis shown in table 6.3 was performed on the absolute forecast error E, the standard error of forecast S_E, and the error as an absolute percentage of the actual values $\%E$.

(a) How many of the absolute errors are within two standard errors of the actual values? How many are within one standard error?

(b) How many of the $\%E$ values are less than 5 percent?

(c) Comment on the quality of the forecasts.

8 The office equipment manufacturer in example 6.4 decided to offer a new two year contract for service on its new office equipment. Data were obtained on the premium X_3 for the two year contract. A new multiplicative model was estimated with the following results:

$$Y = 7.258X_1^{0.144}X_2^{0.078}X_3^{-0.005}$$

(a) Interpret the exponent for promotion expenses and state the meaning of the elasticity measured.

(b) Interpret the exponent for premiums on one year contracts and state the meaning of the elasticity measured.

(c) Interpret the exponent for premiums on two year contracts and state the meaning of the elasticity estimated.

9 In a famous study Ward (1975) presents data on the annual demand Y for processed grapefruit, the annual average price X_1, and the annual advertising expenses X_2. The data for the years studied are summarized in table 6.4.

(a) Use a multiple linear relationship to estimate the demand function.

(b) Interpret the estimated elasticities.

(c) Use the multiplicative form to estimate the demand relationship.

(d) Interpret the estimated elasticities.

TABLE 6.4

Observation	Y (million gallons)	X_1 ($ per gal.)	X_2 ($ million)
7	53.52	1.294	1.837
6	51.34	1.344	1.053
5	49.31	1.332	0.905
4	45.93	1.274	0.462
3	51.65	1.056	0.576
2	38.26	1.102	0.260
1	44.29	0.930	0.363

10 The information in table 6.5 is obtained on the price of the product, the quantity sold, and the cost of advertising.
   (a) Develop and estimate the multiplicative relationship between quantity sold on price and advertising.
   (b) Write out the model in multiplicative form.
   (c) Interpret the meaning of the exponents in terms of elasticities.

TABLE 6.5

Quantity (thousand)	Price ($)	Advertising ($ thousand)
3.7	8.7	22.5
5.4	8.1	32.7
7.4	7.45	39.7
8.0	6.95	42.8
11.3	6.1	47.5
13.1	5.5	53.8
15.0	4.9	59.7
13.2	5.45	53.9
17.6	4.8	60.1
19.4	4.0	65.5
17.5	4.7	59.0
20.5	4.2	65.4
22.1	3.9	67.5
18.5	4.3	60.5
22.5	3.8	67.3
24.3	3.6	72.4

References

Chen, T. P. (1982) A quick glance at four econometric models, *Journal of Business Forecasting, Methods and Systems*, 1 (5), 32.

Dorfman, R. and Steiner, P. O. (1954) Optimal advertising and optimal quality, *American Economic Review*, 44, 826–36.

Elliott, J. W. and Uphoff, H. L. (1972) Predicting the near term profit and loss statement with an econometric model: a feasibility study, *Journal of Accounting Research*, 10(2), Autumn, 259–74.

Goldberger, A. (1964) *Economic Theory*. New York: John Wiley.

Hambor, J. C. (1979) *An Econometric Model of OASDI*. Publication No. (SSA)-79-11776, USHEW/SSA/ORS, Washington, DC.

Kmenta, J. (1986) *Elements of Econometrics*. New York: Macmillan.

Lee, L. D. (1978) A comparison of econometric models. Joint Economic Committee, Congress of the United States, 95, 2. Washington, DC: US Government Printing Office, p. 2.

McNees, S. K. (1981) The recent record of thirteen forecasters, *New England Economic Review*, September–October, 5–21.

Ward, R. W. (1975) Revising the Dorfman–Steiner static advertising theorem: an application to the processed grapefruit industry, *American Journal of Agricultural Economics*, 57 (3).

Further Reading

Fogler, H., Russell, H. and Ganapathy, S. (1982) *Financial Econometrics*, Englewood Cliffs, NJ: Prentice-Hall.

Hambor, J. C. (1984) Econometric models and the study of the economic effects of social security, *Social Security Bulletin*, 47 (10), 3–8.

Intriligator, M. (1978) *Econometric Models, Techniques and Application*. Englewood Cliffs, NJ: Prentice-Hall.

Johnston, J. (1984) *Econometric Methods*. New York: McGraw-Hill.

McNees, S. K. (1985) Which forecast should you use, *New England Economic Review*, July–August, 36–42.

McNees, S. K. and Ries, J. (1983) The track record of macroeconomic forecasts, *New England Economic Review*, November–December, 5–18.

Pindyck, R. S. and Rubinfeld, D. (1976) *Econometric Models and Econometric Forecasts*. New York: McGraw–Hill.

Ramanathan, R. (1989) *Introductory Econometrics With Applications*. San Diego, CA: Harcourt Brace Jovanovich.

The ABC's of econometric forecasting, *Journal of Business Forecasting, Methods and Systems*, 1 (5), Fall 1982.

Appendix   Companies Performing Econometric Services

North America

A. Gary Shilling & Co., 111 Broadway, New York, NY 10006
Center for Economic Research, Chapman College, Orange, CA 92666
Chase Econometrics, 150 Monument Road, Bala Cynwyd, PA 19004
Data Resources Inc, 29 Hartwell Avenue, Lexington, MA 02173

Economic Forecasting, Georgia State University, Atlanta, GA 30303
Informetrica Ltd, PO Box 828, Station B, Ottawa, Ontario, Canada KIP 5P9
Kent Economics and Development Institute, Kent, Ohio 44242
Merrill Lynch Economics, 165 Broadway, New York, NY 10080
UCLA Business Forecasting, Los Angeles, CA 91435
US Department of Commerce, Bureau of Economic Analysis, Washington, DC
Wharton Econometric, 3624 Science Center, Philadelphia, PA 19104
Williams Trend Indicators, 6 Devon Drive, Orangeburg, NY 10962

United Kingdom, Taiwan, and France

Centre for Economic Forecasting, London Business School. Sussex Place, Regents
    Park, London, NW1 4SA, UK
Henley Centre for Forecasting, London, UK
Phillips & Drew, London, UK
Institute of Economics, Taipei, Taiwan, Republic of China 115
Centre d'Observation Economique de la Chambre de Commerce et d'Industrie de
    Paris, Paris, France 75008
Gama, 2 Rue de Rouen, Nanterre, France 92001

PART IV

Advanced Topics in Time Series Analysis

CHAPTER 7

Autocorrelation, Autoregressive Models, and Time Series Analysis

Objectives

In this chapter, we begin the study of advanced time series analysis. The focus of this analysis will be on the selection and identification of a forecasting model that best fits the underlying process that gives rise to the time series. By the end of the chapter you will be able to:

1 Understand the meaning of ARIMA models.
2 Understand the concept of an autoregressive model.
3 Be able to calculate autocorrelation and partial autocorrelation coefficients.
4 Recognize a nonstationary time series.
5 Use the method of differencing to convert a nonstationary to a stationary time series.
6 Recognize a seasonal time series.

Outline

Key Terms

- ARIMA modeling
- Autoregression
- Autoregressive model
- White noise series

- Stationary
- Nonstationary in the mean
- Nonstationary in the variance
- Trend in mean
- Trend in variance
- Order of homogeneity
- Autocorrelation coefficient
- First-order autocorrelation
- Second-order autocorrelation
- Sampling distribution of autocorrelations
- Backshift operator
- Partial autorrelation coefficient

7.1   Introduction

In this chapter and chapters 8 and 9, the focus will be on the identification and selection of a forecasting model based on the analysis of a time series of data. The model selected for forecasting will be the one that best fits the time series. Hence the purpose of this chapter is to introduce the reader to useful concepts in analyzing time series and identifying a model for forecasting. In addition, the reader will be exposed to a general class of models for forecasting time series.

In chapter 2, the models used for forecasting time series were the methods of moving averages and exponential smoothing. Moving averages were shown to be, in one sense, a special form of exponential smoothing. Exponential smoothing methods, however, could be considered an averaging process, since new forecasts are based on a weighted combination of actual values, past errors, and, for some models, past trends. To consider this point, recall that single exponential smoothing models are of the following form:

$$Y_{t+1} = Y_t + \alpha(X_t - Y_t) \tag{7.1}$$

where Y is the forecast and X is the actual value. If we substitute the previous period's forecast

$$Y_t = Y_{t-1} + \alpha(X_{t-1} - Y_{t-1}) \tag{7.2}$$

into (7.1) we have

$$Y_{t+1} = Y_{t-1} + \alpha(X_{t-1} - Y_{t-1}) + \alpha(X_t - Y_t) \tag{7.3}$$

The equation could be further expanded by substituting the expression for Y_{t-1}, $Y_{t-2},\ldots$. The rationale for making such mathematical expansions of (7.1) is clear. After an initial forecast is made, the new forecast becomes the weighted combination of the past error and the initial forecast. The final or resulting forecast Y_{t+1} is close to the real trend in the data because it is an average of negative and positive errors.

In chapter 3, methods of decomposing time series into systematic and nonsystematic (random) components were examined on the principle that one could forecast the recurring systematic patterns of a time series. These components, called seasonal, cyclical, trend, and sometimes trading-day patterns, could be predicted, and a forecaster, in turn, could recombine the components to arrive at a final forecast. Like smoothing methods, the classical decomposition methods presuppose that forecasts are a function of time alone.

Beginning in chapter 4, the methods of developing explanatory or causal methods of forecasting were initially presented. In chapter 4, the method of relating the variation in one dependent variable to an explanatory or independent variable was described. Continuing in chapter 5, the methods of relating one dependent variable to more than one independent variable were considered. These regression methods permit a forecast to relate the dependent variable of interest to those factors that may be associated with the variation in the dependent variable. Stated symbolically, the expression is written as

$$Y = b_0 + b_1X_1 + b_2X_2 + \ldots + b_kX_k \tag{7.4}$$

In chapter 6, the purpose was to present the more sophisticated approach of econometric models. These are multi-equation models which use methods of regression for solving forecasting problems and explain the variation in some endogenous variable(s) of interest.

The focus of this chapter will be on methods and principles of regression as applied directly to the study of time series. In essence, we study a combination of the methodologies and their concepts, emphasizing the *ARIMA modeling* approach.

The abbreviation ARIMA is for "autoregressive integrated moving average" model. Integrated (I) refers to "differencing" of the data series, which is explained in this chapter. The autoregression (AR), differencing (I) and moving-average (MA) portion make up the three numbers following ARIMA. All these terms will become clear as the various time series models are developed in chapters 7 and 8. Finally, MA models are not the same as the concept of "moving averages" discussed in chapter 2.

Equation (7.4) above is a regression relating a dependent variable, such as firm sales, shipments, or inventories, to a set of explanatory (independent) variables. If we define

$$X_1 = Y_{t-1}, \qquad X_2 = Y_{t-2}, \qquad \ldots, \qquad X_k = Y_{t-k}$$

then equation (7.4) becomes

$$Y_t = b_0 + b_1Y_{t-1} + b_2Y_{t-2} + \ldots + b_kY_{t-k} + e_t \tag{7.5}$$

Although equation (7.5) is still a regression, the right-hand side (RHS) variables are merely the values of the dependent variable in previous periods. These variables are time-lagged observations of the dependent variable and the regression of this form is called *autoregression* (AR). If we re-examine the definition of the exponential smoothing formula

$$Y_{t+1} = \alpha X_t + \alpha(1 - \alpha)X_{t-1} + \alpha(1 - \alpha)^2X_{t-2} + \ldots \tag{7.6}$$

we note that this and the autoregressive form are similar. Past values of the forecasts are weighted by the exponential weights α, $\alpha(1 - \alpha)$, $\alpha(1 - \alpha)^2$, etc. These weights take the place of the regression coefficients b_1, b_2,... of the autoregressive scheme.

Autoregressive models differ from other regression models with respect to the assumption of the independence of the error term. Since the independent variables are time-lagged values for the dependent variable the assumption of independent error terms is easily violated. Although the assumption of independent error terms is so easily violated, the problem of determining the appropriate number of past terms of Y to incorporate in (7.5) is not easy to solve.

In the remaining portions of this chapter, we shall study autoregressive models and the problems of estimation to assess their usefulness as a time series forecasting tool.

7.2 Characteristics of Time Series

In chapter 2, we considered a number of models that can be used to predict the future of a time series on the basis of its past behavior. These models were deterministic in that no reference was made to the sources or nature of the underlying randomness in the series. Essentially the models involve extrapolation techniques that have been standard techniques in business and economic forecasting. As we shall see, these techniques do not provide as much forecasting accuracy as the more modern stochastic time series models. Hence, one important question to ask is whether the time series is random.

A simple random model is one where the observation Y_t consists of two parts: these are the overall arithmetic mean μ and a random error component e_t which is independent from period to period (no autocorrelation):

$$Y_t = \mu + e_t \qquad \text{ARIMA}(0,0,0) \tag{7.7}$$

This model is classified as ARIMA(0,0,0). There is no AR portion (Y_t does not depend on Y_{t-1}), there is no differencing, and there is no MA portion (Y_t does not depend on e_{t-1}). It is a completely random stationary series.

If one had a completely random time series, the serial or autocorrelation would be zero. Each succeeding value would not be related to its previous value. A normally distributed random series is often called a *white noise series* and is said to be purely random (all $\rho_R = 0$). However, when autocorrelation is very large, there is a high degree of relation between successive values. By measuring and examining autocorrelation for time lags of more than one period, we would find evidence on how values of a given series are related.

A model that is similar to an AR process because Y_t is a function of Y_{t-1} but the coefficient of Y_{t-1} is equal to unity is

$$Y_t = \mu + Y_{t-1} + e_t \qquad \text{ARIMA}(1,0,0) \tag{7.8}$$

For convenience, this equation can be rewritten as follows:

$$Y_t - Y_{t-1} = \mu + e_t \qquad \text{ARIMA}(1,1,0) \tag{7.9}$$

which is a first-difference series. As we shall see later, there is a reason for finding the first differences of a time series.

ARIMA time series models are designed for stationary time series. A *stationary* time series is one whose basic statistical properties such as the mean or variance remain constant over time. Periodic variations and systematic changes in the mean and variance must first be identified and then removed to build ARIMA models. A series which has no growth or decline, that is, no trend in the mean, is said to be *nonstationary in the mean*.

Similarly when the variance changes over time, that is, the series is heteroscedastic, a time series is said to be *nonstationary in the variance*. A homoscedastic time series is one having no change in the variance over time. As we shall see, knowledge of these statistical properties of a time series will permit us to build ARIMA models better and, in turn, to make more accurate forecasts.

As we develop better ARIMA models, we wish to know whether or not the time series is generated by an underlying process that changes over time. If the underlying process that gives rise to the time series is stationary (does not change over time), we shall find it easy to represent the time series over past and future intervals of time by some simple algebraic model called an ARIMA model. The model will have fixed coefficients estimated from historical observations. However, if the underlying process that gives rise to the time series is nonstationary (changes over time), we shall find it difficult to represent the time series by an ARIMA model. If the underlying process is nonstationary in the mean, then examining the properties of the first-differenced series may make it easy to represent the time series by an ARIMA model.

Among the various ways in which a series encountered in business and economics can be nonstationary is that where the mean or level of the series is not a constant. This situation is known as *trend in mean*. As noted before, if the trend in mean can be effectively removed by differencing the series, then this particular form of nonstationarity can be removed. An example of this process will appear in section 7.8. It is also quite common to find series whose variability is changing over time; this is called *trend in variance*. Such a series can often be made stationary, or approximately so, by taking the logarithms of the time series. Such a transformation (to be discussed in chapter 8) will usually change the trend in variance to a trend in mean. More complicated types of nonstationarity may also be present which require handling techniques of such complexity and mathematical rigor that we shall not consider them here.

If the structured relationship of a model changes over time, that is, the series is nonstationary, we could not utilize the methods of chapters 4 and 5 to forecast future observations. However, we could ask at what point the series becomes stationary. A study of autocorrelations usually indicates that very few time series are stationary. As noted before, however, many of the nonstationary time series encountered have the desirable property that if they are differenced one or more times, the resulting series will be stationary. Examples of this will be demonstrated later. Such a nonstationary series is called homogeneous. The number of times that the original time series is differenced before a stationary series results is known as the *order of homogeneity*.

The basic form of a stationary AR(1) model – ARIMA(1,0,0) – is denoted by

$$(Y_t - \mu) = \phi_1(Y_{t-1} - \mu) + e_t \tag{7.10}$$

where μ is the mean of the Y series. To simplify, we write

$$Y_t = (\mu - \phi_1\mu) + \phi_1 Y_{t-1} + e_t \tag{7.11}$$

and by substitution for $\mu' = \mu - \phi_1\mu$ we have

$$Y_t = \mu' + \phi_1 Y_{t-1} + e_t \qquad \text{ARIMA(1,0,0)} \tag{7.12}$$

Usually, AR models involve a term of the form $(\mu + \phi_1\mu - \phi_2\mu - ...)$ which is generally identified by μ'. Also, note that for the (1,0,0) model, the observation Y_t is related to Y_{t-1}, the previous period's observation. The regression parameter ϕ_1 is restricted to be in the range from -1 to $+1$. The reason for this restriction will be discussed later.

If the AR(1) model is nonstationary, we may wish to transform the model equation to a stationary one by taking first differences. In this case, the model becomes

$$Y_t - Y_{t-1} = \phi_1(Y_{t-1} - Y_{t-2}) + \mu' - \mu' + e_t \qquad (7.13)$$

and

$$\nabla Y_t = \phi_1(\nabla Y_{t-1}) + e_t \qquad \text{ARIMA}(1,1,0) \qquad (7.14)$$

where ∇ indicates the difference between Y in period t and the previous period $t - 1$. We shall be interested in examining models of all the above types and more.

In chapter 3, we examined the seasonality of a series as the repetitive behavior that occurs on a regular calendar basis, usually a year. For example, if a monthly time series Y_t exhibits annual seasonality, then the data points in the series should show some correlation with the corresponding data points that lead or lag by 12 months. Stated differently, the autocorrelation of Y_t, Y_{t-12}, and Y_{t-24}, for example, would be very high. These correlations would exhibit peaks at $k = 12, 24, 36, 48, 60$, and so forth. We should note that seasonality is another form of divergence from stationarity. However, to avoid confusion, we shall use the term seasonality when the time series is nonstationary because of seasonal variation, and use the term nonstationary when the time series is *not* stationary for reasons other than seasonality. Finally, we can observe and identify seasonality by noticing the regular peaks and troughs in the autocorrelation over time. Thus, we wish to identify for each time series whether or not seasonality exists. If it does exist, we need to determine its length.

To sum up, for each time series, we wish to determine the following.

1 Are the data random?
2 Are the data stationary? If they are nonstationary, at what level are they variant with time?
3 Are the data seasonal? If they are seasonal, what is the length of seasonality?

All these characteristics are determined by studying the autocorrelation function for a time series. We shall begin examining the autocorrelation function of a time series in section 7.4.

7.3 A Note on ARIMA Models

Most time series encountered in some forecasting applications are not stationary series. If a nonstationary time series can be made stationary by taking d differences (usually $d = 1$ or 2), the result is a model for the *differenced* series. The original series is referred to as an ARIMA model. The I stands for *integrated* and it is used to suggest "undifferenced."

For an ARIMA model, the order is given by the three letters p, d, and q. The order of the autoregressive component is p, the order of differencing needed to achieve stationarity is d, and the order of the moving-average part is q.

The ARIMA (p, d, q) model is the most general model considered here and is also the most widely used. It is often necessary to take differences to achieve stationarity, but the resulting series may require only an autoregressive component p or a moving-average component q. These models are called *autoregressive integrated* (ARI) or *integrated moving-average* (IMA) models. The term "integrated" is used when differencing is performed to achieve stationarity since the stationary series must be integrated (undifferenced) to recover the original data.

For the purpose of forecasting, we must first identify the appropriate ARIMA model and transform and/or difference the data to produce stationarity. In turn, the diagrams displaying the ordinary autocorrelation coefficients and the partial auto-correlation coefficients for the various patterns of differences that are found in the adjusted data can be contrasted with the basic catalog of theoretical patterns to be discussed in chapter 8. Thus we must begin our study of autocorrelation coefficients and partial autocorrelation coefficients of a time series.

7.4   The Autocorrelation Function

Although it is generally impossible to obtain a complete description of a time series process, the autocorrelation function is extremely useful in helping us to obtain a partial description of the process for developing a forecasting model. Furthermore, the *autocorrelation coefficient* measures the degree of correlation between neighboring data observations in a time series. We begin by defining the autocorrelation with lag k as

$$\rho_k = \frac{E(Y_t - \mu_y)(Y_{t+k} - \mu_y)}{[E(Y_t - \mu_y)^2 \ E(Y_{t+k} - \mu_y)^2]^{1/2}} \tag{7.15}$$

$$\rho_k = \frac{\text{cov}(Y_t, Y_{t+k})}{\sigma_{Y_t} \sigma_{Y_{t+k}}} \tag{7.16}$$

If the numerator and denominator are equal, $\rho_0 = 1$. This will occur when $k = 0$. Some computer software output, for example SAS, will compute the autocorrelation coefficient automatically at $k = 0$.

The autocorrelation coefficient is estimated from sample observations as follows:

$$r_k = \frac{\sum\limits_{t=2}^{n-} (Y_t - \overline{Y}_t)(Y_{t-1} - \overline{Y}_{t-1})}{\left[\sum\limits_{t=1}^{n} (Y_t - \overline{Y}_t)^2 \right]^{1/2} \left[\sum\limits_{t=2}^{n} (Y_{t-1} - \overline{Y}_{t-1})^2 \right]^{1/2}} \tag{7.17}$$

Note carefully the subscript limits in the numerator and denominator here. Since this formula leads to statistical difficulties, a simplifying assumption is made. The series Y_t is assumed to be stationary (in both the mean and the variance). Thus the two means $\overline{Y}_t$ and $\overline{Y}_{t-1}$ can be assumed to be equal (and we shall drop the subscripts, using $\overline{Y} = \overline{Y}_t = \overline{Y}_{t-1}$), and the two standard deviations are estimated only once, using all the known data for Y_t.

Using these simplifying assumptions, equation (7.17) becomes

$$r_k = \sum\limits_{2}^{n} (Y_t - \overline{Y}_t)(Y_{t-1} - \overline{Y}_{t-1}) \bigg/ \sum\limits_{1}^{n} (Y_t - \overline{Y})^2 \tag{7.18}$$

To see how we calculate the autocorrelation coefficient, consider the next example.

Example 7.1

Data for earnings per share are collected for the Gates Learjet Corporation for the years 1970–80. The data, which are presented in table 7.1, are described by the following AR model (an ARIMA(2,0,0)):

$$Y_t = \mu' + \phi_1 Y_{t-1} + \phi_2 Y_{t-2} + e_t \tag{7.19}$$

TABLE 7.1 Time series of earnings per share (Y_t) of Gates Learjet Corporation

(1)	*(2)*	*(3)*	*(4)*
		Lag of	*Lag of*
	Original	*one period*	*two periods*
Period	Y_t	Y_{t-1}	Y_{t-2}
1	0.93	—	—
2	0.78	0.93	—
3	0.83	0.78	0.93
4	1.84	0.83	0.78
5	1.22	1.84	0.83
6	2.21	1.22	1.84
7	1.64	2.21	1.22
8	1.72	1.64	2.21
9	2.22	1.72	1.64
10	2.32	2.22	1.72
11	3.05	2.32	2.22

$$n = 11 \; \overset{11}{\underset{1}{\Sigma}} \; Y_i = 18.76 \; \bar{Y} = 1.71$$

Note: The time series in column 2 is lagged one period (column 3) and, in turn, two periods (column 4).

Source: *Value Line Selection and Opinion*, p. 861.

The AR series of equation (7.19) expresses Y_t as a linear combination of its two preceding values. The time series variables of Y at times $t - 1$ and $t - 2$ are constructed easily by moving the values forward one and two periods respectively. Thus the series for Y_{t-1} loses one value and the series for Y_{t-2} can be calculated rather easily. These autocorrelations will provide evidence about how successive values of the same variable relate to each other. The autocorrelation of Y_t and Y_{t-1} is called *first-order autocorrelation* and the relation between Y_t and Y_{t-2} is called *second-order autocorrelation*.

For the purposes of calculation, we can rewrite the equation above for the autocorrelation coefficient for order 1 as

$$r_1 = \sum_{2}^{n} (Y_t - \bar{Y})(Y_{t-1} - \bar{Y}) \Big/ \sum_{1}^{n} (Y_t - \bar{Y})^2 \tag{7.20}$$

Equation (7.20) is interpreted in the same manner as the correlation coefficient for the relationship of two variables, that is, the autocorrelation coefficient, if squared, is the ratio of the explained variation to the total variation in Y. This indicates whether the autoregression line between Y_t and Y_{t-1} is a better predictor than the mean line of Y_t. The closer r is to ± 1, the better is the autoregression as a predictor.

Before we study how the interpretation of autocorrelation coefficients is used in studying time series, let us see how we use equation (7.20) to calculate r from the original data. For the data of example 7.1, we have

$$r_1 = \frac{(0.93 - 1.71)(0.78 - 1.71) + (0.78 - 1.71)(0.83 - 1.71) + ... + (2.32 - 1.71)(3.05 - 1.71)}{(0.93 - 1.71)^2 + (0.78 - 1.71)^2 + ... + (3.05 - 1.71)^2}$$

$$= 0.427$$

Similarly, we can calculate r_2 as follows:

$$r_2 = \frac{(0.93 - 1.71)(0.83 - 1.71) + (0.78 - 1.71)(1.84 - 1.71) + ... + (2.22 - 1.71)(3.05 - 1.71)}{(0.93 - 1.71)^2 + (0.78 - 1.71)^2 + ... + (3.05 - 1.71)^2}$$

$$= 0.338$$

In a similar manner, we can calculate

$r_3 = 0.024$

$r_4 = -0.011$

$r_5 = 0.020$

and so on.

Finally, equation (7.20) contains properties which make it easier to determine if the series is nonstationary.

7.5   The Sampling Distribution of Autocorrelations

To illustrate the concept of a sampling distribution for a stationary series consider the next sample.

Example 7.2

To illustrate a stationary series, consider a sample of three-digit numbers selected from a table of random digits. The digits range from 000 to 999 and have a mean of 499.5. Also, the probability of selecting any three-digit number is the same and is equal to 1/1000. A sample of 40 numbers is selected from a common table of random numbers to represent observations over a 40 period interval. The data are displayed in table 7.2

In theory, if a time series is a set of completely random and thus independent observations, then the autocorrelation coefficients for all orders must be zero. However, for a random sample of 40 observations, the estimated (sample) autocorrelation coefficient for any order could be different from zero. Since the number of random digits that can be selected is not finite, an infinite number of samples can be

TABLE 7.2 A time series of 40 random observations

Time period	Observation	Time period	Observation
1	457	21	793
2	351	22	239
3	791	23	369
4	558	24	186
5	429	25	523
6	412	26	788
7	795	27	534
8	592	28	120
9	659	29	797
10	703	30	309
11	830	31	500
12	138	32	792
13	695	33	858
14	245	34	615
15	423	35	807
16	682	36	959
17	438	37	349
18	822	38	046
19	614	39	932
20	982	40	725

Source: Data on random numbers selected from Rand
Corporation (1955) *A Million Random Digits With One Hundred
Thousand Normal Deviates.*

selected from this population. Each random sample of 40 observations may have a
different sample autocorrelation coefficient for any order. Furthermore, if a number
of samples of 40 three-digit random numbers were selected and their autocorrelation
coefficients of order 1, 2, 3, 4,..., 16 were averaged, the resulting values would be all
nearly zero. Thus, if k is denoted as the autocorrelation for the population, then
autocorrelations for different samples of observations would form a distribution of
values around k. This distribution would be called the *sampling distribution of
autocorrelations.*

Statistical theory teaches us that the sampling distribution of autocorrelation
coefficients of random data are normal with

$$\mu_{\rho_k} = 0$$

$$\sigma_{\rho_k} = 1/n^{1/2}$$

If r_k is the estimate of ρ_k, then we can use our knowledge of normal distributions to
make interval estimates of the population autocorrelation coefficient p_k. Since the
number n of observations in the random data series of example 7.2 is 40, the
standard error is $1/\sqrt{(40)} = 0.158$. By applying our knowledge of the normal
distribution, we can say that 99.73 percent of sample autocorrelation coefficients lie
with the interval specified by the mean plus or minus three standard errors of the
mean. Similarly, 95.45 percent of all sample autocorrelations lie with two standard
errors of the mean and 68.3 percent of all sample correlation coefficients lie with one

standard error of the mean. We still require to determine at what risk level we are willing to conclude that the data are not random when in reality they are. Stated differently, if we are willing to accept significance limits of two standard errors (95.45 percent), the data can be concluded to be random if the sample autocorrelation coefficients are within the limits

$$-2\sigma_p \leqslant r_k \leqslant + 2\sigma_p$$

$$-2(0.158) \leqslant r_k \leqslant + 2(0.158)$$

$$-0.316 \leqslant r_k \leqslant 0.316$$

Figure 7.1 shows the autocorrelation coefficients for the data of example 7.2 with time lags of 1, 2, 3,...,24. The two lines drawn perpendicular to the horizontal are the limits (plus and minus two standard errors) for a random series (−0.316, +0.316). All 16 sample autocorrelation coefficients lie within the limits of the range, confirming the hypothesis that the time series is random.

```
             -1.0 -0.8 -0.6 -0.4 -0.2  0.0  0.2  0.4  0.6  0.8  1.0
             +----+----+----+----+----+----+----+----+----+----+
   1  -0.034                               XX
   2  -0.146                            XXXXX
   3   0.008                               X
   4  -0.093                              XXX
   5  -0.209                          XXXXXX
   6  -0.042                              XX
   7   0.083                               XXX
   8  -0.060                              XXX
   9  -0.084                              XXX
  10   0.187                               XXXXXX
  11  -0.095                             XXX
  12  -0.144                            XXXXX
  13   0.134                               XXXX
  14   0.048                               XX
  15   0.038                               XX
  16   0.175                               XXXXX
  17  -0.188                           XXXXXX
  18  -0.040                              XX
  19  -0.040                              XX
  20  -0.066                             XXX
  21  -0.086                             XXX
  22   0.067                               XXX
  23   0.105                               XXXX
  24  -0.006                               X
```

FIGURE 7.1 ARIMA (0, 0, 0) autocorrelation coefficients (Note: computer-generated Minitab output)

We could have tested each time lag k separately by the following hypothesis:

$$H_0:\rho_k = 0$$

$$H_A:\rho_k \neq 0$$

However, the limit (or confidence limit) approach is simple and provides the same results. Using this approach, we are able to determine whether any data or time series is random or not.

Finally, we should note that the concept of sampling distribution is as critically important in time series analysis as it is in other applications of statistical theory. The autocorrelation coefficient of order 5 is −0.209. Since this result is based on sample information, we can infer that this value differs from zero because of sampling error. The sampling distribution provides us with a method for concluding whether or not the sample difference is due to sampling error. The value −0.209 indicates that the autocorrelations are not (statistically) different from zero.

If the sample size in example 7.2 was 400 instead of 40, the standard error would be 0.05. By following the same methods, the limits of two standard errors would now be within 0.10 of the mean. In this case, the autocorrelation coefficients of order 2, 5, 10, 12, 13, 16, 17 and 23 have values that lie outside the acceptable limits. Naturally, if the sample size was 400, the sample autocorrelation would also be different. Finally, we should note that success in time series analysis is due in great part to the interpretation of the results from analyzing the autocorrelation coefficients to distinguish the pattern in time series from randomness.

7.6 Are the Data Random?

The procedures of the previous section presented a method for determining whether a given time series was random. Autocorrelation coefficients of several or more time lags are measured and examined to see whether any of them differ significantly from zero. Plotting autocorrelation coefficients as in figure 7.1 permits us to determine whether a pattern exists. There was no pattern in figure 7.1.

In chapter 4, we examined residuals from forecasting models by plotting a time series of them. If a pattern existed in the data, the plot of residuals would exhibit it. In this section, we take this analysis a step further by calculating autocorrelations for the series of residual errors to determine whether they are random.

To consider how fitted models can be examined to see whether the residual errors from forecast are random, examine the next example.

Example 7.3

Data on the dollar value of real estate loans (total for the United States) were examined previously in example 7.2. Forecasts were prepared by single parameter (linear) exponential smoothing and Brown's single parameter model with adjustment for trend. In this example, we wish to estimate the residual from forecast to see if the data are random or not.

Table 7.3 contains the residuals from forecasts for the observed time series. Column 1 of table 7.3 is the difference between observed values (column 1) and predicted values (column 2) from single exponential smoothing in table 2.10. Column 2 of table 7.3 is the difference between column 1 and column 6 (predicted values by Brown's method) of table 2.10. No forecasts are made for periods 1 and 2 by Brown's method; thus, there are no residuals for these periods.

Autocorrelation coefficients can be calculated from the residuals of table 7.3 by the operational equation (7.15). For the data of column 2 (table 7.3) we can see that

TABLE 7.3 Residuals from forecast of
real estate loans time series ($ billions)

Period	(1) Single ES model	(2) Residual from Brown's trend model
1	0.00	XXX
2	0.80	XXX
3	1.40	1.50
4	2.70	2.60
5	2.20	1.40
6	1.80	0.70
7	2.20	1.10
8	2.60	1.30
9	2.90	1.40
10	3.10	1.40
11	3.30	1.30
12	4.20	2.20
13	4.20	1.60
14	4.20	1.40
15	3.40	0.20
16	3.50	0.40
17	4.40	1.30
18	4.30	1.00
19	4.20	0.60
20	4.20	0.40
21	5.00	1.40
22	4.80	0.90
23	4.60	0.50
24	4.50	0.20

there is a pattern in the errors indicating that single exponential smoothing was not the appropriate model for forecasting. Although the pattern in the errors is obvious in this example, in many cases the pattern would not be obvious. Thus the approach to determining whether errors are random or not is to calculate the autocorrelations of the residuals from forecast (the errors).

Figure 7.2 is the plot of the autocorrelations for the residuals of the single exponential smoothing model of example 7.2. Since there were 24 periods the 2σ limits are

$$-2\frac{1}{\sqrt{(24)}} < r_k < 2\frac{1}{\sqrt{(24)}}$$

$$-2(0.204) < r_k < 2(0.204)$$

$$-0.408 < r_k < 0.408$$

From figure 7.2 the autocorrelation associated with time lags one, two, three, and four periods are $0.771, 0.577, 0.443,$ and 0.426 respectively. These values lie outside

```
          −1.0 −0.8 −0.6 −0.4 −0.2   0.0   0.2   0.4   0.6   0.8   1.0
          +----+----+----+----+----+----+----+----+----+----+
   1    0.771                              XXXXXXXXXXXXXXXXXXXXX
   2    0.577                              XXXXXXXXXXXXXXX
   3    0.443                              XXXXXXXXXXXX
   4    0.426                              XXXXXXXXXXXX
   5    0.358                              XXXXXXXXXX
   6    0.217                              XXXXXX
   7    0.121                              XXXX
   8    0.053                              XX
   9   −0.002                              X
  10   −0.090                            XXX
  11   −0.219                          XXXXXX
  12   −0.238                          XXXXXXX
  13   −0.239                          XXXXXXX
  14   −0.235                          XXXXXXX
  15   −0.305                        XXXXXXXXX
  16   −0.362                       XXXXXXXXXX
  17   −0.324                        XXXXXXXXX
  18   −0.309                        XXXXXXXXX
  19   −0.299                        XXXXXXXX
  20   −0.308                        XXXXXXXXX
```

FIGURE 7.2 Autocorrelation coefficients of the residuals from forecast of real estate loans by single exponential smoothing model (Note: computer-generated Minitab output)

the limits, indicating that the error terms are autocorrelated at the specified significance level (about 0.045). This result is not unexpected since the real estate loan data exhibit a trend which single exponential smoothing cannot deal with very well.

Figure 7.3 shows the autocorrelation coefficients for the residual from Brown's exponential model forecast. The 2σ limits for these data are (recall that there are 22 periods here)

$$-2\frac{1}{\sqrt{(22)}} < r_k < 2\frac{1}{\sqrt{(22)}}$$

$$-2(0.213) < r_k < 2(0.213)$$

$$-0.426 < r_k < 0.426$$

Note that there are no autocorrelation coefficients that lie outside the limits of the above interval. Thus no significant autocorrelation is exhibited; the Brown model eliminated the trend completely and produced a residual in which no statistically-significant pattern was present.

These analyses indicate whether a time series of data (or residuals from forecast) is random. The procedure is accomplished by calculating autocorrelation coefficients and plotting them to see whether they are statistically different from zero. The software used for computation of these examples was Minitab on a Prime 750

```
          -1.0 -0.8 -0.6 -0.4 -0.2   0.0   0.2   0.4   0.6   0.8   1.0
            +----+----+----+----+----+----+----+----+----+----+
  1    0.385                              XXXXXXXXXXX
  2   -0.063                           XXX
  3   -0.052                            XX
  4    0.228                              XXXXXXX
  5    0.153                              XXXXX
  6   -0.122                          XXXX
  7   -0.028                            XX
  8    0.258                              XXXXXXX
  9    0.279                              XXXXXXXX
 10   -0.061                           XXX
 11   -0.369                   XXXXXXXXXXX
 12   -0.321                    XXXXXXXXX
 13   -0.019                             X
 14   -0.054                            XX
 15   -0.190                        XXXXXX
 16   -0.158                         XXXXX
 17    0.046                             XX
 18   -0.001                             X
 19   -0.161                         XXXXX
 20   -0.204                        XXXXXX
```

FIGURE 7.3 Autocorrelation coefficients of the residuals from forecast of real estate loans by Brown's trend model (Note: computer-generated Minitab output)

minicomputer. Similar plots and computations are available for other software and computers.

7.7   Are the Data Nonstationary?

A nonseasonal homoscedastic time series is stationary when it contains no evidence of growth or decline, and is nonstationary when a pattern is present. For a nonstationary series the autocorrelation coefficients are typically statistically different from zero for the first several time lags, and only gradually drop to zero or show a spurious pattern as the number of time periods increases. Figure 7.2 is a good example of autocorrelation coefficients for a nonstationary series. Statistically significant autocorrelation coefficients exist for time lags of up to four and the pattern in the residuals drops to zero and then becomes negative, but not significant. A straight line can be drawn through the residuals, indicating a trend.

As pointed out before, when a trend is present in the data, successive values are correlated with each other. Autocorrelation for one time lag is large. However, the autocorrelation for a lag of two periods is not quite as large because one less term is used to calculate the numerator of the autocorrelation coefficient.

If a time series shows statistically significant autocorrelation coefficients for up to two time lags (or more), but not thereafter, the time series is said to be nonrandom but stationary. If the autocorrelations are statistically different from zero for only two time lags, a trend element is not exhibited in the data. However, there is evidence of a pattern other than trend.

7.8   Removing the Trend in the Time Series

Spurious correlations are said to dominate the pattern in the time series when a trend exists. For this reason, trends must be removed before further analysis can take place. One very useful method is that of first differences. Consider the simple series 3, 6, 9, 12, 15, 18, consisting of a nonrandom linear trend. If we subtract consecutive values, 6–3, 9–6, 12–9, 15–12, and 18–15, the result is the first differences, 3, 3, 3, 3, 3. This series is clearly stationary. Thus a new stationary series is created and consists of the differences between successive periods:

$$\nabla Y_t' = Y_{t+1} - Y_t$$

The new series Y_t' contains $n - 1$ values and will be stationary if the trend in the original data Y_t is linear (or order 1).

To express and understand differenced ARIMA models, the concept of the *backshift operator B* must be introduced. This operator has no mathematical meaning other than to facilitate the writing of different types of models that would otherwise be extremely difficult to express. The backshift operator is defined as $B^m Y_t$. For example,

$$BY_t = Y_{t-1} \quad \text{or} \quad Be_t = e_{t-1}$$

$$B^2 Y_t = Y_{t-2} \quad \text{or} \quad B^2 e_t = e_{t-2}$$

$$B^3 Y_t = Y_{t-3} \quad \text{or} \quad B^3 e_t = e_{t-3}$$

$$\vdots$$

$$B^m Y_t = Y_{t-m} \quad \text{or} \quad B^m e_t = e_{t-m}$$

Any ARIMA model can be expressed in terms of the backshift operator. An AR(1) model, ARIMA(1,0,0), is expressed as

$$Y_t = \phi_1 Y_{t-1} + e_t$$

or

$$Y_t - \phi_1 Y_{t-1} = e_t \tag{7.21}$$

However, since $Y_{t-1} = BY_t$, equation (7.21) can be rewritten as

$$Y_t - \phi_1 BY_t = e_t$$

For an AR(2) model $Y_t - \phi_1 Y_{t-1} - \phi_2 Y_{t-2} = e_t$, ARIMA(2,0,0), we can write

$$Y_{t-1} = BY_t$$

and

$$Y_{t-2} = B^2 Y_t$$

which can be rewritten as

$$Y_t - \phi_1 BY_t - \phi_2 B^2 Y_t = e_t$$

and

$$(1 - \phi_1 B - \phi_2 B^2)Y_t = e_t \tag{7.22}$$

If we have an AR(2) model where first differences have been used, ARIMA (2,1,0), the expression is

$$(Y_t - Y_{t-1}) = \phi_1(Y_{t-1} - Y_{t-2}) + \phi_2(Y_{t-2} - Y_{t-3}) + e_t$$

Since $Y_{t-1} = BY_t$, $Y_{t-2} = BY_{t-1}$, and $Y_{t-3} = BY_{t-2}$, the expression can be rewritten as

$$(1 - B)Y_t = \phi_1(1 - B)Y_{t-1} + \phi_2(1 - B)Y_{t-2} + e_t \tag{7.23}$$

Furthermore, since $BY_t = Y_{t-1}$ and $B^2Y_t = Y_{t-2}$, equation (7.20) becomes

$$(1 - B)Y_t = \phi_1(1 - B)BY_t + \phi_2(1 - B)B^2Y_t + e_t$$

or

$$(1 - B)Y_t - \phi_1(1 - B)BY_t - \phi_2(1 - B)B^2Y_t = e_t \tag{7.24}$$

Finally, if $(1 - B)Y_t$ is used as a common factor, equation (7.21) becomes

$$Y_t(1 - B)(1 - \phi_1B - \phi_2B^2) = e_t$$

or

$$(1 - B)(1 - \phi_1B - \phi_2B^2)Y_t = e_t \tag{7.25}$$

Equation (7.22) is the equivalent of a first-differenced AR(2) process.

As we shall see in our discussion of time series techniques, the use of the backshift operator permits us to express a time series model more easily. Both the order and type of process is expressed in terms of the exponent of the backshift operator B and the type of parameter.

Example 7.4

Earnings per share data for the Chase Manhattan Corporation for the years 1965–80 are presented in table 7.4. The first differences are found by subtracting the observation in the preceding period from the observation in the given period. For example,

$$\nabla Y_{1966} = Y_{1965} - Y_{1966}$$

$$= 3.14 - 2.93 = 0.21$$

Thus the data in column 3 of table 7.4 are the differences between the data in columns 2 and 1. These data are thus the first differences of the original time series.

To determine whether the series of first differences produces a stationary series from an original series exhibiting a trend pattern, autocorrelation coefficients for the first differences of the data on earnings per share of Chase Manhattan Corporation are produced. Notice that only the first autocorrelation coefficient is significantly different from zero. The analysis indicates that the series of first-differenced data have been transformed into a stationary form.

If the autocorrelation coefficients of first-differenced data still gradually trail to zero, a stationary state has not been reached. To solve this, we can take the second difference. Second differences are the first differences of the first-differenced data. This is not necessary for the data of example 7.4. For example, the second difference for year 1967 is as follows[1]

---

1   Notice that ∇^2 indicates a second-differenced term.

$$\nabla^2 Y_{1967} = \nabla Y_{1967} - \nabla Y_{1966}$$
$$= 0.21 - 0.21 = 0.00$$

For 1968, we have

$$\nabla^2 Y_{1968} = \nabla Y_{1968} - \nabla Y_{1967}$$
$$= 0.45 - 0.21 = 0.24$$

TABLE 7.4   First differences of earnings per share data of Chase Manhattan Corporation

Year	(1) Y_t	(2) BY_t	(3) $\nabla Y_t = Y_t - BY_t$	(4) $\nabla^2 Y_t = \nabla Y_t - \nabla Y_{t-1}$
1965	2.93	–	–	–
1966	3.14	2.93	0.21	–
1967	3.35	3.14	0.21	0.00
1968	3.80	3.35	0.45	0.24
1969	3.59	3.80	−0.21	−0.66
1970	4.17	3.59	0.58	0.79
1971	4.63	4.17	0.46	−0.12
1972	4.65	4.63	0.02	−0.44
1973	5.15	4.65	0.50	0.48
1974	5.68	5.15	0.53	0.03
1975	4.89	5.68	−0.79	−1.32
1976	3.28	4.89	−1.61	−0.82
1977	3.71	3.28	0.43	2.04
1978	5.59	3.71	1.88	1.45
1979	9.07	5.59	3.48	1.60
1980	10.47	9.07	1.40	−2.08

Notes: ∇ indicates first difference.
   ∇^2 indicates second difference.
   B is backshift operator.

The second differences for the Chase Manhattan time series data are given in column 4 of table 7.4. These data can be used to measure the autocorrelation for the second-differenced time series. The autocorrelation coefficients for the second-differenced time series are presented in figure 7.4. Since no coefficient lies outside the 2σ limits, we can conclude that this series is stationary.

Thus we can sum up the process of achieving stationarity in a time series. First, we calculate the autocorrelations for the original time series and see whether a pattern is present. If the pattern is a trend, then this particular type of pattern suggests nonstationarity. To remove the nonstationarity, the series is transformed to first differences and a second autocorrelation analysis is performed. If stationarity is achieved, the analysis ends. However, if stationarity is not achieved, the second differences are calculated and a new autocorrelation analysis is performed. Achieving stationarity is thus reduced to the rather mechanical task of taking successive differences until the autocorrelations drop to zero with one, two, or three time lags. Usually, we do not go beyond second differences, because time series data usually involve nonstationarities of only the first or second level.

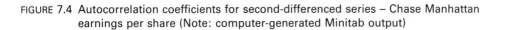

```
           -1.0 -0.8 -0.6 -0.4 -0.2   0.0   0.2   0.4   0.6   0.8   1.0
            +----+----+----+----+----+----+----+----+----+----+----+
  1    0.007                              X
  2   -0.269                        XXXXXXXX
  3   -0.391                    XXXXXXXXXXX
  4    0.053                             XX
  5    0.107                             XXXX
  6   -0.002                              X
  7   -0.005                              X
  8    0.018                              X
  9    0.051                             XX
 10   -0.153                         XXXXX
 11    0.102                             XXXX
 12   -0.027                            XX
 13    0.011                              X
```

FIGURE 7.4 Autocorrelation coefficients for second-differenced series – Chase Manhattan earnings per share (Note: computer-generated Minitab output)

7.9   Are the Data Seasonal?

As demonstrated in chapter 3, seasonality exists when a pattern repeats itself during a particular period of time, usually a year. By examining autocorrelation coefficients, a seasonal pattern can also be recognized. For example, the autocorrelation of 12 month lags would be of high positive value. Furthermore, if the coefficients were significantly different from zero, we would conclude that months one year apart were related or nonrandom.

Autocorrelation analysis applies to the problem of identifying seasonality in stationary data. To recognize seasonality, we measure more than two or three time lags to determine whether they are statistically different from zero. Autocorrelations that are significantly different from zero imply the existence of a pattern. To find seasonality, we must look for significant autocorrelations for higher orders.

Example 7.5

Table 7.5 contains data on a corporation's shipments without capital consumption adjustment, quarterly totals not seasonally adjusted (thousand dollars). The time series data are not seasonally adjusted. Is there significant evidence of seasonality in the time series?

Figure 7.5 shows a plot of the autocorrelation coefficients for the shipment data in table 7.5. Note that the largest autocorrelation coefficients are $r_4 = 0.592$ and $r_8 = 0.422$. These are significant coefficients since the limits at the 2σ level are

$$-2\frac{1}{\sqrt{(24)}} < r_k < 2\frac{1}{\sqrt{(24)}}$$

$$-0.408 < r_k < 0.408$$

Figure 7.5 indicates that this time series is seasonal in the statistical sense. If the data were not seasonal then r_4, r_8, etc. would not have values that lie outside the significance limits.

TABLE 7.5 Shipments of inventory without capital consumption adjustment, quarterly totals not seasonally adjusted ($ thousands)

	Year					
Quarter	1	2	3	4	5	6
1	42.6	46.0	45.9	52.6	54.3	55.0
2	46.4	53.7	55.9	48.7	52.9	54.7
3	48.0	53.3	52.2	50.2	52.6	51.8
4	56.5	67.1	61.0	61.0	60.7	62.0

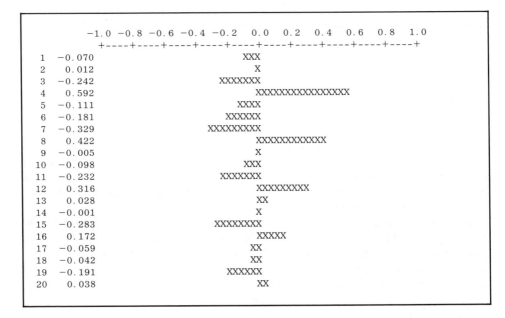

```
          -1.0 -0.8 -0.6 -0.4 -0.2  0.0  0.2  0.4  0.6  0.8  1.0
          +----+----+----+----+----+----+----+----+----+----+
 1  -0.070                            XXX
 2   0.012                             X
 3  -0.242                         XXXXXXX
 4   0.592                             XXXXXXXXXXXXXXXXX
 5  -0.111                           XXXX
 6  -0.181                          XXXXX
 7  -0.329                       XXXXXXXXX
 8   0.422                             XXXXXXXXXXXX
 9  -0.005                             X
10  -0.098                            XXX
11  -0.232                         XXXXXXX
12   0.316                             XXXXXXXXX
13   0.028                            XX
14  -0.001                            X
15  -0.283                       XXXXXXXX
16   0.172                             XXXXX
17  -0.059                            XX
18  -0.042                            XX
19  -0.191                          XXXXXX
20   0.038                            XX
```

FIGURE 7.5 Autocorrelation coefficients for shipments of inventory data
(Note: computer-generated Minitab output)

Seasonality is usually easy to identify when the data do not have a pattern producing nonstationarity. If a pattern is present, it is more difficult to determine the presence of seasonality. In this case the data should first be transformed into a stationary series and then examined for the presence of seasonality.

7.10   Partial Autocorrelation Coefficients

When analyzing a regression model, we may ask about the explanatory power of one independent variable if the effects of other independent variables are held constant.

This may require regressing Y on X_1 (say in a regression model with two independent variables), finding the residual errors, and regressing the residuals against X_2. In the time series analysis of this chapter, there is a similar concept.

Partial autocorrelation coefficients measure the degree of association between Y_t and Y_{t-k} when the effect of other time lags on Y are held constant. As we shall see in later chapters, their purpose is to help identify the best autoregressive moving-average (ARMA) model for forecasting.

A partial autocorrelation permits the forecaster to identify the degree of relationships between current values of a variable and earlier values of the same variable while holding the effects of all other time lags constant. Specifically, it is calculated when we are not aware of the appropriate order of the autoregressive process to fit the time series. This problem is similar to the problem in chapter 5 where we had to decide how many independent variables to include in a multiple regression model.

The *partial autocorrelation coefficient* is defined in terms of the last autoregressive term of an AR model of m lags. The greek letter ϕ is used to denote the partial autocorrelation, and $\hat{\phi}$ is the estimated partial autocorrelation. Thus, ϕ_1, ϕ_2,...,ϕ_{m-1}, ϕ_m are the m partial autocorrelations of the AR(m) model as defined in the following equations:

$$Y_t = \phi_1 Y_{t-1} + e_t \tag{7.26}$$

$$Y_t = \phi_1 Y_{t-1} + \phi_2 Y_{t-2} + e_t \tag{7.27}$$

$$.$$
$$.$$
$$.$$

$$Y_t = \phi_1 Y_{t-1} + \phi_2 Y_{t-2} + ... + \phi_{m-1} Y_{t-m-1} + e_t \tag{7.28}$$

$$Y_t = \phi_1 Y_{t-1} + \phi_2 Y_{t-2} + ... + \phi_{m-1} Y_{t-m-1} + \phi_m Y_{t-m} + e_t \tag{7.29}$$

Solving the above set of equations for ϕ_1, ϕ_2,...,ϕ_{t-m}, ϕ_m permits us to determine their values. The computations are complex and time consuming. A more satisfactory approach is to obtain estimates of $\hat{\phi}_1$, $\hat{\phi}_2$,...,$\hat{\phi}_m$ based on their autocorrelation coefficients. These estimations are made using the method described in appendix A to this chapter and result in

$$\hat{\phi}_1 = \hat{\rho}_1 = r_1$$

The partial autocorrelation of one time lag is ϕ_1 and r_1 is its estimator.

To use information about partial correlations, we must test to determine whether they are significantly different from zero. The null and alternative hypothesis are given as follows:

$$H_0 : \phi_k = 0$$

$$H_A : \phi_k \neq 0$$

If the underlying process generating a given series is an AR(1) model we should understand that only ϕ_1 will be significantly different from zero, while ϕ_2, ϕ_3,..., ϕ_{m-1}, ϕ_m will not be significantly different from zero. In a similar way, when the underlying generating process is AR(2), then only ϕ_1 and ϕ_2 will be statistically significant and all remaining partial autocorrelation will not be significant. In the same way, this principle applies to higher-order AR processes. Finally, if there are p significant partial autocorrelations, then the order is AR(p).

For the purposes of model identification, the partial autocorrelations are examined to determine the order of the process. Furthermore, the order is equal to the number of statistically significant partial autocorrelations.

Partial autocorrelation analysis says nothing about the MA process to be discussed in the next chapter. Partial autocorrelations are constructed to fit only an AR process. Also, they introduce a dependence from one lag to the next which causes them to behave in a manner similar to that of autocorrelations for an AR process. Specifically, partial autocorrelations decline to zero exponentially. When the partial autocorrelations do not fall to random values after p time lags but instead decline to zero exponentially, the true generating process is concluded to be an MA.

Finally, an AR(p) process has only p partial autocorrelations that are statistically different from zero. However, when partial autocorrelations fall off to zero exponentially, the process is said to be an MA.

7.11   Autocorrelation Analysis – A Brief Synopsis

The steps in the study of the autocorrelation of time series can be summarized as follows.

1. Upon calculating and plotting the autocorrelation coefficients of a time series, determine whether they fall off to zero after the second or third time lag. If they do, the series is likely to be stationary in its original form. Look for any patterns. If the autocorrelation trails off to zero (and remains positive), the series is probably stationary, thus go to step 3. If the series is not stationary, go to step 2.
2. If the series is nonstationary, reduce it to first differences and calculate the autocorrelation coefficients. If the new series is stationary, go to step 3. If the new series is still nonstationary, take the first differences again and calculate the autocorrelations. Usually, no more than two differences are required to transform the data into a stationary series. (A procedure to achieve stationarity in the variance is presented in chapter 8.)
3. If the series is stationary, measure and examine their autocorrelations . A quarterly seasonal pattern is suggested if time lags of 4, 8, 12 etc. are significant. Similarly, if r_k for time lags of 12, 24, 36, etc. is significant, then a monthly seasonal pattern is suggested. We shall examine these situations in chapter 9. Finally, if there are no statistically significant autocorrelations, we conclude that the data are random.

One last reminder concerns the measurement of autocorrelations and plotting the coefficients. Many computer software systems, such as the SAS/Econometric and Time Series Library, SPSS-X, and BMDP, are available for such computations. For minicomputers and some microcomputers, Minitab is available in an interactive mode for making these same computations. Another such system is Micro-TSP for microcomputers. The choice is large and the benefits of using such computer software are many.

7.12   Summary

In this chapter, the focus has been on the methods and principles of regression as applied directly to the study of time series.

An autoregression is a regression where the right-hand-side variables are merely the values of the dependent variables in previous periods; they are time-lagged observations.

A complete random or white noise series has no discernible pattern or structure. By measuring and examining autocorrelations for time lags of more than one period, evidence is provided on how values of a given series are related.

If a time series is stationary, we can easily model it via an equation with fixed coefficients estimated from historical observations. A nonstationary series is one where the structural relationships of the model change over time.

If a nonstationary series is differenced one or more times and the differenced series becomes stationary, the series is said to be homogeneous.

The autocorrelation function is extremely useful for describing the generating process used to develop a forecasting model. First-order autocorrelation is the autocorrelation of a time series in period t with the time series observation in period $t - 1$. Similarly, autocorrelation of higher orders refers to correlation with periods $t - 2, t - 3$, etc.

Important questions to ask about a time series are as follows.

1 Are the data random?
2 Are the data nonstationary?
3 Are the data seasonal?

Answers to these questions allow for better forecasting.

A partial autocorrelation coefficient measures the degree of association between an observation Y_t and Y_{t-k}, when the effects of other time lags are held constant. We study partial autocorrelations when we are unaware of the appropriate order of the autoregressive process to fit the time series.

7.13   Exercises

1 Explain in words the meaning of the following autoregressive models.

(a) Earnings per share Y are

$$Y_t = 2.10 + 0.05Y_{t-1} + 0.02Y_{t-2}$$

(b) A price index Y for leather goods and kindred products is

$$Y_t = 97.5 + 0.20Y_{t-1} + 0.05Y_{t-2} + 0.001Y_{t-3}$$

(c) The index of wages of GS 12 federal employees, Y, is given by

$$Y_t = 104.5 + 0.10Y_{t-1} + 0.03Y_{t-2} + 0.0005Y_{t-3} + + 0.00001Y_{t-4}$$

2 (a) For a sample of 81 observations of random data, calculate a 2σ confidence interval for the autocorrelation coefficients.

(b) If all the autocorrelation coefficients lie within the limits of the confidence interval, what conclusion can be drawn?

(c) In an analysis of another series of data, the first six autocorrelation coefficients are statistically different from zero. What conclusion can be drawn about the series?

(d) If r_3, r_7, r_{11}, and r_{15} are statistically different from zero, what conclusion can be drawn about the data?

3 Figure 7.6 contains plots of autocorrelations and partial autocorrelations for the original data of a time series. Identify the potential model in each instance.

4 Figure 7.7 contains a plot of the autocorrelations of an unknown time series. There were 64 observations in the series.

(a) At the 2σ level, what conclusion can be drawn about the time series?

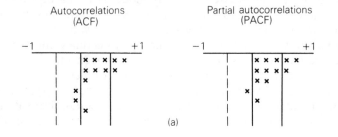

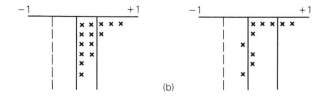

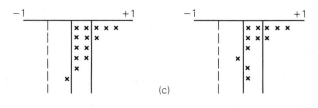

FIGURE 7.6

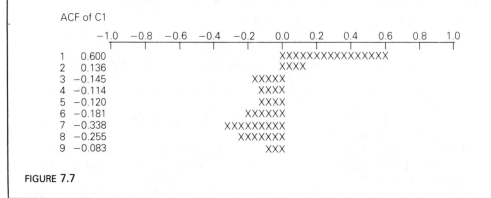

ACF of C1

		−1.0	−0.8	−0.6	−0.4	−0.2	0.0	0.2	0.4	0.6	0.8	1.0
1	0.600						XXXXXXXXXXXXXXXXX					
2	0.136						XXXX					
3	−0.145					XXXXX						
4	−0.114					XXXX						
5	−0.120					XXXX						
6	−0.181					XXXXXX						
7	−0.338				XXXXXXXXX							
8	−0.255				XXXXXXX							
9	−0.083						XXX					

FIGURE 7.7

TABLE 7.6

Period	$\hat{\phi}_k$
1	0.600
2	0.212
3	0.053
4	0.011
5	0.005
6	−0.102
7	0.050
8	−0.047
9	−0.067

(b) If the partial autocorrelations were as given in table 7.6, what conclusions can be drawn about the time series?

5 Table 7.7 contains earnings per share data for three large corporations. By autocorrelation analysis, what can be concluded about these time series?

6 Data listed in table 7.8 are utilization rates in industry (percent, seasonally adjusted). By autocorrelation analysis, what conclusions can be drawn about each series?

TABLE 7.7

Year	Citicorp	Walt Disney	Exxon
1972	0.89	0.32	0.85
1973	1.07	0.37	1.36
1974	1.28	0.38	1.76
1975	1.41	0.48	1.40
1976	1.62	0.58	1.48
1977	1.53	0.63	1.35
1978	1.94	0.76	1.55
1979	2.18	0.88	2.44
1980	2.04	1.04	3.25
1981	2.20	0.93	3.22
1982	2.80	0.75	2.41
1983	3.15	0.68	2.89
1984	3.23	0.75	3.39
1985	3.56	1.29	3.72
1986	3.57	1.82	3.45
1987	4.26	2.85	3.43
1988	4.87	3.80	3.84

7 The data in table 7.9 are for the Index of Industrial Production by various industries obtained from various issues of the *Survey of Current Business*.
(a) Is there evidence of seasonality? At what level?
(b) Is there evidence of trend? At what level?

TABLE 7.8

	Quarter			
	1	2	3	4
1986				
1 Total industry	80.0	79.2	79.3	79.1
2 Mining	78.1	75.6	73.4	73.2
3 Utilities	83.7	79.5	79.8	79.1
4 Manufacturing	80.0	79.5	79.8	79.7
1987				
1 Total industry	79.4	80.7	80.5	80.3
2 Mining	73.3	82.3	81.0	80.2
3 Utilities	81.5	84.4	82.3	83.4
4 Manufacturing	79.9	80.3	80.3	80.0
1988				
1 Total industry	82.4	82.8	83.8	84.1
2 Mining	80.1	81.5	82.3	82.9
3 Utilities	82.3	79.9	81.9	81.3
4 Manufacturing	82.6	83.2	84.0	84.4

Source: *Federal Reserve Bulletin*, various issues.

8 The data in table 7.10 are selected employment data, 1948–86. Study one of the series. Is there evidence of nonstationarity in the original series? If so, take the first differences and find the autocorrelation coefficients for the differenced series. Is there evidence of nonstationarity in the difference series?

9 The data in table 7.11 are for common stock prices, 1949–1988. Study one of the series. Is there evidence of nonstationarity in the series? Can we correct for nonstationarity by finding the first-differenced series?

10 The data in table 7.12 are for personal savings as a percentage of disposable personal income (percent) for the United States. By autocorrelation analysis, is there evidence of seasonality?

11 The data in table 7.13 are for bond yields over the period 1929–88 for the United States. Select one of the time series and, by autocorrelation analysis, indicate whether it is stationary or nonstationary. If nonstationary, try to convert it to a stationary series by differencing.

TABLE 7.9 Industrial production, Federal Reserve Board Index of Quantity Output, not seasonally adjusted (1977 = 100)

	Jan	Feb	Mar	Apr	May	Jun	Jul	Aug	Sep	Oct	Nov	Dec
1985												
Total index	120.0	123.7	124.1	122.9	123.3	127.1	122.2	127.4	129.2	127.0	124.9	122.2
By industry groupings												
Mining and utilities	114.2	116.8	111.8	107.6	106.7	110.6	108.4	111.6	111.4	108.7	108.1	111.8
Manufacturing	121.2	125.2	126.4	125.8	126.5	130.2	124.5	130.4	132.6	130.3	128.2	124.1
Nondurable manufactures	117.1	121.8	122.5	122.4	123.7	128.7	124.6	131.7	134.1	130.6	127.2	122.3
Durable manufactures	124.2	127.6	129.2	128.2	128.5	131.2	124.4	129.4	131.4	130.1	128.8	125.3
1986												
Total index	122.9	124.9	123.1	123.8	123.2	126.9	123.3	127.6	129.1	128.0	125.4	122.4
By industry groupings												
Mining and utilities	113.1	110.8	104.5	101.1	98.5	102.1	102.1	103.8	101.9	99.1	101.4	102.4
Manufacturing	124.7	127.5	126.6	128.1	127.9	131.6	127.3	132.3	134.0	133.4	130.0	126.2
Nondurable manufactures	122.8	126.4	125.4	127.9	128.8	134.7	131.5	137.7	138.1	137.0	132.3	127.9
Durable manufactures	126.1	128.3	127.5	128.2	127.2	129.3	124.3	128.3	131.2	130.8	128.4	125.0
1987												
Total index	123.0	126.9	127.0	126.3	127.4	131.9	128.7	134.3	135.3	135.2	132.7	129.9
By industry groupings												
Mining and utilities	104.6	105.0	100.1	98.1	99.1	103.0	103.9	109.2	106.2	104.7	106.9	108.1
Manufacturing	126.2	131.0	132.1	131.6	132.7	137.4	133.5	139.2	140.9	141.0	137.5	134.0
Nondurable manufactures	127.2	131.9	132.8	133.9	135.4	140.5	138.7	145.0	145.8	143.0	139.1	135.0
Durable manufactures	125.5	130.4	131.6	130.0	130.8	135.3	129.8	135.0	137.3	139.6	136.3	133.3
1988												
Total index	130.8	134.2	134.1	133.9	135.0	139.3	136.3	141.7	143.0	142.2	139.3	136.4
By industry groupings												
Mining and utilities	111.8	111.2	106.1	103.5	101.3	106.5	108.3	112.6	107.9	105.1	106.6	109.4
Manufacturing	134.4	138.5	139.4	139.6	141.3	145.5	141.5	147.2	149.6	149.1	145.4	141.4
Nondurable manufactures	134.2	138.4	139.2	139.8	140.7	146.4	145.1	151.7	152.8	151.2	146.0	141.1
Durable manufactures	134.6	138.6	139.5	139.4	141.6	144.8	138.9	144.0	147.3	147.6	145.0	141.6

Source: Survey of Current Business, various issues.

TABLE 7.10 Civilian labor force participation rate[a]

Year	Total	Both sexes 16–19 years	Males 20 years and over	Females 20 years and over
1948	58.8	52.5	86.6	32.7
1949	58.9	52.2	86.4	33.1
1950	59.2	51.8	86.4	33.9
1951	59.2	52.2	86.3	34.6
1952	59.0	51.3	86.3	34.7
1953	58.9	50.2	86.0	34.4
1954	58.8	48.3	85.5	34.6
1955	59.3	48.9	85.4	35.7
1956	60.0	50.9	85.5	36.9
1957	59.6	49.6	84.8	36.9
1958	59.5	47.4	84.2	37.1
1959	59.3	46.7	83.7	37.1
1960	59.4	47.5	83.3	37.7
1961	59.3	46.9	82.9	38.1
1962	58.8	46.1	82.0	37.9
1963	58.7	45.2	81.4	38.3
1964	58.7	44.5	81.0	38.7
1965	58.9	45.7	80.7	39.3
1966	59.2	48.2	80.4	40.3
1967	59.6	48.4	80.4	41.1
1968	59.6	48.3	80.1	41.6
1969	60.1	49.4	79.8	42.7
1970	60.4	49.9	79.7	43.3
1971	60.2	49.7	79.1	43.4
1972	60.4	51.9	78.9	43.9
1973	60.8	53.7	78.8	44.7
1974	61.3	54.8	78.7	45.7
1975	61.2	54.0	77.9	46.3
1976	61.6	54.5	77.5	47.3
1977	62.3	56.0	77.7	48.4
1978	63.2	57.8	77.9	50.0
1979	63.7	57.9	77.8	50.9
1980	63.8	56.7	77.4	51.5
1981	63.9	55.4	77.0	52.1
1982	64.0	54.1	76.6	52.6
1983	64.0	53.5	76.4	52.9
1984	64.4	53.9	76.4	53.6
1985	64.8	54.5	76.3	54.5
1986	65.3	54.7	76.3	55.3

Note: [a]Civilian labor force as percent of civilian noninstitutional population in group specified.

Source: *Economic Report of the President*, 1987.

TABLE 7.11 Common stock prices 1949–88

Year	Composite	Industrial	Transportation	Utility	Finance	Dow Jones industrial average[c]	Standard & Poor's composite index (1941–3 = 10)[d]
	New York Stock Exchange indexes (Dec 31, 1965 = 50)[b]						
1949	9.02					179.48	15.23
1950	10.87					216.31	18.40
1951	13.08					257.64	22.34
1952	13.81					270.76	24.50
1953	13.67					275.97	24.73
1954	16.19					333.94	29.69
1955	21.54					442.72	40.49
1956	24.40					493.01	46.62
1957	23.67					475.71	44.38
1958	24.56					491.66	46.24
1959	30.73					632.12	57.38
1960	30.01					618.04	55.85
1961	35.37					691.55	66.27
1962	33.49					639.76	62.38
1963	37.51					714.81	69.87
1964	43.76					834.05	81.37
1965	47.39					910.88	88.17
1966	46.15	46.18	50.26	45.41	44.45	873.60	85.26
1967	50.77	51.97	53.51	45.43	49.82	879.12	91.93
1968	55.37	58.00	50.58	44.19	65.85	906.00	98.70
1969	54.67	57.44	46.96	42.80	70.49	876.72	97.84
1970	45.72	48.03	32.14	37.24	60.00	753.19	83.22
1971	54.22	57.92	44.35	39.53	70.38	884.76	98.29
1972	60.29	65.73	50.17	38.48	78.35	950.71	109.20
1973	57.42	63.08	37.74	37.69	70.12	923.88	107.43
1974	43.84	48.08	31.89	29.79	49.67	759.37	82.85
1975	45.73	50.52	31.10	31.50	47.14	802.49	86.16
1976	54.46	60.44	39.57	36.97	52.94	974.92	102.01
1977	53.69	57.86	41.09	40.92	55.25	894.63	98.20
1978	53.70	58.23	43.50	39.22	56.65	820.23	96.02
1979	58.32	64.76	47.34	38.20	61.42	844.40	103.01
1980	68.10	78.70	60.61	37.35	64.25	891.41	118.78
1981	74.02	85.44	72.61	38.91	73.52	932.92	128.05
1982	68.93	78.18	60.41	39.75	71.99	884.36	119.71
1983	92.63	107.45	89.36	47.00	95.34	1,190.34	160.41
1984	92.46	108.01	85.63	46.44	89.28	1,178.48	160.46
1985	108.09	123.79	104.11	56.75	114.21	1,328.23	186.84
1986	136.00	155.85	119.87	71.36	147.20	1,792,76	236.34
1987	161.70	195.31	140.39	74.30	146.48	2,275.99	286.83
1988	149.91	180.95	134.12	71.77	127.26	2,060.82	265.79

[a]Averages of daily closing prices, except New York Stock Exchange data through May 1964 which are averages of weekly closing prices.
[b]Includes all the stocks (more than 1500) listed on the New York Stock Exchange.
[c]Includes 30 stocks.
[d]Includes 500 stocks.

Note: All data relate to stocks listed on the New York Stock Exchange.
Sources: New York Stock Exchange, Dow Jones & Co. Inc., Standard & Poor's Corporation, *Economic Report of the President*, 1989.

TABLE 7.12

					Year						
Month	*1978*	*1979*	*1980*	*1981*	*1982*	*1983*	*1984*	*1985*	*1986*	*1987*	*1988*
Jan	6.7	6.0	5.3	5.4	6.7	5.4	5.6	5.2	4.6	3.9	4.3
Feb	6.7	6.2	5.5	5.4	6.6	5.4	6.1	4.5	5.0	4.4	4.4
Mar	6.4	6.3	5.8	5.7	6.7	5.1	6.5	4.4	5.3	3.3	4.1
Apr	6.1	6.4	6.1	5.9	6.8	4.5	6.1	5.2	5.4	3.4	4.0
May	5.8	6.3	6.1	6.1	6.7	4.0	5.7	5.3	5.5	3.0	3.7
Jun	5.8	6.4	6.1	6.3	6.8	4.0	5.6	6.0	4.9	3.5	4.2
Jul	5.8	6.3	5.9	6.3	7.0	4.5	6.1	4.9	4.4	2.9	4.0
Aug	6.0	5.9	6.1	6.5	6.9	4.9	6.3	4.2	3.6	2.8	4.2
Sep	5.8	5.5	6.0	6.9	6.5	5.1	6.4	3.9	3.5	3.4	4.8
Oct	5.8	5.1	5.9	7.4	6.2	5.2	6.3	4.1	3.6	3.7	4.4
Nov	5.8	5.1	5.5	7.6	6.0	5.3	6.2	4.4	3.6	4.3	4.3
Dec	6.0	5.0	5.4	7.2	5.8	5.2	5.9	4.5	3.9	4.1	4.4

Source: *Survey of Current Business*, various issues.

TABLE 7.13 Bond yields, 1929–88 (percent per annum)

Year and month	US Treasury securities				Corporate bonds (Moody's)		High-grade municipal bonds (Standard & Poor's)	New home mortgage yields (FHLBB)
	Bills (new issues)		*Constant maturities*					
	3 month	*6 month*	*3 year*	*10 year*	*Aaa*	*Baa*		
1929					4.73	5.90	4.27	
1933	0.515				4.49	7.76	4.71	
1939	.023				3.01	4.96	2.76	
1940	.014				2.84	4.75	2.50	
1941	.103				2.77	4.33	2.10	
1942	.326				2.83	4.28	2.36	
1943	.373				2.73	3.91	2.06	
1944	.375				2.72	3.61	1.86	
1945	.375				2.62	3.29	1.67	
1946	.375				2.53	3.05	1.64	
1947	.594				2.61	3.24	2.01	
1948	1.040				2.82	3.47	2.40	
1949	1.102				2.66	3.42	2.21	
1950	1.218				2.62	3.24	1.98	
1951	1.552				2.86	3.41	2.00	
1952	1.766				2.96	3.52	2.19	
1953	1.931		2.47	2.85	3.20	3.74	2.72	
1954	.953		1.63	2.40	2.90	3.51	2.37	
1955	1.753		2.47	2.82	3.06	3.53	2.53	

TABLE 7.13   Bond yields, 1929–88 (percent per annum)

| Year and month | US Treasury securities | | | | Corporate bonds (Moody's) | | High-grade municipal bonds (Standard & Poor's) | New home mortgage yields (FHLBB) |
| | Bills (new issues) | | Constant maturities | | | | | |
	3 month	6 month	3 year	10 year	Aaa	Baa		
1956	2.658		3.19	3.18	3.36	3.88	2.93	
1957	3.267		3.98	3.65	3.89	4.71	3.60	
1958	1.839		2.84	3.32	3.79	4.73	3.56	
1959	3.405	3.832	4.46	4.33	4.38	5.05	3.95	
1960	2.928	3.247	3.98	4.12	4.41	5.19	3.73	
1961	2.378	2.605	3.54	3.88	4.35	5.08	3.46	
1962	2.778	2.908	3.47	3.95	4.33	5.02	3.18	
1963	3.157	3.253	3.67	4.00	4.26	4.86	3.23	5.89
1964	3.549	3.686	4.03	4.19	4.40	4.83	3.22	5.82
1965	3.954	4.055	4.22	4.28	4.49	4.87	3.27	5.81
1966	4.881	5.082	5.23	4.92	5.13	5.67	3.82	6.25
1967	4.321	4.630	5.03	5.07	5.51	6.23	3.98	6.46
1968	5.339	5.470	5.68	5.65	6.18	6.94	4.51	6.97
1969	6.677	6.853	7.02	6.67	7.03	7.81	5.81	7.80
1970	6.458	6.562	7.29	7.35	8.04	9.11	6.51	8.45
1971	4.348	4.511	5.65	6.16	7.39	8.56	5.70	7.74
1972	4.071	4.466	5.72	6.21	7.21	8.16	5.27	7.60
1973	7.041	7.178	6.95	6.84	7.44	8.24	5.18	7.96
1974	7.886	7.926	7.82	7.56	8.57	9.50	6.09	8.92
1975	5.838	6.122	7.49	7.99	8.83	10.61	6.89	9.00
1976	4.989	5.266	6.77	7.61	8.43	9.75	6.49	9.00
1977	5.265	5.510	6.69	7.42	8.02	8.97	5.56	9.02
1978	7.221	7.572	8.29	8.41	8.73	9.49	5.90	9.56
1979	10.041	10.017	9.71	9.44	9.63	10.69	6.39	10.78
1980	11.506	11.374	11.55	11.46	11.94	13.67	8.51	12.66
1981	14.029	13.776	14.44	13.91	14.17	16.04	11.23	14.70
1982	10.686	11.084	12.92	13.00	13.79	16.11	11.57	15.14
1983	8.63	8.75	10.45	11.10	12.04	13.55	9.47	12.57
1984	9.58	9.80	11.89	12.44	12.71	14.19	10.15	12.38
1985	7.48	7.66	9.64	10.62	11.37	12.72	9.18	11.55
1986	5.98	6.03	7.06	7.68	9.02	10.39	7.38	10.17
1987	5.82	6.05	7.68	8.39	9.38	10.58	7.73	9.31
1988	6.69	6.92	8.26	8.85	9.71	10.83	7.76	

Source: Economic Report of the President, 1989.

References

Economic Report of the President, various years. Washington, DC: US Government Printing Office.

Federal Reserve Bulletin, various issues.

Rand Corporation (1955) *A Million Random Digits With One Hundred Thousand Normal Deviates.* Santa Monica, CA: Rand Corporation.

Survey of Current Business, various issues. Washington, DC: Bureau of Economic Analysis, US Department of Commerce.

Value Line Selection and Opinion, January 9, 1981, p. 861. New York: Arnold Bernhard.

Further Reading

Abraham, B. and Ledolter, J. (1983) *Statistical Methods For Forecasting.* New York: John Wiley, chs. 5, 6.

Chatfield, C. (1984) *The Analysis of Time Series, An Introduction.* London: Chapman and Hall.

Cryer, J. (1986) *Time Series Analysis.* Boston, MA: Duxbury, chs 4, 5.

Farnum, N. R. and Stanton, L. W. (1989) *Quantitative Forecasting Methods.* Boston, MA: PWS-Kent, ch. 7.

Granger, C. W. J. (1989) *Forecasting in Business and Economics.* New York: Academic Press, chs 2, 3.

Granger, C. W. J. and Newbold, P. (1986) *Forecasting Economic Time Series.* New York: Academic Press, chs 1, 3.

Hanke, J. R. and Reitsch, A. C. (1989), *Business Forecasting.* Boston, MA: Allyn and Bacon, ch. 10.

Hoff, J. C. (1983) *A Practical Guide To Box–Jenkins Forecasting,* Belmont, CA: Lifetime Learning, chs 1–9.

Makridakis, S., Wheelwright, S. and McGee, V. (1983) *Forecasting: Methods and Applications.* New York: Wiley, ch. 8.

O'Donovan, T. M. (1983) *Short Term Forecasting.* New York: Wiley, chs 2, 3.

Pandit, S. M. and Wu, S. M. (1983) *Time Series and Systems Analysis With Applications.* New York: Wiley, chs 1–4.

Pankratz, A. (1983) *Forecasting with Univariate Box–Jenkins Models.* New York: Wiley, chs 2–7.

Shumway, R. H. (1988) *Applied Statistical Time Series Analysis.* Englewood Cliffs, NJ: Prentice-Hall, ch. 3.

Thomopoulos, N. T. (1980) *Applied Forecasting Methods.* Englewood Cliffs, NJ: Prentice-Hall, ch. 11.

Vandaele, W. (1983) *Applied Time Series and Box–Jenkins Models.* New York: Academic Press.

Appendix A   The Relationship between the Estimated Autoregressive Parameter and the Estimated Autocorrelation Coefficient

Let us consider the autoregressive model of equation (7.26):

$$Y_t = \phi Y_{t-1} + e_t$$

If both sides of this equation are multiplied by Y_{t-1}, the result is

$$Y_{t-1}Y_t = \phi_1 Y_{t-1}Y_t + Y_{t-1}e_t \qquad (7.A1)$$

Taking the expected value of (7.25) yields

$$\theta_1 = \phi_1\theta_0 \qquad (7.A2)$$

since $E(Y_{t-1}Y_t) = \theta_0$ and $E(Y_{t-1}e_t) = 0$ by definition. If both sides of (7.26) are divided by θ_0 the result is

$$\rho_1 = \phi_1 \qquad (7.A3)$$

since $\rho_1 = \theta_1/\theta_0$. Thus, $\phi_1 = \hat{\rho}_1 = r_1$. Stated differently, the partial autocorrelation of one time lag is ϕ_1 and r_1 is its estimator. The general solution to equations (7.26)–(7.29) is a process described by Box and Jenkins (1976) and results in estimates of the partial autocorrelations of up to m time lags.

Appendix B   On Identifying Stationary Autoregressive Time Series Models

In this chapter we noted that autoregressive models are characterized by the behavior of their theoretical autocorrelation coefficients and their theoretical partial autocorrelation coefficients. In turn, if we conclude that the behavior of the theoretical autocorrelation coefficients and theoretical partial autocorrelation coefficients of an observed stationary time series is identical with the behavior of the theoretical autocorrelation and partial autocorrelation coefficients, then it is reasonable to assume tentatively that that particular time series model generates the observed stationary time series. Thus it is very important to understand the behavior of stationary plots of autocorrelation and partial autocorrelation coefficients.

Let us consider a simple ARIMA (1,0,0) model of the form

$$Y_t = \mu + \phi_1 Y_{t-1} + e_t \qquad (7.B1)$$

How do we decide whether this is a stationary model? One way is to write the model in terms of past error terms by substituting Y_{t-1}, Y_{t-2}, etc., a procedure which results in

$$Y_t = \frac{\mu}{1 - \phi_1} + e_t + \phi_1 e_{t-1} + \phi_1 e_{t-2} + \dots \qquad (7.B2)$$

Furthermore, for stationarity to exist the ARIMA(1, 0, 0) model requires that $-1 < \phi_1 < 1$ and the mean of the process be

$$E(Y_t) = \frac{\mu_t}{1 - \phi_1} \qquad (7.B3)$$

Finally, the autocorrelation function for the ARIMA(1,0,0) model is

$$\rho_k = \phi_1^k \tag{7.B4}$$

which indicates that the autocorrelation between observed values declines in an exponential fashion with the number of periods separating them. Figure 7.B1(a) indicates the behavior of the autocorrelation coefficients of a particular stationary autoregressive model. In a similar manner, figure 7.B1(b) indicates the behavior of autocorrelation coefficients for a different ARIMA(1,0,0) model. The autocorrelation for this process is negative for odd lags and positive for even lags. The plot appears very jagged with successive autocorrelation coefficients decaying towards zero. Finally, figure 7.B1(c) indicates a third type of behavior of the autocorrelation coefficients of an ARIMA(1,0,0) model. In this model, the autocorrelation coefficients die down in a damped sine wave fashion. In all these models the plots of the autocorrelation coefficients exhibit a decaying or damping towards zero. In general, a minimum of about 10–15 time lags is necessary to exhibit the apparent decaying processes; often more lags will be required to determine whether the damping process is occurring.

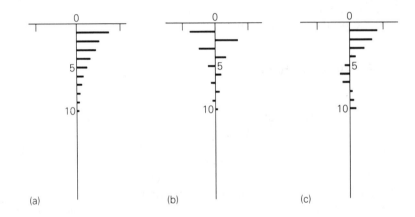

FIGURE 7.B1 Damping patterns for autocorrelation coefficients of autoregressive models: (a) dying down in a damped exponential fashion – no oscillation; (b) dying down in a damped exponential fashion – oscillation; (c) dying down in a damped sine-wave fashion

Before we discuss other models, why does the stationary requirement that $-1 < \phi_1 < 1$ make sense? If $\phi_1 = 1$, the ARIMA(1,0,0) model is a nonstationary random walk. However, if $\phi_1 < 1$, say 2, the observed values of Y_t would behave not only in a nonstationary way but also with explosive growth. Furthermore, after some time periods, the time series would become virtually nonstochastic since the size of the observed values would become extremely large and the residual errors e_t would become negligible in comparison.

For a second-order autoregressive model, ARIMA(2,0,0),

$$Y_t = \mu + \phi_1 Y_{t-1} + \phi_2 Y_{t-1} + \phi_2 Y_{t-2} + e_t \tag{7.B5}$$

Stationarity is assumed if

$$\phi_1 + \phi_2 < 1$$
$$\phi_2 - \phi_1 < 1$$
$$-1 < \phi_2 < 1$$

The range of patterns for the autocorrelation coefficients is more complicated for ARIMA(2,0,0) than for ARIMA(1,0,0). However, usually the autocorrelation coefficients will either be positive as they damp down to zero (figure 7.B1(a)) or they will alternate in sign as they damp down to zero. In special cases (as in $\phi_1 = 1.0$, $\phi_2 = -0.75$), the autocorrelation coefficients will appear as a damped sine wave.[2]

Appendix C   Examples of Micro-TSP Output

In this appendix we give examples of partial output from the command IDENT in Micro-TSP for computing autocorrelations and drawing the autocorrelation func-

```
IDENT RANDOM
Date:            / Time:  10:30
SMPL range:     1 -      40
Number of observations:  40
=================================================================
   Autocorrelations     Partial Autocorrelations        ac        pac
=================================================================

        .     .              .     .          1  -0.034    -0.034
      . ** .              .   ** .            2  -0.146    -0.147
        .     .              .     .          3   0.008    -0.003
      .  * .                .   ** .          4  -0.093    -0.117
      .*** .               .*** .             5  -0.209    -0.224
      .  * .                .    * .          6  -0.042    -0.106
        . * .                .     .          7   0.083     0.001
      .  * .                .   * .           8  -0.060    -0.108
      .  * .                .  ** .           9  -0.084    -0.152
        . ** .                 . * .         10   0.187     0.087
      .  * .                .  ** .          11  -0.095    -0.159
      . ** .                .  ** .          12  -0.144    -0.161
        . ** .                .     .        13   0.134     0.029
        . * .                 .     .        14   0.048    -0.032
        .  .                   . * .         15   0.038     0.071
        . ** .                 . ** .        16   0.175     0.168
      . ** .                .*** .           17  -0.188    -0.261
      . * .                 .     .          18  -0.040     0.037
      . * .                 .     .          19  -0.040    -0.020
      . * .                .  ** .           20  -0.066    -0.140
      . * .                .   * .           21  -0.086    -0.072
        . * .                 .     .        22   0.067     0.022
        . * .                 .   * .        23   0.105    -0.060
        .  .                   .     .       24  -0.006     0.019

=================================================================
                          S. E. of Correlations  0.158
                          ================================
```

FIGURE 7.C1

---

2 For proof of these results, see Nelson (1973, pp. 38–45).

tion. As can be seen the output is similar to Minitab. It should also be noted that the use of the command IDENT in Micro-TSP will draw the partial autocorrelation function automatically. Hence, the software user will have both the ordinary autocorrelation function and the partial autocorrelation function along with their values displayed at the same time.

Figure 7.C1 contains the autocorrelation function that is equivalent to figure 7.1. The time series was labeled RANDOM and is for an ARIMA(0,0,0) model. All autocorrelation coefficients would lie within small distances of the zero midpoint.

Figure 7.C2 contains the autocorrelation function drawn by Micro-TSP for the time series labeled ES. This function is equivalent to figure 7.2 for the time series of the residuals from the forecast of real estate loans by the single exponential smoothing model. The partial autocorrelation function is also automatically drawn by Micro-TSP and appears in this figure.

Figure 7.C3 shows the ordinary and partial autocorrelation functions for the time series labeled BROWN are drawn. This figure is equivalent to figure 7.3, the autocorrelations for the residuals from the forecast of real estate loans by Brown's trend model.

```
IDENT ES
Date:            / Time: 10:39
SMPL range:    1 -    24
Number of observations: 24
================================================================================
    Autocorrelations      Partial Autocorrelations      ac          pac
================================================================================
    .    *********          .    *********       1   0.771        0.771
    .    *******            .  *       .          2   0.577       -0.042
    .    ******             .          .          3   0.443        0.030
    .    ******             .    ***   .          4   0.426        0.210
    .    *****              .  *       .          5   0.358       -0.103
    .    ***  .             .  **      .          6   0.217       -0.192
    .    **   .             .       *  .          7   0.121        0.046
    .    *    .             .  *       .          8   0.053       -0.069
    .         .             .  *       .          9  -0.002       -0.091
    .    *    .             .  *       .         10  -0.090       -0.076
    .  ***    .             .  ***     .         11  -0.219       -0.195
    .  ***    .             .       *  .         12  -0.238        0.114
    .  ***    .             .          .         13  -0.239       -0.030
    .  ***    .             .       *  .         14  -0.235       -0.052
    . ****    .             .       *  .         15  -0.305       -0.100
    *****     .             .       *  .         16  -0.362       -0.077
    . ****    .             .          *         17  -0.324        0.073
    . ****    .             .  **      .         18  -0.309       -0.120
    . ****    .             .          .         19  -0.299       -0.033
    . ****    .             .          .         20  -0.308        0.017
================================================================================

                                    S. E. of Correlations  0.204
                              ==================================================
```

FIGURE 7.C2

```
IDENT BROWN
Date:           / Time: 10:41
SMPL range:     3 -     24
Number of observations: 22
==============================================================================
   Autocorrelations    Partial Autocorrelations        ac        pac
==============================================================================
  .      |*****.    :      .    |*****.    :  1   0.385      0.385
  .    * |     .    :      . *** |     .    :  2  -0.063     -0.248
  .    * |     .    :      .     |*    .    :  3  -0.052      0.093
  .      |***  .    :      .     |*** .    :  4   0.228      0.252
  .      |**   .    :      .    * |    .    :  5   0.153     -0.090
  .    **|     .    :      .    **|    .    :  6  -0.122     -0.133
  .      |     .    :      .     |**   .    :  7  -0.028      0.189
  .      |***  .    :      .     |**   .    :  8   0.258      0.169
  .      |**** .    :      .     |    .     :  9   0.279      0.038
  .    * |     .    :      .    **|    .    : 10  -0.061     -0.135
  .*****|     .    :      . ****|     .    : 11  -0.369     -0.309
  . ****|     .    :      . ***|     .    : 12  -0.321     -0.255
  .      |     .    :      .     |*    .    : 13  -0.019      0.085
  .    * |     .    :      .    * |    .    : 14  -0.054     -0.096
  .   **|     .    :      .     |    .     : 15  -0.190     -0.017
  .   **|     .    :      .     |    .     : 16  -0.158     -0.004
  .      |*    .    :      .    * |    .    : 17   0.046     -0.041
  .      |     .    :      .    * |    .    : 18  -0.001     -0.105
  .   **|     .    :      .     |**   .    : 19  -0.161      0.154
  . ***|     .    :      .     |*    .    : 20  -0.204      0.081
==============================================================================
                                    S. E. of Correlations  0.213
                              ==============================
```

FIGURE 7.C3

References to Appendix

Box, G. E. P. and Jenkins, G. M. (1976) *Time Series Analysis: Forecasting and Control,* revised edn. San Francisco, CA: Holden-Day.

Nelson, C. R. (1973) *Applied Time Series Analysis.* San Francisco, CA: Holden-Day.

CHAPTER 8

Additional Time Series Models and Identification

Objectives

In this chapter, we continue the study of building ARIMA models. The characteristics and form of moving average (MA) and mixed autoregressive moving-average (ARMA) models are discussed. Questions concerning the identification of these and purely seasonal models are considered and answered. By the end of the chapter, you will be able to:

1 Identify nonseasonal time series models.
2 State and explain nonseasonal models.
3 Understand the problems associated with achieving stationarity by differencing and by transformation.
4 Identify purely seasonal models.
5 State and explain purely seasonal models.

Outline

Key Terms

- Moving-average model
- Invertibility
- Autoregressive moving-average model

- Parsimonious model
- Seasonal autoregressive parameter
- Seasonal moving-average parameter
- Seasonal autoregressive moving-average model

8.1   Introduction

In the last chapter, characteristics of a time series were examined to determine its properties. The properties of time series under consideration were as follows: (a) randomness; (b) stationarity; (c) if nonstationary, the level of differencing at which the series becomes stationary; (d) seasonality; (e) if seasonal, the length of the seasonality. Knowledge of these properties will permit us to produce better forecasts.

In this and the next chapter, we shall study approaches to forecasting time series where these properties will be used to build an ARIMA model. To do this, we first study the properties of time series models. In chapter 7, we learned that autoregressive (AR) models express the time series variable Y_t as a linear function of some number of actual past values of Y_t. To continue this study, we shall learn that many moving-average (MA) models provide forecasts of Y based on a linear combination of past errors (residuals). In addition, we find that autoregressive moving-average (ARMA) models are a combination of AR and MA models. They forecast Y as both a linear combination of actual past values and a linear combination of past errors. ARMA or mixed models are said to fit certain time series more adequately than either AR or MA models.

We study these models to enable us to understand and implement Box–Jenkins methodology (chapter 9). The difference between this methodology and previous methods is that Box–Jenkins methodology does not assume anything about the number of terms or the relative weights to be assigned to the terms in the model. The methodology permits forecasters to select the appropriate ARMA, AR, or MA model scientifically after a careful analysis of the statistical properties of the time series. Software systems are used to compute the coefficients of the ARIMA model using a nonlinear least squares technique. Finally, forecasts for future time intervals can be made after tests are conducted concerning the adequacy of the identified model.

To begin, we must continue our study of ARIMA models and how we use our knowledge of autocorrelations and partial autocorrelations to identify these models.

8.2   Moving-average Models

AR(p) models cannot isolate certain data patterns when p is small. However, an alternative model – the *moving-average model* – may isolate the pattern when AR(p) models fail. Wold (1954) showed that any discrete time series can be expressed as an AR model, an MA model, or a combination called an ARMA model. Recent advances in computer technology and software development have permitted forecasters and analysts to utilize ARMA models operationally.

MA models provide predictions of Y_t based on a linear combination of past forecast errors. In contrast, AR models express Y_t as a linear function of p actual past values of Y_t. The general MA model is

$$Y_t = \mu + e_t - \theta_1 e_{t-1} - \theta_2 e_{t-2} - \ldots - \theta_q e_{t-q} \tag{8.1}$$

If $\mu = 0$, we have

$$Y_t = e_t - \theta_1 e_{t-1} - \theta_2 e_{t-2} - \ldots - \theta_q e_{t-q} \tag{8.2}$$

The above equation is expressed without a constant term to be consistent with the previous definition of the AR model (equation (7.29)). Note that the term "moving average" used in this context has nothing to do with the moving averages examined in chapter 2 or those used in chapter 3 in decomposing a time series. Also, the $\theta_1 + \theta_2 + \ldots + \theta_q$ are not necessarily equal to unity nor are the values of the θ_i changing or "moving" as new observations are obtained. Although there may be confusion in the use of this term, we shall continue to use it in this chapter to be consistent with the literature of time series.

The letter q in MA(q) refers to the order of the model. For example, an MA(1) model is

$$Y_t = e_t - \theta_1 e_{t-1} \qquad \text{ARIMA}(0,0,1) \tag{8.3}$$

Note that Y_t is a linear combination of the current and previous uncorrelated (white noise) residuals.

An MA(2) model (without a constant term) is written as

$$Y_t = e_t - \theta_1 e_{t-1} - \theta_2 e_{t-2} \qquad \text{ARIMA}(0,0,2) \tag{8.4}$$

We should note that, although we use the name moving average, the method is similar to the exponential smoothing models of chapter 2 and not to the moving averages of the same chapter.

In chapter 7, we discussed the property of stationarity of a time series model. In modeling MA processes another property called invertibility is required in describing and forecasting a time series. Although we shall not develop the rigorous definition of invertibility, we shall show those conditions for both stationarity and invertibility of a given time series model that can be expressed in terms of the model parameters.

To begin, consider the ARIMA(0,0,1) model

$$Y_t = \mu + e_t - \theta_1 e_{t-1} \tag{8.5}$$

or

$$Y_t = e_t - \theta_1 e_{t-1} \qquad \text{when } \mu = 0 \tag{8.6}$$

It can be shown that, for any value of the parameter θ_1, the ARIMA(0,0,1) model describes the behavior of a stationary time series. Thus there are no conditions that must be imposed on θ_1 to make the model described by equation (8.6) stationary. However, certain conditions are imposed on the parameters of MA models to ensure invertibility. *Invertibility* refers to the possibility of inverting an MA model and expressing it as an AR model of infinite order. An AR model of infinite order has an infinite number of autoregressive coefficients. An MA model is invertible, for example, if the deviation $Y_t - \mu$ does not depend overwhelmingly on deviations in the distant past and this is a reasonable requirement. For an MA(1) model, the invertibility condition is

$$-1 < \theta_1 < 1$$

Knowledge of the stationarity and invertibility conditions on the parameters of a time series model is of paramount importance in estimating the parameters of the model.

We can show that the mean of a time series model ARIMA(0,0,1) is μ and that the theoretical partial autocorrelation function of this trails off to zero in a pattern described by exponential decay. Furthermore, the theoretical autocorrelation function cuts off after a lag of 1. Also, we can show that

$$\rho_k = \begin{cases} \dfrac{-\theta_1}{1 + \theta_1^2} & \text{for } k = 1 \\[2ex] 0 & \text{for } k > 1 \end{cases} \tag{8.7}$$

Knowledge of the relationship between ρ_k and the parameters of a given time series model is important in estimating the parameters of the model. We should notice that in describing the behavior of partial correlations of the ARIMA(0,0,1) model, we say "dying down in a damped exponential fashion." In chapter 9, we shall describe the dying down of both autocorrelation functions and partial autocorrelation functions with words like in a "damped exponential" fashion or in a "damped sine wave" fashion. The meanings of these phrases were described in figure 7.B1. We should note whether it is the autocorrelation functions or the partial autocorrelation functions which die down or cut off. These patterns will permit us to describe a given time series by a particular time series model.

As an example, consider an MA(1) model where $\theta_1 > 0$. In figure 8.1 note that the autocorrelation function (ACF) cuts off after lag 1. This is a characteristic property of the MA(1) or ARIMA(0,0,1) model and means that the memory of an MA(1) model is only one time period long. Stated differently, Y_t is correlated with its predecessor Y_{t-1} and its sucessor Y_{t+1} but not with any other members of the sequence of variables $Y_1, Y_2,\dots$. The theoretical partial autocorrelation function (PACF) dies down to zero as shown in figure 8.1. Exact patterns of the PACF depend on the value of the parameter θ_1. For $\theta_1 > 0$, the pattern dies down with successively smaller negative partial autocorrelations. Finally, the MA(1) model is a simple and useful time series although it is not as widely used as the AR(1) or AR(2) models. It is characterized by the fact that its ACF cuts off after lag 1 and its PACF dies down toward zero.

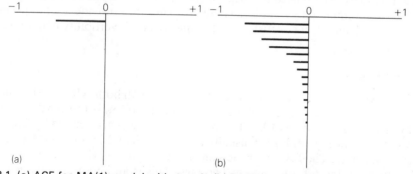

(a)　　　　　　　　　　　　　(b)

FIGURE 8.1　(a) ACF for MA(1) model with $\theta_1 > 0$; (b) PACF for MA(1) model with $\theta_1 > 0$

8.3　Autoregressive Moving-average Models

Autocorrelation patterns may require more complex models. A more general model is a mixture of the AR(p) and MA(q) models and is called an *autoregressive moving-average model* (ARMA model):

$$Y_t = \mu + \phi_1 Y_{t-1} + \phi_2 Y_{t-2} + \ldots + \phi_p Y_{t-p} + e_t -$$

$$\theta_1 e_{t-1} - \theta_2 e_{t-2} - \ldots - \theta_q e_{t-q} \tag{8.8}$$

If $\mu = 0$, then we have

$$Y_t = \phi_1 Y_{t-1} + \ldots + \phi_p Z_{t-p} + e_t - \theta_1 e_{t-1} - \ldots - \theta_q e_{t-q} \tag{8.9}$$

Like the AR(p) model, the ARMA (p,q) model has autocorrelations that diminish as the distance between residuals increases. However, the patterns in the time series that can be described by ARMA(p,q) processes are more general than those of either AR(p) or MA(q) models.

An ARMA(1,1) model is

$$Y_t = \mu + \phi_1 Y_{t-1} + e_t - \phi_1 e_{t-1} \qquad \text{ARIMA(1,0,1)} \tag{8.10}$$

and an ARMA(2,1) model is

$$Y_t = \mu + \phi_1 Y_{t-2} + \phi_2 Y_{t-2} + e_t - \theta_1 e_{t-1} \qquad \text{ARIMA(2,0,1)} \tag{8.11}$$

It can be shown that the mixed ARIMA(1,1) model is stationary if

$$-1 < \phi_1 < 1$$

and is invertible if

$$-1 < \theta_1 < 1$$

The constant of this model is $\mu/(1 - \phi_1)$.

Its theoretical ACF and PACF trail off to zero in a damped exponential fashion. In particular, we can show that

$$\rho_1 = \frac{(1 - \phi_1\theta_1)(\phi_1 - \theta_1)}{1 - \theta_1^2 - 2\theta_1\phi_1} \tag{8.12}$$

$$\rho_2 = \phi_1\rho_1$$

$$\rho_k = \phi_1\rho_{k-1} \qquad \text{for } k \geq 3$$

These relationships are used to solve for the parameters ϕ_1 and θ_1 in terms of ρ_1 and ρ_2 which are estimated by r_1 and r_2. These estimates thus provide a set of preliminary estimates of $\hat\phi$ and $\hat\theta_1$ that satisfy the stationarity and invertibility conditions:

$$-1 < \hat\phi < 1$$

$$-1 < \hat\theta_1 < 1$$

Mixed ARMA processes have theoretical ACFs with both AR and MA characteristics. As an example, the ACF in figure 8.2(a) tails off toward zero with exponential decay. The ACF of an ARMA(1,1) model can also be characterized by damped sine waves. In practice, p and q are usually not larger than 2 in an ARIMA model for nonseasonal data. The PACF for the same model (figure 8.2(b)) tails off toward zero rather than cutting off after one or two lags. This is an important characteristic of ARMA models. Neither the ACF nor the PACF cut off in mixed ARMA models. Finally, it has been found that most of the stationary time series occurring in practice can be fitted by AR(1), AR(2), MA(1), MA(2), ARMA(1,1) or white noise models. In other words, these six models are the only time series models that are customarily needed in practice.

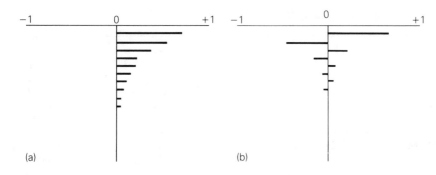

FIGURE 8.2 (a) ACF for ARMA(1,1) model; (b) PACF for ARMA(1,1) model

8.4 A Summary of Modeling Nonseasonal Time Series Models

Up to this point, we have examined common models used to forecast time series by means of Box–Jenkins methods (to be discussed in chapter 9). Before proceeding to consider forecasting methods further, we shall summarize these nonseasonal models and their statistical properties. Table 8.1 summarizes the discussion of general AR, MA, and mixed ARMA models. Conditions for stationarity and invertibility required by each model and a description of the behavior of the theoretical ACFs and PACFs for each model are given in the table.

Table 8.2 summarizes the same stationarity and invertibility conditions for useful specific time series models. The behavior of the theoretical ACFs and PACFs are also summarized. Tables 8.1 and 8.2 are very helpful in identifying the appropriate time series models for Box–Jenkins estimation. For example, if for a stationary time series we concluded that an MA(1) model generated the time series because the autocorrelation coefficient cuts off after lag 1 and the partial autocorrelation was dominated by damped exponential decay, we could estimate the model by a specific Box–Jenkins method. We should point out that if we cannot identify the appropriate model, our estimation may not lead to useful results for the purposes of forecasting.

TABLE 8.1 Identifying general time series models

(1) Model	(2) Stationarity conditions?	(3) Invertibility conditions?	(4) Autocorrelation coefficients	(5) Theoretical function Partial autocorrelation coefficients
1 AR(p)	Yes	No	Dies down	Cuts off after lag p
2 MA(q)	No	Yes	Cuts off after lag q	Dies down
3 ARMA(p,q)	Yes	Yes	Dies down	Dies down

Notes: Time series models

1 AR(p) $Y_t = \mu + \phi_1 Y_{t\text{-}1} + \phi_2 Y_{t\text{-}2} + \ldots + \phi_p Y_{t-p} + e_t$

2 MA(q) $Y_t = \mu + e_t - \theta_1 e_{t-1} - \phi_2 e_{t\text{-}2} - \ldots - \phi_q e_{t-q}$

3 ARMA(p,q) $Y_t = \mu + \phi_1 Y_{t\text{-}1} + \phi_2 Y_{t\text{-}2} + \ldots + \phi_p Y_{t-p} - \theta_1 e_{t-1-1} - \theta_2 e_{t-2} - \ldots - \theta_q e_{t-q} + e_t$

TABLE 8.2   Specific time series models

(1) Model	(2) Stationarity conditions?	(3) Invertibility conditions?	(4) Theoretical function Autocorrelation coefficients	(5) Theoretical function Partial autocorrelation coefficients
1 ARIMA$(1,d,0)$ or AR(1)	$-1<\phi_1<1$	None	Dies down	Cuts off after one lag
2 ARIMA$(2,d,0)$ or AR(2)	$\phi_1 + \phi_2<1$ $\theta_1 - \phi_2<1$ $-1<\theta_2<1$	None	Dies down	Cuts off after two lags
3 ARIMA$(0,d,1)$ or MA(1)	None	$\theta_1 < 1$	Cuts off after one lag	Dies down
4 ARIMA$(0,d,2)$ or MA(2)	None	$\theta_1 + \theta_2 < 1$ $\theta_2 - \theta_1 < 1$ $\theta_2 < 1$	Cuts off after two lags	Dies down
5 ARIMA$(1,d,1)$	$-1 < \phi_1 < 1$	$-1 < \theta_1 < 1$	Dies down	Dies down

It can be seen in table 8.2 that the theoretical ACFs of both AR(1) and AR(2) processes can die down in a damped exponential manner. Hence it is difficult to distinguish between AR(1) and AR(2) models without examining the sample PACFs. To distinguish between AR(1) and AR(2) models, it is important to determine whether the sample PACFs cut off after one or two lags.

In a similar way, we cannot look at only the sample PACFs of MA processes to distinguish between an MA(1) and an MA(2) process. Only by examining the behavior of the sample ACFs to see when they cut off can we distinguish between them. In general, to identify the particular AR(p), MA(q), or ARMA(p,q) process which generated the time series, we must examine the behavior of both the sample ACFs and the sample PACFs. We must try to determine whether the function is decaying or cuts off. Finally, the number of lags of coefficients examined must be large enough to identify whether a particular pattern in the coefficients dominates the movement. In general, at least ten lags should be examined.

The models used in Box–Jenkins methodology contain only a few parameters. None of the models summarized in table 8.2 contain more than three parameters. A goal of developing forecasting models is to obtain *parsimonious models*. Stated differently, we desire forecasting models that adequately describe time series and use only a few parameters. A rule to follow is that if two different models adequately describe a time series equally well, the model with fewer parameters should be chosen for purposes of forecasting. With fewer parameters to estimate, the estimation process is simple, the model is simpler to interpret, and there are often fewer sources of forecast error. Finally, with relatively few parameters, it is less difficult to find parameter estimators which are statistically significant. In chapter 9, we shall see the need for identifying seasonal models as well as the nonseasonal models considered here.

8.5   Backshift Operators for MA and ARMA Models

In chapter 7, the backshift operator B was introduced to enable us to express AR models mathematically. In a similar manner, MA or mixed ARMA models can be expressed in terms of B. For example, an MA(1) model is given by

$$Y_t = e_t - \theta_1 B e_t$$

or

$$Y_t = (1 - \theta_1 B) e_t \qquad \text{ARIMA}(0,0,1) \tag{8.13}$$

An MA(2) model is given by

$$Y_t = (1 - \theta_1 B - \theta_2 B^2) e_t \qquad \text{ARIMA}(0,0,2) \tag{8.14}$$

An MA(2) model for first-differenced data is given by

$$(1 - B)Y_t = (1 - \theta_1 B - \theta_2 B^2) e_t \qquad \text{ARIMA}(0,1,2) \tag{8.15}$$

An ARIMA(1,0,1) model is given by

$$(1 - \phi_1 B)Y_t = (1 - \theta_1 B) e_t \tag{8.16}$$

Finally, an ARIMA(1,1,1) model is given by

$$(1 - B)(1 - \phi_1 B)Y_t = (1 - \theta_1 B) e_t \tag{8.17}$$

8.6   Examples of Nonseasonal Time Series

A time series of 100 observations is analyzed by examining the plots of (ordinary) autocorrelations and partial autocorrelations in figures 8.3 and 8.4. Since the series was generated by a random process, it is known to be stationary. The autocorrelation plot (figure 8.3) gives evidence of stationarity since the autocorrelations drop off rapidly to zero after order 3 or 4. The plot of autocorrelations indicates that there are three significant autocorrelations. After the first three, they rapidly drop off toward zero. Although autocorrelation coefficients for orders 13, 14, and 15 are slightly outside the approximate 2σ limits, we can conclude that this is a stationary time series. From time to time, a forecaster may find some coefficients outside the limits for higher-order coefficients. Unless there are some unusual circumstances it can still be concluded that the series is stationary. In this instance the series is a simulated series generated by a random process for an ARIMA(1,0,0) model. In figure 8.4, the partial autocorrelation of order 1 is large and the remaining coefficients are very close to zero. This indicates that coefficients cut off after order 1. Thus the autocorrelations die down and the partial autocorrelations cut off after order 1, indicating that an ARIMA(1,0,0) process gave rise to the time series observations.

The plots of autocorrelations and partial autocorrelations in figures 8.5 and 8.6 suggest that another ARIMA model generates the time series observations. Figure 8.6 indicates that the partial autocorrelations die down after coefficients of order 3 or 4. Furthermore, the ordinary autocorrelations (figure 8.5) have a large coefficient at order 1 but cut off after the first coefficient. This indicates that the model is stationary and is generated by an ARIMA(0,0,1) model.

ORDER	AUTO– CORR.	S.E. RANDOM MODEL	−1 −.75 −.50 −.25 0 .25 .50 .75 +1
			: ----: -----: ----: ----: ----: ----: ----: -----:
1	0.578	0.099	+ : + *
2	0.303	0.098	+ : +*
3	0.202	0.098	+ : *
4	0.143	0.097	+ : *+
5	0.078	0.097	+ : * +
6	0.054	0.096	+ :* +
7	−0.015	0.095	+ * +
8	0.003	0.095	+ * +
9	0.015	0.094	+ * +
10	−0.032	0.094	+ *: +
11	−0.072	0.093	+ *: +
12	−0.175	0.093	* : +
13	−0.267	0.092	*+ : +
14	−0.261	0.092	*+ : +
15	−0.243	0.091	*+ : +
16	−0.223	0.091	* : +
17	−0.190	0.090	* : +
18	−0.107	0.090	+ * : +
19	−0.084	0.089	+ * : +
20	−0.161	0.089	+* : +
21	−0.085	0.088	+ * : +
22	−0.079	0.087	+* : +
23	−0.077	0.087	+* : +
24	−0.033	0.086	+ *: +
			: ----: -----: ----: ----: ----: ----: ----: -----:
			−1 −.75 −.50 −.25 0 .25 .50 .75 +1

```
                              * :  AUTOCORRELATIONS
                              + :  2 STANDARD ERROR LIMITS  (APPROX.)
   NUMBER OF OBSERVATIONS = 100
```

FIGURE 8.3 Example of ARIMA(1,0,0) model. Ordinary autocorrelations (Note: computer-generated IDA output)

Figures 8.7 and 8.8 are the plots of autocorrelations and partial autocorrelations for a time series of 200 observations generated by another ARIMA model. In this case, the autocorrelations die down after order 5. The partial autocorrelations die down after order 4. Since the plots of both autocorrelations and partial autocorrelations die down and do not cut off, it can be concluded that the time series model that gave rise to these observations was an ARIMA(1,0,1) model. Finally, this series was also generated by a random process with a stationary ARIMA(1,0,1) on the computer.

The purpose of examining these plots is to enable one to understand how the statistical properties of a time series process enables the ARIMA model that gives rise to the process to be identified. In these illustrations, the time series observations were generated on a computer using ARMA models. In practice, a forecaster will not know in advance which ARIMA model gives rise to the time series observations. Hence, the process must be carried out with care.

ORDER	PARTIAL AUTO COR									

```
                  PARTIAL
   ORDER          AUTO COR
                            -1   -.75  -.50  -.25    0    .25   .50   .75    1
                            :-----:----:----:-----:----:----:----:----:
      1           0.5784    -                         :                 *
      2          -0.0474    -                        *:
      3           0.0689    -                         : *
      4           0.0106    -                         *
      5          -0.0244    -                         *
      6           0.0203    -                         *
      7          -0.0839    -                      *  :
      8           0.0662    -                         : *
      9          -0.0048    -                         *
     10          -0.0647    -                        *:
     11          -0.0352    -                        *:
     12          -0.1734    -                     *   :
     13          -0.1250    -                     *   :
     14          -0.0400    -                        *:
     15          -0.0608    -                        *:
     16          -0.0241    -                         *
     17          -0.0338    -                        *:
     18           0.0657    -                         : *
     19          -0.0478    -                        *:
     20          -0.1645    -                     *   :
     21           0.1352    -                         :   *
     22          -0.1020    -                     *   :
     23           0.0026    -                         *
     24           0.0259    -                         : *
```

FIGURE 8.4 Example of ARIMA(1,0,0) model. Partial autocorrelations (Note: computer-generated IDA output)

8.7   Constant Terms in ARIMA Models

The constant term has generally been omitted from the ARIMA models presented in this and the previous chapters. In the absence of a constant term μ, the arithmetic mean of a stationary time series generating the differences $Y_t - Y_{t-1}$ is zero. Hence the mean difference over a long time period will be approximately zero. If this behavior is present in differenced time series, how does it affect undifferenced time series? Stated simply, if a process exhibits no affinity for a mean value, it also exhibits no persistent tendency or trend in either the positive or the negative direction.

Let us now consider the effect of the presence of a constant. The mean or expected value of a process of differences $Y_t - Y_{t-1}$ is given by

$$E(Y_t - Y_{t-1}) = \frac{\mu}{1 - \phi_1 - \ldots - \phi_p} \tag{8.18}$$

This expression indicates that the mean difference over a long time period will not be zero. For example, if the degree of differencing is unity ($d = 1$), the mean change will be greater than zero and the series Y will tend to drift upward. Of course, the

```
                     S.E.
            AUTO-    RANDOM
 ORDER      CORR.    MODEL        -1  -.75 -.50 -.25   0   .25  .50  .75  +1
                                  :----:-----:----:----:----:----:----:----:
    1      -0.407   0.099                         *    +    :         +
    2      -0.164   0.098                            + *    :         +
    3       0.075   0.098                            +    :  *        +
    4       0.008   0.097                            +       *        +
    5       0.007   0.097                            +       *        +
    6       0.019   0.096                            +       *        +
    7       0.044   0.095                            +    :  *        +
    8      -0.163   0.095                            + *    :         +
    9       0.002   0.094                            +       *        +
   10       0.166   0.094                            +    :     *     +
   11      -0.025   0.093                            +       *        +
   12      -0.059   0.093                            +    *:          +
   13      -0.131   0.092                            + *    :         +
   14       0.120   0.092                            +    :  *        +
   15       0.101   0.091                            +    :  *        +
   16      -0.060   0.091                            +    *:          +
   17      -0.125   0.090                            + *    :         +
   18       0.155   0.090                            +    :     *+
   19      -0.069   0.089                            +    *:          +
   20       0.044   0.089                            +    :  *        +
   21      -0.028   0.088                            +    *:          +
   22      -0.053   0.087                           +    *:    +
   23       0.092   0.087                           +    :   *+
   24      -0.095   0.086                           + *  :    +
                                  :----:-----:----:----:----:----:----:----:
                                  -1  -.75 -.50 -.25   0   .25  .50  .75  +1

                             *  :  AUTOCORRELATIONS
                             + : 2 STANDARD ERROR LIMITS  (APPROX.)
 NUMBER OF OBSERVATIONS = 100
```

FIGURE 8.5 Example of ARIMA(0,0,1) model. Ordinary autocorrelations (Note: computer-generated IDA output)

drift, will not always be upward but will move downward sporadically. However, the long-term trend will naturally be in the upward direction. We should be aware that for nonstationary time series what appears to be a trend need not be due to the presence of a constant. For example, upward and downward trends over certain time intervals even appear in time series that are known to be random walks. Thus forecasters must be aware that casual inspection may lead one to conclude that a nonstationary time series exhibits trend although in reality no trend exists.

This statement is even more important if the degree of differencing is two ($d = 2$). In this case, the first differences would be free to wander without any tendency to revert to a mean value. The undifferenced series in this situation often rises rapidly for long time periods only to begin a lengthy downward movement later. One should not conclude hastily that a deterministic trend exists since none is probably present.

The plot of autocorrelations for an ARIMA(0,2,0) model with a mean equal to unity is shown in figure 8.9. This ARIMA model is nonstationary with a positive

```
            PARTIAL
  ORDER    AUTO COR
                         −1   −.75  −.50  −.25    0    .25   .50   .75    1
                         :----:----:----:-----:----:----:----:-----:
    1      −0.4070   −                      *          :
    2      −0.3953   −                      *          :
    3      −0.2545   −                         *       :
    4      −0.2041   −                          *      :
    5      −0.1362   −                           *     :
    6      −0.0644   −                             * :
    7       0.0589   −                               : *
    8      −0.1296   −                          *      :
    9      −0.2071   −                         *       :
   10      −0.0561   −                              *:
   11       0.0107   −                               *
   12       0.0237   −                               *
   13      −0.2055   −                         *       :
   14      −0.1506   −                         *       :
   15       0.0123   −                               *
   16       0.0318   −                               : *
   17      −0.1717   −                         *       :
   18       0.0405   −                               : *
   19       0.0146   −                               *
   20       0.0844   −                               :  *
   21      −0.0725   −                              *:
   22      −0.1327   −                         *       :
   23       0.1183   −                               :  *
   24      −0.0141   −                               *
```

FIGURE 8.6 Example of ARIMA(0,0,1) model. Partial autocorrelations (Note:
        computer-generated IDA output)

```
                         S.E.
                AUTO−   RANDOM
  ORDER        CORR.    MODEL      −1   −.75  −.50  −.25    0    .25   .50   .75   +1
                                   :----:----:----:-----:----:----:----:-----:
    1         −0.851    0.070       *               +   :   +
    2          0.620    0.070                       +   :   +           *
    3         −0.449    0.070              *         +   :   +
    4          0.302    0.070                       +   :   +      *
    5         −0.186    0.069                      *+   :   +
    6          0.114    0.069                       +   :  *+
    7         −0.103    0.069                      +*   :   +
    8          0.130    0.069                       +   :    *
    9         −0.162    0.069                      *    :   +
   10          0.185    0.069                       +   :   +*

                                   −1   −.75  −.50  −.25    0    .25   .50   .75   +1
                                   :----:----:----:-----:----:----:----:-----:
                                   *  :  AUTOCORRELATIONS
                                   +  :  2 STANDARD ERROR LIMITS  (APPROX.)
  NUMBER OF OBSERVATIONS = 200
```

FIGURE 8.7 Example of ARIMA(1,0,1) model. Ordinary autocorrelations (Note:
        computer-generated IDA output)

```
            PARTIAL
   ORDER    AUTO COR
                          -1   -.75  -.50  -.25   0   .25   .50   .75    1
                          :----:-----:----:----:----:----:----:-----:
     1      -0.8508   -              *                :
     2      -0.3763   -                    *          :
     3      -0.1801   -                        *      :
     4      -0.1844   -                        *      :
     5      -0.0739   -                             * :
     6      -0.0084   -                               *
     7      -0.1527   -                         *     :
     8       0.0181   -                               *
     9      -0.0560   -                            *  :
    10      -0.0044   -                               *
```

constant (mean). The series has a very slowly decaying plot of autocorrelations which seem to exhibit a trend of the type just discussed. However, the time series is generated from an ARIMA model that is not deterministic but has a drift as previously described. The undifferenced series will increase rapidly for a long time and later begin to have a protracted decline. By taking first differences and then obtaining second differences (first differences of the first differences), a new plot of the autocorrelations can be found. The plot of the autocorrelations of the second-differenced series (figure 8.10) indicates a random process with virtually all, if not all, low-order coefficients not significantly different from zero, that is, they lie within the 2σ limits.

The point to be noted here is that constant terms in ARIMA models have an effect on the time series generated and, in turn, on the plot of the autocorrelations. Thus, through careful study of the plots, the true underlying ARIMA process that gives rise to the time series observations can be discerned. Furthermore, in practice, we shall not know beforehand what the underlying ARIMA process is that gave rise to the observations as was the case in these illustrations where the data were generated by computer. With real data, a forecaster must carefully analyze the statistical properties of the time series to identify the underlying ARIMA model.

8.8   The Appropriate Degree of Differencing

Business and economic time series usually exhibit nonstationarity so that it will be necessary to obtain first or second differences to identify the underlying ARIMA model. Stated simply, the differencing is necessary to find a stationary ARMA process which gives rise to the time series. We now require to know how much differencing is necessary in order to find the stationary time series.

For nonstationary processes, the autocorrelations will die down very slowly as shown in figure 8.9. But, how slow is slow? Unfortunately, no precise answer to this question is available from the sample autocorrelations alone. In practice, the nature of the time series helps to provide some guidance that can be examined further when

ORDER	AUTO-CORR.	S.E. RANDOM MODEL	-1 -.75 -.50 -.25 0 .25 .50 .75 +1
			:----:-----:----:----:----:----:----:-----:
1	0.970	0.099	+ : + *
2	0.941	0.098	+ : + *
3	0.911	0.098	+ : + *
4	0.881	0.097	+ : + *
5	0.851	0.097	+ : + *
6	0.821	0.096	+ : + *
7	0.792	0.095	+ : + *
8	0.762	0.095	+ : + *
9	0.732	0.094	+ : + *
10	0.703	0.094	+ : + *
11	0.673	0.093	+ : + *
12	0.644	0.093	+ : + *
13	0.615	0.092	+ : + *
14	0.586	0.092	+ : + *
15	0.557	0.091	+ : + *
16	0.528	0.091	+ : + *
17	0.499	0.090	+ : + *
18	0.471	0.090	+ : + *
19	0.442	0.089	+ : + *
20	0.414	0.089	+ : + *
21	0.386	0.088	+ : + *
22	0.358	0.087	+ : + *
23	0.331	0.087	+ : + *
24	0.304	0.086	+ : + *
25	0.277	0.086	+ : + *
26	0.250	0.085	+ : +	*
27	0.224	0.085	+ : + *
28	0.198	0.084	+ : + *
29	0.172	0.083	+ : *
30	0.147	0.083	+ : *
31	0.122	0.082	+ : *+
32	0.098	0.082	+ : *+
33	0.074	0.081	+ :* +
34	0.050	0.080	+ :* +
35	0.027	0.080	+ :* +
36	0.004	0.079	+ * +
37	-0.018	0.079	+ * +
38	-0.040	0.078	+ *: +
39	-0.061	0.077	+ *: +
40	-0.082	0.077	+* : +
41	-0.102	0.076	+* : +
42	-0.121	0.075	+* : +
43	-0.141	0.075	* : +
44	-0.159	0.074	* : +
45	-0.177	0.073	*+ : +
46	-0.194	0.073	*+ : +
47	-0.211	0.072	*+ : +
48	-0.227	0.071	* + : +

```
                      -1  -.75 -.50 -.25   0   .25  .50  .75  +1
                      :----:-----:----:----:----:----:----:-----:
                      *  :  AUTOCORRELATIONS
                      +  :  2 STANDARD ERROR LIMITS  (APPROX.)
```

FIGURE 8.9 ARIMA(0,2,0) model with mean equal to 1. Plot of autocorrelations (Note: computer-generated IDA output)

ORDER	AUTO−CORR.	S.E. RANDOM MODEL	−1	−.75	−.50	−.25	0	.25	.50	.75	+1
			: ---- : ----- : ---- : ---- : ---- : ---- : ---- : ----- :								
1	−0.068	0.099					+	*:	+		
2	0.090	0.099					+	:	* +		
3	−0.089	0.098					+ *	:	+		
4	−0.205	0.098					*	:	+		
5	−0.005	0.097					+	*	+		
6	−0.033	0.097					+	*:	+		
7	0.125	0.096					+	:	*+		
8	−0.047	0.096					+	*:	+		
9	0.056	0.095					+	:*	+		
10	−0.104	0.095					+ *	:	+		
11	0.068	0.094					+	:*	+		
12	−0.020	0.094					+	*	+		
13	0.079	0.093					+	: *	+		
14	0.049	0.093					+	:*	+		
15	−0.152	0.092					+*	:	+		
16	−0.014	0.091					+	*	+		
17	−0.027	0.091					+	*:	+		
18	0.069	0.090					+	:*	+		
19	0.070	0.090					+	:*	+		
20	0.121	0.089					+	: *	+		
			: ---- : ----- : ---- : ---- : ---- : ---- : ---- : ----- :								
			−1	−.75	−.50	−.25	0	.25	.50	.75	+1

* : AUTOCORRELATIONS
+ : 2 STANDARD ERROR LIMITS (APPROX.)

FIGURE 8.10 Second differences of ARIMA(0,2,0) model. Plot of autocorrelations (Note: computer-generated IDA output)

the parameters of the ARIMA model are estimated. If nonstationarity in the data is suspected, then the sample autocorrelations of the first differenced model are plotted and examined for information about the appropriate stationary model. Sometimes second differences will have to be obtained and their sample autocorrelations examined as in figure 8.10. A check on the choice of first or second differences is provided and then the parameter of the identified model is estimated.

Forecasters need only identify the lowest level of differencing for which a stationary model is apparent. This is because further differencing of a stationary series results in series which is also stationary. Overdifferencing a series merely alters the pattern of autocorrelation present in a stationary series and serves only to complicate the identification process.

8.9   Use of the Logarithmic Transformation for Nonstationarity in Variance

Seasonal time series values Y_t, Y_{t-1}, $Y_{t-2}, \ldots$, often exhibit changing variability as time advances. Specifically, time series which exhibit changing variability possess multiplicative seasonal variation of the type discussed in chapter 3. For seasonal time series having this property, it is very often advisable to use the transformation

$$Y_t^* = \ln Y_t \tag{8.19}$$

TABLE 8.3   Specific pure seasonal time series models

(1)	(2)	(3)	(4)	(5) Theoretical function	
Model	Stationarity conditions	Invertibility conditions	Autocorrelation coefficients	Partial autocorrelation coefficients	

(1)	(2)	(3)	(4)	(5)
Model	Stationarity conditions	Invertibility conditions	Autocorrelation coefficients	Partial autocorrelation coefficients
1 ARIMA$(1,D,0)^s$ or SAR(1)	$-1< \phi_s <1$	None	Dies down	Cuts off after one seasonal lag
2 ARIMA$(2,D,0)^s$ or SAR(2)	$\phi_s + \phi_{2s} <1$ $\phi_s - \phi_{2s} <1$ $-1<\phi_{2s}<1$	None	Dies down	Cuts off after two seasonal lags
3 ARIMA $(0,D,1)^s$ or SMA(1)	None	$\theta_s < 1$	Cuts off after one seasonal lag	Dies down
4 ARIMA $(0,D,2)^s$ or SMA(2)	None	$\theta_s + \theta_{2s} < 1$ $\theta_{2s} - \theta_s < 1$ $\theta_{2s} < 1$	Cuts off after two seasonal lags	Dies down
5 ARIMA $(1,D,1)^s$	$-1 < \phi_s < 1$	$-1 < \theta_s < 1$	Dies down	Dies down

to produce values $Y_t^*, Y_{t-1}^*, Y_{t-2}^*, \ldots$ which closely approximate constant variability (additive variation).

Many business and economic time series are characterized by multiplicative seasonal variation. Transforming a nonstationary to a stationary series often requires that the time series first be transformed by equation (8.19) to insure that a stationary model is identified. For example, first differences of US gross national product (GNP) for the past 80 years become more disperse over time. The absolute size of changes increase over time, and this is expected since only the percentage changes from period to period are about the same. Thus, as the level of GNP rises, the size of the changes increases. However, changes in logarithms are essentially percentage changes. Thus, to achieve stationarity, we could transform the GNP series by equation (8.19) and then proceed to examine differences in logarithms.

To see why this result will be obtained consider the following:

$$Y_t^* - Y_{t-1}^* = \ln Y_t - \ln Y_{t-1} \tag{8.20}$$

$$= \ln\left(\frac{Y_t}{Y_{t-1}}\right) \tag{8.21}$$

If, for example, Y_t is $Z \times 100$ percent larger than Y_{t-1}, then

$$Y_t^* - Y_{t-1}^* = \ln\left[\frac{Y_{t-1}(1 + Z)}{Y_{t-1}}\right]$$

$$= \ln(1 + Z)$$

$$\doteq Z \tag{8.22}$$

and Z is a percentage change.

Finally, we should point out that the use of the logarithmic transformation is, in principle, appropriate for many business and economic time series. In practice, it is generally used for data spanning at least several decades.

8.10 Purely Seasonal Models

Seasonal behavior is the most prevalent behavior found in business and economic time series. Business and economic behavior, as we discovered in earlier chapters, is linked in some way to the seasons of the year or to the repetition of some other factor related to the time series. To complete our study of advanced time series analysis, we must look at ARIMA models for seasonal series.

In this chapter, our study is limited to purely seasonal time series. A purely seasonal time series is one that has only seasonal AR or MA parameters. In chapter 9, we shall discuss how the nonseasonal parameters in ARIMA models and seasonal parameters are combined to model both seasonal and nonseasonal time series behavior.

Seasonal autoregressive models are built with parameters called *seasonal autoregressive parameters* (SAR parameters). The SAR parameters represent autoregressive relationships that exist between time series data separated by multiples of the number of periods per season. For example, a model with one SAR parameter is written as follows:

$$Y_t = \phi_s Y_{t-s} + e_t \tag{8.23}$$

$$ARIMA(P,D,Q)^s = ARIMA(1,0,0)^s$$

where s is the number of periods per season. The parameter is called the SAR parameter of order s. The model simply states that any time series Y_t is directly proportional to Y_{t-s}, i.e. to the time series value s periods ago. The value of s would be 12 for monthly data and 4 for quarterly data.

The SAR model can be extended to include more than one SAR parameter. For example, a seasonal AR model with two SAR parameters is written as follows:

$$Y_t = \phi_s Y_{t-s} + \phi_{2s} Y_{t-2s} + e_t \qquad ARIMA(2,0,0)^s \tag{8.24}$$

where the SAR parameters Y_{t-s} and Y_{t-2s} are of order s and $2s$ respectively. For this model, what happens in the current period is directly related to what happened both one and two seasons ago. If $s = 4$, then

$$Y_t = \phi_4 Y_{t-4} + \phi_8 Y_{t-8} + e_t$$

A general seasonal autoregressive model with P SAR parameters is written as follows:

$$Y_t = \phi_s Y_{t-s} + \phi_{2s} Y_{t-2s} + \ldots + \phi_{Ps} Y_{t-Ps} + e_t \tag{8.25}$$

where Y_{t-s} is of order s, Y_{t-2s} is of order $2s,\ldots$, and Y_{t-Ps} is of order Ps. The order of the ARIMA model is Ps.

Seasonal moving-average models are built with *seasonal moving-average parameters* (SMA parameters). SMA parameters represent moving-average relationships that exist among the time series observations separated by a multiple of the number of periods per season. For example, a model with one SMA parameter is written as follows:

$$Y_t = -\theta_s e_{t-s} + e_t \qquad \text{ARIMA}(P, D, Q)^s = \text{ARIMA}(0,0,1)^s \qquad (8.26)$$

The parameter e_{t-s} is called the SMA parameter of order s. The above model states that Y_t is directly related to the random error e_{t-s} that occurred one season ago, that is, s periods ago.

The generalized ARIMA model to include Q SMA parameters is as follows:

$$Y_t = -\theta_s e_{t-s} - \theta_{2s} e_{t-2s} - \ldots - \theta_{Qs} e_{t-Qs} + e_t \qquad (8.27)$$

where e_{t-s} is of order s, e_{t-2s} is of order $2s$,..., and e_{t-Qs} is of order Qs. The order of the model is Qs.

For a mixed *seasonal autoregressive moving-average model,* both SAR and SMA parameters are used in the same way that nonseasonal AR and MA parameters are used. A mixed SAR and SMA model is written as follows:

$$Y_t = \phi_s Y_{t-s} + \ldots + \phi_{Ps} Y_{t-Ps} - \theta_s e_{t-s} - \ldots - \theta_{Qs} e_{t-Qs} + e_t \qquad (8.28)$$

The order of the seasonal ARMA model is expressed in terms of both Ps and Qs.

The identification of seasonal parameters is accomplished by the plotting and careful examination of the autocorrelations and partial autocorrelations of the stationary time series. Like nonseasonal model identification, the appropriate amount of differencing will have to be done and use of the logarithmic transformation may also be necessary if the data are nonstationary in the variance. For purely seasonal models, we shall examine how the theoretical autocorrelation and partial autocorrelation patterns appear.

First, the autocorrelation patterns associated with purely seasonal models are analogous to those for nonseasonal models. The only difference is that the nonzero autocorrelations that form the pattern occur at lags that are multiples of the number of periods per season. In chapter 9, we shall examine the autocorrelation patterns of models that have both nonseasonal and seasonal parameters. Table 8.3 summarizes the identification patterns for specific purely seasonal time series models. Comparison of this table with tables 8.1 and 8.2 reveals similarities. Similar stationarity and invertibility conditions hold for the parameters of purely seasonal models as hold for the nonseasonal models. For purely SAR models, the autocorrelations die down and partial autocorrelations cut off after one seasonal lag for an SAR(1) model and after two seasonal lags for an SAR(2) model. Similarly, the partial autocorrelations die down for SMA models. Also, the autocorrelations cut off after one lag for an SMA(1) model and after two lags for an SMA(2) model. Finally for a mixed model with one SAR and one SMA parameter, both the theoretical autocorrelation function and the partial autocorrelation function die down.

Figure 8.11 shows plots of theoretical autocorrelations and partial autocorrelations for a purely SAR(1) model where the SAR parameter is 0.7. Note that the autocorrelations and partial autocorrelations at lags 1–11 are virtually zero. Only at the seasonal lags, i.e. 12, 24, 36, and 48, would a coefficient have a size which may be significantly different from zero. For the ACF, the coefficients for the seasonal lags die down toward zero. At lag 48, the autocorrelation coefficient is close to zero. For the PACF, the coefficients cut off at a lag of 12 which is the first seasonal lag. Hence, we can conclude that in purely seasonal terms this time series was generated by an SAR(1) model, that is, ARIMA$(1,0,0)^{12}$.

Figure 8.12 shows the plots of the theoretical autocorrelations and partial autocorrelations for an SMA(1) model with a moving average parameter of 0.7.

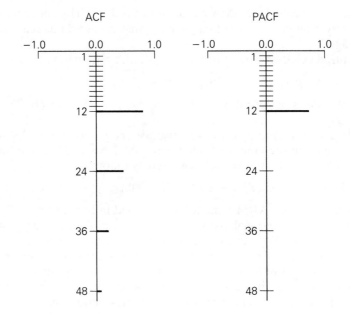

FIGURE 8.11 One SAR parameter of order 12: $Y_t = 0.7Y_{t-12} + e_t$

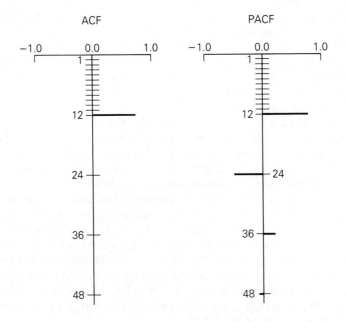

FIGURE 8.12 One SMA parameter of order 12: $Y_t = 0.7e_{t-12} + e_t$

Note that for this purely seasonal model, there are no coefficients different from zero at lags of 1–11. The ACF cuts off at lag 12, the first seasonal lag. For the PACF, we see seasonal coefficients that are dying down in value, i.e., the lags of 12, 24, 36, and 48 are declining in value. Thus the plots indicate that an SMA(1) (ARIMA(0,0,1)^{12}) model generated the time series observations.

Figure 8.13 shows the theoretical autocorrelations and partial autocorrelations for a seasonal ARMA model. For the ACF, a dying down pattern is seen in the seasonal lags (lags of 12, 24, 36, and 48). In the PACF, a different but still decaying pattern is seen in the seasonal lags. There are no nonzero nonseasonal coefficients in either plot. Hence this is a purely seasonal ARMA model with one SAR and one SMA parameter, that is, ARIMA(1,0,1)^{12}.

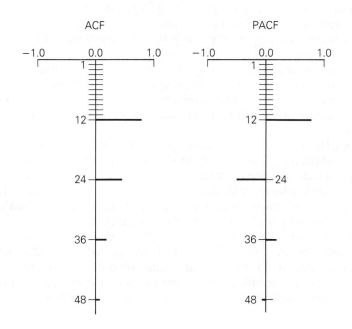

FIGURE 8.13 One SAR and one SMA parameter of order 12

As can be seen from these illustrations, the process of identifying purely seasonal models is very similar to the process of identifying nonseasonal models. In the next chapter, we shall discuss ACF and PACF plots of actual time series. The methods of identification described in this and the previous chapter will become very useful in identifying the patterns discussed in chapter 9. In addition, it will be shown that ARIMA models can have both a nonseasonal and seasonal component. Although these models will be more difficult to identify, the same principles of identification will apply.

8.11 Summary

A moving-average (MA) model provides predictions based on a linear combination of past forecast errors and thus is similar to exponential smoothing models. The order q of the MA model refers to the number of parameters of the model.

If the autocorrelation pattern in the time series residuals requires a more complex model, a mixed model can be estimated. An autoregressive moving-average (ARMA) model of order (p,q) has autocorrelations that diminish as the distance between residuals increases. Also, the patterns in the time series that can be described by ARMA processes are more general than those of either AR(p) or MA(q) models.

Identification of AR(p), MA(q), and mixed ARMA(p,q) time series requires the computation and plotting of the sample autocorrelation function (ACF) (coefficients) and partial autocorrelation function (PACF) (coefficients) of the time series data. If the sample ACFs and PACFs for a time series appear to be generated by a particular time series model, then it is likely that that particular time series model generated the time series data.

Examining plots of theoretical models will enable models for actual time series to be identified better. Through careful examination of the ACF and PACF plots we can discern the true underlying ARIMA process that gives rise to the time series. For example, the influence of the constant term can be found when the ACF and PACF plots are drawn.

Differencing of time series is often necessary to find a stationary time series for the purposes of identification. Forecasters need only to identify the lowest level of differencing for which a stationary model is apparent.

Seasonal time series often exhibit nonstationarity in variance. In these situations, a forecaster must transform the time series to a stationary one by a mathematical transformation. One very useful transformation is natural logarithms.

ARIMA models can be purely seasonal in that only seasonal parameters are present. Examples include SAR, SMA, and seasonal ARMA models where the models include parameters for the seasonal terms. Identification of purely seasonal models is similar to the identification process for nonseasonal models. For purely seasonal models only coefficients at the seasonal lags are examined.

8.12 Exercises

1 The following equation is an AR(2) model:

$$Y_t = 0.7Y_{t-1} + 0.3Y_{t-2}$$

Express the meaning of the coefficients

2 Write the expression for models of the following type:
   (a) AR(2)
   (b) AR(3)
   (c) AR(4)
   (d) AR(n)
   (e) MA(3)

(f) MA(4)

(g) MA(*m*)

(h) ARMA(1,2)

(i) ARMA(2,1)

(j) ARMA(2,2)

3 Write the expression for models of the following type:

(a) SAR(1)

(b) SAR(2)

(c) SMA(2)

(d) seasonal ARMA(1,2)

(e) seasonal ARMA(2,1)

4 Table 8.4 contains information on net domestic investment for nonresidential structures in the United States (billion dollars, 1982). For this data set, use the methods of advanced time series analysis to plot the autocorrelations. Carefully analyze the plot and see if you can identify the nonseasonal ARIMA model that gave rise to the time series.

TABLE 8.4

Year	Y
1970	89.3
1971	76.1
1972	85.3
1973	116.5
1974	106.9
1975	60.8
1976	61.8
1977	85.2
1978	111.6
1979	124.3
1980	101.3
1981	105.5
1982	65.5
1983	50.4
1984	103.3
1985	116.5
1986	80.5
1987	77.7

Source: Economic Report of the President, 1989, p. 327.

5 The data in table 8.5 are the inventory-to-sales ratios for nonfarm business in the United States. For this data set, carefully examine the autocorrelations and see if you can identify the time series.

6 Table 8.6 contains data on producer price indexes for major commodity groups in the United States. Use the methods of autocorrelation analysis to identify the ARIMA model that gave rise to any one of the time series in the table.

TABLE 8.5

Year	Ratio
1972	2.75
1973	2.97
1974	3.45
1975	3.11
1976	3.14
1977	3.10
1978	3.12
1979	3.24
1980	3.26
1981	3.25
1982	3.02
1983	2.87
1984	2.89
1985	2.73
1986	2.61
1987	2.68

Source: *Economic Report of the President*, 1989, p. 328.

7 For the data of table 7.9, plot the autocorrelations of one of the time series. In turn, use the logarithmic transformation and plot the autocorrelations. Compare and contrast the two plots.

8 From the *Survey of Current Business,* find the unemployment rate for the United States for any period. Identify the particular ARIMA process that generated this time series.

9 From *Barron's Weekly Magazine* (or another source) find at least three years' worth of data on monthly closing prices of the Dow–Jones Industrial Average. Identify the ARIMA process that gives rise to this time series.

10 For any time series of your choice, identify the model that generated the time series. Use the summary information described in table 8.2.

11 For the graphs of autocorrelations and partial autocorrelations presented in figure 8.14 identify the ARIMA process that gives rise to each pair of graphs. Explain your answer.

12 In figure 8.15, a series of plots of autocorrelations and partial autocorrelations for purely seasonal time series are illustrated. Identify the ARIMA model that gave rise to each of the time series.

13 Find the annual earnings per share for any firm from a source such as *Value Line*. Calculate the ACF and PACF for this series and identify the time series model that most closely approximates this series.

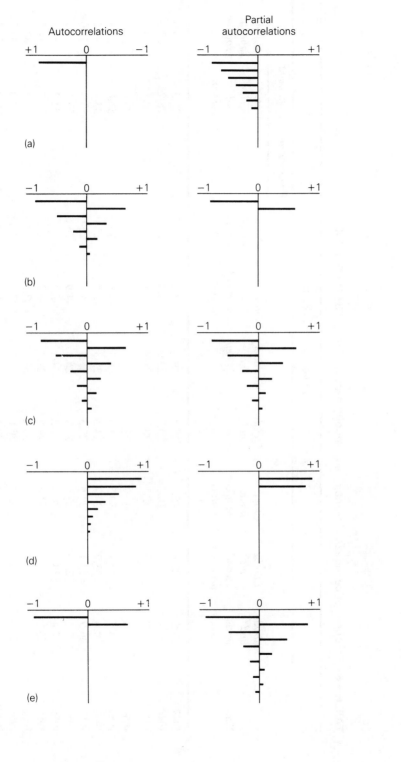

Autocorrelations

Partial
autocorrelations

(a)

(b)

(c)

(d)

(e)

FIGURE 8.14

TABLE 8.6 Producer price indexes for major commodity groups, 1947–1987 (1982 = 100)

Year	Industrial commodities							Transportation equipment		Miscellaneous products
	Rubber and plastic products	Lumber and wood products	Pulp, paper, and allied products	Metals and metal products	Machinery and equipment	Furniture and household durables	Non-metallic mineral products	Total	Motor vehicles and equipment	
1947	29.2	25.8	25.1	18.2	19.3	37.2	20.7		25.5	26.6
1948	30.2	29.5	26.2	20.7	20.9	39.4	22.4		28.2	27.7
1949	29.2	27.3	25.1	20.9	21.9	40.1	23.0		30.1	28.2
1950	35.6	31.4	25.7	22.0	22.6	40.9	23.5		30.0	28.6
1951	34.7	34.1	30.5	24.5	25.3	44.4	25.0		31.6	30.3
1952	39.6	33.2	29.7	24.5	25.3	43.5	25.0		33.4	30.2
1953	36.9	33.1	29.6	25.3	25.9	44.4	26.0		33.3	31.0
1954	37.5	32.5	29.6	25.5	26.3	44.9	26.6		33.4	31.3
1955	42.4	34.1	30.4	27.2	27.2	45.1	27.3		34.3	31.3
1956	43.0	34.6	32.4	29.6	29.3	46.3	28.5		36.3	31.7
1957	42.8	32.8	33.0	30.2	31.4	47.5	29.6		37.9	32.6
1958	42.8	32.5	33.4	30.0	32.1	47.9	29.9		39.0	33.3
1959	42.6	34.7	33.7	30.6	32.8	48.0	30.3		39.9	33.4
1960	42.7	33.5	34.0	30.6	33.0	47.8	30.4		39.3	33.6
1961	41.1	32.0	33.0	30.5	33.0	47.5	30.5		39.2	33.7
1962	39.9	32.2	33.4	30.2	33.0	47.2	30.5		39.2	33.9
1963	40.1	32.8	33.1	30.3	33.1	46.9	30.3		38.9	34.2
1964	39.6	33.5	33.0	31.1	33.3	47.1	30.4		39.1	34.4

Year										
1965	39.7	33.7	33.3	32.0	33.7	46.8	30.4		39.2	34.7
1966	40.5	35.2	34.2	32.8	34.7	47.4	30.7		39.2	35.3
1967	41.4	35.1	34.6	33.2	35.9	48.3	31.2		39.8	36.2
1968	42.8	39.8	35.0	34.0	37.0	49.7	32.4		40.9	37.0
1969	43.6	44.0	36.0	36.0	38.2	50.7	33.6	40.4	41.7	38.1
1970	44.9	39.9	37.5	38.7	40.0	51.9	35.3	41.9	43.3	39.8
1971	45.2	44.7	38.1	39.4	41.4	53.1	38.2	44.2	45.7	40.8
1972	45.3	50.7	39.3	40.9	42.3	53.8	39.4	45.5	47.0	41.5
1973	46.6	62.2	42.3	44.0	43.7	55.7	40.7	46.1	47.4	43.3
1974	56.4	64.5	52.5	57.0	50.0	61.8	47.8	50.3	51.4	48.1
1975	62.2	62.1	59.0	61.5	57.9	67.5	54.4	56.7	57.6	53.4
1976	66.0	72.2	62.1	65.0	61.3	70.3	58.2	60.5	61.2	55.6
1977	69.4	83.0	64.6	69.3	65.2	73.2	62.6	64.6	65.2	59.4
1978	72.4	96.9	67.7	75.3	70.3	77.5	69.6	69.5	70.0	66.7
1979	80.5	105.5	75.9	86.0	76.7	82.8	77.6	75.3	75.8	75.5
1980	90.1	101.5	86.3	95.0	86.0	90.7	88.4	82.9	83.1	93.6
1981	96.4	102.8	94.8	99.6	94.4	95.9	96.7	94.3	94.6	96.1
1982	100.0	100.0	100.0	100.0	100.0	100.0	100.0	100.0	100.0	100.0
1983	100.8	107.9	103.3	101.8	102.7	103.4	101.6	102.8	102.2	104.8
1984	102.3	108.0	110.3	104.8	105.1	105.7	105.4	105.2	104.1	107.0
1985	101.9	106.6	113.3	104.4	107.2	107.1	108.6	107.9	106.4	109.4
1986	101.9	107.2	116.1	103.2	108.8	108.2	110.0	110.5	109.1	111.6
1987	103.0	112.8	121.8	107.1	110.4	109.9	110.0	112.5	111.7	114.9

Source: Economic Report of the President, 1989, p. 383.

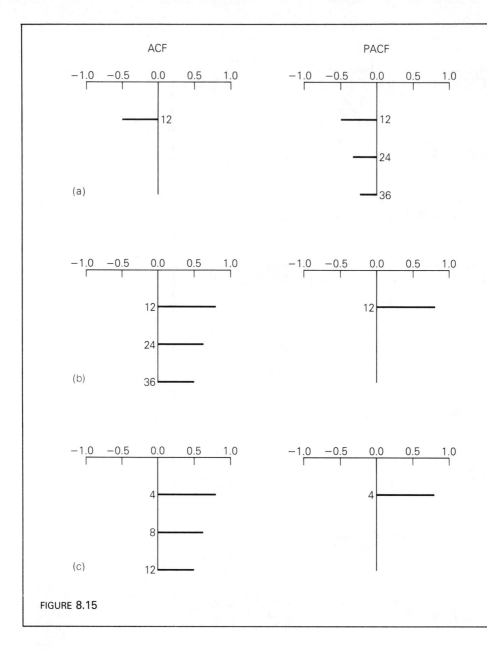

FIGURE 8.15

References

Barron's National Business and Financial Weekly. New York: Dow Jones.

Economic Report of The President, 1989, Washington, DC: US Council of Economic Advisors, US Government Printing Office.

Survey of Current Business, various issues. Washington, DC: US Department of Commerce.

Value Line Selection and Opinion. New York: Arnold Bernhard.

Wold, H. (1954) *A Study In The Analysis of Stationary Time Series.* Stockholm: Almqvist and Wicksell.

Further Reading

Hoff, J. C. (1983), *A Practical Guide to Box–Jenkins Forecasting.* Belmont, CA: Lifetime Learning Press, chs 6, 8–15.

Nelson, C. R. (1973) *Applied Time Series Analysis For Managerial Forecasting,* San Francisco, CA: Holden-Day, chs 3, 4.

O'Donovan, T. M. (1983), *Short-Term Forecasting,* New York: Wiley, chs 2, 3.

CHAPTER 9

Box-Jenkins Methods and ARIMA Modeling

Objectives

The purpose of this chapter is to build ARIMA models using Box–Jenkins methods. This requires the identification, estimation, and diagnostic testing of ARIMA models for time series. You will learn to build ARIMA models for both nonseasonal and seasonal time series models. Since Box–Jenkins methods require extensive use of the computer, examples of computer output are included in the study of time series modeling. By the end of this chapter, you will be able to:

1 From plots of autocorrelations and partial autocorrelations, make tentative identification of the ARIMA model that gave rise to the time series.
2 Estimate the identified ARIMA model.
3 Diagnostically test the model for adequacy.
4 If the model is adequate, forecast using the estimated model.
5 If the estimated model is not adequate, re-identify and reestimate the model.
6 Build ARIMA models for both seasonal and nonseasonal models.

Outline

Key Terms

- Box–Jenkins methodology
- *Q*-statistic
- Transfer function model
- Intervention model
- Multiple time series model

9.1 Introduction

The *Box-Jenkins methodology* (Box and Jenkins, 1976) is a statistically sophisticated way of analyzing and building a forecasting model which best represents a time series. This technique has a number of advantages over other methods of time series analysis. Firstly, it is logical and statistically accurate. Secondly, the method extracts a great deal of information from the historical time series data. Finally, the method results in an increase in forecast accuracy while keeping the number of parameters to a minimum in comparison with similar modeling processes.

In chapter 7 we studied autocorrelation analysis where the purpose was to break down a time series into several important components. By estimating autocorrelation coefficients, for different time lags of a time series, we can answer the following questions about a data set:

1 Are the data random?
2 Is the time series nonstationary?
3 If the series is nonstationary, what is the degree of the process at which it becomes stationary?
4 Are the data seasonal?
5 If it is seasonal, what is the seasonal pattern?

If a series is random, the correlation of a data pair Y_t and Y_{t-1} is about zero. Furthermore, in chapter 7 we learned that autocorrelation coefficients close to zero for the successive values of a time series are not linearly related to each other. The autocorrelation coefficients for the successive values of a time series 3, 6, 9, 12, 15, 18, 21, 24,... would be very high. Stated differently, the relationship between successive values would be strong. By examining autocorrelation coefficients for time lags of more than one period, we can determine additional information concerning the relationship of data in a given time series.

In chapter 7 we examined an autoregressive model with a quarterly seasonal pattern. To identify this pattern, the methodology of autocorrelation analysis suggests that we determine the correlation between Y_t and Y_{t+4}. If the autocorrelation is close to zero, the absence of a quarterly seasonal relationship would be indicated. Similarly, for monthly observations, the autocorrelation of Y_t and Y_{t+12} is studied.

The purpose of the remaining portions of this chapter is to implement our knowledge of autocorrelation analysis along with our knowledge of ARMA processes from chapter 8. Box and Jenkins (1976) have successfully put together a methodology for implementing this acquired knowledge to understand and use single variable (univariate) time series ARIMA models. The basis of their approach

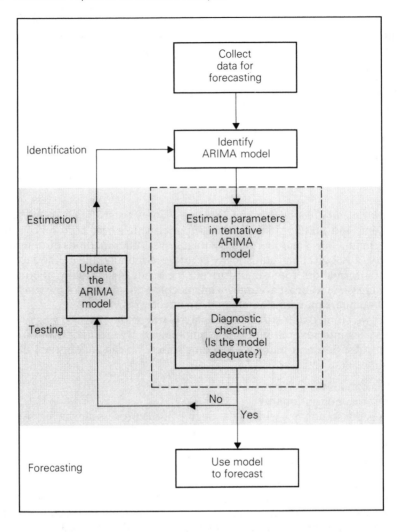

FIGURE 9.1 Schematic representation of the Box–Jenkins process

is described in the schematic diagram of figure 9.1 and consists of four distinct phases.

First, the methodology assumes no particular pattern in the historical data of the time series to be forecast. By an iterative approach, the procedure identifies a possible useful model from a general class of ARMA models. After the estimation, the chosen model is then diagnostically checked against the historical time series to see if it accurately describes the time series. If the residuals between the forecast and actual series are small, randomly distributed, and independent, the chosen ARIMA model is said to be a good fit. However, if the chosen model is *not* satisfactory, the Box–Jenkins process is repeated using another model designed to improve the original one. This process is repeated until a satisfactory model is found.

In this chapter, this four-phase approach will be examined and practical illustrations of univariate time series will be given.

9.2 Identification: Some Preliminary Comments

The purpose of the identification phase is to choose a specific ARMA model from the general class of ARMA(p,q) models denoted as[1]

$$Y_t = \phi_1 Y_{t-1} + \phi_2 Y_{t-2} + \ldots + \phi_p Y_{t-p} + e_t - \theta_1 e_{t-1} - \theta_2 e_{t-2} - \ldots - \theta_q e_{t-q} \tag{9.1}$$

The selection of the appropriate p and q values requires examining the autocorrelation and partial autocorrelation coefficients calculated for the data. In chapter 7, autocorrelation coefficients were explored. However, partial autocorrelations were only briefly mentioned, in chapter 7, and therefore we shall consider this concept before we return to the question of how a specific ARMA model can be selected from among the general ARMA(p,q) class of equation (9.1).

If in equation (9.1), we let $q = 0$ and $p = 0, 1, 2, 3, \ldots ,p$, consecutively, equation (9.1) then becomes

$$Y_t = e_t \tag{9.2}$$

$$Y_t = \phi_1 Y_{t-1} + e_t \tag{9.3}$$

$$Y_t = \phi_1 Y_{t-1} + \phi_2 Y_{t-2} + e_t \tag{9.4}$$

$$Y_t = \phi_1 Y_{t-1} + \phi_2 Y_{t-2} + \phi_3 Y_{t-3} + e_t \tag{9.5}$$

$$Y = \phi_1 Y_{t-1} + \phi_2 Y_{t-2} + \phi_3 Y_{t-3} + \ldots + \phi_p Y_{t-p} + e_t \tag{9.6}$$

When the true order of equation (9.3) is $p = 0$, the parameter ϕ_1 will have a value that is not statistically different from zero. Thus the result would be an AR(0) process and $\phi_1 = 0$. Alternatively, if the true order is $p = 1$, ϕ_2 will not be statistically different from zero. Finally, in general, the pth parameter of an AR(p) process will only be statistically different from zero when the autoregressive (AR) process is at least of order p or higher.

Identifying the order of an AR process can be done by examining its partial autocorrelation coefficients. The order is simply the same as the number of partial autocorrelations statistically different from zero. The partial autocorrelations up through p time lags will be statistically significant, while the remaining coefficients will be approximately equal to zero. This resulting value of p will be the order of the AR process.

Moving-average (MA) processes are not like models (9.3) – (9.6) and the attempt to estimate ϕ_1, ϕ_2, $\phi_3,\ldots,\phi_p$ in such cases is an example of fitting the wrong model to

---

1 For most of this chapter we identify time series models without the constant term μ. As we shall see, this is consistent with the models to be identified in this chapter since differencing removes the constant term.

the data. For an MA process, the different Y_t values are dependent on each other. Since Y_t is a function of Y_{t-1} and e_t, and Y_{t-1} is a function of Y_{t-2} and e_{t-1}, and so on, we would continue to estimate a new parameter ϕ for each equation. Thus an infinite number of ϕ_i terms would be required to fit an AR model to MA data. Partial correlation coefficients for MA data will initially be large and their magnitude will decrease exponentially to zero. Unlike partial autocorrelations for AR processes, the partial autocorrelations of an MA process do not have a cut off after p time lags.

With knowledge of the behavior of autocorrelations and partial autocorrelations discussed and summarized in chapters 7 and 8 in mind, we can begin to illustrate the first stage of the Box–Jenkins analysis.

The first step in model identification is to determine whether or not the series is stationary. If the series is not stationary, it can be converted to a stationary series by the method of differencing. As seen in chapter 7, we generally need only to difference the data to either the first or second degree to convert the series to a stationary one. For the Box–Jenkins analysis, the data must be made stationary and/or invertible and then subsequent computations using the converted data are performed.

Upon obtaining a stationary and/or invertible series, we must identify the form of the model to be used. The form is established by comparing the autocorrelation and partial autocorrelation coefficients of the data to be fitted with the corresponding distributions for the various ARMA models. The most useful theoretical distributions for ARMA models are shown in figures 9.2, 9.3, and 9.4. Note that figure 9.2 is for AR(1) and AR(2) models. Figure 9.3 contains the autocorrelations and partial autocorrelations for MA(1) and MA(2) models. Last, autocorrelations and partial autocorrelations for ARMA(1,1) models are depicted in figure 9.4. These figures are based on the discussions in chapter 8.

Each type of ARIMA process has a unique set of autocorrelations and partial autocorrelations, and we should be able to match the corresponding coefficients of the observed time series to one of the theoretical distributions.

As we shall frequently see, if it is not possible to match the observed time series exactly with the theoretical models, diagnostic tests can be performed in a later step to determine whether the model is adequate. If the preliminary model is not adequate, an alternative model can be specified.

Several observations are worth summarizing at this point. First, if autocorrelations trail off exponentially to zero, an AR model is indicated. Similarly, if the partial autocorrelations trail off to zero then an MA model is indicated. If both autocorrelations and partial autocorrelations trail off to zero then a mixed ARMA model is indicated. Last, the order of the AR model is indicated by the number of partial autocorrelations, and the order of the MA model by the number of autocorrelations that are statistically different from zero.

9.3 Model Estimation and Diagnostic Testing

The second stage of the model building is the estimation or fitting stage. ARIMA models can be fitted by least squares. An iterative nonlinear least squares procedure is applied to the parameter estimates of an ARMA (p,q) model. The method minimizes the sum of squares of errors, Σe_t^2, given the form of the model and the data. This is the least squares method for fitting a model to data. Since the procedure is, in general, nonlinear because of the moving-average terms, the least squares process is nonlinear.

ACF

PACF

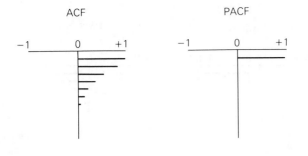

or

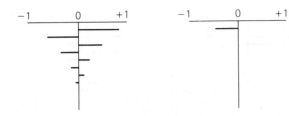

ACF

PACF

or

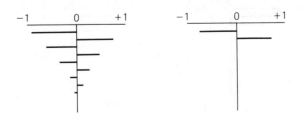

FIGURE 9.2 (a) AR(1) model; (b) AR(2) model

ACF

PACF

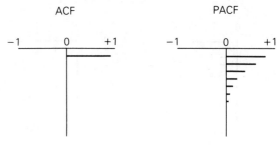

−1   0   +1   −1   0   +1

or

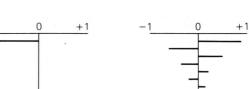

−1   0   +1   −1   0   +1

ACF

PACF

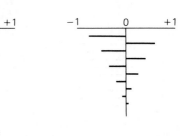

−1   0   +1   −1   0   +1

or

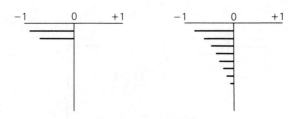

−1   0   +1   −1   0   +1

FIGURE 9.3 (a) MA(1) model; (b) MA(2) model

ACF   PACF

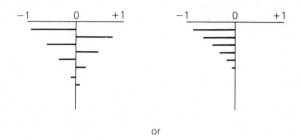

or

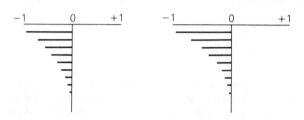

ACF   PACF

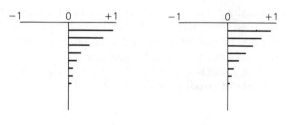

or

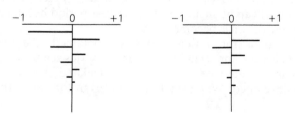

FIGURE 9.4 (a) ARMA(1,1) model; (b) ARMA(1,1) model

Box and Jenkins (1976, ch. 7) suggest a variety of parameter estimation procedures to which interested readers can refer for details. Software programs are available for estimating most low-order ARMA models and for testing the parameters of the model. These programs permit us to assess the precision of the parameter estimates of what are called parsimonious forecasting models. Parsimonious models have fewer rather than more parameters in the model. Since parsimony is a practical as well as a theoretical consideration, forecasters have found that simpler models are best.

Before the model is used for forecasting, it should be checked for adequacy. This diagnostic checking is done by examining the error terms e_t to be sure that they are random. If the error terms are statistically different from zero, the model is not considered adequate. If several autocorrelations are large, we should return to the initial stage, select an alternative model, and then continue the analysis.

To check for adequacy, the autocorrelations of the residuals are diagnostically examined by calculating a χ^2 statistic.[2] The test statistic is the Q *statistic*

$$Q = n(n+2) \sum_{i}^{k} \left(\frac{r_i^2}{n-k} \right) \tag{9.7}$$

which is approximately distributed as a χ^2 with $k - p - q$ degrees of freedom. In this equation, n is the length of the time series, k is the first k autocorrelations being checked, p is the order of the AR process, q is the order of the MA process, and r is the estimated autocorrelation coefficient of the ith residual term. If the calculated value of Q is greater than χ^2 for $k - p - q$ degrees of freedom, then the model should be considered inadequate. The forecaster should then return to selecting an alternative model and continue the Box–Jenkins analysis until a satisfactory model is found.

Both diagnostic procedures aid the analysis to arrive at a final forecasting model, but neither procedure can be considered the final word. For example, if some large deviations from the forecast can be explained adequately as unusual and unrepeatable circumstances, these deviations can be ignored.

Finally, if two or more models are judged to be about equal although no model is an exact fit, the principle of parsimony should prevail.

9.4   Forecasting with ARIMA Models: An Example

Upon the identification and validation of the model, forecasts for one period or several periods ahead can be made. As the forecast period becomes further ahead, the chances of forecast error become larger.

As new observations for a time series are obtained, the model should be re-examined and checked for accuracy. If the time series seems to be changing over time, the parameters of the model should be recalculated or an entirely new model may have to be developed. When small differences in forecast error are observed,

---

2   Ljung and Box (1978) suggest this statistic for determining whether the residuals from an ARIMA model are white noise. This statistic is a useful index of goodness of fit, is relatively simple to use, and is statistically more correct than the Box–Pierce statistic (Box and Pierce, 1970) (see McLeod, 1978; Pankratz, 1983). Computer software such as Minitab, SAS, and others calculate this statistic automatically.

we should only recalculate the model parameters. However, if large differences are observed in the size of the forecast error, this would indicate the need for a new forecasting model. At that time, we should return to the first stage of the Box–Jenkins process.

The index of industrial production (IIP) produced by the Federal Reserve Board is not stationary since the level and slope of the series both change over time. Table 9.1 contains data for the IIP by month for a time period of almost eight years. We are studying IIP numbers which have been previously deseasonalized to avoid the problem associated with the seasonality component of the time series. The first 90 observations are used for identifying, estimating, and diagnostically checking an appropriate model. Observations 91–95 will be used to check on the performance of the forecasting model.

TABLE 9.1   Index of industrial production (1967 = 100), seasonally adjusted

Month	Year	Period	IIP
Jul	1975	1	118.4
Aug	1975	2	121.0
Sep	1975	3	122.1
Oct	1975	4	122.2
Nov	1975	5	123.5
.	.	.	.
.	.	.	.
.	.	.	.
Aug	1982	86	140.5
Sep	1982	87	141.2
Oct	1982	88	138.5
Nov	1982	89	134.8
Dec	1982	90	131.2
Jan	1983	91	133.5
Feb	1983	92	138.1
Mar	1983	93	140.5
Apr	1983	94	141.9
May	1983	95	143.7

Sources: Federal Reserve Bulletin and Survey of Current Business, various issues.

Stage 1 Identification

The first step in identifying a preliminary model is to examine the autocorrelations and partial autocorrelations for the raw data. These values are shown in figures 9.5 and 9.6.

The first 36 autocorrelations are shown in figure 9.5. The autocorrelations, which are very large at first, do not trail off towards zero quickly. They appear to be forming a sine wave pattern, but because the damping process is so slow, we can

		−1.0 −0.8 −0.6 −0.4 −0.2 0.0 0.2 0.4 0.6 0.8 1.0
		+----+----+----+----+----+----+---+---+----+----+
1	0.943	XXXXXXXXXXXXXXXXXXXXXXXX
2	0.889	XXXXXXXXXXXXXXXXXXXXXXX
3	0.834	XXXXXXXXXXXXXXXXXXXXXX
4	0.778	XXXXXXXXXXXXXXXXXXXX
5	0.723	XXXXXXXXXXXXXXXXXXX
6	0.668	XXXXXXXXXXXXXXXXXX
7	0.622	XXXXXXXXXXXXXXXXX
8	0.574	XXXXXXXXXXXXXX
9	0.530	XXXXXXXXXXXXXX
10	0.489	XXXXXXXXXXXXX
11	0.451	XXXXXXXXXXXX
12	0.411	XXXXXXXXXXX
13	0.375	XXXXXXXXXX
14	0.343	XXXXXXXXXX
15	0.313	XXXXXXXXX
16	0.282	XXXXXXXXX
17	0.256	XXXXXXX
18	0.231	XXXXXXX
19	0.199	XXXXXX
20	0.167	XXXXX
21	0.137	XXXX
22	0.110	XXXX
23	0.084	XXX
24	0.059	XX
25	0.036	XX
26	0.012	X
27	−0.013	X
28	−0.041	XX
29	−0.073	XXX
30	−0.111	XXXX
31	−0.157	XXXXX
32	−0.205	XXXXX
33	−0.248	XXXXXX
34	−0.282	XXXXXXX
35	−0.312	XXXXXXXX
36	−0.340	XXXXXXXXX

FIGURE 9.5 Autocorrelation coefficients for the time series: index of industrial production
(Note: computer-generated Minitab output)

conclude that the process is nonstationary. Note that the first 18 coefficients are outside the 2σ limits.[3]

---

3   The 2σ limits are calculated as follows:

$$-\frac{2}{n^{1/2}} < r < +\frac{2}{n^{1/2}}$$

$$-\frac{2}{\sqrt{(90)}} < r < +\frac{2}{\sqrt{(90)}}$$

$$-0.211 < r < 0.211$$

```
                     -1.0 -0.8 -0.6 -0.4 -0.2  0.0  0.2  0.4  0.6  0.8  1.0
                     +----+----+----+----+----+----+---+---+----+----+
   1     0.943                                  XXXXXXXXXXXXXXXXXXXXXXXXX
   2    -0.006                                  X
   3    -0.028                                  XX
   4    -0.045                                  XX
   5    -0.020                                  X
   6    -0.037                                  XX
   7     0.051                                  XX
   8    -0.040                                  XX
   9    -0.003                                  X
  10    -0.001                                  X
  11     0.008                                  X
  12    -0.050                                  XX
  13     0.013                                  X
  14     0.007                                  X
  15    -0.001                                  X
  16    -0.036                                  XX
  17     0.028                                  XX
  18    -0.014                                  X
  19    -0.084                                  XXX
  20    -0.024                                  XX
  21     0.002                                  X
  22    -0.005                                  X
  23    -0.008                                  X
  24    -0.012                                  X
  25    -0.015                                  X
  26    -0.031                                  XX
  27    -0.028                                  XX
  28    -0.061                                  XXX
  29    -0.062                                  XXX
  30    -0.083                                  XXX
  31    -0.114                                  XXXX
  32    -0.084                                  XXX
  33    -0.004                                  X
  34     0.038                                  XX
  35    -0.010                                  X
  36    -0.034                                  XX
```

FIGURE 9.6 Partial autocorrelation coefficients for the time series: index of industrial production (Note: computer-generated Minitab output)

Figure 9.6 contains the plot of partial autocorrelations. The coefficient of order 1 is very large. These figures (often called correlograms) indicate that the time series is nonstationary. The large value for the order 1 partial-autocorrelation coefficient often occurs when the autocorrelations do not rapidly die down. Differencing is necessary at this point to identify the ARIMA model properly.

Upon differencing the ARIMA process to achieve a stationary ARMA process for forecasting, new diagrams of autocorrelation coefficients and partial autocorrelation coefficients are drawn. Figure 9.7 contains the autocorrelation of the first differences. These autocorrelations rapidly trail off towards zero. The partial auto-correlations (figure 9.8) cut off after lag 1. Both these patterns indicate an ARIMA (1,1,0) model. However, this is only a tentative choice.

```
                                  -1.0  -0.8  -0.6  -0.4  -0.2   0.0   0.2   0.4   0.6   0.8   1.0
                                  +----+----+----+----+----+----+---+---+----+----+
     1      0.279                                                 XXXXXXXX
     2      0.227                                                 XXXXXXX
     3      0.153                                                 XXXXX
     4      0.035                                                 XX
     5     -0.076                                              XXX
     6      0.040                                                 XX
     7      0.050                                                 XX
     8      0.006                                                 X
     9      0.019                                                 X
    10      0.013                                                 X
    11      0.031                                                 XX
    12      0.030                                                 XX
    13      0.038                                                 XX
    14     -0.006                                                 X
    15      0.083                                                 XXX
    16      0.041                                                 XX
    17      0.056                                                 XX
    18      0.102                                                 XXXX
    19      0.061                                                 XXX
    20      0.050                                                 XX
    21      0.015                                                 X
    22      0.028                                                 XX
    23      0.005                                                 X
    24     -0.009                                                 X
    25     -0.088                                              XXX
    26     -0.045                                              XX
    27      0.022                                                 XX
    28      0.042                                                 XX
    29      0.162                                                 XXXXX
    30      0.204                                                 XXXXXX
    31      0.205                                                 XXXXXX
    32      0.149                                                 XXXXX
    33      0.048                                                 XX
    34     -0.036                                              XX
    35      0.021                                                 XX
    36     -0.073                                              XXX
```

FIGURE 9.7 Autocorrelation coefficients for first-differenced time series (Note: computer-generated Minitab output)

Stage 2 Estimation

Once the preliminary model is chosen, the estimation stage begins. The estimates must be of the following model:[4]

$$(1 - B)(1 - \phi_1 B)Y_t = e_t \tag{9.8}$$

where the $(1 - B) Y_t$ are the first differences of the original values of table 9.1 expressed in terms of deviations. The purpose of estimation is to find the parameter

---

4 The constant term μ in this example is omitted since we are differencing.

```
               -1.0  -0.8  -0.6  -0.4  -0.2   0.0   0.2   0.4   0.6   0.8   1.0
                +----+----+----+----+----+----+---+----+---+----+----+
    1    0.279                                    XXXXXXXX
    2    0.161                                    XXXXX
    3    0.061                                    XXX
    4   -0.056                                  XX
    5   -0.122                                XXXX
    6    0.088                                    XXX
    7    0.073                                    XXX
    8   -0.019                                   X
    9   -0.020                                   X
   10   -0.015                                   X
   11    0.053                                    XX
   12    0.030                                    XX
   13    0.006                                    X
   14   -0.046                                  XX
   15    0.090                                    XXX
   16    0.023                                    XX
   17    0.027                                    XX
   18    0.060                                    XX
   19   -0.008                                   X
   20    0.025                                    XX
   21   -0.027                                  XX
   22    0.014                                    X
   23    0.007                                    X
   24   -0.025                                  XX
   25   -0.104                                XXXX
   26   -0.012                                   X
   27    0.090                                    XXX
   28    0.060                                    XX
   29    0.141                                    XXXXX
   30    0.088                                    XXX
   31    0.090                                    XXX
   32    0.041                                    XX
   33   -0.087                                 XXX
   34   -0.091                                 XXX
   35    0.045                                    XX
   36   -0.063                                 XXX
```

FIGURE 9.8 Partial autocorrelation coefficients of first-differenced series (Note: computer-generated Minitab output)

estimates that minimize the mean square error (MSE). The process is iterative, and the final value of the parameter estimates may be significantly different from the initialized values of the estimation procedure.

However, the estimates will usually converge on an optimal value for the parameters with a small number of iterations. If the algorithm fails to converge after some specified number of iterations, an examination of the trial values will indicate the direction of changes needed and new initial estimates can be made.[5]

---

5 The method of iterative improvement is based on a powerful algorithm due to Marquardt (1963) and is part of the computational process of many Box–Jenkins software systems.

An AR(1) model is tentatively chosen for the sample data on IIP, and an initial guess of $\phi = -1$ is used.[6] The program converges after five iterations, producing the tentative model with $\phi_1 = 0.3063$ (AR 1).

The final estimate of the model is shown in figure 9.9. The estimate from this model is 0.3063, the standard deviation is 0.1041, and the t ratio (equal to the estimate divided by the standard deviation) is 2.94.[7] The MSE is 2.813. Finally, the computer output produces forecasts with 95 percent confidence limits for periods 91–95. All these estimates and forecasts will be re-examined after we complete stage 2 of the Box–Jenkins method.

Stage 3 Diagnostic Testing

To check the adequacy of the model, we estimate and plot the autocorrelations of the residuals to determine whether they are significantly different from zero (figure 9.10). The limits of the 2σ confidence intervals are

```
Estimates at each iteration
Iteration       SSE         Parameters
    0         258.895        0.100
    1         248.962        0.250
    2         248.170        0.301
    3         248.161        0.306
    4         248.161        0.306
    5         248.161        0.306
Relative change in each estimate less than 0.0010

Final Estimates of Parameters
Type      Estimate   St. Dev.   t-ratio
AR    1    0.3063     0.1041      2.94

Differencing: 1 regular difference
No. of obs.:  Original series 90, after differencing 89
Residuals:    SS = 247.586 (backforecasts excluded)
              MS =   2.813 DF = 88

Modified Box-Pierce chisquare statistic
Lag                    12            24            36            48
Chisquare        6.4 (DF=11)   8.9 (DF=23)   20.0 (DF=35)   30.1 (DF=47)

Forecasts from period 90
                          95 Percent Limits
   Period     Forecast     Lower        Upper
     91        130.097     126.809      133.385
     92        129.759     124.350      135.169
     93        129.656     122.552      136.759
     94        129.624     121.107      138.141
     95        129.614     119.873      139.355
```

FIGURE 9.9 Box–Jenkins estimation of ARIMA(1,1,0) model (Note: computer-generated Minitab output)

---

6 These values are selected using the 1987 version of Minitab. Most software systems operate in a similar manner based on Marquardt's algorithm.

7 This is significant at the 0.01 level.

		-1.0	-0.8	-0.6	-0.4	-0.2	0.0	0.2	0.4	0.6	0.8	1.0
		+----+----+----+----+----+----+---+---+----+----+										
1	-0.066						XXX					
2	0.141						XXXXX					
3	0.109						XXXX					
4	0.019						X					
5	-0.144						XXXXX					
6	0.088						XXX					
7	0.027						XX					
8	-0.014						X					
9	0.027						XX					
10	0.005						X					
11	0.010						X					
12	0.021						XX					
13	0.048						XX					
14	-0.037						XX					
15	0.096						XXX					
16	0.011						X					
17	0.025						XX					
18	0.079						XXX					
19	0.022						XX					
20	0.031						XX					
21	-0.006						X					
22	0.027						XX					
23	-0.002						X					
24	0.019						X					
25	-0.091						XXX					
26	-0.039						XX					
27	0.018						X					
28	-0.020						X					
29	0.105						XXXX					
30	0.122						XXXX					
31	0.132						XXXX					
32	0.107						XXXX					
33	0.037						XX					
34	-0.064						XXX					
35	0.062						XXX					
36	-0.074						XXX					

FIGURE 9.10 Autocorrelation coefficients for the residuals of the fitted ARIMA(1,1,0) model (Note: computer-generated Minitab output)

$$-2\frac{1}{\sqrt{(89)}} \leqslant r \leqslant 2\frac{1}{\sqrt{(89)}}$$
$$-0.212 \leqslant r \leqslant +0.212$$

Hence none of the autocorrelations are significantly different from zero (at 2σ limits), indicating that the model is adequate. Finally, the range of these autocorrelations is from -0.144 to $+0.141$ and shows no particular pattern.

The second test of the adequacy of the model is the Ljung–Box (Q) test (equation (9.7)).[8] When the first $k = 24$ autocorrelations are used for the test, the null and

---

8 In many computer programs the Ljung–Box (Q) test is not identified as such. It is referred to as a χ^2 test or a modified Box–Pierce (Q) test but it is this test statistic. Some programs report the older Box–Pierce test (1970) as well. This test is not as useful.

alternative hypotheses are as follows:

   H_0: the model is adequate
   H_A: the model is not adequate

The number of degrees of freedom (d.f.) is

   d.f. $= k - p - q = 24 - 1 = 23$

From the tabulated value of χ^2 (table A.4 at the end of the book) we find $\chi^2 = 35.1725$ at a significance level of 0.05 for d.f. $= 23$. The calculated value is

$$Q = 90 \times 92 \left[\frac{(-0.066)^2}{89} + \frac{(+0.141)^2}{88} + \dots + \frac{(-0.091)^2}{55} \right]$$
$$= 90 \times 92 \times 0.001075 = 8.9$$

Since the calculated value is less than the tabulated value, we can accept the null hypothesis at the 0.05 level and conclude that the model is adequate.[9] We shall compare the ARIMA (1,1,0) model estimated above with an ARIMA(1,0,0) model (figure 9.11). Stated differently, we shall compare an AR(1) model with differencing of degree 1 with an AR(1) without any differencing. The purpose is to determine which model is the most adequate.

   The results of the two AR(1) models are compared in table 9.2. The value of Q (the Ljung–Box statistic) is smaller for the (1,1,0) differenced model than for the model without differencing. The model with differencing appears more suitable as judged by this measure. If the forecast errors for 1–5 periods into the future are checked, the ARIMA(1,0,0) model has slightly closer estimates. However, the variance in the residuals (MSE) is smaller for the AR(1,1,0) model. Most important is the coefficient for the ARIMA(1,0,0) model, which is 0.9996. This value almost violates the condition for stationarity and hence the model with no differencing is not acceptable for forecasting. Finally, the autocorrelation function (ACF) for the residuals from the (1,0,0) model indicates that r_1 and r_2 are outside the 2σ limits. Thus the model does not yield evidence of stability in the forecasts.

Stage 4: Forecasting

We forecast for five steps ahead using the above ARIMA(1,1,0) model with observation number 31 as the starting value. To begin, we restate the fitted forecast model:

$$(1 - B)(1 - \phi B)Y_t = e_t \tag{9.9}$$

Note the use of the backshift operator to describe the first difference $(1 - B)$ and the AR portion of the model $(1 - \phi_1 B)$. The terms can be multiplied out and rearranged as follows:

$$(1 - \phi_1 B - B + \phi_1 B^2)Y_t = e_t$$

$$Y_t = Y_{t-1} + \phi_1(Y_{t-1} - Y_{t-2}) + e_t \tag{9.10}$$

---

9   Note that Minitab produces Q (χ^2) statistics for 12, 36, and 48 lags as well.

```
              -1.0 -0.8 -0.6 -0.4 -0.2  0.0  0.2  0.4  0.6  0.8  1.0
               +----+----+----+----+----+----+---+---+----+----+
 1    0.277                                     XXXXXXXX
 2    0.226                                     XXXXXXX
 3    0.152                                     XXXXX
 4    0.033                                     XX
 5   -0.077                                  XXX
 6    0.039                                     XX
 7    0.049                                     XX
 8    0.006                                     X
 9    0.018                                     X
10    0.012                                     X
11    0.031                                     XX
12    0.029                                     XX
13    0.037                                     XX
14   -0.006                                     X
15    0.083                                     XXX
16    0.040                                     XX
17    0.056                                     XX
18    0.102                                     XXXX
19    0.060                                     XXX
20    0.049                                     XX
21    0.014                                     X
22    0.028                                     XX
23    0.014                                     X
24   -0.009                                     X
25   -0.089                                  XXX
26   -0.046                                     XX
27    0.021                                     XX
28    0.042                                     XX
29    0.162                                     XXXXX
30    0.204                                     XXXXXX
```

FIGURE 9.11 Autocorrelation coefficients for the residuals of the fitted ARIMA(1,0,0) model (Note: computer-generated Minitab output)

We can now substitute in the equation for $\phi_1 = 0.2178$ and for Y_{t-1} and Y_{t-2}. To forecast for period 91, we write

$$\hat{Y}_{91} = Y_{90} + \phi_1(Y_{90} - Y_{89})$$

with e_t set equal to zero. By substitution we have,

$$\hat{Y}_{91} = 131.2 + 0.3063(131.2 - 134.8)$$

$$= 130.097$$

In a similar manner, we can forecast for more periods ahead.

The result of these forecasts for the first period is a function of the last period's actual observation and the last period's error. All future forecasts (periods 91–95) are based only on predicted values of Y_t since future values of e_t are unknown.

We can now calculate the forecast error and its variance for the ARIMA $(1, 1, 0)$ model to obtain a forecast confidence interval. As we shall see, the forecast

TABLE 9.2 Comparison of two AR (1) models

		ARIMA(1,0,0) no differencing	ARIMA(1,1,0) 1 degree of differencing
Ljung-Box(Q)		18.9	8.9
d.f.		23	23
Forecast errors:			
Period	*Period ahead*		
91	1	−2.36	−3.40
92	2	−7.07	−8.34
93	3	−9.48	−10.84
94	4	−10.93	−12.28
95	5	−12.79	−14.09
Variance of residuals (MSE)		3.073	2.813
AR parameter		0.9996	0.3063
t value		767.26	2.94

confidence interval for Y_t is related to the forecast confidence interval for the differenced series BY_t.

To begin, consider the forecast error for the one-period-ahead forecast $Y_t(1)$:

$$e_t(1) = Y_{t+1} - \hat{Y}_t(1) \tag{9.11}$$

where the circumflex indicates the estimated value. In turn, if we assign $Z_t = Y_t - Y_{t-1}$, then

$$e_t(1) = Y_t + Z_{t+1} - Y_t - \hat{Z}_t(1) = e_{t+1} \tag{9.12}$$

which has a variance σ_e^2. The two-period ahead forecast is given by

$$e_t(2) = Y_{t+2} - \hat{Y}_t(2) \tag{9.13}$$

$$= Y_t + Z_{t+1} + Z_{t+2} - Y_t - \hat{Z}_t(1) - \hat{Z}_t(2)$$

$$= [Z_{t+1} - \hat{Z}_t(1)] + [Z_{t+2} - \hat{Z}_t(2)]$$

$$= (1 + \phi_1)e_{t+1} + e_{t+2} \tag{9.14}$$

This has a variance

$$E[e_t^2(2)] = \sigma_e^2[(1 + \phi_1)^2 + 1] \tag{9.15}$$

Note that the forecast error and its variance are cumulative. The forecast error is equal to the two-period error for $\hat{Z}_t(2)$ in addition to the one-period error for $\hat{Z}_t(1)$. Thus the error in $\hat{Y}_t(2)$ is an accumulation of the forecast errors in $\hat{Z}_t(1)$ and $\hat{Z}_t(2)$:

$$
e_t(n) = \sum_{i=1}^{n} e_{t+1} \sum_{j=0}^{n-i} \phi_1^j
\tag{9.16}
$$

and this has a variance

$$
E[e_t^2(n)] = \sigma_e^2 \sum_{i=1}^{n} \left(\sum_{j=0}^{n-i} \phi_1^j \right)^2
\tag{9.17}
$$

As expected, the error in $\hat{Y}_t(n)$ is an accumulation of errors in $\hat{Z}_t(1)$, $\hat{Z}_t(2),\ldots,\hat{Z}_t(n)$. Thus the confidence interval for $\hat{Y}_t(n)$ grows rapidly since it accounts for the accumulation of forecast errors in the differenced series. It can be seen in figure 9.9 that the width of the 95 percent confidence interval becomes larger as the number of periods ahead forecast increases.

In conclusion, although we examined properties of only a simple ARIMA model, some of our conclusions apply to more complicated (higher-order) ARIMA models. In particular, an MA model of order q has a memory of only q periods, since there are only q error terms. Thus the observed data will affect the forecast only if the lead time n is less than q. An AR model has memory of infinite length, and thus all past observations will have some influence on the forecast, this is true when n is large. Only recent observations, however, will have a large effect. Consequently, in both AR and mixed ARMA models, past observations have only minor effects on the forecast if the lead time is very long. In conclusion, ARIMA models are suitable for short-term forecasting, that is, where the lead time n is not much longer than $p+q$.

Finally, practicing forecasters find it very useful to compare forecasts of several competing fitted time series models as we did in table 9.2. This is particularly helpful if the forecaster is having difficulty in choosing among a variety of possible models. Often the choice is not critical if the forecasts are similar. If the forecasts are dissimilar, an attempt to determine why they are dissimilar should be made. This determination will aid in choosing among the models. For example, we would not choose the ARIMA (1,0,0) model because this AR model would not meet the test for stationarity. Specifically since the autoregressive coefficient is close to unity, the stationarity condition is nearly violated. The Q statistic for this model is 18.9 (24 lags) whereas the Q statistic obtained for the ARIMA (1,1,0) model is 8.9. Thus the ARIMA (1,1,0) model meets the tests for adequacy better than the (1,0,0) model and would be the preferred model for forecasting.

At least 50 observations are usually required for Box–Jenkins estimation. Even more observations are recommended for a seasonal model.

9.5   Forecasting Seasonal Time Series

Many economic time series data available for computerized data bank and publications are seasonally adjusted. These time series are used in models for forecasting trend–cycle components. Econometric regression models are also used where seasonal patterns would otherwise mask the information of interest to the forecaster. In chapter 7, we noted that the study of autocorrelations can provide adequate indication of the relative importance of a seasonal pattern of data.[10]

We may find it desirable to forecast seasonal series that are unadjusted for seasonality. Seasonality varies from year to year, indicating that models based on unadjusted data rather than seasonally adjusted data are likely to be more flexible and useful. If changing seasonality is expected, it is usually preferable to account for it through the development of a properly specified ARIMA model.

For time series that contain a seasonal component that repeats every s observation, a supplement to the nonseasonal ARIMA model can be applied. For a seasonal time series with period s, $s = 12$ for monthly data and $s = 4$ for quarterly data. Seasonal ARIMA$(P,D,Q)^s$ models can be developed for seasonal data in a manner similar to the ordinary ARIMA process.

In a multiplicative ARIMA model, the regular and seasonal autoregressive components, differences, and moving-average components are multiplied together in the general model. Often, most of the p, d, q values are zero in practical illustrations and the resulting models are often quite simple or parsimonious.

A very useful notation for describing the orders of the various components in the multiplicative model is given by

$$(p,d,q) \times (P,D,Q)^s$$

and corresponds to the orders of the regular and seasonal factors respectively.

By representing a time series in terms of a multiplicative model, it is often possible to reduce the number of parameters to be estimated. Also, it is of aid in interpreting the model structure.

Consider a monthly seasonal model that has a seasonal difference (by months) and also, regular and seasonal first-order autoregressive parameters. Thus,

$$(p,d,q) \times (P,D,Q)^s = (1, 0, 0) \times (1, 1, 0)^{12}$$

In terms of Y_t we have

$$Y_t = \phi_1 Y_{t-1} + (1 + \phi_{12}) \, Y_{t-12} - \phi_1(1 + \phi_{12})Y_{t-13}\phi_{12} - Y_{t-24} + \phi_1\phi_{12}Y_{t-25} + e_t$$

(9.18)

Recall that the use of the backshift operator permits us to express the order and type of process in terms of the exponent of B and the type of parameter.

If we are studying seasonal data, an ARMA process may consist of two parts:

1 the regular portion studied earlier in this chapter;
2 the seasonal portion.

For the purposes of identifying a seasonal ARMA process, we divide the process into two parts. To identify the seasonal pattern, we ignore the nonseasonal process and determine whether the seasonality is determined by an AR or an MA process by focusing on the coefficients of the seasonal terms. Suppose that the nonseasonal part is an ARIMA(1,0,1) and the time series show a quarterly seasonal pattern, then the complete model becomes

---

10   In a study by Cholette (1983, p. 13), the conclusion was: "The forecasting error recorded herein with ARIMA forecasting of raw unadjusted series is lower – but not decisively lower – ... However, model identification is a lot easier for raw unadjusted series."

$$(1 - \phi_1 B)(1 - \phi_4 B^4)Y_t = (1 - \theta_1 B)e_t \qquad (9.19)$$

if seasonality is on the AR portion, or

$$(1 - \phi_1 B)Y_t = (1 - \theta_1 B)(1 - \theta_4 B^4)e_t \qquad (9.20)$$

if seasonality is on the MA portion, where

$$(1 - \phi_4 B^4)Y_t = Y_t - \phi_4 B^4 Y_t \qquad (9.21)$$

In a similar manner

$$(1 - \theta_4 B^4)e_t = e_t - \theta_4 B^4 e_t$$

$$= e_t - \theta_4 e_{t-12} \qquad (9.22)$$

Thus the above models include seasonal parameters that use the Y_t or e_t of four quarters ago to take seasonality into account.

An MA(2) seasonal process with one level of differencing is expressed by

$$(1 - B)(1 - B^4)Y_t = (1 - \theta_1 B - \theta_2 B^2)e_t \qquad (9.23)$$

$$\begin{pmatrix} \text{one level} \\ \text{of differencing} \end{pmatrix} \begin{pmatrix} \text{seasonal pattern} \\ \text{in AR} \end{pmatrix} = \begin{pmatrix} \text{MA(2)} \\ \text{nonseasonal} \end{pmatrix}$$

or

$$(1 - B)Y_t = (1 - \theta_1 B - \theta_2 B^2)(1 - \theta_4 B^4)e_t \qquad (9.24)$$

$$\begin{pmatrix} \text{one level} \\ \text{of differencing} \end{pmatrix} = \begin{pmatrix} \text{MA(2)} \\ \text{nonseasonal} \end{pmatrix} \begin{pmatrix} \text{seasonal} \\ \text{parameter in MA} \end{pmatrix}$$

9.6 An Application of Seasonal ARIMA Models

Example 9.1

Data on new plant and equipment expenditures for the United States (billion dollars) for the period third quarter 1967 through second quarter 1982 is collected for forecasting. A seasonal pattern and nonseasonal pattern must be identified for the ARIMA process. A forecast for five periods into the future is to be made on the identified time series model.

To identify whether the data are stationary or not, the autocorrelation coefficients are calculated and plotted in figure 9.12. Since there are 60 observations, the 2σ confidence limits are found to be

$$-2\frac{1}{\sqrt{(60)}} < r < 2\frac{1}{\sqrt{(60)}}$$
$$-0.258 < r < +0.258$$

It can be seen that the data are not stationary in their original form since the coefficients r_1–r_{12} are all significantly different from zero. Also the series does not

```
                    -1.0  -0.8  -0.6  -0.4  -0.2   0.0   0.2   0.4   0.6   0.8   1.0
                    +----+----+----+----+----+----+---+---+----+----+
     1    0.926                                     XXXXXXXXXXXXXXXXXXXXXXXXX
     2    0.902                                     XXXXXXXXXXXXXXXXXXXXXXXXX
     3    0.825                                     XXXXXXXXXXXXXXXXXXXXXXX
     4    0.789                                     XXXXXXXXXXXXXXXXXXXXXX
     5    0.711                                     XXXXXXXXXXXXXXXXXXX
     6    0.677                                     XXXXXXXXXXXXXXXXXX
     7    0.599                                     XXXXXXXXXXXXXXXX
     8    0.557                                     XXXXXXXXXXXXXXX
     9    0.480                                     XXXXXXXXXXXXX
    10    0.441                                     XXXXXXXXXXXX
    11    0.362                                     XXXXXXXXXX
    12    0.317                                     XXXXXXXXX
    13    0.249                                     XXXXXXX
    14    0.212                                     XXXXXX
    15    0.140                                     XXXXX
    16    0.098                                     XXX
    17    0.039                                     XX
    18    0.008                                     X
    19   -0.024                                    XX
    20   -0.034                                    XX
    21   -0.067                                   XXX
    22   -0.074                                   XXX
    23   -0.103                                  XXXX
    24   -0.111                                  XXXX
    25   -0.137                                  XXXX
    26   -0.141                                 XXXXX
    27   -0.166                                 XXXXX
    28   -0.171                                 XXXXX
    29   -0.195                                XXXXXX
    30   -0.200                                XXXXXX
    31   -0.227                               XXXXXXX
    32   -0.236                               XXXXXXX
    33   -0.261                              XXXXXXXX
    34   -0.266                              XXXXXXXX
    35   -0.290                              XXXXXXXX
    36   -0.297                              XXXXXXXX
    37   -0.317                             XXXXXXXXX
    38   -0.320                             XXXXXXXXX
    39   -0.339                             XXXXXXXXX
    40   -0.342                             XXXXXXXXX
    41   -0.356                            XXXXXXXXXX
    42   -0.356                            XXXXXXXXXX
    43   -0.359                            XXXXXXXXXX
    44   -0.344                            XXXXXXXXXX
    45   -0.341                            XXXXXXXXXX
    46   -0.319                             XXXXXXXXX
```

FIGURE 9.12 Autocorrelation coefficients for the time series new plant and equipment
            expenditures (Note: computer-generated Minitab output)

dampen down to zero at any reasonable speed. Since these data are not stationary in their original form, there is no reason for calculating partial autocorrelation coefficients. Hence the next step is to obtain a stationary series.

To obtain a stationary series, the first differences are calculated and a new series is formed. Examination of figure 9.13 indicates a very different pattern for the

```
           -1.0  -0.8  -0.6  -0.4  -0.2   0.0   0.2   0.4   0.6   0.8   1.0
           +----+----+----+----+----+----+---+---+----+----+
   1   -0.564               XXXXXXXXXXXXXXX
   2    0.376                              XXXXXXXXXX
   3   -0.473               XXXXXXXXXXXXX
   4    0.677                              XXXXXXXXXXXXXXXXXXX
   5   -0.472               XXXXXXXXXXXXX
   6    0.336                              XXXXXXXXX
   7   -0.402               XXXXXXXXXXX
   8    0.541                              XXXXXXXXXXXXXXX
   9   -0.409               XXXXXXXXXXX
  10    0.255                              XXXXXXX
  11   -0.342               XXXXXXXXXX
  12    0.403                              XXXXXXXXXXX
  13   -0.306               XXXXXXXXX
  14    0.228                              XXXXXXX
  15   -0.262               XXXXXXXX
  16    0.269                              XXXXXXXX
  17   -0.210                XXXXX
  18    0.169                              XXXX
  19   -0.258               XXXXXXX
  20    0.360                              XXXXXXXXXX
  21   -0.272               XXXXXXXX
  22    0.159                              XXXX
  23   -0.240               XXXXXXX
  24    0.318                              XXXXXXXXX
  25   -0.254               XXXXXXX
  26    0.140                              XXXXX
  27   -0.213               XXXXX
  28    0.283                              XXXXXXXX
  29   -0.243               XXXXXXX
  30    0.125                              XXXX
  31   -0.192               XXXXX
  32    0.234                              XXXXXXX
  33   -0.204               XXXXX
  34    0.109                              XXXX
  35   -0.167               XXXXX
  36    0.205                              XXXXXX
```

FIGURE 9.13 Autocorrelation coefficients for the first-differenced series (Note: computer-generated Minitab output)

autocorrelation coefficients. The (first) differenced series has autocorrelation coefficients distributed in a zigzag pattern around zero, indicating the removal of the period-to-period nonstationarity.[11] However, there are significant coefficients. The coefficients for r_4, r_8, r_{12}, etc. are significant, indicating the existence of a quarterly

---

[11]

$$-\frac{2}{n^{1/2}} < r < + -\frac{2}{n^{1/2}}$$

$$-\frac{2}{\sqrt{(59)}} < r < +\frac{2}{\sqrt{(59)}}$$

$$-0.260 < r < + 0.260$$

		-1.0 -0.8 -0.6 -0.4 -0.2 0.0 0.2 0.4 0.6 0.8 1.0
		+----+----+----+----+----+----+---+---+----+----+
1	-0.564	XXXXXXXXXXXXXXX
2	0.085	XXX
3	-0.341	XXXXXXXXXX
4	0.482	XXXXXXXXXXXXX
5	0.079	XXX
6	-0.007	X
7	-0.045	XX
8	0.104	XXXX
9	0.021	XX
10	-0.105	XXXX
11	-0.079	XXX
12	-0.070	XXX
13	0.033	XX
14	0.057	XX
15	0.056	XX
16	-0.067	XXX
17	0.018	X
18	0.009	X
19	-0.148	XXXXX
20	0.276	XXXXXXXX
21	-0.068	XXX
22	-0.105	XXXX
23	-0.014	X
24	-0.020	X
25	0.010	X
26	-0.068	XXX
27	-0.007	X
28	-0.061	XXX
29	0.007	X
30	0.005	X
31	-0.020	X
32	-0.078	XXX
33	-0.008	X
34	-0.035	XX
35	-0.076	XXX
36	0.126	XXXX

FIGURE 9.14 Partial autocorrelation coefficients for the first-differenced series (Note: computer-generated Minitab output)

seasonal pattern. Also, upon examination of the plot of autocorrelations, a significant coefficient appears at lag 4. A plot of the partial autocorrelation coefficients is given in figure 9.14. The partial autocorrelation cuts off after lag 3, but lag 2 is not significant.

To determine the underlying ARIMA model for the seasonal portion of the time series, any longer-term trend that exists must be removed from the time series. The longer-term trend will be four periods (four quarters). We express a long-term difference as a "seasonal" difference and write it as

$$Y_t - Y_{t-4} = Y_t - B^4 Y_t = (1 - B^4)Y_t \tag{9.25}$$

The original data and the four-period difference are shown in table 9.3. The last column is the difference. From the table, we note that four values are lost and we

TABLE 9.3 Original data and four-period difference

Period	Period after lagging	Original values	Y_t	Y_{t-4}	$(1 - B^4)Y_t$
1	5	16.20	16.09	16.20	−0.11
2	6	18.12	19.03	18.12	0.91
3	7	15.10	16.04	15.10	0.94
4	8	16.85	18.81	16.85	1.96
5	9	16.09	19.25	16.09	3.16
6	10	19.03	21.46	19.03	2.43
⋮	⋮	⋮	⋮	⋮	⋮
54	58	82.31	90.39	82.31	8.08
55	59	69.75	73.80	69.75	4.05
56	60	79.60	84.59	79.60	4.99
57	—	81.75	—	—	—
58	—	90.39	—	—	—
59	—	73.80	—	—	—
60	—	84.59	—	—	—

Note: Data are for new plant and equipment expenditures, United States ($ billions; period 1 is 1967, third quarter).
Source: *Survey of Current Business*, various issues.

must start at Y_5 to take the initial seasonal difference $Y_t - Y_{t-4} - -0.11$. The seasonal difference series has 56 observations. To determine if they are stationary, the autocorrelation coefficients are computed as shown in figure 9.15.

The autocorrelations of the seasonal differences indicate that the series is not stationary. Since a trend will hinder the identification of other patterns, in a similar way a trend will hinder the identification of the seasonal differenced pattern. The data should be stationary before the pattern of the data can be identified. The simplest way to remove the trend element is to combine the seasonal difference shown in figure 9.16 with an ordinary (nonseasonal) difference. Before this is done, it is necessary to examine the partial autocorrelation of the seasonal differences to determine whether an appropriate ARIMA model can be chosen. Figure 9.16 shows the plot of the partial autocorrelation functions (PACFs) for this example. Note that the PACF plot indicates a significant coefficient at lag 1 and lag 5.

Both figures 9.15 and 9.16 indicate a trend in the data. To eliminate the trend, we take the nonseasonal (ordinary) difference in addition to the seasonal difference, which involves differencing more terms. This simultaneous difference is equivalent to

$$(1 - B)(1 - B^4)Y_t \tag{9.26}$$

(one ordinary difference) $\left(\begin{array}{c} \text{one seasonal} \\ \text{term difference} \end{array} \right)$

Figure 9.17 shows the autocorrelation coefficients obtained for the series expressed in equation (9.26). The coefficients are dispersed around the zero level indicating stationarity in the series. Except for r_4, the dispersion appears random,

```
                        -1.0  -0.8  -0.6  -0.4  -0.2   0.0   0.2   0.4   0.6   0.8   1.0
                        +----+----+----+----+----+----+---+---+----+----+
    1     0.813                                      XXXXXXXXXXXXXXXXXXXXXX
    2     0.650                                      XXXXXXXXXXXXXXXXX
    3     0.478                                      XXXXXXXXXXXXX
    4     0.314                                      XXXXXXXXX
    5     0.284                                      XXXXXXXX
    6     0.239                                      XXXXXXX
    7     0.165                                      XXXXX
    8     0.081                                      XXX
    9    -0.000                                      X
   10    -0.054                                      XX
   11    -0.060                                      XX
   12    -0.037                                      XX
   13    -0.031                                      XX
   14    -0.016                                      X
   15    -0.019                                      X
   16    -0.028                                      XX
   17    -0.022                                      XX
   18    -0.018                                      X
   19    -0.021                                      XX
   20    -0.022                                      XX
   21    -0.037                                      XX
   22    -0.058                                      XX
   23    -0.083                                      XXX
   24    -0.094                                      XXX
   25    -0.107                                      XXXX
   26    -0.121                                      XXXX
   27    -0.133                                      XXXX
   28    -0.153                                      XXXXX
   29    -0.178                                      XXXXX
   30    -0.185                                      XXXXXX
   31    -0.187                                      XXXXXX
   32    -0.185                                      XXXXXX
   33    -0.174                                      XXXXX
   34    -0.156                                      XXXXX
   35    -0.151                                      XXXXX
   36    -0.149                                      XXXXX
```

FIGURE 9.15 Autocorrelation coefficients of seasonally differenced series (Note: computer-generated Minitab output)

indicating stationarity at the level of one seasonal difference. By examining the partial autocorrelation coefficients we can begin to finalize our time series model.

Figure 9.18 is a plot of the partial autocorrelations of the series of one difference and one seasonal difference. If we ignore the seasonal coefficients and examine the nonseasonal coefficients, we observe no significant values suggesting an ARIMA(0,1,0) model for the nonseasonal portion. The autocorrelation coefficients also seem to suggest this. The expression for the nonseasonal model is

$$(1 - B) Y_t = e_t \tag{9.27}$$

The next step is to identify the seasonal pattern by examining the coefficients — r_4, r_8, r_{12} and r_{16}. The partial r_4 is significant, and r_8 and r_{12} appear to trail off to zero.

```
                     -1.0 -0.8 -0.6 -0.4 -0.2  0.0  0.2  0.4  0.6  0.8  1.0
                     +----+----+----+----+----+----+---+---+----+----+
 1      0.813                                 XXXXXXXXXXXXXXXXXXXXXX
 2     -0.032                                 XX
 3     -0.121                              XXXX
 4     -0.096                               XXX
 5      0.283                                 XXXXXXXX
 6     -0.055                                 XX
 7     -0.184                            XXXXXX
 8     -0.109                              XXXX
 9      0.081                                 XXX
10      0.008                                 X
11      0.000                                 X
12      0.031                                 XX
13     -0.022                                 XX
14      0.040                                 XX
15     -0.011                                 X
16     -0.012                                 X
17     -0.017                                 X
18      0.004                                 X
19     -0.037                                 XX
20     -0.005                                 X
21     -0.025                                 XX
22     -0.025                                 XX
23     -0.058                                 XX
24      0.030                                 XX
25     -0.028                                 XX
26     -0.056                                 XX
27     -0.033                                 XX
28     -0.014                                 X
29     -0.062                                 XXX
30     -0.009                                 X
31     -0.011                                 X
32     -0.035                                 XX
33     -0.019                                 X
34      0.035                                 XX
35     -0.043                                 XX
36     -0.069                                 XXX
```

FIGURE 9.16 Partial autocorrelation coefficients for seasonally differenced series (Note: computer-generated Minitab output)

The r_4 ordinary autocorrelation is the only one which is significantly different from zero; the r_8, r_{12}, r_{16}, and r_{20} ordinary autocorrelations are virtually zero. All this suggests an MA(1) model for the seasonal parameters as follows:

$$(1 - B^4) \, Y_t = (1 - \theta_4 B^4)e_t \tag{9.28}$$

By combining the nonseasonal equation (9.27) with (9.28) we obtain

$$(1 - B)(1 - B^4)Y_t = (1 - \theta_4 B^4)e_t \tag{9.29}$$

$$\left(\begin{array}{c}\text{ordinary} \\ \text{difference}\end{array}\right)\left(\begin{array}{c}\text{one seasonal} \\ \text{difference}\end{array}\right) = (\text{MA}(1) \text{ seasonal})$$

		-1.0 -0.8 -0.6 -0.4 -0.2 0.0 0.2 0.4 0.6 0.8 1.0
		+----+----+----+----+----+----+---+---+----+----+
1	-0.060	XXX
2	0.022	XX
3	-0.014	X
4	-0.362	XXXXXXXXXX
5	0.037	XX
6	0.072	XXX
7	0.026	XX
8	-0.012	X
9	-0.082	XXX
10	-0.133	XXXX
11	-0.082	XXX
12	0.044	XX
13	-0.019	X
14	0.045	XX
15	0.012	X
16	-0.042	XX
17	0.011	X
18	0.020	XX
19	-0.001	X
20	0.041	XX
21	0.018	X
22	0.008	X
23	-0.036	XX
24	0.007	X
25	0.005	X
26	-0.018	X
27	0.015	X
28	0.006	X
29	-0.054	XX
30	-0.006	X
31	-0.004	X
32	-0.019	X
33	-0.010	X
34	0.031	XX
35	0.014	X
36	0.028	XX

FIGURE 9.17 Autocorrelation coefficients for first-differenced and seasonally differenced series (Note: computer-generated Minitab output)

The steps of the identification stage are now completed. First, the time series was made stationary by taking the appropriate number of ordinary and seasonal term differences. Second, a nonseasonal (0,1,0) model was identified. Finally, a seasonal MA(1) model (0,1,1) was identified. The result is the

$(0,1,0)(0,1,1)^4$ ARIMA model

In the second phase of the Box–Jenkins analysis we estimate the θ_4 parameter by a generalized non-linear estimation process on a computer. The computerized output of the model yields the estimates

$\theta_4 = 0.4653$ MSE = 11.545

		-1.0 -0.8 -0.6 -0.4 -0.2 0.0 0.2 0.4 0.6 0.8 1.0
		+---+---+---+---+---+---+---+---+---+---+---+
1	-0.060	XXX
2	0.019	X
3	-0.012	X
4	-0.366	XXXXXXXXXX
5	-0.007	X
6	0.105	XXXX
7	0.022	XX
8	-0.173	XXXXX
9	-0.095	XXX
10	-0.080	XXX
11	-0.092	XXX
12	-0.042	XX
13	-0.099	XXX
14	-0.054	XX
15	-0.046	XX
16	-0.040	XX
17	-0.051	XX
18	-0.020	X
19	-0.054	XX
20	-0.027	XX
21	-0.022	XX
22	-0.003	X
23	-0.084	XXX
24	-0.024	XX
25	0.004	X
26	-0.038	XX
27	-0.055	XX
28	-0.001	X
29	-0.060	XX
30	-0.053	XX
31	-0.025	XX
32	-0.036	XX
33	-0.091	XXX
34	-0.018	X
35	0.011	X
36	0.010	X

FIGURE 9.18 Partial autocorrelation coefficients for first-differenced and seasonally differenced series (Note: computer-generated Minitab output)

The estimates are noted in figure 9.19.

In figure 9.19, the seasonal MA(1) parameter has a t ratio of 3.50. The ratio is significantly different from zero at the 0.01 level or less. Forecasts for periods 61–65 with the associated confidence limits are also presented.

In figure 9.20, the plot of the autocorrelation coefficients of the residuals from the identified and estimated model is given. Note that no coefficients are outside the 2σ limits. The Ljung–Box statistic is now completed with the following hypotheses:

H_0: the model is adequate

H_A: the model is not adequate

```
Estimates at each iteration
Iteration        SSE        Parameters
    0          699.563        0.100
    1          650.818        0.250
    2          626.603        0.400
    3          624.020        0.460
    4          624.002        0.465
    5          624.001        0.465
Relative change in each estimate less than 0.0010


Final Estimates of Parameters
Number      Type      Estimate    St. Dev.    t-ratio
  1         SMA   4    0.4653      0.1330       3.50


Differencing. 1 regular    1 seasonal differences of order 4
Residuals.     SS = 623.425 (backforecasts excluded)
               DF = 54    MS = 11.545
No. of obs.    Original series 60, after differencing 55


Forecasts from period 60
                            95 Percent Limits
 Period      Forecast       Lower        Upper
   61        86.037        79.376       92.698
   62        94.457        85.037      103.877
   63        80.554        69.017       92.092
   64        90.641        77.319      103.963
   65        92.088        75.296      108.881
```

FIGURE 9.19 Box–Jenkins estimation of ARIMA(0,1,0)(0,1,1)^4 time series model (Note: computer-generated Minitab output)

By the Ljung–Box test, we find

$n = 60$

$k = 24$

$p = 0$

$q = 1$

$d = 5$ one ordinary and four seasonal differences

$$Q = n(n + 2) \sum_{i}^{k} \frac{r_i^2}{n - k} \tag{9.7}$$
$$= 60\,(62)\,(0.001\,860\,2) = 6.9198$$

The χ^2 value for $k - (p + q) = 23$ degrees of freedom is 35.17 at the 5 percent level. Hence we do not have sufficient sample evidence to reject the null hypothesis. Stated

		-1.0 -0.8 -0.6 -0.4 -0.2 0.0 0.2 0.4 0.6 0.8 1.0
		+---+---+---+---+---+---+---+---+---+---+---+
1	-0.106	XXXX
2	0.084	XXX
3	-0.066	XXX
4	0.004	X
5	-0.047	XX
6	0.075	XXX
7	-0.039	XX
8	-0.010	X
9	-0.125	XXXX
10	-0.093	XXX
11	-0.112	XXXX
12	-0.005	X
13	-0.054	XX
14	0.034	XX
15	-0.039	XX
16	-0.092	XXX
17	0.025	XX
18	0.021	XX
19	-0.014	X
20	0.071	XXX
21	0.005	X
22	0.014	X
23	-0.039	XX
24	0.040	XX
25	-0.017	X
26	-0.010	X
27	-0.001	X
28	0.023	XX
29	-0.073	XXX
30	-0.001	X
31	-0.009	X
32	-0.004	X
33	-0.024	XX
34	0.025	XX
35	-0.000	X
36	0.030	XX

FIGURE 9.20 Autocorrelation coefficients for the residuals from the ARIMA$(0,1,0)(0,1,1)^4$ time series model (Note: computer-generated Minitab output)

differently, the ARIMA$(0,1,0)(0,1,1)^4$ model is adequate based on sample evidence. Note that the computation of Q was restricted to 24 lags.

The estimated relationship is complex, involving several terms of Y_t and e_t. Equation (9.29) will be expanded to show how to use past values of Y_t and past errors e_t in making predictions. Equation (9.29) is

$$(1 - B)(1 - B^4)Y_t = (1 - \theta_4 B^4)e_t$$

and

$$(1 - B)(1 - B^4)Y_t = e_t - \theta_4 e_{t-4}$$

and

$$Y_t - Y_{t-1} - Y_{t-4} + Y_{t-5} = e_t - \theta_4 e_{t-4}$$

To use this equation to forecast one period ahead, Y_{t+1}, = the subscripts are increased by 1 throughout, as in the following equation:

$$\hat{Y}_{t+1} = Y_t + Y_{t-3} - Y_{t-4} - \theta_4 e_{t-3} \tag{9.30}$$

(The circumflex is used to indicate that it is an estimate.) Since e_{t+1} will not be known because the expected value of future random errors is assumed to be zero, it is dropped from the equation. From the fitted model, it is possible to replace e_t, e_{t-3}, and e_{t-4} by their empirically determined values. Specifically, the last iteration of Marquardt's algorithm will produce these values for the purpose of forecasting. As we forecast further into the distant future, there will be empirical values for the error terms e after a while and, in turn, their expected values will all be zero.

To forecast for period 61, we have[12]

$$\hat{Y}_{61} = Y_{60} + Y_{57} - Y_{56} - \theta e_{57}$$

$$= 84.59 + 81.75 - 79.60 - 0.4653(1.511)$$

$$= \$86.037 \text{ billion}$$

Forecasts for additional periods can be made in a similar manner.

One last question concerns whether seasonal ARMA models are seasonal in the AR or the MA part. The difficulty is often related to the fact that forecasters usually have neither enough observations nor enough time to compute and plot the numerous ordinary and partial correlations. If it is unclear, forecasters find it advisable to calculate both possibilities.

9.7 Achieving Stationarity in Variance and ARIMA Modeling

Two last concerns when using Box–Jenkins techniques to fit general ARIMA models are (a) fitting monthly time series data and (b) achieving stationarity in the variance of the time series. Both these problems have been addressed before. First, the procedures for identifying and estimating monthly time series data are the same as for identifying and estimating quarterly time series data. Second, the method for achieving stationarity in variance through a logarithmic transformation of the time series data was explored in chapter 7. In this section the method used to identify a monthly seasonal series characterized by nonstationarity in variance will be illustrated.

Example 9.2

Data on traffic flow (in hundreds of thousands) at a sample of airline terminals are collected over a six year period by month. The data are to be modeled and identified, and a forecast for 12 periods (one year) is to be provided.[13] The series is

---

12   We should point out that, because of rounding, this result may only approximate the results of using a computer program.

13   Data for this example were obtained by simulation.

said to be nonstationary in variance because the size of the fluctuations in variance is proportional to the size of observed values (see figure 9.21 where the variation in the observed values increases over time).

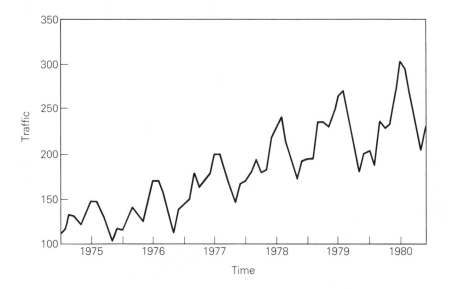

FIGURE 9.21 Traffic flow data

The usual approach to achieving stationarity in variance is to transform the data by taking the natural logarithm of the observed values.[14] Such a transformation is accomplished as follows:

$$\ln Y_t = Y_t \tag{9.31}$$

The size of the fluctuations in the transformed data will not vary with time. In particular, the fluctuations at the very beginning of the time series will be about the same as at the end of the time series. Once we have established the stationarity in variance, the identification can begin. We should be cautious because if stationarity in variance is not achieved, misleading results producing forecasts with large errors will occur.

Once we have established stationarity in variance, we compute and plot the ordinary autocorrelation function (ACF) to determine if we have stationarity in mean. Although not shown here, the ordinary ACF had a large number of low-order autocorrelation coefficients which were outside the 2σ limits. Hence, a first-differenced series was plotted (figure 9.22) indicating significant autocorrelation coefficients at lags of 12, 24, 36, and 48. Note that the values for r_{12}, r_{24}, r_{36} and r_{48} decrease slowly, indicating a trend in the seasonal pattern. Hence we can tentatively identify a model requiring at least one difference in the seasonal as well as the nonseasonal portion of the model.

---

14   We should point out that there are appropriate alternative transformations such as the power function. However, we shall limit our discussion to this transformation.

```
              -1.0 -0.8 -0.6 -0.4 -0.2  0.0  0.2  0.4  0.6  0.8  1.0
              +---+---+---+---+---+---+---+---+---+---+---+
  1   0.124                             XXXX
  2  -0.160                            XXXXX
  3  -0.159                            XXXXX
  4  -0.278                         XXXXXXXX
  5  -0.021                              XX
  6   0.102                             XXXX
  7  -0.078                             XXX
  8  -0.318                        XXXXXXXXX
  9  -0.085                             XXX
 10  -0.130                            XXXX
 11   0.147                             XXXXX
 12   0.708                             XXXXXXXXXXXXXXXXXX
 13   0.146                             XXXXX
 14  -0.178                           XXXXX
 15  -0.094                            XXX
 16  -0.220                          XXXXXX
 17   0.038                              XX
 18   0.078                             XXX
 19  -0.076                             XXX
 20  -0.266                         XXXXXXXX
 21  -0.094                            XXX
 22  -0.058                             XX
 23   0.119                             XXXX
 24   0.530                             XXXXXXXXXXXXXX
 25   0.131                             XXXX
 26  -0.138                            XXXX
 27  -0.091                            XXX
 28  -0.142                           XXXXX
 29  -0.006                              X
 30   0.093                             XXX
 31  -0.083                             XXX
 32  -0.182                           XXXXXX
 33  -0.124                            XXXX
 34  -0.017                              X
 35   0.053                              XX
 36   0.428                             XXXXXXXXXXXX
 37   0.094                             XXX
 38  -0.129                            XXXX
 39  -0.019                              X
 40  -0.088                            XXX
 41  -0.008                              X
 42   0.037                              XX
 43  -0.074                            XXX
 44  -0.165                           XXXXX
 45  -0.017                              X
 46  -0.038                             XX
 47   0.046                              XX
 48   0.303                             XXXXXXXXX
```

FIGURE 9.22 Autocorrelation coefficients of the logarithmic transformed data on airline traffic differenced by one period

```
                   -1.0  -0.8  -0.6  -0.4  -0.2   0.0   0.2   0.4   0.6   0.8   1.0
                   +---+---+---+---+---+---+---+---+---+---+---+
  1    0.378                                     XXXXXXXXXX
  2    0.049                                     XX
  3    0.002                                     X
  4   -0.080                                   XXX
  5    0.179                                     XXXXX
  6    0.266                                     XXXXXXXX
  7    0.071                                     XXX
  8   -0.178                                 XXXXX
  9   -0.065                                   XXX
 10   -0.104                                  XXXX
 11    0.091                                     XXX
 12    0.440                                     XXXXXXXXXXXX
 13    0.013                                     X
 14   -0.166                                 XXXXX
 15   -0.129                                  XXXX
 16   -0.142                                 XXXXX
 17    0.048                                     XX
 18    0.110                                     XXXX
 19   -0.047                                    XX
 20   -0.198                                 XXXXXX
 21   -0.146                                 XXXXX
 22   -0.096                                   XXX
 23    0.058                                     XX
 24    0.361                                     XXXXXXXXXX
 25    0.077                                     XXX
 26   -0.150                                 XXXXX
 27   -0.118                                  XXXX
 28   -0.120                                  XXXX
 29   -0.013                                    X
 30    0.000                                     X
 31   -0.141                                 XXXXX
 32   -0.268                               XXXXXXXX
 33   -0.201                                 XXXXXX
 34   -0.162                                 XXXXX
 35   -0.109                                  XXXX
 36    0.130                                     XXXX
 37   -0.020                                    X
 38   -0.144                                 XXXXX
 39   -0.105                                  XXXX
 40   -0.097                                   XXX
 41    0.006                                     X
 42    0.061                                     XXX
 43   -0.012                                    X
 44   -0.100                                  XXXX
 45   -0.022                                    XX
 46   -0.011                                    X
 47    0.063                                     XXX
 48    0.179                                     XXXXX
```

FIGURE 9.23 Autocorrelation coefficients for transformed traffic data differenced by one period and seasonally differenced by 12 periods

```
                    -1.0 -0.8 -0.6 -0.4 -0.2  0.0  0.2  0.4  0.6  0.8  1.0
                    +---+---+---+---+---+---+---+---+---+---+---+
 1     0.378                                  XXXXXXXXXX
 2    -0.110                              XXXX
 3     0.027                                XX
 4    -0.101                              XXXX
 5     0.297                                  XXXXXXXX
 6     0.092                                XXX
 7    -0.077                               XXX
 8    -0.248                           XXXXXX
 9     0.192                                  XXXXXX
10    -0.182                          XXXXXX
11     0.209                                  XXXXXX
12     0.319                                  XXXXXXXXX
13    -0.321                       XXXXXXXXX
14    -0.077                              XXX
15     0.034                                XX
16    -0.032                               XX
17    -0.089                              XXX
18    -0.030                               XX
19     0.058                                XX
20    -0.025                               XX
21    -0.190                          XXXXXX
22     0.202                                  XXXXXX
23     0.003                                X
24     0.175                                  XXXXX
25    -0.060                              XXX
26    -0.088                              XXX
27    -0.016                                X
28    -0.032                               XX
29    -0.212                          XXXXXX
30    -0.038                               XX
31    -0.102                             XXXX
32     0.007                                X
33    -0.083                              XXX
34    -0.103                             XXXX
35    -0.043                               XX
36    -0.006                                X
37     0.014                                X
38     0.092                                XXX
39    -0.123                             XXXX
40     0.029                                XX
41     0.058                                XX
42    -0.012                                X
43     0.017                                X
44     0.002                                X
45     0.113                                XXXX
46    -0.039                               XX
47     0.053                                XX
48    -0.164                           XXXXX
```

FIGURE 9.24 Partial autocorrelation coefficients for transformed data differenced by one period and seasonally differenced by 12 periods

Ordinary ACFs and PACFs of one ordinary difference and one seasonal difference are drawn for the purposes of model identification (see figures 9.23 and 9.24). The ordinary autocorrelation coefficients have a significant coefficient at r_1 and the partial autocorrelation coefficients have significant coefficients at r_1, r_5 and r_{13} in the nonseasonal portion. This suggests an MA(1) model since the PACF has a wave-like damping down toward zero and the ordinary ACFs cut off at lag 1.

For the seasonal portion, the ACF trails off slowly in terms of 12 period lag autocorrelation coefficients while the partial autocorrelation coefficients drop to zero after one 12 month lag. Tentatively the model appears like a mixed ARMA(1, 1) or AR(1) in the seasonal part; however, both estimation and diagnostic testing indicated that the MA(1) process was more suitable. Often, and especially with the seasonal portion, a forecaster is required to postulate and estimate several models to find the one that is most suitable. The results are as follows for the ARIMA $(0,1,1)(0,1,1)^{12}$ model:

$$\theta_1 = 0.3868$$

$$\theta_{12} = 0.7999$$

$$\text{MSE} = 0.001\ 720\ 5$$

The computer output shown in figure 9.25 indicates that the nonseasonal and seasonal parameter estimates are significantly different from zero at low significance levels since their t ratios are 3.11 and 5.26 respectively. Seven iterations were necessary to achieve the results. To indicate whether this model is adequate for forecasting, two tests for randomness of the residuals are performed. First, the ACFs

```
Estimates at each iteration
  Iteration          SSE              Parameters
      0            0.161495       0.100     0.100
      1            0.140631       0.165     0.250
      2            0.126238       0.217     0.400
      3            0.116564       0.263     0.550
      4            0.106667       0.314     0.700
      5            0.104398       0.379     0.740
      6            0.103071       0.383     0.781
      7            0.102643       0.387     0.800
Unable to reduce sum of squares any further

Final Estimates of Parameters
Type       Estimate    St. Dev.    t-ratio
MA    1      0.3868      0.1245     3.11
SMA  12      0.7999      0.1522     5.26

Differencing: 1 regular, 1 seasonal of order 12
No. of obs.:  Original series 72, after differencing 59
Residuals:    SS = 0.0980686 (backforecasts excluded)
              MS = 0.0017205 DF= 57

Modified Box-Pierce chisquare statistic
  Lag                 12             24              36              48
  Chisquare     6. 0 (DF=10)   18. 7 (DF=22)   32. 7 (DF=34)   43. 0 (DF=46)
```

FIGURE 9.25 Forecast of transformed data, ARIMA$(0,1,1)(0,1,1)^{12}$ model (Note: computer-generated Minitab output)

for the residuals from the model ARIMA$(0,1,1)(0,1,1))^{12}$ are presented in figure 9.26. Note that all the autocorrelation coefficients of the residuals lie within the 2σ limits of 0.4. Hence, ACF is white noise or random. Second the Ljung–Box Q statistic is applied as follows:

$$Q = n(n + 2) \sum_{i}^{k} \frac{r^2}{n - k}$$

$$= 72 \ (74) \ (0.003\ 509\ 8) = 18.7$$

with $k - p - q = 24 - 2 = 22$ degrees of freedom. The critical χ^2 value for 22 degrees of freedom is 33.92 at the 0.05 level.[15] Hence, since the Q statistic is less than the critical χ^2 value, we do not have sufficient evidence to reject the hypothesis that the model is adequate. Thus our fitted model is

$$(1 - B)(1 - B^{12}) \ln Y_t = (1 - \theta_1 B)(1 - \theta_{12} B^{12})e_t \tag{9.32}$$

```
                   -1.0 -0.8 -0.6 -0.4 -0.2  0.0  0.2  0.4  0.6  0.8  1.0
                   +---+---+---+---+---+---+---+---+---+---+---+
    1     0.020                               XX
    2     0.004                               X
    3    -0.243                         XXXXXXX
    4    -0.062                            XXX
    5     0.060                               XX
    6     0.063                               XXX
    7    -0.034                              XX
    8    -0.015                               X
    9     0.037                               XX
   10    -0.016                               X
   11     0.028                               XX
   12    -0.123                           XXXX
   13    -0.019                               X
   14     0.003                               X
   15     0.055                               XX
   16    -0.086                            XXX
   17     0.145                               XXXXX
   18    -0.008                               X
   19     0.008                               X
   20    -0.113                           XXXX
   21    -0.083                            XXX
   22     0.107                               XXXX
   23     0.266                               XXXXXXXX
   24    -0.002                               X
```

FIGURE 9.26 Autocorrelation coefficients of residuals from ARIMA$(0,1,1)(0,1,1)^{12}$ model (Note: computer-generated Minitab output)

---

15   Note that figure 9.25 contains the values obtained for Q at lags 12, 36, and 48 as well as at lag 24.

and the model can also be expressed in the following form:

$$\ln \hat{Y}_t = Y_{t-1} + Y_{t-12} - Y_{t-13} + e_t - \theta_1 e_{t-1} - \theta_{12} e_{t-12} + \theta_1 \theta_{12} e_{t-13} \qquad (9.33)$$

To forecast one period ahead, $\ln \hat{Y}_{t+1}$, we increase the subscripts by 1 throughout as follows:

$$\ln \hat{Y}_{t+1} = Y_t + Y_{t-11} - Y_{t-12} + -\theta_1 e_t - \theta_{12} e_{t-11} + \theta_1 \theta_{12} e_{t-12} \qquad (9.34)$$

We let the e_{t+1} be zero since the expected value of the future random error is zero. For the fitted model, we shall be able to replace the values e_t, e_{t-11}, and e_{t-12} by their empirically determined values. As for the Y values, we know the values Y_t, Y_{t-11} and Y_{t-12} at the start. For future values, the Y values would have to be forecast as well.

For the above model, we can forecast $\ln \hat{Y}_{73}$ by

$$\ln \hat{Y}_{73} = Y_{72} + Y_{61} - Y_{60} - 0.3868 e_{72} - 0.7999 e_{61} + (0.3868)(0.7999) e_{t-60}$$

$$= 5.433\ 72 + 5.318\ 12 - 5.303\ 30 - 0.3868(0.008\ 854)$$
$$- 0.7999(-0.013\ 428) + 0.3094(-0.041\ 296)$$

$$= 5.449\ 92$$

and

$$\hat{Y}_{73} = 232.734$$

In turn, the forecasts for the next 11 periods are

$$\hat{Y}_{74} = 235.945$$
$$\hat{Y}_{75} = 275.644$$
$$\hat{Y}_{76} = 265.347$$
$$\hat{Y}_{77} = 262.994$$
$$\hat{Y}_{78} = 292.525$$
$$\hat{Y}_{79} = 323.190$$
$$\hat{Y}_{80} = 326.373$$
$$\hat{Y}_{81} = 291.241$$
$$\hat{Y}_{82} = 257.226$$
$$\hat{Y}_{83} = 225.466$$
$$\hat{Y}_{84} = 257.055$$

Thus we have made our 12-month-ahead forecast.

9.8   A Brief Synopsis of ARIMA Modeling

So far in this chapter, the problem of building forecasting models for nonseasonal and seasonal data has been examined. The four-stage ARIMA modeling process summarized below has been covered.

1 Identification or specification of forecasting models by the plotting of ordinary and partial correlation coefficients. These plots permit one to make tentative or preliminary guesses at the order of the parameters of the ARMA model. The ARMA model may be either with or without differencing. Note that Box–Jenkins techniques are not completely objective.
2 Parameters are estimated for the preliminary model by using computer modeling software systems such as Minitab, Pack System, SAS, SPSS-X, BMDP, Micro-TSP, etc.
3 The estimated model is checked for adequacy. First, the ordinary autocorrelations are checked to see if the residuals from forecast are white noise (random). If not, the process begins again and a new model is estimated.
4 Forecasts are made of fully identified, estimated, and diagnostically checked models.

Regular ARIMA models can be enlarged to include seasonal data by building a multiplicative ARIMA model. The multiplicative model requires the identification of both a nonseasonal and seasonal model.

Finally, the Box–Jenkins approach to ARIMA modeling provides a very powerful and flexible tool for forecasting. It is an excellent method for forecasting a time series from its own current and historical values. However, some recent studies including those of Brandon et al. (1983), Makridakis and Hibbon (1983), and Jarrett (1989) have indicated that other approaches which are simpler and easier to apply often lead to better forecasts. Pack and Downing (1983) stated that the reason that Box–Jenkins techniques may fail to provide better (more accurate) results than less sophisticated approaches was due to the influence of the following:

1 time series length;
2 time series information (autocorrelation) content;
3 time series outliers or structural changes;
4 averaging results over time series;
5 forecast time origin choice.

If a time series is too short (we usually desire at least 50 observations for nonseasonal Box–Jenkins analysis), the Box–Jenkins estimates are subject to much error. If the time series is uninformative, i.e. there is no discernible pattern in the autocorrelation coefficients, then the Box–Jenkins techniques do not apply as well. An informative historical pattern is of little value if repeated outliers (indicating structural changes) occur at the end of the historical data pattern or during the post-sample period and stop the repetition of the historical pattern. When repeated outliers arise at the end of the historical data or in the post-sample period, this will indicate changes in the pattern of the data which the estimation period cannot pick up. If we compare Box–Jenkins methods with other methods, the averaging of accuracy measures such as MSE presents risks. Averages can cause conflicts in method rankings whenever scale-dependent measures are used. Finally, if we compare Box–Jenkins methods with others where all time series have the same forecast origin, the measures of accuracy will vary depending on the selected time origin. Forecasters must be cautious and not be surprised by the magnitude of variation in forecast accuracy measures resulting from the selection of the time origin. Thus it is often not a fair comparison to compare individual methods with large samples of time series since it is the ability to forecast an individual time series well that is of paramount importance.

Application of the Box–Jenkins methodology requires a great deal of care and sophistication and it should not be applied blindly nor automatically to all kinds of time series. However, the results can be very good in the hands of an intelligent and wise user who aims at a high level of accuracy and an understanding of those processes which generate the series.

9.9   Mutiple Time Series ARIMA Models for Forecasting

Those who practice time series forecasting often criticize single time series analysis and believe that they can produce more successful forecasting models in a multiple series environment. ARIMA modeling by Box–Jenkins methods began in earnest with the publication of their first book in 1970. Published applied research in the 1970s focused on single series applications and many subsequent books, including this one, were limited to single series methodology. The expansion to multiple time series is thus a natural progression, similar to the way in which regression methods began with single regression, and progressed to multiple regression and finally to econometric modeling.

Models for time series forecasting beyond the single series are referred to as (a) transfer function models, (b) intervention models, and (c) multiple time series models. All three of these models involve more than one time series; however, the title "multiple time series" is usually reserved for the third category which is a generalization of the other two categories of forms.

Transfer function models are similar to multiple regression models, with one dependent (or endogenous) variable as a function of one or more independent (or exogenous) time series. The time series for the dependent variable may play a part in the forecast. For the transfer function model form, the time series for the dependent variable does not have any effect on the time series for the independent variable. In this way, the transfer function model can be expressed as a single equation function. The model-fitting methodology follows the identification, estimation, and diagnostic testing steps of figure 9.1. The identification phase focuses on the cross-correlation of time series with each other. Much care is required in applying transfer function methods to avoid between and within series dependence.

Intervention models permit one to account for noncyclical but often repeatable events such as boycotts, wars strikes, or even locusts. All this can be accomplished within the overall ARIMA model structure. Events are represented by a dummy series assuming a value of 0 or 1 corresponding to the occurrence or nonoccurrence of the event being isolated. This dummy series is similar to the use of dummy variables in multiple regression and econometrics. The structure of the ARIMA model is one of a transfer function model with a dummy input series. Phases similar to single series model identification, estimation, and diagnostic checking and testing methodology are employed with some modification. The identification phase is not as straightforward, however. Identification of the time series and representation of specific special events rest to a great extent on graphical or theoretical hypotheses.

Similar to econometric models are *multiple time series models* which involve a system of simultaneous equations. Typically, multiple time series methodology is employed when a single time series model fails to forecast properly. If, as an example, one were to forecast new housing starts for single family dwellings and the single time series model failed, then the forecaster may determine that a new home mortgage interest series would aid the forecasting process. In turn, the forecaster may want the ARIMA model to permit the historical behavior of each time series to affect the other series. If Y_1 and Y_2 represent the two series, a model allowing the joint dependence for AR(1) series could be represented as follows:

$$Y_{1t} = \phi_{11}Y_{1,t-1} + \phi_{12}Y_{2,t-1} + e_{1t}$$

$$Y_{2t} = \phi_{21}Y_{1,t-1} + \phi_{22}Y_{2,t-1} + e_{2t}$$

(9.35)

In the above system, the simultaneous equations express the dependence of current values of each series on the historical values of the other series and on its own historical values. If $\phi_{12} = 0$ or $\phi_{21} = 0$, the relationship becomes one directional and this special case reduces to the transfer function model discussed before.

The extension of ARIMA modeling into the simultaneous equation area is a natural outgrowth of time series research. Extending the philosophy of identification, estimation, and diagnostic checking into that area is not as simple. Jenkins (1979) illustrates a methodology with examples for multiple time series modeling.

Although practical methodology does exist for building time series models of the type discussed in this section, they are beyond the scope of this book. Practical research in new forecasting methods indicates the fusion of the ideas of econometrics and ARIMA modeling. Development of new and better computer software will, of course, enhance and contribute to the use of these techniques. However, it should be noted that complicated econometric models cannot be constructed using the principles of ARIMA modeling given above. Economic theory must be employed to reduce the number of possible models to permit the analyst to simplify the identification process. The future will show, of course, how practical these more complicated methods are to the everyday forecaster.

9.10 Automatic Box–Jenkins Methods

One of the difficulties of employing Box–Jenkins ARIMA modeling is the often lengthy identification phase of the process. Identification is often the most difficult phase to learn for practitioners and often deters users from employing ARIMA modeling techniques. With this in mind, computer software producers have developed methods for permitting the computer software system to generate the identification phase of the Box–Jenkins methods. Although such software appears like an "expert system", in general, these methods employ statistical algorithms for identifying an ARIMA model.

The automatic identification software system reduces the identification phase for the user by incorporating an automatic statistical algorithm. The concept for such an algorithm was developed by Akaike (1974). Pack (1977) produced one of the early computer programs for the analysis of time series for automatic identification. In this and more recently developed software, such as AUTOBJ (Automatic Forecasting Systems, 1986), there is no user intervention. The user only needs to input the time series and the program performs the entire analysis. Usually, these software systems provide for user interaction through a series of key questions. However, the user must understand that these systems are applications of statistical methods to the identification process and are not "expert systems."

Most automatic ARIMA modeling software systems do not require the user to be an experienced modeler. However, he/she should be able to interpret the output. Thus education in ARIMA modeling is necessary.

The underlying ARIMA estimation procedure usually follows closely the formulation of Box and Jenkins (1976). This requires that the time series is fully observed, and missing values will cause both estimation and identification problems. Several forecasting software programs employing multivariate ARIMA techniques handle missing data for ARIMA estimation (Jones, 1980; Kohn and Ansley, 1986). Since these are multivariate procedures they are not compatible with the Box–Jenkins procedures discussed in this chapter.

Model identification is similar to the procedures of stepwise regression (chapter 5). In one software system, AUTOBJ, three options are available. These incorporate a procedure for deleting an AR or MA parameter via a check for sufficiency, that is, the ratio of the parameter estimate to the standard error of the estimate. AR or MA parameters can be added by a check for necessity by examining the ratio of the estimated autocorrelations or partial autocorrelations to their respective standard errors. The last check is for invertibility where a nonseasonal or seasonal difference can be substituted for an AR or MA parameter with roots at or close to the unit circle. Akaike's information theory criterion (Akaike, 1974) or the Bayesian information theory criterion (Lutekepol, 1984) can be employed at this time.

Previous research in this area includes that of Hill and Fildes (1984) and Texter and Ord (1989). They indicated that automatic modeling is appropriate for many time series based on their seasonal samples and the criteria used to make the statistical comparisons. These automatic Box–Jenkins modeling systems include statistical systems designed to produce results that are on average as good as those produced by a competent modeler (Hill and Woodworth, 1980, p. 114). They are not "expert systems" in the sense that the software does not emulate human behavior and employ expert knowledge. However, automatic Box–Jenkins software products are based on scientific statistical theory and analysis which substantially reduces the burden of performing ARIMA modeling.

9.11   Summary

Box–Jenkins methodology is a statistically sophisticated method of analyzing and building a forecasting model which best represents a time series.

The properties of a time series are determined by studying the original data and plots of ordinary and partial autocorrelations. These studies permit one to identify trend, seasonality, and constancy of variance in the time series. The purpose of identification is to choose a specific ARIMA model which may have generated the observed time series.

ARIMA models are fitted by nonlinear least squares. Software programs (Minitab, SAS, Micro-TSP) are available for estimating most low-order models.

To check for the adequacy of the model, the error terms are diagnostically examined to determine whether they are white noise (random). A χ^2 analysis (Ljung–Box test) is also performed to indicate further whether the residuals are white noise or not.

Upon the identification and validation of an ARIMA model, forecasts for one or more periods ahead can be made. As new observations are obtained, the same model can be used to revise forecasts by choosing another time origin.

A nonstationary time series in mean is often made stationary by taking d differences; the result is an ARIMA model for the *differenced series*. If the time series is nonstationary in variance, the series can be stabilized by transforming the original data. The original series is referred to as an ARIMA model. The I stands for *integrated* and is used to suggest undifferencing.

For purposes of forecasting, first identify the appropriate ARIMA model and difference the data to produce stationarity. The model is thereby reduced to one in the ARMA class.

Many time series are seasonal. Seasonality varies from year to year, indicating that models based on unadjusted data rather than seasonally adjusted data are likely to be more flexible and useful for the purpose of identification.

In a multiplicative ARIMA model, the regular and seasonal autoregressive components, differences, and moving-average components are multiplied together in the general model. A very useful notation to describe the orders of the various components in the multiplicative model is given by

$$(p, d, q) \times (P, D, Q)^s$$

For purposes of identifying a seasonal ARIMA process, the nonseasonal process is ignored and we determine whether the seasonality is an AR or an MA process.

Last, although the Box–Jenkins methodology provides a very powerful and flexible tool for building forecasting models, great care and wisdom is required in its application.

Multiple time series modeling may produce better results than the single time series modeling of the type employed in this chapter. It requires more detailed and sophisticated knowledge of time series analysis. In addition, the relation between one time series and another is often the focus of modeling. Finally, more time and care is necessary to generate multiple time series forecasts.

The burden of identification in time series modeling is reduced by employing software systems which automatically identify the underlying ARIMA model that gave rise to the time series. These methods are based on applications of statistical theory for the identification of underlying ARIMA models without user intervention. Programs are available for automatic Box–Jenkins modeling.

9.12   Exercises

1 (a) A sample of 50 observations of data is studied. Calculate the 2σ limits for the autocorrelation coefficients.
   (b) If the data are white noise, how would the autocorrelation coefficients be distributed?
   (c) If coefficients r_{12}, r_{24}, and r_{36} are significantly different from zero, what conclusion can be drawn?
   (d) If the four autocorrelation coefficients are significantly different from zero and the pattern gradually trails to about zero, what conclusion can be drawn?
   (e) How would an MA(2) model be distributed over the interval from time lag 1 to time lag 16?
2 Table 9.4 ordinary and partial correlation coefficients for 100 observations of a time series

TABLE 9.4

Lag	1	2	3	4	5	6	7	8	9	10	11	12
Ordinary	0.56	0.32	0.27	0.24	0.24	0.26	0.14	0.08	0.06	0.04	0.03	0.05
Partial	0.56	−0.12	0.23	0.07	0.09	0.05	−0.10	0.02	−0.05	0.03	−0.04	0.02

Using the usual notions about the behavior of autocorrelation coefficients, draw appropriate conclusions about stationarity and about the behavior of the ordinary and partial autocorrelation coefficients. What tentative model would be most appropriate?

3 Table 9.5 Ordinary and partial correlation coefficients for 100 observations of a time series

TABLE 9.5

Lag	1	2	3	4	5	6	7	8	9	10	11	12
Ordinary	0.62	0.37	0.09	−0.06	−0.08	0.04	0.05	0.17	0.19	0.20	0.18	0.09
Partial	0.62	−0.02	−0.20	−0.05	0.07	−0.02	0.04	0.12	0.03	0.10	−0.04	−0.01

Using the usual notions about the behavior of autocorrelation coefficients, draw appropriate conclusions about stationarity and about the behavior of the ordinary and partial autocorrelation coefficients. What tentative model would be most appropriate?

4 Express the following ARIMA processes in terms of the backshift operator:
  (a) $(1,0,1) \times (1,0,1)^{12}$ (d) $(0,0,1) \times (1,1,1)$
  (b) $(0,1,1) \times (0,1,1)^{4}$ (e) $(0,0,1) \times (1,0,1)$
  (c) $(1,1,1) \times (1,1,0)^{12}$

5 Express the following models in $(p, d, q) \times (P, D, Q)^{s}$ form:
  (a) $(1 - B)(1 - B^{4})Y_{t} = (1 - \theta_{1}B)(1 - \theta_{4}^{4})e_{t}$
  (b) $(1 - B)X_{t} = (1 - \theta_{1}B - \theta_{2}B^{2})e_{t}$
  (c) $(1 - \phi_{1}B)(1 - \phi_{12}B^{12})Y_{t} = (1 - \theta_{1}B)(1 - \theta_{12}B^{12})e_{t}$
  (d) $(1 - \phi_{1}B)Y_{t} = (1 - \theta_{1}B)(1 - \theta_{12}B^{12})e_{t}$

6 Time series data for 50 periods are given in table 9.6.
  Use Box–Jenkins methods to prepare the following.
  (a) A tentative model;
  (b) An estimate of the parameters of the models;
  (c) A diagnostic check of the estimated tentative model. Should a new model be estimated?
  (d) A forecast for period 51.

7 Indicate in table 9.7 whether the distributions of ordinary and partial autocorrelations drop off or trail off to zero for these models.

8 The data in table 9.8 are the observations for the index of industrial production for a major industry division. Perform the following exercises for one of these time series.
  (a) Identify the tentative model.
  (b) Estimate the parameters of the tentative model.
  (c) Diagnostically check the tentative model.
  (d) Forecast two periods ahead.

9 The data in table 9.9 are for corporate profits by industry in the United States (in billion dollars).
  (a) Identify the tentative model.
  (b) Estimate the parameters of the tentative model.

TABLE 9.6

1	599	26	830
2	098	27	254
3	572	28	410
4	874	29	268
5	074	30	961
6	927	31	330
7	294	32	231
8	286	33	028
9	644	34	572
10	361	35	286
11	489	36	168
12	116	37	566
13	532	38	152
14	247	39	056
15	556	40	337
16	705	41	423
17	366	42	158
18	403	43	408
19	528	44	480
20	589	45	982
21	643	46	837
22	643	47	258
23	280	48	695
24	461	49	886
25	981	50	020

TABLE 9.7

	Autocorrelations	
Model	Ordinary	Partial
MA(1)		
AR(1)		
ARMA(1,1)		

(c) Diagnostically check the tentative model. Re-estimate a new model if necessary.
(d) Forecast two periods ahead.
10 The data in table 9.10 are implicit price deflators for personal consumption expenditures.
(a) Determine whether a seasonal model is appropriate.
(b) Identify the tentative model.
(c) Estimate the parameters of the tentative model.
(d) Diagnostically check the model. Re-estimate the model if necessary.
(e) Forecast six periods ahead.

TABLE 9.8 Industrial production indexes, major industry divisions, 1939–1988
(1977 = 100)

Year	Total industrial production	Manufacturing Total	Durable	Nondurable	Mining	Utilities
1977 proportion	100.00	84.21	49.10	35.11	9.83	5.96
1939	16.0	15.8	13.6	17.9	37.6	6.9
1940	18.4	18.6	18.1	18.8	41.8	7.6
1941	23.3	23.8	24.2	22.7	44.4	8.6
1942	26.7	27.7	30.7	23.7	45.7	9.7
1943	32.4	34.5	41.8	25.4	46.8	10.7
1944	34.9	37.3	46.1	26.4	50.2	11.4
1945	29.9	31.2	34.9	26.3	49.2	11.6
1946	25.8	25.9	24.4	27.1	48.3	12.0
1947	29.0	28.9	29.0	28.2	54.6	13.0
1948	30.2	30.0	30.3	29.2	57.4	14.5
1949	28.6	28.3	27.5	28.7	50.9	15.5
1950	33.1	33.0	33.5	31.9	56.9	17.6
1951	35.9	35.6	37.7	33.0	62.4	20.1
1952	37.2	37.1	40.0	33.6	61.9	21.8
1953	40.4	40.4	45.2	35.0	63.5	23.6
1954	38.2	37.8	39.9	35.2	62.3	25.4
1955	43.0	42.6	45.6	39.1	69.5	28.4
1956	44.9	44.4	47.1	41.1	73.1	31.2
1957	45.5	44.9	47.4	41.8	73.2	33.3
1958	42.6	41.7	41.5	42.1	67.1	34.9
1959	47.7	47.0	47.7	46.3	70.2	38.4
1960	48.8	48.0	48.5	47.4	71.6	41.1
1961	49.1	48.1	47.6	48.8	72.1	43.4
1962	53.2	52.4	52.8	51.8	74.1	46.6
1963	56.3	55.5	56.3	54.6	77.1	49.8
1964	60.1	59.3	60.3	58.2	80.2	54.1
1965	66.1	65.7	68.6	62.1	83.1	57.4
1966	72.0	71.7	76.2	66.0	87.6	61.8
1967	73.5	73.1	77.0	68.1	89.3	64.9
1968	77.6	77.2	80.8	72.5	92.7	70.2
1969	81.2	80.6	84.0	76.3	96.4	76.4
1970	78.5	77.0	77.6	76.3	98.9	81.1
1971	79.6	78.2	77.3	79.4	96.4	85.0
1972	87.3	86.4	86.3	86.5	98.4	90.4
1973	94.4	94.0	96.3	90.8	99.3	94.0
1974	93.0	92.6	94.3	90.2	98.8	92.8
1975	84.8	83.4	82.6	84.5	96.6	93.7
1976	92.6	91.9	91.1	93.1	97.4	97.4
1977	100.0	100.0	100.00	100.0	100.0	100.0
1978	106.5	107.1	108.2	105.5	103.6	103.1
1979	110.7	111.5	113.9	108.2	106.4	105.9
1980	108.6	108.2	109.1	107.0	112.4	107.3
1981	111.0	110.5	111.1	109.7	117.5	107.1
1982	103.1	102.2	99.9	105.5	109.3	104.8
1983	109.2	110.2	107.7	113.7	102.9	105.2
1984	121.4	123.4	124.2	122.3	111.1	110.7
1985	123.7	126.4	127.6	124.6	108.9	111.1
1986	125.1	129.1	128.4	130.1	100.4	108.5
1987	129.8	134.7	133.1	136.8	100.7	110.3
1988	137.2	142.7	141.1	143.9	103.4	114.3

Source: Federal Reserve Bulletin.

TABLE 9.9 Corporate profits by industry, 1929–1987 (billions of dollars)

Corporate profits with inventory valuation adjustment and without capital consumption adjustment

Year	Total	Domestic industries Total	Financial[a] Total	Federal reserve banks	Other	Nonfinancial Total	Manu-facturing	Transportation and public utilities	Wholesale and retail trade	Other
1929	10.5	10.2	1.3	0.0	1.3	8.9	5.2	1.8	1.0	0.9
1933	-1.2	-1.2	0.3	0.0	0.3	-1.5	-0.4	0.0	-0.5	-0.7
1939	6.5	6.1	0.8	0.0	0.8	5.3	3.3	1.0	0.7	0.3
1940	9.8	9.6	1.0	0.0	0.9	8.6	5.5	1.3	1.2	0.6
1941	15.4	15.0	1.1	0.0	1.0	14.0	9.5	2.0	1.4	1.1
1942	20.5	20.1	1.2	0.0	1.2	18.9	11.8	3.4	2.2	1.5
1943	24.5	24.1	1.3	0.0	1.3	22.8	13.8	4.4	3.0	1.6
1944	24.0	23.5	1.6	0.1	1.6	21.9	13.2	3.9	3.2	1.6
1945	19.3	18.9	1.7	0.1	1.6	17.3	9.7	2.7	3.3	1.5
1946	19.6	18.9	2.1	0.1	2.0	16.8	9.0	1.8	3.8	2.1
1947	25.9	24.9	1.7	0.1	1.6	23.2	13.6	2.2	4.6	2.9
1948	33.4	32.2	2.6	0.2	2.3	29.6	17.6	3.0	5.5	3.6
1949	31.1	29.9	3.1	0.2	2.9	26.8	16.2	3.0	4.5	3.1
1950	37.9	36.7	3.1	0.2	3.0	33.5	20.9	4.0	5.0	3.6
1951	43.3	41.5	3.6	0.3	3.3	37.9	24.6	4.6	5.0	3.7
1952	40.6	38.7	4.0	0.4	3.7	34.7	21.7	4.9	4.8	3.3
1953	40.2	38.4	4.5	0.4	4.1	33.9	22.0	5.0	3.8	3.1
1954	38.4	36.4	4.6	0.3	4.3	31.8	19.9	4.7	3.8	3.4
1955	47.5	45.1	4.8	0.3	4.5	40.3	26.0	5.6	5.0	3.6
1956	46.9	44.1	5.0	0.5	4.5	39.1	24.7	5.9	4.5	4.1
1957	46.6	43.5	5.2	0.6	4.6	38.3	24.0	5.8	4.4	4.0
1958	41.6	39.1	5.7	0.6	5.1	33.5	19.4	5.9	4.6	3.6
1959	52.3	49.6	6.8	0.7	6.0	42.9	26.4	7.0	5.9	3.6

1960	49.8	46.7	7.2	1.0	6.2	39.5	23.6	7.4	4.9	3.6
1961	50.1	46.8	7.0	0.8	6.3	39.8	23.3	7.8	5.0	3.7
1962	55.2	51.5	7.3	0.9	6.4	44.2	26.0	8.4	5.8	3.9
1963	59.8	55.8	6.8	1.0	5.8	49.0	29.3	9.3	5.9	4.4
1964	66.2	61.8	6.9	1.1	5.8	54.9	32.3	10.0	7.5	5.1
1965	76.2	71.5	7.5	1.4	6.2	64.0	39.3	11.0	8.1	5.6
1966	81.2	76.7	8.5	1.7	6.8	68.2	41.9	11.8	8.2	6.3
1967	78.6	73.9	9.0	2.0	7.0	64.9	38.6	10.7	9.1	6.5
1968	85.4	79.9	10.4	2.5	7.9	69.5	41.4	10.8	10.4	6.9
1969	81.4	74.8	11.2	3.1	8.1	63.7	36.7	10.3	10.5	6.1
1970	69.5	62.6	12.2	3.6	8.6	50.4	26.7	8.2	9.6	5.9
1971	82.7	75.1	14.1	3.3	10.7	61.0	34.3	8.5	11.7	6.5
1972	94.9	85.5	15.4	3.4	12.0	70.2	40.8	9.0	13.4	6.9
1973	107.1	92.6	15.8	4.5	11.2	76.8	46.2	8.5	13.9	8.2
1974	99.4	82.4	14.7	5.7	8.9	67.8	39.8	6.7	12.9	8.3
1975	123.9	109.5	11.2	5.7	5.5	98.3	53.6	10.3	22.2	12.2
1976	155.3	139.3	15.9	6.0	9.9	123.4	70.9	14.8	23.0	14.7
1977	183.3	165.5	21.6	6.2	15.4	143.9	80.6	17.9	27.5	17.8
1978	208.2	186.0	29.1	7.7	21.4	156.8	88.7	20.9	27.3	20.0
1979	214.1	180.4	27.8	9.6	18.2	152.6	87.5	15.2	28.7	21.1
1980	194.0	159.6	21.0	11.5	9.0	138.6	77.1	17.6	21.6	22.4
1981	202.8	173.8	16.5	14.5	1.9	157.3	88.5	19.5	32.5	16.8
1982	159.2	131.2	11.8	15.4	-3.6	119.4	58.0	19.3	34.6	7.5
1983	196.7	166.6	18.1	14.8	3.3	148.5	70.1	28.5	38.9	10.9
1984	234.2	203.3	13.0	16.7	-3.7	190.3	88.8	38.5	51.2	11.8
1985	222.6	191.4	22.8	16.8	6.1	168.6	79.7	33.0	44.1	11.8
1986	244.7	212.8	31.8	16.0	15.8	180.9	79.4	39.2	46.1	16.3
1987	258.7	222.3	30.1	16.0	14.1	192.1	96.8	34.9	42.8	17.6

Notes: [a]Consists of the following industries: banking; credit agencies other than banks; security and commodity brokers, dealers, and services; insurance carriers; regulated investment companies; small business investment companies; and real estate investment trusts.

The industry classification is on a company basis and is based on the 1972 Standard Industrial Classification (SIC) beginning 1948, and on the 1942 SIC prior to 1948.

Source: Survey of Current Business.

TABLE 9.10

Month	1977	1978	(1972 = 100) 1979	1980	1981	1982
Jan	135.8	143.7	155.8	170.8	188.1	202.2
Feb	136.7	144.4	157.1	172.8	189.1	202.1
Mar	137.1	145.2	158.0	174.7	190.5	202.3
Apr	137.7	146.2	159.3	175.9	191.5	202.9
May	138.2	147.8	160.5	177.1	192.8	203.4
Jun	139.1	148.9	161.8	178.4	193.5	205.5
Jul	139.6	149.5	162.9	179.5	195.2	206.9
Aug	140.4	150.4	164.1	181.3	196.2	207.6
Sep	140.8	151.6	165.5	182.9	197.8	208.6
Oct	141.4	152.7	167.0	184.2	198.8	210.0
Nov	142.3	153.7	168.0	185.6	199.9	210.0
Dec	142.9	154.2	169.3	186.8	200.5	210.8

Source: Survey of Current Business, 62(7), 1982, p. 108; 63(3), 1983, p.S-I.

TABLE 9.11 Quarterly shipments from Inventory ($thousand)

Period	Shipments	Period	Shipments
1	127.604	29	94.319
2	143.913	30	51.403
3	71.101	31	27.247
4	118.153	32	0.020
5	65.149	33	56.902
6	8.881	34	81.316
7	56.948	35	12.330
8	32.783	36	21.111
9	73.827	37	65.281
10	5.346	38	86.015
11	16.503	39	44.352
12	6.050	40	32.420
13	28.167	41	106.218
14	16.244	42	88.241
15	33.074	43	44.483
16	6.656	44	41.732
17	46.174	45	53.680
18	26.234	46	25.323
19	19.173	47	72.165
20	6.461	48	99.880
21	37.752	49	102.922
22	10.295	50	111.506
23	9.617	51	172.992
24	1.060	52	137.479
25	49.940		
26	42.926		
27	58.870		
28	63.838		

11 The data in table 9.11 are shipments (thousand dollars) of firms belonging to a United States trade association over a 13 year period by quarter.
(a) Identify the tentative model.
(b) Estimate the parameters of the tentative model.
(c) Diagnostically test the model. Reestimate the model if necessary.
(d) Forecast four periods ahead.
12 Collect quarterly data on profits for any corporation. Identify, estimate, diagnostically check for adequacy, and forecast four periods ahead by Box–Jenkins methodology.
13 Collect monthly data for any time series which has not been deseasonalized. Identify, estimate, diagnostically check for adequacy, and forecast 12 periods ahead by Box–Jenkins methodology.
14 The data in table 9.12 are quarterly totals of orders for a parts manufacturing firm (thousand dollars) over a 13 year period.
(a) Identify the tentative model.
(b) Estimate the parameters of the tentative model.
(c) Diagnostically test the model. Reestimate the model if necessary.
(d) Forecast four periods ahead.

TABLE 9.12 Quarterly totals of orders for a parts manufacturing firm ($thousand), + 13 years

Period	Orders	Period	Orders
1	4.105	27	224.741
2	15.036	28	356.505
3	13.504	29	254.192
4	23.199	30	341.221
5	13.378	31	295.048
6	26.122	32	370.382
7	11.896	33	237.790
8	−26.067	34	309.121
9	−2.309	35	212.465
10	−40.468	36	209.556
11	−17.545	37	120.797
12	−45.174	38	124.047
13	−23.429	39	65.595
14	−29.257	40	23.960
15	−29.487	41	−6.698
16	−38.708	42	−26.580
17	20.534	43	−29.201
18	58.796	44	−27.865
19	67.112	45	−21.845
20	120.146	46	−43.327
21	68.315	47	−56.071
22	80.070	48	−55.916
23	85.701	49	−27.553
24	139.032	50	2.043
25	133.441	51	27.654
26	223.590	52	62.395

Note: Negative values indicate back-orders.

15 The data in table 9.13 are mean monthly earnings per share of certain industrial firms in the United States over a five year period (not seasonally adjusted).
   (a) Identify the tentative model.
   (b) Estimate the parameters of the tentative model.
   (c) Diagnostically test the model. Reestimate the model if necessary.
   (d) Forecast 12 periods ahead.
16 From the *Survey of Current Business*, find the index of industrial production for any industrial grouping. Collect the data for this index for a period of at least six years (not seasonally adjusted data). Use Box–Jenkins methods to forecast six periods ahead.
17 Collect data on the index of consumer prices (not seasonally adjusted) for all items or for a specific item, for example, medical care, over a period of at least six years. Use Box–Jenkins methods to forecast six periods ahead.

TABLE 9.13 Mean Monthly Earnings Per Share
Sample of U.S. Manufacturing Firms

Period	Mean EPS	Period	Mean EPS
1	5.49	31	6.64
2	5.51	32	6.68
3	5.54	33	6.80
4	5.61	34	6.86
5	5.62	35	6.93
6	5.65	36	6.94
7	5.69	37	7.03
8	5.71	38	7.07
9	5.78	39	7.10
10	5.84	40	7.13
11	5.87	41	7.17
12	5.92	42	7.20
13	5.96	43	7.24
14	6.00	44	7.30
15	6.04	45	7.40
16	6.04	46	7.42
17	6.09	47	7.47
18	6.13	48	7.45
19	6.18	49	7.55
20	6.22	50	7.54
21	6.26	51	7.55
22	6.28	52	7.58
23	6.34	53	7.63
24	6.39	54	7.64
25	6.41	55	7.67
26	6.45	56	7.70
27	6.51	57	7.76
28	6.53	58	7.79
29	6.57	59	7.81
30	6.61	60	7.82

Note: Negative values indicate back-orders.

References

Akaike, M. (1974) A new look at the statistical model identification, *IEEE Transactions in Automatic Control*, 716–23.

Automatic Forecasting Systems (1986) *AUTOBJ The Users Guide*. Hatboro, PA: Automatic Forecasting Systems Inc.

Box, G. E. P. and Jenkins, G. M. (1976) *Time Series Analysis, Forecasting and Control*, San Francisco, CA: Holden-Day.

Box, G. E. P. and Pierce, D. A. (1970) 'Distribution of the residual autocorrelations in autoregressive-integrated-moving-average time series models, *Journal of the American Statistical Association*, 65, 1509–26.

Brandon, C., Jarrett, J., and Khumuwala, S. (1983) Revising forecasts of accounting earnings: a comparison with the Box–Jenkins method, *Management Science*, 29(2), February.

Cholette, P. A. (1983) ARIMA forecasting of seasonally adjusted series versus unadjusted series. Presented at the annual meeting of the International Society of Forecasters, June 1983.

Federal Reserve Bulletin, various issues. Washington, DC: US Board of Governors of the Federal Reserve System.

Hill G. W. and Fildes, R. (1984) The accuracy of extrapolation methods: an automatic Box–Jenkins package, SIFT, *Journal of Forecasting*, 3, 319–23

Hill, G. W. and Woodworth, D. (1980) Automatic Box–Jenkins forecasting, *Journal of the Operational Research Society*, 31, 413–22

Jarrett, J. E. (1989) Forecasting monthly earnings per share – time series models, *OMEGA: The International Journal of Management Science*, 17 (1) 37–44.

Jenkins, G. M. (1979) *Practical Experiences with Modeling and Forecasting Time Series*. St Helier, Jersey: Gwilym Jenkins and Partners.

Jones, R. H. (1980) Maximum likelihood fitting of ARMA models to time series with missing observations, *Technometrics*, 22, 389–96.

Kohn, R. and Ansley, C. (1986) Estimation, prediction, and interpolation for ARIMA models with missing data, *Journal of the American Statistical Association*, 81, 751–61.

Ljung, G. M. and Box, G. E. P. (1978) On a measure of lack of fit in time series models, *Biometrika*, 65, 297–308.

Lutekepol, H. (1984) Comparison of criteria for estimating the order of a vector autoregressive process, *Journal of Time Series Analysis*, 6, 35–52

Makridakis, S. and Hibbon, M. (1983) The accuracy of extrapolative methods. Presented at the annual meeting of the International Society of Forecasters, Philadelphia, PA, June 1983.

Marquardt, D. W. (1963) An algorithm for least squares estimation of nonlinear parameters, *Journal of the Society for Industrial and Applied Mathematics*, 11, 431–41.

McLeod, A. I. (1978) On the distribution of residual autocorrelations in Box–Jenkins models, *Journal of the Royal Statistical Society*, Series B, 40 (3), 296–302.

Pack, D. J. (1977) *A Computer Program for the Analysis of Time Series Models using the Box–Jenkins Philosophy*. Hatboro, PA: Automatic Forecasting Systems.

Pack, D. and Downing, D. J. (1983) Why didn't Box–Jenkins win (again)? Presented at the annual meeting of the International Society of Forecasters, Philadelphia, PA, June 1983.

Pankratz, A. (1983) *Forecasting with Univariate Box–Jenkins Models*. New York: Wiley.

Survey of Current Business, various issues. Washington, DC: Bureau of Economic Analysis, US Department of Commerce.

Texter, P. and Ord, K. (1989) Forecasting using automatic identification procedures : a comparative analysis, *International Journal of Forecasting*, 5(4), 209–15.

Further Reading

Abraham, B. and Ledolter, J. (1983) *Statistical Methods for Forecasting*. New York: Wiley, chs 5, 6.

Cleary, J. P. and Levenbach, H. (1982) *The Professional Forecaster: The Forecasting Process Through Data Analysis*. Belmont, CA: Lifetime Learning Publications, chs 17–24.

Cryer, J. D. (1986) *Time Series Analysis*. Boston, MA: Duxbury, chs 6, 7, 8, 9, 10.

Foster, G. (1977) Quarterly accounting data: time series properties and predictive ability results, *Accounting Review*, 52, January, 1–21.

Griffin, P. A. (1977) The time series behavior of quarterly earnings: preliminary evidence, *Journal of Accounting Research*, Spring, 71–83.

Hoff, J. C. (1983) *A Practical Guide to Box–Jenkins Forecasting*. Belmont, CA: Lifetime Learning Press, chs 12–17.

Lorek, K., MacDonald, C. L. and Patz, D. H. (1976) A comparative examination of management forecasts and Box–Jenkins forecasts of earnings, *Accounting Review*, 51, April, 321–30.

Lorek, K. and MacDonald, C. L. (1979) Predicting annual net earnings with quarterly earnings time-series models, *Journal of Accounting Research*, 17, Spring, 190–204.

Makridakis, S. and Wheelwright, S. C. (1983) *Forecasting Methods and Applications*. New York: Wiley, chs 9, 10.

Nelson, C. R. (1973) *Applied Time Series Analysis for Managerial Forecasting*. San Francisco, CA: Holden-Day, chs 6, 7.

O'Donovan, T. M. (1983) *Short Term Forecasting: An Introduction to the Box–Jenkins Approach*. Chichester: Wiley, chs 4, 5, 6.

Appendix

In this appendix the output of SAS PROC ARIMA for modeling time series using the ARIMA procedure is presented. The purpose is to indicate how to interpret computer output from a well-known computer software system. In this way, the computer output will not be a mystery to the user. We should be aware that SAS is just one of the various software systems available for ARIMA modeling, but it does provide us with a way of examining and interpreting output as an illustration.

Data were collected month by month for a six year period (1970–5). The data were transformed by a logarithmic function in order to reduce the influence of nonstationarity in variance and to permit the identification of the ARIMA model to be estimated. To achieve stationarity in mean for both the seasonal and nonseasonal portions, the transformed data were differenced by one lag in both portions. Hence the number of observations for model identification was reduced from 72 to 59 (one for nonseasonal difference and 12 for seasonal difference).

The plot of the autocorrelations from the ARIMA procedure is shown in figure 9.A1. Descriptive information about the time series being modeled is presented as follows:

1 name of variable;
2 periods of differencing;
3 mean of series;
4 standard deviation;
5 number of observations.

The autocorrelations are plotted from lag 0 to lag 24 along with the 2σ limits. Note that we can ignore the lag 0 since the autocorrelation coefficient is 1. The values for the autocorrelation are presented along with the covariances for each lag. The covariance term is the numerator of the autocorrelation coefficient.

In figure 9.Al, significant coefficients are noted at lag 1 (and possibly at lag 3). Seasonality is indicated by the significant coefficient at lag 12.

In figure 9.A2, the partial autocorrelations are plotted along with the 2σ error limits. Note that the partial autocorrelation terms for the nonseasonal part are significant at lags of 1, 3, and 9. They appear to damp down toward zero. Coupled with the information from the autocorrelation plot, a possible MA(1) model in the nonseasonal part is tentatively identified. For the seasonal portion, we find a significant partial autocorrelation at lag 12. This information along with the autocorrelations indicates possibly an ARMA(1,1) or an MA(1) in the seasonal portion. Since several estimations of the data indicate a better fit with the MA(1) model, we shall tentatively judge it to be an MA(1) model. Thus we shall estimate the model

$$ARIMA(0,1,1)(0,1,1)^{12}$$

In figure 9.A3, the ARIMA procedure produces the computational results for the methods outlined by Box and Jenkins (1976). Marquardt's method is used for the nonlinear least squares iterations. The estimate of parameters for the least squares model is given by

$$\theta_1 = 0.358\ 978$$
and
$$\theta_{12} = 0.756\ 628$$

Since no constant term was estimated in this illustration, the model can be written

$$\log Y_t = \log Y_{t-1} + \log Y_{t-12} - \log Y_{t-13} + e_t$$

$$-0.358\ 978 e_{t-1} - 0.756\ 628 e_{t-12} + 0.271\ 613 e_{t-13}$$

The standard error for each parameter estimate is given by STD ERROR. When the estimate is divided by the standard error, the resulting T RATIO is given for each parameter. Since 59 observations are used to produce each estimate (hence, 58 degrees of freedom), both t ratios are significant for a reasonably low significance level (say 0.01). The estimate value is thus stable.

The variance estimate, 0.001 993 74, is the mean square error. Also, the standard error of estimate is the square root of MSE. Correlations of the estimates indicate

ARIMA PROCEDURE

```
NAME OF VARIABLE          = LOGY
PERIODS OF DIFFERENCING = 1. 12

MEAN OF WORKING SERIES = 0. 00176244
STANDARD DEVIATION       =   0. 0560526
NUMBER OF OBSERVATIONS =           59
```

AUTOCORRELATIONS

LAG	COVARIANCE	CORRELATION	−1 9 8 7 6 5 4 3 2 1 0 1 2 3 4 5 6 7 8 9 1
0	0. 0031419	1. 00000	. ********************
1	−. 00096849	−0. 30825	******:
2	. 000253974	0. 08083	. : ** .
3	−. 00092183	−0. 29340	******: .
4	. 000436346	0. 13888	. : *** .
5	. 000052785	0. 01680	. : .
6	. 000218692	0. 06961	. : * .
7	−0. 0004088	−0. 13011	. ***: .
8	−4. 547E−05	−0. 01447	. : .
9	. 000622783	0. 19822	. : **** .
10	−9. 367E−05	−0. 02981	. *: .
11	. 000200284	0. 06375	. : * .
12	−. 00141438	−0. 45017	*********: .
13	. 000507293	0. 16146	. : *** .
14	−7. 714E−05	−0. 02455	. : .
15	. 000617494	0. 19654	. : **** .
16	−. 00066332	−0. 21112	. ****: .
17	. 000409268	0. 13026	. : *** .
18	−. 00012753	−0. 04059	. *: .
19	. 000188098	0. 05987	. : * .
20	−. 00021495	−0. 06841	. *: .
21	−0. 0002926	−0. 09313	. **: .
22	−. 00008917	−0. 02838	. *: .
23	. 000673227	−. 21427	. : **** .
24	. 000192201	0. 06117	. : * .

MARKS TWO STANDARD ERRORS

FIGURE 9.A1 Estimation of an ARIMA$(0,1,1)(0,1,1)^{12}$ model by the SAS software system

that the estimates of θ_1 and θ_{12} are almost uncorrelated since the coefficient is −0.140.

The SAS output produces an autocorrelation check for the residuals to indicate whether the residuals are white noise or not. Ljung–Box χ^2 values are calculated for lags of up to 6, 12, 18 and 24. The χ^2 values, degrees of freedom, and probability of making the error of rejecting the hypothesis that the model is adequate when it is true are given. Note that for all χ^2 values, the probability of making this error is high (467,0.941, etc.). Thus, we would not have sufficient evidence to reject the hypothesis that the estimated model is adequate.

Autocorrelation coefficients for the residuals are printed out but not plotted. Finally, the specifics of the model are stated.

```
                          PARTIAL AUTOCORRELATIONS

  LAG        CORRELATION      -1 9 8 7 6 5 4 3 2 1 0 1 2 3 4 5 6 7 8 9 1
   1         -0.30825                    ******:        .
   2         -0.01567                         .  :      .
   3         -0.30165                    ******:        .
   4         -0.04675                       .  *:       .
   5          0.04905                       .  : *      .
   6          0.01878                       .  :        .
   7         -0.08571                       . **:       .
   8         -0.06138                       .  *:       .
   9          0.22793                       .  :*****
  10          0.04443                       .  : *      .
  11          0.07915                       .  : **     .
  12         -0.37549                 *********:        .
  13         -0.11541                       . **:       .
  14         -0.02857                       .  *:       .
  15         -0.03135                       .  *:       .
  16         -0.12666                       . ***:      .
  17          0.10171                       .  : **     .
  18          0.12969                       .  : ***    .
  19         -0.07562                       . **:       .
  20         -0.04971                       .  *:       .
  21          0.02367                       .  :        .
  22         -0.06765                       .  *:       .
  23          0.20062                       .  :****.
  24         -0.02258                       .  :        .
```

FIGURE 9.A2 Estimation of an ARIMA(0,1,1)(0,1,1)^{12} model by the SAS software system

A plot of the observed, forecast, and fitted values from January 1974 to December 1976 is shown in figure 9.A4. The plot is for the transformed data and includes the following:

1 observed values, asterisk;
2 forecast values, F;
3 lower limit of a 95 percent confidence interval, L;
4 upper limit of a 95 percent confidence interval, U.

The forecast and observed values for 1974 and 1975 appear close except for the second month, which is outside the limit of the confidence interval. Additional research into why this value is outside the interval would be called for if further investigation is warranted. Finally, the values plotted for 1976 are the forecast and limits only. The limits deviate further from the forecast as the number of periods ahead forecast increases.

Finally figure 9.A5 is the plot of the observed and forecast values for variable Y, the original series. The information content in this figure is similar to that in figure 9.A4 except that the data are in the original form. Specifically, the logarithmically transformed data were converted back to the original form.

```
                    AUTOCORRELATION CHECK FOR WHITE NOISE

TO      CHI                                 AUTOCORRELATIONS
LAG   SQUARE    DF    PROB
 6    13.45      6   0.036      -0.308   0.081  -0.293   0.139   0.017   0.070
12    33.35     12   0.001      -0.130  -0.014   0.198  -0.030   0.064  -0.450
18    43.93     18   0.001       0.161  -0.025   0.197  -0.211   0.130  -0.041
24    50.56     24   0.001       0.060  -0.068  -0.093  -0.028   0.214   0.061

                    ARIMA: LEAST SQUARES ESTIMATION

        PARAMETER     ESTIMATE      STD ERROR     T RATIO      LAG

        MA 1,1        0.358978      0.124837       2.88         1
        MA 2,1        0.756628      0.130366       5.80        12


        VARIANCE ESTIMATE    = 0.00199374
        STD ERROR ESTIMATE   =  0.0446513
        NUMBER OF RESIDUALS =     59

                    CORRELATIONS OF THE ESTIMATES

                           MA 1,1      MA 2,1
               MA 1,1       1.000      -0.140
               MA 2,1      -0.140       1.000

                    AUTOCORRELATION CHECK OF RESIDUALS

TO      CHI                                 AUTOCORRELATIONS
LAG   SQUARE    DF    PROB
 6     3.57      4   0.467      -0.004   0.071  -0.185   0.001   0.120   0.036
12     4.14     10   0.941       0.019  -0.008   0.061   0.058   0.007  -0.018
18     9.06     16   0.911      -0.038   0.053   0.096  -0.076   0.197  -0.006
24    17.36     22   0.743       0.043  -0.088  -0.103   0.123   0.216   0.052

            MODEL FOR VARIABLE LOGY
            NC MEAN TERM IN THIS MODEL.
            PERIODS OF DIFFERENCING = 1,12.

            MOVING AVERAGE FACTORS
                         FACTOR 1
            1-.358978B**(1)
                         FACTOR 2
            1-.756628B**(12)
```

FIGURE 9.A3 Estimated ARIMA model and diagnostic check of the residuals

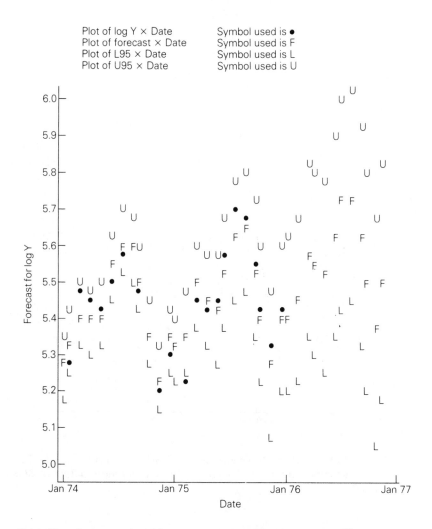

FIGURE 9.A4 Plot of observed and forecast values, ARIMA(0,1,1)(0,1,1)^{12} model, transformed data (Note: 16 observations had missing values or were out of range. Output of SAS PROC PLOT)

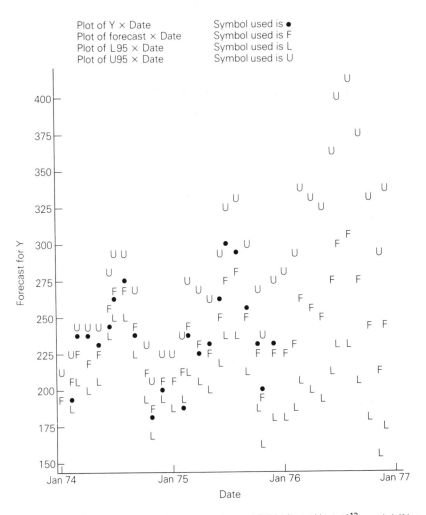

FIGURE 9.A5 Plot of observed and forecast values, ARIMA$(0,1,1)(0,1,1)^{12}$ model (Note: 16 observations had missing values or were out of range. Output of SAS PROC PLOT)

References to Appendix

Box, G. E. P and Jenkins, G. M. (1976) *Time Series Analysis, Forecasting and Control*. San Francisco, CA: Holden-Day.

Marquardt, D. W. (1963) An algorithm for least squares estimation of nonlinear parameters, *Journal of the Society for Industrial and Applied Mathematics*, 11, 431–41.

PART V

Qualitative Forecasting

Forecasting Business Conditions – Some Qualitative Approaches

Objectives

In this chapter, you will be introduced to forecasting methods which are not wholly based on the analysis of numerical data. These techniques often couple judgment with the recognition that economic statisticians can produce useful indicators of changes in business activity. By the end of this chapter, you will have knowledge of the following:

1 Using economic time series to predict changes in economic activity.
2 Using specific time series for forecasting such as gross national product, the index of industrial production, the unemployment rate, the number of housing starts, the consumer price index and the producer price index.
3 Using the index of eleven leading indicators.
4 Using leading indicators to predict recovery and contraction, inflation, and changes in the service sector of the economy.
5 Use of other information such as anticipation surveys and diffusion indexes.
6 Use of the Delphi techniques to predict long-term changes in business and economic activity.

Outline

Key Terms

- Qualitative forecasting
- Business cycles
- Amplitude
- Aggregate economic activity
- Diffusion indexes
- Leading indicator
- Roughly coincident indicator
- Lagging indicator
- Gross national product
- Index of industrial production
- Unemployment rate
- Housing starts
- Consumer price index
- Producer price index
- Index of leading economic indicators
- Anticipation surveys
- Delphi method

10.1   Introduction

Qualitative forecasting consists of techniques which are not wholly dependent upon the analysis of numerical data. They apply when numerical data does not exist, or for very long term forecasts where extrapolations of trends is impossible or unwise, or when turning points in business conditions are to be predicted. These methods are of particular importance because forecasters often do not have numerical data to work with and often have to predict turning points in business and economic activity. Examples of qualitative forecasts include technological forecasting, consumer taste predictions, fashion changes, and changes in long-term social attitudes. These examples usually relate to technological change and to social change where consumers alter or develop new tastes. These longer-term factors can rarely be forecast by quantitative means alone.

Human judgment applies to quantitative forecasts in establishing patterns or relationships in historical time series to select the appropriate quantitative model. Human judgment is also common to all qualitative forecasting and is generally brought to bear by obtaining the views and opinions of experts both within and outside the organization. Often, qualitative forecasts are made along with quantitative forecasts in the selection of appropriate statistical models for forecasting. For example, the demand for natural gas to the year 2000 is usually based on a time series or regression-based model and then qualitative factors are attached to adjust the quantitative part. These factors may include human judgment as to potential competition from other energy sources, changes in consumer tastes, technological developments, and whether energy sources will be needed in the same way.

In previous chapters we have seen that formal quantitative models attempted to separate pattern from randomness in historical time series and then extrapolate the former. These methodologies extrapolate the pattern of the trend–cycle component of the previous years. If the trend–cycle component continues to behave as in the past, forecasting will be relatively accurate. However, there is no way that a typical time series method can predict whether or not a turning point in the data will occur in an upcoming period. Thus in this chapter we shall consider one approach to studying the cyclical component where the purpose is to predict the turning points in economic activity. This approach was developed and is used by the National Bureau of Economic Research, and will be summarized here. The approach couples judgment with an explicit recognition that economic statisticians can produce viable indicators of business activity. In this chapter, we shall not consider those qualitative techniques used to predict changes in technology, consumer tastes, fashion and social behavior, with one exception, the Delphi process. All other techniques are left to books on survey research methods, marketing research and technological forecasting.[1]

10.2 The Cyclical Component

Business cycles are a type of fluctuation found in aggregate economic activity of nations that organize their work in business enterprises: a cycle consists of expansions occurring at about the same time in many economic activities, followed by similarly general recessions, contractions and revivals which merge into the expansion phase of the next cycle; this sequence of changes is recurrent but not periodic; in duration business cycles vary from more than one year to ten or twelve years; they are divisible into shorter cycles of similar character, with amplitudes approximately their own.

(Burns and Mitchell, 1946, p. 3)

The above definition developed by and for the National Bureau of Economic Research (NBER) has been in use for over 40 years. No restrictions are placed upon the length of business expansions or contractions, and even the limits on the period of a full cycle (expansion and contraction) are broad – more than one year to 10 or 12 years.

As well as the length of the cycle, the definition recognizes two other significant features of business cycles – amplitude and scope. No precise numerical magnitudes are cited and, in practice, no precise specifications with respect to amplitude and scope are imposed.

The requirement as to *amplitude* is that expansions and contractions reflect absolute changes in the dissection of "aggregate economic activity." A rise or fall in a measure of a sector of the economy, such as industrial production or manufacturing inventories, is not enough. Nor is a mere slowing down or decline in the rate of growth in total activity enough to qualify as a change in the direction of the economy. Furthermore, the requirement that cycles should not be divisible into shorter cycles means that if a long expansion is interrupted by a decline, the decline should be considered a contraction if, and only if, it is as large as the smallest contraction in the historical record.

The definition of *aggregate economic activity* is also not clear. There is no single measure of the nation's economic activity, whether in terms of income, expenditure, employment, or output over a long period of time on a monthly or quarterly basis, comparable throughout in its coverage or adequate throughout in its statistical

---

1   A brief list of references on these topics is included in the appendix to this chapter.

foundation. Although the coverage and quality of economic data have improved substantially over the years, the specification of a measure of aggregate economic activity is still vague. The best that one can do is to use the best available data at any one time.

At present, gross national product (GNP) is relied upon but there are several problems. Uncertainties are present in the measurement of important sectors of GNP, especially in preliminary figures. Furthermore, increases in the general level of prices may help to increase the value of GNP in current dollars. However, measures of employment and output fall, indicating a period of contraction. Finally, statistical measures of economic activity often move in different directions and no single index is clearly superior to all others.

If such problems exist, what does the NBER do to identify and date business cycles? The procedure consists of two distinguishable parts. First, the NBER identifies whether a period of contraction or expansion has begun. Second, the dates of the peak and the trough are identified. This is done because of the existence of a long and generally accepted historical chronology. An apparent contraction or expansion can be contrasted with earlier contractions and expansions recognized in the chronology. If their character appears similar to the historical contractions and expansions, the NBER will designate the period appropriately.

Three principal types of historical comparisons are made. First, the approximate length of a contraction or expansion in aggregate activity that occurred is compared with earlier contractions or expansions. Second, the relative depth of a contraction or magnitude of an expansion are compared with the declines or expansions of earlier periods. Specific measures of economic activity include GNP in current and constant dollars, employment and unemployment, personal income, and production and output. Third, the same sort of comparison is carried out for other measures called *diffusion indexes* to determine whether the current movement is as widely diffused among different economic activities or among different sectors or industries as on the earlier occasions. Diffusion indexes indicate how widespread a contraction or expansion has become.

All the comparisons mentioned before are tenuous until a contraction or expansion is well under way. Mild contractions or expansions are particularly difficult to identify and often uncertainty exists for many months before the turning point is identified. Furthermore, mere statistical comparisons described before, while necessary, are not the only requirement for an intelligent judgment on the likelihood of a cyclical turning point. Judgments must be coupled with appraisals of the causal factors influencing contractions and expansions and the steps taken by the government to offset contraction and induce expansion.

The dating of peaks and troughs of a business cycle requires the examination of deseasonalized data on economic indicators. These indicators lead, lag, or are roughly coincident with the date of the change in aggregate economic activity. Sometimes these indicators point to a particular month and sometimes the evidence is conflicting and presents a difficult choice. In general, the NBER will choose a particular month in each case rather than indicate a period in which the peak or trough occurred. Thus the users of these dated business cycles should understand that a degree of uncertainty is attached to any particular date. Revisions of the underlying statistical evidence may eventually suggest a different choice. Thus the NBER may from time to time review and change some of the dates. However, for most purposes, small errors or uncertainties in the dates are usually not important. In the next sections we shall see how we can use our knowledge of business cycles and indicators to predict and forecast turning points in time series.

10.3   The Dating of Business Cycles

As stated before, the NBER is the chief agency for dating the peaks (high points) and troughs (low points) in general business activity. Continually the NBER examines data for predicting fluctuations in general business activity with the result being that business cycles or fluctuations are not totally predictable.

The study of business cycles and their causes is beyond the scope of this book but a number of very important observations are worth noting.[2] The recurring sequence of changes, that is, expansion, downturn, contraction, and recovery, is not regular. Phases of business cycles are recurring, but their lengths and intensity vary. Although business cycles are found in modern industrialized nations whose economic activities are organized through the operation of competitive markets, this does not indicate that the market system alone is the cause of business cycles. There is a great diversity of opinion concerning the causes of business cycles. Whatever the causes, fluctuations in business activity affect prices, employment, business failures, costs and profits, spending by consumers, borrowing, interest rates, and tax collections.

Table 10.1 contains a chronology of business cycles in the United States in the post-Second World War era. The source of this table is *Business Conditions Digest*,[3]

TABLE 10.1   Business cycles 1945 to 1989 in the United States

Reference dates		Cycle		Duration in Months	
		Trough to trough	*Peak to Peak*	*Contraction peak to trough*	*Expansion trough to peak*
Trough	*Peak*				
Oct 1945	Nov 1948	88	45	8	37
Oct 1949	Jul 1953	48	56	11	45
May 1954	Aug 1957	55	49	10	39
Apr 1958	Apr 1960	47	32	8	24
Feb 1961	Dec 1969	34	116	10	106
Nov 1970	Nov 1973	117	47	11	36
Mar 1975	Jan 1980	52	74	16	58
Jul 1980	Jul 1981	64	18	7	13
Nov 1982	Jun 1989[a]	28	95	16	80
Mean length		59.22	59.10	10.78	48.67
Standard deviation		27.72	30.90	3.27	28.81
Coefficient of variation (%)		46.1	52.3	30.3	59.2

Notes: [a]As of June, 1989, the peak had not been reached. Coefficient of variation is the standard deviation divided by the mean and multiplied by 100 to yield a percentage.
Source: *Business Conditions Digest*, various issues.

---

2   To study business cycles one should begin by reading Burns and Mitchell (1946), Fels and Hinshaw (1968) and Mitchell (1941) and then proceed to study new ideas in such publications as Bails and Peppers (1982), Dauten and Valentine (1974), Klein and Moore (1982), and Moore (1980).

3   *Business Conditions Digest* was formerly known as *Business Cycle Developments*. This publication contains a wealth of information concerning the forecasting of business conditions.

published by the US Department of Commerce. Note the general lack of periodicity in the cyclical movements. According to NBER definitions, a peak is the month that marks the end of an expansion and the beginning of a downturn. Similarly a trough is the end of the downturn and the beginning of an expansionary period. On examining the data of table 10.1, the variation in the lengths of cycles can easily be seen. The trough-to-trough periods varied in length from 34 months to 117 months with a coefficient of variation of 46.1 percent. Similarly, the peak-to-peak periods varied from 18 months to 116 months in length with a coefficient of variation of 52.3 percent. Contractionary periods demonstrated the smallest variation of from 7 to 16 months with a coefficient of variation of 30.3 percent. However, expansionary periods demonstrated the largest variation from 13 to 106 months with a coefficient of variation of 59.2 percent. Thus there can be no general conclusion concerning the duration of business cycles since the evidence indicates such a wide disparity in the lengths of the periods.

In general, business cycles are not only swings in economic activity but also diffuse themselves throughout the economy. Cycles produce movements called industry and firm cycles as they have differing effects on various sectors of the economy. Individual industry cycles and company cycles have their own unique features. Some industries tend not to be influenced by cycles in aggregate economic activity. In the next section, we shall explore the relationship of business cycles to various sectors of the economy by considering a number of indicators of economic activity.

10.4 The Economic Indicator Approach

Judgment is a major factor in predicting changes or turns in the behavior of economic activity. In predicting cyclical fluctuations, it is necessary to reinforce judgment with various types of economic data.

A large part of the judgmental process of predicting fluctuations in the economy and how they affect individual industries and firms requires the use of significant indicators of general economic activity. For many years, the NBER issued lists of those significant series that usually lead, those that roughly coincide with, and those that usually lag behind the changes in total or aggregate economic activity. These three types of series are denoted indicators by the NBER and one is summarized in table 10.2.

1 *Leading indicators* These series precede upturns and downturns of measures of aggregate economic activity.
2 *Roughly coincident indicators* These series are direct measures of aggregate economic activity or move at roughly the same time as aggregate activity.
3 *Lagging indicators* These series generally reach turning points after the measures of aggregate economic activity.

As well as the NBER indicators, numerous financial newspapers and periodicals produce indicators of economic change. For example, table 10.3 reproduces a list of economic indicators published in the Business and Financial Section of the Sunday *New York Times*. Note that these indicators may permit us to analyze business conditions and interpret them in the process of predicting cyclical upturns and downturns.

While many economic indicators are better than others for predicting economic change, all have their own peculiarities and problems. These economic indicators produce more than merely a picture of the economy. They often form a basis for economic policy decisions at the national as well as the firm level. Finally, they may also signal whether current economic and business policies are working well or not.

10.5   Specific Measures of Economic Activity – Discussion

Gross national product (GNP) is the broadest measure of economic activity showing whether the economy is in a recession or broadly expanding. It is an output measure of all the nation's goods and services divided into four categories as follows:

1 personal consumption – mostly consumer spending;
2 gross private domestic investment – includes business investment in equipment and structures and in housing;
3 net exports of goods and services – the balance of exports and imports;
4 government spending – net purchase of goods and services by the federal, state, and local governments.

GNP measures only the sales of final products such as washing machines and frozen bagels. Hence the value of steel in washing machines and the value of flour and shortening in bagels is assumed to be counted in the sales of the final product. Although this statistic is invaluable in determining changes in business and economic activity, there is one serious flaw in its use. GNP is reported in two forms: nominal GNP which is the total for the quarter and real GNP which is nominal GNP adjusted for inflation. GNP is first reported two weeks following the end of the quarter and is continually revised until a final figure is determined. The continued revision of GNP estimates can cause problems since the revision can be large.

A second serious problem with GNP estimates concerns the current method for deflating net exports. Geoffrey Moore of the Center for Business Cycle Research at Columbia University contends that the current methods distort this figure and because of its relative importance can seriously affect the change in GNP. A plot of GNP for the period 1984–88 is given in figure 10.1

Another measure of change in business activity is the *index of industrial production* (IIP) which measures changes in the output in manufacturing, mining, and electric and gas utilities. This index is issued on a monthly basis by the Board of Governors of the Federal Reserve System. It is seasonally adjusted to remove the effects of the seasonality of production during a year. Furthermore, the IIP is also produced for particular industries.

The index does not measure large sectors of productive activities, that is, agriculture and service industries. Thus a change in economic activity in these industries would not be reflected in the index. However, the IIP is well respected because it covers those industries (manufacturing) which are highly sensitive to downturns in business activity. The actual decline in the economy may be less than the decline in the IIP, since the index covers those sensitive industries usually hardest hit in a recession. Since the Second World War declines in the IIP have usually been much larger than the general decline in GNP during periods of recession. Figure 10.2 shows the IIP over the period January 1985 – February 1989.

Another measure of change in business activity is the *unemployment rate* (figure 10.3) compiled by the Bureau of Labor Statistics. This estimate is the result of a random sample of more than 60 000 households taken during the week each month

TABLE 10.2 Summary of leading, lagging, and roughly coincident indicators: Relationship to the cycle

Cyclical timing	Employment and unemployment (15 series)	Production and income (10 series)	Consumption, trade, orders and deliveries (13 series)	Fixed capital investment (19 series)	Inventories and inventory investment (9 series)	Prices, costs, and profits (18 series)	Money and credit (28 series)
Timing at business cycle peaks							
Leading (L) indicators (61 series)	Marginal employment adjustments (3 series) Job vacancies (2 series) Comprehensive employment (1 series) Comprehensive unemployment (3 series)	Capacity utilization (2 series)	Orders and deliveries (6 series) Consumption and trade (2 series)	Formation of business enterprises (2 series) Business investment commitments (5 series) Residential construction (3 series)	Inventory investment (4 series) Inventories on hand and on order (1 series)	Stock prices (1 series) Sensitive commodity prices (2 series) Profits and profit margins (7 series) Cash flows (2 series)	Money (5 series) Credit flows (5 series) Credit difficulties (2 series) Bank reserves (2 series) Interest rates (1 series)
Roughly coincident (C) indicators (24 series)	Comprehensive employment (1 series)	Comprehensive output and income (4 series) Industrial production (4 series)	Consumption and trade (4 series)	Business investment commitments (1 series) Business investment expenditures (6 series)			Velocity of money (2 series) Interest rates (2 series)
Lagging (Lg) indicators (19 series)	Comprehensive unemployment (2 series)			Business investment expenditures (1 series)	Inventories on hand and on order (4 series)	Unit labor costs and labor share (4 series)	Interest rates (4 series) Outstanding debt (4 series)
Timing unclassified (U) (8 series)	Comprehensive employment (3 series)		Consumption and trade (1 series)	Business investment commitments (1 series)		Sensitive commodity prices (1 series) Profits and profit margins (1 series)	Interest rates (1 series)

Timing at business cycle troughs

	Employment	Production and income	Consumption, trade, orders, and deliveries	Fixed capital investment	Inventories and inventory investment	Prices, costs, and profits	Money and credit
Leading (L) indicators (47 series)	Marginal employment adjustments (1 series)	Industrial production (1 series)	Orders and deliveries (5 series) Consumption and trade (4 series)	Formation of business enterprises (2 series) Business investment commitments (4 series) Residential construction (3 series)	Inventory investment (4 series)	Stock prices (1 series) Sensitive commodity prices (3 series) Profits and profit margins (6 series) Cash flows (2 series)	Money (4 series) Credit flows (5 series) Credit difficulties (2 series)
Roughly coincident (C) indicators (23 series)	Marginal employment adjustments (2 series) Comprehensive employment (4 series)	Comprehensive output and income (4 series) Industrial production (3 series) Capacity utilization (2 series)	Consumption and trade (3 series)	Business investment commitments (1 series)		Profits and profit margins (2 series)	Money (1 series) Velocity of money (1 series)
Lagging (Lg) indicators (41 series)	Job vacancies (2 series) Comprehensive employment (1 series) Comprehensive unemployment (5 series)		Orders and deliveries (1 series)	Business investment commitments (2 series) Business investment expenditures (7 series)	Inventories on hand and on order (5 series)	Unit labor costs and labor share (4 series)	Velocity of money (1 series) Bank reserves (1 series) Interest rates (8 series) Outstanding debt (4 series)
Timing unclassified (U) (1 series)							Bank reserves (1 series)

Source: Business Conditions Digest, June, 1989, p. 2.

TABLE 10.3 Data bank of general economy measures and economic indicators

The economy	*Production*
Gross national product (billions, annual rate)	Steel (thousands of net tons)
Real GNP growth (annual rate, 1982 dollars, percent)	Autos (units)
Corporate after-tax profits (billions, annual rate)	Domestic crude oil (thousands of bbls/day)
Industrial production index (percentage change, monthly and year to year)	Oil imports (crude and products) (thousands of bbls/day, 4-wk moving avg)
Housing starts (thousands of units, annual rate)	Electric power (millions of kilowatt hours)
New orders for durable goods (by manufacturers, in billions)	Coal (bituminous) (thousands of net tons)
Plant and equipment spending (billions, annual rate)	Paperboard (thousands of tons)
Inventory–sales ratio (constant dollars, inventories ÷ sales)	Lumber (millions of feet)
Sales at retail (billions)	Freight car loadings (billions of ton-miles)
Index of leading indicators (percentage change, monthly and year to year)	
Employment (thousands)	
Unemployment (thousands)	
Unemployment rate (percent)	
Merchandise exports (billions)	
Merchandise imports (billions)	
Current account surplus/deficit (goods and services, in billions)	

Prices	*Finance*
GNP price deflator (annual rate, percent)	Federal funds rate (average, percent)
Consumer price index (all urban consumers)	Prime rate (most major banks, percent)
CPI annual rate (percent)	1-month commercial paper (percent)
Producer price index (finished goods, annual rate, percent)	Corporate AA industrial bonds (yield, percent)
Cash wheat price (no. 1 K.C., per bushel)	30-year treasury bonds (yield, percent)
Crude oil, US refiner's cost (composite per barrel)	Money supply growth (M-1B, annual percentage change)
Dow Jones industrial average (Friday close)	Gold (Friday pm London fix, per ounce)

This list comes from the *New York Times*; however, other newspapers have similar lists.

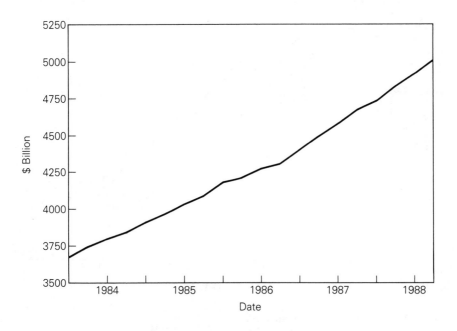

FIGURE 10.1 Gross national product

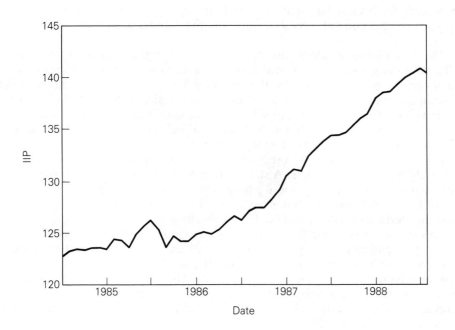

FIGURE 10.2 Index of industrial production (1977 = 100)

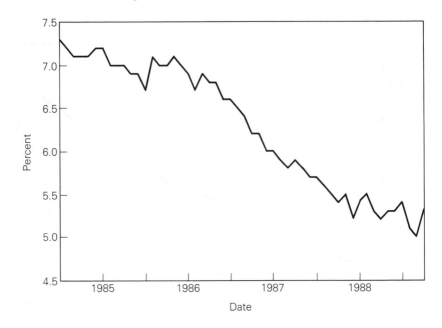

FIGURE 10.3 Unemployment rate, all workers

containing the twelfth day.[4] This household survey reports the size of the adult (over 16 years of age) non-military labor force and the number of workers employed (full time) or not.

The unemployment rate is important because it is representative of joblessness in all parts of the economy. As with all economic statistics, it is criticized because actual joblessness can be distorted by this number. For example, if all part-time and discouraged workers (those employed in positions which do not utilize the extent of their skills, that is, underemployed) were included among the unemployed, the unemployment rate would be much greater. In periods of recession, the number of discouraged workers becomes a more important factor.

Housing starts (figure 10.4), reported monthly, indicate the annual rate of starts of privately owned housing units. A start is counted upon the breaking of ground for a new unit. Completion of the housing project may take many months or years but this factor has no effect on this economic statistic. In turn, this figure is broken down into housing starts for single and multiple unit dwellings.

This statistic is very important since it is a key indicator of activity in the housing industry. Housing is usually the first sector of the economy to decline when the economy is slowed during a recession. Thus the number of housing starts tends to be a leading indicator of general economic activity. However, housing start figures may tend to overstate the activity in the industry. For example, a start can be recorded during a period of economic decline which results in the postponement of the completion of the project.

---

4   This survey is entitled the Current Population Survey and is the prime source of much social economic data. It is timely and provides extremely useful results.

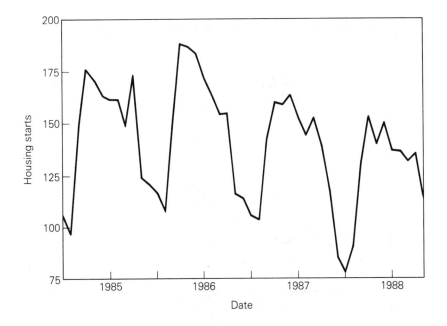

FIGURE 10.4 Housing starts (thousands)

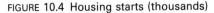

There are several measures of changes in the price level. The *consumer price index* (CPI) and *producer price index* (PPI) are two of the most commonly used. The CPI measures changes in the prices of a fixed market basket of goods and services purchased by the "typical" American consuming household. Some 385 items are included in this market basket with data collected from both primary and secondary sources in 85 metropolitan areas.

The CPI is a Laspeyre type price index having fixed weights for the items included in the index which establish the relative importance of each of them.[5] As of 1981, the housing component is the heaviest weighted component at 45.5 percent whereas transportation is 19 percent and food and beverages is 18.3 percent.

Up until 1978, the CPI recorded only the prices paid by urban wage earners and clerical worker families covering about 40 percent of the population. This index is labeled the CPI-W in contrast with the newer CPI for all urban consumers. The second index, labeled CPI-U, covers about 80 percent of the population and is the one that is generally quoted (figure 10.5).

As a measure of changes in prices, there is a problem with the housing component of the CPI. The rate of inflation has been overstated because the influence of mortgage interest rates and housing prices has been too great. Conversely, the weight for the housing component would understate the rate of inflation when mortgage rates and housing prices are declining. Thus the large weight assigned to the housing component tends to detract from the statistical reliability of the index.

---

5   A Laspeyre type of price index refers to the particular formula used for computing the index. Laspeyre, for whom the index formula was named, produced the weighted-average formula having fixed (or base year) weights.

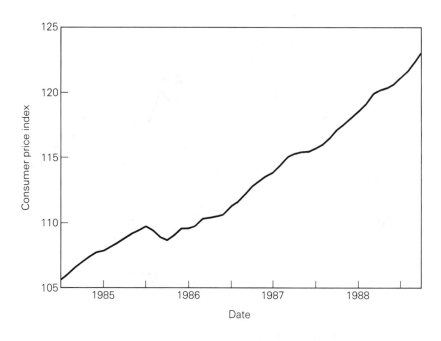

FIGURE 10.5 Consumer price index – all urban consumers (1982–4 = 100)

Weights for components of the CPI are currently based on a (1973–4) Consumer Expenditure Survey. In the period from those dates until today, spending habits have changed. For example, the energy weight makes up a larger portion of the index than is necessary. Recent changes in the index, shifting the emphasis on housing from ownership to a rentai equivalent, have improved the reliability of the index. However, changes always wait until the Bureau of Labor Statistics can finance them, and this is often delayed.

The PPI (figure 10.6) measures price changes of goods that are finished and ready for sale to the ultimate user, either an individual or a business. These goods include items such as farm equipment and machinery that would be sold to business firms, and consumer goods such as food, clothing, automobiles, and household appliances that would be purchased by consumers. Price changes for intermediate goods, that is, flour, motor vehicle parts, cotton yarns, and crude materials (wheat, iron, livestock, crude petroleum) are also included.

About 2800 commodities are included in the PPI in a form similar to the CPI. The index is also of the Laspeyre type with a fixed weight based on past surveys and censuses for business firms. Unlike the CPI, it is not a point-of-sale index. The price quotations are often listed prices which may be at variance from point-of-sale prices during periods of price discounting. Recessionary periods are times when producers tend to engage in price discounts to reduce the size of their inventories of finished goods. Hence, the PPI may tend to understate price reductions in a business recession.

The PPI is not directly comparable with the CPI because it does not contain housing, services, and used car components. Changes in prices for finished goods do not often translate into changes in consumer prices because of the practice of varying

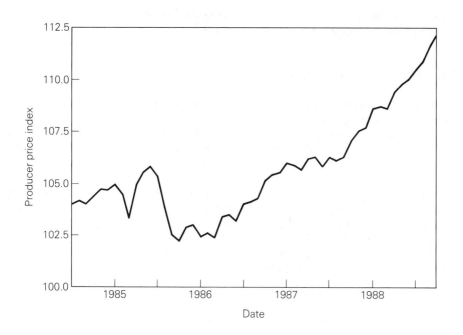

FIGURE 10.6 Producer price index – total finished goods (1982 = 100)

mark-ups on the part of retailers. Hence the PPI is, at best, an imperfect indicator of future changes in the CPI.

Because of the imperfections in the CPI and PPI, several other price indicators are looked at as gauges of inflation. The GNP price deflator and personal consumption expenditure (PCE) deflator are used as indicators of changes in prices of goods or services. These deflators are designed to adjust GNP and PCE for changes in the value of the dollar in estimating the size of the economy. They are directly comparable with the CPI or PPI. These deflators measure both changes in prices and changes in consumption patterns and at times may understate price inflation. The understatement emanates from the decline in the GNP deflator resulting from consumers shifting from high-priced items whose prices are still increasing to products with lower prices with slower increases.

Economic statisticians have tended to favor the GNP and PCE deflators over the CPI because these numbers have shown smaller increases in prices than the CPI in the period from 1980 to 1982 when there were very large increases in the CPI. Furthermore, the PCE deflator contains a measure for housing costs that is like a rental equivalent which the CPI will eventually use.

Use of all the above economic indicators permits the forecaster to predict with a great deal of uncertainty the changes in business and economic activity. No prediction is without risk, but, as Wesley Mitchell observed many years ago, this is not a new problem: "The uncertainty attending forecasts arises chiefly from the imperfections of our knowledge concerning business conditions in the immediate past and in the present" (Mitchell, 1941, p. 175). It is only through the examination of these economic statistics that we can identify past economic cycles and predict future turns in business activity. Unfortunately, no such judgment prediction is without error. In the next section, we shall consider how leading economic indicators can permit us to forecast future turning points.[6]

10.6   The Index of Leading Indicators

The federal government produces from various economic statistics an *index of leading economic indicators* (figure 10.7) designed to predict change in the economy, that is, whether the economy is expanding or declining.[7] This index contains items chosen because historical evidence indicates that they lead swings of the economy in either direction. The components are as follows:

1 average weekly hours of production of nonsupervisory workers, manufacturing;
2 average weekly initial claims for unemployment insurance, state programs;
3 inflation-adjusted new orders for consumer goods and materials;
4 vendor performance – slower deliveries diffusion index;
5 contracts for plant and equipment in 1982 dollars;
6 new private housing units (1967=100);

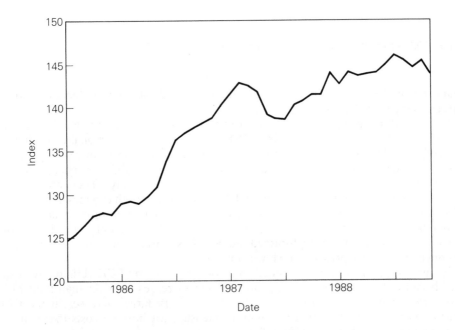

FIGURE 10.7 Index of eleven leading indicators (1982 = 100)

---

6   We should point out that similar economic indicators are produced for many economies. For example, the Federal Reserve Bank of San Francisco produce Pacific Basin Economic Indicators for 12 nations of the Pacific trading area and publishes this information on a periodic basis.

7   The index of leading indicators is revised periodically. Currently, it is based on 11 time series and is often referred to as the index of eleven leading indicators (IELI).

7 changes in manufacturers' unfilled orders;
8 stock prices, 500 common stocks;
9 changes in sensitive materials prices;
10 money supply M2 in 1982 dollars;[8]
11 index of consumer expectations.[9]

Although the index is often used, it is frequently misinterpreted. For example, since the end of the Second World War, this monthly index has declined significantly nine times (a decline of 3 percent or more) but only in six periods did a recession follow. Consequently, the index predicted correctly only two-thirds of the time. Furthermore, in 1973, prior to the beginning of the deepest recessionary period in the post-war era, the index did not fall significantly. The fall was only 1.7 percent before the recession, but the index fell more significantly after the recession took hold.

Finally, the index of leading indicators is subject to monthly revisions. These revisions can alter one's estimate of the timing of a recession or expansion. As with all economic numbers, this index must be used in conjunction with other indexes to identify and predict swings in the economy (figure 10.8).

In practice, forecasters have found that, in general, leading indicators are most useful as pointers to the turning points in a variable. Once a time series is deseasonalized, the leading indicator approach is important in assessing the cyclical aspects of a time series of business data. The reliability that can be placed upon this "lead–lag" analysis must be assessed by the forecasters by using historical data. Some firms have found that leading indicators are quite useful, while others have found them of little help. Thus individual firms and forecasters should assess the relevance of the method to their own circumstances.

In some instances, the forecaster may find a number of specific indicators which have some association with the variable to forecast. These can be used collectively in either multiple regression models (chapter 5) or econometric models (chapter 6). Since the leading indicator approach has been useful to many forecasters, the technique should be pursued for relevance in new situations. In many cases, however, the indicators will be fairly weak. The forecaster, in turn, will have to use other methods and additional judgment in conjunction with this lead–lag analysis.

10.7   Using Indicators as Signals of Recovery and Contraction

The Center for International Business Cycle Research at Columbia University (Director Geoffrey Moore) has been instrumental in developing an early warning system of recovery and contraction. Although the system is not without error, it does indicate how economic indicators can be used with judgment, to predict turning points. The method couples the Department of Commerce's index of leading indicators (discussed before) and its index of coincident indicators in predicting turning points. (The second index includes four components: industrial production, nonfarm employment, real personal income, and total business sales in constant prices.)

---

8   M2 is made up of checking account funds, currency in circulation, and assets of money market funds.

9   The IELI is composed of these series (*Business Conditions Digest*, June 1989, p. 106).

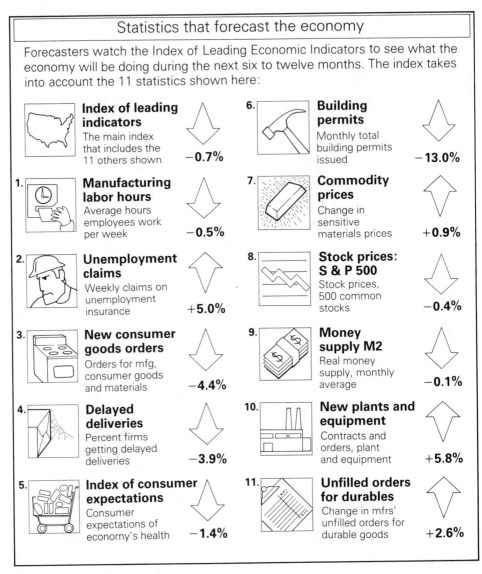

FIGURE 10.8 Index of eleven leading indicators, April 29, 1989
Source: Bureau of Economic Analysis, US Department of Commerce

Both these indexes are relatively free from erratic movements, neither is perfectly smooth, and both have declined during every one of the eight recessions since 1948 and have seldom undergone sustained declines at other times. To implement this early warning system, we first convert the indexes into growth rates. The definition of this rate is the following ratio:

$$\text{growth rate } r = \frac{\text{current month's index}}{\text{average level of the index for the 12 preceding months}} \quad (10.1)$$

In a period of contraction, this growth rate would be less than unity since the indexes themselves decline. In comparison, the growth rate would be greater than unity during an expansionary phase. If the growth rate r is multiplied by 100, it is converted to percentage form. In this way, if $r \times 100 = 95$, we say that there is a 5 percent decline (-5). However, if $r \times 100 = 105$, we say that there is a 5 percent increase $(+5)$. The points at which the growth rate turns positive would therefore signal a recovery. At the same time, the growth rate may turn negative again because of erratic movements or revisions of the index. To meet this problem in a practical manner, we adopt two rules of thumb. First, the growth rate must increase by more than 1 percent to be counted as positive. Second, a reversal is not counted until the retrogression is below -1 percent. Hence, small changes of ± 1 percent are not considered to be early warning signals.

Since the leading index is expected to turn first, the initial signal is based upon it. The second signal of change in the direction of the economy is a change in the growth rate of the coincident index. For an upturn to be signaled, the growth rate in the coincident index must also be greater than 1 percent. At the same time, the leading growth rate must exceed 4.3 percent (a rule of thumb based upon one percentage point greater than the trend in the growth rate of 3.3 recorded in the year prior to July 1982, the time of the early warning signal of recovery). The third signal of a turning point requires a growth rate of 4.3 percent in both the coincident and the leading index. The question now is whether this method predicts turning points adequately or not.

Zarnowitz and Moore (1982) compared the signal dates with the NBER's peak and trough dates to evaluate this procedure. Table 10.4 contains the three signals of recovery and the three signals of recession (downturn). The signals of peaks are denoted P1, P2, and P3, and the trough signals are T1, T2, and T3. Of the troughs, T1 usually occurred within three months of the turn, but rarely before it, T2 usually occurred five or six months after the turn, and T3 occurred about six to eight months after the turning point. There have been no false signals of recovery in the post-war period. However, the analysis is *ex post*, that is, it is based on revised figures

TABLE 10.4   Timing of signals of recovery and contraction

Peak	P1	P2	P3	Trough	T1	T2	T3
No peak	3/51	7/51	–	10/49	8/49	1/50	3/50
7/53	6/53	8/53	9/53	5/54	5/54	11/54	12/54
8/57	1/56	7/53	9/57	4/58	6/58	10/58	11/58
4/60	9/59	6/60	9/60	2/61	3/61	6/61	8/61
No peak	5/62	–	–	11/70	11/70	5/71	12/71
No peak	6/66	–	–	3/75	6/75	9/75	11/75
12/69	6/69	11/69	4/70	7/80	9/80	12/80	4/81
11/73	8/73	1/74	3/74	–	7/82	–	–
1/80	11/78	5/79	3/80				
7/81	6/81	8/81	10/81				
Average lead or lag (in months)	−7	−2	+3	Average lead or lag (in months)	+1	+5	+8

Source: Zarnowitz and Moore (1982, pp. 57–85).

currently available and not on preliminary data that would be available when forecasting.

For the signals of recovery, the P1 signal has preceded the peak. In three instances, however, a recession did not ensue but only a slowdown in growth. P2 occurred either before or within a month or two after the peak. P3 fell within one to five months after the peak. Thus the system is tardy in signaling recovery but this may not be too troublesome if the P3 signal is ignored. The record does seem to indicate that using P1 and P2 will yield sufficiently reliable results.

These signals are useful to business planners and forecasters in industries depending heavily on the business cycle. The signals may prove useful when decisions concerning the appropriate time to reduce or expand production or inventories are to be made, or in instances when capacity is to be changed. Finally, this analysis can be applied to problems in predicting employment cycles and international trade cycles as well as general business cycles (Klein and Moore 1982).

In analyzing the index of leading indicators, we must be very careful to discern what may have caused a change in the index from one month to another. For example, in January 1986 the index declined by 0.6 percent, leading some forecasters to predict a decline in the economy. The drop in the leading index was largely the result of one component – changes in contracts and orders for new plant and equipment. Although the leading index may foreshadow a downturn by one year or more, or sometimes by only a few months, it may sometimes emit a false signal. The suggested recession may have only been a slowdown in one sector of the economy. As the economy of a nation changes, a given index must be revised to reflect the alterations in the economy. Thus the index of leading indicators is constantly under scrutiny and revised periodically. There was no recession in 1986 or 1987 and the dip in the index reflected only a change in one sector of the economy.

No indicator system should be left in the index forever. As we shall see in later sections of this chapter, research is necessary to make the statistical system operate more effectively. In section 10.8, research into predicting inflation is presented and in section 10.9 research into predicting changes in the service sector is discussed. To forecast with greater accuracy, more emphasis must be placed on foreign trade volume and prices, foreign credit and capital flows, and economic indicators from other countries. Import prices obviously have a greater effect on US domestic demand and inflation today than they did 15 years ago. Fuller account of the international sector in leading indexes is necessary.

A new leading index of industrial materials processes, an improved measure of layoff rates, and a monthly ratio of selling prices to unit labor costs are desirable to predict changes in the industrial sector. Additional indicators on bond prices, ratio of sales to inventory, sales of consumer and capital goods, and inventory changes, among others, would provide forecasters with a more complete set of predictive statistical tools. Furthermore, with the growing costs of health and medical care, a leading index for prices in this sector would be advisable.

Leading indicators have many deficiencies that may never be properly fixed. Nevertheless, it is worth trying to improve and fix them because indicators have a long record of success behind them. The index of leading indicators works well because it reflects decisions that subsequently affect production and employment or because it measures factors that influence those decisions. The volume of new consumer goods orders is a leading indicator (included in the index of leading indicators) because production is usually geared to the receipt of new orders. Building permits are included because housing construction tends to follow the issue of new permits to build. The index of consumer expectations is the newest indicator to be added since it reflects consumer confidence and indicates purchase anticipations.

The selection of each of the leading indicators was based on their good performance over time. For example, more than a hundred years of information on stock prices exists, covering more than 20 business cycles. In addition, more than 30 market-oriented nations have an index of leading indicators. Studies of these indexes have shown good results when tested by researchers in forecasting. Thus use of leading indexes is now world-wide and will continue to grow, but much research is necessary to keep these indexes performing well.

10.8   Predicting Inflation by Business Indicators

Predicting the future course of inflation (or the increase in the prices of goods and services without a change in the quality characteristics of these same goods and services) is one of the most perplexing problems confronting business and economic forecasters. This prediction is important because it affects and is related to the most crucial decisions made by business administrators, policy-makers, agency heads, and consumers. The word inflation is very ambiguous because it means different things to different decision-makers. As a decision-maker, one wants to know the changes in the prices of goods and services that one spends one's purchasing power on. To do this, one would have to determine a price index of the market basket of goods and services purchased in either a base year (for a fixed-weight index) or a given year (for a changing-weight index). Since decision-makers do not usually produce specific price indices, we shall focus on the most commonly used index in the United States, that is, the "index of changes in the prices of goods and services purchased by all urban consumers to maintain their level of living," or, more simply, the CPI for all urban consumers.

To predict future values for the CPI, studies have indicated that the largest errors of prediction have occurred around the turning points, that is, the peaks and troughs. Forecast errors made by economic and business forecasters at peaks and troughs in real GNP are often as much as two or three times as large as those made during the sustained periods of expansion and contraction. This may be the result of choosing leading economic indicators designed to predict cyclical change and not to catch the turn in inflation.

In recent years, the Center for International Business Cycle Research has developed a specialized leading indicator to predict speedups and slowdowns in the inflation rate. The index reflects the intensity of demand pressures in the market for labor, the commodity markets, and the capital markets. This index consists of the following time series:

1 percentage of the working-age population that is employed;
2 annual rate of change in prices of industrial materials;
3 annual rate of change in total business, consumer, and federal outstanding debt.

Since 1948, the new index has reached its turning point prior to all the 16 turning points (eight peaks and eight troughs) in the CPI. Sound statistical correlation is a prerequisite for any indicator to be a leading indicator.

In addition to sound statistical analysis, forecasters must be able to show that a sound economic rationale underlies the usefulness of the leading indicator. This rationale is as follows:

1 The percentage employed foreshadows inflation through its implications for both the demand and supply of labor which puts upward pressure on wages, production and distribution costs, and, in turn, prices. Increasing employment, especially with larger numbers of two-income families, puts greater demand on consumer goods and, in turn, upward pressure on consumer prices. On the downslide, the reverse will occur.
2 Industrial materials prices also react promptly to changes in demand and supply. These items are not the same as those included in the CPI but are items such as scrap metal and cotton textiles. Unit labor costs are slow to change and they play a smaller role in industrial materials prices than they do in consumer goods prices. Hence industrial materials prices are more sensitive to changing market conditions and should reflect the effects of these changes much faster than the prices of final goods and services.
3 Finally, since new borrowing by consumers, business, and government is usually undertaken to facilitate the purchase of new goods and services, the rate of change in total outstanding debt should indicate the turning points in inflation. A slowdown in debt accumulation precedes the easing of demand and inflation. Increases in debt accumulation will have the opposite effect.

As indicated in table 10.5, it is apparent that the three series alone do not predict the turning points adequately. However, the composite index does. The individual series all fail in one way or another. The composite index anticipates the CPI trough by a mean of 7.25 months and the peaks by a mean of 10.25 months. The standard deviations for these two distributions are 6.34 and 6.27 months respectively. Thus there is considerable variability in the lead time for this new composite index.

Only the future will tell how well the index performs as a predictive tool. However, we should point out that the index numbers discussed in this section and in other parts of this chapter do provide some very useful tools for forecasting business conditions. Predicting changes in business conditions is particularly difficult to model with sophisticated quantitative tools. Thus forecasters often rely on business indicators and judgment to anticipate changes in specific portions of economic activity, such as inflation, or in general business activity.

10.9 Predicting for the Service Sector by Leading Indicators

The service sector is now accounting for a large and growing portion of the economy of industrial countries such as the United States and the United Kingdom. In the United States, the service sector accounted for about 70 percent of the nonfarm employment and over 65 percent of the economy's output. Furthermore, this rapidly growing sector is replacing all other sectors in growth of job opportunities for new workers.

Along with research in producing leading indicators for inflation and recovery and contraction, research indicates the usefulness of constructing a composite index of aggregate economic activity in the service sector. One such index is currently being developed for the Center for International Business Cycle Research. This new economic indicator for this growing sector of the US economy is important because other economic indicators focus more on manufacturing, mining, and the construction sectors.

The indicator approach to forecasting has a lengthy and successful history. The approach permits a forecaster to classify relevant macroeconomic time series into

TABLE 10.5 Cyclical turning points in the CPI and the lead or lag of four time series

Date turning point	Composite index	Employment percentage	Debt growth rate	Materials prices growth rate
Months of lead (−) or lag (+) at CPI troughs				
7–49	−1	+3	n.a.	−1
3–53	−7	a	n.a.	−12
10–54	−3	−3	−3	a
3–59	−11	−8	−13	−16
6–61	−4	+20	−2	+13
5–67	−1	—	+1	−7
6–72	−19	−15	−26	−15
6–76	−12	−12	−12	−17
Mean	−7.25	−2.50	−9.17	−7.86
Standard deviation	6.34	12.76	9.99	10.81
Months of lead (−) and lag (+) at CPI peaks				
2–51	−3	a	n.a.	−1
10–53	−7	−7	n.a.	−12
8–57	−20	−12	−23	a
10–59	−3	+8	−2	−16
10–66	66	−9	−40	+13
2–70	−10	−2	−10	−7
9–74	−18	−6	−18	−15
3–80	−12	−3	−21	−17
Mean	−10.25	3.67	−19.0	−7.86
Standard deviation	6.27	6.71	12.9	10.81

Notes: [a]There was no turn in the indicator.
n.a., not available. This particular series began in 1954.
Source: Data were collected from the Morgan Guaranty Trust Company of New York, *Morgan Guarantee Survey*, July 1983, p. 9.

leading, roughly coincident, and lagging indicators. The coincident index is used to represent the level of economic activity. Research on the coincident indicator focuses on the identification of an appropriate turning-point chronology by which time series indicators can be classified. Once the identification step is completed, a set of four leading indicators is identified, and a composite index is constructed from them. The resulting services leading indicator is useful if it leads the chronology of turning points of the coincident index of services.

Leading indicator research methodology requires that the service growth chronology be identified first. The second step is to choose time series for the leading index of the service sector. The final selection of the series for inclusion in the index is based on consistency. Specifically, the following question is asked: are the growth rates in the individual indicators consistently leading the turning points in the services growth chronology? The following time series were selected for inclusion in the leading index:

1 profit margins in service industries;
2 Stock price index of service companies;

3 Construction contracts for commercial buildings, floor space;
4 Average working week in service industries.

Research by the International Center for Business Cycle Research indicated that the lead–lag record was sufficiently strong to indicate their usefulness as components of an index of leading indicators.

Studies of this leading indicator index suggest that it is a fairly consistent leader of both the growth rate chronology and the coincident index. On average, the index leads the chronology by seven months at peaks and by four months at troughs (by the median). Studies have shown that, with the exception of two instances, the index led the turning points in the coincident time series. Table 10.6 contains the lead–lag record of the services leading index.

TABLE 10.6   Lead/lag record of the services leading index in the United States, 1949–1988: leads (−) and lags (+) of growth rates, in months

Services growth chronology		Leading index, services	
P	T	P	T
	10/49		0
8/50	2/54	−2	−3
11/55	4/58	−9	−6
6/59	3/61	−5	−12
11/65	11/70	−29	−6
3/73	4/75	−24	−8
4/78	5/80	−33	−2
4/81	1/82	−1	0
10/83		−4	
Median:			
P·T		−7	−4
P and T		−6	
Mean:			
P·T		−13	−5
P and T		−9	

Source: Layton and Moore (1989, p. 384).

With the acceptable performance of this leading index of the service sector, it will be quite useful in anticipating future fluctuations in the growth of the service sector. Thus, as well as studies of leading indicators of inflation and recession and recovery, a forecaster can find many useful applications for them in making judgmental or qualitative forecasts. In particular, the development of indicators of changes in business activity in the service sector enable forecasters to focus attention on predicting events which have not been considered in as much detail as in the past.

10.10   Using Anticipation Surveys

Surveys of consumer buying intentions and business capital spending plans are examples of scientific sampling (usually stratified random sampling) aimed at providing information to forecasters and business planners. These samples are called *anticipation surveys*. The major types are as follows:

1 business capital investment plans;
2 business expectations of inventory level and product demand (sales);
3 consumer buying plans and attitudes.

These anticipation surveys aim at providing inputs into the prediction of the cycle. However, their forecasting accuracy is often not very good. This is often because anticipations and consumer and business decisions are not necessarily the same.

The best-known survey of consumer attitudes and buying plans is conducted by the Institute for Social Research at the University of Michigan. This survey collects data on consumer opinions and consumer buying plans. Although it cannot be relied upon to predict turning points accurately, it is more useful than relying on historical data of consumer purchases and attitudes.

Two of the most widely used business investment surveys are the McGraw-Hill Survey of Business Capital Spending Plans published in *Business Week* and the US Office of Business Economics and the Securities and Exchange Commission (OBE–SEC) Survey. The McGraw-Hill survey is more timely but the OBE–SEC survey has been found to be more statistically accurate.

A third type of survey conducted by the OBE–SEC concerns inventory and product demand anticipations. The accuracy of this survey with regard to demand product is not high since those sampled are not necessarily good predictors of future sales. Anticipatory data on inventories have been more accurate and more useful.

Although survey results often do not accurately predict turning points in business activity their promptness does suggest some possibilities for increasing forecasting accuracy. They can be used along with or as proxies for quantitative economic indicators.

In recent years, the Institute for Social Research at the University of Michigan has conducted more research into its surveys of consumers to produce the index of consumer sentiment. This index is based on questionnaire responses to monthly surveys of consumer attitudes. These periodic surveys provide regular assessments of consumer attitudes and expectations. They are often employed to evaluate business trends and prospects in the consumer-driven economy of the United States. The purpose of the surveys is to explore why changes in consumer attitudes and expectations occur and how these changes influence spending and saving decisions.

Figure 10.9 shows a saw-toothed pattern in the index of consumer expectations, which is the expectations component of the index of consumer sentiment. Fore-casters analyze the movement in this time series based on anticipation surveys to predict changes in the economy. As noted before, the index of consumer expectations is one of the eleven statistical time series which make up the index of leading indicators produced by the US Department of Commerce. This series was selected on the basis of its performance in predicting turning points in the economy. By performance, we mean economic significance, statistical adequacy, consistency of timing at cyclical peaks and troughs, conformity to business expansions and

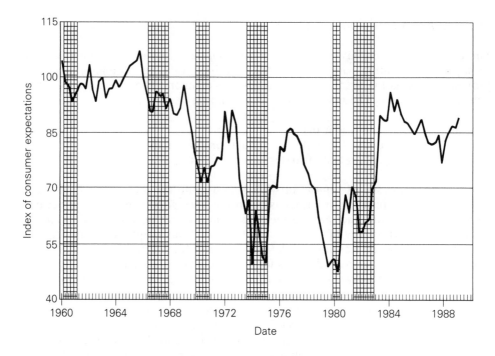

FIGURE 10.9 Index of consumer expectations: comparison of index with changes in the
economy (Note: shaded regions are contractions)
Source: Institute of Social Research, The University of Michigan, Ann Arbor, MI

contractions, and prompt availability. Like other indicators of change in the business economy, no one indicator or survey alone can predict perfectly. However, anticipation surveys along with other indicators can aid a forecaster in discerning trends and changes in the economy or some sector of the economy.

10.11   Diffusion Indexes

Diffusion indexes published in *Business Conditions Digest* attempt to measure how widely spread the existing stage of the cycle is. Specifically, they examine the changes in the degree of dispersion of a contraction or recovery rather than changes in the total.

These indexes are rates of changes and tend to anticipate the change in the direction of the aggregates themselves. For example, a diffusion index may consist of 12 subtotals for individual industries which, when added together, equal aggregate national employment. In general, aggregate employment is rising: more than half of the individual industries are experiencing rising employment and less than half are experiencing declining employment. If total employment is declining, the reverse would be true. If total employment is rising rapidly, then the great majority of the individual industries would be rising. Again, if total employment is falling rapidly, the opposite is true. The percentage of industries experiencing rising employment will change its direction well before a change of direction in aggregate employment, that is, the percentage statistics will begin declining when the *rate of increase* in total employment slows. When the rate of increase in aggregate employment stops (stable employment), the percentage will continue falling below 50 percent as aggregate employment begins declining. At the opposite end of the cycle, the percentage of series expanding will be lowest when the rate of decline in the aggregate is greatest, and the percentage will actually begin rising when the rate of decline in the aggregate slows.

The diffusion index measures the percentage of industries increasing, that is, the range of the index is from 0 to 100. The value of 50 is the neutral midpoint indicating a balance of expansive and contractive forces at work in the business system as a whole. A crossing of the midpoint is a very important event in the index since it indicates a reversal of a cyclical phase. However, diffusion indexes are erratic in behavior and may yield invalid signals by crossing the midpoint in either direction as a result of irregularity. Thus, diffusion indexes are limited tools marked by a considerable abstraction from reality. They cannot appropriately recognize a number of independent events which more general forecasting approaches can specifically embody. Finally, the lead of a diffusion index over the aggregate economic system tends to be variable so that conclusions are often difficult to draw.

Despite their shortcomings, the diffusion indexes allow for useful observations of the breadth and vigor of a cyclical movement. They provide an informative method for testing the depth of recovery and contraction. This is important since cyclical movements act in different ways in different sectors of the economy. In the next section, we shall see how this occurred in two sectors of the economy.

10.12   Studies of Cyclical Behavior: Some Case Studies

Cyclical behavior within an industry or sector is studied to see how changes in general business activity diffuse through a sector of the economy. Two such case studies are described in the next two examples.

Example 10.1

Duke and Brand (1981) studied the cyclical behavior of productivity in the machine tool industry. Their results indicate some useful observations concerning how the industry operates during economic downturns and recovery periods.

For example, during the severe economic downturns of the latter part of the Eisenhower administration (1957–8 and 1960–1), productivity growth was slow in part because of the industry's tendency to retain skilled workers during downturns. Computers and other electronic equipment did aid productivity but diffusion of such innovations was slow.

The diffusion of new technologies and innovations was slow in this industry because of the predominance of small firms producing small batches of frequently complex machinery and components. The industry is labor intensive, and the mass production techniques made possible by machine tools are of little use in building them. Slowdowns are a deterrent to increased productivity and only accelerating demand for machine tools will induce new investment in numerically controlled machine tool production. Under the spur of strong demand (an economic upturn), including investment in a recurrently labor-short industry will result in great productivity.

The above study indicates that a business cycle has specific effects on the industry studied. These effects may not be the same in other industries. To consider another industry, read the next short case history.

Example 10.2

Prices of industrial metals (copper, zinc, and lead) are influenced by the fluctuations in economic activity. For example, figure 10.10 indicates the monthly average price per pound (in cents) for the period 1973–81 and how it fluctuates during periods of downturn and expansion in general economic activity.

During the 1974–5 recession, the prices of metals climbed and metal producers tended to stockpile inventories of metals. After the recession, prices did not recover as producers worked off huge inventories. Producers had greatly underestimated the severity of the depression.

Beginning in the fall of 1981, a downturn in the nation's economy commenced. Unlike the period 1974–5, inventories of copper, zinc, and lead are much lower, indicating that these metals are poised for increases in prices. The relative smallness of the inventories can be the result of severe factors. First, inventory investments were kept low by metal producers based on their experience during the 1974–5 recession and its aftermath. Second, the high level of interest rates induced producers to invest less funds in stockpiling inventories.

By examining the effects of slackening economic activity on these metals industries in the past, producers have learned to adapt and alter their business strategies. Careful business planning by lead, zinc, and copper producers has permitted them to be in a much better economic position. Hence forecasting the prices of these metals becomes easier because of the acquired knowledge gained through the approach of relating general swings in business activity to the specific practices of firms in particular industries such as metals.

Industry analyses during periods of economic recovery and economic downturn provide forecasters with knowledge of special and very important facts about the

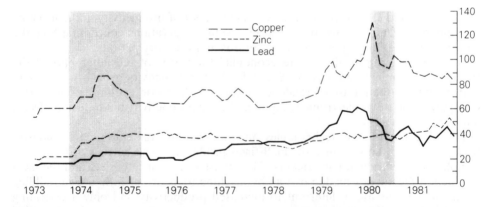

FIGURE 10.10 Prices of copper, lead, and zinc and the business cycle (Note: prices of metals are monthly averages in cents per pound. Shaded areas are periods of economic downturn as defined by the National Bureau of Economic Research (NBER))

industries and firms under study. Knowledge of these facts can permit the forecaster to predict turning points for an industry or firm. Special knowledge of how an industry behaves during different phases of the cycle thus provides forecasters with the ability to make predictions that are not otherwise possible.

10.13 The Delphi Method and Long-term Forecasting

Up to this point, we have considered methods of judgmental forecasting with short- and medium-term time horizons. A fairly common judgmental procedure for long-term forecasting is the *Delphi method*. This method consists of organizing a group of "experts" who will give their own views and opinions as to the future direction of business conditions, business activity, technology, product development, or market changes. These views include (a) predictions on the usefulness of new products, (b) the desirability of new products, (c) the direction of existing product lines, and (d) the desirability of abandoning existing products, product lines, and/or technologies. To insure that their opinions are their own, the experts are kept apart. However, the experts are informed periodically about the "average" or "typical" opinion. Upon review of the opinions of all experts, a consensus or median forecast of the future is put together by the person in charge of the Delphi forecasting.

To illustrate the Delphi forecasting process, let us consider the method as a series of discrete steps.

1 A panel of experts is employed for forecasting by a particular firm, agency, or institution which wishes to have a long-term forecast of economic activity made. These experts come from outside as well as inside the organization. If the problem under consideration is very complex, such as the need for new laser technology in medicine, the experts may be authoritative only on various subsections of the problem. One expert may be a physicist who is an expert on laser technology while another may be a surgeon who is an expert on complex eye surgery. In very complex problems the panel may be divided into several subpanels, each having authority on one or more subsections of the problem. The individual subpanels thus focus on various subsections to which they have the knowledge to contribute.
2 The experts are given the write-up and are presented (often orally as well as by written report) with the business forecasting problem. A typical scenario would be to predict new product technology utilizing laser concepts up to the year 2000. Another scenario could be to predict the acceptance of a new product or product line five years or more in the future. Usually, the experts respond in writing with their opinions expressed separately to minimize the probability of bias that is common to small group behavior. For example, if two experts were to interact in some way, it is likely that one would persuade the other about the wisdom of his/her prediction or opinion. The experts are instructed to forecast by any method they wish and incorporate in their projections any assumptions that they believe are relevant. Naturally, the Delphi process may specify the various methods and assumptions within which the experts are asked to operate. At the conclusion, the experts return their completed forecast scenarios to the coordinator of the Delphi process.
3 Upon receipt of all the forecast scenarios, the coordinator ranks the returns and the assumptions used in the returns. Each expert is, in turn, sent a second problem questionnaire asking if they would also give reasons why their final responses

differ from the "typical" or "median" forecast. The second questionnaire usually asks for more precise quantification of their final forecast. This follow-up stage is continually replicated until the experts no longer change their opinion in any significant manner. The purpose of the repetition is to narrow the range of options open to the experts and allow the coordinator to focus on the likely technological advances or other variables under consideration. One major disadvantage of asking the experts to revise their forecasts is that their judgment is influenced by others. The problem here is that the influence may move an expert to change a very accurate prediction because of the errors of others.

Although the use of expert subjective opinion by the Delphi method has proven to be popular in many organizations, there are many critics of its use. One difficulty in using the Delphi method is actually to explain the problem situation to a great many experts in the panel. If the problem is not adequately explained, the expert is often not able to understand what he/she is required to do.

The coordinator has a difficult job to rank the qualitative answers received from the respondents. In some cases, this may prove to be nearly impossible and result in the bias of the coordinator entering the process directly. When the panel of experts is small, group bias may lead to erroneous predictions. A well-developed Delphi system should minimize this bias, but it can be a serious problem when Delphi is initialized.

Selecting a panel of experts can be an exhausting and expensive process. Many leading authorities from universities, private foundations, industry, and government are usually employed. A great deal of care is required in the selection process since there is a tendency to use the same experts on many panels. One such expert told the author how he became resistant to the process after he was asked to participate on a large number of panels. He believed that his opinions had started to lose their reliability. If this persists in any one organization, the Delphi process tends to lead to the same conclusions all the time. Finally, the main difference between Delphi and other subjective (qualitative) methods is the use of many independent opinions in the process of forecasting. Obviously, this has both benefits and disadvantages, as noted above.

10.14 Summary

Qualitative approaches to forecasting consist of techniques which are not wholly dependent upon the analysis of numerical data.

The NBER approach to predicting business cycles couples judgment with an explicit recognition that economic statisticians can produce viable indicators of business activity.

A business cycle consists of expansion occurring at about the same time in many economic activities followed by similarly general recessions, contractions, and revivals which merge into the expansionary phase of the next cycle.

No single measure of the nation's economic activity is available, whether in terms of income, expenditures, employment, or output over a long period of time on a monthly or quarterly basis, that is comparable throughout its coverage or adequate throughout in its statistical foundation.

Cycles are characterized by periods of expansion (recovery), contraction (recession or downturn), peaks, and troughs. Phases of business cycles are recurring but their lengths and intensity vary.

A large part of the judgmental process of predicting fluctuations in the economy and how they affect individual industries and firms requires the use of significant indicators of general economic activity. Specific measures of economic activity include gross national product (GNP), the index of industrial production (IIP), the unemployment rate, the number of housing starts, the consumer price index (CPI), and the producer price index (PPI).

The index of leading indicators contains 11 items chosen because historical evidence indicates that they lead swings of the economy in either direction.

Early warning systems based on the growth rate in leading and coincident indicators provide forecasters with a tool for predicting, with some accuracy, changes in general economic conditions. An early warning system based on a composite index of employment percentage, industrial materials prices and outstanding debt was developed to predict changes in inflation as measured by the CPI. Finally, a composite leading index for the service sector has been developed.

Surveys of consumers and business decision-makers can provide useful information concerning their buying and investment plans and intentions. However, such surveys have not been found to be foolproof in predicting turning points in general economic activities. They can be of use when combined with other indicators.

A diffusion index indicates the dispersion of a cyclical movement in specific sectors of the economy.

Studies of industry and firm behavior during business cycles can produce specific knowledge concerning the behavior of prices, productivity, employment, and other factors during different phases of the cycle. Such information is invaluable in a wise and rational prediction of behavior of a firm or industry during the cycle.

The Delphi process is a method by which expert judgment is used to forecast future changes in technology and product development, among other activities. It requires the careful use of a small group of experts in various disciplines.

10.15   Exercises

Unlike previous chapters, numerical exercises are not of particular importance in understanding this chapter.

1 Choose a specific economic variable for any industry or sector of the economy. Plot the data over a lengthy period (at least ten years) on a graph. Try and determine whether this economic time series precedes, is roughly coincident, or lags the peaks and troughs of the cycle. (Recall that dates of the cycle can be found in *Business Conditions Digest* and in this chapter.)

2 For the latest 12 month period, collect data on the index of leading indicators and the index of roughly coincident indicators. Use the early warning system analysis to determine if there are signals of recovery or contraction.

3 For any particular sector of the consumer price index or producer price index, collect data over a lengthy period (at least ten years). Plot the data and comment on the behavior of series during the phases of the cycle.

4 For any particular sector of the index of industrial production, collect data over a lengthy period (at least ten years). Comment on the behavior of this economic time series during specific phases of the business cycle.

5 For any economic time series, choose a lengthy period to be studied. Comment on the behavior of this time series during different phases of the cycle.

6 Examine a recent issue of *Business Conditions Digest* and determine for a particular sector of the economy the meaning of the diffusion index.

7 Track the business forecasts in a publication such as *Fortune, Business Week*, or another business periodical against later reported figures. Is the track record of the periodical optimistic, pessimistic, or on target? Discuss.

8 Track prices of industrial metals, commodities, or construction costs over a ten year period. Discuss the way that the time series behaves during periods of expansion and contraction. Does the time series anticipate or follow turning points? Why?

9 Collect data on production in a particular industry, for a period of five years or more, from the *Survey of Current Business*. Collect data for the same period from the index of leading indicators. Discuss the movement of the production data as it relates (or does not relate) to the index of leading indicators.

10 Track the consumer price index (for all urban consumers) and the composite index of inflation over a period of five years. Does the composite index lead the CPI? By how long? Discuss.

11 A small island in the Caribbean sea, named Moa-Moa, has two sources of income. The first is generated from tourists from the United States and the second is the sales of a rare fruit, largely to Puerto Rico. In Puerto Rico, the fruit is made into a sweet fruit drink, most of which is exported to the United States. Suggest a leading, a roughly coincident, and a lagging indicator for the Moa-Moa economy.

12 Do you believe that any of the following time series would be good indicators of anything?
(a) The number of requests for Sears catalogs.
(b) The number of business failures in the State of Texas.
(c) The number of speeding and other moving violations issued on Florida's turnpike.
(d) The number of building permits issued in the State of California.
(e) The number of children born to local stockbrokers in the State of Virginia.

13 Diego Diego is a ruler of a small island paradise 3000 miles southwest of San Francisco. He wishes to put controls on the money supply in his nation to stem the hard currency outflow. As a college graduate, fluent in several languages, he read a book on business forecasting suggesting the following three methods to predict inflation:
(a) A composite index which predicts change in the CPI for all urban American consumers.
(b) Box–Jenkins ARIMA modeling.
(c) Econometric methods.
Of the three methods which would provide the best forecasts for Diego Diego's island paradise? Discuss and suggest why your choice will produce the best method for analyzing the effects of changes in monetary policy on the island.

References

Bails, D. G. and Peppers, L. C. (1982) *Business Fluctuations; Forecasting Techniques and Applications*. Englewood Cliffs, NJ: Prentice-Hall.

Burns, A. F. and Mitchell, W. C. (1946) *Measuring Business Cycles*. New York: National Bureau of Economic Research.

Business Conditions Digest, various issues. Washington, DC: US Department of Commerce.

Dauten, C. A. and Valentine, L. M. (1974) *Business Cycles and Forecasting*. Cincinnati, OH: Southwestern.

Duke, J. and Brand, H. (1981) Cyclical behavior of productivity in the machine tool industry, *Monthly Labour Review*, 104, November, 27–34.

Fels, R. and Hinshaw, C. E. (1968) *Forecasting and Recognizing Business Cycle Turning Points*. New York: Columbia University Press for the National Bureau of Economic Research.

Klein, P. A. and Moore, G. H. (1982) The leading indicator approach to economic forecasting – retrospect and prospect, *Journal of Forecasting*, 2(2), 119–36.

Layton, A. P. and Moore, G. H. (1989) Leading indicators for the service sector, *Journal of Business and Economic Statistics,* 7(3), 379–86.

Mitchell, W. C. (1941) *Business Cycles and their Causes*. Berkeley, CA: University of California Press.

Moore, G. H. (1980) *Business Cycles Inflation and Forecasting*. Cambridge, MA: Ballinger.

Morgan Guaranty Trust Company of New York (1983) *Morgan Guarantee Survey*, July, 9.

Survey of Current Business, various issues. Washington, DC: US Department of Commerce.

Zarnowitz, V. and Moore, G. H. (1982) Sequential signals of recession and recovery, *Journal of Business*, 35(1), 57–85.

Further Reading

Angle, E. W. (1980) *Keys for Business Forecasting*. Richmond, VA: Federal Reserve Bank of Richmond.

Baldwin, G. H. (1982) The Delphi technique and the forecasting of specific fringe benefits, *Futures*, August, 319–24.

Banerji, A., and Boschan, C. (1989), Constructing a time-consistent composite index: an eclectic approach. Working paper, Center for International Business Cycle Research. Columbia University.

Boehm, E. A. and Moore, G. H. (1984) New economic indicators for Australia, 1949–1984, *Australian Economic Review*, 34–56.

Cohen, M. (1966) Surveys and forecasting. In W. F. Butler and R. A. Kavesh (eds), *How Business Economists Forecast*. Englewood Cliffs, NJ: Prentice-Hall.

Gershuny, J. I. and Miles, I. D. (1983) *The New Service Economy*. New York: Praeger.

Granger, C. W. J. (1989) *Forecasting in Business and Economics*. New York: Academic Press, ch. 7.

Handbook of Cyclical Indicators: A Supplement to the Business Conditions Digest, Washington, DC: US Department of Commerce, 1984.

Kennessey, Z. (1988) *Methodology of the Experimental Service Index*. Washington, DC: Federal Reserve Board, Output and Capacity Series.

Klein, P. A. and Moore, G. H. (1985) *Monitoring Growth Cycles in Market-oriented Countries*. Cambridge, MA: Ballinger.

Laumer, H. and Ziegler, M. (eds) (1982) *International Research on Business Cycle Surveys*. London: Gower.

Layton, A. P. (1987), Australian and U.S. growth cycle linkages, 1967–1983, *Journal of Macroeconomics*, 9, 31–44.

Lempert, L. H. (1966) Leading indicators. In W. F. Butler and R. A. Kavesh (eds), *How Business Economists Forecast*. Englewood Cliffs, NJ: Prentice-Hall, 31–47.

Moore, G. H. (1987) The service industries and the business cycle, *Business Economics*, 22, 12–17.

Sackman, H. (1975) *Delphi Critique*. Lexington, MA: Lexington Books.

Sommers, A. T. (1966) Diffusion indexes. In W. F. Butler and R. A. Kovesh (eds), *How Business Economists Forecast*. Englewood Cliffs, NJ: Prentice-Hall, 48–54.

Stekler, O. and Schepsman, M. (1973) Forecasting with an index of leading indicators, *Journal of the American Statistical Association*, 68, 291–5.

Appendix   Books on Related Methods used for Forecasting

Sample Surveys

Cochran, W. G. (1977) *Sampling Techniques*, 3rd edn. New York: Wiley.

Deming, W. E. (1960) *Sample Design in Business Research*. New York: Wiley.

Hess, I. (1985) *Sampling for Social Research Surveys, 1974–1980*. Ann Arbor, MI: Institute for Social Research.

Jessen, R. J. (1978) *Statistical Survey Techniques*. New York: Wiley.

Kish, L. (1965) *Survey Sampling*. New York: Wiley.

Sanquist, J. A. and Dunkelberg, W. C. (1977) *Survey and Opinion Research: Procedures for Processing and Analysis*. Englewood Cliffs, NJ: Prentice-Hall.

Schaeffer, R. L., Menderhall, W., and Ott, L. (1986) *Elementary Survey Sampling*, 3rd edn. North Scituate, MA: Duxbury.

Sudman, S. (1976) *Applied Sampling*. New York: Academic Press.

Williams, B. (1978) *A Sampler on Sampling*. New York: Wiley.

Yates, F. (1981) *Sampling Methods for Censuses and Surveys*. London: Griffin.

Market and Marketing Research

Dodge, H. R., Fullerton, S. D. and Rink, D. R. (1982) *Marketing Research*. Columbus, OH: Charles E. Merrill.

Douglas, S. and Craig, S. (1983) *International Marketing Research*. Englewood Cliffs, NJ: Prentice-Hall.

Ferber, R. (ed.) (1974) *Handbook of Marketing Research*. New York: McGraw-Hill.

Green, P. E., Tull, D. S. and Albaum, G. (1988) *Research for Marketing Decisions*, 5th edn. Englewood Cliffs, NJ: Prentice-Hall.

Kinnear, T. C. and Taylor, J. R. (1987) *Marketing Research: An Applied Approach*. New York: McGraw-Hill.

Petersen, R. A. (1982) *Marketing Research*. Plano, TX: Business Publications.

Tull, D. S. and Hawkins, D. I. (1987) *Marketing Research: Measurement and Method*. New York: Macmillan.

Technological Forecasting

Ayres, R. U. (1969) *Technological Forecasting and Long-Range Planning*, New York: McGraw-Hill.

Blohm, H. and Steinbuch, K. (1973) *Technological Forecasting in Practice*. Lexington, MA: Lexington Books.

Blohm, H., Steinbuch, K. and Schoeman, M. E. F. (eds) (1973) *A Guide to Practical Technological Forecasting*. Englewood Cliffs, NJ: Prentice-Hall.

Cetron, M. (1971) *Industrial Applications of Technological Forecasting*. New York: Wiley.

Martino, J. P. (1985) *Technological Forecasting for Decision Making*. New York: Elsevier.

National Science Foundation (1977) *The Study of the Future: An Agenda for Research* (NSF/RA-770036). Washington, DC: US Government Printing Office.

PART VI

Issues In Forecasting

CHAPTER 11

Forecast Evaluation, Revision, and Business Planning and Control

Objectives

The purpose of this book is to introduce to management and educate would-be forecasters in the wide variety of forecasting methods available today. In this chapter, the key link between forecasting and management is explored. You will see that forecasting is a process which contributes to the managerial goals of planning and control. In addition, by the end of this chapter you will be introduced to methods for evaluating past forecasts and revising forecasts to improve accuracy. In particular, you will be able to:

1 Statistically test for the presence of bias.
2 Measure accuracy by five measures of forecast error.
3 Analyze the sources of forecast error.
4 Revise a forecast to improve accuracy.

Outline

11.1 Introduction

11.2 Forecasting's Place in Management (Summary)

11.3 Criteria for Choosing a Forecasting Technique

11.4 Analyzing Forecast Error

11.5 Improving Business Forecasts: A Case Study

11.6 Forecasting and Information Systems

11.7 Data Sources and their Limitations

11.8 Database Management Systems

11.9 Forecasting Consulting and Data Banks

11.10 Managing the Forecasting Function

11.11 Summary

Key Terms

- Bias
- Mean Error
- Root Mean Square Error

- *U* statistic
- Decomposing MSE
- Optimal Linear Forecasting

11.1 Introduction

The purpose of this book has been to outline for the reader the most common and useful forecasting techniques available to business management, policy-makers, and those involved in decision support in all areas. At the beginning, the reader was introduced to extrapolative techniques called moving averages and exponential smoothing. As these models were shown to be restricted, adaptive and more sophisticated smoothing and moving average models were introduced.

In chapter 3 the methods of time series decomposition were introduced. Decomposition methods permitted the forecaster to separate the systematic components – trend cycle, seasonal, trading day – from the randomness in time series data. Chapters 4 and 5 introduced the useful methods of regression and correlation. These methods permit the forecaster to separate pattern from randomness in data by relating the time series variable to one or more explanatory variables in building a model. These methods were extended to building a general system of linear systems called an econometric model. This multi-equation causal model provided a method by which forecasters can predict the outcome of various policy actions and permit business to be able to develop strategies in keeping with those outcomes. These models are based on economic theories and estimated by the methods of regression for multi-equation systems.

Chapters 7, 8, and 9 were concerned with the statistically based methods of time series analysis known as autoregressive integrated moving-average (ARIMA) processes. The essence of this approach is similar to exponential smoothing and decomposition methods in that these processes are based on historical time series analysis. However, the ARIMA approach employed unique methods for identifying patterns in such time series and extrapolating them into the future. Chapters 7 and 8 presented the basis for ARIMA schemes and included a study of autocorrelation analysis, stationarity, invertibility, and seasonality, and defined autoregressive (AR), moving-average (MA), and autoregressive moving-average (ARMA) processes. A method for estimating these models, called adaptive filtering, was also outlined. Finally, Box–Jenkins methods were studied in chapter 9. These methods were found to embody statistical techniques for analyzing, identifying, and forecasting time series.

Since the problem of predicting cycles or turning points is an elusive one for quantitative techniques, chapter 10 outlined judgmental methods used to study these movements in time series. This study embodied those methods of the National Bureau for Economic Research (NBER) and the Center for International Business Cycle Research, the use of leading indicators, and other subjective methods. The purpose of the study of these methods was to permit the forecaster to combine judgment with the results of quantitative forecasts.

By understanding the methods of forecasting, the forecaster can influence administrative decision-making and planning. The purpose of this chapter is to serve the reader in defining several important issues surrounding the effective use of a forecast in an organization.

These problems include those of information management, data procurement and data handling and preparation. In particular, we wish to minimize the tasks associated with information management and succeed in making the forecasting function an integral part of the strategic decision-making of a firm.

Before the information management function is discussed, the nature of planning and its relation to forecasting and forecasting methodologies must be examined. We must integrate the forecasting methods with the purposes of planning and control.

11.2   Forecasting's Place in Management (Summary)

Two key functions of management for any enterprise or institution are planning and control. Firms must plan for the future, and planning for the future involves a series of steps. One such series of steps is as follows.

1 Determine the product and geographic markets where the firm can achieve the goals of profit maximization and, perhaps, the largest contribution to society.
2 Forecast demand in these markets under different conditions of promotion, price, competition, and general economic activity.
3 Forecast the costs of production and marketing different levels of output under conditions of changing technology and input prices.
4 Choose the best plan of operations, that is, the one that maximizes the well-being of the firm.
5 Implement personnel training, capital construction, and acquisition programs to carry out the general corporate plan.

Once the corporate plan has been established, it is carried out in the operating or control phase of corporate activity. Planning and control are thus closely related and are not usually separable. The process of control is geared to the corporate plan. If the forecasts of demand or input costs are in error, the plan can be adjusted based on revised forecasts. If forecasts are seriously in error, then the plan will be inoperable and the control phase will break down.

Since forecasting has a key role in business planning it is not surprising that management emphasizes its importance. In the preceding chapters, we have examined a large number of forecasting techniques. In summary, the problem facing the forecaster is to decide which is the most appropriate, given the environment of business planning and control.

11.3   Criteria for Choosing a Forecasting Technique

If forecasting is to be an integral part of the planning and control activities of a firm, the selection of a forecasting technique should be based on criteria which are sensible and wise. Geurts (1981–2) summarized the selection criteria as follows:

1 ease of use and expense;
2 lack of bias;
3 least forecasting error.

The forecaster should be guided as to ease of use by past experience and the number of items to be forecast. If the number is large, exponential and extrapolative methods are preferable since econometric and Box–Jenkins techniques require a separate model for each item. Extrapolative techniques are easier to use, less expensive to implement, and easier for unsophisticated management to interpret.

Econometric techniques generally have huge data requirements and are more expensive in computer usage than Box–Jenkins methods. Hence the popularity of

Box–Jenkins methods with professional forecasters is largely due to their relative ease of use and low cost.

A good technique should be free from *bias*, that is, it should not consistently overforecast nor underforecast. Bias leads to serious managerial problems. Business plans would obviously be wrong if the forecasts that they are based on are in error. A common way of checking for the bias in forecasting is to keep a check on the errors by recording the overforecasts (+) and underforecasts (−). If there is a consistent number of overforecasts (+) or underforecasts (−), bias exists. Stated simply, if we find this consistency, then the *mean error* (ME)

$$ME = \sum \frac{Y - \hat{Y}}{N} \tag{11.1}$$

is not equal to zero and bias exists. A periodic count of just the signs of the forecast error will indicate whether the ME is not zero and bias is likely to be present. It was shown in chapter 2, that simple moving-average and single exponential smoothing techniques often resulted in forecasts that were biased in one direction or another for nonstationary time series. If bias is likely to be present, a suggestion was to see whether there is a significant difference between the expected number of positive signs and the observed number of positive signs. This suggestion employs a χ^2 test as follows:

$$\chi^2 = \sum \frac{(O_i - E_i)^2}{E_i} \tag{11.2}$$

where O and E are observed and expected values. In equation (11.2) the expected number of positive (or negative) signs of the errors equals 0.50 of all errors. To see how this statistic applies consider the next example.

Example 11.1

In example 2.2, data on manufacturing inventories (1972 dollars by month, seasonally adjusted) for the United States for 1981 was used to forecast. The observed and forecast values are contained in table 2.3 of chapter 2. For periods 2–11, the following errors were found: +0.3, +0.5, +0.7, +0.8, +0.3, +0.7, +1.4, +1.5, +1.2, and +0.4. Thus, there are eleven plus signs and zero minus signs. It is likely that biased forecasts exist. Can we test this assumption? Yes, by the χ^2 test denoted before.

The following summarizes the method assuming that no bias exists and 0.50 of the forecasts are 1 plus and 0.50 are minus:

	Observed	Expected
+	11	0.50 × 11 = 5.5
−	0	0.50 × 11 = 5.5
Total	11	11.0

Since there are two categories, the number of degrees of freedom is one (one less than the number of categories). The hypotheses are as follows:

H$_o$: there are an equal number of positive and negative forecasts
H$_A$: the number of positive and negative forecasts are not equal

With one degree of freedom and assuming a 5 percent risk of rejecting a true null hypothesis, the critical χ^2 value is 3.841. Thus, we would conclude that the number of positive and negative forecasts are not equal if the sample χ^2 value exceeds 3.841. The computations are

$$\chi^2 = \frac{(0 - 5.5)^2}{5.5} + \frac{(0 - 5.5)^2}{5.5} = 11.0$$

Hence, at the 0.05 risk level, we can conclude that the numbers of overforecasts and underforecasts (positive and negative forecasts) are not equal for this data set. This result was expected and the χ^2 statistic merely confirms our previous observations.

The final and perhaps the most important criterion for selecting forecasting models is accuracy. Accuracy is the absence of error, and error is defined by

$$e_t = Y_t - \hat{Y}_t \tag{11.3}$$

Y_t and $\hat{Y}_t$ are observed (actual) and predicted values. Choosing a measure of forecast accuracy (the absence of error) is related to the environment of the decision-maker and the goals of evaluating forecasts. A rich literature exists and the reader is advised to examine, among others, Beaver et al. (1979), Brandon and Jarrett (1974, 1977, 1979, 1986), Brandon et al. (1983), Copeland and Marioni (1972), Demski and Feltham (1972), Harris (1966), Jenkins (1983), Makridakis et al. (1982), Malcolm and Fraser (1977), and Salamon and Smith (1977). Since the demand for forecast evaluations emanates from the users as well as the preparers of forecasts, the goal of evaluating forecasts is to produce the best business decisions. Users and preparers of forecasts evaluate historical performance as the basis of judging future accuracy.

The purpose of evaluating the accuracy of forecasts is to find the best forecasting techniques. Forecasters define measures of accuracy in operational terms, that is, the measure is quantitative. Also, the measure reflects the consequences associated with forecasting errors resulting from predictions that are unequal to their realizations. The proximity of the forecast to the actual or realized value reflects the seriousness of these consequences in terms of either gain or loss. By gain or loss, we refer to a measurement system which incorporates the severity of forecast errors. Thus, several measures of forecast error are commonly used.

Mean absolute percentage error (MAPE) as defined in chapter 2 is[1]

$$\text{MAPE} = \frac{1}{n} \sum \frac{e_t}{\hat{Y}_t} \times 100 \tag{11.4}$$

MAPE measures the severity of forecast errors as the absolute value of the difference between prediction and realization relative to the realization. This measure is appropriate whenever the error is linear and symmetric.

Mean square error (MSE), defined initially in chapter 2, is given by

$$\text{MSE} = \frac{\Sigma e_t^2}{n} \tag{11.5}$$

---

1   Note that $\hat{Y}$ is the forecast (predicted) value for Y. In chapter 2 the forecast value was denoted by F.

MSE measures accuracy as the quadratic loss or how larger errors contribute disproportionately to inaccuracy when compared with small errors. Often, we take the square root of MSE as follows:

$$(MSE)^{1/2} = \left(\frac{\Sigma e^2}{n}\right)^{1/2}$$

(11.6)

which is called the *root mean square error* (RMS). Some prefer RMS over MSE because RMS has the same units of measurement as the realized series and is thus easier to interpret. The implied distribution of errors is quadratic since the error increases in proportion to the square of the error. A disadvantage of RMS and MSE is that they are absolute measures and penalize severely for large errors.

One final measure of accuracy, which is entitled the U statistic and was developed by Theil (1965, pp. 32–8), is defined by

$$U = \left(\frac{MSE}{S_Y^2 + S_{\hat{Y}}^2}\right)^{1/2}$$

(11.7)

The U *statistic* is the ratio of the square root of MSE divided by the sum of the variances of the observed and predicted values. If the technique forecasts perfectly ($e_t = 0$ for all t), $U = 0$. Alternatively, if $U = 1$, the technique is generating erroneous forecasts. In figure 11.1, the actual changes in the data are measured along the vertical axis, and forecast changes are measured along the horizontal axis. The 45° line represents the perfect forecast, that is, when $U = 0$. Areas IB and IIIB are areas of underprediction of observed changes ($Y - \hat{Y} > 0$). In a similar way,

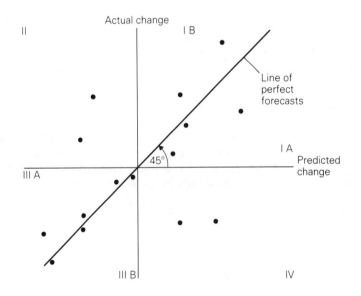

FIGURE 11.1 A comparison of predicted and observed changes in a forecast

areas IA are areas of overprediction of observed changes $(Y - \hat{Y} < 0)$. If most of the points fall in these areas, then $0 \leqslant U \leqslant 1$. Finally, areas II and IV are regions of turning-point error; that is, the model predicted an increase when in fact there was a decrease (IV), and a decrease when there was an increase (II). If the majority of points lie in these quadrants, U approaches unity, indicating that the technique employed to generate the predicted changes is not satisfactory. However, we should note that Theil's U statistic cannot be examined in isolation. Consider the next example.

Example 11.2

In example 2.9, data on new plant and equipment expenditures, total nonfarm business (billion dollars, unadjusted) was forecast using Winters' linear and seasonal exponential smoothing model. The data for the observed and forecast values were presented in table 2.13 and are presented again in table 11.1 without the inter-mediate values used for calculating the forecast. At this point, we shall evaluate this forecast by the definition of bias and measures of accuracy (or forecast error) as follows:

$$ME = \frac{(66.8 - 66.8) + (68.4 - 67.9) + \ldots}{11}$$

$$= 0.064$$

$$MAPE = \frac{(|66.8 - 66.8|/66.8) + (|68.4 - 67.9|/67.9) + \ldots}{11}$$

$$= 0.012 \quad \text{or} \quad 1.2 \text{ percent}$$

TABLE 11.1   Original values, forecasts, and errors for the data of example 2.9

(1)	(2) Observed	(3)	(4)	(5)
Period t	values Y	Forecast $\hat{Y}$	Error $e = Y - \hat{Y}$	$(Error)^2$ e^2
2	66.8	66.8	0.0	0.00
3	68.4	67.9	0.5	0.25
4	78.0	76.2	1.8	3.24
5	65.2	63.9	1.3	1.69
6	74.0	74.1	−0.1	0.01
7	74.1	75.7	−1.6	2.56
8	82.3	84.6	−2.3	5.29
9	69.8	69.8	0.0	0.00
10	79.6	79.7	−0.1	0.01
11	81.8	80.6	1.2	1.44
12	90.4	90.4	0.0	0.00

$$\text{MSE} = \frac{(66.8 - 66.8)^2 + (68.4 - 67.9)^2 + \ldots}{11}$$

$$= 1.317$$

$$\text{RMS} = 1.148$$

Since each measure of forecast error (accuracy) has a different formula, each measure results in a different value. The value of ME is negative indicating that on average, the forecast, was smaller than the observed values, the bias. For MAPE, the value was small in comparison with the values of the observations. MSE measures the mean of the square of the error terms. Large errors have a disproportionate weight in measuring the size of the error. Theil's U statistic is calculated as follows:

$$U = \left(\frac{\text{MSE}}{S_Y^2 + S_{\hat{Y}}^2}\right)^{1/2}$$

$$= \left(\frac{1.317}{(7.7452)^2 + (8.0709)^2}\right)^{1/2}$$

$$= 0.1026$$

A value of 0.1026 indicates that the forecasting method is not generating perfect prediction. However, the value of U is closer to zero than to unity, indicating that the forecasts are generally good.

It is impossible to evaluate any of the above measures in isolation. If ME, MAPE, and MSE are smaller for one forecast than for another, the former would be more accurate. Similarly, if a second forecast achieved a U value greater than 0.1026, then the first method would be best.

Finally, the forecaster, when determining the best forecasting model to use, must be aware that ME, MAPE, MSE, or Theil's U statistic are not enough to distinguish between models.

An analysis of bias should also be part of the procedure to determine the best forecasting model. Equally important is the criterion of ease and expense of usage. By considering all criteria, the forecaster can choose the "best" model for forecasting.

11.4 Analyzing Forecast Error

An important feature of MSE is that error increases disproportionately, that is, quadratically, as the forecast deviates from the observed values, reflecting the increased seriousness and consequences of large errors. If we consider MSE as a measure of forecast accuracy, the MSE function can be decomposed as follows:

$$\text{MSE} = (Y - \hat{Y})^2 + S_Y^2 + S_{\hat{Y}}^2 - 2rS\,YS_{\hat{Y}}$$

$$(11.8)$$

where Y and $\hat{Y}$ are the means of observed and predicted values, S_Y^2 and $S_{\hat{Y}}^2$ are the variances of observed and predicted values, and r is the coefficient of correlation between observed and predicted values.

To find those conditions under which forecast error is minimized, we find[2]

$$\overline{\hat{Y}} = \overline{Y}$$

and

$$S_{\hat{Y}} = rS_Y$$

To achieve minimum forecast error, the forecast model must be unbiased and the standard deviation of the forecasts should be equal to the product of the correlation of forecasts and observed values and the standard deviation of the observed values. Furthermore, if $r = 1$, that is, perfect positive correlation, the standard deviation of forecast and observed values are the same.

If both the above conditions hold, MSE is zero and Theil's U statistic is zero, and the forecasts are perfect. This conclusion is important because it indicates a method by which one can improve forecast performance, specifically by *decomposing MSE* into its components and examining the proportion of the total error attributable to each source of error. Several forecast evaluations and researchers (Granger and Newbold, 1973; Jorgenson et al., 1970; Mincer and Zarnowitz, 1969; Theil, 1971) suggested the following indices which indicate the relative importance of each source of error:

$$E^m = \frac{(\overline{Y} - \overline{\hat{Y}})^2}{\text{MSE}} \tag{11.9}$$

$$E^s = \frac{(S_Y - S_{\hat{Y}})^2}{\text{MSE}} \tag{11.10}$$

$$E^c = \frac{2(1 - r)S_Y S_{\hat{Y}}}{\text{MSE}} \tag{11.11}$$

$$E^m + E^s + E^c = 1 \tag{11.12}$$

Note that the first component, E^m, is the proportion of error attributable to bias. The second component, E^s, is the proportion of error due to differences in the

---

2   To find the conditions under which forecast error is minimized, we first evaluate the partial derivatives of the MSE with respect to the mean of the predicted and actual (observed) values:

$$\frac{\partial(\text{MSE})}{\partial \overline{\hat{Y}}} = -2(\overline{Y} - \overline{\hat{Y}})$$

$$\frac{\partial(\text{MSE})}{\partial S_{\hat{Y}}} = -2(S_{\hat{Y}} - rS_Y)$$

$$\frac{\partial(\text{MSE})}{\partial r} = -2S_Y S_{\hat{Y}}$$

To optimize, each of the three partial derivatives is set equal to zero.

standard deviations of predicted and observed values. The third component, E^c, is the proportion of error due to the inability of the forecaster to estimate the correlation between the observed and predicted series. The two sources of errors can be reduced over time but the covariance portion is more difficult to handle and is not easy to control (Theil, 1971, p. 32).

Many have studied the usefulness of the decomposition to determine how management and forecasters can improve forecasting accuracy. Granger and New-bold (1973) studied this process by comparing it with an autoregressive process as follows:

$$Y_t = \phi_1 \hat{Y}_{t-1} + e_t \qquad 0 \leqslant \phi_1 \leqslant 1 \tag{11.13}$$

The equation is an AR(1) process with the optimal next-period predictor being

$$\hat{Y} = \overline{e}_t = 0 \tag{11.14}$$

As the number of observations approaches infinity, the means of the predicted and observed series converge $(\overline{Y} = \overline{\hat{Y}})$ and the first proportion E^m approaches zero. This is the result observed when the MSE and U statistics are optimized with respect to the mean of the predictor $\hat{Y}$. Furthermore, as the number of observations increases, the variance component approaches $1 - \phi$ and the mean square approaches $1 + \phi$ such that

$$E^s \rightarrow \frac{1 - \phi}{1 + \phi} \tag{11.15}$$

The third proportion approaches 2 as follows:

$$E^c \rightarrow \frac{2}{1 + \phi} \tag{11.16}$$

As the parameter ϕ varies from zero to unity, then E^s and E^c take different values with the restriction that $E^s + E^c = 1$. Thus Granger and Newbold (1973, p. 45) concluded that the interpretation of these quantities is impossible.

Fortunately, a second decomposition of MSE leads to a more meaningful method for improving forecast performance. The alternative decomposition is as follows:

$$\text{MSE} = (\overline{\hat{Y}} - \overline{Y})^2 + (S_{\hat{Y}} - rS_Y)^2 + (1 - r^2)S_Y^2 \tag{11.17}$$

This decomposition is restated in terms of the relative importance of each source of error:

$$E^m = (\frac{\overline{Y} - \overline{\hat{Y}})^2}{\text{MSE}} \tag{11.18}$$

$$E^r = \frac{(S_{\hat{Y}} - rS_Y)^2}{\text{MSE}} \tag{11.19}$$

$$E^d = \frac{(1 - r^2)S_Y^2}{\text{MSE}} \tag{11.20}$$

where E^m is the proportion of error associated with bias, E^r is the slope component, and E^d is the residual or random component. Furthermore,

$$E^m + E^s + E^d = 1 \qquad (11.21)$$

This decomposition is more appropriate for an AR(1) model because E^m and E^r fall to zero as the number of observations increases. Furthermore, these results are obtained when one utilizes the methods of Theil's *optimal linear forecasting* (OLF) method (Theil, 1971) where the mean and slope component are removed based upon a regression of the actual values of a series on the predicted values. The remaining error becomes the residual component which is a standard error of regression. In this case, the size of the MSE equals the complement of the coefficient of determination between the predicted and observed values and the variance of the predicted series. Since the numerator of E is

$$(1 - r^2)S_Y^2 = S_Y^2 - \frac{S_{Y\hat{Y}}^2}{S_{\hat{Y}}^2} \qquad (11.22)$$

the residual component is recognized as the difference between the variance of the actual series less the ratio of the covariance of the observed and predicted series to the variance of the predicted series. When all the forecasts equal the observed values, then the linear regression of observed values on predicted values will produce a bias or slope error of zero. In that case, the slope of the regression is unity, the intercept is zero, and the line is the line of perfect forecast noted in figure 11.1.

The net effect of this second decomposition is to allow the forecaster and the management to identify the sources of controllable error, that is, the mean and slope portions, and to provide a method for their elimination over time.

Example 11.3

The results of an empirical study of the usefulness of Theil's OLF method (Brandon and Jarrett, 1979) indicated better forecasting when OLF was employed in comparison to the no revision case. Seven models were employed to forecast over a four-year-ahead time horizon. A comparison was made between the no revision and OLF revision methods to indicate if revision may be useful. The results are summarized in table 11.2.

The sample selected for this study consisted of 50 firms with earnings per share data (EPS) over a 15 year period. The historical time series permitted EPS forecasts using seven different extrapolative models. Each method was corrected by the OLF method and comparisons were made.

Three measures of accuracy, ME, MAPE, and MSE, were used to determine which method, no revision or OLF, performed better. On the basis of the study, the revision technique (OLF) is clearly superior to forecasts obtained without revision. Similar results were obtained by Brandon et al. (1983) and Brandon and Jarrett (1986).

Thus on the basis of both theoretical and empirical studies revising forecasts can enable forecaster and management to improve their forecast performance. The particular functional form of the forecasting model had no effect on the general

TABLE 11.2   Number of times method achieved best result for three measures of accuracy

Measure of accuracy	Year	Number of times achieved best results	
		No revision	OLF method
ME	1	1	5
	2	2	5
	3	0	6
	4	0	5
MAPE	1	0	7
	2	0	7
	3	0	7
	4	0	7
MSE	1	0	7
	2	0	7
	3	0	7
	4	0	7

Source: Brandon and Jarrett (1979, p. 216).

observations. However, the empirical study is limited to the forecasting models employed, the time period covered, and the sample of firms observed in the study. Stated differently, forecasters may find situations where the forecast error is relatively small and there would not be any clear benefit from using the OLF forecast revision technique.

11.5   Improving Business Forecasts: A Case Study

Example 11.4

In examples 2.9 and 11.2, data on new plant and equipment, total nonfarm business (billion dollars, unadjusted) were forecast by Winters' linear and seasonal exponential smoothing model. Data for observed and forecast values are summarized in table 11.1.

The forecast error will now be decomposed to find bias E^m, the slope component E^r, and the residual component E^d. The purpose is to identify the sources of controllable error. In turn, the Theil method for providing improved forecasts will be followed. Finally, the revised forecasts will be analyzed to ascertain the effectiveness of the forecast improvement process.

The following values were calculated for the data in table 11.1:

$$\overline{Y} = 75.491 \qquad \overline{\hat{Y}} = 75.427$$

$$S_Y = 7.7452 \qquad S_{\hat{Y}} = 8.0709$$

$$r = 0.989 \qquad MSE = 1.317 \qquad b_1 = 0.94937$$

We now find the decomposed MSE values:

$$E^m = \frac{(\overline{Y} - \overline{\hat{Y}})^2}{MSE} = \frac{(75.491 - 75.427)^2}{1.317} = 0.003$$

$$E^r = \frac{(S_{\hat{Y}} - rS_Y)^2}{MSE} = \frac{(8.0709) - (0.989)(7.7452))^2}{1.317} = 0.128$$

$$E^d = \frac{(1 - r^2)S_Y^2}{MSE} = \frac{(1 - (0.989)^2)(7.7452)^2}{1.317} = 0.869$$

or

$$E^d = 1 - E^m - E^r = 1 - 0.003 - 0.128 = 0.869$$

The above values indicate that 0.3 percent (0.003) of the total error (MSE) is associated with bias and 12.8 percent (0.128) is associated with the slope component.

The sum of the above two components represents the total percentage of forecast error (MSE) that can be reduced by improving the accuracy of the forecasts.

To revise forecasts, we utilize the OLF technique developed by Theil (1971). This method increases overall accuracy over time by reducing the proportion of error attributable to the controllable components E^m and E^r.

The OLF is calculated by linear regression of the observed values on the predicted values in the following way:

$$Y = a + b\hat{Y} \tag{11.23}$$

The corrected forecast $\hat{Y}_c$ is estimated using the estimates from equation (11.23) in the form:

$$\hat{Y}_c = a + b\hat{Y} \tag{11.24}$$

This technique is designed to produce corrected forecasts whose intercept approaches zero and whose slope approaches unity.

Now, using equation (11.23) we obtain the following regression estimate:

$$\hat{Y}_c = 3.887 + 0.94937 \ \hat{Y}$$
$$\phantom{\hat{Y}_c = } (1.10) \quad (20.34)$$

The values for the intercept and slope are 3.882 and 0.94937 respectively. The t statistics are presented in parentheses. It is obvious that a t statistic of 1.10 would require the forecasters not to reject the hypothesis that the intercept parameter is zero. A t statistic of 20.34 indicates that the slope parameter is significantly different from zero. Recall that the corrected forecasts should have an intercept approaching zero and a slope approaching unity. The above results are consistent with the design of the Theil OLF technique.

To analyze the improvement we calculate

$$ME = 0$$

$$MAPE = 1.1 \text{ percent}$$

$$MSE = 1.161$$

$$RMS = 1.078$$

$$U = 0.0989$$

If we compare these measures of forecast error with the same measures before the OLF technique was applied, that is,

$$ME = 0.064$$

$$MAPE = 1.2 \text{ percent}$$

$$MSE = 1.317$$

$$RMS = 1.148$$

$$U = 0.1026$$

we note that all these measures are smaller after the application of OLF. Furthermore, if we decompose MSE into its components we have

$$E^m = \frac{(\overline{Y}_c - Y)^2}{MSE} = \frac{75.491 - 75.491}{1.317} = 0$$

$$E^r = \frac{(S_Y - rS_Y)^2}{MSE} = \frac{(7.6623 - (0.989) 7.7452)^2}{1.317} = 0.00$$

Therefore

$$E^d \hat{=} 1.0$$

Thus, the corrected forecasts are free of error associated with bias and slope. The OLF provides improved forecasts. Studies have shown that the particular functional form of the forecast model had no effect on the general observation that the OLF revision produces more accurate forecasts (Brandon and Jarrett, 1974, 1979; Brandon et al., 1983). Most important, the OLF produces revised forecasts that are uniformly more accurate than the original unadjusted forecasts.

The steps in utilizing the OLF technique can be summarized as follows.

1 Fit initial forecast model and calculate forecast error.
2 Fit the OLF regression model and diagnostically test the parameters of OLF regression.
3 Forecast for the future by employing initial model and OLF correction.
4 Examine to see whether the revised forecast is more accurate than initial forecasts by comparing forecast errors before and after OLF is applied.

11.6 Forecasting and Information Systems

To forecast, a forecaster must consider the availability of numerical information. This relates to both the variable being forecast and the independent variable used in building forecasting models (that is, for use in causal models or as indicators of cyclical turning points). The importance of data is that they have a major role in determining the type of forecasting model to use as well as a significant impact on the accuracy of the forecast.

As noted earlier, corporate plans involve the goal of increasing the firm's total wealth which may not be forecastable. In approaching an assignment, a forecaster may elect to focus on unit sales in the forecasting model and from this produce a forecast of total revenues and perhaps profits and EPS. Thus forecasters often focus on variables which they can forecast in order to produce results of prime interest to management. Specific guidelines for determining which variable to forecast are not available, except to use one's *a priori* knowledge and experience. Forecasters should be cognizant of the purpose for which the forecast is required since this will aid in the utilization of suitable time series and forecasting models. In analyzing the purpose for which the forecast is required, the forecaster should consider the factors of (a) ease of use and expense, (b) lack of bias, and (c) achieving the least forecasting error. By considering these factors and the knowledge of data sources, the forecaster will determine an appropriate forecasting technique to use.

Numerical information or data are classified to insure that a system for collecting, storing and utilizing such information can be developed. Usually such data are classified into three types as follows.

Existing Accounting Information

Accounting information is the record of the firm's financial transactions and activities and forms accessible data to utilize. Most accounting systems, however, categorize transactions into various groupings and these are invariably difficult to disaggregate should the grouping be inappropriate for the forecast. For example, sales are usually lumped together with no record of unit sales or prices of the items sold. This is inappropriate for forecasting when forecasters wish to know unit sales, revenues by product or at least product group, and often a geographic split of sales in order to produce information for market planning.

In a similar manner, hospital accounting systems allocate various administrative and fixed costs to various revenue-producing departments. The procedures tend to distort costs of operating these departments and often produce ineffective forecasts of hospital costs by department and for the entire hospital.

The net result of accounting practices is to produce an information system of limited value. One has to be aware of these limitations when choosing a forecasting model.

Data which are not part of the firm's accounting/management information system

This usually covers situations where numerical information is located in the accounting/management information system but in aggregated form, or the data may not be in the accounting/management information system at all. Obtaining the data is often expensive and a great deal of care is required in administering its collection. The primary benefit of gathering original data is that they can be made suitable for the particular forecasting technique chosen on this occasion. If the forecasts are likely to be required on an ongoing basis then the data gathering should be incorporated into a forecasting decision support system (DSS).

The notion of a DSS for forecasting is certainly not new but has become much easier to implement in recent years. Improvement in data management languages such as SAS coupled with its forecasting capabilities have made this very possible to implement on mainframe computers. SPSS-X (Statistical Package for the Social Sciences), which was originally developed as a tool to collect and gather survey data, has added data management and report writing features. FOCUS is a third language with report writing, data management, and statistical capabilities. However, this language is much weaker than the other two in its array of forecasting models and users tend not to find it user-friendly. However, it does have some query capabilities. Today, there are some excellent DSS software systems such as MODEL, EXPRESS, COMSHARE's System W, FAME and IFPS which are used by large corporations. These software systems are at the frontier of business forecasting containing many statistical and forecasting options. Also, they may contain Monte Carlo simulation methods, optimization techniques, and the ability to perform sensitivity analysis of model parameters. These software are very transparent to the user and aid forecasters in preparing forecasts and business plans. Recent years have also seen the rapid development of desk-top personal computers which may permit forecasters to develop DSSs. Software is available on these machines for information storage and retrieval and for forecasting. Many personal computer software packages (Micro-TSP, Minitab, SYSTAT, and SAS) can interact with files created by other software (Lotus 1-2-3 and other spreadsheets) to permit users to have a forecasting decision support system on a personal computer. Also, other microcomputer forecasting systems interact with spreadsheet software to provide forecasters with a total system for forecasting, database, plotting, and word processing. In general, new developments in software have given forecasters capabilities which were not available until recent years.

The use of published data

The use of publicly available data is generally inexpensive with the main cost being that of employing someone to interpret the vast array of statistics that are produced. Published data, as we have seen throughout this text, often provide information on variables employed in causal modeling. Short-term forecasting by extrapolative and time series techniques rarely requires the use of published data apart from being a comparison yardstick on which to assess the usefulness of forecasts. In the next section, we shall consider the limitations on the use of publicly available data.

11.7   Data Sources and their Limitations

The accuracy of all data should be assessed prior to use. For published data, the problem of assessing accuracy is difficult because the forecaster does not control the procedures involved with collecting and recording the data. One major investigation by Morgenstern (1963) on the accuracy of economic observations classified errors originating from the major sources.

1 *Sampling error* Samples are used to gather and collect data on economic phenomena. Forecasters should be fully accomplished in understanding the theory underlying scientific sampling in order to assess the existence, magnitude, and sources of sampling error involved in all probability sampling designs.
2 *Measurement errors* These errors arise when large amounts of data are collected. In practice, most economic data that are reported are later revised because of the initial measurement errors that are made.

3 *Questionnaire error and bias* Many data are derived from responses to question-naires and a variety of errors and biases can arise. These are often due to improperly designed questions, ill-trained interviewers, and poorly controlled interviewing techniques.

4 *Aggregated data may be unsuitable* The problems involved with aggregation include the following: (a) aggregation is not always explicitly stated, (b) even if stated, the quantitative breakdown is not usually given, and (c) more than one time period may have been used in compiling the statistics.

Forecasters have a choice in dealing with published data. Either they use them or they do not. The choice is based on how well the data aided the forecasting process in the past. However, the forecaster should be aware of the possible shortcomings in published data and should monitor their usefulness for purposes of forecasting.

11.8   Database Management Systems

As noted before, the past 20 years have seen a tremendous increase in the development of accounting/management information systems (MIS). While MIS is largely out of the control of the forecaster, the forecaster and MIS manager should be cognizant of each other's goals. In this way, an advanced MIS can be collecting information of use in forecasting. The advanced MIS can collect, store, and retrieve information concerning firm transactions. Each transaction is recorded separately along with its characteristics. For example, a sale is characterized by customer, type of product sold, date of transaction, color of product, location where sold, etc. From this overall database, specific categories can be constructed such as sales by color of product, sales of a particular product at a particular location, and so on.

The database management system described above has several benefits to the forecaster. Forecasts can be made by product, location, or any category format desired. Also, forecasting models can be continually appraised if current disaggre-gated data are available. Finally, if an MIS is built in order for users to interact with it, then the MIS can be made part of a forecasting DSS especially when query languages with forecasting capabilities (SAS and SPSS-X) can be used to interact with the MIS. Some software for use on personal computers are a complete database, graphics, and statistical system. Thus both MIS and forecasting personnel can make valuable contributions to management.

11.9   Forecasting Consulting and Data Banks

In recent years, significant growth has occurred in data banks and forecasting consulting bureaus. Many of these services were started by academic economists and statisticians who produced large-scale econometric models for use by large corporate clients. As time went by, these agencies both grew in number and in the scope of the services they provided. In general, they offer three basic services: forecasts, data banks, and economic consultation. In total, these services provide a forecasting DSS.

Forecasting services provided usually include predictions of macroeconomic variables such as GNP and product accounts, employment and unemployment roles, interest rates, and monetary statistics. These forecasts are, in turn, broken down into forecasts for economic sectors and industries. Finally, the service bureaus can provide firm forecasts on a custom basis.

These forecasting services have created large sets of data on macroeconomic as well as sector, industry and firm variables. The databases contain historical and current numerical information on thousands of economic activities. Individual firms can access these databases for their own macroeconomic forecasting or when they need data on a more convenient and timely basis than is available from published reports.

The economic consultation services enables a firm to complete its forecast DSS. Companies requiring expert advice on the use of their own forecasting models can acquire this service from these consulting agencies. Furthermore, these service bureaus can provide advice to management for the planning and control activities of the firm.

Forecast users are, of course, very concerned with the accuracy of these forecast service bureaus. However, it is difficult to compare the past performance of forecast bureaus because forecast users do not have precise, known, and identical interests. This is particularly important because these forecast service bureaus use different methods, forecast a large number of variables, the variables vary for each forecaster, and the time horizons vary for each forecaster. Even if we were to focus on a single variable and horizon, it is difficult to establish a definitive ranking among forecasters. The noncomparability arises because forecasters issue their forecasts at various times within each quarter and thus they have access to different amounts of information. This timing disparity can be of crucial significance in comparing certain variables. One such study (McNees, 1981) did make a set of comparisons but no general conclusion concerning the accuracy of 13 service bureaus could be made. In later studies McNees (1988) contended that accuracy keeps improving although forecasts are not infallible.

11.10   Managing the Forecasting Function

Business forecasting has benefited by great advances in statistics and computer support in the last few decades. In this book we have emphasized the nature and availability of forecasting methods and the sources of error that may occur. Although managers are aware of the importance of improved forecasts, few keep up with the wide range of forecasting techniques available.

Forecasts are critical imputs to a wide variety of business plans and investment decisions. However, after many years of teaching and consulting, this forecaster has come to realize that many firms and organizations simply do not forecast. They rely on information from others and even hunches and guesses as to future demand for product, inventory and production levels, and the like. Often these same organizations will reject forecasts because they feel that the future holds no important change or there is sufficient time after the fact to react to any significant change. This notion is often coincident with firms who have not suffered harshly in recent times from the losses associated with insufficient demand or excessive inventories. Unless these firms are in great deal of difficulty, they will not change their bad habits.

Since the purpose of forecasting is to assist management in their planning requirements for marketing efforts, personnel, production, services, and finances, what can be done by forecasters to achieve the stated purpose? To say it another way, how can forecasters help managers to achieve their goals?

Forecasting in any environment is unique but a few points should be considered before starting a new forecasting program in an organization. First, determine the purpose for which the forecast is intended. The forecaster's efforts will benefit the organization best if it is known, for example, that the forecast will be used as a guide for setting production levels. Second, if the purpose of the forecast is to predict demand for a product or product group, a separate forecast for each product or product group will be made. Third, an initial forecast which may be crude and simple should start the forecasting program. Forecasting programs are often a progressive process beginning simply and ending possibly in an elaborate system including outside consultants. Fourth, forecasts should be reviewed often and revised as new information is obtained. Finally, the effects of changes in the competitive environment on a firm's forecasts must be specifically assessed. These changes in the economic environment could be incorporated into the forecasting model.

For forecasts to be an effective management tool, management's needs must be met. An industry forecast as well as an all-firm forecast is often an essential element in the forecasting program. A clear brief statement of the assumptions of the forecasting model should be made. Forecasts should not be unduly qualified. A clear statement as to the forecast horizon is necessary. Management is entitled to have forecasts that are not altered very often. Most managers prefer not to see details on techniques used but it is also very easy to underestimate the knowledge and abilities of many managers. Finally, forecasts are to be checked against reality, that is, accuracy should be measured.

All the above will not guarantee success of the forecasting program, but gaining acceptance of forecasts will be eased. Forecasting is hard work, but financial reward from reasonable success is often quick and measurable. Today, there are a number of financially and professionally successful analysts on Wall Street who started by forecasting stock market trends and writing research reports based on business forecasts. Furthermore, success in the past (especially recent past) breeds greater acceptance of future forecasts (Zehren, 1987).

11.11 Summary

The purpose of this book has been to outline the most common and useful forecasting techniques available to business management.

Key functions of management are planning and control. Forecasting has an integral role in the planning and control activities of a firm.

Criteria for choosing a forecasting technique include the following:

1 ease of use and expense;
2 lack of bias;
3 least forecasting error.

The presence of bias can be tested for by a χ^2 statistic.

Measures of forecast error (accuracy) include mean error (ME), mean absolute percentage error (MAPE), mean square error (MSE), root mean square error (RMS) and Theil's U statistic.

MSE can be decomposed to analyze the sources of forecast error. One such method for revising forecasts to improve forecast performance is Theil's optimal linear forecasting procedure.

The importance of gathering, collecting, and storing data for use in forecasting cannot be understated. Numerical information includes existing accounting information, data which are not part of the existing accounting/management information system, and published data.

The usefulness of published data is limited by sampling error, measurement errors, questionnaire error and bias, and the fact that aggregated data may be unsuitable.

Forecasters should interact with MIS managers to insure that databases contain information which is useful for forecasting.

To have a successful forecasting program, forecasters must meet the needs of management.

11.12 Exercises

1 For the data of table 2.6 (chapter 2), test to determine whether bias exists in the forecasts produced by adaptive-response-rate single exponential smoothing. Choose $\alpha = 0.05$.

2 For the data of table 2.10 (chapter 2), test to determine whether bias exists in the forecasts produced by Brown's linear exponential smoothing. Choose $\alpha = 0.05$.

3 For the data of table 2.14 (chapter 2), test to determine whether bias exists in the forecasts produced by Winters' seasonal exponential smoothing model. Choose $\alpha = 0.05$.

4 For the data cited in exercise 1, calculate ME, MAPE, MSE, and Theil's U statistic.

5 For the data cited in exercise 2, calculate ME, MAPE, MSE, RMS, and Theil's U statistic.

6 For the data cited in exercise 3, calculate ME, MAPE, MSE, RMS and Theil's U statistic.

7 For the data of exercise 1, calculate E^m and E^r. Interpret these values.

8 For the data of exercise 2, calculate E^m and E^r. Interpret these results.

9 For the data of exercise 3, calculate E^m and E^r. Interpret these results.

10 Based on the results of exercises 1, 4, and 7, and your perception of the methods used, comment on the usefulness of ARRSES in forecasting the observed values in table 2.6.

11 Based on the results of exercises 2, 5, and 8, and your perception of the methods used, comment on the usefulness of Brown's single-parameter linear exponential smoothing in forecasting the observed values of table 2.10

12 Based on the results of exercises 3, 6, and 9, and your perception of the methods used, comment on the usefulness of Winters' method in forecasting the observed values of table 2.14.

13 Revise the following forecasts by the OLF method and recalculate E^m, E^r, and E^d.
(a) The forecast for the data of table 2.6.
(b) The forecast for the data of table 2.10.
(c) The forecast for the data of table 2.14.

14 Investigate the academic computing center at your university to determine whether DSS systems exist. Determine if the DSS software contains all the forecasting methods described in this book. What methods are not included? Does the DSS system permit the user to test the sensitivity of model parameters?

Are the computing center personnel who advise students and other university users well versed in the statistical methods available in the DSS? How does one access the DSS?

15 Planning for future course schedules at a university is an extremely difficult task. Interview a department chairperson or MBA program director and ask how he/she plans for student and faculty needs. How does this person interact with a database, predict student enrolment, and interact with a computer DSS for forecasting and scheduling purposes?

16 Interview a college bookstore manager and query him/her about how plans are made to order textbooks for the following semester. What is the information system used? Is a DSS available for his/her use? How does the manager handle situations when too few books are ordered or if too many are ordered? Are the prediction errors costly and to whom, e.g. the bookstore manager, student, faculty?

17 For a business firm, determine what constitutes the management information system for the purpose of forecasting sales, earnings, or costs. How does the person in charge of business planning and/or forecasting interact with the information system? Is there a DSS software system available for use? What are its qualities and deficiencies?

18 Gather the forecasts of EPS made by a forecasting service such as Value Line for 25 firms or more. Compare the forecasts with actual EPS by calculating MSE and its three components. Revise the forecasts by the OLF technique. Does the OLF improve the forecasting performance of the earnings forecasting service? Which component(s) of MSE changed after the OLF technique was applied?

References

Beaver, W., Clarke, R., and Wright, W. F. (1979) The association between unsystematic security returns and the magnitude of earnings forecast errors. *Journal of Accounting Research* 17(2), Autumn, 316–40.

Brandon, C. H. and Jarrett, J. E. (1974) Accuracy of forecasts in annual reports. *Financial Review* 29–45.

Brandon, C. H. and Jarrett, J. E. (1977) On the accuracy of externally published forecasts. *Review of Business and Economic Research* 13, Fall, 35–47.

Brandon, C. H. and Jarrett, J. E. (1979) Revising earnings per share forecasts: an empirical test. *Management Science* 25(3), 211–20.

Brandon, C. H. and Jarrett, J. E. (1986) Improving accuracy of forecasts by a cost-effective method. *Futures* 18 (1), 78–83.

Brandon, C. H., Jarrett, J. E., and Khumuwala, S. B. (1983) Revising forecasts of accounting earnings: a comparison with the Box–Jenkins method. *Management Science* 29(2), 256–64.

Copeland, R. M. and Marioni, R. J. (1972) Executives' forecast of earnings per share versus forecasts of naive models. *Journal of Business* 15, October, 492–512.

Demski, J. S. and Feltham, G. A. (1972) Forecast evaluation, *Accounting Review* 47, July, 533–48.

Geurts, M.D. (1981–2) Four criteria by which to choose the best forecasting technique. *Journal of Business Forecasting Methods and Systems* 1(2), 6–8.

Granger, C. W. J. and Newbold, P. (1973) Some comments on the evaluation of economic forecasts. *Applied Economics* 5, 35–47.

Harris, L. (1966) A decision theoretic approach on deciding when a sophisticated forecasting technique is needed. *Management Science* 12, October 66–9.

Jenkins, G. M. (1983) Some practical aspects of forecasting in organizations. *Journal of Forecasting* 1(1), 3–22.

Jorgenson, D. W., Hunter, J. and Nadiri, M. I. (1970) The predictive performance of econometric models of quarterly investment behavior. *Econometrica*, March, 213–24.

Makridakis, S., Andersen, A., Carbone, R., Fildes, R., Hibon, M., Lewandowski, R., Newton, J., Parzen, E., and Winkler, R. (1982) The accuracy of extrapolation (time series) methods: results of a forecasting competition. *Journal of Forecasting* 1(2), 111–53.

Malcolm, R. R. and Fraser, D. R. (1977) Further evidence on the accuracy of analysts. Earnings forecasts; a comparison among analysts. *Journal of Economics and Business* 29, Summer/Spring, 193–7.

McNees, S. K. (1981) The recent record of thirteen forecasters. *New England Economic Review*, September/October, 5–21.

McNees, S. K. (1988) The accuracy keeps improving. *New York Times* 10 January 1988. Section 3, p. 2.

Mincer, J. and Zarnowitz, V. (1969) The evaluation of economic forecasts. In J. Mincer (ed.), *Economic Forecasts and Expectations*, New York: National Bureau of Economic Research.

Morgenstern, O. (1963) *On the Accuracy of Economic Observations*, Princeton, NJ: Princeton University Press.

Salamon, G. L. and Smith, D. E. (1977) Additional evidence on the time series properties of reported earnings per share: Comment. *Journal of Finance* 32, December, 1975–1801.

Theil, H. (1965) *Economic Forecasts and Policy*. Amsterdam: North-Holland.

Theil, H. (1971) *Applied Economic Forecasting*. Amsterdam: North-Holland.

Zehren, C. V. (1987) Elaine Garzarelli: from researcher to market guru. *Providence Journal*, 26 July, 1987, pp. F1, F18.

Further Reading

Brandon, C. H., Jarrett, J. E., and Khumuwala, S. B. (1986) Comparing forecast accuracy for exponential smoothing models of earnings per share data for financial decision making. *Decision Science*, 17(1), 186–94.

Jarrett, J. E. (1989) Forecasting monthly earnings per share – time series models. *OMEGA: The International Journal of Management Science* 17(1), 37–44.

McNees, S. (1986) Forecasting accuracy of alternative techniques: a comparison of US macroeconomic forecasts. *Journal of Business and Economic Statistics* 4(1), 5–15.

Schnarrs, S. P. (1986) A comparison of extrapolation models on yearly sales forecasts. *International Journal of Forecasting*, 2(1), 71–86.

APPENDIX

Statistical Tables for Forecasting

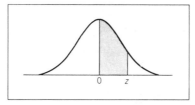

TABLE A.1 Normal Curve Areas

z	.00	.01	.02	.03	.04	.05	.06	.07	.08	.09
0.0	.0000	.0040	.0080	.0120	.0160	.0199	.0239	.0279	.0319	.0359
0.1	.0398	.0438	.0478	.0517	.0557	.0596	.0636	.0675	.0714	.0753
0.2	.0793	.0832	.0871	.0910	.0948	.0987	.1026	.1064	.1103	.1141
0.3	.1179	.1217	.1255	.1293	.1331	.1368	.1406	.1443	.1480	.1517
0.4	.1554	.1591	.1628	.1664	.1700	.1736	.1772	.1808	.1844	.1879
0.5	.1915	.1950	.1985	.2019	.2054	.2088	.2123	.2157	.2190	.2224
0.6	.2257	.2291	.2324	.2357	.2389	.2422	.2454	.2486	.2517	.2549
0.7	.2580	.2611	.2642	.2673	.2704	.2734	.2764	.2794	.2823	.2852
0.8	.2881	.2910	.2939	.2967	.2995	.3023	.3051	.3078	.3106	.3133
0.9	.3159	.3186	.3212	.3238	.3264	.3289	.3315	.3340	.3365	.3389
1.0	.3413	.3438	.3461	.3485	.3508	.3531	.3554	.3577	.3599	.3621
1.1	.3643	.3665	.3686	.3708	.3729	.3749	.3770	.3790	.3810	.3830
1.2	.3849	.3869	.3888	.3907	.3925	.3944	.3962	.3980	.3997	.4015
1.3	.4032	.4049	.4066	.4082	.4099	.4115	.4131	.4147	.4162	.4177
1.4	.4192	.4207	.4222	.4236	.4251	.4265	.4279	.4292	.4306	.4319
1.5	.4332	.4345	.4357	.4370	.4382	.4394	.4406	.4418	.4429	.4441
1.6	.4452	.4463	.4474	.4484	.4495	.4505	.4515	.4525	.4535	.4545
1.7	.4554	.4564	.4573	.4582	.4591	.4599	.4608	.4616	.4625	.4633
1.8	.4641	.4649	.4656	.4664	.4671	.4678	.4686	.4693	.4699	.4706
1.9	.4713	.4719	.4726	.4732	.4738	.4744	.4750	.4756	.4761	.4767
2.0	.4772	.4778	.4783	.4788	.4793	.4798	.4803	.4808	.4812	.4817
2.1	.4821	.4826	.4830	.4834	.4838	.4842	.4846	.4850	.4854	.4857
2.2	.4861	.4864	.4868	.4871	.4875	.4878	.4881	.4884	.4887	.4890
2.3	.4893	.4896	.4898	.4901	.4904	.4906	.4909	.4911	.4913	.4916
2.4	.4918	.4920	.4922	.4925	.4927	.4929	.4931	.4932	.4934	.4936
2.5	.4938	.4940	.4941	.4943	.4945	.4946	.4948	.4949	.4951	.4952
2.6	.4953	.4955	.4956	.4957	.4959	.4960	.4961	.4962	.4963	.4964
2.7	.4965	.4966	.4967	.4968	.4969	.4970	.4971	.4972	.4973	.4974
2.8	.4974	.4975	.4976	.4977	.4977	.4978	.4979	.4979	.4980	.4981
2.9	.4981	.4982	.4982	.4983	.4984	.4984	.4985	.4985	.4986	.4986
3.0	.4987	.4987	.4987	.4988	.4988	.4989	.4989	.4989	.4990	.4990

Source: abridged from Table 1, A. Hald, *Statistical Tables and Formulas*, Wiley, New York, 1952. Reproduced by permission of the publisher.

TABLE A.2   Critical Values of *t*

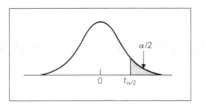

d.f.	$t_{.10}$	$t_{.05}$	$t_{.025}$	$t_{.01}$	$t_{.005}$
1	3.078	6.314	12.706	31.821	63.657
2	1.886	2.920	4.303	6.965	9.925
3	1.638	2.353	3.182	4.541	5.841
4	1.533	2.132	2.776	3.747	4.604
5	1.476	2.015	2.571	3.365	4.032
6	1.440	1.943	2.447	3.143	3.707
7	1.415	1.895	2.365	2.998	3.499
8	1.397	1.860	2.306	2.896	3.355
9	1.383	1.833	2.262	2.821	3.250
10	1.372	1.812	2.228	2.764	3.169
11	1.363	1.796	2.201	2.718	3.106
12	1.356	1.782	2.179	2.681	3.055
13	1.350	1.771	2.160	2.650	3.012
14	1.345	1.761	2.145	2.624	2.977
15	1.341	1.753	2.131	2.602	2.947
16	1.337	1.746	2.120	2.583	2.921
17	1.333	1.740	2.110	2.567	2.898
18	1.330	1.734	2.101	2.552	2.878
19	1.328	1.729	2.093	2.539	2.861
20	1.325	1.725	2.086	2.528	2.845
21	1.323	1.721	2.080	2.518	2.831
22	1.321	1.717	2.074	2.508	2.819
23	1.319	1.714	2.069	2.500	2.807
24	1.318	1.711	2.064	2.492	2.797
25	1.316	1.708	2.060	2.485	2.787
26	1.315	1.706	2.056	2.479	2.779
27	1.314	1.703	2.052	2.473	2.771
28	1.313	1.701	2.048	2.467	2.763
29	1.311	1.699	2.045	2.462	2.756
inf.	1.282	1.645	1.960	2.326	2.576

Source: M. Merrington, Table of percentage points of the *t*-distribution, *Biometrika*, 32, 300, 1941. Reproduced by permission of Biometrika Trustees.

TABLE A.3(a)   Critical Values of the *F* Distribution

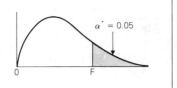

Degrees of freedom

		Numerator							
	1	*2*	*3*	*4*	*5*	*6*	*7*	*8*	*9*
1	161.4	199.5	215.7	224.6	230.2	234.0	236.8	238.9	240.5
2	18.51	19.00	19.16	19.25	19.30	19.33	19.35	19.37	19.38
3	10.13	9.55	9.28	9.12	9.01	8.94	8.89	8.85	8.81
4	7.71	6.94	6.59	6.39	6.26	6.16	6.09	6.04	6.00
5	6.61	5.79	5.41	4.19	5.05	4.95	4.88	4.82	4.77
6	5.99	5.14	4.76	4.53	4.39	4.28	4.21	4.15	4.10
7	5.59	4.74	4.35	4.12	3.97	3.87	3.79	3.73	3.68
8	5.32	4.46	4.07	3.84	3.69	3.58	3.50	3.44	3.39
9	5.12	4.26	3.86	3.63	3.48	3.37	3.29	3.23	3.18
10	4.96	4.10	3.71	3.48	3.33	3.22	3.14	3.07	3.02
11	4.84	3.98	3.59	3.36	3.20	3.09	3.01	2.95	2.90
12	4.75	3.89	3.49	3.26	3.11	3.00	2.91	2.85	2.80
13	4.67	3.81	3.41	3.18	3.03	2.92	2.83	2.77	2.71
14	4.60	3.74	3.34	3.11	2.96	2.85	2.76	2.70	2.65
15	4.54	3.68	3.29	3.06	2.90	2.79	2.71	2.64	2.59
16	4.49	3.63	3.24	3.01	2.85	2.74	2.66	2.59	2.54
17	4.45	3.59	3.20	2.96	2.81	2.70	2.61	2.55	2.49
18	4.41	3.55	3.16	2.93	2.77	2.66	2.58	2.51	2.46
19	4.38	3.52	3.13	2.90	2.74	2.63	2.54	2.48	2.42
20	4.35	3.49	3.10	2.87	2.71	2.60	2.51	2.45	2.39
21	4.32	3.47	3.07	2.84	2.68	2.57	2.49	2.42	2.37
22	4.30	3.44	3.05	2.82	2.66	2.55	2.46	2.40	2.34
23	4.28	3.42	3.03	2.80	2.64	2.53	2.44	2.37	2.32
24	4.26	3.40	3.01	2.78	2.62	2.51	2.42	2.36	2.30
25	4.24	3.39	2.99	2.76	2.60	2.49	2.40	2.34	2.28
26	4.23	3.37	2.98	2.74	2.59	2.47	2.39	2.32	2.27
27	4.21	3.35	2.96	2.73	2.57	2.46	2.37	2.31	2.25
28	4.20	3.34	2.95	2.71	2.56	2.45	2.36	2.29	2.24
29	4.18	3.33	2.93	2.70	2.55	2.43	2.35	2.28	2.22
30	4.17	3.32	2.92	2.69	2.53	2.42	2.33	2.27	2.21
40	4.08	3.23	2.84	2.61	2.45	2.34	2.25	2.18	2.12
60	4.00	3.15	2.76	2.53	2.37	2.25	2.17	2.10	2.04
120	3.92	3.07	2.68	2.45	2.29	2.17	2.09	2.02	1.96
∞	3.84	3.00	2.60	2.37	2.21	2.10	2.01	1.94	1.88

Denominator

				Numerator						
10	*12*	*15*	*20*	*24*	*30*	*40*	*60*	*120*	∞	
241.9	243.9	245.9	248.0	249.1	250.1	251.1	252.2	253.3	254.3	1
19.40	19.41	19.43	19.45	19.45	19.46	19.47	19.48	19.49	19.50	2
8.79	8.74	8.70	8.66	8.64	8.62	8.59	8.57	8.55	8.53	3
5.96	5.91	5.86	5.80	5.77	5.75	5.72	5.69	5.66	5.63	4
4.74	4.68	4.62	4.56	4.53	4.50	4.46	4.43	4.40	4.36	5
4.06	4.00	3.94	3.87	3.84	3.81	3.77	3.74	3.70	3.67	6
3.64	3.57	3.51	3.44	3.41	3.38	3.34	3.30	3.27	3.23	7
3.35	3.28	3.22	3.15	3.12	3.08	3.04	3.01	2.97	2.93	8
3.14	3.07	3.01	2.94	2.90	2.86	2.83	2.79	2.75	2.71	9
2.98	2.91	2.85	2.77	2.74	2.70	2.66	2.62	2.58	2.54	10
2.85	2.79	2.72	2.65	2.61	2.57	2.53	2.49	2.45	2.40	11
2.75	2.69	2.62	2.54	2.51	2.47	2.43	2.38	2.34	2.30	12
2.67	2.60	2.53	2.46	2.42	2.38	2.34	2.30	2.25	2.21	13
2.60	2.53	2.46	2.39	2.35	2.31	2.27	2.22	2.18	2.13	14
2.54	2.48	2.40	2.33	2.29	2.25	2.20	2.16	2.11	2.07	15
2.49	2.42	2.35	2.28	2.24	2.19	2.15	2.11	2.06	2.01	16
2.45	2.38	2.31	2.23	2.19	2.15	2.10	2.06	2.01	1.96	17
2.41	2.34	2.27	2.19	2.15	2.11	2.06	2.02	1.97	1.92	18
2.38	2.31	2.23	2.16	2.11	2.07	2.03	1.98	1.93	1.88	19
2.35	2.28	2.20	2.12	2.08	2.04	1.99	1.95	1.90	1.84	20
2.32	2.25	2.18	2.10	2.05	2.01	1.96	1.92	1.87	1.81	21
2.30	2.23	2.15	2.07	2.03	1.98	1.94	1.89	1.84	1.78	22
2.27	2.20	2.13	2.05	2.01	1.96	1.91	1.86	1.81	1.76	23
2.25	2.18	2.11	2.03	1.98	1.94	1.89	1.84	1.79	1.73	24
2.24	2.16	2.09	2.01	1.96	1.92	1.87	1.82	1.77	1.71	25
2.22	2.15	2.07	1.99	1.95	1.90	1.85	1.80	1.75	1.69	26
2.20	2.13	2.06	1.97	1.93	1.88	1.84	1.79	1.73	1.67	27
2.19	2.12	2.04	1.96	1.91	1.87	1.82	1.77	1.71	1.65	28
2.18	2.10	2.03	1.94	1.90	1.85	1.81	1.75	1.70	1.64	29
2.16	2.09	2.01	1.93	1.89	1.84	1.79	1.74	1.68	1.62	30
2.08	2.00	1.92	1.84	1.79	1.74	1.69	1.64	1.58	1.51	40
1.99	1.92	1.84	1.75	1.70	1.65	1.59	1.53	1.47	1.39	60
1.91	1.83	1.75	1.66	1.61	1.55	1.50	1.43	1.35	1.25	120
1.83	1.75	1.67	1.57	1.52	1.46	1.39	1.32	1.22	1.00	∞

Denominator (left vertical label)

Source: M. Merrington and C. Thompson, Tables of percentage points of the inverted beta (*F*)-distribution, *Biometrika*, 33, 73–88, 1943. Reproduced by permission of Biometrika Trustees.

TABLE A.3(b) Critical Values of the *F* Distribution

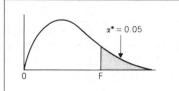

$z^* = 0.05$

Degrees of freedom

					Numerator				
	1	*2*	*3*	*4*	*5*	*6*	*7*	*8*	*9*
1	4052	4999.5	5403	5625	5764	5859	5928	5981	6022
2	98.50	99.00	99.17	99.25	99.30	99.33	99.36	99.37	99.39
3	34.12	30.82	29.46	28.71	28.24	27.91	27.67	27.49	27.35
4	21.20	18.00	16.69	15.98	15.52	15.21	14.98	14.80	14.66
5	16.26	13.27	12.06	11.39	10.97	10.67	10.46	10.29	10.16
6	13.75	10.92	9.78	9.15	8.75	8.47	8.26	8.10	7.98
7	12.25	9.55	8.45	7.85	7.46	7.19	6.99	6.84	6.72
8	11.26	8.65	7.59	7.01	6.63	6.37	6.18	6.03	5.91
9	10.56	8.02	6.99	6.42	6.06	5.80	5.61	5.47	5.35
10	10.04	7.56	6.55	5.99	5.64	5.39	5.20	5.06	4.94
11	9.65	7.21	6.22	5.67	5.32	5.07	4.89	4.74	4.63
12	9.33	6.93	5.95	5.41	5.06	4.82	4.64	4.50	4.39
13	9.07	6.70	5.74	5.21	4.86	4.62	4.44	4.30	4.19
14	8.86	6.51	5.56	5.04	4.69	4.46	4.28	4.14	4.03
15	8.68	6.36	5.42	4.89	4.56	4.32	4.14	4.00	3.89
16	8.53	6.23	5.29	4.77	4.44	4.20	4.03	3.89	3.78
17	8.40	6.11	5.18	4.67	4.34	4.10	3.93	3.79	3.68
18	8.29	6.01	5.09	4.58	4.25	4.01	3.84	3.71	3.60
19	8.18	5.93	5.01	4.50	4.17	3.94	3.77	3.63	3.52
20	8.10	5.85	4.94	4.43	4.10	3.87	3.70	3.56	3.46
21	8.02	5.78	4.87	4.37	4.04	3.81	3.64	3.51	3.40
22	7.95	5.72	4.82	4.31	3.99	3.76	3.59	3.45	3.35
23	7.88	5.66	4.76	4.26	3.94	3.71	3.54	3.41	3.30
24	7.82	5.61	4.72	4.22	3.90	3.67	3.50	3.36	3.26
25	7.77	5.57	4.68	4.18	3.85	3.63	3.46	3.32	3.22
26	7.72	5.53	4.64	4.14	3.82	3.59	3.42	3.29	3.18
27	7.68	5.49	4.60	4.11	3.78	3.56	3.39	3.26	3.15
28	7.64	5.45	4.57	4.07	3.75	3.53	3.36	3.23	3.12
29	7.60	5.42	4.54	4.04	3.73	3.50	3.33	3.20	3.09
30	7.56	5.39	4.51	4.02	3.70	3.47	3.30	3.17	3.07
40	7.31	5.18	4.31	3.83	3.51	3.29	3.12	2.99	2.89
60	7.08	4.98	4.13	3.65	3.34	3.12	2.95	2.82	2.72
120	6.85	4.79	3.95	3.48	3.17	2.96	2.79	2.66	2.56
∞	6.63	4.61	3.78	3.32	3.02	2.80	2.64	2.51	2.41

Denominator

Denominator	Numerator 10	12	15	20	24	30	40	60	120	∞
1	6056	6106	6157	6209	6235	6261	6287	6313	6339	6366
2	99.40	99.42	99.43	99.45	99.46	99.47	99.47	99.48	99.49	99.50
3	27.23	27.05	26.87	26.69	26.60	26.50	26.41	26.32	26.22	26.13
4	14.55	14.37	14.20	14.02	13.93	13.84	13.75	13.65	13.56	13.46
5	10.05	9.89	9.72	9.55	9.47	9.38	9.29	9.20	9.11	9.02
6	7.87	7.72	7.56	7.40	7.31	7.23	7.14	7.06	6.97	6.88
7	6.62	6.47	6.31	6.16	6.07	5.99	5.91	5.82	5.74	5.65
8	5.81	5.67	5.52	5.36	5.28	5.20	5.12	5.03	4.95	4.86
9	5.26	5.11	4.96	4.81	4.73	4.65	4.57	4.48	4.40	4.31
10	4.85	4.71	4.56	4.41	4.33	4.25	4.17	4.08	4.00	3.91
11	4.54	4.40	4.25	4.10	4.02	3.94	3.86	3.78	3.69	3.60
12	4.30	4.16	4.01	3.86	3.78	3.70	3.62	3.54	3.45	3.36
13	4.10	3.96	3.82	3.66	3.59	3.51	3.43	3.34	3.25	3.17
14	3.94	3.80	3.66	3.51	3.43	3.35	3.27	3.18	3.09	3.00
15	3.80	3.67	3.52	3.37	3.29	3.21	3.13	3.05	2.96	2.87
16	3.69	3.55	3.41	3.26	3.18	3.10	3.02	2.93	2.84	2.75
17	3.59	3.46	3.31	3.16	3.08	3.00	2.92	2.83	2.75	2.65
18	3.51	3.37	3.23	3.08	3.00	2.92	2.84	2.75	2.66	2.57
19	3.43	3.30	3.15	3.00	2.92	2.84	2.76	2.67	2.58	2.49
20	3.37	3.23	3.09	2.94	2.86	2.78	2.69	2.61	2.52	2.42
21	3.31	3.17	3.03	2.88	2.80	2.72	2.64	2.55	2.46	2.36
22	3.26	3.12	2.98	2.83	2.75	2.67	2.58	2.50	2.40	2.31
23	3.21	3.07	2.93	2.78	2.70	2.62	2.54	2.45	2.35	2.26
24	3.17	3.03	2.89	2.74	2.66	2.58	2.49	2.40	2.31	2.21
25	3.13	2.99	2.85	2.70	2.62	2.54	2.45	2.36	2.27	2.17
26	3.09	2.96	2.81	2.66	2.58	2.50	2.42	2.33	2.23	2.13
27	3.06	2.93	2.78	2.63	2.55	2.47	2.38	2.29	2.20	2.10
28	3.03	2.90	2.75	2.60	2.52	2.44	2.35	2.26	2.17	2.06
29	3.00	2.87	2.73	2.57	2.49	2.41	2.33	2.23	2.14	2.03
30	2.98	2.84	2.70	2.55	2.47	2.39	2.30	2.21	2.11	2.01
40	2.80	2.66	2.52	2.37	2.29	2.20	2.11	2.02	1.92	1.80
60	2.63	2.50	2.35	2.20	2.12	2.03	1.94	1.84	1.73	1.60
120	2.47	2.34	2.19	2.03	1.95	1.86	1.76	1.66	1.53	1.38
∞	2.32	2.18	2.04	1.88	1.79	1.70	1.59	1.47	1.32	1.00

Source: M. Merrington and C. M. Thompson, Tables of percentage points of the inverted beta (F)-distribution. *Biometrika*, 33, 73–88, 1943. Reproduced by permission of Biometrika Trustees.

TABLE A.4 Critical Values of χ^2

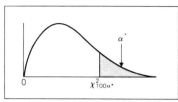

$\chi^2(10)$	$\chi^2(5)$	$\chi^2(2.5)$	$\chi^2(1)$	$\chi^2(.5)$	d.f.
2.70554	3.84146	5.02389	6.63490	7.87944	1
4.60517	5.99147	7.37776	9.21034	10.5966	2
6.25139	7.81473	9.34840	11.3449	12.8381	3
7.77944	9.48773	11.1433	13.2767	14.8602	4
9.23635	11.0705	12.8325	15.0863	16.7496	5
10.6446	12.5916	14.4494	16.8119	18.5476	6
12.0170	14.0671	16.0128	18.4753	20.2777	7
13.3616	15.5073	17.5346	20.0902	21.9550	8
14.6837	16.9190	19.0228	21.6660	23.5893	9
15.9871	18.3070	20.4831	23.2093	25.1882	10
17.2750	19.6751	21.9200	24.7250	26.7569	11
18.5494	21.0261	23.3367	26.2170	28.2995	12
19.8119	22.3621	24.7356	27.6882	29.8194	13
21.0642	23.6848	26.1190	29.1413	31.3193	14
22.3072	24.9958	27.4884	30.5779	32.8013	15
23.5418	26.2962	28.8454	31.9999	34.2672	16
24.7690	27.5871	30.1910	33.4087	35.7185	17
25.9894	28.8693	31.5264	34.8053	37.1564	18
27.2036	30.1435	32.8523	36.1908	38.5822	19
28.4120	31.4104	34.1696	37.5662	39.9968	20
29.6151	32.6705	35.4789	38.9321	41.4010	21
30.8133	33.9244	36.7807	40.2894	42.7956	22
32.0069	35.1725	38.0757	41.6384	44.1813	23
33.1963	36.4151	39.3641	42.9798	45.5585	24
34.3816	37.6525	40.6465	44.3141	46.9278	25
35.5631	38.8852	41.9232	45.6417	48.2899	26
36.7412	40.1133	43.1944	46.9630	49.6449	27
37.9159	41.3372	44.4607	48.2782	50.9933	28
39.0875	42.5569	45.7222	49.5879	52.3356	29
40.2560	43.7729	46.9792	50.8922	53.6720	30
51.8050	55.7585	59.3417	63.6907	66.7659	40
63.1671	67.5048	71.4202	76.1539	79.4900	50
74.3970	79.0819	83.2976	88.3794	91.9517	60
85.5271	90.5312	95.0231	100.425	104.215	70
96.5782	101.879	106.629	112.329	116.321	80
107.565	113.145	118.136	124.116	128.299	90
118.498	124.342	129.561	135.807	140.169	100

Source: C. M. Thompson, Tables of the percentage points of the χ^2-distribution, *Biometrika*, 32, 188–9, 1941. Reproduced by permission of Biometrika Trustees.

TABLE A.5(a) Values of the Durbin–Watson Statistic

1 percent significance points of L and U

	Number of independent (explanatory) variables k																			
	1		2		3		4		5		6		7		8		9		10	
n	L	U	L	U	L	U	L	U	L	U	L	U	L	U	L	U	L	U	L	U
6	0.390	1.142	----	----																
7	0.435	1.036	0.294	1.676	----	----														
8	0.497	1.003	0.345	1.489	0.229	2.012	----	----												
9	0.554	0.998	0.408	1.389	0.279	1.875	0.183	2.433	----	----										
10	0.604	1.001	0.466	1.333	0.340	1.733	0.230	2.193	0.150	2.690	----	----								
11	0.653	1.010	0.519	1.297	0.396	1.640	0.286	2.030	0.193	2.453	0.124	2.892	----	----						
12	0.697	1.023	0.569	1.274	0.449	1.575	0.339	1.913	0.244	2.280	0.164	2.665	0.105	3.053	----	----				
13	0.738	1.038	0.616	1.261	0.499	1.526	0.391	1.826	0.294	2.150	0.211	2.490	0.140	2.838	0.090	3.182	----	----		
14	0.776	1.054	0.660	1.254	0.547	1.490	0.441	1.757	0.343	2.049	0.257	2.354	0.183	2.667	0.122	2.981	0.078	3.287	----	----
15	0.811	1.070	0.700	1.252	0.591	1.464	0.488	1.704	0.391	1.967	0.303	2.244	0.226	2.530	0.161	2.817	0.107	3.101	0.068	3.374
16	0.844	1.086	0.737	1.252	0.633	1.446	0.532	1.663	0.437	1.900	0.349	2.153	0.269	2.416	0.200	2.681	0.142	2.944	0.094	3.201
17	0.874	1.102	0.772	1.255	0.672	1.432	0.574	1.630	0.480	1.847	0.393	2.078	0.313	2.319	0.241	2.566	0.179	2.811	0.127	3.053
18	0.902	1.118	0.805	1.259	0.708	1.422	0.613	1.604	0.522	1.803	0.435	2.015	0.355	2.238	0.282	2.467	0.216	2.697	0.160	2.925
19	0.928	1.132	0.835	1.265	0.742	1.415	0.650	1.584	0.561	1.767	0.476	1.963	0.396	2.169	0.322	2.381	0.255	2.597	0.196	2.813
20	0.952	1.147	0.863	1.271	0.773	1.411	0.685	1.567	0.598	1.737	0.515	1.918	0.436	2.110	0.362	2.308	0.294	2.510	0.232	2.714
21	0.975	1.161	0.890	1.277	0.803	1.408	0.718	1.554	0.633	1.712	0.552	1.881	0.474	2.059	0.400	2.244	0.331	2.434	0.268	2.625
22	0.997	1.174	0.914	1.284	0.831	1.407	0.748	1.543	0.667	1.691	0.587	1.849	0.510	2.015	0.437	2.188	0.368	2.367	0.304	2.548
23	1.018	1.187	0.938	1.291	0.858	1.407	0.777	1.534	0.698	1.673	0.620	1.821	0.545	1.977	0.473	2.140	0.404	2.308	0.340	2.479
24	1.037	1.199	0.960	1.298	0.882	1.407	0.805	1.528	0.728	1.658	0.652	1.797	0.578	1.944	0.507	2.097	0.439	2.255	0.375	2.417
25	1.055	1.211	0.981	1.305	0.906	1.409	0.831	1.523	0.756	1.645	0.682	1.776	0.610	1.915	0.540	2.059	0.473	2.209	0.409	2.362
26	1.072	1.222	1.001	1.312	0.928	1.411	0.855	1.518	0.783	1.635	0.711	1.759	0.640	1.889	0.572	2.026	0.505	2.168	0.441	2.313
27	1.089	1.233	1.019	1.319	0.949	1.413	0.878	1.515	0.808	1.626	0.738	1.743	0.669	1.867	0.602	1.997	0.536	2.131	0.473	2.269
28	1.104	1.244	1.037	1.325	0.969	1.415	0.900	1.513	0.832	1.618	0.764	1.729	0.696	1.847	0.630	1.970	0.566	2.098	0.504	2.229
29	1.119	1.254	1.054	1.332	0.988	1.418	0.921	1.512	0.855	1.611	0.788	1.718	0.723	1.830	0.658	1.947	0.595	2.068	0.533	2.193

30	1.133	1.263	1.070	1.339	1.006	1.421	0.941	1.511	0.877	1.606	0.812	1.707	0.748	1.814	0.684	1.925	0.622	2.041	0.562	2.160
31	1.147	1.273	1.085	1.345	1.023	1.425	0.960	1.510	0.897	1.601	0.834	1.698	0.772	1.800	0.710	1.906	0.649	2.017	0.589	2.131
32	1.160	1.282	1.100	1.352	1.040	1.428	0.979	1.510	0.917	1.597	0.856	1.690	0.794	1.788	0.734	1.889	0.674	1.995	0.615	2.104
33	1.172	1.291	1.114	1.358	1.055	1.432	0.996	1.510	0.936	1.594	0.876	1.683	0.816	1.776	0.757	1.874	0.698	1.975	0.641	2.080
34	1.184	1.299	1.128	1.364	1.070	1.435	1.012	1.511	0.954	1.591	0.896	1.677	0.837	1.766	0.779	1.860	0.722	1.957	0.665	2.057
35	1.195	1.307	1.140	1.370	1.085	1.439	1.028	1.512	0.971	1.589	0.914	1.671	0.857	1.757	0.800	1.847	0.744	1.940	0.689	2.037
36	1.206	1.315	1.153	1.376	1.098	1.442	1.043	1.513	0.988	1.588	0.932	1.666	0.877	1.749	0.821	1.836	0.766	1.925	0.711	2.018
37	1.217	1.323	1.165	1.382	1.112	1.446	1.058	1.514	1.004	1.586	0.950	1.662	0.895	1.742	0.841	1.825	0.787	1.911	0.733	2.001
38	1.227	1.330	1.176	1.388	1.124	1.449	1.072	1.515	1.019	1.585	0.966	1.658	0.913	1.735	0.860	1.816	0.807	1.899	0.754	1.985
39	1.237	1.337	1.187	1.393	1.137	1.453	1.085	1.517	1.034	1.584	0.982	1.655	0.930	1.729	0.878	1.807	0.826	1.887	0.774	1.970
40	1.246	1.344	1.198	1.398	1.148	1.457	1.098	1.518	1.048	1.584	0.997	1.652	0.946	1.724	0.895	1.799	0.844	1.876	0.789	1.956
45	1.288	1.376	1.245	1.423	1.201	1.474	1.156	1.528	1.111	1.584	1.065	1.643	1.019	1.704	0.974	1.768	0.927	1.834	0.881	1.902
50	1.324	1.403	1.285	1.446	1.245	1.491	1.205	1.538	1.164	1.587	1.123	1.639	1.081	1.692	1.039	1.748	0.997	1.805	0.955	1.864
55	1.356	1.427	1.320	1.466	1.284	1.506	1.247	1.548	1.209	1.592	1.172	1.638	1.134	1.685	1.095	1.734	1.057	1.785	1.018	1.837
60	1.383	1.449	1.350	1.484	1.317	1.520	1.283	1.558	1.249	1.598	1.214	1.639	1.179	1.682	1.144	1.726	1.108	1.771	1.072	1.817
65	1.407	1.468	1.377	1.500	1.346	1.534	1.315	1.568	1.283	1.604	1.251	1.642	1.218	1.680	1.186	1.720	1.153	1.761	1.120	1.802
70	1.429	1.485	1.400	1.515	1.372	1.546	1.343	1.578	1.313	1.611	1.283	1.645	1.253	1.680	1.223	1.716	1.192	1.754	1.162	1.792
75	1.448	1.501	1.422	1.529	1.395	1.557	1.368	1.587	1.340	1.617	1.313	1.646	1.284	1.682	1.256	1.716	1.227	1.746	1.199	1.785
80	1.466	1.515	1.441	1.541	1.416	1.568	1.390	1.595	1.364	1.624	1.338	1.653	1.312	1.683	1.285	1.714	1.259	1.745	1.232	1.777
85	1.482	1.528	1.458	1.553	1.435	1.578	1.411	1.603	1.386	1.630	1.362	1.657	1.337	1.685	1.312	1.714	1.287	1.743	1.262	1.773
90	1.496	1.540	1.474	1.563	1.452	1.587	1.429	1.611	1.406	1.636	1.383	1.661	1.360	1.687	1.336	1.714	1.312	1.741	1.288	1.769
95	1.510	1.552	1.489	1.573	1.468	1.596	1.446	1.618	1.425	1.642	1.403	1.666	1.381	1.690	1.358	1.715	1.336	1.741	1.313	1.767
100	1.522	1.562	1.503	1.583	1.482	1.604	1.462	1.625	1.441	1.647	1.421	1.670	1.400	1.693	1.378	1.717	1.357	1.741	1.335	1.765
150	1.611	1.637	1.598	1.651	1.584	1.665	1.571	1.679	1.557	1.693	1.543	1.708	1.530	1.722	1.515	1.737	1.501	1.752	1.486	1.767
200	1.664	1.684	1.653	1.693	1.643	1.704	1.633	1.715	1.623	1.725	1.613	1.735	1.603	1.746	1.592	1.757	1.582	1.768	1.571	1.779

Source: N. E. Savin and K. D. White, The Durbin–Watson test for serial correlation with extreme sample sizes or many regressors, *Econometrica*, 45 (8), 1992. November 1977. Reproduced with permission of the Econometrics Society.

TABLE A.5(b) Values of the Durbin–Watson Statistic

5 percent significance points of L and U

											Number of independent (explanatory) variables k										
	1		2		3		4		5		6		7		8		9		10	
n	L	U	L	U	L	U	L	U	L	U	L	U	L	U	L	U	L	U	L	U
6	0.610	1.400																		
7	0.700	1.356	0.467	1.896																
8	0.763	1.332	0.559	1.777	0.368	2.287														
9	0.824	1.320	0.629	1.699	0.455	2.128	0.296	2.588												
10	0.879	1.320	0.697	1.641	0.525	2.016	0.376	2.414	0.243	2.822										
11	0.927	1.324	0.758	1.604	0.595	1.928	0.444	2.283	0.316	2.645	0.203	3.005								
12	0.971	1.331	0.812	1.579	0.658	1.864	0.512	2.177	0.379	2.506	0.268	2.832	0.171	3.149						
13	1.010	1.340	0.861	1.562	0.715	1.816	0.574	2.094	0.445	2.390	0.328	2.692	0.230	2.985	0.147	3.266				
14	1.045	1.350	0.905	1.551	0.767	1.779	0.632	2.030	0.505	2.296	0.389	2.572	0.286	2.848	0.200	3.111	0.127	3.360		
15	1.077	1.361	0.946	1.543	0.814	1.750	0.685	1.977	0.562	2.220	0.447	2.472	0.343	2.727	0.251	2.979	0.175	3.216	0.111	3.438
16	1.106	1.371	0.982	1.539	0.857	1.728	0.734	1.935	0.615	2.157	0.502	2.388	0.398	2.624	0.304	2.860	0.222	3.090	0.155	3.304
17	1.133	1.381	1.015	1.536	0.897	1.710	0.779	1.900	0.664	2.104	0.554	2.318	0.451	2.537	0.356	2.757	0.272	2.975	0.198	3.184
18	1.158	1.391	1.046	1.535	0.933	1.696	0.820	1.872	0.710	2.060	0.603	2.257	0.502	2.461	0.407	2.667	0.321	2.873	0.244	3.073
19	1.180	1.401	1.074	1.536	0.967	1.685	0.859	1.848	0.752	2.023	0.649	2.206	0.549	2.396	0.456	2.589	0.369	2.783	0.290	2.974
20	1.201	1.411	1.100	1.537	0.998	1.676	0.894	1.828	0.792	1.991	0.692	2.162	0.595	2.339	0.502	2.521	0.416	2.704	0.336	2.885
21	1.221	1.420	1.125	1.538	1.026	1.669	0.927	1.812	0.829	1.964	0.732	2.124	0.637	2.290	0.547	2.460	0.461	2.633	0.380	2.806
22	1.239	1.429	1.147	1.541	1.053	1.664	0.958	1.797	0.863	1.940	0.769	2.090	0.677	2.246	0.588	2.407	0.504	2.571	0.424	2.734
23	1.257	1.437	1.168	1.543	1.078	1.660	0.986	1.785	0.895	1.920	0.804	2.061	0.715	2.208	0.628	2.360	0.545	2.514	0.465	2.670
24	1.273	1.446	1.188	1.546	1.101	1.656	1.013	1.775	0.925	1.902	0.837	2.035	0.751	2.174	0.666	2.318	0.584	2.464	0.506	2.613
25	1.288	1.454	1.206	1.550	1.123	1.654	1.038	1.767	0.953	1.886	0.868	2.012	0.784	2.144	0.702	2.280	0.621	2.419	0.544	2.560
26	1.302	1.461	1.224	1.553	1.143	1.652	1.062	1.759	0.979	1.873	0.897	1.992	0.816	2.117	0.735	2.246	0.657	2.379	0.581	2.513
27	1.316	1.469	1.240	1.556	1.162	1.651	1.084	1.753	1.004	1.861	0.925	1.974	0.845	2.093	0.767	2.216	0.691	2.342	0.616	2.470
28	1.328	1.476	1.255	1.560	1.181	1.650	1.104	1.747	1.028	1.850	0.951	1.958	0.874	2.071	0.798	2.188	0.723	2.309	0.650	2.431
29	1.341	1.483	1.270	1.563	1.198	1.650	1.124	1.743	1.050	1.841	0.975	1.944	0.900	2.052	0.826	2.164	0.753	2.278	0.682	2.396

n																				
30	1.352	1.489	1.284	1.567	1.214	1.650	1.143	1.739	1.071	1.833	0.998	1.931	0.926	2.034	0.854	2.141	0.782	2.251	0.712	2.363
31	1.363	1.496	1.297	1.570	1.229	1.650	1.160	1.735	1.090	1.825	1.020	1.920	0.950	2.018	0.879	2.120	0.810	2.226	0.741	2.333
32	1.373	1.502	1.309	1.574	1.244	1.650	1.177	1.732	1.109	1.819	1.041	1.909	0.972	2.004	0.904	2.102	0.836	2.203	0.769	2.306
33	1.383	1.508	1.321	1.577	1.258	1.651	1.193	1.730	1.127	1.813	1.061	1.900	0.994	1.991	0.927	2.085	0.861	2.181	0.795	2.281
34	1.393	1.514	1.333	1.580	1.271	1.652	1.208	1.728	1.144	1.808	1.080	1.891	1.015	1.979	0.950	2.069	0.885	2.162	0.821	2.257
35	1.402	1.519	1.343	1.584	1.283	1.653	1.222	1.726	1.160	1.803	1.097	1.884	1.034	1.967	0.971	2.054	0.908	2.144	0.845	2.236
36	1.411	1.525	1.354	1.587	1.295	1.654	1.236	1.724	1.175	1.799	1.114	1.877	1.053	1.957	0.991	2.041	0.930	2.127	0.868	2.216
37	1.419	1.530	1.364	1.590	1.307	1.655	1.249	1.723	1.190	1.795	1.131	1.870	1.071	1.948	1.011	2.029	0.951	2.112	0.891	2.198
38	1.427	1.535	1.373	1.594	1.318	1.656	1.261	1.722	1.204	1.792	1.146	1.864	1.088	1.939	1.029	2.017	0.970	2.098	0.912	2.180
39	1.435	1.540	1.382	1.597	1.328	1.658	1.273	1.722	1.218	1.789	1.161	1.859	1.104	1.932	1.047	2.007	0.990	2.085	0.932	2.164
40	1.442	1.544	1.391	1.600	1.338	1.659	1.285	1.721	1.230	1.786	1.175	1.854	1.120	1.924	1.064	1.997	1.008	2.072	0.945	2.149
45	1.475	1.566	1.430	1.615	1.383	1.666	1.336	1.720	1.287	1.776	1.238	1.835	1.189	1.895	1.139	1.958	1.089	2.022	1.038	2.088
50	1.503	1.585	1.462	1.628	1.421	1.674	1.378	1.721	1.335	1.771	1.291	1.822	1.246	1.875	1.201	1.930	1.156	1.986	1.110	2.044
55	1.528	1.601	1.490	1.641	1.452	1.681	1.414	1.724	1.374	1.768	1.334	1.814	1.294	1.861	1.253	1.909	1.212	1.959	1.170	2.010
60	1.549	1.616	1.514	1.652	1.480	1.689	1.444	1.727	1.408	1.767	1.372	1.808	1.335	1.850	1.298	1.894	1.260	1.939	1.222	1.984
65	1.567	1.629	1.536	1.662	1.503	1.696	1.471	1.731	1.438	1.767	1.404	1.805	1.370	1.843	1.336	1.882	1.301	1.923	1.266	1.964
70	1.583	1.641	1.554	1.672	1.525	1.703	1.494	1.735	1.464	1.768	1.433	1.802	1.401	1.837	1.369	1.873	1.337	1.910	1.305	1.948
75	1.598	1.652	1.571	1.680	1.543	1.709	1.515	1.739	1.487	1.770	1.458	1.801	1.428	1.834	1.399	1.867	1.369	1.901	1.339	1.935
80	1.611	1.662	1.586	1.688	1.560	1.715	1.534	1.743	1.507	1.772	1.480	1.801	1.453	1.831	1.425	1.861	1.397	1.893	1.369	1.925
85	1.624	1.671	1.600	1.696	1.575	1.721	1.550	1.747	1.525	1.774	1.500	1.801	1.474	1.829	1.448	1.857	1.422	1.886	1.396	1.916
90	1.635	1.679	1.612	1.703	1.589	1.726	1.566	1.751	1.542	1.776	1.518	1.801	1.494	1.827	1.469	1.854	1.445	1.881	1.420	1.909
95	1.645	1.687	1.623	1.709	1.602	1.732	1.579	1.755	1.557	1.778	1.535	1.802	1.512	1.827	1.489	1.852	1.465	1.877	1.442	1.903
100	1.654	1.694	1.634	1.715	1.613	1.736	1.592	1.758	1.571	1.780	1.550	1.803	1.528	1.826	1.506	1.850	1.484	1.874	1.462	1.898
150	1.720	1.746	1.706	1.760	1.693	1.774	1.679	1.788	1.665	1.802	1.651	1.817	1.637	1.832	1.622	1.847	1.608	1.862	1.594	1.877
200	1.758	1.778	1.748	1.789	1.738	1.799	1.728	1.810	1.718	1.820	1.707	1.831	1.697	1.841	1.686	1.852	1.675	1.863	1.665	1.874

Source: N. E. Savin and K. D. White, The Durbin–Watson test for serial correlation with extreme sample sizes or many regressors, *Econometrica*, 45 (8), 1994, November 1977. Reproduced with permission of the Econometrics Society.

Solutions to Selected Exercises

This section is designed to accompany the text and aid students in the understanding of the many methods discussed in this book.

The final answers obtained by instructors and students may not always agree with my solution down to the last digit because of different rounding procedures. Computer software systems such as recent versions of Minitab, SAS and Micro-TSP were used to obtain most of the numerical solutions. IDA was used in chapter 9 and the computer program in the appendix to chapter 2 was used for the solutions to chapter 2. Unless my computer's rounding procedures are duplicated, there is likely to be an occasional disagreement between results. Although I carefully checked all the solutions several times, I will be surprised if no errors remain undetected. For these I offer my apologies and hope that errors are rare.

Chapter 2

9 (a) $F_{25} = 5.80$, MSE $= 0.535$, MAPE $= 5.47$.
   (b) $F_{25} = 6.05$, MSE $= 0.500$, MAPE $= 7.18$.
   (c) $F_{25} = 5.90$, MSE $= 0.473$, MAPE $= 7.18$
   (d) Calculated above.
   (e) Single exponential smoothing with $\alpha = 0.30$.
   (f) Single moving average with $n = 3$.

11 (a) $F_{20} = 318.479$.
   (b) MSE $= 179.07$
   (c) Yes.
   (d) MAPE $= 4.618$; yes.

13 $F_{11} = 29.0$, MSE $= 30.33$; smaller MSE for Brown's method than single exponential smoothing (MSE is 53.03 when $\alpha = 0.2$).

15 (a) If $\alpha = 0.2$, $F_{10} = 41.13$, MSE $= 874.78$
   (b) If $\alpha = 0.2$, $F_{10} = 86.11$, MSE $= 153.80$
   (c) Quadratic exponential smoothing.

17 (a) $F_{25} = 115.29$, MSE $= 32.05$, MAPE $= 4.13$
   (b) $F_{25} = 105.40$, MSE $= 37.93$, MAPE $= 4.71$.
   (c) By MSE and MAPE, Winters' method is better.

19 (b) $F_{20} = 1581.27$, MSE $= 208419$, MAPE $= 32.41$
   (c) $F_{20} = 2049.04$, MSE $= 76746$, MAPE $= 20.51$.
   (d) Holt's method is better with fitted values closer to actual values.

Chapter 3

1 (a) Trend.
  (b) Cycle, trend.
  (c) Trend.
  (d) Seasonal.
  (e) Trend.
  (f) Cycle.
  (g) Seasonal.

3 (a) Sales are 5 percent larger than average in January because of seasonal variation; sales are 20 percent smaller than average in February because of seasonal variation.
  (b) -3.4, 11.5, -13.3, -6.3, 6.7, -3.2, 6.9, -14.7, 3.0, -8.3, -7.6.
  (c) 133.3, 181.3, 152.9, 144.2, 148.1, 147.1, 158.2, 161.1, 161.9, 161.8, 168.2, 171.1.
  (d) 26.4, -18.5, -6.0, 2.6, -0.7, 7.0, 1.8, 0.5, -0.1, 3.8, 1.7.

5 (a) \$225 000.
  (b) \$25 000.

7 (a) Actual usage of electric light and power is depressed by 28.5 percent because of a downturn.
  (b) Actual usage of electric light and power is increased by 15 percent because of an upturn.

9 (b) Seasonal indexes are as follows:

Quarter	I	II	III	IV
Canada	99.78	100.12	100.99	99.11
France	99.53	101.20	99.12	100.14
FRG	99.60	102.66	100.74	97.11

  (d) Deseasonalized series.
  (e) Seasonal index numbers are the same after 1984.

11 For detrended series
   $\hat{Y} = 76.299 - 0.236X$
   (origin at December 1983 $= 0$).

13 (b) $\hat{Y} = -1796.3 + 1492.8X$
      (origin at 1971 $= 0$).
   (c) $\hat{Y} = 135.0 + 527.2X + 87.8X^2$
      (origin at 1971 $= 0$).

15 (b) ln $\hat{Y}$ = 4.386 + 0.026X
  (base e logarithms).
  (c) 4.426, 4.952 or 137.9, 141.5.

17 (a) $\hat{Y}$ = 672.07 + 72.94X
  (b) $\hat{Y}$ = 68.297 + 0.5065X
  (origin at January 15, 1971).
  (c) 135.16 for January 1982.

19 (b) One-year-ahead seasonal index numbers are 99.842, 99.395, 100.003, 100.055, 99.589, 101.508, 100.092, 98.475, 100.501, 101.261, 99.477, 99.458.

23 Annual forecast is $18.9 million; quarterly forecasts (million dollars) for the beginning of each quarter are 4.4, 5.2, 4.4, and 4.9.

Chapter 4

1 (a) At X = 0, Y is −1750.
  (b) For every change of income by $1, there is an associated change in the same direction of 6.5 cents.
  (c) Y = − $125.00.

3 (a) 73.3 percent. No, statistics cannot prove causation.
  (b) 42.6 percent. No, statistics cannot prove causation.
  (c) In study 1, 75 percent of the variation in deposits is associated with the linear regression on interest rates.
      In study 2, 82 percent of the variation in deposits is associated with the linear regression on family income.
      No, more information or study is needed.

5 (b) $\hat{Y}$ = −9104.89 + 2.2504X
  (1971 = 0).
  (c) t = 20.87 and the null hypothesis is rejected at the 0.01 level.
  (d) F = 435.67 and the null hypothesis is rejected at the 0.05 level.
  (e) t = −11.80 and the null hypothesis is rejected at the 0.05 level.
  (f) Possible nonlinear relationship or serial correlation.
  (g) 0.982.

7 (b) Private business sector
      $\hat{Y}$ = −518.73 + 6.4246X_t
      Manufacturing
      Y = −192.99 + 3.0186 X_t

  (c) Private business sector: t = 10.94, reject null hypothesis.
      Manufacturing: t = 11.61, reject null hypothesis.
  (d) Private business sector: t = −8.87, reject null hypothesis.
      Manufacturing: t = −7.11, reject null hypothesis.
  (e) Private business sector: 0.882, 0.939.
      Manufacturing: 0.894, 0.945.

(f) Private business sector: DW $= 0.627$, reject null hypothesis
   Manufacturing: DW $= 0.395$, reject null hypothesis
(g) Private business sector:
   $\hat{Y}_t = 0.9916\,Y_{t-1} + 6.26 \times 10^{-14}\,(1-0.9916) + (X_t - 0.9916X_{t-1})$
   Manufacturing:
   $\hat{Y}_t = 0.9951\,Y_{t-1} + 1882(1-0.9951) - 0.7123\,(X_t - 0.9951X_{t-1})$

9 (a) (i) $\hat{Y}_t = 182.62 + 5.0557X_t$
       (ii) $\hat{Y}_t = -2223.20 + 0.7831X_t$
   (b) (i) $S_e = 61.98$
       (ii) $S_e = 59.21$
       Regression on income is better.
   (c) (i) $R^2 = 0.934$
       (ii) $R^2 = 0.940$
   (d) (i) DW $= 0.975$; test is inconclusive at the 0.05 level.
       (ii) DW $= 1.109$; test is inconclusive at the 0.05 level.
   (e) (i) $\hat{Y}_t = 0.534Y_{t-1} + 214.14(1- 0.534) + 4.863(X_t - 0.534X_{t-1})$
       (ii) $\hat{Y}_t = 0.182Y_{t-1} - 2634.13(1-0.182) + 0.877(X_t - 0.182X_{t-1})$
   (f) (i) $S_e = 60.87$
       (ii) $S_e = 52.91$
       S_e is smaller after correcting for serial correlation.

13 (a),(b)

X	$\hat{Y}$	95 percent confidence interval
5000	1697.5	(1557.7, 1827.4)
6000	2475.7	(2183.2, 2768.2)
7000	3258.8	(2806.0, 3711.7)

15 (a) $\hat{Y}_t = 1.13 + 0.121X_t$
   (b) $F = 148.10$; reject null hypothesis.
   (c) $t = -6.70$; reject null hypothesis. Yes.
   (d) $t = 12.17$; reject null hypothesis. Yes.
   (e) $\hat{Y} = £1.7738$ thousand.
       99 percent interval for mean (1.4940, 2.0536).
       99 percent interval for individual (1.0922, 2.4554)
       (in thousand pounds sterling)
   (g) 0.914, 0.956

Chapter 5

1 (a) For every change of one day in the average length of stay, there is an associated change of $12 in cost per patient day. For every change of one unit in the occupancy rate, there is an associated change of $110 in cost per patient day.
   (b) $259.

3 (a),(b)

Mean square	F
0.002 975	4.46
0.000 667	

(c) Critical $F = 4.53$; hence do not reject the null hypothesis.

(d) 96.67 percent of the variation in the dependent variable is associated with the linear regression on the independent variables.

5 (a) $\hat{Y} = 3.014 - 0.214X_1 + 1.027X_2 + 0.479X_3$

(b) If X_1, X_2, and X_3 are zero, then $\hat{Y}$ is 3.014.

(c) For every unit change in X_1, there is an associated change of 0.214 in the opposite direction in Y. For every unit change in X_2, there is an associated change of 1.027 in Y. For every unit change in X_3, there is an associated change of 0.479 in Y.

(d) For β_1, reject at the 0.011 level. For β_2, reject at the 0.001 level. For β_3, do not reject at any reasonable level of significance.

(e) $F = 16.67$.

(f) Reject at both the 0.01 and 0.05 levels.

7 (a) $\overline{R}^2 = 1$. There is a perfect association between the dependent variable and the independent variables.

(b) $\overline{R}^2$ becomes smaller.

9 (a) $\hat{Y} = -20\ 855 + 273.30X_1 + 0.0549X_2$

(b) For every change of a million automobile registrations, there is an associated change of \$273.3 thousand in tire sales. For every change of one million dollars in disposable personal income, there is an associated change of \$.0549 (thousand) in tire sales.

(c) For β_1, reject the null hypothesis at the 0.01 level or less. For β_2, do not reject the null hypothesis at any level.

(d) 99.2 percent.

(e) $F = 412.83$. Reject the null hypothesis at the 0.01 level or less.

(f) Since we did not reject $\beta_2 = 0$, variable X_2 should not be included in the regression.

11 Only variable PPI should be entered into the regression model by the stepwise procedure. The model equation is $\hat{Y} = -840.80 + 9.0426X_1$. For every change of one unit in PPI, there is an associated change of \$9.0426 in the cost of heating per day.

13 (a) $\hat{Y} = 30.376 - 3.121X_1 - 0.221X_2$
where X_1 is price and X_2 is gender.

(b) $F = 230.16$; reject the null hypothesis at the 0.05 and 0.01 levels.

(c) For β_1, $t = -21.2$; hence reject the null hypothesis.
For β_2, $t = -0.58$; do not reject the null hypothesis.

(d) Change in quantity sold is associated with changes in price. Change in quantity sold is not associated with gender differences.

15 Only variable X_1 (new housing units) entered the regression model by stepwise procedures:
$\hat{Y} = 3535.15 + 1.2003\ X_1$

Appendix A to chapter 5

1 (a) $\hat{Y} = -10.877 + 7.056X$
   (b) $\hat{Y} = 15.593 - 1.768X + 0.519X^2$
   (c) $\hat{Y} = 5.722 + 4.300X - 0.347X^2 + 0.034X^3$
   (d) Cubic model, 1.599.
   (e) Cubic model, 0.998.
   (f) Yes, $t = 6.394$ (0.0001).
   (g) Yes, $t = -2.530$ (0.0264).
   (h) Cubic model.
   (i) 109.1, 116.1, 123.2 for linear model; 135.5, 151.9, 169.4 for quadratic model; 145.4, 168.8, 195.1 for cubic model.

3 (a) $\hat{Y} = 8.228 - 2.517X + 0.481X^2$
   (b) To interpret change for the quadratic model, we find the first derivative, $-2.517 + 0.962X$. At first the change is in the negative direction until X is large enough for change to be increasingly positive.

Chapter 6

1 (a) Y, M, N
   (b) X, Z, U
   (c) X and Z are right-hand-side variables in two equations. Y is a left-hand-side variable in one equation and a right-hand-side variable in another equation.

3 (a) If b_3 and b_4 are zero, $Y_2 = b_1Y_1 + e_2$
      Note also that the first equation is $Y_1 = a_1Y_2 + e_1$
   (b) If $C_1 = ab_3/(1-ab_1)$, $C_2 = ab_4/(1-ab_1)$, and $u = ae_2/(1-ab_1 + e_1)$, then $Y_1 = C_1Z_1 + C_2Z_2 + u$.

5 (a) $C_1 = 450.45$, $I_1 = 369.419$.
   (b) $C_2 = 416.805$, $I_1 = 367.672$.
   (c) C, I are endogenous; G is exogenous.

7 (a) Seven are within two standard errors; four are within one standard error.
   (b) Four

9 (a) $\hat{Y} = 41.88 + 0.04X_1 + 7.479X_2$
   (b) At observation 1, for example, the elasticity with respect to price is

$$E = 0.04 \times \frac{0.930}{44.29} = 0.000\ 839\ 9$$

The elasticity with respect to advertising is

$$E = 7.479 \times \frac{0.363}{44.29} = 0.0613$$

(c) $\ln \hat{Y} = 3.976 - 0.209\ln X_1 + 0.181\ln X_2$
$\hat{Y} = 3.976 X_1^{-0.209} X_2^{-0.181}$

(d) Point elasticities are 0.209 for price and 0.181 for advertising.

Chapter 7

1 (a) For earnings per share (EPS), there is a change of $0.05 associated with a change of one period in EPS lagged one period; the change is $0.02 associated with a unit change in EPS lagged two periods.

(b) For the price index for leather goods and kindred products (index), there is a change of $0.20 associated with a unit change in the index lagged one period, a change of $0.05 associated with a unit change in the index lagged two periods, and a change of $0.001 associated with a unit change in the index lagged three periods.

(c) For the index of wages of GS12 federal employees (index), there is an associated change of $0.10 for a unit change in the index lagged one period, a $0.03 change associated with a unit change in the index lagged two periods, a $0.0005 change associated with a unit change in the index lagged three periods, and a $0.000001 change associated with a unit change in the index lagged four periods.

3 (a) (1,d,1)
  (b) (1,d,0)
  (c) (1,d,1)

5

Period	Citicorp	Autocorrelations Walt Disney	Exxon
1	0.767	0.621	0.750
2	0.572	0.292	0.536
3	0.450	0.087	0.436
4	0.303	−0.040	0.324
5	0.174	−0.046	0.196
6	0.010	−0.020	0.017
7	−0.118	0.010	−0.132
8	−0.177	−0.051	−0.290
9	−0.241	−0.099	−0.354
10	−0.340	−0.154	−0.353

Citicorp and Exxon are nonstationary. Walt Disney is possibly an autoregressive model.

7 (a) Yes, one difference.
  (b) Yes, 12 periods.

9 New York Stock Exchange Composite: the time series is nonstationary; a first difference will transform the data set to a stationary time series.

11 Three month treasury bills (1939–89): the data set is nonstationary; a first difference will transform the data set to a stationary time series.

Chapter 8

1 For a one-period change in Y lagged one period, there is an associated change of 0.3 in Y. For a one-period change in Y lagged two periods, there is an associated change of 0.3 in Y.

3 (a) $Y_t = \mu + \phi Y_{t-s} + e_t$
  (b) $Y_t = \mu + \phi_1 Y_{t-s} + \phi_2 Y_{t-2s} + e_t$
  (c) $Y_t = \mu + e_t - \theta_1 e_{t-s} - \theta_2 e_{t-2s}$
  (d) $Y_t = \mu + \phi_1 Y_{t-s} + e_t - \theta_1 e_{t-s} - \theta_2 e_{t-2s}$
  (e) $Y_t = \mu + \phi_1 Y_{t-s} + \phi_2 Y_{t-2s} + e_t - \theta_1 e_{t-s}$

5 ARIMA(1,1,1).

7 The plot of autocorrelations of the total index time series and the plot of autocorrelations of the logarithmic transformation of the same time series are very similar.

11 (a) ARIMA(0,d,1).
   (b) ARIMA(2,d,0).
   (c) ARIMA(1,d,1).
   (d) ARIMA(2,d,0).
   (e) ARIMA(0,d,2).

Chapter 9

1 (a) $\pm$ 0.283.
  (b) Randomly and normally distributed.
  (c) The time series is seasonal and may require seasonal differencing.
  (d) Most likely stationary unless the gradual pattern is very slow when the data are nonstationary.
  (e) Ordinary autocorrelations will cut off after two lags and partial autocorrelations will die down.

3 Time series is stationary. The ARIMA(1,0,0) model appears because autocorrelations die down and partial autocorrelations cut off after one lag.

5 (a) ARIMA(0,1,1)(0,1,1)^4.
  (b) ARIMA(0,1,2).
  (c) ARIMA(1,1,1)(1,1,1)^{12}.
  (d) ARIMA(1,0,1)(0,0,1)^{12}.

7

	Autocorrelations	
	Ordinary	Partial
MA(1)	Drop	Trail
AR(1)	Trail	Drop
ARMA(1,1)	Trail	Trail

9 Total (1939–87)
   (a) ARIMA(0,1,0) with a constant.
   (b) $\hat{Y}_t = 5.254 + Y_{t-1}$ (by IDA).
   (c) $Q = 11.7$ for 24 lags.
   (d) 263.95 and 269.21.

11 (a) ARIMA(0,1,1).
   (b) $\hat{Y}_t = Y_{t-1} - 0.503e_{t-1}$ (by IDA).
   (c) $Q = 20.9$ with 24 lags.
   (d) 137.1, 137.1, 137.1, 137.1.

15 (a) $(0,1,0)(0,1,1)^{12}$.
   (b) $\hat{Y}_t = Y_{t-1} + Y_{t-12} - Y_{t-13} - 0.880e_{t-12}$ (by IDA).
   (c) $Q = 18.2$ at 24 lags.
   (d) Forecasts are 7.90, 7.93, 7.97, 7.99, 8.03, 8.06, 8.10, 8.15, 8.24, 8.27, 8.32, 8.33.

Chapter 10

11 Leading indicator – sales of sweet fruit drink in the United States; coincident indicator – tourist arrivals; lagging indicator – shipments of rare fruit to Puerto Rico.

13 CPI would not be a good indicator of changes in money supply of the island nation. ARIMA modeling can predict short-term changes in money supply. If the model is prudently constructed, econometric methods may give the best overall forecasts. If it is not prudently constructed, the model is of little value.

Chapter 11

1 $\chi^2 = 4.45$; reject null hypothesis.

3 $\chi^2 = 0.83$; do not reject null hypothesis.

5 ME $= 1.13$, MAPE $= 1.02$, MSE $= 1.63$, RMS $= 1.27$, $U = 0.127$.

7 $\overline{Y} = 146.9$ $\overline{\hat{Y}} = 146.66$
   $S_Y = 0.81$ $S_{\hat{Y}} = 0.88$
   $r = 0.883$ MSE $= 0.212729$
   $E^m = 0.271$ $E^\tau = 0.128$

9 $\overline{Y} = 75.35$ $\overline{\hat{Y}} = 75.42$
   $S_Y = 7.40$ $S_{\hat{Y}} = 7.70$
   $r = 0.987$ MSE $= 1.39500$
   $E^m = 0.0035$ $E^\tau = 0.1043$

11 Since errors are small, bias does exist but is small. Brown's method will result in small errors in the downside direction. The results are for this data set only.

13 (a) $\hat{Y}_c = 28.3 + 0.809\hat{Y}$

$E^m = 0$

$E^r = \dfrac{(0.71556 - 0.883 \times 0.80994)^2}{0.13088} = 0.0000011,$

$E^d \doteq 1.0$

(b) $\hat{Y}_c = 6.73 + 0.950Y$

$E^m = 0$

$E^r = \dfrac{(6.8937 - 0.997 \times 6.9113)^2}{0.23143} = 0.0000424$

$E^d \doteq 0$

(c) $\hat{Y}_c = 6.73 + 0.950\hat{Y}$

$E^m = 0$

$E^r = \dfrac{(7.309 - 0.987 \times 7.4009^2)}{1.2530} = 0.000015$

$E^d \doteq 1.0$

INDEX